Ius Gentium: Comparative Perspectives on Law and Justice

Volume 54

More information about this series at http://www.springer.com/series/7888

Neil Andrews

Arbitration and Contract Law

Common Law Perspectives

Springer

Neil Andrews
Faculty of Law
Cambridge, UK

ISSN 1534-6781 ISSN 2214-9902 (electronic)
Ius Gentium: Comparative Perspectives on Law and Justice
ISBN 978-3-319-27142-2 ISBN 978-3-319-27144-6 (eBook)
DOI 10.1007/978-3-319-27144-6

Library of Congress Control Number: 2015960935

Printed on acid-free paper

This Springer imprint is published by Springer Nature
The registered company is Springer International Publishing AG Switzerland

For Liz, Sam, Hannah, and Ruby

Preface

Arbitration and the Three Dimensions of Consent

Arbitration and agreement are inter-linked in three respects: (i) the agreement to arbitrate is itself a contract; (ii) there is scope (subject to clear consensual exclusion) in England for monitoring the arbitral tribunal's fidelity and accuracy in applying substantive English contract law; and (iii) the subject matter of the arbitration is nearly always a 'contractual' matter. These three elements underlie this work. They appear as Part I (arbitration is founded on agreement), Part II (monitoring accuracy), and Part III (synopsis of the contractual rules frequently encountered within arbitration).

Arbitration Is a Consensual Process. Nearly all commercial arbitrations arise from an arbitration agreement voluntarily reached by both parties. Occasionally, arbitration is made available under statute and is not voluntary. Another exception is when arbitration is made available under Treaty in favour of third party corporate investors. It can be safely assumed, however, that arbitration has as one of its pillars the fundamental concept of party consent. It is hoped that the wider legal community will find interesting and useful this study of the working out within English law of the notion that arbitration arises from agreement.

Monitoring the Tribunal's Application of Contract Law. English law takes seriously (although in a balanced way) the need to maintain links between the practice of arbitral decision-making on points of English contract law and the wider interest of the legal community (a global audience) in studying progress within the substantive body of contract law. This is examined in Part II (notably Chap. 8). By contrast, as explained in Chap. 9, the enforcing court has less opportunity to monitor a foreign arbitral tribunal's compliance with contract law. Even so, various contractual issues can be examined by the enforcing court: whether the arbitration agreement is valid, what is its scope, and who are the relevant parties.

Central Contractual Doctrines. The subject matter of disputes submitted to arbitration is substantially concerned with contract law: the arbitral tribunal receiving a claim or allegation that the parties had a contract, or remain bound by one, or were negotiating one, or that one party failed properly to negotiate one, or receiving the submission that the agreement should be interpreted in a certain way, or that one party has breached the agreement and is now liable to pay compensation or to be rendered subject to some other remedy. Chapters 10, 11, 12, 13, 14, 15, 16, and 17 provide a synopsis of English contract law. Here the aim has not been to provide an encyclopaedia of contract law. Instead these succinct chapters provide a means of navigating the detailed rules and of identifying the main doctrines likely to engage the attention of advisors and arbitrators. It is hoped that these synoptic chapters will be of help to: (1) foreign lawyers or English non-lawyers unfamiliar with the details of English contract law; (2) English lawyers who have lost their orientation because of the complexity of contract law; and (3) arbitral tribunals in search of solid ground.

Ten Leading Points Within English Arbitration Law

1. *Supervisory Court*. The Commercial Court is the main court appointed to oversee issues arising under the Arbitration Act 1996 (but some arbitration matters will come before the Mercantile Courts, and the Technology and Construction Court, or the Chancery Division, and county courts).
2. *Main Statute*. The law of arbitration in England was substantially codified by the Arbitration Act 1996, which must be read in the light of the Departmental Advisory Committee's report. Unlike many other nations, England has not adopted the UNCITRAL Model Law. The main deviation from the Model Law is section 69 of the Arbitration Act 1996 (**8.01**), which permits appeals (subject to the High Court's permission) from awards where there is alleged to have been an error of *English* law. Part 1 of the Arbitration Act 1996 applies when the 'seat' of the arbitration proceedings is in England and Wales or Northern Ireland (**3.01**). Even if the seat is not England and Wales or Northern Ireland, the 1996 Act will apply to various matters, notably: (i) the grant of a stay of legal proceedings, and (ii) enforcement of an award. The parties' consensual autonomy is a leading feature of the 1996 Act, section 1 of which states: the parties should be free to agree how their disputes are resolved, subject only to such safeguards as are necessary in the public interest. But this is qualified by the 'mandatory' provisions listed in Schedule 1 to the 1996 Act. The 1996 Act also imposes duties upon both the arbitral tribunal and the parties to ensure fairness, efficiency, and an appropriate degree of speediness (**6.25**). The 1996 Act also emphasises that English courts should not interfere excessively in the conduct of the arbitration process. However, in cases of urgency the court can provide relief for the purpose of preserving evidence or assets.
3. *Law Governing the Arbitration Agreement*. The Court of Appeal in *Sulamerica Cia Nacional de Seguros SA* v. *Enesa Engenharia SA* (2012) (**3.17**) held that the arbitration agreement will be subject to the law of the seat only if the parties have neither expressly nor impliedly nominated a different law to govern that agreement.

4. *Separability*. Section 7 of the 1996 Act, adopting the concept of 'separability' (or 'severability'), provides that the main contract's invalidity does *not necessarily* entail the invalidity of the arbitration agreement (see Lord Hoffmann in *Fiona Trust and Holding Corporation* v. *Privalov* (2007) for details, also known as *Premium Nafta Products Ltd* v. *Fili Shipping Co Ltd*) (**2.47 ff**).
5. *Religious Affiliation of Arbitrators*. In *Jivraj* v. *Hashwani* (2011) (**5.32**) the United Kingdom Supreme Court held that appointment of arbitrators is not governed by the European employment provisions prohibiting selection by reference to religion.
6. *Upholding Arbitration Agreements*. A party to an arbitration agreement ('the applicant') can apply to the court for a stay of English court proceedings if such proceedings have been brought against him (**4.02**). The Supreme Court in the *AES* case (2013) (**4.13** and **4.17**) confirmed that the English courts have power to issue anti-suit injunctions to prevent a party to an arbitration agreement from acting inconsistently with that exclusive commitment to arbitrate rather than to litigate. But the European Court of Justice's decision in *Allianz SpA* v. *West Tankers* (2009) (**4.22**) prevents the Common Law anti-suit injunction from being issued to counter breach of arbitration clauses by the commencement of inconsistent *court* litigation within the *same* European jurisdictional zone. In the *Gazprom* case (2015) (**4.24**), the European Court of Justice confirmed the central feature of the *West Tankers* case (2009): that it is incompatible with the Jurisdiction Regulation for the court of a Member State to issue a decision prohibiting the respondent from continuing, or initiating, civil or commercial proceedings covered by the Jurisdiction Regulation (2012) (effective from 10 January 2015) in another Member State.
7. *Confidentiality*. The Court of Appeal's decision in *Michael Wilson & Partners Ltd* v. *Emmott* (2008) (**7.02**) confirms that an implied obligation of confidentiality governs all documents 'prepared for', 'used', and 'disclosed during' arbitration proceedings governed by English law.
8. *Challenges to the Award*. The High Court can hear a challenge to an award where it is alleged that the tribunal lacked jurisdiction (section 67, 1996 Act), or that there has been a 'serious irregularity affecting the tribunal, the proceedings or the award' (section 68, 1996 Act). Neither section 67 nor 68 can be excluded by agreement. However, the House of Lords in the *Lesotho* case (2005) (**9.09 and 17.04 ff**) noted that a 'mere' error of fact or law within the tribunal's jurisdiction does not justify resort to section 68. Although there can be no appeal from an English award to the High Court on a point of foreign law, section 69 (**8.04**) permits an appeal to occur on a matter of English law if the court itself gives permission. Careful wording is required to exclude section 69.
9. *Res Judicata*. The Privy Council in *Associated Electric & Gas Insurance Services Ltd* v. *European Reinsurance Co of Zurich* (2003) (**7.08 ff**) held that issue estoppel can arise in arbitration, and this will be binding on a second arbitration panel seised with a matter on a related topic between the same parties.

10. *Cross-border Enforcement of Awards*. The Supreme Court in *Dallah Real Estate & Tourism Holding Co* v. *Pakistan* (2010) (**9.36**) held that a foreign award (given in Paris) could not be recognised and enforced in England (under the New York Convention (1958), enacted as section 103, Arbitration Act 1996), because the arbitral tribunal had incorrectly determined that the Pakistan Government was a party to the relevant arbitration agreement. But a French court, applying its domestic arbitration law, as distinct from the New York Convention (1958), later upheld the same award.

Cambridge, UK
October 2015

Neil Andrews

Contents

Part I
Arbitration: A Consensual Process

Chapter 1
The Landscape of International Commercial Arbitration

Abstract Chapters 1–7 cover the main features of the arbitral process from the perspective of the parties' agreement, the court's supportive function, and overarching standards or values of impartiality, fairness, efficiency and expedition.

Chapter 1 begins with examination of the reasons why parties might prefer to pursue arbitration rather than the court system for the resolution of their differences. The second section examines the 'Three Pillars' of commercial arbitration: agreement; autonomy from judicial interference (substantial, not complete); cross-border enforcement of awards.

1.1 Arbitration's Perceived Advantages

1.01 Here we will consider six main advantages associated with arbitration (as distinct from use of court proceedings): (i) neutrality, (ii) expertise, (iii) procedural flexibility, (iv) finality, (v) superior cross-border enforcement, and (vi) confidentiality. Factors (i), (ii), (iii), (iv), and (vi) are interests normally shared by claimant and defendant. But factor (v) is a claimant's interest.

1.02 But how do these factors withstand sceptical scrutiny? All things considered, factors (i) (neutrality), (ii) (expertise), (iv) (finality) and (v) (superior cross-border enforcement) seem most important.[1]

1.03 *Factor (i), Neutrality*.[2] Here the attraction is that the seat of the arbitration can be a neutral jurisdiction, for example, London, Paris, Stockholm, or Zurich, the

[1] D Wong, 'The Rise of the International Commercial Court…' (2014) 33 CJQ 205 at 205–206 identifies (i) (ii) (v) and (vi).

[2] AH Baum, 'International Arbitration: the Path Towards Uniform Procedures', in G Aksen, et al (eds), *Global Reflections on International Law, Commerce and Dispute Resolution: Liber Amicorum in Honour of Robert Briner* (ICC, Paris, 2004), 51–52; AF Lowenfeld, 'The Party-Appointed Arbitrator: Further Reflections', in LW Newman and RD Hill (eds), *The Leading Arbitrators' Guide to International Arbitration* (3rd edn, New York, 2014), chapter 19, at 473, however, suggests that 'rooting for the home team' by a party-appointed arbitrator' is 'not much in evidence'; CA Rogers and JC Jeng, 'The Ethics of International Arbitrators', in Newman and Hill, *op cit*, chapter 7, at 191–192 ('to say that all arbitrators are equally "neutral" is mostly a triumph of rhetoric'), and 199–200; party-appointed arbitrators 'serve as an "interpreter" of language, of legal culture, and of law for the benefit of fellow adjudicators', F Gelinas, 'The Independence of

N. Andrews, *Arbitration and Contract Law*, Ius Gentium: Comparative Perspectives on Law and Justice 54, DOI 10.1007/978-3-319-27144-6_1

parties being based in (for example) China and the USA. Neutrality can be reinforced, if the tribunal consist of three members, by each party appointing his own co-arbitrator (for example, a Chinese and American), and the President being neither Chinese nor American. But given that the parties could elect to have the dispute litigated in a neutral court, for example, in London or Paris, what additional benefit is secured by the nationally selected wing-arbitrators? In fact 'neutrality' is an imponderable element. Böchstiegel even predicts that technical excellence and reliability might eclipse considerations of securing local representation on the arbitral tribunal: 'parties seem less inclined to select arbitrators from their own legal background but rather…from any region of the world whom they consider best equipped to for particular case.'[3]

1.04 *Factor (ii), Expertise*. Arbitrators can be selected for their expertise in technical areas, such as engineering, economics, science, the 'customs of the sea', or commercial law.[4] This factor can be important in some technical fields. But it does not in all contexts render arbitration overwhelmingly superior. This is because courts can be informed by expert opinion. Furthermore, specialist courts develop familiarity with certain branches of commerce and even technology. But Born notes the potential for disaster: 'many national courts are distressingly inappropriate choices for resolving international commercial disputes'.[5] And the (expensive) three-member arbitral panel might be attractive: 'hardly any national courts can

International Arbitrators and Judges: Tampered With or Well Tempered' (2011) 24 New York Int'l LR 1, 26; I Lee, 'Practice and Predicament: Nationalism, Nationality, and National-Affiliation in International Commercial Arbitration' (2007) 31 Fordham Int'l LJ 603 (also noting religious affiliation—and see end of this note); and for practice in ICSID matters, CA Rogers and JC Jeng, *ibid,* 199–200. On English arbitration's willingness to allow appointment by reference to national or religious criteria, see *Jivraj* v. *Hashwani* [2011] UKSC 40; [2011] 1 WLR 1872, on which *Andrews on Civil Processes*, vol 2, *Arbitration and Mediation* (Intersentia, Cambridge, Antwerp, Portland, 2013), 9.25 ff; and on connections between potential arbitrators and parties based on 'residence' and 'other relationships' (and not just nationality), ICC Rules (2012), Article 13(1).

[3] K-H Böchstiegel, 'Perspectives on Future Developments in International Arbitration', in LW Newman and RD Hill (eds), *The Leading Arbitrators' Guide to International Arbitration* (3rd edn, New York, 2014), chapter 12, at 330.

[4] eg, Heidelberg Conference (2011), National Report (a series of national reports on arbitration filed with the author): Viktória Harsági (Hungary): 'Judges of state courts are (or can be) highly qualified legal experts; however, they cannot be expected to have detailed knowledge of international trade practices.' David Steward (London, Singapore, and Hong Kong): 'There is a common perception that an arbitration tribunal's decision will be more grounded in commercial considerations than that of a judge....In some commodity trade arbitrations, the tribunal may decide not to apply the law strictly and to make an award that reflects its view of what the trade would regard as fair. This is generally recognised and accepted by the parties, who submit to the judgment of others who know how the market works.' Natalie Moore (England): 'In the field of shipping, clients often prefer their dispute to be referred to "three commercial men sitting in London" (as the arbitration clause is often worded) who are familiar with shipping matters… The decision making is likely to be more rough and ready, but my clients (charterers, ship-owners, insurers etc) seem to accept that this is the traditional way of litigating shipping disputes.'

[5] Gary Born, *International Arbitration and Forum Selection Agreements: Drafting and Enforcing* (4th edn, Kluwer, Netherlands, 2013), 8.

offer the breadth of resources and experience possessed by a tribunal of three experienced international arbitrators.'[6]

1.05 *Factor (iii), Procedural Flexibility.* This has ceased to be a major distinguishing feature. The practices of court proceedings within both the Common Law and other traditions have been absorbed into modern cosmopolitan arbitral practice. Common lawyers will recognise within modern arbitral practice the familiar patterns and techniques of written submissions, documentary disclosure, witness statements, expert opinions, oral examination of witnesses, including cross-examination by opposing parties, elaborately reasoned awards. The rules of institutional arbitration, much less detailed than most national procedural codes, have elastically accommodated these practices. As Jan Paulsson notes, 'modern practitioners have a adopted a cosmopolitan approach which converges in a range of shared practices' and 'remarkable procedural commonalities'.[7] And Gary Born comments: 'most developed nations have rejected the view that arbitrators sitting there must apply local judicial procedural laws', adding, however, 'there continues to be a tendency, particularly among less experienced international arbitrators, to look to local judicial procedures as their starting point in determining arbitral procedures.'[8]

1.06 *Factor (iv): Finality.* There is (in general) no appeal from arbitral awards (furthermore, respondents to a 2006 poll strongly opposed intra-arbitral appeals).[9] Arbitration is an escape from judicial appeals. Given the baroque and entrenched appellate arrangements in many legal systems, the arbitration community's decision to walk away from appeals is plainly sound. Arbitration can involve high stakes. No doubt, errors of fact are beyond further scrutiny. But what if the tribunal has misapplied the applicable law? As Jan Paulsson says, 'To give [an arbitral tribunal] the power to make a final and unreviewable decision may be a frightening thing'.[10] But he dismisses the idea of appeal to national courts[11] and he notes how difficult and expensive ('daunting') an intra-arbitral 'appeal' by a large arbitral panel would be.[12] In fact arbitral 'finality' is a highly contestable 'advantage'. Born notes the tactical see-saw nature of arbitral finality: one party's final victory is the opponent's irreversible defeat.[13] The arbitration community, and users of that system, are opposed to squandering the advantage of insulation from the national court process by admitting appeals on the merits from arbitral decisions to courts. The price that is

---

[6] *ibid*, 9.

[7] J Paulsson, *The Idea of Arbitration* (Oxford University Press, 2013), 179.

[8] Gary Born, *International Arbitration and Forum Selection Agreements: Drafting and Enforcing* (4th edn, Kluwer, Netherlands, 2013), 70.

[9] Queen Mary College (London) Survey of Arbitration Users (2006): 'International Arbitration: Corporate Attitudes and Practices <http://www.arbitration.qmul.ac.uk/docs/123295.pdf>, p 15 (over 90 % opposed; poll of 103 counsel, mostly internal, concerned with arbitration).

[10] J Paulsson, *The Idea of Arbitration* (Oxford University Press, 2013), 291.

[11] *ibid.*

[12] *ibid.* at 292–293.

[13] Gary Born, *International Arbitration and Forum Selection Agreements: Drafting and Enforcing* (4th edn, Kluwer, Netherlands, 2013), 5 to 6.

paid for such insulation is that arbitral awards are virtually final, subject only to restricted grounds of review (**8.01**), which are aimed at ensuring the jurisdictional validity of the arbitration submission, the correct appointment of the tribunal, and compliance with the applicable procedure, and stop far short of permitting appellate re-examination of the award's substantive or factual merits.

1.07 *Factor (v): Superior Cross-border Enforcement.* Taking a global perspective, foreign awards are more easily enforced than foreign judgments.[14] Born comments: 'there are significant obstacles to obtaining effective enforcement of foreign court judgments in many cases'.[15] But this point is losing strength or it might even have become a non-point within the European Union and between well-established major trading nations who have bilateral arrangements[16] (admittedly in the wider world enforcement of foreign judgments is underdeveloped).[17] Certainly, the New York Convention (1958) is not the fast-route to enforcement which some had supposed (for examples of problematic enforcement under the NYC (1958), see **9.36** on the *Dallah* litigation and **9.31** on the *Yukos* saga). Furthermore, Jan Paulsson (2014) gave this verdict on the New York Convention (1958): 'Some of the largest countries in the world have signed the New York Convention but are incapable of demonstrating an acceptable record of judicial compliance with its terms.'[18] He adds[19]: 'Enforcement of foreign arbitral awards may be described as routine only in countries that have well-established institutional traditions and mature legal orders.' Were it otherwise, why would there be an established practice of award-holders settling for significant percentage reductions of the amount of award?[20]

---

[14] Identified as the weakest feature of the arrangements for the Singapore International Commercial Court, D Wong, 'The Rise of the International Commercial Court…' (2014) 33 CJQ 205,226; see also Singapore International Commercial Court Committee (2013): <https://www.mlaw.gov.sg/content/dam/minlaw/corp/News/Annex%20A%20-%20SICC%20Committee%20Report.pdf>), paras 42 ff.

[15] BORN (2013), 152, and generally chapter 6; and see pp 10–11.

[16] C Bühring-Uhle, *Arbitration and Mediation in International Business* (2nd edn, Kluwer, The Hague, 2006), 60, 66, 68.

[17] On the Hague Convention on Choice of Court Agreements (2005), Gary Born, *International Arbitration and Forum Selection Agreements: Drafting and Enforcing* (4th edn, Kluwer, Netherlands, 2013), 24. Hence the exhortation in *American Law Institute/UNIDROIT'S Principles of Transnational Civil Procedure* (Cambridge University Press, 2006), Principle 30: '*Recognition: A final judgment awarded in another forum in a proceeding substantially compatible with these Principles must be recognized and enforced unless substantive public policy requires otherwise. A provisional remedy must be recognized in the same terms.* Comment: P-30B …a judgment given in a proceeding substantially compatible with these Principles ordinarily should have the same effect as judgments rendered after a proceeding under the laws of the recognizing state. Principle 30 is therefore a principle of equal treatment… Only the limited exception for non-recognition based on substantive public policy is allowed when the foreign proceedings were conducted in substantial accordance with these principles.'

[18] J Paulsson, *The Idea of Arbitration* (Oxford University Press, 2013), 264.

[19] *ibid.*

[20] Queen Mary College (London) Survey of Arbitration Users (2008): 'Corporate Attitudes and Practices: Recognition and Enforcement of Foreign Awards' <http://www.arbitration.qmul.ac.uk/

1.08 *Factor (vi): Confidentiality.*[21] Although England has endorsed arbitral confidentiality,[22] not all legal systems have promoted that feature[23] (further on this factor see chapter 7). Globally, it has been said that arbitral confidentiality has 'suffered considerable damage'.[24] A 2006 poll of 53 leading arbitration practitioners records that confidentiality was third in the list of perceived advantages (after neutrality of the forum and cross-border enforcement of awards).[25] Born (2014)

---

docs/123294.pdf>: p 9 ('54 % of the corporations surveyed negotiated a settlement amounting to over 50 % of the award; 35 % settled for an amount in excess of 75 % of the award.'

[21] *Andrews on Civil Processes*, vol 2, *Arbitration and Mediation* (Intersentia, Cambridge, Antwerp, Portland, 2013), chapter 8; M Pryles, 'Confidentiality', in LW Newman and RD Hill (eds), *The Leading Arbitrators' Guide to International Arbitration* (3rd edn, New York, 2014), chapter 5; noting, at 110 n 2, another's conclusion that confidentiality was in fact the most important factor: H Bagner, 'Confidentiality- A Fundamental Principle in Commercial Arbitration' (2001) 18 Jo of Int'l Arbitration 243; generally, I Smeureanu, *Confidentiality in International Commercial Arbitration* (Kluwer, Deventer, 2011).

[22] *Andrews, ibid.*

[23] Gary Born, *International Arbitration and Forum Selection Agreements: Drafting and Enforcing* (4th edn, Kluwer, Netherlands, 2013), 11–12; M Pryles, 'Confidentiality', in LW Newman and RD Hill (eds), *The Leading Arbitrators' Guide to International Arbitration* (3rd edn, New York, 2014), chapter 5; UNCITRAL's *Notes on Organizing Arbitral Proceedings* (2012 edn), paragraph 31; CA Rogers and JC Jeng, 'The Ethics of International Arbitrators', in Newman and Hill, *op cit*, chapter 7, at 203; *Redfern and Hunter on International Arbitration* (6th edn, Oxford University Press, 2015), 2.161 ff, noting *Esso Australia Resources Ltd* v. *Plowman* (1995) 193 CLR 10, H Ct Aust (criticised P Neill, 'Confidentiality in Arbitration' (1996) 12 Arb Int 287; and considered by Pryles, *op cit.* at 111–122); *Commonwealth of Australia* v. *Cockatoo Dockyard Pty Ltd* (1995) 36 NSWLR 662; on US decisions, *Redfern and Hunter*, *op cit*, at 2.173 ff and M Pryles, 'Confidentiality', in Newman and Hill, *op cit*, chapter 5, at 137–140; on Swedish law, *Redfern and Hunter*, *op cit*, 2.176 and Pryles, *op cit*, at 140–142; French law, *Redfern and Hunter*, *op cit*, 2.182 and Pryles, *op cit.*, at 142; ICSID decisions, *Redfern and Hunter*, *op cit*, 2.184 ff; World Intellectual Property Organization decisions, *Redfern and Hunter*, *op cit*, 2.193 to 2.195 and on other institutional rules 2.190 to 2.192, Pryles, *op cit*, 150–151. And for the NZ Arbitration Act, 1996, section 14, Pryles, *op cit.*, at 143. For analysis of institutional rules, Pryles, *op cit*, at 147 ff. And on the movement towards 'transparency' in certain spheres of arbitration, see the new Article 1(4) on transparency in UNCITRAL Arbitration Rules (2013) <http://www.uncitral.org/pdf/english/texts/arbitration/arb-rules-2013/UNCITRAL-Arbitration-Rules-2013-e.pdf> more generally on transparency, K-H Böchstiegel, 'Perspectives on Future Developments in International Arbitration', in Newman and Hill, *op cit*, chapter 12, at 327; and A Malatesta and R Sali (eds), *The Rise of Transparency in International Arbitration: The Case for the Anonymous Publication of Arbitration Awards* (Juris, New York, 2013) (also containing surveys of systems and institutional rules by various contributors); earlier, concerning publication of anonymous awards, J Lew, 'The Case for the Publication of Arbitration Awards', in JC Schultz and A van den Berg (eds), *The Article of Arbitration: Essays on International Arbitration, Liber Amicorum Pieter Sanders* (Kluwer, Deventer, 1982), 223.

[24] M Hunter and A Phillips, 'The Duties of an Arbitrator', in LW Newman and RD Hill (eds), *The Leading Arbitrators' Guide to International Arbitration* (3rd edn, New York, 2014), chapter 20, at 486.

[25] C Bühring-Uhle, *Arbitration and Mediation in International Business* (2nd edn, Kluwer, The Hague, 2006), 107–109.

summarises the position by noting 'empirical'[26] and 'anecdotal'[27] support for 'confidentiality' as having 'substantial value'; but he also notes[28] that 'different jurisdictions have arrived at materially different salutations…and institutional rules continue to provide divergent treatments of the subject of confidentiality.' The Queen Mary College (2010) report found that 65 % of respondents did not regard the absence of confidentiality in court proceedings as a 'principal' reason for choosing arbitration.[29] Some foreign court systems might be prepared to display flexibility. For example, in Singapore the International Commercial Court might be prepared to hold some hearings *in camera*.[30] Born also notes that court proceedings are more likely to attract media attention than confidential arbitral proceedings: media bias in favour of local parties might become significant.[31] Conversely, disclosure of a local party's embarrassing malpractices might engender local hostility.[32]

1.2 The Three Pillars of International Commercial Arbitration

1.09 (i) *Agreement.*[33] Nearly all commercial arbitration presupposes an arbitration agreement (exceptions arise where arbitration is mandatory, that is, to the exclusion of other forms of dispute resolution, according to national statute, or where the opportunity for arbitration is created under Treaty). Therefore, this is the first fundamental element of arbitration. This might involve an *ex ante* arbitration agreement, following by a reference to arbitration. Or it might involve an 'after-the-event' arbitration reference. The agreement defines the scope of the arbitral tribunal's powers. The notion of consensus is especially prominent in the Arbitration Act 1996 (section 1(b), *the parties should be free to agree how their disputes are resolved,*

[26] Gary Born, *International Commercial Arbitration* (2nd edn, Kluwer, Netherlands, 2014) (3 vols), 2781 n 6 (adopting the preceding note's findings and Queen Mary College (London) Survey of Arbitration Users (2006): 'International Arbitration: Corporate Attitudes and Practices <http://www.arbitration.qmul.ac.uk/docs/123295.pdf>: p 6 (54 %, citing 'privacy') (wrongly citing Queen Mary College 2008) and Queen Mary College (London) Survey of Arbitration Users (2010): 'Choices in International Arbitration' <http://www.arbitration.qmul.ac.uk/docs/123290.pdf> chart 25 p 29 (62 % saying 'very important').

[27] Gary Born, *op cit*, 2781 n 7.

[28] *ibid*, 2783.

[29] Queen Mary College (London) Survey of Arbitration Users (2010): 'Choices in International Arbitration' <http://www.arbitration.qmul.ac.uk/docs/123290.pdf> Chart 28 p 30 (136 respondents, mostly 'counsel', international or external).

[30] Singapore International Commercial Court Committee (2013), paras 32 and 33 <https://www.mlaw.gov.sg/content/dam/minlaw/corp/News/Annex%20A%20-%20SICC%20Committee%20Report.pdf>.

[31] Gary Born, *International Arbitration and Forum Selection Agreements: Drafting and Enforcing* (4th edn, Kluwer, Netherlands, 2013), 5.

[32] *ibid.*

[33] Andrea Marco Steingruber, *Consent in International Arbitration* (Oxford University Press, 2012).

subject only to such safeguards as are necessary in the public interest). But that statute also makes clear that there are matters beyond the pale of party control. These are the 'non-negotiable' *mandatory* norms listed in Schedule 1 to the Arbitration Act 1996. Notable examples of arbitral norms or mechanisms which cannot be excluded by party agreement are:

section 9 (the English court's duty to stay English court proceedings, unless the arbitration agreement is 'null and void, inoperative, or incapable of being performed': **4.02**);
section 24 (power to apply to the court to remove an arbitrator, on specified statutory grounds);
section 29 (general civil immunity of arbitrator acting without bad faith: **5.27**); and
sections 67 and 68 (respectively supervision, on party application, of the jurisdiction of the tribunal and of the procedural regularity of the process: **8.01**).

Conversely, the parties are at liberty to exclude section 69 of the Arbitration Act 1996, provided clear language is used: **8.21**.

1.10 Agreement enables the parties to select arbitrators, and generally to determine how the process will be conducted. Therefore agreement underpins these leading features (already mentioned) of arbitration:

(a) *neutrality*: parties are especially attracted to arbitration because it offers the chance to reduce or eliminate the national advantage of 'home territory' enjoyed by a resident litigant when conducting a case in court; thus, when agreeing arrangements for arbitration, the seat can be chosen in a neutral jurisdiction, or at least non-local arbitral tribunal members can be selected to achieve a balance; in short, 'neutrality' (national, regional, political, and cultural) is a leading reason for choosing arbitration (**1.03**);
(b) *flexible process*: arbitration offers the prospect of flexible procedural arrangements (**1.05**);
(c) *confidentiality*: arbitral procedures are presumed to be confidential (**7.01** and **1.08**); but this can be varied by party consensus; in English law the basis of confidentiality is an implied term of the arbitration agreement.

1.11 The parties' 'freedom of contract'(see also, in the context of English contract law, principle 1 at **10.04**) is a leading feature of the Arbitration Act 1996 (as noted in section 1 of: *the parties should be free to agree how their disputes are resolved, subject only to such safeguards as are necessary in the public interest*). This freedom enables them to determine, or at least influence, how the repertoire of procedural measures should be applied in their particular case. Parties to arbitration can shape their 'alternative' to ordinary court procedure.[34]

1.12 However, the parties' autonomy is qualified by the Arbitration Act 1996s 'mandatory' provisions, that is, matters which cannot be consensually excluded

---

[34] That the parties' agreement takes priority over the arbitrator's regulation of the proceedings is emphasised, and elaborated, by the Departmental Advisory Committee Report (1996), at [154] to [162], and [173] to [175]; generally on this topic, GA Bermann and LA Mistelis (eds), *Mandatory Rules in International Arbitration* (Juris, New York, 2011).

(conversely, *Russell* supplies a helpful checklist of non-mandatory issues which can be modified by party agreement).[35] The mandatory matters include the fundamental values of impartiality and a reasonable opportunity to participate in the proceedings (*audi alteram partem*).[36] Such core elements of protection ensure that the parties are recipients of civilised justice. Furthermore, an award will be enforceable transnationally only if basic standards of procedural fairness have been respected.[37] Schedule 1 specifies the relevant 'mandatory' provisions.[38] At first sight, these mandatory provisions might appear to be completely miscellaneous. However, they can be grouped under six headings, namely provisions which: (i) enable the English courts to enforce arbitration agreements[39]; (ii) concern matters of timing[40]; (iii) enable the court to preserve the integrity of the arbitral process[41]; (iv) enable the court to provide support for that process[42]; (v) prescribe the core responsibilities of the arbitral participants[43]; (vi) confer immunity upon arbitrators[44]; or (vii) otherwise protect the arbitrator from unfairness.[45]

---

[35] *Russell on Arbitration* (24th edn, London, 2015), 2.066.

[36] On impartiality, **6.01**.

[37] New York Convention on the Recognition and Enforcement of Foreign Arbitral Awards (1958), Article V1(b).

[38] Sections 9 to 11, Arbitration Act 1996 (stay of legal proceedings); section 12 (power of court to extend agreed time limits); section 13 (application of Limitation Acts); section 24 (power of court to remove arbitrator); section 26(1) (effect of death of arbitrator); section 28 (liability of parties for fees and expenses of arbitrators); section 29 (immunity of arbitrator); section 31 (objection to substantive jurisdiction of tribunal); section 33 (general duty of tribunal); section 37(2) (items to be treated as expenses of arbitrators); section 40 (general duty of parties); section 43 (securing the attendance of witnesses); section 56 (power to withhold award in case of non-payment); section 60 (effectiveness of agreement for payment of costs in any event); section 66 (enforcement of award); sections 67 and 68 (challenging the award: substantive jurisdiction and serious irregularity), and sections 70 and 71 (supplementary provisions; effect of order of court) so far as relating to those sections; section 72 (saving for rights of person who takes no part in proceedings); section 73 (loss of right to object); section 74 (immunity of arbitral institutions, etc); section 75 (charge to secure payment of solicitors' costs).

[39] Sections 9 and 11, Arbitration Act 1996 (stay of legal proceedings).

[40] Section 12, *ibid* ('limitation' under general law); section 13 (time limits otherwise imposed).

[41] Section 24, *ibid* (power of court to remove arbitrator); section 31 (objection to substantive jurisdiction of tribunal); sections 67 and 68 (challenging the award: substantive jurisdiction and serious irregularity).

[42] Section 43, *ibid* (securing the attendance of witnesses); section 66 (enforcement of awards).

[43] Sections 33 and 40, *ibid.*

[44] Section 29, *ibid* (immunity of arbitrators if acting otherwise than in bad faith, and subject to a qualification concerning resignation); section 74 (immunity of arbitral institutions, etc).

[45] Section 28, *ibid* (liability of parties for fees and expenses of arbitrators); section 37(2) (items to be treated as expenses of arbitrators); section 56 (power to withhold award in case of non-payment); section 26(1) (effect of death of arbitrator is made mandatory out of an abundance of caution—it is doubtful whether parties can contemplate an award from the grave (or graves)); furthermore, section 26(2) (also rendered mandatory) deals with the distinct question of the death of a person by whom an arbitrator was appointed—such an appointor's death does not revoke the appointee's authority.

1.13 (ii) *Arbitral Autonomy (Restricted Judicial Intervention)*. This is the second fundamental element of arbitration: that the arbitral process should be substantially free from judicial interference.[46] The main manifestations of this principle are:

(a) (judicial support and restraint: the courts provide support for the system of arbitration, but they are not expected to intervene excessively during the process); the 'pro-arbitration' sentiment has grown; but it is too early to say that it has become the dominant judicial attitude.
(b) *Kompetenz-Kompetenz*: arbitral tribunals enjoy the capacity to make a provisional determination of the validity and scope of their (suggested) jurisdiction (**2.52**);
(c) *confidentiality*: the courts respect and give effect to the implied consensual status of confidentiality; this covers both the process, notably the parties' contentions and evidence, and the award (**7.01**);
(d) *finality*: arbitral awards are not subject to appeal on the factual merits (**8.19** and **8.20**) or on points of foreign law (**8.19**); but in England there is a restricted possibility of the High Court hearing an appeal on a point of English law (for examination of section 69 of the Arbitration Act 1996, **8.04**).

1.14 In many states, and not only England,[47] the courts support arbitration and do not regard it with suspicion.[48] Perhaps, to quote the Marriage Service within the 1549 *Book of Common Prayer* (England), we might even speak of an indissoluble contract between courts and arbitration, importing a mutual obligation '*to have and to holde from this day forwarde, for better, for wurse, for richer, for poorer, in sickenes, and in health, to love and to cherishe, til death us departe.*' The marriage between courts and arbitration is at times tempestuous (compare the *West Tankers* affair: **4.22**), at other times harmonious. But the relationship is always interesting. The marriage has not broken down: too many depend on its success. (Or, as one

---

[46] eg, (including rich citation of other literature), Luca Radicati di Brozolo, 'The Impact of National Law and Courts on International Commercial Arbitration': Mythology, Physiology, Pathology, Remedies and Trends' (2011) 3 *Cahiers de l'Arbitrage: Paris Jo of Int'l Arbitration* 663, and 'The Control System of Arbitral Awards' (2011) ICCA Congress Series 74; Wang Shengchang and Cao Lijun, 'The Role of National Courts and *Lex Fori* in International Commercial Arbitration', in LA Mistelis and JDM Lew (eds), *Pervasive Problems in International Arbitration* (The Hague, 2006), 155–184; H Alvarez, 'Autonomy of the International Arbitration Process', *ibid,* at 119–140; JDM Lew, 'Achieving the Dream: Autonomous Arbitration?', in JDM Lew and LA Mistelis (eds), *Arbitration Insights: Twenty Years of the Annual Lecture of the School of International Arbitration* (The Hague, 2007), 455–484; compare, for emphasis on the fact and utility of measured national support, SC Boyd, 'The Role of National Law and National Courts in England', in JDM Lew (ed), *Contemporary Problems in International Arbitration* (London, 1986), 149–163; and JMH Hunter, 'Judicial Assistance for the Arbitrator', *ibid,* 195–206.

[47] J Paulsson, 'Interference by National Courts', in LW Newman and RD Hill (eds), *The Leading Arbitrators' Guide to International Arbitration* (3rd edn, New York, 2014), chapter 2.

[48] *Redfern and Hunter on International Arbitration* (6th edn, Oxford University Press, 2015), 7.04 ff.

arbitrator suggested,[49] 'arbitration and the courts are joined at the hip': an allusion, in particular, to the need for awards to be enforced).

1.15 However, the Arbitration Act 1996 makes clear that arbitral autonomy must be accorded respect. at the same time the Act states that there are limits to arbitral autonomy: *in matters governed by this Part the court should not intervene except as provided by this Part.* (section 1(c), 1996 Act), Ultimately the arbitration system's authority and effectiveness require judicial support. Such support can be national, for example, assistance in enforcing arbitral agreements, and provisional relief, especially before arbitral proceedings begin, appointment or removal of arbitrators, the gathering of evidence from recalcitrant witnesses. Such judicial orders are normally made available by the courts of the 'seat'. But at the enforcement stage there is also a need for international judicial co-operation and multi-state support, principally in accordance with the New York Convention (1958). Courts not only assist, they also recognise legitimate restrictions. They are responsible for the maintenance of the rule of law and compliance with the tribunal's arbitral mandate. And so courts can ensure that arbitrators do not distort their jurisdictional licence by purporting to decide matters not referred to the tribunal, or by applying legal rules not authorised by that mandate. Nor can the tribunal illegitimately treat non-parties as parties if they are not indeed true parties to the arbitration agreement. Another example of legitimate judicial intrusion upon the seclusion of arbitration is that confidentiality has its limits. For there are situations where the wider interests of justice justify, indeed require, disclosure of information ordinarily protected by arbitral confidentiality (**7.11**).

1.16 (iii) *International Enforcement*. This is the third fundamental element of arbitration. It is widely recognised that the New York Convention (1958) ('NYC (1958)') provides an invaluable mechanism for international enforcement of arbitral awards (**9.01**). That instrument also links with 'autonomy': for there are restricted grounds upon which the enforcing court is permitted to decline recognition or enforcement (Article V of the NYC (1958): **9.07**). The NYC (1958) also links with the concept of 'agreement'. For it is an obvious feature of an arbitration agreement (unless expressly qualified) that the parties have not merely agreed to pursue that form of dispute resolution to the exclusion of other available forms,[50] but the parties have further agreed that they will abide by the result and give effect to the award.[51] In the absence of spontaneous compliance with the award, the NYC (1958) strengthens the award-creditor's hand, by enabling that party to seek enforcement in a foreign state (other than the seat where the award was granted). But there is a further connection between the third fundamental element, international enforcement, and the first fundamental element, agreement. The NYC (1958) permits the enforcing court to decline recognition or enforcement if the arbitral tribunal has not respected

[49] CIArb symposium, Cambridge, July 2015.

[50] Such an exclusive undertaking is 'enforced' by stays—and the English court has no discretion in this matter, according to section 9(4), Arbitration Act 1996, **4.02**DOUBLEHYPHEN- or the exclusive undertaking can be positively enforced by other judicial remedies, notably anti-suit injunctions: **4.11**.

[51] *Mustill & Boyd, Commercial Arbitation* (2nd edn, London, 1989), 103.

the agreed limits of the arbitration reference, because that tribunal has wrongly attributed jurisdiction to itself, or it was not constituted in accordance with the parties' agreement, or a supposed party is not truly a party to the arbitration reference, or the terms of the reference have been misapplied (for example, the tribunal has applied remedies excluded by the arbitration reference, or it has based itself on a system of law which is not consistent with the parties' agreement).

1.3 Need for a Transnational 'Mentality' in the Conduct of International Arbitration

1.17 Pierre Lalive (1923–2014), drawing on extensive experience of international commercial arbitration, long ago castigated some lawyers, notably counsel, for bringing to the arbitral chamber blinkered minds and inappropriately national forensic techniques[52]:

> *'...in any important or complex international arbitration case, each side should preferably be represented by an "international" team of counsel (and/or consultants), by which I do not mean only a team composed of different nationalities or legal backgrounds, but also and foremost counsel trained in comparative and foreign law and specially trained to deal with international arbitral cases.'*

He added[53]:

> *'Many international arbitrators I know frequently note with regret the lack of "international and comparative outlook", the lack of "arbitral feeling and diplomacy" evinced by too many counsel, who merely transpose into international arbitration proceedings their traditional national recipes and the "aggressive" tactics which they use in their own courts.'*

Bibliography

International Commercial Arbitration

AIJA (1994) Evidence in arbitration proceedings. AIJA Publications, London. Association Internationale des Jeunes Avocats
Aksen G et al (eds) (2005) Global reflections on international law, commerce and dispute resolution: liber amicorum in honour of Robert Briner. ICC Publications, Paris
Andrea Marco Steingruber (2012) Consent in international arbitration. Oxford University Press, Oxford

[52] 'International arbitration-teaching and research', in JDM Lew (ed), *Contemporary Problems in International Arbitration* (London, 1986), 16, at 17; see also JDM Lew, 'Fusion of Common Law and Civil Law Traditions in International Arbitration', in P Wautelet, T Kruger, G Coppens (eds), *The Practice of Arbitration: Essays in Honour of Hans van Houtte* (Hart, Oxford, 2012), 1 to 14.
[53] *ibid.*

Bachand F, Gélinas F (eds) (2013) The UNCITRAL model Law after 25 years: global perspectives on international commercial arbitration. Juris, New York
Berger B, Schneider ME (eds) (2014) Inside the black box: how arbitral tribunals operate and reach their decisions. Juris, New York
Bermann GA, Mistelis LA (eds) (2011) Mandatory rules in international arbitration. Juris, New York
Blackaby N, Partasides C (eds) (2009) Redfern and Hunter on international arbitration, 5th edn, Oxford University Press
Born G (2010) International arbitration: cases and materials. Wolters Kluwer, Aspen
Born G (2013) International arbitration and forum selection agreements: drafting and enforcing, 4th edn. Kluwer, The Hague
Born G (2014) International arbitration: law and practice, vol 3, 2nd edn. Kluwer, Deventer
Bray D, Bray HL (eds) (2013) Post-hearing issues in international arbitration. Juris, New York
Brekoulakis S (2010) Third parties in international commercial arbitration. Oxford University Press, Oxford
Buhring-Uhle C, Kirchhoff L, Scherer G (2006) Arbitration and mediation in international business, 2nd edn. Kluwer, The Hague
Cadiet L, Jeuland E, Clay T (eds) (2005) Médiation et Arbitrage: Alternative Dispute Resolution-Alternative a la justice ou justice alternative? Perspectives comparatives. Lexis Nexis: Litec, Paris
Carbonneau TE (2014) The law and practice of arbitration, 5th edn. Juris, New York
Collier J, Lowe V (1999) The settlement of disputes in international law. Oxford University Press, Oxford
Craig WL, Park WW, Paulsson J (2000) International chamber of commerce arbitration, 3rd edn. Oceana/ICC Publishing, Dobbs Ferry
Croft C, Kee C, Waincymer J (2013) A guide to the UNCITRAL arbitration rules. Cambridge University Press, Cambridge
Draetta U (2011) Behind the scenes in international arbitration. Juris, New York
Drahozal CR, Naimark RW (eds) (2005) Towards a science of international arbitration: collected empirical research. Kluwer, Deventer
Esplugues C, Barona S (eds) (2014) Global perspectives on ADR. Intersentia, Cambridge/Antwerp/Portland. (mediation and arbitration)
Finizio SP, Speller D (2010) A practical guide to international commercial arbitration: assessment, planning and strategy. City and Financial Publishing, London
Fouchard P, Gaillard E, Goldman B (1999) International commercial arbitration. Gaillard E, Savage J (eds). Kluwer, The Hague
Gaillard E (ed) (2005) Anti-suit injunctions in international arbitration. Juris, New York
Gaillard E (ed) (2010) The review of international arbitral awards. Juris, New York
Gaitis JM (ed) (2014) The college of commercial arbitrators' guide to best practices in commercial arbitration. Juris, New York
Greenberg S, Kee C, Weeramantry JR (2011) International Commercial Arbitration: An Asia-Pacific Perspective. Cambridge University Press, Cambridge. (2nd edn, forthcoming)
Hanotiau B (2005) Complex arbitrations: multiparty, multicontract, multi-issue and class actions. Kluwer, The Hague
Heilbron H (2008) A practical guide to international arbitration in London. Informa, London
ICCA's guide to the interpretation of the 1958 New York Convention (2011) (International Council for Commercial Arbitration). Available: http://www.arbitration-icca.org
Karton J (2013) The culture of international arbitration and the evolution of contract law. Oxford University Press, Oxford
Kun F (2013) Arbitration in China: a legal and cultural analysis. Hart Publishing, Cambridge
Lew JDM (ed) (1987) Contemporary problems in international arbitration. Kluwer, The Hague
Lew JDM (ed) (2001) International arbitration law library series set (many volumes). Kluwer, The Hague

Lew JDM, Mistelis L, Kröll S (2003) Comparative international commercial arbitration. Kluwer, The Hague
Lew JDM, Mistelis LA (eds) (2007) Arbitration insights: twenty years of the annual lecture of the school of international arbitration. Kluwer, The Hague
Luttrell S (2009) Bias challenges in international commercial arbitration. Kluwer, The Hague
Mistelis LA, Lew JDM (eds) (2006) Pervasive problems in international arbitration. Kluwer, The Hague
Newman LW, Hill RD (eds) (2014) The leading arbitrators' guide to international arbitration, 3rd edn. Juris, New York.
Newman LW, Ong C (eds) (2014) Interim measures in international arbitration. Juris, New York
Newman LW, Radine MJ (eds) (2014) Soft law in international arbitration. Juris, New York
Mistelis LA, Brekoulakis SL (eds) (2009). Arbitrability: international and comparative perspectives. Kluwer, The Hague
Moses ML (2012) The principles and practice of international commercial arbitration, 2nd edn. Cambridge University Press, New York
Park WW (2006) Arbitration of international business disputes: studies in law and practice. Oxford University Press, Oxford
Paulsson J, Sanders P, van den Berg AJ (eds) (2012), International handbook on commercial arbitration. Kluwer, The Hague
Poudret JF, Besson S (2007) Comparative law of international arbitration, 2nd edn. Thomson, London
Rovine AW (ed) (2012) Contemporary issues in international arbitration and mediation: the Fordham papers 2011. Martinus Nijhoff, Leiden
Sanders P (2004) The work of UNCITRAL on arbitration and conciliation, 2nd edn. Kluwer, The Hague
Schreuer C et al (eds) (2009) The ICSID convention: a commentary, 2nd edn. Cambridge University Press, Cambridge
Schütze RA (ed) (2013) Institutional arbitration: article-by-article commentary. Beck/Hart/Nomos, Munich
Schwebel SM (1987) International arbitration: three salient problems. Grotius Publications, Cambridge
Smeureanu I (2011) Confidentiality in international commercial arbitration. Kluwer, Deventer
Smit RH et al (eds) (2013) Comparison of international arbitration rules, 4th edn. Juris, New York
Tercier P (ed) (2011) Post-award issues. Juris, New York
van den Berg AJ (ed) (2012) Arbitration: the next fifty years. Kluwer, Deventer
Wautelet P, Kruger T, Coppens G (eds) (2012) The practice of arbitration: essays in Honour of Hans van Houtte. Hart, Oxford
Webster T (2015) Handbook of UNCITRAL arbitration, 2nd edn. Sweet & Maxwell, London
Weigand FB (2010) Practitioner's handbook on international commercial arbitration. Oxford University Press, Oxford

English Arbitration

Ambrose C, Maxwell K, Parry A (2010) London maritime arbitration, 3rd edn. Informa, London
Chitty on Contracts (2015) 31st edn. London, vol 2, ch 32
Dicey, Morris, and Collins on the Conflict of Laws (2012) 15th edn. LA Collins (gen ed), London. Ch 16 (and referring to other literature)
Heilbron H (2008) A practical guide to international arbitration in London. Informa, London
Jacobs R, Masters L, Stanley P (2011) Liability insurance in international arbitration: the Bermuda form, 2nd edn. Hart, Oxford

Joseph D (2015) Jurisdiction and arbitration agreements and their enforcement, 3rd edn. Sweet & Maxwell, London
Merkin R (2014) Arbitration law. Lloyd's of London Press, London. Looseleaf updating service
Mustill M, Boyd S (2001) Commercial arbitration: companion volume. Butterworths, London. Updating Commercial Arbitration (2nd edn)
Russell on Arbitration (2015) D Sutton et al. (eds) 24th edn. Sweet & Maxwell, London
Tackaberry J, Marriott A (eds) (2003) Bernstein's handbook of arbitration and dispute resolution practice., 4th edn. Thomson, London
Tweeddale A, Tweeddale K (2005) Arbitration of commercial disputes: international and english law and practice. Oxford University Press, Oxford 2005; paperback 2007
Wade S, Clifford P, Clanchy J (2015) A commentary on the LCIA arbitration rules 2014. Sweet & Maxwell, London

Arbitration in Other Systems

China: Kun F (2013) Arbitration in China: a legal and cultural analysis. Hart Publishing, Cambridge
China: Yang F (2015) Foreign-related arbitration in China. Cambridge University Press (2 vols)
French Law: Delvolvé, Pointon and Rouche (2003) French arbitration law and practice, 2nd edn. Kluwer, The Hague
French Law: Vidal D (2004) Droit francais de la'arbitrage commercial international. Guilino Editeurs, Paris (bilingual edition)
Roman Law: Roebuck D (2004) Roman arbitration. Holo Books, Oxford
Spanish arbitration law: Barona-Vilar S (2011) The legal framework of arbitration in spain…'. 16 ZZP Int 407
USA: Brunet E, Speidel RE, Sternlight JR, Ware SL (2006) Arbitration law in America: A critical assessment. Cambridge University Press, New York
USA: Carbonneau TE (2014) The law and practice of arbitration, 5th edn. Juris, New York
USA: Gaitis JM (ed) (2014) The college of commercial arbitrators' guide to best practices in commercial arbitration. Juris, New York

Arbitration: Theory and Fundamental Analysis

Gaillard E (2010) Legal theory of international arbitration. Martinus Nijhoff, Leiden/Boston
Paulsson J (2013) The idea of arbitration. Oxford University Press, Oxford

Chapter 2
Arbitration Agreements: Validity and Interpretation

Abstract At the heart of this chapter is the legal framework for establishing a valid arbitration agreement. Such an agreement must be in writing and sufficiently certain. But it might form part of a wider dispute-resolution clause which includes an obligation to engage in preliminary negotiation or to consider mediation, before proceeding to arbitration.

2.1 Introduction[1]

2.01 This chapter encompasses many points which arise from the central questions: is there a valid arbitration; what matters does it cover; and who are the parties? An 'arbitration agreement' involves (i) an advance commitment to arbitrate (followed by an *ex post facto* agreement to make a submission), or (ii) an agreement (not preceded by the anticipatory commitment mentioned at (i)) to refer a specific dispute to arbitration once such a dispute has arisen (of these two forms, (i) is more common). There can also be ancillary agreements concerning the need for negotiation or mediation prior to arbitration.

2.2 What Type of Dispute-Resolution Clause?

2.02 The assumption made in this work is that the parties have elected to pursue arbitration rather than to use the courts for the conduct of the main proceedings (for a variation, where one party has an option to opt out of the court process and commence arbitration proceedings, or the converse option, see, respectively, 2.08 and 2.09 below).

[1] G Born, *International Arbitration and Forum Selection Agreements: Drafting and Enforcing* (4th edn, Kluwer, Netherlands, 2013); A Briggs, *Agreements on Jurisdiction and Choice of Law* (Oxford University Press, 2008), chapter 12; D Joseph, *Jurisdiction and Arbitration Agreements and Their Enforcement* (3rd edn, London, 2015); CR Drahozal and RW Naimark (eds), *Towards a Science of International Arbitration: Collected Empirical Research* (Kluwer, 2005) (Part 3, 'Arbitration Clauses); Andrea Marco Steingruber, *Consent in International Arbitration* (Oxford University Press, 2012).

N. Andrews, *Arbitration and Contract Law*, Ius Gentium: Comparative Perspectives on Law and Justice 54, DOI 10.1007/978-3-319-27144-6_2

2.03 Nevertheless some brief remarks are necessary concerning court selection clauses (jurisdiction clauses). Sometimes the court acquires jurisdiction as a result of an exclusive jurisdiction agreement[2] (or a non-exclusive jurisdiction agreement),[3] or at any rate, the defendant's submission to the foreign court's jurisdiction.[4] An exclusive jurisdiction clause stipulates that legal disputes arising from the relevant transaction can only be litigated in the nominated jurisdiction, for example, the courts of London or Hong Kong.[5] A non-exclusive jurisdiction clause confers jurisdiction on the relevant nominated courts even though, in the absence of such a clause, that jurisdiction would not have been available to the parties.[6] An intermediate species is an exclusive jurisdiction clause requiring party A to right sue in forum X, where the defendant B has its place of business, if A chooses to become the claimant and, conversely, requiring party B to bring suit in forum Y, where defendant A has its place of business, if B chooses to become the claimant.[7] Another variation is for the bulk of disputes arising from a transaction to be subject to an exclusive jurisdiction clause, but particular categories of dispute to be excepted from that clause.[8] A further variation, a so-called 'asymmetrical' or 'one-sided' forum selection clause (either court/arbitration or arbitration/court), is for the parties to agree (for example) 'that all disputes relating to this Agreement shall be resolved exclusively in the Courts of Xanadu, unless party A chooses to bring action in Ruritania'[9] (and see 2.09 below on arbitration/court option clauses).

2.04 The stakes are high because the choice between court proceedings and arbitration can affect the result. As Gary Born notes[10]:

---

[2] G Born, *International Arbitration and Forum Selection Agreements: Drafting and Enforcing* (4th edn, Kluwer, Netherlands, 2013), chapter 2; A Briggs, *Agreements on Jurisdiction and Choice of Law* (Oxford University Press, 2008); D Joseph, *Jurisdiction and Arbitration Agreements and Their Enforcement* (3rd edn, London, 2015); A Briggs, 'The Subtle Variety of Jurisdiction Agreements' [2012] LMCLQ 364–381; T Hartley, *Choice-of-Court Agreements Under the European and International Instruments* (Oxford University Press, 2013); *Dicey, Morris and Collins on the Conflicts of Laws* (15th edn, London, 2012), 12–098 ff; see also RG Fentiman, *International Commercial Litigation* (2nd edn, Oxford University Press, 2015), 2.05 ff.

[3] The latter permits but does not require proceedings to be brought in the nominated forum; but there are complexities: *Dicey, Morris and Collins on the Conflicts of Laws* (15th edn, London, 2012), 12–107 and 12–108.

[4] *Dicey, Morris and Collins on the Conflicts of Laws* (15th edn, London, 2012), 11–124 ff.

[5] e.g., *Nomura International plc v. Banca Monte dei Paschi Di Siena Spa* [2013] EWHC 3187 (Comm); [2014] 1 WLR 1584 at [16], [17], [80] to [83], Eder J.

[6] *Deutsche Bank AG v. Highland Crusader Offshore Partners LP* [2009] EWCA Civ 725; [2010] 1 WLR 1023, at [50], [64], [105] and [106].

[7] G Born, *International Arbitration and Forum Selection Agreements: Drafting and Enforcing* (4th edn, Kluwer, Netherlands, 2013), 30–31: 'Although there is relatively limited precedent, national courts that have considered the issue have in principle upheld the enforceability of such clauses.'

[8] ibid, 27, commenting that these clauses can generate disputes concerning the scope of the excepted category.

[9] ibid, 29.

[10] ibid, 1.

> *'Almost every international commercial controversy poses a critical preliminary question—"Where, and by whom, will this dispute be decided?" The answer...often decisively affects a dispute's eventual outcome. It can mean the difference between winning and losing, between de minimis damages and a [very large monetary] award.'*

Careful and perceptive negotiation of the appropriate dispute-resolution provision is unusual and receives little attention. It is the Cinderella clause.

2.05 Problems have arisen when a breach (or a connected set of breaches) of contract (or connected contracts) is susceptible to court proceedings or arbitration, so that the court has to consider the problem of parallel and fragmented litigation.[11]

2.06 Another difficulty is when the main transaction is subject to one form of dispute resolution, but the guarantee agreement between the relevant creditor and a third party surety is subject to a different form of dispute resolution.[12]

2.07 *'Hybrid' 'Unilateral' 'Optional', 'Non-mutual' or 'Asymmetrical' Dispute-resolution Clauses Valid under English law.*[13] Such a clause enables one party to opt out of court proceedings in England by taking the case to arbitration or, conversely, such a clause can permit a party to opt out of arbitration and instead bring proceedings before an English court. However, Moore-Bick LJ in the *Sulamerica* case (2012)[14] indicated that the parties must spell out such a one-sided variation. This is because this type of arrangement is quite exceptional. There are two permutations: court proceedings, with an unilateral escape clause to arbitration; and the converse.

2.08 *Court/Arbitration Option.* In *NB Three Shipping Ltd* v. *Harebell Shipping Ltd* (2004) Morison J upheld[15] the following clause: '*The courts of England shall*

---

[11] *Deutsche Bank AG v. Tongkah Harbour Public Co Ltd* [2011] EWHC 2251 (QB); [2012] 1 All ER (Comm) 194; [2011] Arb LR 20, at [29], Blair J; *Sebastian Holdings Inc v. Deutsche Bank AG* [2010] EWCA Civ 998; [2011] 2 All ER (Comm) 245; [2011] 1 Lloyd's Rep 106, at [39] to [49], per Thomas LJ (considering, notably *Satyam Computer Services Ltd v. Upaid Systems Ltd* [2008] EWCA Civ 487; [2008] 2 All ER (Comm) 465; *UBS AG v. HSH Nordbank AG* [2009] EWCA Civ 585; [2010] 1 All ER (Comm) 727; [2009] 2 Lloyd's Rep 272).

[12] *Deutsche Bank AG v. Tongkah Harbour Public Co Ltd* [2011] EWHC 2251 (QB); [2012] 1 All ER (Comm) 194; [2011] Arb LR 20, at [30], Blair J (permitting the guarantee court claim to run separately from the main arbitration claim).

[13] *NB Three Shipping Ltd v. Harebell Shipping Ltd* [2004] EWHC 2001(Comm); [2005] 1 All ER (Comm) 200; [2005] 1 Lloyd's Rep 509, Morison J (applied in *Deutsche Bank AG v. Tongkah Harbour Public Co Ltd* [2011] EWHC 2251 (QB); [2012] 1 All ER (Comm) 194; [2011] Arb LR 20, Blair J); *Law Debenture Trust Corp plc v. Elektrim Finance BV and others* [2005] EWHC 1412 (Ch); [2005] 2 All ER (Comm) 476; [2005] 2 Lloyd's Rep 755, Mann J; on this topic, S Nesbitt and H Quinlan, 'The Status and Operation of Unilateral or Optional Arbitration Clauses' (2006) 22 Arbitration International 133; D Joseph, *Jurisdiction and Arbitration Agreements and Their Enforcement* (3rd edn, London, 2015), 4.31; R Merkin, *Arbitration Law* (London, 2014), 3.16, 8.16; *Russell on Arbitration* (24th edn, London, 2015), 2.018 and 2.019; see drafting suggestions in G Born, *International Arbitration and Forum Selection Agreements: Drafting and Enforcing* (4th edn, Kluwer, Netherlands, 2013), 28–9, 121–2.

[14] [2012] EWCA Civ 638; [2013] 1 WLR 102, at [30].

[15] *NB Three Shipping Ltd v. Harebell Shipping Ltd* [2004] EWHC 2001(Comm); [2005] 1 All ER (Comm) 200; [2005] 1 Lloyd's Rep 509, Morison J (applied in *Deutsche Bank AG v. Tongkah*

have jurisdiction to settle any disputes which may arise out of or in connection with this Charterparty but the Owner shall have the option of bringing any dispute hereunder to arbitration.' Here the charterer commenced court proceedings, but the owner's application for a stay under section 9, Arbitration Act 1996 was sustained, effect being given to the owner's right to elect to arbitrate instead. Morison J added[16] that the owner's option to choose arbitration '*would cease to be available if Owners took a step in the [court] action or they otherwise led Charterers to believe on reasonable grounds that the option to stay would not be exercised...*').

2.09 *Arbitration/Court Option.* In *Law Debenture Trust Corp plc* v. *Elektrim Finance BV* (2005)[17] the parties had agreed an arbitration clause under UNCITRAL Arbitration Rules, the seat being London. But one of the parties was given the option to use London court proceedings instead, if he so chose: Clause 29.7 provided that: '*Notwithstanding [the preceding agreement to arbitrate], [X, one of the parties, shall have] the exclusive benefit [and]...exclusive right, at their option, to apply to the courts of England, who shall have non-exclusive jurisdiction to settle any disputes which may arise out of or in connection with these presents ....*').

2.3 Arbitration Agreements and Contractual Imbalance

2.10 Furthermore, dispute-resolution clauses, including arbitration agreements, are nearly always an exercise in unequal power. Procedural choice (jurisdiction clauses, arbitration clauses, and variants) is seldom founded on equality of party strength. As we shall see, English law takes a stand in protecting consumers (see (1) below), but otherwise the validity of an arbitration agreement depends on the ordinary principles of contract law, such as the doctrines concerning incorporation (13.14), misrepresentation (12.01), and duress (12.19). Consider these examples of contractual imbalance in the context of arbitration agreements:

(1) *Company* v. *Individual*: Suppose that an academic author signs a publishing contract which is governed by the law of Erewhon.[18] The contract has been

---

Harbour Public Co Ltd [2011] EWHC 2251 (QB); [2012] 1 All ER (Comm) 194; [2011] Arb LR 20, Blair J).

[16] *NB Three Shipping*, ibid, at [11].

[17] [2005] EWHC 1412 (Ch); [2005] 2 All ER (Comm) 476; [2005] 2 Lloyd's Rep 755, Mann J.

[18] A Briggs, *Agreements on Jurisdiction and Choice of Law* (Oxford University Press, 2008), chapters 10 and 11; A Briggs, in AS Burrows and E Peel (eds), *Contract Terms* (Oxford University Press, 2007), chapter 15; on the *Rome I Regulation, Dicey, Morris and Collins on the Conflicts of Laws* (15th edn, London, 2012), chapters 32 and 33 (on Regulation (EC) No 593/2008); RG Fentiman, *International Commercial Litigation* (2nd edn, Oxford University Press, 2015), chapters 4 and 5. Where the chosen substantive law is foreign, that is, not the substantive system of the relevant forum, the problem of 'proof of foreign law' will arise: Dicey, Morris and Collins on the Conflicts of Laws (15th edn, London, 2012), chapter 9; RG Fentiman, *International Commercial Litigation* (2nd edn, Oxford, 2015), chapter 20 (and literature cited at 666 n 1); R Fentiman, 'Law, Foreign Laws, and Facts' (2006) 59 Current Legal Problems 391; Neil Andrews, *English Civil*

drawn up by the foreign publishing company situated in Erewhon and that company has inserted a clause stipulating that Erewhon will be the seat of an arbitration conducted under the laws of Erewhon (the publisher, but only that party, also has the 'asymmetrical' option whether to proceed by court proceedings rather than by arbitration).[19] Here there is significant inequality of power. The asymmetrical arbitration/jurisdiction clause is inserted by the powerful publishing house for its sole convenience and to secure home advantage. It should be noted that English law regards as necessarily 'unfair' an arbitration agreement which purports to bind a 'consumer' (whether or not a natural person) and relates to a pecuniary claim for less than £5,000.[20]

(2) *Big Company* v. *Small Company*: A commercial agent, based in America, agrees to solicit custom from the US Navy on behalf of a principal, a UK company. The agent's work will be done in the USA, where the goods will also be received by the US Navy. The agent accepts the principal's proposed arbitration clause which provides that any dispute arising will be heard by an arbitral tribunal whose seat will be Geneva. Here the arbitration agreement is not negotiated. Ostensibly the parties have opted for neutrality, but there is a significant inequality of power between the UK company and the USA commercial agent. The clause has been inserted on the initiative of the UK company. The parties have opted for 'neutrality': both parties will be playing 'away'. But it is more likely that the agent will wish to sue the principal, rather than vice versa. Geneva is an expensive venue and, for reasons of expense and distance, will not be attractive to the American agent.

(3) *Sovereign State* v. *Big Company*. Suppose that a sovereign state, Ruritania, contracts with Gush Oil Inc, a major foreign oil company, registered in Oceania, for the extraction of oil and gas from land in Ruritania. The transaction is governed by Ruritanian law. In the event of a dispute, the seat of the arbitration will be in Yonderstate. Here both parties are powerful legal entities. Again, the parties have opted for 'neutrality': both parties will be playing 'away'. But even a powerful corporation might not be able to match the resources of a large state (conversely, some small states might be weaker than large companies). The arbitration will prove expensive for both parties. But Ruritania, if sued by Gush

---

Justice and Remedies: Progress and Challenges: the Nagoya Lectures (Shinzan Sha Publishers, Tokyo, 2007), chapter 5; Neil Andrews, 'English Civil Proceedings: Proof of Foreign Law', in R Stürner and M Kawano (eds), *International Contract Litigation, Arbitration and Judicial Responsibility in Transnational Disputes* (Mohr Siebeck, Tübingen, Germany, 2011), 243–252; *Harley v Smith* [2010] EWCA Civ 78; [2010] CP Rep 33; on the Singapore International Commercial Court's innovative approach to proof of foreign law, D Wong, 'The Rise of the International Commercial Court…' (2014) 33 CJQ 205, 210, 214, 221–222.

[19] See text below on 'asymmetrical' clauses.

[20] Sections 89 to 91, Arbitration Act 1996 (as amended by Schedule 4, paras 30 to 33, Consumer Rights Act 2015); unless the claim is for a sum greater than £5,000 (Unfair Arbitration Agreements (Specified Amount) Order 1999 (SI 1999/2167); generally, R Merkin, *Arbitration Law* (London, 2014), 1.50 ff.

Oil Inc, has vast resources to delay the rendering of an award and its enforcement.

(4) *Shifting Economic Strength*. Power can shift during the life of a transaction. Suppose that, 6 years ago, a promising Ruritanian tennis-player, not yet a 'star', signed a promotion agreement which provided that the promoter, based in the United States of Xanadu, would gain 10 % of the player's sponsorship revenue. The agreement is terminable upon a 2-year notice by either party. There is an arbitration clause with the seat in Xanadu. At the time that the dispute falls for reference to arbitration, the player has become a very wealthy star, much richer than the promoter. And the tennis-player now lives (mostly) in Xanadu,[21] although he remains a Ruritanian citizen. Here the balance of advantage has tilted towards the tennis-player. His foreign status is nominal. He is now at home in Xanadu. Even an expensive arbitration holds no terror for him.

2.4 Drafting Issues

2.11 It is prudent to draft the arbitration agreement in some detail to avoid the danger of uncertainty and confusion. *Russell* (2015) supplies a helpful checklist of issues that might be addressed[22]:

(i) Have the parties been properly identified?
(ii) Is there a clear reference to arbitration?
(iii) What disputes are referred to arbitration?
(iv) Where is the seat of the arbitration?
(v) What is the law governing the substance of the dispute?
(vi) What is the law of the arbitration agreement?
(vii) Is there a choice of the procedural law to be applied by the arbitral tribunal?
(viii) How will the tribunal be appointed?
(ix) Is there an appointing authority?
(x) Is the tribunal to have any particular attributes or qualifications?
(xi) How many members of the tribunal will there be?
(xii) Are procedural and/or evidential rules or the rules of an institution to be adopted?
(xiii) What will be the language of the arbitration?
(xiv) Should the tribunal be given power to make provisional awards under section 39, Arbitration Act 1996?
(xv) Confidentiality: scope for specific provision;

[21] A variation on the facts of *Cody v Murray* [2013] EWHC 3448 (Ch) (no arbitration clause, but a tennis-player who became successful).

[22] *Russell on Arbitration* (24th edn, London, 2015), 2.066.

(xvi) Should determinations of preliminary points of law (section 45(1), Arbitration Act 1996) or appeals on points of English law (section 69, Arbitration Act 1996) be excluded?
(xvii) Is a waiver of sovereign immunity required?
(xviii) Should there be provision of multi-party arbitration, consolidation, or concurrent hearings?

There are also helpful practical comments on this matter in *Finizio and Speller* (2010).[23]

2.12 If the parties wish to nominate, for example, the LCIA (London Court of International Arbitration),[24] the following standard arbitration clause for future disputes is offered on its website[25]:

> *Future Disputes*
>
> *'Any dispute arising out of or in connection with this contract, including any question regarding its existence, validity or termination, shall be referred to and finally resolved by arbitration under the LCIA Rules, which Rules are deemed to be incorporated by reference into this clause.*
>
> *The number of arbitrators shall be [one/three].*
>
> *The seat, or legal place, of arbitration shall be [City and/or Country]. The language to be used in the arbitral proceedings shall be []. The governing law of the contract shall be the substantive law of [].'* (This next note cites LCIA's standard arbitration clause for existing disputes).[26]

2.13 *Over-Complex and Confused Dispute-Resolution Clauses*. Sometimes the dispute-resolution clause is confusing, convoluted, and poorly structured. In a development contract, which came to the author's attention, a composite dispute-resolution clause comprised these elements: (i) expert determination on technical matters arising under the construction phase of the development and concerning the adequacy of steps taken to procure planning permission; (ii) arbitration (although, curiously, 'not on points of law or matters of interpretation of the written contract'); (iii) High Court proceedings. The remedy sought at the time of the relevant dispute was specific performance (to compel a party to complete certain building obligations). But it was unclear whether that remedy was within the scope of the arbitral

---

[23] SP Finizio and D Speller, *A Practical Guide to International Commercial Arbitration: Assessment, Planning and Strategy* (London, 2010), chapter 2 ('drafting an agreement to arbitrate').

[24] On the interesting nineteenth century roots of this arbitral institution, http://www.lcia.org/LCIA/Our_History.aspx

[25] http://www.lcia.org/Dispute_Resolution_Services/LCIA_Recommended_Clauses.aspx (on the interesting nineteenth century roots of this arbitral institution, http://www.lcia.org/LCIA/Our_History.aspx).

[26] ibid: 'Existing disputes: A dispute having arisen between the parties concerning [], the parties hereby agree that the dispute shall be referred to and finally resolved by arbitration under the LCIA Rules. The number of arbitrators shall be [one/three]. The seat, or legal place, of arbitration shall be [City and/or Country]. The language to be used in the arbitral proceedings shall be []. The governing law of the contract [is/shall be] the substantive law of [].'

tribunal because of the 'land exception' to the availability of specific performance under section 48(5)(b) of the Arbitration Act 1996.[27]

2.5 Need for a Written Arbitration Agreement

2.14 *English Law*. Writing tends to prove easier to verify than the evidence of human memory or other ephemeral evidence. Such written evidence is helpful in verifying (a) that an agreement was made; (b) in determining whether it was intended to be binding; (c) fixing the relevant parties; (d) revealing the more precise contents and limits of the agreement.

2.15 The English Arbitration Act 1996 requires the arbitration agreement (including an individual 'submission agreement')[28] to be in writing[29] (including procedural amplification of the arbitration agreement during the course of a reference).[30] An unwritten arbitration agreement is not lacking in legal effect; but it will not be governed by the Act.[31] Although the Arbitration Act 1996 requires the arbitration agreement to be in writing, the position is very liberal indeed. Thus (i) the agreement need not be signed by the parties; (ii) and the agreement can be made orally but recorded in writing; according to section 5(6), 'written' or 'in writing' include 'its being recorded by any means', which will include electronic usages, such as e-mail; if not made in writing, the agreement can be 'evidenced in writing' provided the agreement 'is recorded by one of the parties, or by a third party, with the authority of the parties to the agreement', section 5(4)).[32]

2.16 In essence, the following elements apply for the purpose of the Arbitration Act 1996:

---

[27] *Telia Sonera AB v. Hilcourt (Docklands) Ltd* [2003] EHWC 3540, at [17] and [36], per Etherton J (considered, *Lesley McCaughan v. Belwood Homes Limited* [2011] NIMaster 11, at [11]); VV Veeder, 'Compound Interest and Specific Performance: "Arbitral Imperium" and ss 49 and 48 of the English Arbitration Act 1996', in *Interest, Auxiliary and Alternative Remedies in International Arbitration* (L Levy and F De Ly, eds) (ICC Institute of World Business Law, ICC Publishing, 2008), 81, at 83–89. But the parties can expressly extend the tribunal's powers to include the grant of specific performance in respect of land.

[28] Viz, an agreement to submit a particular dispute to arbitration once the dispute has already arisen.

[29] Section 5, Arbitration Act 1996.

[30] Section 5(1): … [A]nd any other agreement between the parties as to any matter is effective for the purposes of this Part only if in writing; Mustill & Boyd, *Commercial Arbitration: Companion Volume* (London, 2001), 20.

[31] The Departmental Advisory Committee Report (1996), paragraph 32; section 81(2)(b), Arbitration Act 1996; Mustill & Boyd, *Commercial Arbitration: Companion Volume* (London, 2001), 21, 371.

[32] Mustill & Boyd, *Commercial Arbitration: Companion Volume* (London, 2001), 263, note that a non-literal audio recording or filming of an oral agreement would satisfy the test; qury whether a voice mail message will be enough (it is submitted, by Andrews, that it will be, provided the message consummates, and thus records in reproducible audio form, the acceptance of an offer to arbitrate, or the message recites earlier agreed terms).

(a) there is no need for the agreement to be signed by the parties, or indeed signed at all[33]; (b) writing includes the information '*being recorded by any means*'[34];(c) the agreement can be:(i) itself made in writing[35]; or (ii) formed by exchanging written communications[36]; or (iii) evidenced in writing[37]; or (iv) made by reference[38] (and see paragraph at (v) below) to written terms (containing an arbitration agreement)[39]; or (v) it can result from the exchange of written submissions in arbitral or legal proceedings '*in which the existence of an agreement otherwise than in writing is alleged by one party against another party and denied by the other party in his response*'[40] (category (v) is, in effect, an example of estoppel by convention, on which generally see 10.15 at section (iii)(c)).

2.17 However, an arbitration agreement not in writing might be valid at Common Law, that is, outside the scope of the 1996 Act. An unwritten arbitration agreement is not lacking in legal effect; but it will not be governed by the Act.[41]

2.18 The modern principles for the interpretation of written contracts in English law apply to jurisdiction and arbitration agreements, including the court's power to recast botched text when the true intention is readily discernible.[42]

2.19 *Seat England and Wales: English Courts Alone can Determine whether the Writing Requirement is Satisfied.* If the seat is England and Wales or Northern Ireland, the English (etc) court (or the arbitral tribunal under section 30 of the 1996 Act) will determine the issue whether there is a valid arbitration agreement, that is, whether there has been compliance with the writing requirement of section 5 of the Arbitration Act 1996. The better view is that section 5 is the exclusive test and that

---

[33] Section 5(2)(a), Arbitration Act 1996.

[34] Section 5(6), ibid.

[35] Section 5(2)(a), ibid.

[36] Section 5(2)(b), ibid.

[37] Section 5(2)(c), ibid; section 5(4) explains that this can be an oral agreement which is (1) recorded by one party, or (2) by a third party, where (1) or (2) occurs with the authority of the parties to the agreement. Query whether all the terms have to be evidenced in writing? Such a view was taken on identical wording in another context in *RJT Consulting v. DM Engineering (Northern Ireland) Ltd* [2002] EWCA Civ 270; *Carillion Construction Ltd v. Devonport Royal Dockyard Ltd* [2005] EWCA Civ 1358.

[38] *Sea Trade Maritime Corp v. Hellenic Mutual War Risks Association (Bermuda) Ltd ('The Athena')* [2006] EWHC 2530 (Comm); [2007] 1 All ER (Comm) 183; [2007] 1 Lloyd's Rep 280, per Langley J, at [65] and [81]; considered in *Habas Sinai Ve Tibbi Gazlar Isthisal Endustri AS v. Sometal SAL* [2010] EWHC 29 (Comm); [2010] 1 All ER (Comm) 1143; [2010] 1 Lloyd's Rep 661, at [13], per Christopher Clarke J (distinguishing four categories of incorporation; the passage is too long to quote here); on these first instance decisions, see the note by Andrew and Keren Tweeddale (2010) 76 Arbitration 656–60.

[39] Section 5(3), ibid; on the need for an oral agreement to be capable of being treated as written when it is made by reference to written terms, notably in the context of salvage agreements: The Departmental Advisory Committee Report (1996), at [36].

[40] Section 5(5), ibid.

[41] The Departmental Advisory Committee Report (1996), at [32]; section 81(2)(b), Arbitration Act 1996; Mustill & Boyd, *Commercial Arbitration: Companion Volume* (London, 2001), 21, 371.

[42] *British American Insurance (Kenya) Ltd v. Matelec SAL* [2013] EWHC 3278 (Comm), Walker J.

there is no scope for referring the matter (additionally) to a different foreign test of written formality, in the event that the arbitration agreement is subject to non-English law.

2.20 *XL Insurance Case (2001)*. This last proposition must be amplified. It is arguable that the following case is authority that the putative foreign system of law might not apply because the English courts will treat the fact that England is the arbitral seat as itself a consensual preclusion of any further investigation (beyond satisfaction of the English requirements within section 5) of the arbitration agreement's compliance with formalities. In *XL Insurance Ltd* v. *Owens Corning* (2001) Toulson J did not find that the arbitration agreement was subject to foreign law.[43] Instead he simply held that an arbitration clause, stipulating that the seat should be in London, was validly made 'in writing' for the purpose of section 5.[44] In the *XL* case the main contract was subject to US law, but there had been no choice of law concerning the arbitration agreement. However, London was expressly made the seat of the arbitration. Once the seat is identified as London (under section 3, Arbitration Act 1996) then section 5 will be applied to determine whether the arbitration agreement is validly in writing for the purpose of the 1996 Act (in the absence of contrary provision; Toulson J unconvincingly suggesting[45] that section 5 is not a mandatory provision—see section 4(1) and Schedule 1). And so the issue whether the arbitration agreement was in writing fell to be decided in accordance with the section 5 test and by the English arbitral tribunal and the English High Court.[46] And so Toulson J granted anti-suit relief against the respondent to prevent it pursuing New York proceedings designed to demonstrate that the arbitration agreement failed to satisfy a more exacting New York test of written formality.

2.12 *Support for the XL Insurance Case (2001)*. Toulson J's analysis in the *XL* case (2001), see the preceding paragraph, was approved in the *Sulamerica* case (2012) by both Moore-Bick[47] and by Lord Neuberger MR.[48] It is submitted that the *XL* case (2001) shows that, once the seat is held to be England, the next issue is whether the English definition of 'written' or 'in writing' is satisfied for the purpose of section 5 of the 1996 Act. Section 5 is mandatory not in the sense that it is amongst the mandatory provisions listed in the Schedule to the 1996 Act, but in the fundamental sense that section 5 expressly requires an arbitration clause to be in writing if the Act is to govern the relevant arbitral proceedings. If section 5 is satis-

---

[43] [2001] CLC 914.

[44] [2001] CLC 914, 924.

[45] D Joseph, *Jurisdiction and Arbitration Agreements and Their Enforcement* (3rd edn, London, 2015), 3.49 challenges this, saying that section 5(1) makes clear that the 1996 Act will apply only if the agreement is in writing for the purpose of section 5.

[46] [2001] CLC 914, 924, per Toulson J.

[47] *Sulamerica Cia Nacional de Seguros SA v. Enesa Engenharia SA* [2012] EWCA Civ 638; [2013] 1 WLR 102, at [29].

[48] ibid, at [55].

fied, the result is to ensure availability of the English court as the supervisory and supportive court. There should not be a second-level possibility of impugning the arbitration agreement under the non-English law governing the arbitration agreement; for that would involve a split in functions between the supervisory court and a foreign court; and the undesirability of such a splitting of functions was affirmed by the Court of Appeal in *C* v. *D* (2007).[49]

2.22 *The Writing Requirement under the New York Convention (1958).* Article II(1) of the New York Convention (1958) (generally on the NYC (1958), see 9.01) refers to 'an agreement in writing under which the parties undertake to submit to arbitration all or any differences which have arisen or which may arise between them in respect of a defined legal relationship, whether contractual or not, concerning a subject matter capable of settlement by arbitration.' For this purpose, Article II(2) makes clear that '"agreement in writing" shall include an arbitral clause in a contract or an arbitration agreement, signed by the parties or contained in an exchange of letters or telegrams.' As *Redfern & Hunter* note 'the general view' is that Article II(2) does not apply the requirement of party signature to all arbitration agreements, because the signature requirement does not apply to the second limb of that paragraph: '[an arbitral clause] contained in an exchange of letters or telegrams.'[50]

2.23 *The Writing Requirement under the UNCITRAL Model Law.* The English definition of 'in writing' (see 2.14 above) is 'much wider than the Model Law', Option I, Article 7(2).[51]

2.24 Option 1 of the UNCITRAL Model Law concerns an 'arbitration agreement'. There is no reference to signature.[52] Article 7(1) defines this as: '*an agreement by the parties to submit to arbitration all or certain disputes which have arisen or which may arise between them in respect of a defined legal relationship, whether contractual or not. An arbitration agreement may be in the form of an arbitration clause in a contract or in the form of a separate agreement.*'

Article 7(2) of the UNCITRAL Model Law states that: 'The arbitration agreement shall be in writing'. But this is misleading: the arbitration agreement does not itself have to be in writing; and instead it is enough that 'its content is recorded in any form'. Thus Article 7(3) adds: '*An arbitration agreement is in writing if its content is recorded in any form, whether or not the arbitration agreement or contract has been concluded orally, by conduct, or by other means.*' Article 7(4) amplifies this by referring to a non-tangible 'electronic communication' which is accessible and 'useable for subsequent reference':

> *'The requirement that an arbitration agreement be in writing is met by an electronic communication if the information contained therein is accessible so as to be useable for subsequent reference; "electronic communication" means any communication that the parties*

---

[49] [2007] EWCA Civ 1282; [2008] 1 Lloyd's Rep 239.

[50] *Redfern and Hunter on International Arbitration* (6th edn, Oxford University Press, 2015), 2.15 nn 23 and 24.

[51] Mustill & Boyd, *Commercial Arbitration: Companion Volume* (London, 2001), 20.

[52] Unlike the first limb of the provision within the NYC (1958), Article II.2.

make by means of data messages; "data message" means information generated, sent, received or stored by electronic, magnetic, optical or similar means, including, but not limited to, electronic data interchange [ED], electronic mail, telegram, telex or telecopy.'

The existence of an arbitration agreement can arise as an example of estoppel by convention (10.15, paragraph (iii)(c) above). Thus Article 7(5) provides: '*Furthermore, an arbitration agreement is in writing if it is contained in an exchange of statements of claim and defence in which the existence of an agreement is alleged by one party and not denied by the other.*'

Finally, the incorporation method is also noted. Article 7(6) states: '*The reference in a contract to any document containing an arbitration clause constitutes an arbitration agreement in writing, provided that the reference is such as to make that clause part of the contract.*'

2.25 There is an 'oral option' under the UNCITRAL Model Law. However, this is treacherous because writing is a requirement under the New York Convention (1958).[53] Option II of the UNCITRAL Model Law recognises a formless arbitration agreement: '*an agreement by the parties to submit to arbitration all or certain disputes which have arisen or which may arise between them in respect of a defined legal relationship, whether contractual or not.*'

2.6 Judicial Interpretation of Arbitration Agreements

2.26 Arbitration agreements, if subject to English law (3.17), are governed by the principles of interpretation formulated in the *Investors Compensation Scheme* case (1998),[54] including the proposition (confirmed in *Chartbrook Ltd* v. *Persimmon Homes Ltd*, 2009)[55] that Common Law interpretation can involve giving effect to intended meaning when it is obvious that something has gone wrong with the contractual language and it is also clear how that should be reconstituted.

2.27 The following four interpretative propositions are identified by *Lewison on the Interpretation of Contracts* (2015) as established features in English law:

(1) *incorporation*[56]: '*Whether a contract incorporates an arbitration clause is a question of construction of the contract. Where the arbitration clause is contained in a party's standard terms or in the terms of a previous contract between the same parties, general words of incorporation will generally suffice. But*

[53] *Redfern and Hunter on International Arbitration* (6th edn, Oxford University Press, 2015), 2.16 ff; noting that writing is a requirement, however, under the New York Convention (1958), Art's II(1) and (2), IV ('supply' of the original agreement or a copy), and V(1)(a) ('thereon' is an anachronistic physical allusion to a hard-copy document).

[54] *Nine Gladys Road Ltd v. Kersh* [2004] EWHC 1080. On the principles of interpretation under the *Investors Compensation Scheme v. West Bromwich Building Society* [1998] 1 WLR 896, 912–3, HL, per Lord Hoffmann, see the large literature cited at 14.02.

[55] [2009] UKHL 38; [2009] 1 AC 1101.

[56] (6th edn, London, 2015), 18.01.

where the arbitration clause is contained in a contract between different parties, or between one of them and a third party, clearer words are necessary.'

(2) *contractual commitment*[57]: *'If the contract gives a reasonably clear indication that arbitration is envisaged by both parties as a means of dispute resolution, it will be interpreted as binding on them to refer disputes to arbitration even though the clause is not expressed in mandatory terms.'*

(3) *material scope*[58]: *'If the contract gives a reasonably clear indication that arbitration is envisaged by both parties as a means of dispute resolution, it will be interpreted as binding on them to refer disputes to arbitration even though the clause is not expressed in mandatory terms.'*

(4) *authentic nature of the purported arbitration agreement* (see also the next paragraph on the *Sulamerica* case, 2012)[59]: *'Whether a clause providing for dispute resolution is an arbitration agreement or some other form of dispute resolution is a question of interpretation of the agreement. The indicia of arbitration are (a) there is a dispute or a difference between the parties which has been formulated in some way or another; (b) the dispute or difference has been remitted by the parties to the person to resolve in such a manner that he called upon to exercise a judicial function; (c) where appropriate, the parties must have been provided with an opportunity to present evidence and/or submissions in support of their respective claims in the dispute; (d) the parties have agreed to accept his decision.'*

2.28 *Arbitration Clause Taking Precedence over a Court Jurisdiction Clause.* The decision in *Sulamerica Cia Nacional de Seguros SA* v. *Enesa Engenharia SA* (2012) (on this topic, see further 2.34 below) demonstrates that an arbitration clause will take precedence, even though there is a co-existing jurisdiction clause. In this case the Court of Appeal held that the arbitration clause covered both disputes concerning liability and quantum of damages and that the jurisdiction clause nominating Brazilian courts had to yield to this London arbitration clause.[60]

2.29 The scope of arbitration agreements was an issue in *Fiona Trust and Holding Corporation* v. *Privalov* (also known as *Premium Nafta Products Ltd* v. *Fili Shipping Co Ltd*) (2007). In that case the arbitration agreement empowered the tribunal to determine 'any dispute arising under this charter'. Lord Hoffmann emphasised[61] the need to '*start from the assumption that the parties, as rational businessmen, are likely to have intended any dispute arising out of the relationship into which they have entered or purported to enter to be decided by the same tribunal.*' Similarly, Lord Hope protested at the now discredited case law which had

---

[57] ibid, 18.02.

[58] ibid, 18.03.

[59] ibid, 18.04.

[60] [2012] EWCA Civ 638; [2012] 1 Lloyd's Rep 671; [2012] Lloyd's Rep IR 405, at [5], and [40] and [41].

[61] [2007] UKHL 40; [2007] 4 All ER 951; [2008] 1 Lloyd's Rep 254, at [13]; and applauding the liberal approach formulated by Longmore LJ in the lower appeal court at [2007] EWCA Civ 20; [2007] 2 Lloyd's Rep 267, at [17].

drawn '*fussy distinctions as to what the words "arising under" and "arising out of" may mean*'.[62] He also emphasised the need to construe the arbitration agreement liberally with a view to empowering the tribunal to determine a broad range of matters.[63]

2.30 The *Fiona Trust* case (2007) attractively consolidates within the English case law a modern pattern of liberal interpretation of arbitration agreements (a pattern noted by Clarke LJ in *Capital Trust Investments Ltd* v. *Radio Design TJ AB*, 2002).[64] The phrase 'arising out of' was held to encompass not just contractual claims but tortious claims for misrepresentation and fraud. And Clarke LJ noted other cases[65] in which the same phrase had been held to be elastic enough to cover issues of rectification and declarations of non-liability. Similarly, the Court of Appeal in *AMEC Civil Engineering Ltd* v. *Secretary of State for Transport* (2005)[66] adopted a liberal interpretation of the phrase 'dispute or difference' and held that such a matter had arisen, justifying immediate referral of that issue to arbitration so as to comply with a tight time limitation, even though an engineer's decision was still pending. In this case Sir Anthony May said[67]:

> *'... "Dispute or difference" seems to me to be less hard-edged than "dispute" alone...In many instances, it will be quite clear that there is a dispute. ...Commercial good sense does not suggest that the clause should be construed with legalistic rigidity so as to impede the parties from starting timely arbitration proceedings...This leads me to lean in favour of an inclusive interpretation of what amounts to a dispute or difference.*

2.7 Need for a Clear Commitment to Arbitrate

2.31 An arbitration clause (according to English tradition) is regarded as a species of agreement subject to ordinary contractual doctrines, including certainty (11.01 ff), interpretation (14.00 ff), and remedies for breach of contract (chapter 17).[68]

2.32 The doctrine of contractual certainty is applied liberally to arbitration agreements. It is enough that arbitration is mentioned and that London (as is customary, or England and Wales) is identifiable as the seat. Thus an agreement for 'arbitration in London'[69] would be upheld: failing party agreement on selection of

---

62 [2007] UKHL 40; [2007] 4 All ER 951; [2008] 1 Lloyd's Rep 254, at [27].

63 ibid, at [26] to [28].

64 [2002] EWCA Civ 135; [2002] 2 All ER 159; [2002] 1 All ER (Comm) 514; [2002] CLC 787, at [50] to [52].

65 ibid, at [52], citing *Ashville Investments Ltd v. Elmer Construction Ltd* [1989] QB 488, CA, and *Harbour Assurance Co (UK) Ltd v. Kansa General International Insurance Co Ltd* [1993] QB 701, CA.

66 [2005] EWCA Civ 291; [2015] 1 WLR 2339.

67 ibid, at [31].

68 *Lewison on the Interpretation of Contracts* (6th edn, 2015), 18.01 ff.

69 Such a sparse agreement was upheld in *Naviera Amazonica Peruana v. Cie Internacional de Seguros del Peru* [1988] 1 Lloyd's Rep 116, 118–9, CA, per Kerr LJ.

the arbitrator, the court can appoint an arbitrator.[70] Here are examples of laconic and summary arbitration agreements which have been judicially upheld: 'arbitration to be settled in London'[71]; '& arbitration…in London'[72]; and 'arbitration, if any, by ICC rules in London'[73]; and 'suitable arbitration clause'.[74]

2.33 Secondly, it is not necessary for the words 'arbitration' or 'arbitrator(s)' to be mentioned, provided it can be inferred that the parties are not intending the dispute to be resolved by some non-arbitral mechanism such as (a) expert determination (decision without having to hear argument from the parties), or (b) adjudication within the construction zone, or (c) mediation without arbitration, or, of course, (d) court adjudication. *Lewison on the Interpretation of Contracts* (2015) formulates this principle of construction[75]:

> *'…The indicia of arbitration are (a) there is a dispute or a difference between the parties which has been formulated in some way or another; (b) the dispute or difference has been remitted by the parties to the person to resolve in such a manner that he is called upon to exercise a judicial function; (c) where appropriate, the parties must have been provided with an opportunity to present evidence and/or submissions in support of their respective claims in the dispute; (d) the parties have agreed to accept his decision.'*

2.34 Thirdly, the courts will infer a binding commitment to arbitration, even if the language is not explicitly mandatory. *Lewison on the Interpretation of Contracts* (2015) formulates this principle[76]: *'If the contract gives a reasonably clear indication that arbitration is envisaged by both parties as a means of dispute resolution, it will be interpreted as binding on them to refer disputes to arbitration even though the clause is not expressed in mandatory terms.'*

2.35 Finally, English courts will regard the parties' agreement to arbitrate as mandatory, even though the dispute resolution clause additionally nominates a court jurisdiction as the exclusive forum. In this situation the parties' reference to court proceedings will be regarded as intended to operate as a supervisory and supplementary 'back-up' or, if the arbitration aborts, as a safety-net.[77]

---

[70] Section 18(3)(d), Arbitration Act 1996 (England).

[71] *Tritonia Shipping Inc v. South Nelson Products Corp* [1966] 1 Lloyd's Rep 238, CA.

[72] *Transamerican Ocean Contractors Inc v. Transchemical Rotterdam BV* [1978] 1 Lloyd's Rep 617, CA.

[73] *Mangistaumunaigaz Oil Production Association v. United World Trade Inc* [1995] 1 Lloyd's Rep 617, Potter J.

[74] *Hobbs Padgett & Co (Reinsurance) Ltd v. Kirkland Ltd* [1969] 2 Lloyd's Rep 547, CA (clause not void for uncertainty).

[75] (6th edn, 2015), 18.02 and 18.04, respectively.

[76] (6th edn, 2015), 18.02.

[77] *Sulamerica Cia Nacional de Seguros SA v. Enesa Engenharia SA* [2012] EWCA Civ 638; [2012] 1 Lloyd's Rep 671; [2012] Lloyd's Rep IR 405, at [5], [40], [41], demonstrates that an arbitration clause will take precedence, even though there is a co-existing jurisdiction clause; in this case the Court of Appeal held that the arbitration clause covered both disputes concerning liability and quantum of damages; the jurisdiction clause nominating Brazilian courts had to yield to this London arbitration clause.

2.36 This raises the question: what are the potential supportive functions of the court vis-a-vis arbitration? The first function, identified by Blair J in *U&M Mining Zambia Ltd* v. *Konkola Copper Mines plc* (2013)[78], is that a party might need to bring pre-arbitration court proceedings in which it seeks protective relief or an interim injunction. Blair J said that such recourse is not incompatible with an arbitration clause (citing also the LCIA rules in this respect: now the LCIA Rules (2014) (London Court of International Arbitration).[79]

2.37 Six further supportive judicial functions were suggested by Cooke J (at first instance) in *Sulamerica CIA Nacional De Seguros SA* v. *Enesa Engenharia SA* (2012)[80]:

> *'[Despite an operative arbitration clause, an exclusive jurisdiction provision] enables the parties to found jurisdiction in a court in Brazil to (1) declare the arbitrable nature of the dispute, (2) to compel arbitration, (3) to declare the validity of the award, (4) to enforce the award, or (5) to confirm the jurisdiction of the Brazilian courts on the merits in the event that the parties agree to dispense with arbitration. (6) It specifically operates to prevent the parties proceeding in another court on the merits.'* (Numbering added).

As for the enforcement function (see (4) in the preceding quotation), in the *U&M Mining Zambia* case (2013)[81] Blair J saw no incompatibility between a clause granting Zambian courts exclusive jurisdiction specifically with respect to enforcement and an arbitration clause rendering London the seat of the proceedings). He said[82]:

> *'The fact that clause 9.10 provides that the High Court of Zambia shall have exclusive jurisdiction to execute the arbitration award merely reflects the fact that both parties are Zambian companies, and so far as the evidence in this case is concerned, their assets are to be found in Zambia.'*

But such a clause is not to be recommended because it would be foolhardy to grant exclusive jurisdiction to a particular court in respect of enforcement, given the mobility of corporate assets and the vagaries of different systems of enforcement law.

2.38 However, it should be noted that a more exacting degree of certainty applies to mediation agreements. The Court of Appeal in *Sulamerica Cia Nacional de Seguros SA* v. *Enesa Engenharia SA* (2012) made clear that contractual reference to mediation as a desirable mechanism is not the enough,[83] and that the doctrine of certainty requires a mediation clause to provide a clear commitment to mediation,

---

[78] [2013] EWHC 260 (Comm); [2013] 2 Lloyd's Rep 218; [2013] 1 CLC 456.

[79] Article 25.3 of the LCIA rules (2014).

[80] [2012] EWHC 42 (Comm), at [48]; that case proceeded to the Court of Appeal, in *Sulamerica Cia Nacional de Seguros SA v. Enesa Engenharia SA* [2012] EWCA Civ 638; [2013] 1 WLR 102, but this aspect of Cooke J's judgment was not critically revisited because Moore-Bick LJ considered at [42] to [46] that this issue was outside the scope of the permission for appeal to the Court of Appeal.

[81] [2013] EWHC 260 (Comm); [2013] 2 Lloyd's Rep 218; [2013] 1 CLC 456, at [69].

[82] ibid, at [69].

[83] [2012] EWCA Civ 638; [2012] 1 Lloyd's Rep 671.

and a criterion for the selection of a mediator and an express or implied definition or selection of a mediation procedure.

2.8 Expert Determination Clauses and Other Forms of Dispute Resolution

2.39 Expert determination concerns a reference of a technical issue to an impartial third party. For example, a request might be made to obtain the expert's valuation of company assets or commercial property.[84] The expert's decision will be binding on the parties. But the expert determination process takes place outside the Arbitration Act 1996. This is significant for at least three reasons. First, an arbitrator is required to reach a decision following rival presentations of factual evidence and/or law, whereas an expert determination involves no such rival set of submissions. Secondly, an arbitral tribunal enjoys immunity (5.27), whereas an expert determination exposes the expert to possible liability in negligence.[85] Thirdly, an arbitral award can be subject to challenge under the English legislation, but an expert determination lies outside that legislation and there is only a very restricted power[86] to review the determination.

2.40 An expert determination clause can be combined with an arbitration agreement, as on the facts of the 'Channel Tunnel' construction dispute, *Channel Tunnel Group Ltd* v. *Balfour Beatty Construction Ltd* (1993).[87] Christopher Clarke J in *Thames Valley Power Ltd* v. *Total Gas & Power Ltd* (2005) held that the court might stay English court proceedings if they would involve a failure to adhere to an undertaking to refer the matter to 'expert determination'.[88] But on the facts of this case he exercised his discretion by deciding not to award a 'stay' because of the need for speed and also because he could see no substantive merit in the defaulting party's case.

---

[84] J Kendall, C Freedman, J Farrell, *Expert Determination* (4th edn, London, 2008); on mediation and experts, L Blom-Cooper (ed), *Experts in Civil Courts* (Oxford University Press, 2006), chapter 10. *Russell on Arbitration* (24th edn, London, 2015), 2.029 to 2.032; *Halifax Life Ltd v. Equitable Life Association Co* [2007] EWHC 503; *David Wilson Homes Ltd v. Surrey Services Ltd* [2001] 1 All ER (Comm) 449; *Re British Aviation Insurance Co* [2005] EWHC 1621, at [130] to [132]; *Veba Oil Supply & Trading GmbH v. Petrotrade Inc* [2001] EWCA Civ 1832; *Nikko Homes Ltd v. MEPC plc* [1991] 28 EG 86; [1991] 2 EGLR 103; *Worrall v. Topp* [2007] EWHC 1809.

[85] *Arenson v. Arenson* [1977] AC 405, HL.

[86] *Veba Oil Supply & Trading GmbH v. Petrotrade* Inc [2001] EWCA Civ 1832.

[87] [1993] AC 334, 345–6, HL (clause 67).

[88] [2005] EWHC 2208 (Comm); [2006] 1 Lloyd's Rep 441, at [6], for the terms of the relevant force majeure clause.

2.41 Five other styles of dispute resolution should be mentioned.[89]

(i) '*Ombudsmen*'[90]: such neutrals (who might or might not be officials paid out of public funds) administer justice, often on a 'documents-only' basis, in a range of specific fields, for example, pensions or investments disputes.

(ii) '*Adjudication*' (in English Construction disputes): statute also allows experts to make swift decisions if disputes arise during the course of a building project; these decisions are initially provisional; they become binding if, within a short period, neither party seeks to re-open the determination (by litigation or arbitration).[91]

(iii) '*Dispute Review Boards*': major international construction projects often involve such decision-makers, which becomes binding unless it is reversed by arbitration or a court decision.[92]

(iv) '*Early Neutral Evaluation*'[93]: this involves a neutral third party, often a lawyer, providing a non-binding verdict on the merits of the dispute. In particular, within the English Commercial Court, the parties can consent to a High Court judge providing such an 'early neutral evaluation'.[94]

(v) '*Mini-trial*': this is an adjunct to mediation. A 'mini-trial' can create a 'stronger feeling of having had a day in court than mediation', and 'a better opportunity to assess the performance of key witnesses'.[95] As leading commentators have said: *'in essence lawyers or other advisors for each party present a mini-version of their case to a panel consisting of a senior executive of their client and of the other party…The procedure may take place without a neutral's*

[89] For comment on this gamut of techniques within the Construction Industry, Sir Rupert Jackson, 'The Role of Alternative Dispute Resolution in Furthering the Aims of the Civil Litigation Costs Review' (RICS Expert Witness Conference, 8 March 2012), at 4.1 ff: http://www.judiciary.gov.uk/Resources/JCO/Documents/Speeches/lj-jackson-speech-eleventh-lecture-implementation-programme.pdf

[90] On the rise of informal litigation regimes governing disputes in the banking, building societies, investment, insurance, and pensions industries, E Ferran, 'Dispute Resolution Mechanisms in the UK Financial Sector' (2002) 21 CJQ 135; R Nobles, 'Access to Justice through Ombudsmen: the Courts' Response to the Pensions Ombudsman' (2002) 21 CJQ 94; Lord Woolf, Access to Justice: Interim Report (1995) 111, at [40]; T Buck, R Kirkham, B Thompson, *The Ombudsman Enterprise and Administrative Justice* (Farnham, 2011) (reviewed (2012) 75 MLR 299).

[91] P Coulson, *Coulson on Construction Adjudication* (3rd edn, Oxford University Press, 2015), on accelerated resolution of construction disputes (so-called 'Adjudication') under Part II, Housing Grants, Construction and Regeneration Act 1996.

[92] *Redfern and Hunter on International Arbitration* (5th edn, Oxford University Press, 2009), 1.145 ff (text not appearing in 6th edn, 2015).

[93] K Mackie, D Miles, W Marsh, T Allen, *The ADR Practice Guide* (3rd edn, 2007), 3.2.2.3.

[94] *The Admiralty and Commercial Courts Guide* (9th edn, London, 2011), section G2; for comment, Neil Andrews, *English Civil Justice and Remedies: Progress and Challenges: Nagoya Lectures* (Shinzan Sha Publishers, Tokyo, 2007) 3.23.

[95] *The ADR Practice Guide* (2000), at 13.2 (observation not made in 2007 edn).

involvement but will usually be more effective if a capable neutral chairs the presentation stage.'[96]

2.9 Agreements to Engage in Negotiation or Mediation Before Arbitration

2.42 *Negotiation as a Condition Precedent to Arbitration.* In *Emirates Trading Agency LLC* v. *Prime Mineral Exports Private Ltd* (2014)[97] Teare J upheld a negotiation clause (forming part of a wider dispute resolution clause), restricted to a fixed period of 4 weeks, requiring the parties to conduct 'friendly' negotiations as the mandatory prelude to commencing arbitration proceedings. He decided that the negotiation clause operates as a condition precedent to valid arbitral proceedings. But he held that, on the facts, there had been no failure to comply with this requirement. And so the relevant arbitration (held in London, commenced in June 2010, before a three member panel, and under ICC rules) had been commenced validly.

2.43 Teare J encapsulated his decision as follows.[98]

> *'an obligation to seek to resolve a dispute by friendly discussions in good faith has an identifiable standard, namely, fair, honest and genuine discussions aimed at resolving a dispute... Enforcement of such an agreement when found as part of a dispute resolution clause is in the public interest, first, because commercial men expect the court to enforce obligations which they have freely undertaken and, second, because the object of the agreement is to avoid what might otherwise be an expensive and time consuming arbitration.'*

2.44 Teare J held that in this context the negotiation agreement will include an implied obligation that each party will conduct '*fair, honest and genuine discussions aimed at resolving a dispute*', and that this is contractually certain.[99] If compensation is sought, damages for loss of a chance are available. Teare J distinguished[100] *Walford* v. *Miles* (1992)[101] in which the House of Lords had held that an agreement to negotiate in good faith or reasonably was void for uncertainty. The *Walford* case had been concerned with a negotiation commitment within an agreement which was 'subject to contract', the main agreement not yet having been established. Teare J cited extensively from an Australian decision.[102] He also noted developments in

[96] K Mackie, D Miles, W Marsh, T Allen, *The ADR Practice Guide* (2000), 13.1 (not in 2007 edn).

[97] [2014] EWHC 2104 (Comm), notably at [59] to [64], distinguishing *Walford v. Miles* [1992] 2 AC 128, 140, HL on the basis that it was not concerned with a negotiation clause incorporated into a dispute resolution clause.

[98] [2014] EWHC 2104 (Comm), at [64].

[99] ibid, at [64].

[100] ibid, at [29] and [59].

[101] [1992] 2 AC 128, HL.

[102] [2014] EWHC 2104 (Comm), at [42] to [46], citing *United Group Rail Services v. Rail Corporation New South Wales* (2009) 127 Con LR 202.

Singapore.[103] Finally, he cited ICSID (investment disputes, arbitral tribunal case law) support[104] for negotiation obligations contained in dispute resolution clauses.

2.45 *Negotiation Obligation without a Time-limit?* In the *Emirates* case (2014), Teare J decided that there is no problem of uncertainty where a clause requires parties to engage in 'friendly' discussions, and impliedly in good faith.[105] And he seemed prepared to recognise as binding an obligation to negotiation in good faith without a time limit. But a range of alleged misconduct during negotiations is easily imagined: from total refusal to engage, use of fraudulent misrepresentations, manifestly insincere proposals, bad faith tactics designed to slow down the process or to exhaust the opponent, half-truths, deliberate non-disclosure. Is there really a solidly '*identifiable standard*' of '*fair, honest and genuine discussions*'? Or is this a recipe instead for protracted and messy *ex post facto* inquiries into allegedly bad faith negotiation? Perhaps the better approach would be to treat a negotiation clause within a dispute resolution clause as non-legally binding (on the basis of uncertainty) except when it clearly specifies a fixed period of pause as mandatory before commencement of arbitral proceedings. And so a clause stipulating that the parties '*will conduct good faith and friendly settlement negotiations prior to commencing arbitration*' should be void for uncertainty; but a clause stating that '*(i) once a dispute has arisen, neither party will commence arbitration proceedings within 4 weeks and before he has notified the other of the existence of a dispute and his intention to pursue arbitration; and (ii) during those 4 weeks the parties will be at liberty to try to reach an amicable conclusion or accommodation.*' Element (i) is certain; and element (ii) is merely exhortatory and so does not create a problem of uncertainty.

2.46 *Which Law Governs the Negotiation Clause*? It will not always be clear whether the arbitration clause and the negotiation clause are subject to the same law. In the interest of clarity, the law governing the arbitration agreement should be spelt out, and similarly that law (which need not be the same) applicable to all other parts of the dispute resolution clause (see 3.17 concerning the law governing the arbitration agreement).

2.47 *Mediation as a Condition Precedent to Arbitration.* The English courts have given effect to mediation agreements (for example, by staying premature court proceedings),[106] provided[107] (i) there is a binding commitment to mediate (ii) the

---

[103] *Emirates Trading Agency LLC v. Prime Mineral Exports Private Ltd* [2014] EWHC 2104 (Comm), [2014] EWHC 2104 (Comm), at [54], citing *International Research Corp plc v. Lufthansa Systems Asia Pacific Pte Ltd* [2012] SGHC 226 (upheld on the legal analysis, [2013] SGCA 55 at [54] to [63]).

[104] [2014] EWHC 2104 (Comm), at [57], citing *Tulip Real Estate Investment and development Netherlands BV v. Republic of Turkey* (ICSID Case No ARB/11/28) at paragraphs 56–72.

[105] [2014] EWHC 2104 (Comm), at [64].

[106] *Cable & Wireless v. IBM* [2002] EWHC 2059 (Comm), [2002] CLC 1319, Colman J.

[107] [2014] EWHC 2104 (Comm), at [32] and [33], noting the approval in *Sulamerica Cia Nacional de Seguros SA v. Enesa Engenharia SA* [2012] EWCA Civ 638; [2013] 1 WLR 102 of *Holloway v. Chancery Mead* [2007] EWHC 2495 (TCC), [2008] 1 All ER (Comm) 653, at [83], per Ramsey J; for similar analysis in Australia, *Aiton Australia Pty Ltd v. Transfield Pty Ltd* (1999) 153 FLR

mediator is nominated or ascertainable and (iii) there is a complete or ascertainable mediation procedure. If arbitration is subject to a prior (attempt at) mediation, this appears to create a condition precedent to valid commencement of English arbitration proceedings. And so the parties must raise and consider the possibility of mediation. Hildyard J's discussion in *Wah* v. *Grant Thornton International Ltd* (2012) of a cognate provision, intended to create a condition precedent to arbitration proceedings, is consistent with this.[108] Similarly, Teare J in the *Emirates* case (2014) noted (with approval)[109] a decision in Singapore which directly recognised this analysis. No problem of certainty will arise if the mediation clause refers to a well-established institutional 'model' set of mediation rules, as in *Cable & Wireless* v. *IBM United Kingdom Ltd* (2002),[110] where the mediation clause incorporated an institutional set of mediation rules, containing a detailed process.

2.10 'Separability' of the Arbitration Agreement from the Main Contract

2.48 The (possible or actual) invalidity of the main contract does *not necessarily* entail the invalidity of the arbitration agreement (see the remarks of Lord Hoffmann in *Fiona Trust and Holding Corporation* v. *Privalov* (2007); and see 2.49 and 2.52 for details).[111] This is because the arbitration agreement has a life independent of its parent, the main contract. It follows that the arbitration agreement *might be valid* even though the main contract (the so-called 'matrix contract') is invalid (void, voidable, terminated for frustration or breach) or the main contract did not come into existence. The notion of 'separability' (or 'severability') is 'an international

236, at [69]; and *Elizabeth Bay Developments Pty v. Boral Building Services Pty Ltd* (1995) 36 NSWLR 709, 715, Giles J: *Lewison on the Interpretation of Contracts* (5th 6th edn, 2015) 18.08.

[108] [2012] EWHC 3198 (Ch); [2013] 1 All ER (Comm) 1226; [2013] 1 Lloyd's Rep 11.

[109] *Emirates Trading Agency LLC v. Prime Mineral Exports Private Ltd* [2014] EWHC 2104 (Comm), [2014] EWHC 2104 (Comm), at [54] and [55], citing *International Research Corp plc v. Lufthansa Systems Asia Pacific Pte Ltd* [2012] SGHC 226 (upheld on the legal analysis, [2013] SGCA 55 at [54] to [63]).

[110] [2002] EWHC 2059 (Comm); [2002] 2 All ER (Comm) 1041, at [21] per Colman J.

[111] Also known as *Premium Nafta Products Ltd v. Fili Shipping Co Ltd* [2007] UKHL 40; [2007] 4 All ER 951; [2008] 1 Lloyd's Rep 254, notably Lord Hoffmann's speech at [17] to [19]; considered in *JSC BTA Bank v. Ablyazov* [2011] EWHC 587 (Comm), Christopher Clarke J (granting a stay of English civil proceedings because an arbitration agreement had been shown to exist by the party seeking the stay, and the party seeking to oppose the stay had not shown that this clause had been avoided on the ground of non-disclosure).

concept'[112] now clearly absorbed into English law.[113] Section 7 of the Arbitration Act 1996 states:

> *'Unless otherwise agreed by the parties, an arbitration agreement which forms or was intended to form part of another agreement (whether or not in writing) shall not be regarded as invalid, non-existent or ineffective because that other agreement is invalid, or did not come into existence or has become ineffective, and it shall for that purpose be treated as a distinct agreement.'*

Lord Hoffmann in the *Fiona Trust* case (2007) explained[114]:

> *'This section shows a recognition by Parliament that... businessmen frequently do want the question of whether their contract was valid, or came into existence, or has become ineffective, submitted to arbitration and that the law should not place conceptual obstacles in their way.'*

2.49 In the *Fiona Trust* case (2007), shipowners had begun London court proceedings. These claimants alleged that charterparties had been validly rescinded on the basis of the charterers' receipt of bribes at the inception of the transactions. Damages were also sought. Conversely, the charterers had invoked arbitration agreements in the relevant eight charterparties. The arbitrators were asked to determine whether the charterparties had been validly rescinded[115] for bribery. The House of Lords held that the arbitral tribunal retained power, in accordance with the 'separability' principle, to determine whether the main contract had been procured by bribery.[116] The same would apply if the issue arose whether agents had exceeded their authority in entering into relevant contracts falling within the scope of the arbitration agreement. The result in the *Fiona Trust* case (2007) was that the arbitration would proceed and the parallel High Court claim by the owners would be stayed *in so far as it concerned the question whether the transactions could be rescinded for bribery* (claims for monetary relief in respect of bribery would be tried in that court in due course).

---

[112] *JSC BTA Bank v. Ablyazov* [2011] EWHC 587 (Comm); [2011] 2 Lloyd's Rep 129, at [44], per Christopher Clarke J; *Redfern and Hunter on International Arbitration* (5th edn, Oxford University Press, 2009), 2.102 ff; UNCITRAL Model Law, Article 16(1); SM Schwebel, *International Arbitration: Three Salient Problems* (Grotius Publications, Cambridge, 1987), Part 1, 'The Severability of the Arbitration Agreement', 1–60; D Joseph, *Jurisdiction and Arbitration Agreements and their Enforcement* (3rd edn, London, 2015), 4.36 ff.

[113] Leggatt LJ in the Harbour Assurance case [1993] QB 701, 716–7, CA, the Harbour Assurance case noted Steyn J's citation (at first instance in the Harbour litigation, [1992] 1 Lloyd's Rep 81; Financial Times, October 15, 1991) of the seminal comparative and transnational analysis in SM Schwebel, *International Arbitration: Three Salient Problems* (Grotius Publications, Cambridge, 1987), 1–60. But Steyn J had erred in not extending the separability principle to the context of a disputed substantive plea of illegality.

[114] [2007] UKHL 40; [2007] 4 All ER 951; [2008] 1 Lloyd's Rep 254, at [10].

[115] A Berg (2007) 123 LQR 352, 356 contends that the purported main contract must be void and not voidable if A has bribed B's agent to agree terms favourable to A, when A knows that B has not authorised its agent to accept such terms.

[116] [2007] UKHL 40; [2007] 4 All ER 951; [2008] 1 Lloyd's Rep 254, at [19], per Lord Hoffmann.

2.50 Christopher Clarke J in *JSC BTA Bank* v. *Ablyazov* (2011)[117] said that the 'separability' principle justified referring to the arbitral tribunal the question whether the main transaction and the arbitration agreement might be voidable[118] and, if so, obtaining its avoidance. Until the issue concerning voidability was established, and the transaction avoided, it could not be said that the disputed arbitration agreement was '*null and void, inoperative, or incapable of being performed'* for the purpose of section 9(4) of the Arbitration Act 1996. Accordingly, the judge granted a stay of court proceedings.[119]

2.51 *'Separability' and a Disputed Issue of Illegality*. Consistent with the 'separability' principle, the Court of Appeal held in the *Harbour Assurance case* (1993) that an arbitration clause would subsist even though the issue (or one of the issues) referred by the parties to arbitration is whether the main contract is (whether wholly or partly) void for illegality.[120] Leggatt LJ attractively explained[121]:

> *'because the arbitration agreement is separable from the contract containing it, it has a life of its own, which continues while the fate of the contract is being determined. Where the contract is alleged to have been invalidated by statute, the essential question must be whether the statute was intended to strike down the submission to arbitration. ...The arbitration agreement, if sufficiently widely drawn, is from its nature intended by the parties to govern any dispute that may arise between them, including a dispute about the initial illegality of the contract. ...Otherwise it would put it in the power of one contracting party to prevent arbitration from taking place simply by alleging that the contract was void for initial illegality.'*

In the same case Hoffmann LJ carefully analysed and illustrated the nature of an arbitration clause's 'separate' or 'collateral' or 'ancillary' status[122]:

> *'The flaw in the logic [of those opposed to the 'separability' principle]...lies in the ambiguity of the proposition that the arbitration clause "formed part" of the [main] agreement... [It] is always essential to have regard to the reason why the question is being asked. There is no single concept of "forming part" which will provide the answer in every case.'*

Hoffmann LJ noted the juridical turning point in the English cases on this topic:

> *'But the reign of false logic came to an end with the decision of the House of Lords in Heyman* v. *Darwins Ltd. [1942] AC 356, HL. This case decided that an accepted repudiation or frustration, while it might bring the contract to an end in the sense of discharging*

---

[117] [2011] EWHC 587 (Comm); [2011] 2 Lloyd's Rep 129, at [49].

[118] The main grounds of voidability in English contract law are: misrepresentation; duress; undue influence (an equitable doctrine); unconscionable transactions (an equitable doctrine); and the non-disclosure doctrine in the field of insurance law: on these various doctrines, N Andrews, *Contract Law* (2nd edn, Cambridge University Press, 2015), chapters 9 to 11; and see text below at chapter 12.

[119] On stays under section 9 of the Arbitration Act 1996, 4.02.

[120] *Harbour Assurance Co (UK) Ltd v. Kansa General International Insurance Co Ltd* [1993] QB 701, CA, per Ralph Gibson LJ, at 712c-f, Leggatt LJ, at 719 and Hoffmann LJ, at 723f-724e; explained by Colman J in *Westacre Investments Inc v. Jugoimport SDPR Holding Co Ltd* [1999] QB 740, 756–757.

[121] *Harbour Assurance* case [1993] QB 701, 716–7, CA, per Leggatt LJ.

[122] ibid, at 722–3 (these quotations form a continuous passage).

the parties from further performance of their primary obligations, did not affect the enforceability of an arbitration clause.. In the context of the repudiation or frustration rules...there was no reason to treat the obligation to submit to arbitration as discharged, and such a conclusion would have severely reduced the value of the clause...'

2.52 *Qualifications upon 'Separability'*. However, in the House of Lords' decision in *Fiona Trust and Holding Corporation* v. *Privalov* (2007)[123] Lord Hoffmann persuasively suggested that there are two fundamental types of defective consent where the arbitration clause will necessarily founder because it is not supported by any consensus. Thus he said: (i) that the 'separability' principle would not provide a basis for the arbitral tribunal to determine whether the main contract had been forged, since forgery would also invalidate the arbitration agreement[124]; (ii) on the same principle, he further suggested that the total absence of authority to act as agent would nullify both the main contract and the arbitration agreement.[125] Situations (i) and (ii) can be rationalised as examples of identical defects vitiating both the main transaction and the arbitration agreement.

2.53 *Connection between the Principles of Kompetenz-Kompetenz and 'Separability'*. The *Kompetenz-Kompetenz* principle enables the arbitral tribunal to make at least a provisional assessment of its own competence or jurisdiction in the relevant matter. However, the arbitral tribunal's jurisdictional determination is not conclusive. Instead in most arbitration systems, the question whether the arbitral tribunal does indeed have jurisdiction in the relevant reference is an issue which can be reviewed by the court. And so arbitrators have the 'first crack' at determining whether there is a valid arbitration reference, who are the parties to the arbitration agreement, and what is the scope of that agreement or reference. The principle of 'separability' (the arbitral agreement's validity is not dependent on the main transaction's validity) operates alongside the related principle of *Kompetenz-Kompetenz*.

2.54 Combination of the principles of *Kompetenz-Kompetenz* and separability enables the arbitral tribunal to provide a preliminary opinion on whether the arbitration clause is valid and to fix it scope. But this opinion can be challenged before the national courts. This is certainly possible under the English Arbitration Act 1996, notably section 67. Another possibility is that the arbitral tribunal's opinion might be re-considered during the process of foreign enforcement under the New York Convention (1958).

---

[123] [2007] UKHL 40; [2007] 4 All ER 951; [2008] 1 Lloyd's Rep 254; on which L Flannery (2007) NLJ 1756; A Rushworth (2008) 124 LQR 195; A Briggs [2008] LMCLQ 1–5.

[124] ibid, at [17]; for an instance, *Albon (t/a NA Carriage Co) v. Naza Motor Trading Sdn Bhd* [2007] EWCA Civ 1124; [2008] 1 All ER (Comm) 351; [2008] 1 Lloyd's Rep 1; [2007] 2 CLC 782 (High Court justified in determining issue of forged signature, rather than permitting arbitrators to decide this issue).

[125] *Fiona Trust* case [2007] UKHL 40; [2007] 4 All ER 951; [2008] 1 Lloyd's Rep 254, at [18].

2.11 Parties to Arbitration: Joinder and Consolidation

2.55 This is a difficult topic.[126] The ensuing discussion will proceed from first principle. The basic proposition is that it is not possible for the arbitral tribunal to require joinder or consolidation of related arbitration references, or to add third parties, unless all parties consent, such consent having been given immediately before the relevant procedural variation or in anticipation (for example, by agreeing to institutional rules which permit this).[127] For example, the LCIA Rules (2014) (London Court of International Arbitration) permit (1) 'one or more third persons to be joined in the arbitration as a party'[128] or (2) 'the consolidation of the arbitration with one or more other arbitrations into a single arbitration subject to the LCIA Rules'.[129] But (1) this requires the applicant party and the third party to consent in writing[130]; and (2) requires all relevant parties to consent in writing to the proposed consolidation.[131] This is to be contrasted with the English court's active and mandatory power to order joinder of related claims, including claims between different parties.[132]

2.56 Principles Relevant to the Joinder and Consolidation Issue.

(i) *Party Consent: the Voluntary Principle.* Arbitration rests on consent between the parties (unless a special statutory exception exists). Consent, which must be real and free, is fundamental. This is the voluntary principle. The alternative is statute but any such mandatory arbitration is an exception to, or violation of, the voluntary principle (but see 2.57 for refinement of this point).

[126] Section 35, Arbitration Act 1996; Departmental Advisory Committee Report (1996), at [177] ff; S Brekoulakis, *Third Parties in International Commercial Arbitration* (Oxford University Press, 2010); B Hanotiau, *Complex Arbitrations: Multiparty, Multicontract, Multi-Issue and Class Actions* (The Hague, 2005); D Joseph, *Jurisdiction and Arbitration Agreements and their Enforcement* (3rd edn, London, 2015), chapter 7; Jan Kleinheisterkamp, 'Lord Mustill and the courts of tennis – *Dallah v. Pakistan* in England, France and Utopia' (2012) 75 MLR 639, 640 n 3; A Melnyk (2003) Int ALR 59–63; *Redfern and Hunter on International Arbitration* (5th edn, Oxford University Press, 2009), 2.59 ff; *Russell on Arbitration* (24th edn, London, 2015), 3.058; Andrea Marco Steingruber, *Consent in International Arbitration* (Oxford University Press, 2012); N Voser, 'Multi-Party Disputes and Joinder of Third Parties' (2008) ICCA Congress Series.

[127] *The Bay Hotel and Resort v. Cavalier Constructions Co* [2001] UKPC 34, at [44] to [49], per Lord Cooke (giving the Advice of the Privy Council).

[128] LCIA Rules (2014), Article 22(1)(viii).

[129] ibid, Article 22(1)(ix).

[130] ibid, Article 22(1)(viii).

[131] ibid, Article 22(1)(ix).

[132] CPR 3.1(2)(e) to (j); noted Andrews on Civil Processes (Intersentia, Cambridge, Antwerp, Portland, 2013), volume 1, Court Proceedings, 6.55 ff.

(ii) *Consumer Protection*. English legislation[133] ensures that consumers (whether, in this context, an individual or a legal person)[134] is not bound by an arbitration agreement in respect of a claim for £5,000 or less.
(iii) *Procedural Privity Principle*. The award is binding only between the parties to the arbitration.[135]
(iv) *Enforcement Only Against the True Party*. Enforcement of an award against a non-party will fail, under either the New York Convention (1958) system, or the local system of enforcing domestic awards. But as the *Dallah* litigation shows, the issue whether the award-debtor is truly a non-party can require the enforcing court to consider proof of intricate foreign law (9.36).

2.57 *What is 'Party Consent'?* The manifestation of consent in orthodox arbitral practice is a written arbitration agreement. This provides a direct nexus linking the relevant party to the proposed arbitral proceedings. But an alternative and more liberal consensual framework would be to treat as sufficient a party's *ex ante* consent to have disputes subject to a nominated arbitration system or institution. This would be the warrant for a party being subject to procedural arrangements necessary in the interest of economy and fairness to ensure the fair disposal of subsequent arbitral proceedings. But that possible development has yet to be ratified by the arbitral community. The matter could be conceptualised as party accession to a multilateral contract administered by the relevant arbitral authority or perhaps groups of arbitral authorities. The analogy in English contract law would be cases liberally recognising party membership of complex contracts (yachting contests[136] and unincorporated associations).[137]

2.58 *Consolidation of Concurrent Proceedings*. Section 35 of the Arbitration Act 1996 empowers the tribunal to permit separate arbitration proceedings to be consolidated or that concurrent proceedings will be held. But the consent of all parties is required to either form of procedural mutation.

2.59 *Joinder Must be Voluntary*. Where the arbitration is between A and B, and A wishes to add X, but X is not a party to any arbitration agreement, it is clear that

---

[133] Sections 89 to 91, Arbitration Act 1996 (as amended by the Consumer Rights Act 2015, schedule 4, paras 30 to 33); unless the claim is for a sum greater than £5,000 (Unfair Arbitration Agreements (Specified Amount) Order 1999 (SI 1999/2167); generally, R Merkin, *Arbitration Law* (London, 2014), 1.50 ff.

[134] Section 90, Arbitation Act 1996.

[135] eg, *Golden Ocean Group Ltd v. Humpuss etc* [2013] EWHC 1240 (Comm), Popplewell J; but see R Merkin, *Arbitration Law* (London, 2014), 17.17, for possible qualifications in the case law; section 82(2), Arbitration Act 1996 extends this to 'the persons claiming under them', such as executors or assignees. But if A loses as against B in an arbitration, it might exceptionally be an abuse of process for A to re-open the central issue by suing C in court proceedings in a related case; but such a finding of abuse of process will be exceptional, *Michael Wilson & Partners v. Sinclair* [2012] EWHC 2560 (Comm), Teare J; *Arts & Antiques Ltd v. Richards* [2013] EWHC 3361 (Comm), Popplewell J; Merkin, *Arbitration Law* (London, 2014), 17.25.1.

[136] *Clarke v. Dunraven ('The Satanita')* [1897] AC 59, HL) 'The Satanita' [1897] AC 59, 63, HL.

[137] *Re Recher* [1972] Ch 526, per Brightman J (unincorporated association; multi-party contractual matrix).

X is not compellable to join the arbitration as a co-respondent. X could be added as a party only if A, B, and X consent. This is another manifestation of the voluntary principle (2.56 and 2.57).

2.60 *No Power to Order Consolidation.* There is no parallel in the field of arbitration to court-directed consolidation; but *in principle* an arbitral tribunal could be consensually clothed with the power to engage in these techniques whether (a) by specific agreement in a master contract to which all prospective disputants are party or (b) by virtue of the institutional rules[138] to which the parties might have assented when making their arbitration agreement.

2.61 *Opt-in Multi-party Arbitration. Absence of arbitral tribunal power to order consolidation.* Again *in principle* an arbitral tribunal could be consensually clothed with the power to engage in that type of enlarged form of arbitration. This would be consistent with the voluntary principle because each party would need positively to opt-in.

2.62 *Representative Proceedings and Opt-out Systems.* Where the class of potential claimants (perhaps respondents) is large, it might be desirable to have representative arbitral proceedings. Are they possible? The voluntary principle would require the representative to be party to an arbitration agreement; and the persons represented would also need to have agreed to such proceedings and to this particular mechanism; such agreement (in writing) would need to occur in advance or at the time of submission of the dispute to arbitration. Awards would be declared binding on both the representative and the represented. Although objections to such awards might be made by either represented persons (who have lost or not won well enough) or the defeated respondent, such a jurisdictional objection would appear to be unsound. There will have been no breach of the consensual principle: each type of objector will in fact not have been taken by surprise and will have consented in writing to this type of process. A positive award would appear to be enforceable under the law of the seat, and be accorded *res judicata* effect also. Whether it would be upheld within the NYC (1958) system might be less straightforward.

2.63 *Section 8(1), Contracts (Rights of Third Parties) Act 1999.*[139] Section 8(1) empowers third party T to sue party A in arbitration proceedings if the contract between parties A and B confers a direct right of action on T to obtain a benefit (such as the payment of money by A to T). In fact third party T becomes subject to a procedural constraint: T's capacity to realise the substantive benefit of party A's promise is *prima facie* confined to arbitration, unless A waives that requirement (as

---

[138] For institutional rules permitting 'sting awards' under GAFTA rules, r 5, and related commodity rules, R Merkin, *Arbitration Law* (London, 2014), 17.10; and in the construction industry, ibid, 17.10.1 (on the latter, notably, Jackson J in *City & General (Holborn) Ltd v. AYH plc* [2005] EWHC 2494 (TCC); but for the position in the Federation of Civil Engineering Contractors Rules, cl 18(1), *Lafarge Aggregates v. Shepherd Hill Civil Engineering Ltd* [2001] 1 WLR 162, HL.

[139] For critical comment on section 8, 1999 Act, VV Veeder, 'On Reforming the English Arbitration Act 1996?', in J Lowry and L Mistelis, *Commercial Law: Perspectives and Practice* (London, 2006), 243, at 14.12, noting on this point also Diamond, 'The Third Man: the 1999 Act Sets Back Separability' (2011) Arb Int 211; and AS Burrows [2000] LMCLQ 540, 551 (as for section 8(2), Veeder, ibid, n 16, says that it is 'beyond judicial repair').

where A commences active judicial proceedings, or A submits to T's commencement of court proceedings).[140] Section 8(1) is thus structured so that third party T's access to arbitration is dependent on T having the prospect of gaining some positive or independent benefit under the party A/party B contract, such as a payment. The identity of third party T must be clearly ascertainable, although T need not be named.

2.64 Section 8(1) was applied in *Nisshin Shipping Co Ltd* v. *Cleaves & Co Ltd* (2003).[141] In this case party B had chartered party A's ship and third party T had brokered this deal. The charterparty stated that T should receive a specified commission payable by A. The charterparty further provided that 'any dispute arising' between A and B should be referred to arbitration (rather than to litigation in the courts). On the facts of this case, and as conceded by counsel on the basis of House of Lords authority directly in point,[142] T also had (in addition to the 1999 Act right of action) a right under a trust of a promise to sue A (B having defaulted in his trustee duty to sue A on T's behalf). Colman J held that T's action under the 1999 Act could (and indeed should) be brought by arbitration, as stated in section 8(1). The arbitration would then be between T and A. There would be no need for T to join B as a party to the arbitration reference. But section 8(1) would not help T to bring the trust of a promise claim because that subsection is only concerned with claims against A founded on section 1 of the 1999 Act. And so an action by T under the trust of a promise doctrine could not be arbitrated (the arbitration clause only applying as between A and B, and so the arbitrator would lack jurisdiction to hear a claim brought by T). If T chose to sue A under a trust of a promise in court proceedings, joinder of A, B and T would be required (unless waived by A). Would A be entitled to a stay of those proceedings by contending that B would be in breach of the arbitration agreement by participating in those court proceedings? The better view is that B's participation as co-defendant is not enough; the substance of the claim is between T and A, and B's reluctant involvement (the need for which A could in any event waive) should not justify a stay of the proceedings.

2.65 *Section 8(2), Contracts (Rights of Third Parties) Act 1999.* Under section 8(2) the right to arbitrate can be conferred as an autonomous right by A and B on T (contrast section 8(1) of the 1999 Act, noted at 2.63 above, where T's involvement

---

140 *Nisshin Shipping Co Ltd v. Cleaves & Co Ltd* [2003] EWHC 2602 (Comm); [2004] 1 Lloyd's Rep 38 (criticised, J Hayton [2011] LMCLQ 565); see also R Merkin, *Arbitration Law* (London, 2014), 17.51, 17.52 on the section 8(1) issue whether the A/T arbitration is to be combined with a possible A/B arbitration. But Toulson LJ in *Fortress Value Recovery Fund I LCC v. Blue Skye Special Opportunities Fund LLP* [2013] EWCA Civ 367; [2013] 1 WLR 3466, at [45], suggests that A can waive the requirement that T should proceed by arbitration: 'In summary, section 8(1) allows for [A] to give T an enforceable substantive right, subject to a procedural condition on which [A] may but need not insist. By contrast, section 8(2) allows for [A] to give T an enforceable procedural right, which T may but need not exercise (since the right is unilateral).'

141 [2004] 1 Lloyd's Rep 38.

142 *Les Affréteurs Réunis SA v. Leopold Walford (London) Ltd* [1919] AC 801, HL (applying *Robertson v. Wait* (1853) 8 Ex 299 which had given effect to an implied trust of a promise in this mercantile context).

in arbitration as against A follows from the promise by A of a substantive benefit to T, such as payment of money by party A to the third party T). A right created under section 8(2) confers on third party T the unilateral power to insist[143] that any dispute between T and A (the party who has conferred this section 8(2) autonomous arbitration right) should proceed to arbitration. But T could decide not to exercise that last point and instead could proceed by court proceedings or acquiesce in court proceedings brought against T by A. Section 8(2) is thus structured so that T's access to arbitration is in effect a floating right, exercisable (and waivable) by T should any dispute arise between T and A. The identity of T must be clearly ascertainable, although T need not be named. This provision would appear capable, therefore, of empowering a range of prospective parties to gain the right to arbitrate. But section 8(2) does not place the relevant targeted third parties under an obligation to arbitrate; and so it cannot be used to exclude access to courts.

2.66 It is possible that an arbitration right carved out under section 8(2) could be useful in the context which gave rise to a notorious contractual saga, culminating in the House of Lords' decision in the *Panatown* case (2001).[144] In this case a clause stipulated for arbitration between parties A and B, parties to a building contract. But the economically interested third party, T, the owner of the land, was not party to that arbitration agreement. The action in court brought by party B against party A proved abortive because the House of Lords held that party B could not recover substantial damages on behalf of the third party T. The reason for that was that T had a direct contractual action against party A. That direct right of action arose under a deed. That deed imposed a duty of care on party A in the performance of the building contract. The covenantee under the deed was T. Party A and party T had specially entered this side agreement at the time the main building contract had been formed. In this context, the solution would be to stipulate in favour of third party T, within the contract between A and B, that any action brought by T would be capable of being arbitrated. This would create a right to arbitrate in favour of T under section 8(2) of the 1999 Act. Another solution would be to insert an arbitration clause into the deed between A and T.

2.12 Termination of Arbitration Agreements

2.67 Is an arbitration agreement capable of being (a) terminated for breach, or (b) for frustration, or (c) otherwise (such as by an express termination clause),[145] in accordance with general principles of contractual doctrine? The clear answer to (a)

---

[143] Toulson LJ in *Fortress Value Recovery Fund I LCC v. Blue Skye Special Opportunities Fund LLP* [2013] EWCA Civ 367; [2013] 1 WLR 3466, at [45] (but this right had not been conferred in the present case).

[144] *Alfred McAlpine Construction Ltd v. Panatown* [2001] 1 AC 518, HL; noted B Coote (2001) 117 LQR 81; AS Burrows (2001) 1 Univ of Oxford Commonwealth LJ 107.

[145] Neil Andrews, *Contract Law* (2nd edn, Cambridge University Press, 2015), 17.25 ff; Neil H Andrews, MA Clarke, AM Tettenborn, G Virgo, *Contractual Duties: Performance, Breach, Termination and Remedies* (London, 2012) (breach and performance section by Neil Andrews),

is 'yes', and the same answer is probably applicable to (b) and (c). Christopher Clarke J's statement in *AP Moller-Maersk A/S (t/a Maersk Line)* v. *Sonaec Villas Cen Sad Fadoul* (2010) is consistent with this[146]:

> *'it is now established that an arbitration agreement is a contract collateral to the main contract, and that it may survive the termination of the latter. Thus, if it is alleged that the contract, although once existing, has come to an end by the acceptance of a repudiation or frustration, or through the operation of a termination provision in the contract itself or the failure of a condition precedent, the arbitration clause may still operate: see Mustill and Boyd, Commercial Arbitration (2nd edn) pages 110–112.'*

That case did not concern an arbitration agreement, but rather an exclusive jurisdiction clause. But the same principles were treated as applicable to the latter context.[147] Similarly, Beatson J in *Dubai Islamic Bank PJSC* v. *PSI Energy Holding Co BSC (2011)* said[148]: '*the normal contractual principles which have been applied to arbitration clauses are equally applicable to jurisdiction clauses.*'

2.68 The Commercial Court has consistently accepted that arbitration agreements governed by English law are subject to traditional contractual analysis, including the possibility of termination for repudiatory breach.[149] Furthermore, as traced by Lord Goff in *Food Corp of India* v. *Antclizo Shipping Corp ('The Antclizo')* (1988),[150] three is a line of cases from the 1980s (three decisions of the House of

---

chapter 9; K Lewison, *Interpretation of Contracts* (6th edn, London, 2015), 17.15 to 17.17.; G McMeel, *The Construction of Contracts: Interpretation, Implication and Rectification* (2nd edn, Oxford University Press, 2011), 23.02 ff; E Peel, 'The Termination Paradox' [2013] LMCLQ 519–543; J Randall, 'Express Termination Clauses' [2014] CLJ 113–141; R Hooley, 'Express Termination Clauses', in G Virgo and S Worthington (eds), *Commercial Remedies: Resolving Controversies* (Cambridge University Press, 2016); JE Stannard and D Capper, *Termination for Breach of Contract* (Oxford University Press, 2014), chapter 8; S Whittaker, 'Termination Clauses', in AS Burrows and E Peel (eds), *Contract Terms* (Oxford University Press, 2007), chapter 13 (discussion of many related decisions concerning 'material breach' and similar contract drafting).

146 [2010] EWHC 355 (Comm); [2010] 2 All ER (Comm) 1159; [2011] 1 Lloyd's Rep 1, at [32].

147 ibid, at [33].

148 [2011] EWHC 1019 (Comm); [2011] 1 CLC 595, at [49].

149 [2007] EWHC 1363 (Comm); [2007] 2 Lloyd's Rep 493; [2007] 1 CLC 920, Cooke J (noted J Levy (2007) NLJ 1036); at [15], citing *World Pride Shipping Ltd v. Daiichi Chuo Kisen Kaisha ('The Golden Anne')* [1984] 2 Lloyd's Rep 489, Lloyd J (Comm Ct); *Rederi Kommanditselskaabet Merc-Scandia IV v. Couniniotis SA ('The Mercanaut')* [1980] 2 Lloyd's Rep 183, Lloyd J (Comm Ct) and *Downing v. Al Tameer Establishment* [2002] EWCA Civ 721; [2002] 2 All ER (Comm) 545, at [21], [25] and [26]; also noting the seminal 'contractual' analysis of arbitration agreements in *Bremer Vulcan v. South India Shipping Corporation Limited* [1981] AC 909, HL; *'The Hannah Blumenthal'* [1983] 1 AC 854, HL; *'The Splendid Sun'* [1981] QB 694, CA; and *'The Leonidas D'* [1985] 1 WLR 925, CA (on this stream of authority, Mustill & Boyd, *Commercial Arbitration: Companion Volume* (London, 2001), 503 ff).

150 [1988] 1 WLR 603.

Lords on three occasions,[151] and two before the Court of Appeal)[152] in which various contractual doctrines were applied to determine whether arbitration submission agreements had been terminated (the relevant doctrines considered in these cases included (i) implied terms[153]; (ii) repudiatory breach[154]; (iii) frustration[155]; (iv) mutual abandonment by inaction).[156] These elaborate doctrinal discussions too placed in response to the problem of stale arbitration references and the absence of a power, whether vested in the arbitral tribunal or the supervisory court, to terminate such references on the basis that, in view of the protracted delay, no fair or satisfactory hearing was possible. Eventually Parliament intervened by transposing into the arbitration context the concept of dismissal of litigation for 'want of prosecution'. In fact developments within the ordinary court context rendered that procedural device somewhat anachronistic. The law on this topic is not entirely satisfactory, but the problem of grossly delayed arbitration references appears to have abated in England.

2.69 There is more recent evidence of the contractual framework within which the arbitration agreement, including submission agreements, will be analysed. In *Bea Hotels NV* v. *Bellway LLC* (2007) both sides accepted that there can be a repudiation of an agreement to arbitrate and that the general principles of contractual breach and termination apply (see further on this case 2.70 below).[157] Similarly, the Court of Appeal in *Downing* v. *Al Tameer Establishment* (2002)[158] endorsed this analysis (as noted by Beatson J in *Dubai Islamic Bank PJSC* v. *PSI Energy Holding Co BSC*, 2011).[159] Potter LJ in the *Downing* case (2002) said[160]:

> *'the court approaches the question of whether or not a party has lost the right to arbitrate... by applying the traditional principles of the law of contract and, in particular, the doctrine of repudiation whereby if one party, by words or conduct, demonstrates an intention no*

---

[151] *Bremer Vulkan Schiffbau und Maschinenfabrik v. South India Shipping Corporation Ltd* [1981] AC 909, HL; *Paal Wilson & Co A/S v. Parternreederei Hannah Blumenthal ('The Hannah Blumenthal')* [1983] 1 AC 854, HL; *Food Corp of India v. Antclizo Shipping Corp ('The Antclizo')* [1988] 1 WLR 603, HL.

[152] *Allied Marine Transport Ltd. v. Vale do Rio Doce Navegacao SA ('The Leonidas D')* [1985] 1 WLR 925, CA; *Andre et Cie v. Marine Transocean Ltd ('The Splendid Sun')* [1981] QB 694, CA.

[153] *Bremer Vulkan Schiffbau und Maschinenfabrik v. South India Shipping Corporation Ltd* [1981] AC 909, HL; *Food Corp of India v. Antclizo Shipping Corp ('The Antclizo')* [1988] 1 WLR 603, HL.

[154] *Bremer* case [1981] AC 909, HL.

[155] *Paal Wilson & Co A/S v. Parternreederei Hannah Blumenthal ('The Hannah Blumenthal')* [1983] 1 AC 854, HL.

[156] *Andre et Cie v. Marine Transocean Ltd ('The Splendid Sun')* [1981] QB 694, CA (abandonment established); *Allied Marine Transport Ltd. v. Vale do Rio Doce Navegacao SA ('The Leonidas D')* [1985] 1 WLR 925, CA (abandonment not established).

[157] [2007] EWHC 1363 (Comm); [2007] 2 Lloyd's Rep 493; [2007] 1 CLC 920, at [13].

[158] [2002] EWCA Civ 721; [2002] 2 All ER (Comm) 545; see Potter LJ at [25] (too long to cite here).

[159] [2011] EWHC 1019 (Comm); [2011] 1 CLC 595, at [55].

[160] [2002] EWCA Civ 721; [2002] 2 All ER (Comm) 545, at [25].

longer to be bound by the contract, it is open to the other party to accept such demonstration as a repudiation and thereby to bring the contract to an end...[In] appropriate circumstances, a party may be held to have repudiated by anticipatory breach, and/or by an unequivocal rejection of any obligation to arbitrate, before such arbitration has been instituted by the other party to the agreement.'

2.70 Cooke J in *Bea Hotels NV* v. *Bellway LLC* (2007) held that the bringing of court proceedings in Israel did not constitute a repudiatory breach of an arbitration agreement[161] (lucidly re-examined by Beatson J in *Dubai Islamic Bank PJSC* v. *PSI Energy Holding Co BSC* (2011), see below). Cooke J concluded that there had been no repudiatory breach of the agreement to refer[162] the relevant dispute to arbitration because it was plain from the Israeli pleadings that Bellway (the arbitration claimant) was procedurally ring-fencing the matters raised in the arbitration and that the Israeli proceedings would not trench on that topic as between these parties.[163] Cooke J's test was summarised by Beatson J in *Dubai Islamic Bank PJSC* v. *PSI Energy Holding Co BSC* (2011),[164] following counsel's agreement, as follows:

'It was common ground (see Cooke J at [13]) that: (a) It was not repudiatory merely to bring proceedings in breach of an arbitration agreement even if the claims pursued in those proceedings were plainly ones which were subject to the arbitration agreement; (b) It was only a repudiatory breach where bringing the other proceedings was done in circumstances that showed that the party in question no longer intended to be bound to arbitrate; and (c) Such an intention could not lightly be inferred and could only be inferred from conduct which was clear and unequivocal.'

2.71 The repudiatory breach analysis also applies to failure to comply with an exclusive jurisdiction clause, as noted by Beatson J in *Dubai Islamic Bank PJSC* v. *PSI Energy Holding Co BSC* (2011)[165] (this case contains a careful review of the authorities).[166] Beatson J also noted that there can be a binding and unequivocal 'election' not to proceed in accordance with such a jurisdiction clause, or some species of estoppel can arise following such a statement. But neither waiver by election nor estoppel by representation or conduct was made out on the facts.[167]

---

[161] [2007] EWHC 1363 (Comm); [2007] 2 Lloyd's Rep 493; [2007] 1 CLC 920, at [13] (too long to cite here); at [15] citing *World Pride Shipping Ltd v. Daiichi Chuo Kisen Kaisha ('The Golden Anne')* [1984] 2 Lloyd's Rep 489, Lloyd J (Comm Ct); *Rederi Kommanditselskaabet Merc-Scandia IV v. Couniniotis SA ('The Mercanaut')* [1980] 2 Lloyd's Rep 183, Lloyd J (Comm Ct).

[162] *Bea* case, ibid, at [12].

[163] ibid, at [24].

[164] [2011] EWHC 1019 (Comm); [2011] 1 CLC 595, at [52].

[165] ibid.

[166] ibid, at [49] ff, considering *Rederi Kommanditselskaabet Merc-Scandia IV v. Couniniotis SA ('The Mercanaut')* [1980] 2 Lloyd's Rep 183, Lloyd J (Comm Ct); *World Pride Shipping Ltd v. Daiichi Chuo Kisen Kaisha ('The Golden Anne')* [1984] 2 Lloyd's Rep 489, Lloyd J (Comm Ct); *Downing v. Al Tameer Establishment* [2002] EWCA Civ 721; [2002] 2 All ER (Comm) 545; and *Bea Hotels NV v. Bellway LLC* [2007] EWHC 1363 (Comm); [2007] 2 Lloyd's Rep 493; [2007] 1 CLC 920.

[167] [2011] EWHC 1019 (Comm); [2011] 1 CLC 595, at [66] ff.

2.72 However, the repudiatory breach analysis does not extend to 'Adjudication' of construction disputes (arising from the building industry) under the statutory scheme of accelerated provisional determination (statute also allows experts to make swift decisions if disputes arise during the course of a building project; these decisions are initially provisional; they become binding if, within a short period, neither party seeks to re-open the determination).[168] Akenhead J so held in *Lanes Group plc* v. *Galliford Try Infrastructure Ltd* (2011), sitting in the Technology and Construction Court.[169] He held that the inability of parties to contract out of this statutory regime is incompatible with a party losing the benefit of such protection[170]: '*the statute requires in an unqualified way that a party to such contract "has the right" "at any time" to refer a dispute to adjudication. The party cannot lose its right to adjudicate by in some way "repudiating" the adjudication agreement and the concept of repudiation does not apply to statutory rights.*'

[168] P Coulson, *Coulson on Construction Adjudication* (3rd edn, Oxford University Press, 2015); Part II, Housing Grants, Construction and Regeneration Act 1996.

[169] [2011] EWHC 1035 (TCC); [2011] 1 CLC 937; [2011] BLR 438.

[170] ibid, at [25].

Chapter 3
'The Seat' and the Laws Affecting the Arbitration

Abstract Arbitration must be centred upon a nominated legal jurisdiction, the 'seat' of the process. The law governing the substance of the dispute might be different from that applicable to the arbitration agreement and, in turn, another law might govern the conduct of the arbitration. There is a further question concerning the types of matter which can be validly assigned to arbitration ('arbitrability').

3.1 Introduction[1]

3.01 The following must be differentiated: (i) the law governing the substantive dispute; (ii) the seat of the arbitration; (iii) the arbitration agreement (or individual arbitration submission); (iv) the procedure applicable to the arbitration, including the national law supporting that system (*lex arbitri* – the law of the seat of arbitration, or *lex fori* – the law of the forum or jurisdiction in which the arbitral seat is located); and (v) the language(s) of the arbitration.[2]

3.02 Different laws might govern: the law applicable to the substance of the dispute; the arbitration agreement (or individual arbitration submission, see next paragraph); and the procedure applicable to the arbitration reference, including the supporting domestic law (the so-called curial law or procedural law or *lex fori*).[3]

3.03 There is a distinction between (A) the overarching arbitration agreement ('continuous agreement') and (B) the subsidiary agreement to submit a particular

---

[1] E Gaillard, 'The Role of the Arbitrator in Determining the Applicable Law', in LW Newman and RD Hill (eds), *The Leading Arbitrators' Guide to International Arbitration* (3rd edn, New York, 2014), chapter 18; JC Kessedjian, 'Determination and Application of Relevant National and International Laws and Rules', in LA Mistelis and JDM Lew (eds), *Pervasive Problems in International Arbitration* (The Hague, 2006), 71–88; LA Collins, 'The Law Governing the Agreement and Procedure in International Arbitration in England', 126–140, in JDM Lew (ed), *Contemporary Problems in International Arbitration* (London, 1986).

[2] Selection of the language for the reference is an important and practical modality of the arbitration, which must be relevant to choice of arbitrators and counsel; on this topic the rules of the LCIA (London Court of International Arbitration) provide a detailed code for determining which language shall be adopted by the tribunal: LCIA Arbitration Rules (2014), Article 17.

[3] *Naviera Amazonica Peruana* v. *Cie Internacional de Seguros del Peru* [1988] 1 Lloyd's Rep 116, 119, CA, *per* Kerr LJ.

N. Andrews, *Arbitration and Contract Law*, Ius Gentium: Comparative Perspectives on Law and Justice 54, DOI 10.1007/978-3-319-27144-6_3

dispute to arbitration ('individual agreement').[4] There is the possibility that the law governing (A) might be different from that governing (B).[5] The division between A and B was examined by Aikens J in *Dubai Islamic Bank PJSC* v. *Paymentech Merchant Services Inc* (2001)[6] and by Beatson J in *Serbia* v. *Imagesat International NV* (2009).[7]

3.04 The law chosen to govern the arbitration agreement will not necessarily indicate the law governing the arbitration proceedings (*lex arbitri* – the law of the place of arbitration; and *lex fori* – the law of the forum or jurisdiction in which the arbitral seat is located).[8]

3.05 As Kerr LJ remarked in *Naviera Amazonica Peruana* v. *Cie Internacional de Seguros del Peru* (1988), 'occasionally, but rarely' not only will the law governing the substance differ from that governing the arbitration agreement and the arbitral process, but the law applicable to the arbitration agreement might differ also from that governing the arbitral process.[9] For example, the dispute-resolution clause might state that:

(a) Ruritanian law governs the main transaction;
(b) Utopian law governs the arbitration agreement;
(c) the law of Erewhon governs the procedure applicable to the arbitration reference, including the supporting domestic arbitral (or 'supervisory') law, and
(d) that the nominated seat or venue (where 'venue' is used as a synonym for seat) is also Erewhon.

3.2 The Law Governing the Substance of the Dispute

3.06 *English Law.* If the seat is England, the substance of the dispute considered in most arbitration references will be governed by English law either because that is the set of norms explicitly chosen by the parties or because, in the absence of such express choice, that system is in any event held to be applicable.[10]

3.07 *Foreign Law Governing the Substance of the Dispute.* It is possible that the applicable substantive law of the dispute will be a foreign set of laws.[11] If so,

---

[4] *Black Clawson International* v. *Papierwerke Waldhof-Aschaffenburg AG* [1981] 2 Lloyd's Rep 446, 455, *per* Mustill J.

[5] *ibid,* at 455.

[6] [2001] CLC 173, at [33] to [35].

[7] [2009] EWHC 2853 (Comm); [2010] 2 All ER (Comm) 571; [2010] 1 Lloyd's Rep 324, at [66] (illuminating but too long to cite here).

[8] *Union of India* v. *McDonnell Douglas* [1993] 2 Lloyd's Rep 48, 50, *per* Saville J, citing *James Miller & Partners* v. *Whitworth Street Estates (Manchester) Ltd* [1970] AC 583, HL.

[9] *Union of India, ibid,* at 119.

[10] Section 46(1)(a), Arbitration Act 1996; section 46(3), *ibid*; *Mustill & Boyd, Commercial Arbitration: Companion Volume* (London, 2001), 327.

[11] Again in accordance with express choice or conflicts rules: section 46(1)(a), Arbitration Act 1996; section 46(3), *ibid*; *Mustill & Boyd, Commercial Arbitration: Companion Volume* (London, 2001), 327.

Thomas J in *Hussmann (Europe) Ltd* v. *Al Ameen Development & Trade Co* (2000)[12] offered guidance on the possibility that a tribunal might actively seek to inform itself concerning aspects of foreign law[13]:

> '*The correct course to have been followed by the tribunal was to have asked the parties whether there were any points where the law of Saudi Arabia differed from the law of England and Wales or to have itself raised with the parties specific points on which they might need assistance. Certainly it would have been better if the tribunal had sought the views of the parties on the issues raised before instructing [the foreign legal expert] and discussed with the parties the terms in which he should be instructed.*'

Thomas J held that the tribunal had not acted wrongly in *seeking such an opinion* because section 37(1) of the Arbitration Act 1996 permits a tribunal to appoint its own expert(s). But Thomas J held that the tribunal had erred when it failed, contrary to section 37(1)(b), to allow the parties to comment on this advice. However, the tribunal's rejection of the foreign expert's opinion meant that no serious injustice resulted.[14]

3.08 *Non-Law*: The English legislation[15] also enables the parties to agree that the substance of the dispute will be subject to norms drawn from general principles of equity or norms founded on religious law,[16] including (it would appear) *lex mercatoria* (a suggested body of settled transnational contractual principles, or a contractual *ius gentium*; but on this topic, opinions divide; there are sceptics and enthusiasts, romantics and hard-boiled pragmatists; and the literature is extensive).[17]

---

[12] See the long passage at [2000] CLC 1243, at [41] to [44].

[13] *ibid*, at [43].

[14] *ibid*, at [44].

[15] See the reference in section 46(1)(b), Arbitration Act 1996 to '*such other considerations as are agreed by them or determined by the tribunal*'; *Mustill & Boyd, Commercial Arbitration: Companion Volume* (London, 2001), 326–8 and 124–127.

[16] (i) This renders arbitration practice under English rules more flexible that other contractual choices of law (see remainder of this note); this was acknowledged in *Halpern* v. *Halpern (No 2)* [2007] EWCA Civ 291; [2008] QB 195; (ii) the Rome I Regulation on the law applicable to contractual obligations, (EC) 593/2008, applicable to contracts formed after 17 December, 2009, does not permit the parties to choose a non-State law (*Dicey, Morris and Collins on the Conflict of Laws* (15th edn, London, 2012), vol 2, 32–049, 32–050; RG Fentiman, *International Commercial Litigation* (2nd edn, Oxford University Press, 2015), 5.28 to 5.30); see also *Halpern* case, at [21] ff and [37]); (iii) the Rome I Regulation, see Article 1(2)(e), does not does not apply to 'arbitration agreements' (as distinct from the matrix or main transaction), *Dicey* (15th edn, London, 2012), vol 2, 32–021; (iv) however, the provisions of Jewish law (or other elements of non-State law) might be incorporated as terms of a contract otherwise governed by national law, and thus be taken into account when interpreting the relevant contract: *Halpern* case, at [30] ff.

[17] For extensive literature, J Braithwaite, 'Standard Form Contracts as Transnational Law: Evidence from the Derivatives Markets' (2012) 75 MLR 779, nn 1–33, citing, notably, Lord Mustill, 'The new *Lex Mercatoria*: the First Twenty-five Years' (1988) 4 Arbitration International 86 (a sceptic); K Berger, *The Creeping Codification of the New Lex Mercatoria* (2nd edn, Kluwer, The Hague, 2010); see also B Goldman, 'The Applicable Law: General Principles of Law-the *Lex Mercatoria*', in JDM Lew (ed), *Contemporary Problems in International Arbitration* (London, 1986), 113.

Similarly, the English courts will respect a foreign arbitration agreement in which the arbitral tribunal is required to apply such fluid principles.[18]

3.09 *Arbitral Tribunal Deciding Points of International Law*. In *Serbia* v. *Imagesat International NV* (2009)[19] Beatson J (as he then was) concluded that *Ecuador* v. *Occidental Exploration & Production Co* (2005)[20] establishes that arbitration conducted under the Arbitration Act 1996 can involve issues which would not be justiciable by the English courts, applying Common Law principles. The *Ecuador* case (2005) supported the conclusion that the issue whether Serbia was a (valid or effective) party to the relevant arbitration reference (or had become one by submission to the reference) was justiciable by an arbitrator. That matter could be decided within the arbitration even though the question whether Serbia was a successor state or a continuator state might be non-justiciable in the ordinary courts. Furthermore, that preliminary issue—whether Serbia had become a valid and effective party to the arbitration reference—fell within the arbitrator's jurisdiction. Accordingly, the partial award on this preliminary matter could be re-examined by the High Court under section 67 of the Arbitration Act (appeals to the High Court concerning the arbitral tribunal's jurisdiction).

3.3 The Seat of the Arbitration

3.10 *Relevance of the Seat*. The seat will have an important bearing on the processes of ascertaining both the law governing the arbitration agreement and the law governing the arbitration process, or the 'curial law'. In the absence of explicit designation of the law governing these various matters, the relevance of the seat was considered by the Court of Appeal in *Sulamerica Cia Nacional de Seguros SA* v. *Enesa Engenharia SA* (2012) (on which see also **03.17 ff**)[21]; and by Clarke J in

---

[18] e.g., *Weissfisch* v. *Julius* [2006] EWCA Civ 218; [2006] 2 All ER (Comm) 504; [2006] 1 Lloyd's Rep 716; [2006] 1 CLC 424 (on which **4.15**); in this case the arbitrator, Anthony Julius, an English solicitor, was appointed to conduct arbitration with its seat in Geneva; Lord Phillips CJ at [7] cited the relevant clause: '*The Arbitrator will have the discretion to act ex aequo et bono whenever he may find it suitable or equitable, paying due regard in all circumstances to the parties' equal treatment and their right to be heard in fair adversarial proceedings.*'

[19] [2009] EWHC 2853 (Comm); [2010] 2 All ER (Comm) 571; [2010] 1 Lloyd's Rep 324, at [114] ff.

[20] [2005] EWCA Civ 1116; [2006] QB 432, at [32] ff, *per* Mance LJ. (A later issue, also concerning jurisdiction, went to the Court of Appeal under section 67, Arbitration Act 1996: *Ecuador* v. *Occidental Exploration & Production Co* [2007] EWCA Civ 656; [2007] 2 Lloyd's Rep 352; [2007] 2 CLC 16).

[21] [2012] EWCA Civ 638; [2012] 1 Lloyd's Rep 671; [2012] Lloyd's Rep IR 405.

ABB Lummus Global Ltd v. *Keppel Fels Ltd* (1999)[22] and by Aikens J in *Dubai Islamic Bank PJSC* v. *Paymentech Merchant Services Inc* (2001).[23]

3.11 In England and Wales, and also Northern Ireland, the 'juridical seat of the arbitration' is determined as follows:

(i) It can be 'designated' (a) 'by the parties to the arbitration agreement', or (b) 'by any arbitral or other institution or person vested by the parties with powers in that regard', or (c) 'by the arbitral tribunal if so authorised by the parties'; or
(ii) in the absence of (i) (a) to (c), the seat can be 'determined… having regard to the parties' agreement and all the relevant circumstances'.[24]

3.12 If the seat is England and Wales, or Northern Ireland, the provisions of Part 1 of the Arbitration Act 1996 apply.

3.13 Even if the seat is within one of those territories, or 'no seat has been designated or determined', the Arbitration Act 1996 will apply to the following matters (Clarke J in *ABB Lummus Global Ltd* v. *Keppel Fels Ltd* (1999) considered the structure of these provisions of the Arbitration Act 1996)[25]:

(i) the grant of a stay of legal proceedings[26];
(ii) enforcement of an award[27];
(iii) unless this is 'inappropriate', securing attendance of witnesses[28];
(iv) unless this is 'inappropriate', various supportive powers concerning, for example, taking of evidence, preservation of evidence, etc.[29];
(v) the court can exercise any of the powers contained within Part 1 of the Arbitration Act 1996 if '*by reason of a connection with England and Wale or Northern Ireland the court is satisfied that it is appropriate to do so*'[30]; (vi) the provision on the 'separability' of the arbitration agreement (**2.47**)[31]; and
(vi) the provision on the death of a party.[32]

---

[22] [1999] 2 Lloyd's Rep 24, considering *James Miller & Partners* v. *Whitworth Street Estates (Manchester) Ltd* [1970] AC 583, HL; *Black Clawson International* v. *Papierwerke Waldhof-Aschaffenburg AG* [1981] 2 Lloyd's Rep 446, Mustill J; *Naviera Amazonica Peruana* v. *Cie Internacional de Seguros del Peru* [1988] 1 Lloyd's Rep 116, CA; and *Union of India* v. *McDonnell Douglas* [1993] 2 Lloyd's Rep 48, Saville J.

[23] [2001] CLC 173, also noting (besides the cases listed in the preceding note) Lord Mustill's analysis in *Channel Tunnel Group Ltd* v. *Balfour Beatty Construction Ltd* [1993] AC 334, 357, HL.

[24] Section 3, Arbitration Act 1996. For an example of judicial determination under (ii), see Aikens J's decision in *Dubai Islamic Bank PJSC* v. *Paymentech Merchant Services Inc* [2001] CLC 173.

[25] [1999] 2 Lloyd's Rep 24, 33 col 1 to 34 col 2.

[26] Section 2(2)(a), *ibid*, referring to sections 9 to 11.

[27] Section 2(2)(b), *ibid*, referring to section 66.

[28] Section 2(3)(a), *ibid*, referring to section 43.

[29] Section 2(3)(b), *ibid*, referring to section 44.

[30] Section 2(4), *ibid*.

[31] Section 2(5), *ibid*, referring to section 7.

[32] Section 2(5), *ibid*, referring to section 8.

3.14 *Change of Seat.* Although the English Arbitration Act 1996 is silent on the question whether the seat can be changed from that which was originally designated or determined, Clarke J in *ABB Lummus Global Ltd* v. *Keppel Fels Ltd* (1999)[33] and Aikens J in *Dubai Islamic Bank PJSC* v. *Paymentech Merchant Services Inc* (2001)[34] accepted that the parties can by agreement vary the seat. Aikens J in the latter case also held that the determination or designation of a seat must be carried out so as to operate from the inception of arbitration proceedings, and that thereafter it can change (at least under English principles) only if the parties agree to a change of seat (as distinct from a mere change of the place where the proceedings might in fact occur: such 'peripatetic' proceedings, without a change of seat, are not uncommon).[35]

3.15 *No Change of Seat, but Change of Venue for Conduct of Part of Proceedings.* As just mentioned, a different point arises when the parties wish, or the tribunal proposes, that arbitration proceedings should take place in a place other than the designated or determined seat. Section 34(2) of the Arbitration Act 1996 empowers the tribunal to decide (subject to the parties' right to agree otherwise) 'when and where any part of the proceedings is to be held'. It is not uncommon for a seat to be established in jurisdiction X, but for the hearing (or hearings) to take place in another location, for the convenience of the parties or tribunal. As Saville J noted: '*This does not mean that the "seat" of the arbitration changes with each change of country. The legal place of the arbitration remains the same even if the physical place changes from time to time, unless of course the parties agree to change it.*'[36] The Court of Appeal in *Naviera Amazonica Peruana* v. *Cie Internacional de Seguros del Peru* (1988) also acknowledged that the place where the arbitration is held might in fact change, from time to time, for reasons of convenience.[37] But the court also made clear that such a physical change of hearing venue is not the same as a change of the legal seat.[38]

3.16 *Possible Change of Seat in Extreme Circumstances.* Pierre Lalive, a leading international arbitrator, supports the view that in exceptional circumstances the arbitral tribunal, or its governing institution, or perhaps a court, could change the seat of an arbitration if it had become 'unduly difficult' to conduct the proceedings in the originally nominated seat.[39] But his remarks were not made in the context of the English arbitration legislation and this point awaits clarification in this jurisdiction.

---

[33] [1999] 2 Lloyd's Rep 24.

[34] [2001] CLC 173.

[35] *ibid.*

[36] *Union of India* v. *McDonnell Douglas* [1993] 2 Lloyd's Rep 48, 50, col 2, *per* Saville J, noting *Naviera Amazonica Peruana* v. *Cie Internacional de Seguros del Peru* [1988] 1 Lloyd's Rep 116, 121.

[37] *Naviera Amazonica Peruana* v. *Cie Internacional de Seguros del Peru* [1988] 1 Lloyd's Rep 116, 120–1, CA, *per* Kerr LJ.

[38] *ibid.*

[39] P Lalive, 'On the Transfer of Seat in International Arbitration…', in JAR Nafziger and SC Symeonides (eds), *Law and Justice in a Multistate World: Essays in Honor of Arthur von Mehren* (Ardsley, New York, 2002), 515.

3.4 The Law Governing the Arbitration Agreement

3.17 English law applies the following three-pronged test to determine which law governs the arbitration agreement:

(a) the law expressly selected by the parties to govern the arbitration agreement; failing which
(b) the law which has been impliedly selected to govern the arbitration agreement (the inference will be that the law is normally the same as the law governing the substance of the dispute) or (in default of (a) or (b) supplying the answer); failing which
(c) the arbitration agreement will be governed by the law of the seat, on the basis that this is the law which has the closest and most real connection with the arbitration agreement.

This three-stage analysis was accepted in *Amin Rasheed Shipping Corp* v. *Kuwait Insurance Co (The Al Wahab)* (1984),[40] confirmed by the Court of Appeal in *Sulamerica Cia Nacional de Seguros SA* v. *Enesa Engenharia SA* (2012),[41] and further examined in the *Arsanovia* case (2012)[42] (in this last case Andrew Smith J noted[43] that the Court of Appeal in the *Sulamerica* case (2012)[44] had rejected the *dicta* of Longmore LJ *C* v. *D* (2007)[45] who had gone straight from the first question to the third question, excising the middle question).[46]

3.18 In the *Arsanovia* case (2012), the tests were presented by Andrew Smith J as follows:

(i) *Express Designation.* This is the question whether there has been an express choice of law concerning the arbitration agreement (Andrew Smith J in the *Arsanovia* case (2012) added *dicta* suggesting that in the case before him it might have been arguable that there had been a sufficiently clear nomination of India as the expressly applicable law governing the arbitration agreement)[47];

---

[40] [1984] AC 50, 61, HL, *per* Lord Diplock; and [1983] 1 WLR 228, 233, CA, *per* Sir John Donaldson MR, and 246–7, Goff LJ; [1982] 1 WLR 961, 967, *per* Bingham J).

[41] [2012] EWCA Civ 638; [2013] 1 WLR 102, at [9], *per* Moore-Bick LJ; supported by Lord Neuberger MR at [62]; at [48], Hallett LJ agreeing.

[42] *Arsanovia Ltd* v. *Cruz City 1 Mauritius Holdings* [2012] EWHC 3702 (Comm); [2013] 2 All ER (Comm) 1; [2013] 1 Lloyd's Rep 235 at [8].

[43] *ibid*, at [13].

[44] *Sulamerica Cia Nacional de Seguros SA* v. *Enesa Engenharia SA* [2012] EWCA Civ 638; [2013] 1 WLR 102.

[45] *C* v. *D* [2007] EWCA Civ 1282; [2008] 1 Lloyd's Rep 239, at [21] to [29]. On the status of Longmore LJ's comments as *dicta*, see Andrew Smith J at *Arsanovia* case [2012] EWHC 3702 (Comm); [2013] 2 All ER (Comm) 1; [2013] 1 Lloyd's Rep 235 at [11].

[46] Andrew Smith J in the *Arsanovia* case [2012] EWHC 3702 (Comm); [2013] 2 All ER (Comm) 1; [2013] 1 Lloyd's Rep 235, at [12].

[47] *ibid*, at [22].

(ii) *Implied Designation.* This test arises (in default of express designation) because English law gives **presumptive effect to the same law as that chosen by the parties to govern the main transaction** (for example, where the main transaction is expressly governed by the law of Utopia, there will be an implication that the arbitration agreement is also subject to the law of Utopia). **Choice of a seat in England, and hence in a territory other than Utopia, is not sufficient to displace this presumption.**[48] Where the seat is England and the arbitration clause expressly excludes a particular aspect of a foreign arbitral system, that partial exclusion of the foreign arbitral system might (as in the *Arsanovia* case) be interpreted as impliedly adopting the remainder of the foreign arbitral system.[49]

(iii) *Default Rule: Closest and Most Real Connection.* It is only if the court discerns no express or implied agreement concerning the law applicable to the arbitration agreement that the court will apply the default rule: that the arbitration agreement will be governed by the law of the seat, on the basis that this is the law which has the closest and most real connection with the arbitration agreement.[50]

3.19 *In the Sulamerica Case* (2012), the seat was London and it was held that there had been neither an express nor an implied nomination of Brazilian law to govern the arbitration agreement. Moore-Bick LJ concluded that the following three factors (individually or collectively) did not impliedly render the arbitration agreement subject to Brazilian law[51]:

(i) the parties' choice of Brazilian law to govern a (disputed) mediation agreement;
(ii) nomination of the Brazil courts as the exclusive jurisdiction (it appears for fall-back purposes, if the other modes of dispute resolution failed); and
(iii) the fact that Brazilian law also expressly governed the substantive transaction.

And so the third limb of the test applied: that the law governing the arbitration agreement should be the law of the seat (here England).[52] Moore-Bick LJ in the *Sulamerica* case (2012)[53] noted that the operation of this third test was fortified by the fact that if Brazilian law applied to the arbitration agreement, rather than English law, the arbitration agreement would be commercially ineffective, because the parties would not be *ex ante* obliged to pursue arbitration. The parties would instead have to consent to the making of a reference to arbitration at the time when such a reference is proposed by the other. But this would be unworkable in most cases because consent would be lacking.

[48] *ibid*, at [16] and [19] and [21].

[49] *ibid*, at [13], [20], and [24].

[50] *Arsanovia* case [2012] EWHC 3702 (Comm); [2013] 2 All ER (Comm) 1; [2013] 1 Lloyd's Rep 235 at [13] and [24].

[51] [2012] EWCA Civ 638; [2013] 1 WLR 102, at [31].

[52] *ibid*, at [32].

[53] *ibid*,, at [30].

3.20 *The Law Governing the Arbitration Agreement: Should there be a Stronger Default Rule in Favour of the Seat?* The current law is, as mentioned, that the arbitration agreement should normally match the law governing the substantive agreement on the basis of the second 'implied' limb of the threefold test set out above.[54] However, Moore-Bick LJ in the *Sulamerica* case (2012) noted[55] that a different direction was indicated by a leading textbook (*Mustill & Boyd, Commercial Arbitration*, 1989)[56] and by Longmore LJ in *C* v. *D* (2007)[57] and Toulson J in *XL Insurance Ltd* (2001).[58] Also in the *Sulamerica* case (2012), Lord Neuberger MR (as he then was) noted the same shift in the case law discussion.[59] Thus, by contrast, Longmore LJ suggested (this suggestion is not English law) in *C* v. *D* (2007) that English law should incline in favour of treating the law of the seat as the law applicable to the arbitration agreement unless there has been an express choice to the contrary.[60] That tension had been identified (and left unresolved) by Lord Neuberger MR in the *Sulamerica* case.[61] It appears unlikely that a third Court of Appeal will deviate from the *Sulamerica* case. But the Supreme Court has the power to overrule the *Sulamerica* case and abandon the middle category of an implied selection on the presumption that this is the law governing the substance of the dispute.

3.21 *Criticism of the* C v. D *Law of Seat Approach.* Lord Neuberger MR in the *Sulamercia* case noted Joseph's 'powerful' textbook criticism of *C* v. *D* (2007).[62] Also in the *Sulamerica* case Moore-Bick LJ summarised, with qualified approval, that criticism.[63] In essence, the points made by Joseph in his textbook are:

(i) *continuity*: pre- *C* v. *D* case law favoured the *Sulamerica* approach, and that case law was not considered in *C* v. *D*; [64]

---

[54] *ibid,* at [11] ff, noting comments by Lord Mustill in *Channel Tunnel Group Ltd* v. *Balfour Beatty Construction Ltd* [1993] AC 334, 357–8, HL; by Mustill J in *Black Clawson International Ltd* v. *Papierwerke Waldhof-Aschaffenburg AG* [1982] 2 Lloyd's Rep 446, 456, col. 1; by Colman J in *Sonatrach Petroleum Corp* v. *Ferrell International Ltd* [2002] 1 All ER (Comm) 627, at [32]; by Potter J in *Sumitomo Heavy Industries Ltd* v. *Oil & Natural Gas Commission* [1994] 1 Lloyd's Rep 45, 57, col. 1; and by Cooke J in *Leibinger* v. *Stryker Trauma GmbH* [2005] EWHC 690 (Comm).

[55] [2012] EWCA Civ 638; [2013] 1 WLR 102, at [17].

[56] (2nd edn, London, 1989), 63.

[57] *Sulamerica* case [2012] EWCA Civ 638; [2013] 1 WLR 102, at [20] and [21], commenting on Longmore LJ's discussion in *C* v. *D* [2007] EWCA Civ 1282, [2008] 1 All ER (Comm) 1001.

[58] *Sulamerica* case, *ibid,* at [19], commenting on *XL Insurance* Ltd [2001] 1 All ER (Comm) 530; [2000] 2 Lloyd's Rep 500.

[59] *Sulamerica* case, *ibid,* at [61].

[60] *C* v. *D* [2007] EWCA Civ 1282; [2008] 1 Lloyd's Rep 239, at [21] to [29].

[61] *Sulamerica* case, *ibid,* at [49] ff, notably at [56] to [59].

[62] *ibid,* at [58], noting D Joseph, *Jurisdiction and Arbitration Agreements and Their Enforcement* (2nd edn, London, 2010), paras 6.33–6.41; see now on this topic Joseph (3rd edn, 2015), 6.29 ff; for a sixpoint distillation of the case law, Hamblen J in the *Habas Sinai* case [2013] EWHC 4071 (Comm); [2014] 1 Lloyd's Rep 479, at [101]; see also A Briggs, *Private International Law in English Courts* (Oxford Uiviersity Press, 2014), 14.38 ff.

[63] *Sulamerica* case, *ibid,* at [24].

[64] Thus the *Sulamerica* case vindicates Colman J in *Sonatrach Petroleum Corp (BVI)* v. *Ferrell International Ltd* [2002] 1 All ER (Comm) 627, at [32], cited by Moore-Bick LJ in the *Sulamerica*

(ii) *overlapping issues of validity and identification of parties*: considerations of forensic economy and consistency support the presumption that the main contract and the arbitration agreement should be governed by the same substantive law[65];
(iii) *exaggeration of the claim that there is close and real connection between the arbitration agreement and the law of the seat*: Jacob contends that there is no real problem if the proper law of the arbitration agreement is different from the law of the seat.[66]
(iv) *wider dispute resolution clauses:* arbitration clauses might subsist within more complex multi-level dispute clauses, including mediation and expert determination clauses, so that a mismatch between the proper law of the main agreement and the dispute-resolution clause will become more problematic[67] (but this point was explicitly doubted by Lord Neuberger MR in the *Sulamerica* case).[68]

3.22 *Relevant Arguments if the Approach in the Sulamerica Case is Re-examined.* The Supreme Court might prefer the approach suggested in *C* v. *D* and thus reformulate the law as follows:

(i) there should be a strong presumption that the arbitration agreement should be governed by the law of the seat; and this default position should be displaced only by express and clear choice of a different set of laws to govern the arbitration agreement;
(ii) (a) the middle category of 'implied agreements' designating the law applicable to arbitration agreements should be eliminated; but if this middle category is instead retained, the law should act on the opposite presumption: (b) that the arbitration agreement is to be governed by the same law as that of the seat, unless there are unusual and strong contrary indications.

Arguably, the following factors tilt the matter in favour of that re-formulation (preferably (ii) (a), that is, elimination of the middle category; failing which (ii) (b), that is, a presumption that, in the absence of express designation of the law applicable to the arbitration agreement, the law governing it will be that of the seat).

First, the current presumption that the law applicable to the arbitration agreement should be presumed to be the same as the law governing the substance of the dispute (the main transaction) seems to be an anachronistic approach for it clashes with the modern and transnationally accepted doctrine known as the 'separability' principle

---

case, at [13] (and Moore-Bick LJ cited at [14] similar comments by Potter J in *Sumitomo Heavy Industries Ltd v. Oil and Natural Gas Commission [1994] 1 Lloyd's Rep 45,* and by Cooke J in *Leibinger* v. *Stryker Trauma GmbH* [2006] EWHC 690 (Comm)); similarly, Saville J's decision in *Union of India* v. *McDonnell Douglas* [1993] 2 Lloyd's Rep 48, as noted by D Joseph, *Jurisdiction and Arbitration Agreements and Their Enforcement* (2nd edn, London, 2010), 6.37 (discussion not presented in 3rd edn, 2015).

[65] D Joseph, *ibid,* at 6.41 (not presented in 3rd edn, 2015).

[66] *ibid*, at 6.41 (not presented in 3rd edn, 2015).

[67] *ibid.*

[68] [2012] EWCA Civ 638; [2013] 1 WLR 102 at [60]: '*The fact that the mediation agreement...[is] governed by Brazilian law does not necessarily mean that any subsequent arbitration must be similarly so governed.*'

(**2.47**), namely, that the arbitration agreement is juridically distinct from the main transaction.[69]

Secondly, English courts now acknowledge that the law of the seat is the law with which the arbitration agreement has 'the closest and most real connection'.[70] There is ample support for this approach, as noted in the *Sumamerica* case,[71] in the various provisions of the Arbitration Act 1996. That statute applies the law of the seat to determine these matters: section 5—arbitration agreement to be in writing[72]; section 7—separability principle; section 8—arbitration agreement not discharged by death of a party; section 12—power of court to extend time for commencement of arbitration; section 13—interaction of English arbitration and the Limitation Act 1980. Furthermore, in the *Sulamerica* case (2012) Lord Neuberger MR noted the modern emphasis upon the significance of the 'separability' principle[73] and of the 'closest and most real connection' test in this context.[74]

Thirdly, the search for an implied intention is something of a 'will of the wisp', producing lengthy debate.

Fourthly, as noted by *Mustill & Boyd*,[75] the New York Convention on the Recognition and Enforcement of Foreign Arbitral Awards (1958) adopts the presumption that (in the absence of clear contrary indication by the parties) the law governing the arbitration agreement should be the law of the seat. Thus Article V.1(a) of the NYC (1958) provides: '*The parties to the [arbitration] agreement... were, under the law applicable to them, under some incapacity, or* ***the said agreement is not valid under the law to which the parties have subjected it or, failing any indication thereon, under the law of country where the award was made.***' Similarly, in Scots law the law of the seat governs the arbitration agreement, unless the parties have expressly stipulated for some other law.[76]

Finally, it would be forensically easier for the court of the seat to consider the arbitration agreement using the law with which it is most familiar; it could then avoid the uncertainty and complexity created by conflicting expert opinions on

---

[69] See Moore-Bick LJ noted in *Sulamerica Cia Nacional de Seguros SA* v. *Enesa Engenharia SA* [2012] EWCA Civ 638; [2013] 1 WLR 102, at [9].

[70] e.g., the authorities cited by Andrew Smith J in *Arsanovia Ltd* v. *Cruz City 1 Mauritius Holdings* [2012] EWHC 3702 (Comm); [2013] 2 All ER (Comm) 1; [2013] 1 Lloyd's Rep 235, at [24].

[71] These provisions were noted in the *Sulamerica* case, [2012] EWCA Civ 638; [2013] 1 WLR 102, *per* Moore-Bick LJ at [29] and Lord Neuberger MR at [55].

[72] Considered by Toulson J in *XL Insurance Ltd* v. *Owens Corning* [2001] 1 All ER (Comm) 530; [2000] 2 Lloyd's Rep 500; [2001] CP Rep 22; [2001] CLC 914; Toulson J's analysis was approved in the *Sulamerica* case by both Moore-Bick [2012] EWCA Civ 638; [2013] 1 WLR 102, at [29] and by Lord Neuberger MR, at [55].

[73] [2012] EWCA Civ 638; [2013] 1 WLR 102, at [55].

[74] *ibid*, at [55].

[75] *Commercial Arbitration* (2nd edn, London, 1989), 63.

[76] Section 6, Arbitration (Scotland) Act 2010: *Law governing arbitration agreement: Where—(a) the parties to an arbitration agreement agree that an arbitration under that agreement is to be seated in Scotland, but (b) the arbitration agreement does not specify the law which is to govern it, then, unless the parties otherwise agree, the arbitration agreement is to be governed by Scots law.*

aspects of foreign law (for an example of the complexities arising from proof of foreign law concerning the arbitration agreement, see *Dallah Real Estate & Tourism Holding Co* v. *Pakistan* (2010), **9.36**).[77] Some foreign national systems of arbitral law are much less developed than English law and are more likely, therefore, to provide unclear or even surprising approaches to the ascertainment, construction, and implementation etc., of arbitration agreements.

3.5 The Law of the Arbitral Process: Procedural and Curial Laws

3.23 A line of cases[78] establish that the curial or procedural law of the arbitration seat (or lex fori) should be the regulatory arbitration law applicable within the jurisdiction where that seat is situated. For example, the law concerning supervision of arbitral proceedings and concerning the validity of the award should derive from the national law of the relevant seat. This will avoid conflicts of approaches between the courts of the law of the seat and foreign courts. And so where the parties have stated that the seat of the arbitration shall be Utopia, it will be implicit that they intend that the arbitration proceedings should be conducted within the curial or procedural framework of Utopian law.[79] This presumptive approach will avoid, therefore, divergence between the seat and the procedural law governing the reference.[80]

3.24 The Court of Appeal in *Naviera Amazonica Peruana* v. *Cie Internacional de Seguros del Peru* (1988) held that specification of arbitration 'under the conditions and laws of London' was sufficient to specify (adopting commercial notions of reasonable implication) that the seat would be London and that the procedural law applicable to the reference would be English arbitration law[81] (the parties had also agreed to a conflicting choice of forum, specifying the Peruvian courts in Lima, but the English court held that this had been effectively overridden by the arbitration agreement).[82] The English court rejected a 'jurisdictional split' which would have involved holding the arbitration in Peru in accordance with English arbitration rules,

[77] [2010] UKSC 46; [2011] 1 AC 763.

[78] *Black Clawson International* v. *Papierwerke Waldhof-Aschaffenburg AG* [1981] 2 Lloyd's Rep 446, Mustill J; *Naviera Amazonica Peruana* v. *Cie Internacional de Seguros del Peru* [1988] 1 Lloyd's Rep 116, CA; *Union of India* v. *McDonnell Douglas* [1993] 2 Lloyd's Rep 48, Saville J; *ABB Lummus Global Ltd* v. *Keppel Fels Ltd* [1999] 2 Lloyd's Rep 24, Clarke J.

[79] *Union of India* v. *McDonnell Douglas* [1993] 2 Lloyd's Rep 48, 50, *per* Saville J; *Naviera Amazonica Peruana* v. *Cie Internacional de Seguros del Peru* [1988] 1 Lloyd's Rep 116,120, CA; noting also *Black Clawson International* v. *Papierwerke Waldhof-Aschaffenburg AG* [1981] 2 Lloyd's Rep 446, 453, *per* Mustill J.

[80] *Union of India* v. *McDonnell Douglas* [1993] 2 Lloyd's Rep 48, 51, *per* Saville J.

[81] [1988] 1 Lloyd's Rep 116.

[82] *ibid,* at 121.

but subject to the ultimate supervision of the Peruvian courts.[83] The upshot of the case was that the arbitration would take place in London and that the (English) Commercial Court would be available to assist in the appointment of an arbitrator.

3.25 Similarly, Mustill J in *Black Clawson International* v. *Papierwerke Waldhof-Aschaffenburg AG* (1981)[84] held that the parties' specification that the arbitration reference should be conducted in Zurich ('the arbitration shall take place in Zurich') meant that the English courts should not be treated as retaining a supervisory jurisdiction over that process (despite the arbitration agreement stating that the arbitration should be 'deemed to be submission to arbitration within the meaning of [the then applicable Arbitration statutes] of England'). To allow the English supervisory arbitration machinery to apply to arbitration proceedings taking place in Zurich would give rise to the possibility of conflict between the Swiss process (for it was there that the arbitration had its seat) and the English High Court. In this case Mustill J had determined, therefore, that the seat of the arbitration was Switzerland, and that the English courts had no supervisory responsibility. That approach was preferred to an alternative view, that the process should be regarded as an English arbitration, London being the seat, but with a venue in Switzerland.

3.26 However, it is not impossible that the curial law (that is, the relevant judicial system of supervision) applicable to the relevant arbitration might differ from the municipal curial law of the relevant seat. This was acknowledged by Hobhouse J in *Dallal* v. *Bank Mellat* in the context of a special tribunal instituted by agreement between the US and Iran (the Iran-US Claims Tribunal), but his remarks should be understood as influenced by that special arrangement.[85]

3.6 'Arbitrability': Disputes Beyond the Pale of Arbitration[86]

3.27 Not all civil disputes or issues are capable of being subject to arbitration. Section 81(1)(a) of the Arbitration Act 1996 refers to 'matters which are not capable of settlement by arbitration'. Section 81(1)(c) of the Arbitration Act 1996 refers to 'the refusal or recognition or enforcement of an arbitral award on grounds of public policy' (on that topic, **9.11**).[87]As noted at **9.07**, Article V(2)(a) of the New York Convention (1958) grants a ground for non-recognition of foreign awards which is based on the concept of 'arbitrability'. Although no more than a passing observation,

---

[83] *ibid,* at 120, and 121.

[84] [1981] 2 Lloyd's Rep 446.

[85] [1986] QB 441, 458.

[86] *Mustill & Boyd, Commercial Arbitration: Companion Volume* (London, 2001), 70–82, containing references to literature; *Redfern and Hunter on International Arbitration* (6th edn, Oxford University Press, 2015), 2.124 ff; LA Mistelis and Stavros L Brekoulakis (eds), *Arbitrability: International and Comparative Perspectives* (The Hague, 2009).

[87] Similarly, section 103(3), Arbitration Act 1996, in the context of recognition or enforcement of a New York Convention (1958) award.

in his Opinion in the *Gazprom* case, Advocate General Wathelet[88] thought that it is possible[89] that the appropriate ground of non-recognition in that case would have been Article V(2)(a), namely non-arbitrability of the corporate investigation which had been initiated before the Lithuanian courts.

3.28 Some situations clearly lie beyond the pale of arbitration. It is obvious, for example, that it would not be possible to use arbitration to determine matters affecting the welfare of children.

3.29 But an open mind might be taken to questions of matrimonial finance not affecting children. In this context there is in fact a demand for arbitration in England, because this consensual process would be very likely to be both quicker and cheaper than the court process regulating divorce and financial orders. Furthermore, arbitration would be confidential. The legal impediment is that the family court's jurisdiction cannot be ousted.[90] And so an arbitration award would need to be clothed as a consent order, requiring the court to ratify. This issue remains to be worked through.

3.30 Another context in which arbitration would be problematic, and probably unavailable, is planning law. Such issues, although arising between individual landowners and planning authorities, are not merely bilateral contests: they have an obvious impact on third parties, and affected persons, sometimes the public at large, are given wide scope to participate or intervene and make objections.

3.31 Many of these matters can be expressed as a matter of public policy. But there are also issues which lie beyond the competence of arbitrators because they lack the remedial powers to make determinations which will affect third parties. On this basis it is clear that winding-up petitions (in the sphere of company law) cannot be the subject of arbitration. Only the court has power to make such complex determinations.

3.32 *Mustill & Boyd* (2001),[91] although acknowledging the principled and legislative fact that there are certain matters not susceptible to arbitration, suggested attractively that:

> '*the policy of English law, as of arbitration law worldwide, is to encourage and support arbitration as a means of settling commercial disputes, and particular international commercial disputes. Doctrinaire disapproval of procedures on the margin of arbitrability is not the way forward. If the parties have chosen any method which they intend to be a form of arbitration they should be allowed, and if possible compelled, to affirm their choice.*'

3.33 *'Arbitrability': English Discussion.* The leading English case on this topic is *Fulham Football Club (1987) Ltd* v. *Richards* (2011)[92] (a decision which is consistent with the approach adopted in the same context by an Australian court).[93]

---

[88] Opinion of Advocate General Wathelet (delivered 4 December 2014), at [130] to [152].

[89] *ibid*, at [165].

[90] For this restriction, section 34(1)(a), Matrimonial Causes Act 1973; on which *Radmacher* v. *Granatino* [2010] UKSC 42; [2011] 1 AC 534, at [2], [154].

[91] *Commercial Arbitration: Companion Volume* (2001), 75.

[92] [2011] EWCA Civ 855; [2012] Ch 333; Longmore, Patten, and Rix LJJ (latter at [97]) held that section 1(b) of the Arbitration Act 1996 requires courts to lean in favour of a wide consensual power to refer matters to arbitration, subject only to points of public interest.

[93] *ibid*, at [79], noting *ACD Tridon Inc* v. *Tridon Australia Pty Ltd* [2002] NSWSC 896.

3.34 The *Fulham Football Club* case (2011) arose from these facts. A leading footballer, Peter Crouch, an English international player, had been placed on the transfer list by his club, Portsmouth Football Club. The Portsmouth club was in financial difficulty. Fulham FC wanted to sign him. But he was sold instead to Tottenham Hotspurs FC. Fulham FC was aggrieved that, Sir David Richards, the Chairman (and a director) of the Premiership (the top league, consisting of 20 clubs, in which all three clubs were then playing) had intervened as an agent on behalf of the transferor and transferee clubs. Fulham FC contended that this had been a breach of his fiduciary duty to be even-handed towards all the Premiership clubs. The same club claimed that the transfer to Tottenham had taken place only because of Sir David's (allegedly) illicit intervention. Fulham contended that it had been the victim of 'unfair prejudice'[94] under the company legislation. Each football club within the Premiership had a right as shareholder of the Premiership, a company, to exercise its statutory rights under that legislation.[95] And so Fulham petitioned, by court proceedings, for an injunction to exclude Richards from his position within the Premiership. Such proceedings would take place in public. Sir David Richards was prepared to accede as a party to arbitration. He and the Premiership sought from the High Court a stay[96] of the court proceedings in recognition of an arbitration agreement, of wide scope,[97] contained within the Premiership rules. The Court of Appeal granted the stay, holding (i) that there was no reason of public policy[98] why the arbitral tribunal should not adjudicate on these matters; (ii) and that there was no statutory reservation (express[99] or implied)[100] of the courts' exclusive jurisdiction in this matter; and (iii) the court distinguished the legislative regime concerning winding-up petitions, where the court's jurisdiction is exclusive.[101] In short, this was a circumscribed issue, within the tribunal's remedial competence, not pregnant with third party ramification, not rooted in a dark issue of public policy which should be

[94] [2011] EWCA Civ 855; [2012] Ch 333, at [59], noting Lord Hoffmann's exegesis on this provision in *O'Neill* v. *Phillips* [1999] 1 WLR 1092, 1098G–1099B, HL.

[95] Section 994, Companies Act 2006; and on the court's wide remedial powers, section 996, Companies Act 2006: cited [2011] EWCA Civ 855; [2012] Ch 333, at [45].

[96] Section 9(4), Arbitration Act 1996.

[97] Longmore LJ was satisfied it was sufficiently wide: [2011] EWCA Civ 855; [2012] Ch 333, at [95].

[98] *ibid*, at [78] *per* Patten LJ; and at [97] to [104] *per* Longmore LJ; overruling *Exeter City AFC Ltd* v. *Football Conference Ltd* [2004] EWHC 831 (Ch), [2004] 1 WLR 2910, Judge Weeks QC (which had conflicted with *Re Vocam Europe Ltd* [1998] BCC 396, Rimer J, the latter case was here affirmed).

[99] [2011] EWCA Civ 855; [2012] Ch 333, at [96], *per* Longmore LJ; and Patten LJ at [42], contrasting sections 34–36, Matrimonial Causes Act 1973; section 203, Employment Rights Act 1996 and section 144(1), Equality Act 2010 (discussed in *Clyde & Co LLP* v. *Van Winkelhof* [2011] EWHC 668 (QB)).

[100] [2011] EWCA Civ 855; [2012] Ch 333, at [85] to [88], *per* Patten LJ; at [96] *per* Longmore LJ.

[101] *ibid*, at [52] and [53], noting section 122(1)(g), Insolvency Act 1986 (and citing *Re Crigglestone Coal Co Ltd* [1906] 2 Ch 327; and noting Lord Hoffmann's comments on insolvency proceedings in *Cambridge Gas Transport Co* v. *Official Committee of Unsecured Creditors of Navigator Holdings plc* [2006] UKPC 26; [2007] 1 AC 508, at [14]).

monopolised by state courts. As Patten LJ explained (here the passage has been divided into four segments)[102]:

(1) arbitral substantive competence: '*...determination of whether there has been unfair prejudice consisting of the breach of an agreement or some other unconscionable behaviour is plainly capable of being decided by an arbitrator*'
(2) remedial competence: '*an arbitration tribunal ...would have the power to grant the [injunction] sought by Fulham in its section 994*[103] *petition...*'
(3) no State monopoly or special advantage: '*Nor does the determination of issues of this kind call for some kind of state intervention in the affairs of the company which only a court can sanction.*'
(4) third-parties not affected: '*[Fulham's complaint]...is an essentially contractual dispute which does not necessarily engage the rights of creditors or impinge on any statutory safeguards imposed for the benefit of third parties. The...only issue between the parties is whether Sir David has acted in breach of the FA and FAPL Rules in relation to the transfer of a Premier League player.*'

3.35 The Court of Appeal in the *Fulham Football Club* cited the following leading commentators on the issue of 'arbitrability'[104]:

(i) comments of *Mustill & Boyd* (1989)[105]:

> '*The types of remedies which the arbitrator can award are limited by considerations of public policy and by the fact that he is appointed by the parties and not by the state. For example, he cannot impose a fine or a term of imprisonment, commit a person for contempt or issue a writ of subpoena; nor can he make an award which is binding on third parties or affects the public at large, such as a judgment in rem against a ship, an assessment of the rateable value of land, a divorce decree, a winding-up order...*'

(ii) comments by Gary Born[106]:

> '*Although the better view is that the [New York Convention (1958)] imposes limits on Contracting States' applications of the non-arbitrability doctrine, the types of claims that are non-arbitrable differ from nation to nation....The types of disputes which are non-arbitrable nonetheless almost always arise from a common set of considerations. The non-arbitrability doctrine rests on the notion that some matters so pervasively involve public rights, or interests of third parties, which are the subjects of uniquely governmental authority, that agreements to resolve such disputes by "`private" arbitration should not be given effect.*'

---

[102] [2011] EWCA Civ 855; [2012] Ch 333, at [77].

[103] Section 994, Companies Act 2006; on the court's wide remedial powers, section 996, Companies Act 2006: cited [2011] EWCA Civ 855; [2012] 1 All ER 414; [2011] BCC 910, at [45].

[104] [2011] EWCA Civ 855; [2012] Ch 333, at [38] and [39].

[105] *Commercial Arbitration* (2nd edn, London, 1989), 149; much more detailed, but not cited by the court is Mustill and Boyd's further discussion in *Commercial Arbitration*: *Companion Volume* (2001), 70–82, containing references to literature.

[106] G Born, *International Commercial Arbitration* (Kluwer, Deventer, 2009), 768.

Chapter 4
Upholding the Agreement to Arbitrate

Abstract The two main ways in which arbitration agreements are upheld by the courts are: staying of court proceedings which are inconsistent with the commitment to arbitrate; the grant of anti-suit injunctions to stop a person from proceeding in a way which is similarly inconsistent with that commitment. Other topics include the grant of freezing relief by courts in support of arbitration proceedings or the judicial award of other interim orders to 'hold the ring' while arbitral proceedings are commenced.

4.1 Introduction

4.01 These are the main points made in this chapter:

(i) An arbitration clause creates an implicit 'negative' right not to be sued other than in accordance with an arbitration clause to which the applicant and respondent are party.

(ii) A stay of judicial proceedings is the primary mechanism for 'giving effect' to an arbitration agreement. And the New York Convention (1958) requires contracting states to give effect to arbitration agreements.

(iii) English courts (subject to (iv) below) might issue an injunction to stop a party pursuing litigation or arbitration outside England if that conduct is a violation of an arbitration agreement in respect of which the English court has jurisdiction to 'police' compliance. Furthermore the English courts can also grant a declaration in this context, whether independently of, or (as will be more usual) in addition to, an anti-suit injunction.

(iv) But where the infringing litigation, brought in breach of an arbitration clause or exclusive jurisdiction clause, occurs within a EU Member, anti-suit relief is not permitted. In the *West Tankers* case (2009), the ECJ held that an anti-suit injunction cannot be granted to stop the (English) respondent from commencing or continuing to pursue court litigation in another Member State

N. Andrews, *Arbitration and Contract Law*, Ius Gentium: Comparative Perspectives on Law and Justice 54, DOI 10.1007/978-3-319-27144-6_4

within the EU.[1] Outside the geographical zone of this restriction, however, the English courts retain the power to issue anti-injunctive relief, for example, if the offending proceedings are brought in New York, or Singapore, these being jurisdictions outside the European judicial area.

(v) The power exercisable by the English courts to issue anti-suit relief is derived from the general power conferred under section 37(1) of the Senior Courts Act 1981, and that provision is the sole basis (section 44 of the Arbitration Act 1996 is not applicable for this purpose on this point see Lord Mance in the *AES* case (2013) at [48], quoted in the text below at 4.24).

(vi) Where the English court makes an anti-suit decision on the basis that a valid arbitration clause has been shown to exist, that decision will create an issue estoppel[2] on this point as between those parties. It follows that an arbitral tribunal with a seat in England (or, even if the seat of the arbitration is outside England, an arbitral tribunal willing to recognise Common Law principles of *res judicata*) would give effect to this estoppel if the point arose in a dispute between the same parties.

(vii) Damages can be awarded in English law for breach of an arbitration agreement.

(viii) The High Court can issue a declaration under section 66 of the Arbitration Act 1996 in enforcement of an arbitral award's declaratory award, because section 66 is not confined to coercive forms of enforcement.

(ix) The chapter ends with discussion of protective and other interim relief granted by the courts in support of arbitration.

4.2 Staying English Court Proceedings

4.02 A stay of judicial proceedings is the primary mechanism for 'giving effect' to an arbitration agreement.[3] An important transnational provision is Article II.3 of the New York Convention (1958), which states:

> '*The court of a Contracting State, when seised of an action in manner in respect of which the parties have made an agreement within the meaning of this article [viz an arbitration agreement], shall, at the request of one of the parties, refer the parties to arbitration, unless*

[1] *Allianz SpA etc.* v. *West Tankers, 'The Front Comor'* (C-185/07) [2009] 1 AC 1138, ECJ; confirmed in *Gazprom OAO* case (Grand Chamber, ECJ, 13 May 2015) (Case C-536/13): see **4.22**.

[2] *Andrews on Civil Processes* (Intersentia, Cambridge, Antwerp, Portland, 2013), vol 1, *Court Proceedings*, chapter 16.

[3] Mustill & Boyd, *Commercial Arbitration: Companion Volume* (London, 2001), 267: '*A stay of legal proceedings is the principal means by which an arbitration agreement is enforced, there being no direct power to compel a party, by mandatory injunction, to appoint an arbitrator or to bring his claim by arbitration. A negative injunction is not, since the Judicature Acts [1873–5], the proper remedy for stopping court proceedings in England and Wales, although an injunction may, in a proper case, be granted to stay foreign proceedings brought in breach of an agreement to arbitrate.*' D Joseph, *Jurisdiction and Arbitration Agreements and Their Enforcement* (3rd edn, London, 2015), chapter 11.

it finds that the said agreement is null and void, inoperative or incapable of being performed.'

4.03 A party to an arbitration agreement ('the applicant') can apply to the English court for a stay of English court proceedings if such proceedings have been brought against him, either as a defendant to the main claim, or as a claimant who is subject to a counterclaim.[4] The court does not have discretion when deciding whether to grant a stay. It *must* grant the stay unless it is satisfied that the arbitration agreement is 'null and void, inoperative, or incapable of being performed.'[5]

4.04 But it might be show that an arbitration clause, although valid, does not in fact cover the type of dispute which is before the English courts. For example, a stay of English proceedings was refused by Morison J in *Abu Dhabi Investment Co* v. *H Clarkson & Co Ltd* (2006).[6] The claim in the English Commercial Court concerned allegations of pre-contractual misrepresentation regarding a joint venture. The transaction contained an arbitration agreement. The agreement, including this clause, was subject to the law of the United Arab Emirates ('UAE'). Morison J heard party-appointed experts on the arbitration law of the UAE. Surprisingly, it emerged that UAE arbitration law would not permit the jurisdiction of the UAE courts to be ousted by arbitration if the cause of action concerned not a direct contractual claim but a pre-contractual wrong, such as the misrepresentation alleged in this case.[7]

4.05 *Has the Rubicon been Crossed?* The applicant must have already taken '*the appropriate procedural step (if any) to acknowledge the legal proceedings before him*'.[8] But the applicant must not have taken '*any step in those [court] proceedings to answer the substantive claim*' (crossing the Rubicon).[9] Here the test is whether the defendant taken a step in the proceedings which indicates clearly that he has elected to abandon arbitration and instead he has decided to respond on the merits to the court proceedings? In the following three cases, the defendant had not taken any such fateful step in court proceedings so as to have precluded resort to, or insistence on use of, arbitration by obtaining a stay:

(1) The Court of Appeal in *Patel* v. *Patel* (2000) held that a defendant had not abandoned arbitration when he applied to have a default judgment set aside and then

[4] Section 9(1), Arbitration Act 1996; as noted by Lord Woolf in *Patel* v. *Patel* [2000] QB 551, 556, CA, the provision is based on Article 8(1) of the UNCITRAL Model Law; and on Article II.3 (cited in the text above) of the New York Convention (1958); and indeed the phrase '*null and void, inoperative, or incapable of being performed*' in section 9(4) of the Act (see below) is a literal adoption of those instruments.

[5] Section 9(4), Arbitration Act 1996.

[6] [2006] EWHC 1252 (Comm); [2006] 2 Lloyd's Rep 381.

[7] *ibid,* at [27].

[8] Section 9(3), Arbitration Act 1996.

[9] Section 9(3), *ibid*; Mustill & Boyd, *Commercial Arbitration: Companion Volume* (London, 2001), 270-1; see also *Roussel-Uclaf* v. *Searle* [1978] 1 Lloyd's Rep 225, 231-2, Graham J (defendant resisting application for interim injunction; this did not involve 'some positive act by way of offence on the part of the defendant', who was instead 'merely parrying a blow').

made the 'otiose' statement in his summons to the court that: '*the default judgment dated 23 March 1998 be set aside unconditionally and the defendant be given leave to defend this action.*'[10] The Court of Appeal was satisfied that there was no indication, when this otiose phrase was read in context, that the defendant was intending to abandon the stipulated arbitration route.

(2) In *Capital Trust Investments Ltd* v. *Radio Design TJ AB* (2002)[11] the Court of Appeal held that the defendant in court proceedings had not crossed the Rubicon for the purpose of section 9(3) because its responses to the claim had not created any suspicion that the defendant was abandoning the stipulated route of arbitration. Here the defendant had (i) applied for a stay and (ii) also applied for summary judgment against the claimant on the *express basis* that this application would be necessary only if the application under (i) were refused.

(3) Similarly, Sales J held in *Bilta (UK) Ltd* v. *Nazir* (2010)[12] that a defendant had not 'crossed the Rubicon' by applying to the court for an extension of time within which to serve a defence. It was clear to the opponent that the defendant's motive[13] in doing so was to create more time within which to determine whether the relevant dispute was covered by the relevant arbitration agreement.

4.06 In the case of a multi-tier dispute-resolution clause, which stipulates that there should be a 'tiered' series of responses to a dispute (for example, different levels of negotiation, then mediation, and only then arbitration), the applicant can seek a stay even though the pre-arbitral steps have not yet been 'exhausted'.[14]

4.07 Finally, if the court refuses a stay, section 9(5) of the Arbitration Act 1996 makes clear that the claimant will not be subject to a procedural 'Catch 22'. Such an unjust log-jam would arise if (i) the parties have agreed that an arbitral award will be a condition precedent to any legal proceedings (a so-called *Scott* v. *Avery* clause),[15] but (ii) the claimant is now unable to bring such arbitral proceedings because the court proceedings are taking place, and (iii) at the same time those court proceedings will not progress because of the *Scott* v. *Avery* clause clogging them.[16]

4.08 *Inherent Jurisdiction to Grant a Stay.* Apart from section 9 of the Arbitration Act 1996, just examined, the court can issue a stay under its inherent jurisdiction (this power is preserved in section 49(3) of the Senior Courts Act 1981).[17] The inherent power is wider because the court can grant a stay in favour of

---

[10] [2000] QB 551, 556, CA.

[11] [2002] EWCA Civ 135; [2002] 2 All ER 159; [2002] 1 All ER (Comm) 514; [2002] CLC 787, at [60] to [64].

[12] [2010] EWHC 1086 (Ch); [2010] Bus LR 1634; [2010] 2 Lloyd's Rep 29.

[13] *ibid,* at [31].

[14] Section 9(2), Arbitration Act 1996.

[15] Mustill & Boyd, *Commercial Arbitration* (2nd edn, London, 1989), chapter 13, examining the eponymous case, (1856) 5 HL Cas 811.

[16] Mustill & Boyd, *Commercial Arbitration: Companion Volume* (London, 2001), 272; the Departmental Advisory Committee Report (1996), at [57].

[17] Section 49(3), Senior Courts Act 1981.

an applicant (normally the defendant in the English proceedings) even though that applicant is not party to the relevant arbitration agreement. This was the position in *Reichhold Norway ASA* v. *Goldman Sachs International* (2000).[18] Here London court proceedings subsisted between RN and GS, and the related (Norwegian) arbitration was between RN and J. J had sold shares to RN. GS had supported J's sale, but had not been in privity of contract with RN. The English Court of Appeal granted the stay because the two matters were closely related and the arbitration would not take more than 1 year.

4.09 However, the *Reichhold Norway* case (2000) was distinguished by Henderson J in *Mabey & Johnson Ltd* v. *Danos* (2007),[19] where no stay was granted in favour of a civil action defendant who was not party to parallel arbitration proceedings. As for the court proceedings, party A alleged fraud and was suing D Co, and human agents, X, Y, and Z (four co-defendants). The arbitration was confined to A and D Co and a stay was granted in favour of D Co But X sought a stay of the remaining claim by A against X (and Y and Z). The application for this stay was made under the court's inherent jurisdiction (section 9(1) of the Arbitration Act 1996 did not apply because X was not party to an arbitration agreement). Henderson J refused X's application for a stay, noting especially that '*there are powerful considerations which tell against a stay*',[20] especially the need for public trial in England of these allegations of fraud.[21]

4.10 In *A* v. *B* (2006),[22] Colman J granted a stay of English proceedings in which a disgruntled party to a Swiss arbitration agreement sought an injunction *against the arbitrator* and a declaration that the arbitration was fundamentally vitiated and ineffective. Colman J held that the stay should be granted: these English proceedings were a direct invasion of the Swiss arbitral proceedings and that the Swiss courts should be allowed to exercise supervision over the Swiss arbitral process and the relevant award.[23] Colman J's stay of the *claim against the arbitrator* was issued under the court's inherent jurisdiction, preserved by section 49(3) of the Senior Courts Act 1981. Section 9(1) of the Arbitration Act 1996 was not the source of this stay. This is because that provision requires the applicant for the stay to be both (i) a party to the arbitration agreement (satisfied here) and (ii) the person 'against whom [English] legal proceedings are brought'. Element (ii) was not satisfied because the English civil proceedings were directed at the arbitrator and not at one of the arbitration parties. As for English proceedings against the other *arbitration party*, Colman J was satisfied that this claim should not proceed. He set aside leave to serve out of the jurisdiction vis-à-vis that arbitration party. In substance this decision not to allow that party to be served out of the jurisdiction was a vindication

---

[18] [2000] 1 WLR 173, CA.

[19] [2007] EWHC 1094 (Ch).

[20] *ibid,* at [35].

[21] *ibid,* at [37].

[22] [2006] EWHC 2006 (Comm); [2007] 1 All ER (Comm) 591; [2007] 1 Lloyd's Rep 237; [2007] 2 CLC 157.

[23] *ibid,* at [112].

of the Swiss arbitration agreement, and functionally analogous to a stay of the civil proceedings (although a stay is suspensory rather than a final dismissal).

4.3 Anti-suit Injunctions in Support of Arbitration Agreements[24]

4.11 *Nature of the Relief.* The English courts have a long-established jurisdiction to compel a defendant, over whom the court has jurisdiction, to refrain from commencing, or continuing, foreign civil proceedings, or from participating in arbitration, if that litigious activity (foreign litigation or English or foreign arbitration) will involve a breach of an exclusive jurisdiction clause nominating England as the only chosen forum or a breach of an arbitration agreement. The court's power to issue anti-suit relief derives from its general power to issue injunction in section 37(1) of the Senior Courts Act 1981.[25] The Court of Appeal made such an order as long ago as 1911 in support of an arbitration agreement.[26] In *Noble Assurance Co* v. *Gerling-Konzern General Insurance Co* (2007) Toulson LJ, drawing on House of Lords authorities, distilled these criteria governing anti-suit relief in general (whether in support of exclusive jurisdiction clauses or arbitration agreements)[27]:

> '*(1) The jurisdiction [to issue anti-suit relief] is to be exercised when the ends of justice require it. (2) Where the court decides to grant an injunction restraining proceedings in a foreign court, its order is directed not against the foreign court but against the parties so proceeding or threatening to proceed. (3) An injunction will only be issued restraining a party who is amenable to the jurisdiction of the court, against whom an injunction will be*

[24](All the works cited here, except those published since 2014, ante-date the *AES* case [2013] UKSC 35; [2013] 1 WLR 1889): *Dicey, Morris and Collins on the Conflict of Laws* (15th edn, London, 2012), 16-088 ff; E Gaillard (ed), *Anti-Suit Injunctions in International Arbitration* (Juris, New York, 2005); S Gee, *Commercial Injunctions* (5th edn, London, 2006), chapter 14 (6th edn expected late 2015); D Joseph, *Jurisdiction and Arbitration Agreements and Their Enforcement* (3rd edn, London, 2015), chapter 12; T Raphael, *The Anti-Suit Injunction* (Oxford University Press, 2008), especially chapter 7, and see chapter 4; *Redfern and Hunter on International Arbitration* (6th edn, Oxford University Press, 2015), 5.132 to 5.137; *Russell on Arbitration* (24th edn, London, 2015), 7-043 ff.

[25]Section 37(1), Senior Courts Act states: '*The High Court may by order (whether interlocutory or final) grant an injunction or appoint a receiver in all cases in which it appears to the court to be just and convenient to do so.*'

[26]Lord Mance in *AES Ust-Kamenogorsk Hydropower Plant LLP* v. *Ust-Kamenogorsk Hydropower Plant* [2013] UKSC 35; [2013] 1 WLR 1889, at [24] cited *Pena Copper Mines Ltd* v. *Rio Tinto Co Ltd* (1911) 105 LT 846, CA, as amongst the early, if not the first, instance of this type of anti-suit injunction in the context of arbitration agreements.

[27][2007] EWHC 253 (Comm); [2007] 1 CLC 85; [2008] Lloyd's Rep IR 1, at [85], *per* Toulson LJ sitting at first instance in the Commercial Court, citing Lord Bingham's approval in *Donohue* v. *Armco* [2001] UKHL 64; [2002] 1 All ER 749, at [19] of Lord Goff's remarks in *Société Nationale Industrielle Aerospatiale* v. *Lee Kui JAK* [1987] AC 871, 892, PC. And Toulson LJ cited Rix LJ in *Glencore International AG* v. *Exter Shipping Ltd* [2002] EWCA Civ 528; [2002] 2 All ER (Comm) 1; [2002] CLC 1, at [42] and [43]; see also Rix LJ in *Star Reefers Pool Inc* v. *JFC Group Co Ltd* [2012] EWCA Civ 14, at [25] (noted M Ahmed (2012) 31 CJQ 267).

an effective remedy. (4) Since such an order indirectly affects the foreign court, the jurisdiction is one which must be exercised with caution.'

4.12 The English anti-suit injunction is directed at parties and not at foreign courts, and the relief is granted with appropriate caution. As Lord Sumption said in *Stichting Shell Pensioenfonds* v. *Krys* (2014)[28]:

> '*The fundamental principle applicable to all anti-suit injunctions.... is that the court does not purport to interfere with any foreign court, but may act personally on a defendant by restraining him from commencing or continuing proceedings in a foreign court where the ends of justice require.*'

Lord Sumption added[29]:

> '*As with any injunction, this is subject to the court's discretion to refuse relief if in the particular circumstances it would not serve the ends of justice. It is neither possible nor desirable to identify what circumstances might have that effect. But it has often, and rightly, been said that the jurisdiction to grant anti-suit injunctions is to be exercised with caution.*'

Consistent with this, Advocate General Wathelet, in his Opinion (2014) given in the *Gazprom* case (2015), acknowledged that the injunction does operate *in personam*[30] (noting that the same analysis had been emphasised by the House of Lords in *Turner* v. *Grovit* (2001)[31]; where the House of Lords made a reference to the European Court of Justice). In that case Lord Hobhouse began by noting the scope for terminological confusion[32]: '*Certain preconceptions and misunderstandings still tend to persist as to the nature of the type of restraining order made in the present case and the grounds upon which it can be [sought]...*' He noted that the injunction operates only against the individual defendant[33]: '*When an English court makes a restraining order, it is making an order which is addressed only to a party which is before it. The order is not directed against the foreign court...*' He further noted that the English courts adopt a cautious approach to such personal injunctions[34]: '... *since such an order indirectly affects the foreign court, the jurisdiction must be exercised with caution and only if the ends of justice so require...*'

---

[28] [2014] UKPC 41; [2015] AC 616, at [17]; these remarks concern anti-suit relief generally; the *Shell* case concerned prevention of foreign litigation which would distract from and perhaps conflict with efficient insolvency proceedings in the relevant host jurisdiction. Lord Sumption cited as follows Sir John Leach V-C in *Bushby* v. *Munday* (1821) 5 Madd 297, 307; 56 ER 908: '... *this Court does not pretend to any interference with the other Court; it acts upon the Defendant by punishment for his contempt in his disobedience to the order of the Court...*'

[29] [2014] UKPC 41; [2015] AC 616, at [41].

[30] Opinion of Advocate General Wathelet (delivered 4 December 2014), at [64], citing [2001] UKHL 65; [2002] 1 WLR 107, at [23], *per* Lord Hobhouse, and *Société Nationale Industrielle Aerospatiale* v. *Lee Kui Jak* [1987] 1 AC 871, 892, PC, *per* Lord Goff.

[31] [2001] UKHL 65; [2002] 1 WLR 107; Neil Andrews, 'Injunctions in Support of Civil Proceedings and Arbitration', in R Stürner and M Kawano (eds), *Comparative Studies on Enforcement and Provisional Measures* (Mohr Siebeck, Tübingen, Germany, 2011), 319–344.

[32] [2001] UKHL 65; [2002] 1 WLR 107, at [22].

[33] *ibid,* at [23].

[34] *ibid,* at [24].

4.13 The operation of anti-suit injunctions to support arbitration clauses was further examined by the Supreme Court of the United Kingdom in *AES Ust-Kamenogorsk Hydropower Plant LLP* v. *Ust-Kamenogorsk Hydropower Plant* (2013), which made three important observations. First, it held[35] that anti-suit injunctions can be awarded *by the courts* under section 37 of the Senior Courts Act 1981 (the general power to issue injunctions). Secondly, it noted that the injunction gives effect to an implicit negative undertaking in any arbitration agreement that both parties will exclusively pursue arbitration, forsaking all other modes, and that the injunction operates to uphold that commitment.[36] Such injunctions are the ordinary remedial response to a contractual breach where damages are not an adequate remedy because they would involve compensation for a wrong 'after the horse has bolted'. Thirdly, there is no need to locate the court's power to issue anti-suit injunctions as part of the internal law of arbitration (that internal law is (partially) codified in the Arbitration Act 1996). And so the limitations upon judicial injunctions for support of pending and imminent arbitration contained in section 44 of the Arbitration Act 1996 Act are irrelevant to an application of an anti-suit injunction, Lord Mance commenting on this last point[37]:

> '*Where an injunction is sought to restrain foreign proceedings in breach of an arbitration agreement...the source of the power...is to be found* ***not in section 44 of the 1996 Act****, but in section 37 of the 1981 Act. Such an injunction is* ***not "for the purposes of and in relation to arbitral proceedings", but for the purposes of and in relation to the negative promise contained in the arbitration agreement not to bring foreign proceedings, which applies and is enforceable regardless of whether or not arbitral proceedings are on foot or proposed.*** (Emphasis added).'

4.14 Where an arbitral panel has been appointed, there is another potential source: arbitrators (as explained by the European Court of Justice in the *Gazprom* case (2015),[38] on which see **4.24**) also possess power to issue *final* anti-suit injunctions and (with the parties' agreement) to issue interim anti-suit injunctions.[39] For this reason Lord Mance recognised in the *AES* case (2013) the need for sensitivity in exercise of the power contained in section 37 of the 1981 Act[40]:

> '*The general power provided by section 37 of the 1981 Act must be exercised sensitively and, in particular, with due regard for the scheme and terms of the 1996 Act when any arbitration is on foot or proposed. It is also open to a court under section 37, if it thinks fit,*

---

[35] *AES* case [2013] UKSC 35; [2013] 1 WLR 1889.

[36] Arbitration clauses or exclusive jurisdiction clauses create a reciprocal duty to use only the nominated seat/forum and a reciprocal duty not to arbitrate/litigate elsewhere: *AMT Futures Ltd* v. *Marzillier* [2014] EWHC 1085 (Comm), at [36], *per* Popplewell J (reversed on a different point, [2015] EWCA Civ 143; [2015] 3 WLR 282; [2015] ILPr 20).

[37] *AES* case [2013] UKSC 35; [2013] 1 WLR 1889, at [48]; see also [55] to [57] and [60].

[38] *Gazprom OAO* case (Grand Chamber, ECJ, 13 May 2015) (Case C-536/13).

[39] (i) final relief, section 48(5), Arbitration Act 1996; (ii) interim anti-suit relief, section 39(1),(4), Arbitration Act 1996; T Raphael, *The Anti-Suit Injunction* (Oxford University Press, 2008), 7.39 to 7.41.

[40] *AES* case [2013] UKSC 35; [2013] 1 WLR 1889, at [60].

to grant any injunction on an interim basis, pending the outcome of current or proposed arbitration proceedings, rather than a final basis.'

4.15 Anti-suit injunctions to restrain foreign arbitration are not justified if the parties have validly agreed that there shall be a foreign arbitration. If there is a valid arbitration agreement, and the relevant arbitration has a foreign seat, it would be contrary to the New York Convention (1958) to restrain such foreign arbitration. For this reason no English ant-suit injunction was granted to restrain Swiss arbitration in *Weissfisch* v. *Julius* (2006).[41] (For the sequel, which came before Colman J in *A* v. *B* (2006),[42] see **04.10**).

4.16 However, in *Albon (t/a NA Carriage Co)* v. *Naza Motor Trading Sdn Bhd* (2007) the parties had agreed that English anti-suit proceedings would take priority over the foreign arbitration proceedings, and the applicant had alleged that the foreign arbitration agreement was a forgery.[43] Longmore LJ explained[44]: '*It is... arguable that the agreement to arbitrate has been forged in order to defeat proceedings properly brought in England and...it is at present agreed that the English court will determine that question. The autonomy of the arbitrators has thus already been undermined because they are, in any event, precluded for the present from determining that question.*'

4.17 *Examples of Anti-Suit Injunctions in Support of Arbitration.* Four examples will be given in this and the following three paragraphs. First, the Supreme Court in *AES Ust-Kamenogorsk Hydropower Plant LLP* v. *Ust-Kamenogorsk Hydropower Plant* (2013)[45] (**4.13** above for that case's main points) upheld a declaration[46] that there was a binding arbitration agreement and also upheld an anti-suit injunction despite the fact that a non-EU court (in Kazakhstan) had declared that the purported clause was contrary to its domestic foreign policy. In this context the foreign decision is not binding on the English courts.[47] AES held the concession rights to run a hydro-electric plant in Kazakhstan, and party U owned the plant. The substance of the concession agreement was governed by Kazakh law, but the same agreement included an arbitration clause, nominating London as the seat, and incorporating ICC rules. Party U, the owner of the hydro-electric plant, brought court proceedings against AES in Kazakhstan, alleging that AES had breached its

---

[41] [2006] EWCA Civ 218; [2006] 2 All ER (Comm) 504; [2006] 1 Lloyd's Rep 716, at [33], *per* Lord Phillips CJ, giving the court's judgment; noted H Seriki (2006) JBL 541-4.

[42] [2006] EWHC 2006 (Comm); [2007] 1 All ER (Comm) 591; [2007] 1 Lloyd's Rep 237.

[43] [2007] EWCA Civ 1124; [2008] 1 All ER (Comm) 351; [2008] 1 Lloyd's Rep 1; [2007] 2 CLC 782.

[44] *ibid,* at [17].

[45] [2013] UKSC 35; [2013] 1 WLR 1889.

[46] Although declaratory relief is not mentioned within section 37, Senior Courts Act 1981, the Supreme Court in the present proceedings appears to have regarded declaratory powers to be part of its inherent jurisdiction.

[47] Applying section 32, Civil Jurisdiction and Judgments Act 1982 (section 32(4) creates a different approach where the foreign decision is made within the Jurisdiction Regulation (the Brussels Regulation) or the Lugano Convention systems).

contractual duties by failing to supply information concerning concession assets. In response, AES obtained from Burton J in the English Commercial Court a final order restraining party U, the owner of the hydro-electric plant, from continuing or bringing court proceedings in Kazakhstan. The English court also held that the foreign court had been wrong to characterise the English claimant's conduct before the foreign court as involving a submission to those proceedings, and the foreign court's decision on this issue of submission was in any event not binding on the English courts.[48]

4.18 This is the second example. The English Court of Appeal in *C* v. *D* (2007) granted an anti-suit injunction to prevent foreign proceedings and in support of a 'London arbitration' clause.[49] The court held that an English anti-suit injunction was appropriate to restrain a party from bringing proceedings in New York designed to 'second guess' the London arbitration award's application of New York insurance law (contained in a 'partial award'). The English court held that it would be improper, and a 'recipe for chaos', to allow this award to be challenged in New York proceedings. Instead the English arbitral award could only be challenged in accordance with the judicial remedies prescribed and regulated under the (restrictive) scheme contained in the English Arbitration Act 1996. In short, '*a choice of seat for the arbitration must be a choice of forum for remedies seeking to attack the award*'.[50] In fact an appeal from an award to the London High Court on a question of law is confined to errors of *English* law (questions of foreign law not covered).[51]

4.19 A third example is *Midgulf International Ltd* v. *Groupe Chimiche Tunisien* (2010),[52] where the Court of Appeal held that Tunisian proceedings commenced with a view to determining that no arbitration agreement existed were an attempt to undermine the efficacy of that arbitration agreement. The English court had jurisdiction over the Tunisian claimant and an injunction should be granted.

4.20 The fourth example is Hamblen J's decision in *Niagara Maritime SA* v. *Tianjin Iron & Steel Group Co Ltd* (2011),[53] where he granted an anti-suit injunction to restrain the defendant from pursuing Chinese court proceedings, which were subject to a pending appeal, because this Chinese litigation was inconsistent with a clearly valid and effective London arbitration agreement. There was no doubt that

[48] See on this last point, section 33, Civil Jurisdiction and Judgments Act 1982.

[49] *C* v. *D* [2007] EWCA Civ 1282; [2008] 1 Lloyd's Rep 239; on the so-called 'Bermuda Form', R Jacobs, L Masters, P Stanley, *Liability Insurance in International Arbitration: The Bermuda Form* (2nd edn, Hart, Oxford, 2011).

[50] *C* v. *D* [2007] EWCA Civ 1282; [2008] 1 Lloyd's Rep 239, at [17], *per* Longmore LJ.

[51] This is the result of the definition of 'question of law' in section 82(1), Arbitration Act 1996; that definition fixes the scope of section 69, Arbitration Act 1996 (appeal to court on a 'question of law arising out of an award made in the [arbitration] proceedings'); equally, if the award has applied non-English law to the substantive agreement, consistent with a choice of law clause (see section 46(1), Arbitration Act 1996), there will be no possibility of appeal under section 69.

[52] [2010] EWCA Civ 66; [2010] 2 Lloyd's Rep 543; [2010] 1 CLC 113, at [50] to [52] and [69], *per* Toulson LJ.

[53] [2011] EWHC 3035 (Comm); [2011] Arb LR 54.

the arbitration agreement had been validly incorporated into the parties' main contract.[54]

4.21 *Anti-suit Injunctions Issued by English Courts vis-a-vis Litigation Outside the European Judicial Area.* The Supreme Court in *AES Ust-Kamenogorsk Hydropower Plant LLP* v. *Ust-Kamenogorsk Hydropower Plant* (2013)[55] confirmed that the European Court of Justice's decision in the *West Tankers* case (*Allianz SpA etc.* v. *West Tankers, 'The Front Comor'* 2009)[56] does not preclude use of anti-suit injunctions against parties contemplating bringing, or already actively pursuing, proceedings in the courts of a country which is not a Member State of the European Community or of the Lugano system.

4.22 *Judicial Anti-suit Injunctions Banished between Member States of the European Union.* Many civil law jurisdictions do not follow suit and are distinctly anti-anti suit orders.[57] It has become obvious that on the topic of anti-suit relief the Common Law and civilian traditions are at odds. Within Europe matters came to a head when the European Court of Justice in *Allianz SpA etc.* v. *West Tankers, 'The Front Comor'* (2009)[58] held that English courts cannot issue anti-suit injunctions vis-a-vis courts proceedings in Member States. This prohibition applies to all forms of anti-suit injunction where the relief is targeted at a party bringing courts proceedings in a Member State. The prohibition includes, therefore, attempts to restrain a party to an arbitration agreement from continuing such wrongful judicial proceedings in the courts of a Member State within the European Judicial Area. In the *West Tankers* case (2009), the European Court of Justice concluded that:

> '*It is incompatible with the Council Regulation (EC) No 44/2001 of 22 December 2000 [now the Jurisdiction Regulation (2012) (the relevant parts of which take effect on 10 January 2015)] on jurisdiction and the recognition and enforcement of judgments in civil and commercial matters for a court of a Member State to make an order to restrain a person from commencing or continuing proceedings before the courts of another Member State on the ground that such proceedings would be contrary to an arbitration agreement.*'

4.23 According to this decision, an anti-suit injunction, although directed at the litigant rather than the foreign court, would indirectly strip the foreign court of the power to rule on its own jurisdiction under the same Regulation. This would offend the European axiom that every Member State's court, when seised in a civil or commercial matter concerning the Regulation, must be accorded jurisdiction to determine for itself whether it does in fact have jurisdiction to hear the substantive

[54] *ibid,* at [16] and [17].

[55] [2013] UKSC 35; [2013] 1 WLR 1889.

[56] *Allianz SpA etc.* v. *West Tankers* (C-185/07) [2009] 1 AC 1138; [2009] 1 All ER (Comm) 435; [2009] 1 Lloyd's Rep 413; [2009] 1 CLC 96; [2009] ILPr 20; *The Times*, 13 February, 2009; noted E Peel (2009) 125 LQR 365.

[57] However, for discussion by a leading French and transnational commentator, E Gaillard, 'Reflections on the Use of Anti-Suit Injunctions in International Arbitration', in LA Mistelis and JDM Lew (eds), *Pervasive Problems in International Arbitration* (The Hague, 2006), 201–214.

[58] *Allianz SpA etc.* v. *West Tankers, 'The Front Comor'* (C-185/07) [2009] 1 AC 1138.

dispute before it.[59] Also underpinning the European Court of Justice's hostility to anti-suit relief might be the pragmatic perception that, even if experienced London High Court judges might apply anti-suit injunctions only when such relief is clearly justified, the courts of other Member States might not be so reliable.[60] A further reason for the European Court of Justice opposing `anti-suit' orders is the prospect of conflicting anti-suit orders from different Member States. As the European Court of Justice said in *Turner* v. *Grovit* (2004)[61]:

> '*The possibility cannot be excluded that, even if an injunction had been issued in one contracting state, a decision might nevertheless be given by a court of another contracting state. Similarly, the possibility cannot be excluded that the courts of two contracting states that allowed such measures might issue contradictory injunctions.*'

4.24 *West Tankers Remains Applicable after the Brussels 1 Regulation (recast) (2015).* The European Court of Justice in the *Gazprom* case (2015)[62] did not endorse Advocate General Wathelet's Opinion[63] that *West Tankers* has been impliedly reversed by Recital 12 of the Brussels 1 Regulation (recast) (see content of this note[64] for full text). It follows that **courts in Member States** still lack capacity to

---

[59] *ibid*, at [28], [29], citing *Erich Gasser GmbH* v. *Misat Srl Case C-116/02* [2003] 1 ECR 14693; [2005] QB 1; [2004] 1 Lloyd's Rep 222; *Overseas Union Insurance Ltd* v. *New Hampshire Co Case C-351/89* [1991] 1 ECR I-3317; [1992] QB 434; [1992] 2 All ER 138; [1992] 1 Lloyd's Rep 204.

[60] Observation communicated to the author at a European colloquium.

[61] [2005] 1 AC 101; [2004] ECR I-3565, at [30].

[62] *Gazprom OAO* case (Grand Chamber, ECJ, 13 May 2015) (Case C-536/13).

[63] Opinion of Advocate General Wathelet (delivered 4 December 2014), at [130] to [152].

[64] In detail, recital (12) of the Jurisdiction Regulation (2012) (effective 10 January 2015) provides:

'*This Regulation should not apply to arbitration. Nothing in this Regulation should prevent the courts of a Member State, when seised of an action in a matter in respect of which the parties have entered into an arbitration agreement, from referring the parties to arbitration, from staying or dismissing the proceedings, or from examining whether the arbitration agreement is null and void, inoperative or incapable of being performed, in accordance with their national law.*

A ruling given by a court of a Member State as to whether or not an arbitration agreement is null and void, inoperative or incapable of being performed should not be subject to the rules of recognition and enforcement laid down in this Regulation, regardless of whether the court decided on this as a principal issue or as an incidental question.

On the other hand, where a court, exercising jurisdiction under this Regulation or under national law, has determined that an arbitration agreement is null and void, inoperative or incapable of being performed, this should not preclude that court's judgment on the substance of the matter from being recognised and, as the case may be, enforced in accordance with this Regulation. This should be without prejudice to the competence of the courts of the Member States to decide on the recognition and enforcement of arbitral awards in accordance with the Convention on the Recognition and Enforcement of Foreign Arbitral Awards, done at New York on 10 June 1958 ('The 1958 New York Convention'), which takes precedence over this Regulation.

This Regulation should not apply to any action or ancillary proceedings relating to, in particular, the establishment of the arbitral tribunal, the powers of the arbitrators, the conduct of the arbitration procedure or any other aspects of such a procedure, nor to any action or judgment concerning the annulment, review, appeal, recognition or enforcement of an arbitral award.'

issue anti-suit injunctions to uphold arbitration clauses. In the *Gazprom* case (2015),[65] the European Court of Justice, confirming the *West Tankers* case (2009), noted that it is incompatible with the Jurisdiction Regulation for the court of a Member State to issue a decision prohibiting the respondent from continuing, or initiating, civil or commercial proceedings covered by the Jurisdiction Regulation[66] in another Member State. This is because the latter court must be permitted to determine for itself whether it has jurisdiction[67] and this includes determining whether there is a valid arbitration clause in respect of the relevant civil or commercial matter.[68]

4.25 *Arbitral Award Affirming Arbitration Clause's Binding Quality.* The European Court of Justice in the *Gazprom* case (2015) distinguished[69] the grant by an arbitral tribunal of an anti-suit order from the issue by a Member State court of an anti-suit injunction (as in the *West Tankers* case). A Member State court does not act inconsistently with the Jurisdiction Regulation if it decides to recognise or enforce such an arbitral award. The result of such recognition might be that the relevant Member State court decides not to receive or continue to hear a civil or commercial matter (wholly or partially). Such a decision by a Member State court to give effect to a prohibitory arbitral award (an arbitral anti-suit order) is compatible with the Jurisdiction Regulation. The various reasons made by the European Court of Justice in support of this last point are:

(a) issues of arbitration fall outside the scope of the Jurisdiction Regulation,[70] so that any decision on such a matter made by one Member State court cannot be binding under the same Regulation on the courts of other Member States (instead[71] the New York Convention on the Recognition and Enforcement of Foreign Arbitral Awards (1958) governs recognition of foreign arbitral awards); in other words, if (for example) an English court recognised and gave effect to an arbitral award, the latter declaring that only arbitral proceedings should be pursued with respect to the relevant dispute, the English court's recognition or

---

[65] *Gazprom OAO* case (Grand Chamber, ECJ, 13 May 2015) (Case C-536/13).

[66] The *Gazprom* case (2015) was decided under the pre-2012 Jurisdiction Regulation, Council Regulation (EC) No 44/2001 of 22 December 2000 on jurisdiction and the recognition and enforcement of judgments in civil and commercial matters, but it is clear from the Opinion of Advocate General Wathelet (delivered 4 December 2014) that Recital 12 in the preamble to the Brussels 1 Regulation (recast) (Regulation (EU) No 1215/2012 of the European Parliament and of the Council of 12 December 2012 on jurisdiction and the recognition and enforcement of judgments in civil and commercial matters) is a 'retroactive interpretative law', which 'explains how [the arbitration] exclusion must be and always should have been interpreted' (*per* A-G Wathelet, Opinion, 4 December 2014, at [91] ff).

[67] *Gazprom OAO* case (Grand Chamber, ECJ, 13 May 2015) (Case C-536/13), at [32] and [33].

[68] *ibid*, at [34].

[69] *ibid*, at [35].

[70] *ibid*, at [36] (and at [28]).

[71] *ibid*, at [42] and [43].

enforcement decision would not be binding under the Jurisdiction Regulation on another member State court; and

(b) the prohibitive arbitral award is unobjectionable under the Jurisdiction Regulation because the arbitral tribunal is not a Member State court; and so the arbitral award involves no attempt **by a Member State court** to preclude or constrain (whether directly or indirectly) another Member State court's determination concerning its jurisdiction; there is no conflict **between courts** in the matter of jurisdiction[72]; and

(c) the arbitral tribunal, unlike the Member State court in the *West Tankers* context, has no direct power to issue penalties against the party who fails to comply with the anti-suit prohibition[73]; this means that the party who is subject to an arbitral tribunal's prohibition has an opportunity to contest[74] whether the prohibitive arbitral award should be recognised and enforced (in the case of a foreign arbitral award by applying the New York Convention's criteria).[75]

4.26 *Member State Court Decision Concerning the Matrix Agreement is Binding under the Brussels 1 Regulation (recast) (2015).* A judgment **on the substance of a case** (for example, granting or denying damages for breach of the underlying and main transaction) is binding even though the Member State's decision involved a preliminary decision rejecting the suggestion that the matter was subject to a valid arbitration clause. This ratifies the English decision in *Youell* v. *La Reunion Aerienne* (2009).[76]

4.27 The Brussels 1 Regulation (recast) (2015) provides that a Member State court's ruling whether an arbitration clause exists or is valid, etc., is not subject to the EU rules concerning recognition and enforcement of judgments. This is so 'regardless of whether the court decided on this as a principal issue or as an incidental question.' This reverses the English decision in *National Navigation Co* v. *Endesa Generacion SA ('The Wadi Sudr')* (2009).[77]

4.28 *Is the Arbitral Tribunal Bound by Issue Estoppel under English Res Judicata Principles?* This is the question whether **an arbitral tribunal** (whose seat is England) is precluded by the English principle of issue estoppel[78] from re-opening a Member Court decision, made between the same parties, in which an arbitration agreement has been held to be valid or invalid. That form of estoppel would operate quite independently of the Brussels 1 Regulation (recast) (2015). In *National*

---

[72] *ibid*, at [37].

[73] *ibid*, at [40].

[74] *ibid*, at [38].

[75] *ibid*, at [38], [41], [42], [43].

[76] [2009] EWCA Civ 175; *The Times*, 27 March 2009, at [32].

[77] [2009] EWCA Civ 1397; [2010] 2 All ER (Comm) 1243; [2010] 1 Lloyd's Rep 193.

[78] *Andrews on Civil Processes* (Intersentia, Cambridge, Antwerp, Portland, 2013), vol 1, *Court Proceedings*, chapter 16.

Navigation Co v. *Endesa Generacion SA ('The Wadi Sudr')* (2009)[79] the English Court of Appeal supported this analysis:

> *'...arbitrators are not therefore bound by the [the Brussels 1 Regulation (recast) (2015)] themselves to recognise judgments of the courts of Member States of the EU, but it does not follow that foreign judgments, whether of the courts of Member States or other countries, can be disregarded in arbitration proceedings. A judgment of a foreign court which is regarded under English [law] as having jurisdiction and which is final and conclusive on the merits is entitled to recognition at common law...It follows, therefore, that arbitrators applying English law are bound to give effect to that rule. There is nothing new in this; it has long been recognised that a judgment of a foreign court can give rise to estoppel by res judicata – see, for example, 'The Sennar' (No 2) [1985] 1 WLR 490 – and the principle is routinely applied in arbitration proceedings.*

4.29 *Anti-Enforcement Injunctions.* The Court of Appeal *in Bank St Petersburg* v. *Arkhangelsky* (2014)[80] held that the English courts can grant an injunction against the respondent designed to prevent him from pursuing enforcement, including all relevant enforcement proceedings in any part of the world, which would undermine the exclusivity of the relevant exclusive jurisdiction agreement ('EJC'). That case does not concern an arbitration agreement, but it appears that the analogy between an EJC and an arbitration clause would be applied. In essence, both types of clause create mutual restrictions[81] upon inconsistent forms of litigation, arbitration, or related proceedings.

4.4 Damages for Breach of Arbitration Agreements

4.30 Under English law, a party in breach of an arbitration agreement can be ordered to pay compensation[82] to the innocent party for the latter's loss. In England an arbitration agreement is regarded as a species of contract. Accordingly, (i) an English court would recognise an English arbitral tribunal's award of compensatory damages for the expenses incurred following breach of an arbitration agreement (the cost of defending and seeking to repel foreign proceedings brought in breach of the clause)[83]; or (ii) the award of compensatory damages might be made directly by

---

[79] [2009] EWCA Civ 1397; [2010] 2 All ER (Comm) 1243; [2010] 1 Lloyd's Rep 193, at [118], *per* Moore-Bick LJ (noted, H Seriki, (2010) 7 JBL 541-55); overruling Burton J in *CMA SA Hyundai MIPO Dockyard Co Ltd* [2008] EWHC 2791(Comm); [2009] Lloyd's Rep 213.

[80] *Bank St Petersburg* case, [2014] EWCA Civ 593; [2014] 1 WLR 4360.

[81] Arbitration clauses or exclusive jurisdiction clauses create a duty to use only the nominated seat for the arbitral process/nominated forum for the court proceedings and a duty not to arbitrate/litigate elsewhere: *AMT Futures Ltd* v. *Marzillier* [2014] EWHC 1085 (Comm), at [36], *per* Popplewell J (reversed on a different point, [2015] EWCA Civ 143; [2015] QB 699).

[82] Under English law, punitive damages are not available for breach of contract: **17.17**, at paragraph (iv).

[83] Lord Hobhouse in *Donohue* v. *Armco Inc* {2001] UKHL 64; [2002] 1 Lloyd's Rep 425, at [48], [75] assumed that, in the analogous situation of a breach of an exclusive jurisdiction clause, the

a court in England. In *Mantovani* v. *Carapelli Spa* (1980) the Court of Appeal approved both propositions (i) and (ii).[84] The possibility of damages was also noted by Colman J at first instance in the *West Tankers* case.[85]

4.31 Proposition (i), just noted, is supported by *CMA SA Hyundai MIPO Dockyard Co Ltd* (2008).[86] A party to a shipbuilding company (that party having joined as a party to this agreement following novation) breached a London arbitration agreement by continuing French court proceedings which had been wrongly commenced before the novation. Burton J in the (London) Commercial Court upheld the London arbitral tribunal's award covering these points: (1) the arbitration agreement covered the subject-matter of the French judicial proceedings; and so the relevant arbitration party was in breach of the arbitration agreement by failing to discontinue the French court proceedings, once it had become privy to the arbitration agreement, following the novation process; (2) the damages to be awarded for breach of the arbitration agreement were the amount of the judgment paid by the innocent party in response to the French judgment, the costs of fighting the French proceedings, and management time wasted during those improper proceedings.

4.32 The prospect of compensatory damages for breach of arbitration agreements was also raised by the Common Lawyers at the London discussion of experts, May 2009.[87] The question posed was whether the European Court of Justice might regard (i) a Member State court's award of such damages or (ii) the court's enforcement of an arbitral tribunal's award of such damages) as another infringement of 'mutual trust', tending to interfere indirectly with Member State courts' decisions whether to recognise jurisdiction in the relevant substantive matter. But the better view is that neither (i) nor (ii) would constitute a violation of the Brussels 1 Regulation (recast) (2015) and indeed both types of judicial decision fall outside that system, as Recital 12, cited above in the footnote at **4.25**, indicates. Moreover, compensatory damages are not coercive in the way in which anti-suit injunctions inhibit resort to courts.

4.33 *Indemnity Costs in respect of Court Proceedings Undertaken in Breach of a Binding Arbitration Agreement.* Breach of an arbitration agreement will normally justify the English court in granting an order for indemnity costs[88] in respect of the costs incurred in obtaining either a stay of English civil proceedings or anti-suit

---

innocent party would have a claim for breach of the contract, giving him at any rate compensation for costs not awarded in the relevant foreign jurisdiction; generally on this topic, D Joseph, *Jurisdiction and Arbitration Agreements and Their Enforcement* (3rd edn, London, 2015), chapter 14.

[84] [1980] 1 Lloyd's Rep 375, CA; *CMA CGM SS* v. *Hyundai Mipo Dockyard Co* [2008] EWHC 2791; [2009] 1 Lloyd's Rep 213, where Burton J awarded damages for breach of an arbitration agreement.

[85] Colman J in *West Tanker* case [2005] EWHC 454 (Comm); [2005] 2 Lloyd's Rep 257, at [66], [67], [69].

[86] [2008] EWHC 2791(Comm); [2009] Lloyd's Rep 213.

[87] British Institute of International and Comparative Law, 12 May 2009.

[88] Indemnity costs are more generously assessed in favour of the receiving party than standard basis costs, because the control of 'proportionality' does not apply to the indemnity measure: for details,

relief, since this stay or anti-suit relief will have been sought to enforce the arbitration agreement.[89]

4.34 *Tortious Liability of Third Party which Induced Breach of a Dispute-Resolution Clause.* In *AMT Futures Ltd* v. *Marzillier* (2015)[90] parties A and B had agreed a jurisdiction clause (the underlying contract concerned investment deals), in which England was nominated as the exclusive forum. In breach of this exclusive jurisdiction clause, B (in fact circa 70 investors) sued A in Germany. Party A brought a claim in tort against B's German lawyers, alleging that the latter committed the tort of inducing breach of contract, by instigating, or assisting in, the German litigation. On the issue whether the tortious 'harm' on these facts occurred in England or Germany, the Court of Appeal, with reluctance, concluded that it was in Germany. This was because this was the place where the litigation was brought. And so the court held that in this context the tortious harm occurred in the foreign jurisdiction (Germany) where the offending proceedings were brought, in breach of an exclusive jurisdiction clause nominating England.[91] The harm consisted in legal costs and settlement payments incurred as a result of the offending foreign proceedings (in Germany).

4.35 The preceding type of tort claim could be brought against third parties similarly involved in breach of an arbitration clause.

4.5 Inconsistent Foreign Decisions Concerning the Arbitration Agreement

4.36 The Supreme Court in *AES Ust-Kamenogorsk Hydropower Plant LLP* v. *Ust-Kamenogorsk Hydropower Plant* (2013)[92] noted that a non-EU foreign court's decision denying that there is a valid arbitration clause is not binding on the English courts. The result was that the English court would not recognise a Kazakhstan court's decision declaring that the London arbitration clause was ineffective and that this clause operated contrary to Kazakh public policy.[93] And in fact this foreign decision was regarded as wrong. The relevant provision in the United Kingdom is section 32 of the Civil Jurisdiction and Judgments Act 1982 ('CJJA 1982'). Outside the Brussels or Lugano territories (as in the present case, where the relevant foreign court, a Kazakh court, was non-EU and non-Lugano), if a valid arbitration clause

Andrews on Civil Processes (Intersentia, Cambridge, Antwerp, Portland, 2013), vol 1, *Court Proceedings*, chapter 18.

[89] *A* v. *B (No 2)* [2007] 1 Lloyd's Rep 358 (Colman J), especially at [10].

[90] [2015] EWCA Civ 143; [2015] 3 WLR 282; [2015] ILPr 20 (reversing Popplewell J).

[91] *ibid.*

[92] [2013] UKSC 35; [2013] 1 WLR 1889.

[93] *AES* case [2013] UKSC 35; [2013] 1 WLR 1889, at [9], [10], [61] (noting that the impact of section 32 of the 1982 had been considered in the courts below); see especially Rix LJ in [2011] EWCA Civ 647; [2012] 1 WLR 920, at [149] and [150].

appears to exist, but foreign proceedings are brought in apparent breach of that clause ('*the bringing of those proceedings in that court was contrary to an agreement under which the dispute in question was to be settled otherwise than by proceedings in the courts of that country*', section 32(1)(a) CJJA 1982), the English court is entitled to investigate afresh the status of the purported arbitration clause. The foreign court's decision that this arbitration agreement is void, invalid or unenforceable is not binding on the English court ('*shall not be recognised or enforced in the United Kingdom*', section 32(1) CJJA 1982).

4.37 Another provision, section 33 of the CJJA Act 1982, states that a party to an (apparent) arbitration clause will not be taken to have submitted to a foreign court's determination of the validity of the arbitration clause even though that party contested that issue of validity in proceedings heard by that foreign court.

4.38 The position is slightly different where the foreign court is an EU Member State court. Within the EU the position can be summarised as follows (see text above at **4.22 ff** for elaboration):

(i) A substantive decision by an EU Member State court (for example, the award of damages in a civil or commercial matter) would need to be recognised and enforced in England even though that foreign court's assertion of jurisdiction seemed (from an English perspective) to override or be inconsistent with an apparent arbitration clause.
(ii) However, the EU Jurisdiction Regulation (2012) (the relevant parts of which take effect on 10 January 2015) makes clear that a Member State's decision concerning (a) the validity, etc., or (b) invalidity, etc., of a purported arbitration clause will not constitute a judgment requiring recognition and enforcement under the Jurisdiction Regulation.
(iii) The rule just stated at (ii)(b) applies even though the incidental determination that there was no valid arbitration clause formed a preliminary stage in the rendering of a substantive decision by the Member State court (as mentioned at (i), the substantive decision will constitute a judgment requiring recognition and enforcement under the Jurisdiction Regulation).

4.6 English Court Ratifying Arbitral Tribunal's Negative Declaratory Award

4.39 In a sequel to the *West Tankers* saga (see above at **4.22** on the European Court of Justice's decision), the (English) Court of Appeal in the *West Tankers* decision (2012) held that the High Court can issue a declaration under section 66 of the Arbitration Act 1996 in enforcement of an arbitral award, because that provision is not confined to coercive forms of enforcement.[94] This case concerned judicial

[94] *West Tankers Inc* v. *Allianz SpA ('The Front Comor')* [2012] EWCA Civ 27; [2012] 2 All ER (Comm) 113; [2012] 1 Lloyd's Rep 398; [2012] CP Rep 19; [2012] 1 CLC 312; 140 Con LR 45;

enforcement of an award made by an arbitral tribunal, sitting in London. This was an award on the substance of a dispute but in the form of a negative declaration: that X was not liable to Y. In the (English) Court of Appeal in the *West Tankers* decision (2012), Toulson LJ attractively explained that *the arbitral tribunal's* declaratory award creates rights either by way of monetary entitlement or at least by way of *res judicata*, and that the court's (subsequent) embodiment of that right involves enforcement in the wider sense[95]:

> '...*Judges may give force to an arbitral award by a number of means, including by applying the doctrine of issue estoppel. The argument that in such cases the court is not enforcing an award but only the rights determined by an award is an over subtle and unconvincing distinction. ...In the present case...the owners want to enforce the award through res judicata, and for that purpose they seek to have the award entered as a judgment.*'

4.40 Toulson LJ in the (English) *West Tankers* decision (2012) noted the two routes to such enforcement, either by the modern statutory route of leave under section 66 of the Arbitration Act 1996, or by the now older (and less common) Common Law route[96]:

> '*At common law a party to an arbitration who has obtained a declaratory award in his favour could bring an action on the award and the court, if it thought appropriate, could itself make a declaration in the same terms. The purpose of section 66 is to provide a simpler alternative route to bringing an action on the award, although the latter possibility is expressly preserved by section 66 (4). I cannot see why in an appropriate case the court may not give leave [under section 66(1) to (3)] for an arbitral award to be enforced in the same manner as might be achieved by an action on the award and so give leave for judgment to be entered in the terms of the award.*'

4.41 Finally, Toulson LJ in the (English) *West Tankers* decision (2012) noted that the court's decision to give a declaration in support of the award involves no 'rubber-stamping', but is instead a judicial act based on assessment of the validity of the declaration[97]:

> '...*the language of [section 66(1) to (3)] is permissive. It does not involve an administrative rubber stamping exercise. The court has to make a judicial determination whether it is appropriate to enter a judgment in the terms of the award. There might be some serious question raised as to the validity of the award or for some other reason the court might not be persuaded that the interests of justice favoured the order being made, for example because it thought it unnecessary.*'

[2012] ILP 19, at [36] to [38], upholding Field J at first instance ([2011] EWHC 829 (Comm); [2011] 2 All ER (Comm) 1), and approving at [28], [34], and [39], Beatson J in *African Fertilizers and Chemicals NIG Ltd* v. *BD Shipsnavo GmbH & Co Reederei KG* [2011] EWHC 2452 (Comm); [2011] 2 Lloyd's Rep 531; [2011] ILPr 38; [2011] 2 Lloyd's Rep 117; [2011] 1 CLC 553.

[95] [2012] EWCA Civ 27; [2012] 2 All ER (Comm) 113; [2012] 1 Lloyd's Rep 398; [2012] CP Rep 19; [2012] 1 CLC 312; 140 Con LR 45; [2012] ILP 19, at [36].

[96] *ibid*, at [37].

[97] *ibid*, at [38].

4.7 Protective Relief Granted by Courts in Support of Arbitration

4.42 The most important type of relief under this heading is the freezing injunction.[98] But under English arbitration law *the arbitral tribunal* cannot grant freezing relief.[99] A 2006 report recommended no change.[100] And so it is necessary to invoke the assistance of the courts. When arbitral proceedings are not pending, nor in immediate prospect, and the case is one of 'urgency', section 44(3) of the Arbitration Act 1996 empowers the High Court to grant such relief.[101] Although (whether or not arbitration is pending), section 44 of the Arbitration Act 1996 and section 37(1),(3) of the Senior Courts Act 1981 appear to overlap in this regard,[102] the court should not use the general power contained in the Senior Courts Act 1981 '*to get round the limitations of section 44*' (to adopt Rix LJ's helpful comments in the Court of Appeal in the *AES* case).[103]

4.43 Finally, what if the arbitral proceedings are, or are likely to be, outside England? The combination of sections 44 and 2(3)(b) of Arbitration Act 1996[104]

---

[98] *Andrews on Civil Processes* (Intersentia, Cambridge, Antwerp, Portland, 2013), vol 1, *Court Proceedings*, chapter 21; S Gee, *Commercial Injunctions* (5th edn, 2006), ch 2 (6th edn expected); M Hoyle, *Freezing and Search Orders* (4th edn, 2006); *Zuckerman on Civil Procedure* (3rd edn, 2013), 10.201 ff; IS Goldrein (ed), *Commercial Litigation: Pre-emptive Remedies* (updated service), Part A, section 2; for extensive bibliographical details on this topic, Neil Andrews 'Provisional and Protective Measures: Towards a Uniform Provisional Order' (2001) Uniform L Rev (Rev dr unif) vol VI, 931-49 (this article contains analysis of a possible 'blue-print' for an international code or practice relating to freezing relief, preservation of evidence, and asset disclosure orders). P McGrath, 'The Freezing Order: A Constantly Evolving Jurisdiction' (2012) 31 CJQ 12.

[99] Section 39(1), Arbitration Act 1996 precludes the arbitrator from granting a 'provisional' order if it is of a type which cannot be granted as final relief by the arbitrator; there is no such thing as a final freezing injunction, because this type of order is intrinsically ancillary to the adjudication of the merits, as Mustill & Boyd, *Commercial Arbitration; Companion Volume* (2001), 330-1 correctly observe, see also, *ibid,* at 314-5, also citing the DAC Report, at [201] to [203] ('these draconian powers are best left to be applied by the Courts'); see also T Raphael, *The Anti-Suit Injunction* (Oxford University Press, 2008), 7.39 n 102; but *the court* has a power to issue a freezing injunction under section 44(3), Arbitration Act 1996 in cases of 'urgency', on the application of a party or 'proposed' party; in the absence of 'urgency' the court can grant freezing relief only if the parties or arbitrator requests: section 44(4), Arbitration Act 1996.

[100] 'Report (2006) on the Arbitration Act 1996', at [49] to [54].

The report is accessible at www.idrc.co.uk/aa96survey/Report_on_Arbitration_Act_1996.pdf.

[101] DAC Report (1996), at [214].

[102] *AES Ust-Kamenogorsk Hydropower Plant LLP* v. *Ust-Kamenogorsk Hydropower Plant JSC* [2011] EWCA Civ 647; [2012] 1 WLR 920; [2012] Bus LR 330; [2012] 1 All ER (Comm) 845; [2011] 2 Lloyd's Rep 233; [2011] 2 CLC 51, at [56]: '*Section 37 is a general power, not specifically tailored to situations where there is either an arbitration agreement or an exclusive choice of court clause.*'

[103] *AES Ust-Kamenogorsk Hydropower Plant LLP* v. *Ust-Kamenogorsk Hydropower Plant JSC* [2011] EWCA Civ 647; [2012] 1 WLR 920; [2012] Bus LR 330; [2012] 1 All ER (Comm) 845; [2011] 2 Lloyd's Rep 233; [2011] 2 CLC 51, at [96], *per* Rix LJ.

[104] Section 44, Arbitration Act 1996.

empowers the court to grant freezing relief in support of arbitration, including arbitration taking place or likely to place outside England, even if the seat of the arbitration is not[105] England or Wales. But there must be (a) 'urgency' (as required by section 44(3) of the 1996 Act), (b) connecting links with England (the respondent's residence or presence or some of the respondent's assets are situated in England),[106] and (c) the grant of such relief must not be inappropriate (section 2(3), Arbitration Act 1996).

4.44 In *Mobil Cerro Negro Ltd* v. *Petroleos De Venezuela SA* (2008)[107] Walker J emphasised that worldwide freezing orders are made 'only sparingly' in support of arbitration.[108] In January 2008, the English court had granted Mobil Cerro Negro (Mobil) a temporary worldwide freezing order covering assets of up to US $12 billion against the Venezuelan national oil company, Petroleos de Venezuela SA (PDVSA). This order was to support International Chamber of Commerce arbitration taking place between Mobil and PDVSA. The seat of the arbitration was New York, and the parties were Bahamian and Venezuelan. The governing law of the main contract was Venezuelan. PDVSA successfully applied to set aside the London freezing order. In the *Mobil* case (2008) Walker J found that there was no evidence that the respondent was likely to dissipate its assets. But he gave three *additional* reasons for setting aside the freezing injunction[109]: (1) '*Mobil cannot surmount the... hurdle [in section 44(3) of the Arbitration Act 1996 and] show that the case is one of "urgency"*'; (2) '*in the absence of any exceptional feature such as fraud, [Mobil] would have had to demonstrate a link with this jurisdiction in the form of substantial assets of PDV located here*' but '*Mobil cannot demonstrate such a link*'; and (3) '*in the absence of any exceptional feature such as fraud, and in the absence of substantial assets of PDV located here, the fact that the seat of the arbitration is not here makes it inappropriate to grant an order under section 2(3) of the Arbitration Act 1996...*'

4.45 *Freezing Relief in Support of Enforcement Proceedings in Respect of an Arbitration Award.* An illustration is *Linsen International Ltd* v. *Humpuss Sea Transport PTE Ltd* (2011).[110] Here the applicant obtained freezing relief against the first and second defendants (in support of enforcement (under section 66, Arbitration Act 1996) of arbitration awards entered in England. The practical importance of such relief is not confined to the applicant's 'substantive' protection against

---

[105] Section 2(3)(b), Arbitration Act 1996.

[106] The leading discussion of such links is *Motorola Credit Corporation* v. *Uzan* [2004] 1 WLR 113, CA; on which *Andrews on Civil Processes* (Intersentia, Cambridge, Antwerp, Portland, 2013), vol 1, *Court Proceedings*, 21.30 ff.

[107] [2008] EWHC 532 (Comm); [2008] 2 All ER (Comm) 1034; [2008] 1 Lloyd's Rep 684; [2008] 1 CLC 542; noted Adam Johnson (2008) CJQ 433-44; see also *ETI Euro Telecom International NV* v. *Republic of Bolivia* [2008] EWCA Civ 880; [2009] 1 WLR 665.

[108] [2008] EWHC 532 (Comm), at [5].

[109] *ibid*, at [28].

[110] [2011] EWCA Civ 1042; on this case *Andrews on Civil Processes* (Intersentia, Cambridge, Antwerp, Portland, 2013), vol 1, *Court Proceedings*, 21.22 and 21.23.

dissipation of the respondent's assets (although that is important), but extends crucially to obtaining a worldwide inventory of the respondent's assets. Such information is of great forensic importance when chasing mercurial assets.[111]

4.8 Other Interim Relief Granted by the Courts in Support of Arbitation

4.46 The courts have power to issue interim injunctions other than for the purpose of anti-suit prohibition or the preservation of assets or evidence.[112]

4.47 Where the seat of a proposed arbitration is England, the English courts are more likely to provide interim relief. For example, the Court of Appeal in *Cetelem SA* v. *Roust Holdings Ltd* (2005)[113] held that section 44(3) of the Arbitration Act 1996 empowers the court to issue an interim mandatory order requiring the respondent to produce documents necessary for the completion of the transaction which will form the subject-matter of the arbitration. Otherwise the respondent could stultify the proposed transaction (involving transfer of shares), and there would be no assets available to form the subject-matter of the dispute.

4.48 In *Hiscox Underwriting Ltd* v. *Dickson Manchester & Co Ltd* (2004)[114] Cooke J held that, even where an arbitral tribunal has been appointed, 'urgency' (as required by section 44(3) of the Arbitration Act 1996) can justify the court in issuing interim relief, because the tribunal is not yet ready to deal with the relevant pressing issue.

4.49 In the 'Channel Tunnel' construction dispute, *Channel Tunnel Group Ltd* v. *Balfour Beatty Construction Ltd* (1993),[115] the House of Lords acknowledged the jurisdiction of English courts to issue interim injunctions to support arbitration, even if the seat of the arbitration were not England. But the House of Lords refused on the facts to issue an interim injunction, in favour of the employer, to prevent the contractor from stopping work on the tunnel project.[116] In that case, the parties' dispute-resolution clause included a prior stage of expert determination,[117] and a

[111] On asset disclosure orders, *Andrews, ibid,* 21.18.

[112] For a global survey, LW Newman and C Ong (eds), *Interim Measures in International Arbitration* (Juris, New York, 2014).

[113] [2005] EWCA Civ 618; [2005] 1 WLR 3555 (noted in *AES Ust-Kamenogorsk Hydropower Plant LLP* v. *Ust-Kamenogorsk Hydropower Plant* [2013] UKSC 35; [2013] 1 WLR 1889, at [46]).

[114] [2004] EWHC 479 (Comm); [2004] 1 All ER (Comm) 753; [2004] 2 Lloyd's Rep 438, Cooke J (noted in *AES* case, *ibid*, at [46]).

[115] [1993] AC 334, 345-6, HL (clause 67).

[116] See now the even clearer statutory power to grant a stay in this context under section 9(1)(2), Arbitration Act 1996, on which Mustill & Boyd, *Commercial Arbitration; Companion Volume* (2001), 268 ff.

[117] J Kendall, C Freedman, J Farrell, *Expert Determination* (4th edn, London, 2008); A Agapiou and B Clark, 'An Empirical Analysis of Scottish Construction Lawyers' Interaction with Mediation…' (2012) CJQ 494; on mediation and experts, L Blom-Cooper (ed), *Experts in Civil Courts* (Oxford University Press, 2006), chapter 10. See also P Coulson, *Coulson on Construction*

second stage of arbitration.[118] The defendants, a consortium of contractors, were subject to the personal jurisdiction of the English court. The House of Lords noted that the English High Court's general power to issue an injunction, including an interim injunction, is available in principle to support a foreign arbitration (the seat of the channel tunnel arbitration would be Brussels, Belgium). The case was borderline. The House of Lords noted that the dispute required urgent resolution but the privatised dispute mechanism would be slow. However, countervailing factors, tipping the balance against the English court intervening, were: the seat of the proposed arbitration was located in a neutral forum, Belgium, and the more obviously suitable court to issue the requested injunction would be Belgian[119]; the proposed interim injunction would trench upon the substance of the intended arbitral tribunal's issues, namely whether there had been a breach of the construction contract and, if so, what remedy should be granted; national courts should be slow to venture into a zone of decision-making reserved for arbitration.

Adjudication (3rd edn, Oxford University Press, 2015) on accelerated resolution of construction disputes (so-called 'adjudication') under Part II, Housing Grants, Construction and Regeneration Act 1996.

[118] Clause 67 provided: '*...If any dispute or difference shall arise between the employer and the contractor during the progress of the works..., [it] shall at the instance of either the employer or the contractor in the first place be referred...to be settled by a panel of three persons (acting as independent experts but not as arbitrators)... [If] either the employer or the contractor be dissatisfied with any unanimous decision of the [expert] panel... [that party] may... notify the other party... that the dispute or difference is to be referred to arbitration.*'

[119] [1993] AC 334, 368, HL, *per* Lord Mustill.

Chapter 5
Appointing the Tribunal

Abstract Courts can assist the arbitral process by enabling the proposed tribunal to be properly constituted. Thereafter, the courts might need to fill gaps in the tribunal's membership. Arbitral tribunals in England are typically either a sole arbitrator or a panel of three. The courts are the ultimate 'police-men' of problems arise concerning payment of arbitrators and the limits of arbitral immunity.

5.1 Introduction

5.01 Appointing the tribunal can be a prolonged and delicate process, ultimately supported by the supervisory court (section 5.2 of the chapter). Related to this is the problem which arises if a tribunal member dies, resigns, or is removed, and needs to be replaced (section 5.3) (the topics of payment of arbitrators, section 5.4, and their immunity, section 5.5, are also conveniently discussed in this chapter).

5.02 Other questions arise. Should there be more than one arbitrator (sole arbitrators are not uncommon in English arbitration proceedings, section 5.6 below) or an arbitral panel, comprising three or perhaps even five members? In the international context, where the parties are resident or active in different jurisdictions, there is a considerable advantage in ensuring that a sole arbitrator, or the chair of a panel of arbitrators, is a citizen of a third country.[1] And what if it is proposed to adopt a religious criterion for the selection and appointment of the tribunal (see section 5.7 below)? In England this criterion is lawful.

[1] *Redfern and Hunter on International Arbitration* (6th edn, Oxford University Press, 2015), 4.61 ff.

N. Andrews, *Arbitration and Contract Law*, Ius Gentium: Comparative Perspectives on Law and Justice 54, DOI 10.1007/978-3-319-27144-6_5

5.2 Appointment Machinery

5.03 The parties can agree[2] on the procedure for appointing the arbitral panel, including any chairman or umpire[3] (on the umpire system, see **5.05** below).[4] In the absence of such agreement, the Act prescribes the process and time-table for: (i) appointment of a single arbitrator[5]; or (ii) two arbitrators[6]; or (iii) three arbitrators[7]; or (iv) two arbitrators and an umpire[8]; or (v) otherwise.[9] Modes (i) and (iii) will be the most frequent.

5.04 *Three Arbitrators.* Section 17 of the Arbitration Act 1996 governs failure by a party to appoint his own arbitrator, where it is contemplated that there will be a tribunal of three (or two),[10] the central passage being section 17(1), which states:

> *(1) Unless the parties otherwise agree, where each of two parties to an arbitration agreement is to appoint an arbitrator and one party ("the party in default") refuses to do so, or fails to do so within the time specified, the other party, having duly appointed his arbitrator, may give notice in writing to the party in default that he proposes to appoint his arbitrator to act as sole arbitrator.*

In that situation, the defaulting party must play 'catch up', in accordance with section 17(2) to (4) in order to attempt to retrieve the situation.

5.05 *The Umpire System.* The umpire's task is to cut the Gordian knot if a tribunal, comprising an even number of members, normally two, is divided and no unanimity can be achieved, or, where the number is four or more, no majority emerges.[11] Section 21(4) of the Arbitration Act 1996 provides: *Decisions, orders and awards shall be made by the other arbitrators unless and until they cannot agree on a matter relating to the arbitration. In that event they shall forthwith give notice in writing to the parties and the umpire, whereupon the umpire shall replace them as the tribunal with power to make decisions, orders and awards as if he were sole arbitrator.* And section 21(3) makes clear that the default procedure (that is, in the absence of contrary agreement) is that the umpire: *shall attend the proceedings and be supplied with the same documents and other materials as are supplied to the other arbitrators.* Commenting on the umpire system, an Anglo-eccentricity, *Mustill & Boyd* explain[12]:

---

[2] Section 16(1), Arbitration Act 1996.

[3] Section 21, *ibid.*

[4] *Mustill & Boyd, Commercial Arbitration: Companion Volume* (London, 2001), 287, note that an umpire in England is not a chairman, unlike the practice in the USA: see further text at **5.05** below.

[5] Section 16(3), Arbitration Act 1996.

[6] Section 16(4), *ibid.*

[7] Section 16(5), *ibid.*

[8] Section 16(6), *ibid.*

[9] Section 16(7), *ibid.*

[10] *Mustill & Boyd, Commercial Arbitration: Companion Volume* (London, 2001), 282–3.

[11] Section 21, Arbitration Act 1996 regulaters this type of arbitration.

[12] *Mustill & Boyd, Commercial Arbitration: Companion Volume* (London, 2001), 286.

'A tribunal consisting of two arbitrators and an umpire is a well-established feature of English arbitration practice, but little understood outside England and a frequent cause of misunderstanding, particularly in the United States, where an "umpire" is simply a chairman. At common law an umpire has no power to make decisions until the arbitrators disagree on any matter relating to the reference. Once this happens, the arbitrators cease to have the power to make decisions, and the umpire takes over in their place. Subsection 21(4) states this in legislation for the first time.'

5.06 *The Judicial Safety-Net: Appointment According to Judicial Directions.* Section 18 of the Arbitration Act 1996 (which reflects the general scheme of the Model Law)[13] provides the safety-net of judicial involvement in the process of appointing arbitrators where the agreed mechanism has failed. The court will have due regard to agreed qualifications.[14] The central provision is section 18(3), which states that the court has power: '...*(a) to give directions as to the making of any necessary appointments; (b) to direct that the tribunal shall be constituted by such appointments (or any one or more of them) as have been made; (c) to revoke any appointments already made; (d) to make any necessary appointments itself.*'

5.07 The Court of Appeal in *Itochu Corporation* v. *Johann MK Blumenthal GMBH & Co KG* (2012)[15] held that an arbitration agreement providing for adjudication by 'arbitrators', but without specifying how many, would result in the appointment of a sole arbitrator. The relevant clause stated that the parties' contract 'shall be submitted to arbitration held in London in accordance with English law, and the award given by the arbitrators shall be final and binding on both parties'. The court, giving directions under section 18(2) and (3) of the Arbitration Act 1996, applied the default provision contained in section 15(3) of the same statute. The paradoxical result was that the tribunal consisted of a sole arbitrator: this plainly makes a nonsense of the parties' use of the plural 'arbitrators' in the clause.[16]

A better approach would be to imply a term that the number of arbitrators, if the plural is used without qualification, should be three which is the standard number in international commercial arbitration. The attraction of the implied term approach is that it would lead to a tribunal of more than one. The implied term can be carried into effect by reference to sections 16(5) and 17, or (if section 17 were not invoked by a party), section 18. This would have involved the following steps: (i) the implied

---

[13] As noted by the Departmental Advisory Committee's Report (1996), at [87] to [89]; UNCITRAL Model Law on International Commercial Arbitration (1985, amended 2006), Article 11(3) to (5). The court's power, on application, to appoint a sole arbitrator, where the parties have failed to do so, in fact ante-dates the Arbitration Act 1996: see section 10, Arbitration Act 1950, as amended (on these legislative antecedents, *Mustill & Boyd, Commercial Arbitration* (2nd edn, London, 1989), 659–60).

[14] *Mustill & Boyd, Commercial Arbitration: Companion Volume* (London, 2001), 284–5; and cautioning against expansion of the *dictum* in *R Durtnell & Sons* v. *Secretary of State for Trade and Industry* [2001] 1 All ER (Comm) 41; [2001] 1 Lloyd's Rep 275.

[15] [2012] EWCA Civ 996; notable passages are [18], [28] and [31], *per* Gross LJ.

[16] *ibid,* at [31], *per* Gross LJ.

term required a tribunal of three; (ii) the parties had an opportunity to appoint an arbitrator each; (iii) these party-appointed arbitrators might have agreed the third arbitrator under section 16(5)(b); (iv) if, however, one party failed to appoint an arbitrator, the other might have given notice that his appointee should become the sole arbitrator, in accordance with section 17(2); (v) if that appointment under 17(2) was successfully challenged (section 17(3) allows such a challenge), or if the section 17 route was not taken, the court could ultimately give directions under section 18 concerning appointment of the three-arbitrator panel.

5.08 *How Long Does the Appointment Process Take? Redfern and Hunter* suggest[17] that the process of appointing the tribunal normally takes at least 2 months. This explains institutional interest in developing expedited systems of appointment and other expedients to provide interim measures.[18]

5.3 Absent Members: Gap-Filling

5.09 Section 27 of the Arbitration Act 1996 governs the filling of (or decision not to fill) vacancies which occur when an arbitrator ceases to hold office. For reasons of space, the reader is referred to the rule and commentary.[19] Arbitrators might have ceased to hold office because their authority has been revoked,[20] or they have resigned,[21] or been removed,[22] or they have died.[23]

5.10 *Resignation.* The arbitrator can become civilly liable for resigning his appointment: under section 25 of the Arbitration Act 1996, resignation is an exception to the arbitrator's general immunity, on which **5.27** below (this immunity being granted by section 29 of the Arbitration Act 1996; and the immunity applies to non-'bad faith' omissions or culpable conduct). More generally, section 25 of the Arbitration Act 1996 governs the process of resignation. The parties might have stipulated already, whether *ex ante* or after-the-event, what would be the consequences of resignation, both with respect to fees and expenses and 'any liability… incurred by him' as a result of the resignation.[24] In the absence of such agreement, the arbitrator can apply to the court for 'relief from any liability thereby incurred by him' and for an order 'as it thinks fit' concerning payment or re-payment of fees and expenses.[25]

---

[17] *Redfern and Hunter on International Arbitration* (6th edn, Oxford University Press, 2015), 4.02.

[18] *ibid,* at 4.03.

[19] *Mustill & Boyd, Commercial Arbitration: Companion Volume* (London, 2001), 293–4.

[20] Section 23, Arbitration Act 1996.

[21] Section 25, *ibid.*

[22] Section 24, *ibid.*

[23] Section 26(1), *ibid.*

[24] Section 25(1), Arbitration Act 1996.

[25] Section 25(3) and (4).

5.11 *Death.* The arbitrator's death terminates his authority.[26] Companies cannot die, but the English legislation assumes that an arbitrator will be a natural person, although the body appointing an arbitrator might be a partnership or a company or association.[27]

5.12 *Party Revocation of Arbitral Authority.* Section 23 of the Arbitration Act 1996 provides that the parties can only revoke the arbitrator(s)' authority by 'acting jointly' or 'by an arbitral or other institution or person vested by the parties with powers in that regard' (once more, for reasons of space, the reader is referred to the rule and commentary[28]; the court will have due regard to agreed qualifications).

5.13 *Removal of Arbitrator by the Court.*[29] Section 24(1) of the Arbitration Act 1996 lists four grounds upon which an arbitrator can be removed:

> *(a) that circumstances exist that give rise to justifiable doubts as to his impartiality* [see discussion at **6.01**]; *(b) that he does not possess the qualifications required by the arbitration agreement; (c) that he is physically or mentally incapable of conducting the proceedings or there are justifiable doubts as to his capacity to do so; (d) that he has refused or failed—(i) properly to conduct the proceedings, or (ii) to use all reasonable despatch in conducting the proceedings or making an award, and that substantial injustice has been or will be caused to the applicant.*

5.14 On application by a party, removal can be made by the nominated arbitral body or third person,[30] or by the court. For example, in *Norbrook Laboratories* v. *Tank* (2006),[31] Colman J held that a sole arbitrator had committed a serious irregularity, causing a real injustice, when he had independently contacted three witnesses without giving the parties an opportunity to discover what evidence he was receiving from them. The award was set aside under section 68 of the Arbitration Act 1996, and Colman J ordered, under section 24, that he be removed from any further conduct of the proceedings.[32] In the meantime, pending such removal, the arbitral tribunal might continue to act, and might even make an award.[33]

5.15 *Tribunal's Position Pending Filling of Vacancy.* If (i) a sole arbitrator ceases to hold office, then the court can appoint a new arbitrator under section 18, in the absence of the parties having agreed on the method of appointment or on the appointment of an individual (under section 27(1) of the Arbitration Act 1996). The new sole arbitrator will then have to decide, in accordance with section 27(4), whether to carry over the previous proceedings, and if so to what extent: *(4) The tribunal (when reconstituted) shall determine whether and if so to what extent the*

---

[26] Section 26(1), Arbitration Act 1996.

[27] On this last point, *Russell on Arbitration* (24th edn, London, 2015), 4.013.

[28] *Mustill & Boyd, Commercial Arbitration: Companion Volume* (London, 2001), 288–9.

[29] *Russell on Arbitration* (24th edn, London, 2015), 7.116 ff.

[30] Section 24(2), Arbitration Act 1996; on this provision, *Mustill & Boyd, Commercial Arbitration: Companion Volume* (London, 2001), 290–1.

[31] [2006] EWHC 1055 (Comm); [2006] 2 Lloyd's Rep 485; [2006] BLR 412, at [139], [142], and [154] to [156].

[32] *ibid,* at [156] on both points.

[33] Section 24(3), Arbitration Act 1996.

previous proceedings should stand. Similarly (ii), if a member of a panel ceases to hold office, then the court can appoint a new arbitrator under section 18, again, in the absence of the parties having agreed on the method of appointment or on the appointment of an individual (under section 27(1) of the Arbitration Act 1996). Again, the newly constituted tribunal will then have to decide in accordance with section 27(4) whether to carry over the previous proceedings, and if so to what extent.

5.16 It is obvious that in situation (i), where a sole arbitrator ceases to hold office, the tribunal will have temporarily become inactive, pending appointment of a new sole arbitrator ('inactive', the sense, that it cannot operate in the transitional period between that cessation and a replacement, because the tribunal requires some human agency). By contrast, in situation (ii), where the original tribunal consists of more than one member (normally three members), there is scope for the parties, in exercise of the wide power of agreement acknowledged by section 27(1)(a), to dispense with a replacement panel member. There might be a temptation to do so if the arbitration has already reached an advanced stage and the parties recognise and agree that the remaining members are competent to continue. However, in this last situation, there are perils. If only two members survive, and the parties further agree that one of the remaining members should act as (or continue to act as) a chairman, section 20(4) of the Arbitration Act 1996 should be noted: *The view of the chairman shall prevail in relation to a decision, order or award in respect of which there is neither unanimity nor a majority under subsection (3).* Such an award will hardly carry conviction, even if in a technical sense it is a valid award.

5.17 But if no chairman is agreed, and only two members survive, it appears that section 22 will render a 'split decision' (where the split is even) ineffective, so that no valid award will result (for a similar problem in the English Court of Appeal, when a two-judge panel split, see *Farley* v. *Skinner*, 1999, where a second Court of Appeal decision was required).[34] The relevant portion of section 22(2) states: '*…decisions, orders and awards shall be made by all or a majority of the* arbitrators.' In the light of these perils, the prudent course is not to trust to luck, hoping that two panel members will reach unanimous decisions, and instead to replenish the tribunal and to fill the vacancy.

5.18 As for international commercial arbitration (other than governed by the English Arbitration Act 1996), *Redfern and Hunter* note a general preference for the tribunal to be allowed to proceed, especially if the vacancy occurs towards the conclusion of the process.[35]

---

[34] *Farley* v. *Skinner (No 1)* (CA: 30 November 1999, where Judge and Hale LJJ could not agree); requiring a second appeal to the Court of Appeal (*Farley* v. *Skinner (No 1)* [2000] Lloyd's Rep PN 516; [2000] PNLR 441), from which there was a final appeal to the House of Lords: [2001] UKHL 49; [2002] 2 AC 732.

[35] *Redfern and Hunter on International Arbitration* (6th edn, Oxford University Press, 2015), 4.154 ff; SM Schwebel, *International Arbitration: Three Salient Problems* (Grotius Publications, Cambridge, 1987), Part III, 'The Authority of Truncated International Tribunals', 144–296 (antedating the English Arbitration Act 1996).

5.4 Payment of Arbitrators and Determination of Party Costs[36]

5.19 Here there are two matters: (i) the question whether the arbitrator (or tribunal) is entitled to fees and expenses, or entitled to keep payments made in respect of these; and (ii) the question of payment of costs as between the parties to the reference. These will be examined in turn.

5.20 Those technically qualified to graduate (or to receive postgraduate degrees), and now proposing to gain their degree, are unable to receive their degrees in the University of Cambridge unless they have paid their university and college bills. A Rite of Passage is thus subject to a prior Right to Payment. On a similar basis, the arbitral tribunal can withhold the award if it has not yet been paid in full for their fees and expenses.[37]

5.21 The court can determine a dispute over fees and expenses.[38] It would not seem to matter whether the fees have yet to be paid or whether they have already been paid, because the criterion to determine whether they are 'excessive' should apply uniformly. This appears to be the judicial approach, even though the criteria are only set out in connection with the second context.

5.22 In a case where the fees had been paid in order to obtain the award (this is the usual case), in *Hussmann (Europe) Ltd* v. *Al Ameen Development & Trade Co* (2000),[39] Thomas J examined closely the fees submitted by a tribunal and held that they were not excessive, although the number of hours spent was surprisingly high and the fee claim was, therefore, borderline. It might be significant that the chairman in this case was a judge who had been permitted to act gratuitously, although his 'fee' would be paid to the Treasury. There was certainly no suggestion that the hours claimed had not genuinely been worked.

5.23 In *United Tyre Co Ltd* v. *Born* (2004)[40] the Court of Appeal considered a preliminary issue concerning delay in the bringing of an application under section 28(3) for adjustment of a fee. Again in this case (as is usual) the fee had already been paid in order to obtain the award. The fee greatly exceeded the value of the claim and the number of hours claimed, in addition to secretarial hours, was surprisingly high.

---

[36] *Mustill & Boyd, Commercial Arbitration: Companion Volume* (London, 2001), 294–8 and 344–8, provide intricate analysis of these interrelated topics; for a transnational perspective, *Redfern and Hunter on International Arbitration* (6th edn, Oxford University Press, 2015), 9.85 ff; see also T Rohner and M Lazopoulos, 'Respondent's Refusal to Pay its Share of the Advance on Costs' (2011) 29 ASA Bulletin 549–73.

[37] Section 56(1), Arbitration Act 1996; section 53(2) to (6) contains detailed machinery for resolution of problems in this regard by reference to the court; section 28 governs the parties' joint and several liability to pay the arbitrators for '*such reasonable fees and expenses (if any) as are appropriate in the circumstances*'.

[38] Section 28(2) and (3), Arbitration Act 1996.

[39] [2000] CLC 1243, at [58] ff.

[40] [2004] EWCA Civ 1236.

5.24 The Court of Appeal in *United Tyre Co Ltd* v. *Born* (2004) noted the Departmental Advisory Committee's report (1996) on the machinery for review of arbitration fees.[41] The court held that the first instance judge had been correct to entertain the challenge, and that the claimant's delay in bringing this challenge had not been such as to preclude the court from hearing it. The outcome on the substantive issue of the level of the fee is not reported, but the report contains hints that it was probably excessive. Munby J, sitting with Mance LJ in the Court of Appeal, said[42]: '*It was for the claimant to establish two things. First, that the fees claimed were "excessive" and, secondly, that it is "reasonable in the circumstances to order repayment".*'

5.25 *Award of costs as between the parties.* The starting–point is that section 60 of the Arbitration Act 1996 imposes this restriction on an *ex ante* costs agreement: *An agreement which has the effect that a party is to pay the whole or part of the costs of the arbitration in any event is only valid if made after the dispute in question has arisen.*[43] On section 60 (just cited), Park comments[44]:

> '*This provision casts a wide net, serving not only as an anti-abuse mechanism to prevent "you-pay-in-any-event" clauses from discouraging claims by weaker parties, but it also catches otherwise reasonable arrangements among sophisticated business managers to split arbitrator compensation on a 50/50 basis and to mandate that each side cover its own legal expenses.*'

Subject to section 60, the parties are free to agree what costs are recoverable.[45]

5.26 The next possibility is that the tribunal might apply *ex ante* a cap on the recoverable fees.[46] Otherwise, the matter is left to the tribunal or court's *ex post facto* determination applying these criteria:

(i) the '*general principle that costs should follow the event except where it appears to the tribunal that in the circumstances this is not appropriate in relation to the whole or part of the costs*'[47];

(ii) unless the tribunal or court '*determines otherwise, the recoverable costs... shall be determined on the basis that there shall be allowed a reasonable amount in respect of all costs reasonably incurred, and any doubt as to whether costs were reasonably incurred or were reasonable in amount shall be resolved in favour of the paying party*'[48]; and

---

[41] The Departmental Advisory Committee Report (1996), at [124].

[42] *ibid,* at [27].

[43] Section 60, Arbitration Act 1996.

[44] William W Park, 'The Four Musketeers of Arbitral Duty', in Y Derains and L Lévy (eds), 'Is Arbitration Only as Good as the Arbitrator?' (2011) 8 *ICC Dossiers* 25, 36.

[45] Section 63(1), Arbitration Act 1996.

[46] Section 65, *ibid.*

[47] Section 61(2), *ibid.*

[48] Section 63(5)(a) and(b), *ibid.*

(iii) '*Unless otherwise agreed by the parties, the recoverable costs... shall include in respect of the fees and expenses of the arbitrators only such reasonable fees and expenses as are appropriate in the circumstances.*'[49]

5.5 Arbitrators' Immunity[50]

5.27 Section 29 of the Arbitration Act 1996 confers a generous measure of civil immunity upon an arbitrator (or arbitral institution) who or which is acting (or failing to act), provide the culpability does not involve 'bad faith'. These last words connote, in the opinion of leading commentators, 'conscious and deliberate fault'.[51] But liability can arise from resigning his appointment (under section 25). Here the immunity does not apply. It is not clear that a mediation is covered by this immunity, even when the mediation is conducted by a third party neutral who was appointed as an arbitrator.[52]

5.6 One or More Arbitrators?

5.28 In English arbitration law, the default size of the tribunal number is one arbitrator, as the Arbitration Act 1996 demonstrates[53]: '*If there is not agreement as to the number of arbitrators, the tribunal shall consist of a sole arbitrator.*' If a multimember tribunal is chosen, the more usual course will be for it to consist of three members.[54] One arbitrator will be appointed by party A, the other by party B, and the third chosen by parties A and B.[55] The third appointee will sit as Chair (or 'President').[56]

---

[49] Section 64(1), *ibid.*

[50] For the position outside England, *Redfern and Hunter on International Arbitration* (6th edn, Oxford University Press, 2015), 5.54 ff; JDM Lew (ed), *The Immunity of Arbitrators* (Lloyd's of London Press, 1990); Hausmaninger, 'Civil Liability og Arbitrators—Comparative Analysis and Proposals for Reform' (1990) Jo of Intern'l Arbitration 7.

[51] *Mustill & Boyd, Commercial Arbitration: Companion Volume* (London, 2001), 300.

[52] On 'med-arb' in general, *Andrews on Civil Processes* vol 1, *Arbitration and Mediation* (Intersentia, Cambridge, Antwerp, Portland, 2013), chapter 2.

[53] Section 15(3), Arbitration Act 1996; '*The Lapad*' [2004] EWHC 1273 (Comm).

[54] For an argument that this should be the implied term basis of a clause which stipulates a tribunal of 'arbitrators' but does not specify the precise number, see the critique of *Itochu Corporation* v. *Johann MK Blumenthal GMBH & Co KG* (2012) at **5.07**.

[55] Section 16(5), Arbitration Act 1996. Professor Taniguchi (Rikkyo University symposium on arbitration and mediation, Tokyo, 20 June 2012) suggested that each of the parties (i) has a right to veto a proposal of a third arbitrator made by the parties's appointees; (ii) subject to that, the parties' appointees can select the third party arbitrator.

[56] Section 16(5), Arbitration Act 1996; PM Patocchi and R Briner, 'The Role of the President of the Arbitral Tribunal', in LW Newman and RD Hill (eds), *The Leading Arbitrators' Guide to*

5.29 The single arbitrator remains common in England. The LCIA Rules (2014) (London Court of International Arbitration) reflect this.[57] This arrangement was favoured by a majority of respondents to consultation on the 1996 Bill. The ICC Rules (2012)[58] also state that, in the absence of contrary agreement, an arbitration agreement will be taken to involve appointment of a sole arbitrator (under those Rules), although this presumption can be rebutted if the ICC thinks that on the facts a three member panel might be 'appropriate'.

5.30 There are arguments in favour of using sole arbitrators. Such an arrangement is cheaper. Another benefit is that the sole arbitrator is less inclined to strike a crude compromise between rival submissions and positions. A minor advantage is that the sole arbitrator system works well if there are more than two parties, because in that situation appointment of a three member panel can be cumbersome.[59]

5.31 But there are countervailing points. First, the burden of making a decision in a heavy case can be considerable, and the sole decision-maker might not always be on top form, even if the individual's general reputation is strong. There is safety in numbers. Furthermore, a three arbitrator panel allows each side to select their appointee, the third member being quite insulated from unilateral choice. The party-appointee system can foster (i) a sense that each party has a 'judge of its choice'; (ii) and a further sense of 'investment in the arbitration'; and (iii) that (certainly in an international context) the parties' appointees can help resolve linguistic and cultural differences, and avoid misperceptions. Finally, the sole arbitrator might be imposed on the parties by an institutional arbitration system (as agreed by the parties) if the parties have not nominated the arbitrator, or, in default, by the court (**5.06**).

5.7 Criteria for Selection of the Arbitral Tribunal

5.32 *Competence.* Arbitrators should not be chosen if they are manifestly disqualified by reason of age, infirmity or criminality.[60] The Arbitration (Scotland) Act 2010 states that only a person possessing legal capacity, and provided that

---

International Arbitration (3rd edn, New York, 2014), chapter 10.

[57] LCIA Rules (2014), Article 5.8. But the UNCITRAL Model Law, Article 10(2), adopts the three member tribunal as its starting-point.

[58] Article 12.2, ICC Rules (2012): http://www.iccwbo.org/Products-and-Services/Arbitration-and-ADR/Arbitration/Rules-of-arbitration/Download-ICC-Rules-of-Arbitration/ICC-Rules-of-Arbitration-in-several-languages/.

[59] *Mustill & Boyd, Commercial Arbitration: Companion Volume* (London, 2001), 280–1.

[60] cf under Hungarian law, as V Harsági notes (Hungary: National Report for the Heidelberg conference, summer 2011): '*The following may not be arbitrators: a) those under 24 years of age; b) those who have been barred from public affairs by a final court judgment; c) those who have been placed under curatorship by the court; d) those who have been sentenced to imprisonment, until they are dispensed from the disadvantages attached to a criminal record. [Arbitration Act, §§ 11–12].*'

person is 16 or older, can be appointed as an arbitrator,[61] and it further provides that only a natural person (as distinct from a corporation, etc) can act as an arbitrator.[62]

5.33 *Religious or Ethnic Criteria for Appointment of Arbitrator(s).* In *Jivraj* v. *Hashwani* (2011)[63] the United Kingdom Supreme Court held that the appointment of arbitrators is not governed by the European employment provisions prohibiting selection by reference to religion and, therefore, such a criterion is lawful.

5.34 In *Jivraj* v. *Hashwani* (2011) the parties had established a joint venture in 1981 for the purpose of investing in property. The agreement contained an arbitration agreement, providing for the appointment of three arbitrators: each party would select one arbitrator, and the third would be the President of the HH Aga Khan National Council for the United Kingdom. The arbitrators selected by the parties were to be respected members of, and holders of high office in, the Ismaili community. In 2008 a long-standing financial dispute arising from the termination of the parties' joint venture arose. The claimant commenced an arbitration reference under the arbitration agreement. And that party appointed Sir Anthony Colman, a retired judge of the Commercial Court, to sit as his nominated arbitrator, even though he is not a member of the Ismaili community.

5.35 The claimant applied to the High Court under the Arbitration Act 1996[64] to obtain confirmation that Sir Anthony Colman could be validly appointed. The claimant contended that the arbitration agreement could not be applied so as to impose a criterion based on religious affiliation,[65] (or indeed 'belief, disability, age or sexual orientation'; or, under the latest expanded list: 'age; disability; gender reassignment; marriage and civil partnership; pregnancy and maternity; race; religion or belief; sex; sexual orientation').[66] The defendant made a counter-application to the High Court for a declaration that the claimant's appointee was invalid because he was not of the Ismaili community.[67] At first instance, Steel J found in favour of the defendant, namely that the claimant was not free to deviate from the religious criterion contained in the arbitration agreement. His decision was ultimately upheld by the Supreme Court (overturning the Court of Appeal's decision that the religious criterion ran contrary to discrimination law). In essence, therefore,

[61] Rule 4, the Scottish Arbitration Rules, at Schedule 1 of the Arbitration (Scotland) Act 2010: *An individual is ineligible to act as an arbitrator if the individual is— (a) aged under 16, or (b) an incapable adult (within the meaning of section 1(6) of the Adults with Incapacity (Scotland) Act 2000.*

[62] *ibid,* at rule 3.

[63] [2011] UKSC 40; [2011] 1 WLR 1872.

[64] Under section 18(3)(a), Arbitration Act 1996.

[65] Now under the Equality Act 2010; formerly the Employment Equality (Religion or Belief) Regulations 2003 (SI 2003/1660) (implementing EU Council Directive 2000/78/EC; the 2003 Regulations were revoked by section 211 and Schedule 27, Part 2 of the Equality Act 2010 on 1 October 2010).

[66] [2011] UKSC 40; [2011] 1 WLR 1872, at [6], citing Article 1, EU Council Directive 2000/78/EC; see now section 4, Equality Act 2010, for the list of 'protected characteristics'.

[67] Under section 72(1)(b), Arbitration Act 1996 (challenging whether the arbitration tribunal had been properly constituted).

the Supreme Court held that statutory employment discrimination law does not apply to the appointment and conduct of arbitrators under English law.

5.36 The relevant discrimination law presupposes that the discrimination occurs during the course of 'employment'. But arbitrators do not have an 'employer': at any rate, the parties appointing arbitrators are not the 'employer' of the arbitrator or arbitration panel. On this last point, Lord Clarke of Stone-cum-Ebony and the other members of the Supreme Court in *Jivraj* v. *Hashwani* (2011) agreed that an arbitrator did not have the parties as their 'employer'. Lord Clarke continued[68]:

> *'The arbitrator is in critical respects independent of the parties. His functions and duties require him to rise above the partisan interests of the parties and not to act in, or so as to further, the particular interests of either party. As the International Chamber of Commerce (the "ICC") puts it, he must determine how to resolve their competing interests. He is in no sense in a position of subordination to the parties; rather the contrary. He is in effect a quasi-judicial adjudicator.'*

5.37 Lord Clarke added[69]:

> *'In England his role is spelled out in the Arbitration Act 1996. By section 33, he has a duty to act fairly and impartially as between the parties and to adopt procedures suitable to the circumstances of the particular case so as to provide a fair means of determination of the issues between the parties... Once an arbitrator has been appointed, at any rate in the absence of agreement between them, the parties effectively have no control over him. Unless the parties agree, an arbitrator may only be removed in exceptional circumstances...'*

Lord Mance, in a concurring judgment, approved Gary Born's characterisation of the legal connection between appointing parties and the arbitral tribunal as '*sui generis*'.[70]

5.38 Finally, in *Jivraj* v. *Hashwani* (2011), Lord Clarke observed that members of communities might feel more comfortable and 'confident' if arbitral proceedings are conducted by adjudicators familiar with their special ways of dealing, notably their community traditions and values[71]: *'The parties could properly regard arbitration before three Ismailis as likely to involve a procedure in which the parties could have confidence and as likely to lead to conclusions of fact in which they could have particular confidence.'*

---

[68] *ibid*, at [41].

[69] *ibid*, at [42].

[70] *ibid*, at [77].

[71] *ibid*, at [70].

Chapter 6
The Tribunal's Integrity: Impartiality and Procedural Responsibilities

Abstract Arbitrators, even if appointed by rival parties, must be impartial. This chapter explores the scope of that requirement. The tribunal is also charged with overall procedural responsibility to secure a fair, efficient, and speedy process. The parties must co-operate in helping to advance those aims.

6.1 Impartiality and Independence of Arbitrators[1]

6.01 *The Need for Impartiality: English Practice*. It is clear that an arbitral tribunal should be impartial. An arbitrator should not have any pecuniary interest in the outcome of the case, nor have or display actual or apparent bias.[2] In England, the impartiality of the arbitrator is mandatory.[3] Section 24(1)(a) of the Arbitration Act 1996 allows a party to arbitral proceedings to apply to the High Court to remove an arbitrator on the ground (amongst other possible grounds) that '*circumstances exist that give rise to justifiable doubts as to his impartiality*'.

6.02 The following five English cases illuminate the topic of apparent bias.

---

[1] G Eastwood, 'A Real Danger of Confusion? The English Law Relating to Bias in Arbitrators' (2001) 17 Arb Int 287–301; M Gearing, '"A Judge in His Own Cause?": Actual or Unconscious Bias of Arbitrators' (2000) Int'l ALR 46 to 51; AF Lowenfeld, 'The Party-Appointed Arbitrator: Further Reflections', in LW Newman and RD Hill (eds), *The Leading Arbitrators' Guide to International Arbitration* (3rd edn, New York, 2014), chapter 19; S Luttrell, *Bias Challenges in International Commercial Arbitration* (The Hague, 2009); *Redfern and Hunter on International Arbitration* (6th edn, Oxford University Press, 2015), 4.75 ff; M Smith, 'The Impartiality of the Party-Appointed Arbitrator' (1990) 6 Arb Int 320–42; Lord Steyn, 'England: the Independence and/or Impartiality of Arbitrators in International Commercial Arbitration' (2007) ICC International Court of Arbitration Bulletin (Independence of Arbitrators: Special Supplement), 91; J van Compernolle and G Tarzia (eds), *L'impartialité du juge et de l'arbitre: Étude de droit comparé* (Bruylant Publishers, 2006); VV Veeder (in French), in L Cadiet, E Jeuland and T Clay (eds), *Médiation et Arbitrage: Alternative Dispute Resolution-Alternative a la justice ou justice alternative? Perspectives comparatives* (Paris, 2005), 219.

[2] *AT & T Corporation* v. *Saudi Cable* [2000] 2 All ER (Comm) 625, CA (no finding of pecuniary interest or apparent bias).

[3] Section 4(1) and Schedule 1, Arbitration Act 1996, referring to section 24.

N. Andrews, *Arbitration and Contract Law*, Ius Gentium: Comparative Perspectives on Law and Justice 54, DOI 10.1007/978-3-319-27144-6_6

(1) English courts have held that an arbitrator retains impartiality despite having the same chambers affiliation as an advocate representing a party (case 1: below). In *Laker Airways Inc* v. *FLS Aerospace Ltd* (2000)[4] Rix J held that no appearance of bias arose when the arbitrator was from the same set of chambers as counsel for a party to the arbitration reference. However, foreign clients and lawyers cannot suppress their scepticism, as Herbert Smith (London) note: '*Whilst this is not usually considered an issue in England, it can cause disquiet amongst parties and practitioners from other parts of the world, and in one ICSID case*[5] *has resulted in the tribunal directing that one of the parties refrain from using counsel from the same chambers as the president of the tribunal.*'
(2) There is no automatic disqualification of *the other members of an arbitral tribunal* when an individual arbitrator is removed by the court, or recuses himself, on the basis of lack of impartiality. In *ASM Shipping Ltd* v. *Harris* (2007)[6] Andrew Smith J held that the remaining two arbitrators had not been infected by X QC's apparent bias, even though they had 'aligned themselves' with his refusal to recuse themselves.
(3) But business links between an arbitrator and a party, even a party's associated company, will be strong enough to give rise to an appearance of bias. In *Save and Prosper Pensions Ltd* v. *Homebase Ltd* (2001)[7] an arbitrator in a rent review was removed under section 24 of the Arbitration Act 1996 because his firm had been instructed by a company which was an associated company of a party to the present arbitration.
(4) It is also unacceptable if an arbitrator has acquired, in a different capacity, confidential information concerning alleged misconduct by a party. In *Sphere Drake Insurance* v. *American Reliable Insurance Co* (2004)[8] an arbitrator was required to recuse himself because, in a different capacity, as expert consultant, he had earlier received confidential information relating to alleged misconduct by a party to the current arbitration.
(5) It is also unacceptable if an arbitrator had previously acted as an advocate in earlier proceedings, and during that earlier role as advocate had a direct forensic confrontation with a party's leading witnesses on a sensitive issue involving

---

[4] [2000] 1 WLR 113. Similarly, *in court proceedings*, the Court of Appeal in *Smith* v. *Kvaerner Cementation Foundations Ltd* [2007] 1 WLR 370; [2006] EWCA Civ 242, at [17] held that there is no lack of impartiality where a party's barrister is a member of the same chambers as the Recorder, a part-time judge, in a civil case: but apparent bias arose because of the close business connection between the defendant and the judge; waiver had not occurred because the aggrieved party had not known all the facts.

[5] Herbert Smith (London): citing *Hrvatska Elektroprivreda, d.d.* v. *Republic of Slovenia* (ICSID Case No ARB/05/24), Tribunal's Ruling regarding the participation of David Mildon QC in further stages of the proceedings, 6 May 2008, available at http://icsid.worldbank.org/ICSID/FrontServlet.

[6] [2007] EWHC 1513 (Comm); [2008] 1 Lloyd's Rep 61.

[7] [2001] L & TR 11 (Judge Rich QC, Chancery Division).

[8] [2004] EWHC 796 (Comm), at [32] and [43], Cooke J.

alleged misconduct. In *ASM Shipping Ltd* v. *TTMI Ltd* (2005)[9] one of the arbitrators, X QC, had earlier acted as counsel in an arbitration in which there had been an allegation of impropriety made by X QC's client, a charterer, against the owner's witness, M. In the later arbitration, a similar complaint was made concerning the same witness. Morison J held[10] that this gave rise to an objective appearance of bias, and that the arbitrator X should have recused himself. This was a 'serious irregularity' (under section 68 of the Arbitration Act 1996). It gave rise to a successful challenge to an award. But by calling for the award (a partial award on a preliminary point), knowing of this problem, the complainant had waived the objection vis-à-vis that award. However, as for the remainder of the arbitration, X QC should stand down. The judgment contains a helpful summary of the general approach to allegations of apparent bias.[11]

6.03 The *IBA Guidelines on Conflicts of Interest in International Arbitration* (2014). This document distinguishes the following four categories: (i) a 'non-waivable' red list; (ii) a 'waivable' red list; (iii) an orange list; and (iv) a green list. Category (i) involves automatic disqualification. Matters falling within category (ii) are 'waivable' in the sense that these issues can be passed over by agreement of the parties, following disclosure of the relevant problem. Matters within category (iii) are to be disclosed and might or might not give rise to problems. Category (iv) covers aspects which, being innocuous, do not need to be disclosed. The *IBA Guidelines* are influential and illuminating, but neither binding nor exhaustive. As Morison J noted in *ASM Shipping Ltd* v. *TTMI Ltd* (2005; see also **6.02** on this case)[12]: '*The IBA guidelines do not purport to be comprehensive and, as the Working Party added, nor could they be. "The Guidelines are to be applied with robust common-sense and without pedantic and unduly formulaic interpretation.*"

6.04 Walter Rechberger (Vienna) has noted the following recurrent problematic types of proximity between parties and prospective arbitrators;

(i) the arbitrator(s) and counsel are in the same law practice or firm or chambers;
(ii) the pre-appointment 'beauty contest' (Rechberger says that there should not be any probing of the arbitrators on their factual or legal disposition; there are various controls, such as meeting on the arbitrator's 'soil'; the meeting should not be over lunch or dinner; both parties should be present—but some laxity is tolerated by the *IBA Guidelines on Conflicts of Interest in International*

---

[9] [2005] EWHC 2238 (Comm); [2006] 2 All ER (Comm) 122; [2006] 1 Lloyd's Rep 375; [2006] 1 CLC. 656.

[10] *ibid*, at [43].

[11] *ibid*, at [39].

[12] '*The IBA guidelines do not purport to be comprehensive…*', *per* Morison J in *ASM Shipping Ltd* v. *TTMI Ltd* [2005] EWHC 2238 (Comm); [2006] 2 All ER (Comm) 122; [2006] 1 Lloyd's Rep 375, at [43].

Arbitration (2014) see **6.24**, placing exploratory contact to establish availability, and possible choice of a chairperson, on the (innocuous) 'Green List');

(iii) repeated appointment of an arbitrator by the same law firm or by the same party[13] (see further **6.11** below). Roman Khodykin (Russia) notes judicial insistence in Russia that arbitrators should disclose 'whether they have been appointed by a party too frequently'.[14] But in all jurisdictions it is common practice for arbitrators to be selected by parties on the basis of their 'track-record' (a) with respect to former arbitral proceedings involving the appointing party or (b) proceedings between different parties. As for (a), the matter is further discussed at **6.11**. As for (b), this factor cannot be prohibited, given the fundamental feature of party choice. But within the court system, provided there is a significant pool of judges who are randomly selected to cases without party influence or control, it becomes (virtually) impossible for a party to cherry-pick an individual judge (or set of judges).

6.05 *Party-Appointed Arbitrators*. But parties often exercise the right to appoint each 'side-arbitrator', the third being either nominated by the relevant arbitral institution or by the first two appointed arbitrators. This is intended to conduce to neutrality, selection by reference to expertise, and equality of 'representation' within the tribunal. Within this framework, the arbitrator is nevertheless expected to be 'impartial' (in all nations, including England), and 'independent' (in all jurisdictions, except England, independence is an additional requirement; but in England it was considered that 'independence' is otiose and that 'impartiality' covers the whole ground of potential complaint; but see the criticism of this English view at **6.15**). The common modern practice is that the same requirements of impartiality and independence apply equally to the party-appointed panel members and to the third and entirely neutral chairman or president.

6.06 Hogan Lovells (London) emphasise the wisdom of securing an impartial tribunal:

> '*Arbitration benefits from a pool of experienced arbitrators who have a reputation for impartiality and independence and are likely to be appointed to sit on tribunals. Choosing arbitrators with an established impartial reputation can significantly assist a party because*: (*a*) *the appointment of an unbiased or impartial arbitrator will likely not threaten the enforcement and recognition of an award*; *and* (*b*) *the views of an arbitrator who is seen by his fellow co-arbitrators to be unbiased or impartial will more readily be taken into consideration than a person viewed as partial to their appointing party*.'

---

[13] W Rechberger (Hong Kong symposium on judicial independence, City University, 23 March 2012), also noted that Norwegian arbitration law, Article 13(4), allows the parties to derogate from impartiality and independence: examples are employer representatives on one side, and fellow employees on the other hand. Another example is where partisan experts are chosen. The parties cannot challenge under the UNCITRAL Model Law because both parties will be aware of this ground of partiality. This is rationalised as consistent with freedom of contract. However, it would be problematic if the award were challenged under the New York Convention (1958).

[14] Khodykin (Russia: National Report for the Heidelberg conference, summer, 2011): '*Arbitrators should also disclose if they have been appointed by a party too frequently* (*Decree of the Moscow Okrug Federal Arbitrazh Court dated 13 October 2008 No KG-A40/9254-08*).'

6.07 Similarly, *Redfern and Hunter* spell out the folly of appointing one's own arbitrator to act as a puppet or partisan ally, by requiring or expecting that this appointee will follow slavishly the instructions or perceived interests of the appointing party[15]: '*Deliberate appointment of a partisan arbitrator is counter-productive, because the [other arbitrators] will very soon perceive what is happening and the influence of the partisan arbitrator during the tribunal's deliberations will be diminished.*'

6.08 The system of unilateral appointments has been criticised by some leading commentators. A notable attack on this system is Jan Paulsson's lecture 'Moral Hazard in International Dispute Resolution' (2010),[16] in which he proposed that panel members should be appointed instead by arbitral institutions. He also advocated a more professional arrangement amongst arbitral institutions, so that prospective arbitrators are chosen who have manifest integrity and appropriate qualifications and experience.

6.09 There is also the issue of the remuneration of party-appointed arbitrators. Admittedly, the fee payable in a particular case is not directly dependent on the nature of their eventual decision: it is payable irrespective of who wins the case; and the level of the fee is not adjusted according to the amount or terms of the award. Furthermore, arbitrators are not normally salaried employees but are instead appointed separately for each arbitration reference. There is also no ladder of promotion which might induce arbitrators to be wary of making 'unattractive' decisions. Nevertheless, there is a structural problem: the independence of arbitral tribunals is jeopardised by the fact that an arbitrator might be actuated by the prospect of future economic gain (attracting more arbitration appointments) and avoiding financial loss (losing a stream of anticipated arbitral appointments). This financial incentive to act in a certain way need not, therefore, stem from any pre-existing tie between the arbitrator (prospective or sitting) and the appointing party.

6.10 Possible responses to the problems of arbitrators trying to attract more work, by slanting their decisions to attract (or avoid alienating) particular law firms or parties are:

(i) special criteria for selection might be adopted:

  (a) arbitrators are selected from a special pool of economically independent lawyers or experts; these will be people of established integrity and probity; or

[15] *Redfern and Hunter on International Arbitration* (6th edn, London, 2015), 4.76.

[16] Delivered at the University of Miami, 29 April 2010: (2010) 25 ICSID Review 339 (available at: http://www.arbitration-icca.org/media/0/12773749999020/paulsson_moral_hazard.pdf); J Paulsson, *The Idea of Arbitration* (Oxford University Press, 2013), chapter 5; and further comment by Joseph Mathews, (2010) 25 ICSID Review, at 356 and David D Branson, (2010) 25 ICSID Review, 367; see also David D Branson, 'American Party-Appointed Arbitrators: Not the Three Monkeys' (2004) 30 U Dayton L Rev 1.

(b) appointed randomly or without party-influence or party–choice, by a prestigious arbitral institution maintaining a list of tried-and-tested arbitrators of probity and skill; or
(c) arbitrators are full-time judges permitted to sit as arbitrators; (possible under the English procedural rules, but virtually[17] dormant in practice[18]; the more recent Scottish arbitration legislation has also prescribed such a mechanism)[19]; or
(d) a system of sole arbitrators is used, with guarantees that parties cannot influence the selection of an arbitrator for a particular case;

(ii) arbitrators might be exhorted to rise above economic considerations and to respect the higher duty of adjudicative integrity; (this overlaps with approaches (i)(a) and (c), use of a cadre of super-respected appointees);
(iii) arbitrators might act for free or *pro bono*; or donate their fee to charity;
(iv) arbitrators might persuade themselves that their long-term economic prospects are enhanced if they acquire a reputation for punctilious independence, demonstrating this characteristic by strict adherence to the pure merits of each dispute, and stopping their ears to the siren-call of 'short-term fee income' (unless the short-term 'return' in a series of very lucrative appointments will greatly exceed the gains from a longer string of middling value appointments);
(v) arbitrators might be prevented from acting for the same party or law firm for more than a specified number of occasions within a specified period.

6.11 Approach (v) is adopted by the *IBA Guidelines on Conflicts of Interest in International Arbitration* (2014): that arbitrators cannot act for the same party or law firm for more than a specified number of occasions within a specified period.

(a) Article 3.1.3 states: '*The arbitrator has within the past three years been appointed as arbitrator on two or more occasions by one of the parties or as an affiliate of one of the parties.*' (This situation is on the *IBA* 'Orange list', and so this is a factor to be disclosed and might or might not give rise to problems.) In *Tidewater Inc* v. *Venezuela* (2010)[20] Venezuela appointed arbitrator S; S had been appointed by that State on two[21] other occasions, although in one of those instances more than three years before. The other members of the

[17] For an exotic example of an appeal to the Court of Appeal from such a judge-arbitrator decision, *Henry Boot Construction Ltd* v. *Alstom Combined Cycles Ltd* [2005] EWCA Civ 814; [2005] 1 WLR 3850.

[18] Section 93, Arbitration Act 1996, enabling a Commercial Court judge (with the Lord Chief Justice's permission), or an official referee (now a judge of the Technology and Construction Court), to sit as a judge-arbitrator; fees are payable to the High Court.

[19] Section 25, Arbitration (Scotland) Act 2010.

[20] ICSID Case No ARB/10/3, 23 December 2010.

[21] *ibid*, at [8]: '…I have been nominated by Venezuela in two other cases, in the last 6 years, for which the Tribunal is constituted… Also, I have accepted a nomination in a new case, this year, for which the tribunal is *not yet constituted… ICSID Case No ARB/10/9.*' Therefore, the *Tidewater*

tribunal declared that the challenging party would need to show that the prospect of continued and regular appointments might have created a relationship of influence on the arbitrator's judgement or that the arbitrator would have been influenced by factors outside the case record by virtue of the knowledge derived from the earlier cases. But no such influence was proved here,[22] a finding which has attracted criticism.[23]

(b) Article 3.1.5 (also on the *IBA* 'Orange' list) states: '*The arbitrator currently serves, or has served within the past three years, as arbitrator in another arbitration on a related issue involving one of the parties or an affiliate of one of the parties.*' However, in note 5 to the *Guidelines* it is conceded that: '*It may be the practice in certain kinds of arbitration, such as maritime, sports or commodities arbitration, to draw arbitrators from a smaller or specialised pool of individuals. If in such fields it is the custom and practice for parties frequently to appoint the same arbitrator in different cases, no disclosure of this fact is required, where all parties in the arbitration should be familiar with such custom and practice.*' This sensible qualification was emphasised by Philip Yang at the Hong Kong symposium on judicial and arbitral independence, City University, March 2012.[24]

6.12 *Independence Not a Separate Requirement in English Arbitration Law*. In England, lack of independence is not a ground for removal of an arbitrator. By contrast, courts are expected to be both impartial and independent. As Lord Hope commented in the House of Lords in *Porter* v. *Magill* (2001),[25] 'there is a close relationship between the concept of independence and that of impartiality', and he quoted from the European Court of Human Rights in *Findlay* v. *United Kingdom* (1997)[26]:

> '*The Court recalls that in order to establish whether a tribunal can be considered as "independent", regard must be had inter alia to the manner of appointment of its members and their term of office, the existence of guarantees against outside pressures and the question whether the body presents an appearance of independence.... The concepts of independence and objective impartiality are closely linked ...*'

---

case (2010) was only the third case when she was nominated. However, at the time of this decision she had already accepted a further appointment by Venezuela.

[22] *ibid*, at [64]: '*...the mere fact of holding three other arbitral appointments by the same party does not, without more, indicate a manifest lack of independence or impartiality...*'

[23] **P Ashford, 'Arbitrators' Repeat Appointments and Conflicts of Interest', criticising this case:** http://www.crippslink.com/index.php?option=com_content&view=article&id=1146:arbitrators-repeat-appointments-and-conflicts-of-interest&catid=16:international-arbitration-publications&Itemid=537.

[24] Professsor Philip Yang, commodity and maritime arbitrator, and visiting professor at City University, Hong Kong, noted [*In*] *smaller venues there will be only a dozen or so experienced arbitrators available*; *very soon the IBA 'ration' will be used up*; *in fact some arbitrators in these zones of dispute might be holding more than 200 cases at a time, often from the same small pool of firms*'.

[25] [2001] UKHL 67; [2002] 2 AC 357, at [88].

[26] (1997) 24 EHRR 221, 244, at [73].

6.13 And Lord Bingham wrote, in *The Business of Judging* (2000):

> *'Impartiality and independence may not be synonyms, but there is a very close blood-tie between them: for a judge who is truly impartial, deciding each case on the merits as they appear to him or her, is of necessity independent.'*[27]

6.14 However, the Departmental Advisory Committee's Report (1996, commenting on the Arbitration Bill 1996) contains a sustained argument[28] that a separate ground of 'lack of independence' is otiose. The Committee said that lack of independence will manifest itself as lack of impartiality: but if the tribunal is impartial there is no further ground of complaint.[29] The same report expressed anxiety that 'independence', if recognised as a separate and additional ground, would overstimulate objections to the appointment or continued involvement of individual arbitrators, based on tenuous arguments imputing lack of complete neutrality.[30]

6.15 *Independence a Separate Requirement Outside England.* Leading arbitration institutions prescribe a double requirement, of 'impartiality' and 'independence', for example, ICC Arbitration Rules (2012), Article 11(1), and LCIA (2014), Article 5.3. The UNCITRAL Model Law on International Commercial Arbitration, Article 12, requires prospective arbitrators to disclose 'circumstances likely to give rise to justifiable doubts' concerning arbitrators' 'impartiality *or independence*'. Impartiality and independence are not used as synonyms but as distinct concepts, although having some field of overlap. There is no need to show actual bias, but merely a risk of bias: 'circumstances likely to give rise to justifiable doubts' concerning arbitrators' 'impartiality or independence'. The *IBA Guidelines on Conflicts of Interest in International Arbitration* (2014)[31] refer to the requirement that arbitrators should be both 'impartial' and 'independent', although this fundamental document contains no explication of the relationship between these terms: '*(1) GENERAL PRINCIPLE: Every arbitrator shall be impartial and independent of the parties at the time of accepting an appointment to serve and shall remain so until the final award has been rendered or the proceedings have otherwise finally terminated.*' Another important 'soft law' document, although focused mainly on state courts, is the *American Law Institute/UNIDROIT's 'Principles of Transnational Civil Procedure'*, which recommends, in language suggesting some notion of the (partial) separation of impartiality and independence[32]: '*The court and the judges should have judicial independence to decide the dispute according to the facts and the law, including* ***freedom from improper internal and external influence****.*' (Emphasis

---

[27] T Bingham, *The Business of Judging* (Oxford University Press, 2000), 59.

[28] The Departmental Advisory Committee Report (1996), at [100] ff; available in Appendix 1 to *Mustill & Boyd, Commercial Arbitration: Companion Volume* (London, 2001).

[29] *ibid*, at [101] and [102].

[30] *ibid*, at [102].

[31] See also remarks in JDM Lew, L Mistelis, S Kröll, *Comparative International Commercial Arbitration* (Kluwer, The Hague, 2003), 11.19.

[32] Principle 1.1, *American Law Institute/UNIDROIT'S Principles of Transnational Civil Procedure* (Cambridge University Press, 2006), 17.

added.) And these *Principles* continue[33]: '*Judges should have reasonable tenure in office…*' Finally, on this topic, the *Principles* state[34]: '*The court should be impartial. A judge or other person having decisional authority must not participate if there is reasonable ground to doubt such person's impartiality.*'

6.16 The Departmental Advisory Committee (1996) also noted the connection between a wide notion of independence, in the sense of openness to a reasoned debate, and the expertise of the chosen arbitral tribunal[35]: '*There may well be situations in which parties desire their arbitrators to have familiarity with a specific field, rather than being entirely independent.*'[36] The *IBA Guidelines on Conflicts of Interest in International Arbitration* (2014) address this issue. Article 4.1.1 in the (innocuous) 'Green List' states: '*The arbitrator has previously published a legal opinion (such as a law review article or public lecture) concerning an issue which also arises in the arbitration (but this opinion is not focused on the case).*' However, the divining rod of the *IBA Guidelines* starts to quiver when the arbitrator has entered the more immediate fray (Article 3.5.2): '*The arbitrator has publicly advocated a specific position regarding the case that is being arbitrated, whether in a published paper, or speech, or otherwise.*' The latter type of intervention into the public domain falls within the 'Orange list', that is, it is a matter which should be disclosed and might or might not give rise to problems.

6.17 *In Favour of Independence as a Separate Criterion.* A case can be made for recognition of the notion of 'independence', despite the stubborn objection (**6.14**) of the English Departmental Advisory Committee's Report (2006) that this element is otiose.[37] The concept of 'impartiality' is wide. But it is arguably not wide enough to embrace all possible sources of corrupting influence, including background intimidation (other than by the parties or their lawyers), and subtler and insidious economic factors (see **6.09** above). As for external interference with the tribunal's task of conducting a fair hearing and delivering a dispassionate award. The tribunal should not suffer any form of overt or covert intimidation or inducement to decide the case other than by strict reference to the factual and legal merits of the case. In particular, there should not be any threat that the arbitrator will be at personal risk of harm, or that others will be subject to harm, unless a decision is made in favour of a party. It is possible that such threats might be made by persons other than a party to the arbitration, and without that party being associated with the threat. In some corrupt or oppressive countries, it might be hard for arbitrators

---

[33] *ibid*, at Principle 1.2.

[34] *ibid*, at Principle 1.3.

[35] The Departmental Advisory Committee Report (1996), at [100] ff; available in Appendix 1 to *Mustill & Boyd*, *Commercial Arbitration*: *Companion Volume* (London, 2001), at [103].

[36] On the question of arbitrators' special expertise, *Checkpoint Ltd* v. *Strathclyde Pension Fund* [2003] EWCA Civ 84; [2003] L & TR 22; [2003] 1 EGLR 1; [2003] NPC 23.

[37] The Departmental Advisory Committee Report (1996), at [100] ff; available in Appendix 1 to *Mustill & Boyd*, *Commercial Arbitration*: *Companion Volume* (London, 2001); see also JDM Lew, L Mistelis, S Kröll, *Comparative International Commercial Arbitration* (Kluwer, The Hague, 2003), 11.29.

domiciled there, or having families or friends who reside there, to feel entirely free to decide important arbitral matters affecting leading industrialists, financiers, politicians, other officials, or state companies. The sense of foreboding might be pervasive or it might be reinforced by specific threats.

6.2 Procedural Responsibilities of the Tribunal

6.18 *Fundamental Statutory Requirements*. The Arbitration Act 1996 contains these fundamental statements of the tribunals' responsibilities and of the bilateral relations between the parties and the tribunal, and the trilateral relations between the parties, the tribunal, and the court:

> *Section 1: General principles: The provisions of [Part 1 of the Act] are founded on the following principles, and shall be construed accordingly—(a) the object of arbitration is to obtain the fair resolution of disputes by an impartial tribunal without unnecessary delay or expense; (b) the parties should be free to agree how their disputes are resolved, subject only to such safeguards as are necessary in the public interest; (c) in matters covered by [Part 1 of the Act] the court should not intervene except as provided by [Part 1].*
>
> *Section 33(1): General duty of the tribunal: (1) The tribunal shall— (a) act fairly and impartially as between the parties, giving each party reasonable opportunity of putting his case and dealing with that of his opponent; (b) adopt procedures suitable to the circumstance of the particular case, avoiding unnecessary delay or expense, so as to provide a fair means for the resolution of the matters falling to be determined..*
>
> *Section 40(1): General duty of the parties: (1) The parties shall do all things necessary for the proper and expeditious conduct of the arbitral proceedings.*

6.19 *The Principle of Party Procedural Co-operation*. The Arbitration Act 1996 imposes duties upon both the arbitral panel[38] and the parties to ensure fairness, efficiency, and an appropriate degree of speediness.[39] Each party is obliged to 'do all things necessary for the proper and expeditious conduct of the arbitral proceedings'.[40] A party cannot refuse to co-operate in the resolution of the dispute. The parties must help the arbitrator to reach an accurate decision after employing a fair, efficient, and speedy process.

6.20 *Arbitral Due Process*. Arbitration shares with court adjudication two core procedural values or principles: impartiality of the arbitrator, and a duty to hear the other's case.[41] Thus each member of the neutral arbitral tribunal must preserve his appearance of impartiality (**6.01**). The arbitrator must examine the dispute judiciously and reach a decision (an 'award'). The arbitrator should not become enthusiastic in pursuing their initial perception of the case's merits before all the relevant

[38] M Hunter and A Philip, 'The Duties of an Arbitrator', LW Newman and RD Hill (eds), *The Leading Arbitrators' Guide to International Arbitration* (3rd edn, New York, 2014), chapter 20.

[39] *Mustill & Boyd, Commercial Arbitration: Companion Volume* (London, 2001), 30–37, discussing respectively sections 33 and 40, Arbitration Act 1996.

[40] Section 40(1), Arbitration Act 1996.

[41] A Pullé, 'Securing Natural Justice in Arbitration Proceedings' (2012) 20 Asia Pacific L Rev 63.

material is assembled.[42] Furthermore, the parties must enjoy an equal opportunity to present their cases. In reaching decision, the tribunal must respect the parties' right to present points of claim and defence, to adduce evidence, and to make submissions concerning substantive norms.[43]This range of procedural constraints might conveniently be expressed as the requirement of arbitral 'due process' (in preference to the 'duty to act judicially').[44] Claudia Perri (Brazil) notes the requirement that Brazilian arbitration must be conducted in accordance with constitutional norms requiring 'due process'.[45] And Rolf Stürner encapsulates the requirements of fair process applicable in Germany[46]:

> '... *[T]here are indispensable requirements of a fair procedure which limit the tribunal's freedom of discretion. The most important principles are the equality of the parties (§ 1042(1) ZPO), the right to be heard and the right to be represented by a counsel admitted to the courts (§ 1042(2) ZPO). Especially the right to be heard protects the parties from orders which limit their right to present their case and to give evidence arbitrarily, and it forces the tribunal to consider all factual assertions carefully against the background of the applicable legal theory for the solution of the dispute. It is my experience as a judge of a state court of appeals during many years that an infringement of the right to be heard is the most important ground for the denial of enforceability.*'

6.21 The way in which the arbitral proceedings are conducted might engender a justified sense that the tribunal is less than impartial. For this reason, unilateral contact between arbitrators and a party is to be avoided.[47] Such contact will often involve (i) breach of the duty to treat both parties equally and to hear both sides, and (ii) this type of contact might expose the arbitrator to the charge that he appears biased.

6.22 As for (i), Megaw LJ said in *Government of Ceylon* v. *Chandris* (1963)[48]:

---

[42] Arguably, this might be a special problem in the case of 'med-arb', where the arbitrator acquires early acquaintance with the case, before taking on the mantle of arbitrator: on 'med-arb' in general, *Andrews on Civil Processes* vol 1, *Arbitration and Mediation* (Intersentia, Cambridge, Antwerp, Portland, 2013), chapter 2.

[43] The singular 'arbitrator' is used throughout, rather than 'tribunal'; although English arbitration is accustomed to arbitration panels consisting of two or more (normally, nowadays, an uneven number), most references are heard by a single arbitrator.

[44] *Redfern and Hunter on International Arbitration* (6th edn, Oxford University Press, 2015), 5.70ff, noting the range of principles of 'due process'; see also, *ibid*, 10.53 ff in the context of judicial challenges before national courts on the ground of procedural irregularity.

[45] Perri (Brazil: National Report for the Heidelberg conference, summer 2011): ' *The law itself provides for a limitation to the powers of the arbitrator, who must establish (and conduct) the proceeding in compliance with the constitutional principle of the due process of law ('CFB' – Brazilian Constitution, art. 5, LIV and LV c/c art. 21, Par. 2, of the 'LAB'), under penalty of the award being revoked by means of a claim for annulment (art. 32, VIII c/c art. 33, both in the 'LAB').*'

[46] R Stürner (Germany: National Report for the Heidelberg conference, summer 2011).

[47] *Norbrook Laboratories* v. *Tank* [2006] EWHC 1055 (Comm); [2006] 2 Lloyd's Rep 485; [2006] BLR 412, at [137], Colman J (unilateral telephone conversations; but no substantial injustice occurred on the facts).

[48] [1963] 1 Lloyd's Rep 214, 225–6.

> '*It is… a basic principle, in arbitrations as much as in litigation in the Courts (other than, of course, ex parte proceedings), that no one with judicial responsibility may receive evidence, documentary or otherwise, from one party without the other party knowing that the evidence is being tendered and being offered an opportunity to consider it, object to it, or make submissions on it. No custom or practice may override that basic principle.*'

6.23 In *Norbrook Laboratories* v. *Tank* (2006),[49] Colman J held that a sole arbitrator had committed a serious irregularity, causing a real injustice, when he had independently contacted three witnesses without giving the parties an opportunity to discover what evidence he had received from them, and without allowing them an opportunity to challenge this evidence. This procedural breach vitiated the award, which was set aside under section 68 on the grounds of 'serious irregularity'. This misconduct also justified an order to remove the arbitrator from any further conduct of the proceedings, under section 24 of the Arbitration Act 1996.[50]

6.24 By contrast, it is unavoidable that, prior to appointment of arbitrators, there will be pre-appointment unilateral contact between a party and a prospective party-appointed arbitrator for the purpose of arranging that proposed appointment. Such contact does not normally found a basis for impugning that arbitrator's appointment on the basis of bias.[51] This point is acknowledged by Article 4.4.1 of the *IBA Guidelines on Conflicts of Interest in International Arbitration* (2014) (placing these points of contact in the 'Green' list of innocuous connections between parties and arbitrators). This states:

> '*The arbitrator has had an initial contact with a party, or an affiliate of a party (or their counsel) prior to appointment, if this contact is limited to the arbitrator's availability and qualifications to serve, or to the names of possible candidates for a chairperson, and did not address the merits or procedural aspects of the dispute, other than to provide the arbitrator with a basic understanding of the case.*' (See also comments by Rechberger at **6.04** above)

6.25 *Procedural Expedition.* The Arbitration Act 1996 seeks to balance efficiency and fairness. It obliges arbitrators to promote a speedy and economical resolution of the dispute. This is subject to the constraints of fairness and party-agreement: *The tribunal shall… adopt procedures suitable to the circumstance of the particular case, avoiding unnecessary delay or expense, so as to provide a fair means for the resolution of the matters falling to be determined.*[52] (Emphasis added.) Cynics might regard this as the rhetoric of arbitral efficiency. The English legislation enforces the duty to achieve a speedy outcome: '*The tribunal shall… adopt procedures suitable to the circumstance of the particular case, avoiding unnecessary delay or expense, so as to provide a fair means for the resolution of the matters falling to be*

[49] [2006] EWHC 1055 (Comm); [2006] 2 Lloyd's Rep 485; [2006] BLR 412, at [139], [142], and [154] to [156].

[50] *ibid*, [156] on both points.

[51] *Russell on Arbitration* (24th edn, London, 2015), 5-039 citing Hong Kong discussion and other materials.

[52] Section 33(1)(b), Arbitration Act 1996.

determined.'[53] In many parts of the world, arbitration is chosen to avoid the local court system, which can be glacially slow, administered by a judiciary which is corrupt, incompetent, commercially naive, nationally biased, and long since past its 'sell-by-date'.

6.26 *Intelligible Reasoning*. There is an expectation that arbitral awards will be reasoned. In England it is clear that the arbitrator should give reasons in support of his award, unless the parties have 'contracted out' of this requirement.[54] In England there is a (heavily qualified) power to challenge the award before the court on the basis of an error of English law (**8.04**)[55] (but not on foreign law or findings of fact).

6.27 *Park's Four Main Arbitral Duties*. In a penetrating study, William W Park (Boston, USA) identifies four leading duties of arbitrators: (1) rendering an accurate award; (2) respect for procedural fairness; (3) efficiency, by balancing goals (1) and (2) and the reduction of cost and delay; (4) promoting an enforceable award.[56]

6.28 *Accuracy*. Park further comments: '*the arbitrator should get as near as reasonably possible to an understanding of what actually happened between the litigants and how pertinent legal norms apply to the controverted events.*'[57] As for the risk of error, Park says simply: 'the possibility that an arbitrator will make a mistake, or be less than efficient, remains a risk assumed by both sides',[58] adding '*true enough, any error of law might be cast as a disregard of arbitral jurisdiction, in the sense that the litigants do not expressly empower an arbitrator to make a mistake*';[59] however, he continues: '*the parties asked an arbitrator, not a judge, to decide the case, thereby assuming the risk that the arbitrator might get it wrong*'.[60]

6.29 *Procedural Fairness*. Park makes a three-fold division: (a) '*the responsibility to hear both sides*'[61]; (b) an obligation to '*respect the contours of arbitral jurisdiction or, to put the duty in the negative, to avoid decisions which constitute an excess of authority...either under the contract or by reason of some public policy constraint*'[62]; (c) compliance with '*the general duty of impartiality and*

---

[53] Section 33(1)(b), Arbitration Act 1996.

[54] Section 69, Arbitration Act 1996; if 'reasons' are dispensed with, by agreement, there is no such right of appeal: section 69(1), Arbitration Act 1996: *An agreement to dispense with reasons for the tribunal's award shall be considered an agreement to exclude the court's jurisdiction under this section*...; and section 45(1), Arbitration Act 1996.

[55] Section 69, Arbitration Act 1996.

[56] William W Park, 'The Four Musketeers of Arbitral Duty' in Y Derains and L Lévy (eds), 'Is Arbitration Only as Good as the Arbitrator?' (2011) 8 *ICC Dossiers* 25, 26–7.

[57] *ibid*, at 26.

[58] *ibid*, at 26.

[59] *ibid*, at 33.

[60] *ibid*, at 33.

[61] Park cites a French case, *ibid*, at 28, where an arbitral tribunal was held to have acted wrongly by imposing a legal analysis not explored with the parties during the hearing; see further case law on this problem, *ibid*, 41 at nn 18, 19 (A Pullé, 'Securing Natural Justice in Arbitration Proceedings' (2012) 20 Asia Pacific L Rev 63).

[62] William W Park, 'The Four Musketeers of Arbitral Duty' in Y Derains and L Lévy (eds), 'Is Arbitration Only as Good as the Arbitrator?' (2011) 8 *ICC Dossiers* 25, 29–36, analysing the US

independence'.[63] *He also suggests that 'overly intricate procedural safeguards can paralyze proceedings'.*[64]

6.30 *Efficiency.* Park suggests that '*too much efficiency may mean too little accuracy'.*[65]

6.31 *Promoting an Enforceable Award.* Park comments that victorious parties '*hope that the arbitral process will lead to something more than a piece of paper*'; and he suggests that '*they expect arbitrators to avoid giving reasons for annulment ort non-recognition to any authority called to review the award'.*[66] He also notes that some institutional arbitration rules emphasise this duty.[67] Finally, Park, after noting American[68] and English[69] court decisions on the mandatory status of anti-trust law, comments: '*an arbitrator must satisfy norms both at the arbitral seat, where proceedings take place, and at the recognition forum, where the winner goes to attach assets'.*[70]

Supreme Court's majority decision in *Stolt-Nielsen* v. *AnimalFeeds* (2010) in which an arbitral tribunal was held to have erred by permitting consolidation of related claims against the same party to take place, ostensibly on the basis of party consent, but—according to the majority—without any convincing consensual support: 130S Ct 1758 (2010).

[63] *ibid*, at 26.

[64] *ibid*, at 27.

[65] *ibid*, at 27.

[66] *ibid*, at 27.

[67] *ibid*, n 11, citing Article 35 ICC Rules; and Article 32.2, LCIA Rules.

[68] *ibid*, at 36, noting *Mitsubishi Motors* v. *Soler Chrysler-Plymouth* 473 US 614 (1985).

[69] *ibid*, at 37, *Accentuate Ltd* v. *Asigra Inc* [2009] EWHC 2655 (QB); [2010] 2 All ER (Comm) 738; [2009] 2 Lloyd's Rep 599; [2010] Eu LR 260.

[70] Park, *ibid*, at 36.

Chapter 7
Confidentiality and the Arbitral Process

Abstract English law treats confidentiality as a legal obligation arising as an integral aspect of the arbitration agreement (on the basis of an implied term). This chapter is concerned with the scope of that obligation and with the occasions when the courts will relax arbitral confidentiality, in the interests of the wider justice system.

7.1 Introduction[1]

7.01 This topic was not covered by the Arbitration Act 1996 because the Departmental Advisory Committee (1996) regarded the subject as too fluid for consolidation.[2] That report stated that recognition of exceptions to confidentiality would need to be worked out by the courts on a case-by-case basis.[3] As we shall see, there is no clearly delineated set of exceptions. This topic continues to be molten. Indeed, the exceptions have been described as 'manifestly legion and unsettled in part'.[4]

---

[1] F De Ly, L Radicati di Brozolo and M Friedman, 'Confidentiality in International Commercial Arbitration' (report by International Commercial Committee, International Law Association, Hague conference, August 2010: available at http://www.ila-hq.org); F Dessemontet, 'Arbitration and Confidentiality' (1996) 7 Am Rev Int'l Arb 299; P Neill, 'Confidentiality in Arbitration' (1996) 12 Arb Int 287; K Noussia, *Confidentiality in International Commercial Arbitration* (Springer, Dordrecht, Heidelberg, New York, London, 2010); M Pryles, 'Confidentiality', in LW Newman and RD Hill (eds), *The Leading Arbitrators' Guide to International Arbitration* (3rd edn, New York, 2014), chapter 5; Rogers and Miller, 'Non-Confidential Arbitration Proceedings' (1996) 12 Arb Int 319; M Pryles, 'Confidentiality', in LW Newman and RD Hill (eds), *The Leading Arbitrators' Guide to International Arbitration* (3rd edn, New York, 2014), chapter 5I Smeureanu, *Confidentiality in International Commercial Arbitration* (Kluwer, Netherlands, 2011); VV Veeder, 'The Transparency of International Arbitration: Process and Substance' (concerning confidentiality), in LA Mistelis and JDM Lew (eds), *Pervasive Problems in International Arbitration* (The Hague, 2006), 89–102; Hong-Lin Yu, 'Duty of Confidentiality: Myth and Reality' (2012) 31 CJQ 68; various authors, (1995) 11 Arb Int 3, 319.

[2] The Departmental Advisory Committee on Arbitration Law, Report on the Arbitration Bill, 1996 ('DAC report'), at [10] ff; reprinted in M Mustill and S Boyd, *Commercial Arbitration: Companion Volume* (2001), Appendix 1.

[3] DAC report, at [17].

[4] *ibid,* at [16].

N. Andrews, *Arbitration and Contract Law*, Ius Gentium: Comparative Perspectives on Law and Justice 54, DOI 10.1007/978-3-319-27144-6_7

7.2 Implied Term Analysis

7.02 The Court of Appeal's decision in *Michael Wilson & Partners Ltd* v. *Emmott* (2008)[5] confirms that an obligation of confidentiality arises as a matter of law (on the basis of an 'implied term in law') in arbitration references conducted in accordance with English law. This implied term has been recognised for some time. For example, the Court of Appeal in *Ali Shipping Corporation* v. *Shipyard Trogir* (1999)[6] had said that this term is '*an essential corollary of the privacy of arbitration proceedings*'.[7] (For a Scottish decision adopting the same analysis, see *Gray Construction Limited* v. *Harley Haddow LLP* (2012),[8] on which **7.21** below).

7.03 In passing, it should be noted that Lord Hobhouse in the Privy Council in *Associated Electric & Gas Insurance Services Ltd* v. *European Reinsurance Co of Zurich* (2003)[9] (on this case, **7.08**) was critical of the 'implied term' as the juridical basis of confidentiality in this field: '*Generalisations and the formulation of detailed implied terms are not appropriate*.'[10] But an alternative legal construct was not suggested by him.

7.3 Scope of Protection

7.04 The implied term analysis, ratified by the Court of Appeal in *Michael Wilson & Partners Ltd* v. *Emmott* (2008),[11] governs all documents 'prepared for', 'used', and 'disclosed during' arbitration proceedings governed by English law.

7.05 Lawrence Collins LJ in the *Michael Wilson* case (2008) summarised the position as follows[12]:

> '*There is an obligation, implied by law and arising out of the nature of arbitration, on both parties not to disclose or use for any other purpose any documents prepared for and used in the arbitration, or disclosed or produced in the course of the arbitration, or transcripts or notes of the evidence in the arbitration or the award, and not to disclose in any other way what evidence has been given by any witness in the arbitration. The obligation is not limited to commercially confidential information in the traditional sense. ... [T]his is in reality a substantive rule of arbitration law reached through the device of an implied term.*'

---

[5] [2008] EWCA Civ 184; [2008] 2 All ER (Comm) 193; [2008] 1 Lloyd's Rep 616; noted H Dundas, 'Confidentiality in English Arbitration: The Final Word? *Emmott* v. *Michael Wilson & Partners*' (2008) 74 Arbitration 458–66.

[6] [1999] 1 WLR 314, CA.

[7] *ibid*, at 326 D.

[8] [2012] CSOH 92, at [5].

[9] [2003] UKPC 11; [2003] 1 WLR 1041.

[10] *ibid*, at [20].

[11] [2008] EWCA Civ 184; [2008] 2 All ER (Comm) 193; [2008] 1 Lloyd's Rep 616.

[12] *ibid*, at [105] and [106].

7.06 In some circumstances, there will also be an intrinsic ground of confidentiality attaching to documents, or information, for example, when the relevant information is a trade secret. Lawrence Collins LJ in the *Michael Wilson* case (2008) also noted that the broad topic of arbitral confidentiality involves a mix of (i) privacy, (ii) 'intrinsic' confidentiality in specific documents (such as in trade secrets), and (iii) procedural confidentiality imported under the rubric of the implied duty to maintain arbitral confidentiality.[13]

7.07 *Injunction to Maintain Confidentiality.* In *Insurance Company* v. *Lloyd's Syndicate* (1994)[14] Colman J granted an injunction to prevent a party to arbitration from showing an arbitration award to directly interested reinsurers in the relevant 'market' (viz third parties) because such disclosure would involve breach of an implied confidentiality clause. Injunctive relief is the primary relief to enforce a negative contractual stipulation, whether it be an express term not to do something or an implied term to the same effect.

7.08 *Express Confidentiality Clause.* In *Associated Electric & Gas Insurance Services Ltd* v. *European Reinsurance Co of Zurich* (2003)[15] the Privy Council held (upholding the Court of Appeal of Bermuda) that no injunction should be granted to restrain a party to arbitration A (the so-called 'Boyd arbitration', having been chaired by Stewart Boyd QC) from referring to the award in that arbitration in a second arbitration, B, (the so-called 'Rowe arbitration'). The arbitration agreement included a detailed confidentiality clause, part of which stated:

> *[C]lause 30. The parties, their lawyers, and the court of arbitration agree as a general principle to maintain the privacy and confidentiality of the arbitration. In particular they agree that the contents of the briefs or other documents prepared and filed in the course of this proceeding, as well as the contents of the underlying claim documents, testimony, affidavits, any transcripts, and the arbitration result will not be disclosed at any time to any individual or entity, in whole or in part, which is not a party to the arbitration between Aegis and European Re.*

7.09 In the *Associated Electric* case (2003) the *two arbitrations were between the same parties*, and both references concerned re-insurance transactions, although they were separate disputes. An injunction in these circumstances would preclude the party who had been victorious on this issue from asserting that victory by way of issue estoppel (**10.15** section (iii) (g)).

7.10 Giving the court's advice in the *Associated Electric* case (2003), Lord Hobhouse attractively explained[16] that the grant of an injunction in this intense fashion would run counter to the fundamental obligation that the parties will abide by the arbitration award and allow it to be enforced. 'Enforcement' in a full sense must include a party relying upon a final decision by way of issue estoppel (generally on that concept, **10.15** section (iii) (g)). It would fall, therefore, to the Rowe arbitration

---

[13] *ibid,* at [79].

[14] [1994] CLC 1303, 1309-10 (noting *Doherty* v. *Allman* (1878) 3 App Cas 709, 720, HL, *per* Lord Cairns LC; on this topic **17.27**, at paragraph (vii)).

[15] [2003] UKPC 11; [2003] 1 WLR 1041.

[16] *ibid,* at [9] to [15].

to decide whether the ingredients of issue estoppel were made out in the dispute. In this respect, the Rowe arbitration would not take place 'in the dark'. (The Court of Appeal in the *West Tankers* decision (2012) (**4.39**) adopted the reasoning of Lord Hobhouse in order to support the conclusion that the High Court can issue a declaration under section 66 of the Arbitration Act 1996, in enforcement of an arbitral award itself involving a declaration, because section 66 is not confined to coercive forms of enforcement).[17]

7.4 Judicial Relaxation of Confidentiality

7.11 '*Exceptions to Confidentiality*'. The English courts recognise various exceptional contexts in which it is necessary or appropriate to relax confidentiality. Lawrence Collins LJ summarised the position as follows[18]:

> *'The principal cases in which disclosure will be permissible are these: the first is where there is consent, express or implied; second, where there is an order, or leave of the court (but that does not mean that the court has a general discretion to lift the obligation of confidentiality); third, where it is reasonably necessary for the protection of the legitimate interests of an arbitrating party*[19]*; fourth, where the interests of justice require disclosure, and also (perhaps) where the public interest requires disclosure'.* Adding[20]: *'The interests of justice are not confined to the interests of justice in England. The international dimension of the present case demands a broader view.'*

7.12 In particular, the decision in *Michael Wilson & Partners Ltd* v. *Emmott* (2008) (noted in detail in the following paragraph) shows that the English courts will be prepared to relax confidentiality in order to prevent another court, whether in England or elsewhere, from being misled concerning an issue, provided the parallel court proceedings arise from similar events and there is a sufficient connexion between the parties to the relevant arbitration and the parties to the relevant parallel litigation.

7.13 In the *Michael Wilson* case (2008) MWP, a law firm specialising in international commercial arbitration, was a party to arbitration in London and party to court litigation in several jurisdictions (Jersey, Colorado, British Virgin Islands, 'BVI', and New South Wales, 'NSW') involving former associates of MWP, namely

[17] *West Tankers Inc* v. *Allianz SpA ('The Front Comor')* [2012] EWCA Civ 27, at [36] to [38].

[18] *Michael Wilson & Partners Ltd* v. *Emmott* [2008] EWCA Civ 184; [2008] 2 All ER (Comm) 193; [2008] 1 Lloyd's Rep 616, at [107].

[19] *ibid*, at [101], *per* Lawrence Collins LJ: '*[Disclosure is] permissible when, and to the extent to which, it was reasonably necessary for the establishment or protection of an arbitrating party's legal rights vis-à-vis a third party in order to found a cause of action against that third party or to defend a claim, or counterclaim, brought by that third party. It would be this exception which would apply where insurers have to be informed about the details of arbitral proceedings...*'

[20] *ibid*, at [111].

E (Emmott), N (Nicholls) and S (Slater). All this litigation concerned the same basic claim by MWP that these former members of its staff had conspired to steal business from MWP. There was an obvious inconsistency, and hence relevance, in the fact that, in the London arbitration, MWP had abandoned allegations of fraud committed by these three, but MWP retained this allegation on the same facts in the NSW and BVI court litigation. The English Court of Appeal held that these facts justified permitting E, one of the parties to the English arbitration, to disclose material generated during that arbitration. Such disclosure was justified because of the danger that the NSW and BVI courts might otherwise be misled. It did not matter that E was not party to the relevant foreign court proceedings. It was enough that those proceedings concerned the same 'substratum of facts' as the arbitration.

7.14 *Institutional Rules on Confidentiality.* Other legal systems might be less supportive of confidentiality than the English courts. Indeed, *Redfern and Hunter* note the tendency for legal systems to recognise only a qualified right to arbitral confidentiality[21]:

> '*It is increasingly necessary to rely on an express provision of the [relevant institutional] rules... or to enter into a specific confidentiality agreement as part of the agreement to arbitrate or at the outset of proceedings (and it seems that this may be overridden in some jurisdictions if the relevant court considered it to be in the public interest that it should be).*'

7.15 Against this background, therefore, the following institutional rules will be helpful: Article 30 of the LCIA Rules (2014) (London Court of International Arbitration) states:

> 30.1 *The parties undertake as a general principle to keep confidential all awards in the arbitration, together with all materials in the arbitration created for the purpose of the arbitration and all other documents produced by another party in the proceedings not otherwise in the public domain, save and to the extent that disclosure may be required of a party by legal duty, to protect or pursue a legal right, or to enforce or challenge an award in legal proceedings before a state court or other legal authority.*
>
> 30.2 *The deliberations of the Arbitral Tribunal shall remain confidential to its members, save as required by any applicable law and to the extent that disclosure of an arbitrator's refusal to participate in the arbitration is required of the other members of the Arbitral Tribunal under Articles 10, 12, 26 and 27.*
>
> 30.3 *The LCIA does not publish any award or any part of an award without the prior written consent of all parties and the Arbitral Tribunal.*

7.16 By contrast, the 2012 version of the ICC Arbitration Rules provides a more diluted regime:

> Article 22.3: *Upon the request of any party, the arbitral tribunal may make orders concerning the confidentiality of the arbitration proceedings or of any other matters in connection with the arbitration and may take measures for protecting trade secrets and confidential information.*

---

[21] *Redfern and Hunter on International Arbitration* (6th edn, Oxford University Press, 2015), 2.196.

Article 26.3: *The arbitral tribunal shall be in full control of the hearings, at which all the parties shall be entitled to be present. Save with the approval of the arbitral tribunal and the parties, persons not involved in the proceedings shall not be admitted.*

Article 34.2: This provides for additional copies of the award to be sent 'to the parties, but to no one else.'

7.5 Judicial Proceedings Within the High Court: Hearings and Judgment

7.17 In *Department of Economics, Policy and Development of the City of Moscow* v. *Bankers Trust Co* (2004)[22] the Court of Appeal noted the restriction on publicity (CPR 62.10)[23] applicable to High Court proceedings in arbitration matters, that is, concerning court proceedings under the Arbitration Act 1996. The Court of Appeal held that a judge's refusal (or grant) of an application for permission to appeal to the High Court on the basis of an alleged serious irregularity did not have to be publicised as an open transcript or electronically accessible judgment. Mance LJ said[24]: '*[the Arbitration Act 1996 and CPR 62.10] rest clearly on the philosophy of party autonomy in modern arbitration law, combined with the assumption that parties value English arbitration for its privacy and confidentiality.*'[25]And he noted the emphasis upon maintaining the privacy of the original arbitration reference,[26] and parties '*expectations regarding privacy and confidentiality when agreeing to arbitrate.*'[27] He also noted that the principle of publicity applies with special force to judgments, especially if they will illuminate aspects of practice and law[28]: Finally, Mance LJ said[29]: '*judges framing judgments are accustomed to concentrate on essentials, to avoid where possible unnecessary disclosure of sensitive material and in some cases to anonymise.*'

---

[22] [2004] EWCA Civ 314; [2005] QB 207 (discussed in *North Shore Ventures Ltd* v. *Anstead Holdings Inc (No 2)* [2011] EWHC 910 (Ch); [2011] 1 WLR 2265, at [18] ff, *per* Floyd J).

[23] CPR 62.10.

[24] [2004] EWCA Civ 314; [2005] QB 207, at [30].

[25] Similarly, *Glidepath BV* v. *Thompson* [2005] EWHC 818 (Comm); [2005] 2 Lloyd's Rep 549, at [19], *per* Colman J (endorsement of the need to maintain confidentiality in arbitration practice, despite judicial proceedings designed to grant injunctive relief, prior to the grant of a stay under section 9, Arbitration Act 1996).

[26] [2004] EWCA Civ 314; [2005] QB 207, at [32].

[27] *ibid,* at [34].

[28] [2004] EWCA Civ 314; [2005] QB 207, at [39].

[29] *ibid,* at [40].

7.6 Confidentiality: Non-English Developments

7.18 The judgments in *Michael Wilson & Partners Ltd* v. *Emmott* (2008)[30] contain rich citation of the English case law,[31] and foreign courts' decisions,[32] as well as the relevant rules adopted by leading arbitration bodies[33] on the question of 'privacy of hearings'[34] 'confidentiality of documentation',[35] 'confidentiality of awards',[36] and literature discussing these rules.[37]

7.19 As the (English) Departmental Advisory Committee (1996) noted, Australian decisions have been perceived in England as troublingly ungenerous in their protection of arbitral confidentiality: England and Australia have here parted company.[38]

7.20 Since the *Michael Wilson* case (2008), there has been some development of this topic in Scotland: an important judicial decision (*Gray Construction Limited*

---

[30] [2008] EWCA Civ 184; [2008] 2 All ER (Comm) 193; [2008] 1 Lloyd's Rep 616.

[31] Most recent cases first: *Associated Electric and Gas Insurance Services Ltd* v. *European Reinsurance Co of Zurich* [2003] UKPC 11; [2003] 1 WLR 1041; *Glidepath BV* v. *Thompson* [2005] 2 Lloyd's Rep 549, Colman J; *Department of Economics, Policy and Development of the City of Moscow* v. *Bankers Trust Co* [2004] EWCA Civ 314; [2005] QB 207; *Ali Shipping Corporation* v. *Shiphard Trogir* [1999] 1 WLR 314, CA; *Insurance Co* v. *Lloyd's Syndicate* [1995] 1 Lloyd's Rep 272; *London and Leeds Estates Ltd* v. *Paribas Ltd* [1995] 1 EGLR 102; [1995] EG 134, Mance J; *Hassneh Insurance Co of Israel* v. *Mew* [1993] 2 Lloyd's Rep 242; *Dolling-Baker* v. *Merrett* [1990] 1 WLR 1205; *Oxford Shipping Co Ltd* v. *Nippon Kaisha ('The Eastern Saga')* [1984] 3 All ER 835, Leggatt J.

[32] Lawrence Collins LJ, in *Michael Wilson & Partners Ltd* v. *Emmott* [2008] EWCA Civ 184; [2008] 2 All ER (Comm) 193; [2008] 1 Lloyd's Rep 616, at [74], citing various foreign cases. *Redfern and Hunter on International Arbitration* (6th edn, Oxford University Press, 2015), 2.161 ff, noting *Esso Australia Resources Ltd* v. *Plowman* (1995) 193 CLR 10, H Ct Aust (criticised P Neill, 'Confidentiality in Arbitration' (1996) 12 Arb Int 287); *Commonwealth of Australia* v. *Cockatoo Dockyard Pty Ltd* (1995) 36 NSWLR 662; on US decisions, *Redfern and Hunter, ibid,* at 2.173; on Swedish law, *ibid,* 2.176; French law, *ibid,* 2.182; ICSID decisions, *ibid,* 2.185 ff; institutional rules, 2.190 ff.

[33] *Michael Wilson* case (2008), Lawrence Collins LJ at [66], citing *ICC Commission on Arbitration, Forum on ICC Rules/Court: Report on Confidentiality as a Purported Obligation of the Parties in Arbitration* (2002); Fouchard, Gaillard and Goldman, *International Commercial Arbitration* (1999), paragraph 1412; Lew, Mistelis and Kröll, *Comparative International Commercial Arbitration* (2003), 24–99 ff; for other references, *Redfern and Hunter on International Arbitration* (6th edn, Oxford University Press, 2015), 2.163, 2.164.

[34] *Michael Wilson* case (2008), Lawrence Collins LJ at [64].

[35] *ibid,* at [67] to [70].

[36] *ibid,* at [65].

[37] *ibid,* at [66].

[38] The Departmental Advisory Committee on Arbitration Law, Report on the Arbitration Bill, 1996 ('the DAC report'), at [13] and [16], noting noting *Esso Australia Resources Ltd* v. *Plowman* (1995) 193 CLR 10, H Ct Aust (criticised P Neill, 'Confidentiality in Arbitration' (1996) 12 Arb Int 287); *Commonwealth of Australia* v. *Cockatoo Dockyard Pty Ltd* (1995) 36 NSWLR 662.

v. *Harley Haddow LLP* (2012), on which **7.21** below),[39] and legislation (the Arbitration (Scotland) Act 2010), containing a codification of the whole topic.[40] In Particular, Rule 25 of the Arbitration (Scotland) Act 2010 provides a comprehensive statement of arbitral confidentiality.[41]

> *(1) Disclosure by the tribunal, any arbitrator or a party of confidential information relating to the arbitration is to be actionable as a breach of an obligation of confidence unless the disclosure—(a) is authorised, expressly or impliedly, by the parties (or can reasonably be considered as having been so authorised), (b) is required by the tribunal or is otherwise made to assist or enable the tribunal to conduct the arbitration,(c) is required—(i) in order to comply with any enactment or rule of law, (ii) for the proper performance of the discloser's public functions, or (iii) in order to enable any public body or office-holder to perform public functions properly, (d) can reasonably be considered as being needed to protect a party's lawful interests, (e) is in the public interest, (f) is necessary in the interests of justice, or (g) is made in circumstances in which the discloser would have absolute privilege had the disclosed information been defamatory.*
>
> *... (4) "Confidential information", in relation to an arbitration, means any information relating to—(a) the dispute, (b) the arbitral proceedings, (c) the award, or (d) any civil proceedings relating to the arbitration in respect of which an order has been granted under section 15 of this Act, which is not, and has never been, in the public domain.*

Of course, Scots law remains separate from English law, so that these Scottish materials are merely of comparative interest. Nevertheless, the analysis of various exceptions to confidentiality is attractive.

7.21 The pre- Arbitration (Scotland) Act 2010 Scottish decision in *Gray Construction Limited* v. *Harley Haddow LLP* (2012) is a convincing illustration. In that case Lord Hodge, in the Outer House of the Court of Session, held that Scots law mirrors the implied term analysis adopted in English arbitration law (on which **7.02** above).[42] He also held that the court will allow confidentiality to be lifted in favour of a party to the relevant arbitration to enable that party to sustain properly a legal claim in related proceedings between that party and a third party.[43] He generalised this point by referring to the 'public interest in the administration of justice'.[44]

On the facts of this case, G succeeded in its application for the lifting of confidentiality in documents created during an arbitration reference between G and N G made this application in order to rely on this information in court proceedings between G and HH. In the latter proceedings, G was seeking damages from HH. This compensation included the amount of a settlement concluded by G and N during the relevant arbitral proceedings. The court proceedings brought by G, a construction company, were against HH, engineering consultants. The case concerned defective foundations in houses in Dunfermline. In the arbitration between G and N, N had

---

[39] [2012] CSOH 92 (Outer House of the Court of Session, Lord Hodge).

[40] *ibid*, at [6], noting the Scottish Arbitration Rules, at Schedule 1 of the Arbitration (Scotland) Act 2010 (see next note).

[41] Rule 25, Scottish Arbitration Rules, at Schedule 1 of the Arbitration (Scotland) Act 2010.

[42] [2012] CSOH 92, at [5].

[43] *ibid*, at [6].

[44] *ibid*, at [9].

claimed c £360,000 damages in respect of these defects, and the parties, G and N, had settled on a sum of £110,000, payable by G to N.[45] In these circumstances, the Scottish court held that it was fair and reasonable for G to be allowed to use this confidential information in order to demonstrate that the settlement between G and N had been objectively reasonable[46] (the decision ante-dates the Scottish statutory codification of arbitral confidentiality).[47]

---

[45] *ibid,* at [1].

[46] *ibid,* at [3].

[47] *ibid,* at [6], noting that the Scottish Arbitration Rules, at Schedule 1 of the Arbitration (Scotland) Act 2010 would yield the same result

Part II
Monitoring the Tribunal's Application of Contract Law

Chapter 8
Awards Disclosing Errors of English Law

Abstract In the Second Part of this work (the present chapter and the next), the reader is provided with material relevant to the monitoring of the arbitral award's compliance with the applicable substantive contract law. This is taken seriously in England. A party can seek permission from the Commercial Court to receive an appeal from an award concerning a point of substantive English law. Such permission is sparingly granted, in accordance with demanding criteria. Furthermore, the parties can (and often do) by agreement exclude this possibility of appeal. Appeals on a point of substantive law are a special feature of the system of arbitration in England. Other systems might regard this with suspicion. But the author considers that the balance has been attractively struck between the value of finality and arbitral autonomy and the competing interest in monitoring the substantive accuracy of arbitral adjudication on points of law.

8.1 Introduction

8.01 Section 69 of the Arbitration Act 1996 confers power to challenge the award before the Commercial Court on the basis of an error of English law.[1] In fact section 69 is one of three possible grounds of challenge. The triad consists of these elements: (A) lack of jurisdiction (section 67), or (B) the assertion that the arbitral panel has been guilty of 'serious irregularity affecting the tribunal, the proceedings or the award' (section 68), or (C) on the basis of an error of (English) law.[2] Ground (C), under section 69, can be excluded by agreement. But grounds (A) and (B) are mandatory: they cannot be excluded by party agreement. As for (A) (that is,

---

[1] Section 69(2)(3), Arbitration Act 1996; the report by VV Veeder and A Sander (2009: see end of this note) notes (Schedule 8, p 8 of the report) that the Commercial Court, in London, considered 36 applications in 2006, and granted leave in 9; in 2007, 58, leave granted in 13; in 2008, 57, leave granted in 14; disclosing an average of 50 a year, with permission granted in 12; report available at: http://www.lmaa.org.uk/uploads/documents/First%20Interim%20Report%20Mance%2024%2005%202009.pdf.

[2] Section 69(2)(3), Arbitration Act 1996.

N. Andrews, *Arbitration and Contract Law*, Ius Gentium: Comparative Perspectives on Law and Justice 54, DOI 10.1007/978-3-319-27144-6_8

disputes concerning the tribunal's jurisdiction),[3] this matter is mainly subject in English law to a challenge under section 67 of the Arbitration Act 1996. In fact there are five routes for considering this issue[4]:

Section 67: the court might be asked to pronounce *ex post facto* on the tribunal's decision concerning its substantive jurisdiction; or

Section 30: the tribunal itself might first make a 'ruling' on the same issue, following an 'objection' made by an alleged party; or

Section 32: the court might be asked to give a decision on the question of the tribunal's jurisdiction; or

Section 72: a party, having stood aloof[5] from the proceedings, might apply to the court for relief, essentially complaining that he is not subject to the relevant arbitral proceedings.

At the Stage of Enforcement: the question of jurisdiction might arise during the stage of seeking recognition or enforcement of the award, under the English legislation,[6] or, in the case of a relevant foreign court, for example, under the New York Convention (1958) (**9.01**).

8.02 All three bases of challenge (sections 67–69) are subject to the need to exhaust other routes for obtaining relief,[7] for example by asking the tribunal to correct or clarify its award.[8] There is a 28 day period[9] for seeking such corrections, commencing on the date of the award.[10] But this period can be extended by the court.[11]

---

[3] On that topic generally, *Andrews on Civil Processes* volume 2, *Arbitration and Mediation* (Intersentia, Cambridge, Antwerp, Portland, 2013), 18.14 ff; S Jarvin and A Leventhal, 'Objections to Jurisdiction', in LW Newman and RD Hill (eds), *The Leading Arbitrators' Guide to International Arbitration* (3rd edn, New York, 2014), chapter 22.

[4] A careful overview is by Rix LJ in *AES Ust-Kamenogorsk Hydropower Plant LLP* v. *Ust-Kamenogorsk Hydropower Plant JSC* [2011] EWCA Civ 647; [2012] 1 WLR 920, at [82].

[5] The principles governing such a non-participating party's capacity to resist enforcement of an award are examined in *London Steam Ship Owners Mutual Insurance Association Ltd* v. *Spain ('The Prestige')* [2013] EWHC 2840 (Comm); [2014] 1 All ER (Comm) 300; [2014] 1 Lloyd's Rep 137, Walker J.

[6] Section 66(3), Arbitration Act 1996 expressly refers to the question of substantive jurisdiction; this provision operates subject to the possibility that the right to object has been lost, on which see section 73.

[7] Section 70(2), Arbitration Act 1996.

[8] *Omnibridge Consulting Ltd* v. *Clearsprings (Management) Ltd* [2004] EWHC 2276 (Comm), at [62]; section 70(1),(2) of the Arbitration Act 1996.

[9] An application for correction of the award, or the giving of an additional award, under section 57, Arbitration Act 1996, must be made 'within 28 days of the date of the award or such longer period as the parties may agree' (section 57(4)); an application or appeal under sections 67, 68, 69 must be made 'within 28 days of the date of the award or, if there has been any arbitral process of appeal or review, of the date when the applicant or appellant was notified of the result of that process' (section 70(3)).

[10] The date of the award is that stated by the arbitrators (section 52(5), Arbitration Act 1996).

[11] The court has power to extend the 28 day time limit under the general power contained in section 79(1), Arbitration Act 1996.

8.03 In *Torch Offshore LLC* v. *Cable Shipping Inc* (2004)[12] Cooke J held that preclusion will occur if a party has not sought from the tribunal a 'correction' where the reasoning on an issue is defective. In the *Buyuk* case (2010)[13] Gavin Kealey QC, sitting as a Deputy High Court judge, held that a distinction must be drawn between (a) a tribunal's complete failure to deal with an issue presented to it by the parties (such a failure can give rise to a challenge under section 68, namely a 'serious irregularity', if the failure has produced 'serious injustice') and (b) a confusing or incomplete treatment in the award of an issue. As for (b), the same judge noted a sub-division between instances (i) where the award does not make clear whether the tribunal has postponed its decision on a particular issue and (ii) where the award is obscure on how it has been decided.[14]

8.2 General Features of the Gateway Under Section 69

8.04 Permission to appeal under sections 67–69 from the High Court (for qualifications concerning other courts, see the end of this paragraph) to the Court of Appeal can only be given by the High Court itself,[15] unless (i) the High Court decision was made outside the court's jurisdiction,[16] or (ii) consideration of the issue of permission involved an unfair process,[17] or (iii) there is a preliminary issue whether section 69 applies at all or whether the parties have excluded it.[18] The reason for exception (iii) is this: '*there is a distinction between those cases where the court is assisting or overseeing the arbitration process and the cases where the question is whether the jurisdiction of the court has been excluded.*'[19] The Commercial Court is the main court appointed by statute to oversee issues arising under the Arbitration Act 1996. But some arbitration matters will come before the Mercantile Courts, and

[12] [2004] EWHC 787 (Comm); [2004] 2 All ER (Comm) 365; [2004] 2 Lloyd's Rep 446, at [28].

[13] *Buyuk Camlica Shipping Trading and Industry Co Inc* v. *Progress Bulk Carriers Ltd* [2010] EHWC 442 (Comm); [2011] Bus LR D 99, at [42] and [43].

[14] *ibid*, at [43].

[15] *Cetelem SA* v. *Roust Holdings Ltd* [2005] EWCA Civ 618; [2005] 1 WLR 3555, at [20].

[16] In *Cetelem*, *ibid*, it was held that a decision made by the High Court under section 44(3) which was made outside the court's jurisdiction was not subject to section 44(7) and so the Court of Appeal could entertain an appeal.

[17] *CGU International Insurance plc* v. *Astra Zeneca Insurance Co Ltd* [2006] EWCA Civ 1340; [2007] 1 All ER (Comm) 501; [2007] 1 Lloyd's Rep 142, at [98], *per* Rix LJ.

[18] *Sukuman Ltd* v. *Commonwealth Secretariat* [2007] EWCA Civ 243; [2007] 3 All ER 342; [2007] 2 Lloyd's Rep 87 (held that an exclusion clause, accompanying an arbitration agreement, had been validly incorporated into the parties' agreement; the resulting arbitration award could not be challenged under section 69, Arbitration Act, because the parties had in writing excluded that possibility; such exclusion was not contrary to Article 6 of the European Convention on Human Rights).

[19] *ibid*, at [30].

the Technology and Construction Court,[20] or the Chancery Division,[21] and county courts.[22]

8.05 Unless both parties agree to an appeal,[23] the High Court, acting as its own 'gate-keeper', is required to apply specified restrictive criteria, in effect a statutory 'filter', to determine whether to grant permission for such an appeal on a point of English law[24]:

> *Leave to appeal shall be given only if the court is satisfied—(a) that the determination of the question will substantially affect the rights of one or more of the parties, (b) that the question is one which the tribunal was asked to determine, (c) that, on the basis of the findings of fact in the award—(i) the decision of the tribunal on the question is obviously wrong, or (ii) the question is one of general public importance and the decision of the tribunal is at least open to serious doubt, and (d) that, despite the agreement of the parties to resolve the matter by arbitration, it is just and proper in all the circumstances for the court to determine the question.*

8.06 Commenting generally on section 69 of the 1996 Act (appeals to the High Court from arbitration awards on points of pure English law), Rix LJ said in *CGU International Insurance plc* v. *Astra Zeneca Insurance Co Ltd* (2006)[25]: *'Section 69 is concerned with appeals from arbitration awards. It enacts a concern, in the interests of party autonomy, privacy and finality, that such awards should not be readily transferred to the courts for appellate review.'*

8.07 *Court of Appeal Closed Off unless High Court Judge Grants Permission.* The policy of the law is to lean against second appeals[26] from arbitration decisions, that is, from the High Court and then to the Court of Appeal. That policy was noted in the *Itochu* case (2012),[27] the *Amec* case (2011),[28] and earlier in *Sukuman Ltd* v.

---

[20] (1) CPR 62.1(3): *Part 58 (Commercial Court) applies to arbitration claims in the Commercial Court, Part 59 (Mercantile Court) applies to arbitration claims in the Mercantile Court and Part 60 (Technology and Construction Court claims) applies to arbitration claims in the Technology and Construction Court, except where this Part provides otherwise;* (2) PD (61), paragraph 2.3(2); (3) Section O, *The Admiralty and Commercial Courts Guide* (9th edn, London, 2011); (4) High Court and County Courts (Allocation of Arbitration Proceedings) Order 1996/3215.

[21] PD (61), paragraph 2.3(2): matters '*relating to a landlord and tenant or partnership dispute must be issued in the Chancery Division of the High Court*'.

[22] High Court and County Courts (Allocation of Arbitration Proceedings) Order 1996/3215.

[23] Walker J in *Royal & Sun Alliance Insurance plc* v. *BAE Systems (Operations) Ltd* [2008] EWHC 743 (Comm); [2008] 1 Lloyd's Rep 712, at [29]; case is noted in the report by VV Veeder and A Sander (2009), at [13] and [14]; report available at: http://www.lmaa.org.uk/uploads/documents/First%20Interim%20Report%20Mance%2024%2005%202009.pdf.

[24] Section 69(3), Arbitration Act 1996.

[25] [2006] EWCA Civ 1340; [2007] 1 All ER (Comm) 501; [2007] 1 Lloyd's Rep 142; [2007] CP Rep 4, at [3], *per* Rix LJ.

[26] For a trenchant examination of this topic, J Hill, 'Onward Appeals under the Arbitration Act 1996' (2012) 31 CJQ 194.

[27] *Itochu Corporation* v. *Johann M.K. Blumenthal GMBH & Co KG* [2012] EWCA Civ 996, at [18], *per* Gross LJ.

[28] *AMEC Civil Engineering Ltd* v. *Secretary of State for Transport* [2005] EWCA Civ 291; [2005] 1 WLR 2339, at [9], *per* Sir Anthony May, criticising Jackson J's grant of permission for a second appeal under section 67, Arbitration Act 1996.

Commonwealth Secretariat (2007).[29] Permission to appeal under section 69 from the High Court to the Court of Appeal can only be given by the High Court itself. Thus section 69(6) states that: *The leave of the court is required for any appeal from a decision of the court under this section to grant or refuse leave to appeal.*[30] That restriction applies equally to (i) a refusal to grant permission for an appeal to the High Court (or to the grant of such permission) and (ii) to the refusal (or grant) of permission to appeal from a decision made after the High Court, having granted permission at stage (i), has heard an appeal under section 69 (but see the next paragraph for a qualification).

8.08 *'The Residual Jurisdiction' of the Court of Appeal.* In *North Range Shipping Ltd* v. *Seatrans Shipping Corporation* (2002)[31] the Court of Appeal said that civil judges, even when performing such instinctive assessments as the decision whether to grant permission to appeal, must respect minimal requirements of 'reasoning'. And so the High Court judge in the present context must indicate the essence of the judge's reasons for refusing permission.[32] This 'last ditch' opportunity to test the procedural integrity of the judge's decision has become known as the 'residual jurisdiction'[33] of the Court of Appeal to examine High Court decisions in this context.

8.09 Rix LJ in *CGU International Insurance plc* v. *Astra Zeneca Insurance Co Ltd* (2006) noted that the *North Range* case is concerned not just (as on its facts) with the allegation that the High Court judge's decision is procedurally flawed because it discloses no adequate reasoning (although that reasoning need only be cursory), but that the process whereby that decision was made was procedurally unjust[34]:

> *'If, as is accepted, there is a residual jurisdiction in this court to set aside a judge's decision for misconduct then there can be no reason in principle why the same relief should not be available in the case of unfairness. Each is directed at the integrity of the decision-making process or the decision-maker, which the courts must be vigilant to protect, and does not directly involve an attack on the decision itself.'*

8.10 If the High Court judge has granted permission to examine the arbitration award under section 69, and has made a substantive decision, but the High Court judge then refuses (or perhaps grants) permission under section 69(8) for a further

---

[29] [2007] EWCA Civ 243; [2007] 3 All ER 342; [2007] 2 Lloyd's Rep 87; [2007] 1 CLC 282, at [15], *per* Waller LJ.

[30] *Cetelem SA* v. *Roust Holdings Ltd* [2005] EWCA Civ 618; [2005] 1 WLR 3555, at [20]; but in the *Cetelem* case itself, concerning section 44(3) and 44(7), it was held that a decision made by the High Court under section 44(3) which was made outside the court's jurisdiction was not subject to section 44(7) and so the Court of Appeal could entertain an appeal.

[31] [2002] 1 WLR 2397, CA, at [21] and [22].

[32] *ibid*, at [27], *per* Tuckey LJ (this passage is trenchant and should be closely examined).

[33] *CGU International Insurance plc* v. *Astra Zeneca Insurance Co Ltd* [2006] EWCA Civ 1340; [2007] 1 All ER (Comm) 501; [2007] 1 Lloyd's Rep 142, at [48] ff, *per* Rix LJ; and *per* Arden LJ in *BLCT (13096) Ltd* v. *J Sainsbury plc* [2003] EWCA Civ 884; [2004] 1 CLC 24, at [22] and [31].

[34] *ibid*, at [49], where Rix LJ cited Tuckey LJ in *North Range Shipping Ltd* v. *Seatrans Shipping Corporation* [2002] 1 WLR 2397, CA, at [14].

appeal to the Court of Appeal, the latter court has held that the appellate court can intervene only if there is a breach of fairness in this 'permission' process. This involves the Court of Appeal's 'residual jurisdiction': an opportunity for last-ditch attack on a decision on the ground that it is procedurally vitiated, rather than it is insecure or even demonstrably wrong on the factual or legal merits. Indeed in this context the Court of Appeal has said that the residual discretion is highly restricted: it is not enough to show that the judge's decision was merely perverse or that he had erred in law.[35] An example might be that suggested by Arden LJ in one case[36]: the High Court judge's decision not to recuse himself on grounds of bias. Another example might be the judge's declaration: 'I will deal with the issue of permission myself and I do not need to receive any information from either party on that point'. Similar breaches of procedural fairness are not difficult to invent in theory. But they are rarer than hen's teeth or trophy victories by the full English (male) football team in leading international tournaments.[37]

8.11 The English court is also given a circumscribed power under section 45 of the Arbitration Act 1996 to decide a point of law (that is, a point of English law)[38] arising in the proceedings before the making of the main award. Section 45 can be excluded by agreement and there is a restriction on appeal to the Court of Appeal, as noted *en passant* by Waller LJ in *Sukuman Ltd* v. *Commonwealth Secretariat* (2007).[39] According to *Mustill & Boyd*, the court should assert sovereign command of the section 45 gateway and, where appropriate, decide to override the parties' agreement to obtain a judicial ruling.[40] But there is no clear textual support for the argument just cited. (By contrast, for the purpose of section 69, it has been decided that the High Court *must* hear an appeal on a point of English law if the parties agree to such an appeal[41]: it is arguably regrettable that the court lacks sovereign command of the gateway under section 69).

[35] *CGU International Insurance plc* v. *Astra Zeneca Insurance Co Ltd* [2006] EWCA Civ 1340; [2007] 1 All ER (Comm) 501; [2007] 1 Lloyd's Rep 142, at [98], *per* Rix LJ.

[36] Arden LJ's brief discussion in a 2003 case was cited by Rix LJ in *CGU International Insurance plc* v. *Astra Zeneca Insurance Co Ltd* [2006] EWCA Civ 1340, at [52].

[37] The foreign (or non-English) reader should note that the last such trophy victory was the World Cup in 1966.

[38] Section 82(1), Arbitration Act 1996.

[39] [2007] EWCA Civ 243; [2007] 3 All ER 342; [2007] 2 Lloyd's Rep 87, at [9].

[40] *Mustill & Boyd, Commercial Arbitration: Companion Volume* (London, 2001), 326.

[41] Walker J in *Royal & Sun Alliance Insurance plc* v. *BAE Systems (Operations) Ltd* [2008] EWHC 743 (Comm); [2008] 1 Lloyd's Rep 712; [2008] 1 CLC 711; [2008] Bus LR D127, at [29], construing section 69(2), Arbitration Act 1996: '*An appeal shall not be brought under this section except—(a) with the agreement of all the other parties to the proceedings, or (b) with the leave of the court.*'

8.3 Key to the Section 69 Lock: A Point of English Law

8.12 Issues of construction of written contracts can fall within the scope of 'law'.[42]

8.13 Sometimes the arbitration will also or instead be asked to determine the correct interpretation of the arbitration agreement, but this will normally attract protection under section 67, rather than section 69.[43]

8.14 In *Trustees of Edmond Stern Settlement* v. *Simon Levy* (2007) Judge Coulson QC, in the Technology and Construction Court, said that one-off contracts are unlikely to raise issues of sufficient general importance to warrant permission being granted under section 69.[44] More generally, he noted that interpretation of written contracts is often a matter of impression, involving reference to relevant 'factual matrix' material. For this reason, the High Court should be slow to second-guess that type of decision.[45]

8.15 Where the governing substantive law is English, the arbitral tribunal is obliged to adhere to English principles governing interpretation of written contracts.[46] It follows that the tribunal must not engage in equitable re-writing of the agreement[47]:

> *'The tribunal does not have a judicial discretion" to decide on a commercially sensible solution...nor does it have the right to rewrite a contractual provision...so that it accords with what the tribunal thinks the parties ought to have agreed, irrespective of their intentions as deduced from the terms of the contract, properly construed.'*

8.16 It appears that the courts will be slow to construe the arbitration clause as authorising a looser approach. For example, in *Home & Overseas Insurance Co Ltd* v. *Mentor Insurance Co (UK) Ltd* (1990)[48] the arbitration agreement stated: '*The arbitrators...shall interpret this reinsurance as an honourable engagement and they shall make their award with a view to effecting the general purpose of this reinsurance in a reasonable manner rather than in accordance with a literal interpretation of the language*.' The Court of Appeal held that this merely affirmed the commercial style of English interpretation of contracts (notably the approach endorsed by Lord Diplock in '*The Antaios*', 1985).[49]

---

[42] e.g., *Henry Boot Construction Ltd* v. *Alstom Combined Cycles Ltd* [2005] EWCA Civ 814; [2005] 1 WLR 3850.

[43] *AMEC Civil Engineering Ltd* v. *Secretary of State for Transport* [2005] EWCA Civ 291; [2005] 1 WLR 2339 (in fact a point of interpretation of the arbitration agreement will normally give rise to a challenge under the jurisdiction head, within section 67, Arbitration Act 1996).

[44] [2007] EWHC 1187 (TCC), at [11] and 13], *per* Judge Coulson QC (as he then was).

[45] *ibid.*

[46] For literature on the principles of interpretation, **14.02**.

[47] This restrictive approach was noted, after a review of several authorities, in *Omnibridge Consulting Ltd* v. *Clearsprings (Management) Ltd* [2004] EWHC 2276 (Comm), at [52] (Siberry QC, deputy High Court judge).

[48] [1990] 1 WLR 153,161-2, CA, *per* Parker LJ; however, Lloyd LJ at 164-5 contemplated that arbitrators might be inclined to be more 'lenient' in their approach to contractual language.

[49] [1985] AC 191, HL; and see the present text below at **14.10** to **14.23**.

8.17 There is some judicial suggestion that (i) the date of formation (if extrinsic to the text) falls outside section 69; (ii) similarly, issues of rectification; and (iii) issues concerning the incorporation of side agreements. However, of these, only (i) seems clearly to involve an issue of fact, rather than law.[50]

8.18 Another case decides, persuasively, that a question of reasonableness, detached from the text of a written contract, but arising in connection with a written contract, is an issue of fact.[51]

8.19 An aggrieved party cannot bring an appeal from an award on the basis that the arbitral tribunal has committed an error of fact or that it has misidentified or misapplied a point of foreign law.[52] Furthermore, as the Court of Appeal decided in *C* v. *D* (2007),[53] if the seat of the arbitration is England and Wales, a party cannot evade this last limitation by seeking a declaration from a foreign court that the English award on a point of foreign law involves a misunderstanding or misapplication of that foreign law.

8.20 Findings of fact should not be dressed up as issues of law.[54] The arbitral tribunal's findings of fact cannot be attacked under section 69 by contending that there is no evidence at all to support them, or by similar intellectual devices.[55]

---

[50] The following case must be treated with caution as far as propositions (ii) and (ii) are concerned: *The Council of the City of Plymouth* v. *D R Jones (Yeovil) Ltd* [2005] EWHC 2356, *per* Coulson J at [20], suggesting (persuasively) that the question (extrinsic to the text of the written contract) of the contract's date of formation was a question of fact and not of law; less convincingly at [26] and [39] suggesting that the question whether the written contract should be open to rectification on the basis of shared error was an issue of fact (the more persuasive analysis is that such an issue is quintessentially one of establishing the integrity of the text and, therefore, a matter of law); suggesting further at [32] to [34] that the issue whether the written agreement includes other documents, not expressly included in the main text, is a question of fact; again this view seems doubtful.

[51] *London Underground Ltd* v. *Citylink Telecommunications Ltd* [2007] EWHC 1749 (TCC); [2007] 2 All ER (Comm) 694; [2007] BLR 391; 114 Con LR 1, at [250] ff, *per* Ramsey J.

[52] This is the result of the definition of 'question of law' in section 82(1), Arbitration Act 1996; affecting scope of section 69, Arbitration Act 1996 (appeal to court on a 'question of law arising out of an award made in the [arbitration] proceedings'; choice of substantive law covered by section 46(1), Arbitration Act 1996.

[53] *C* v. *D* [2007] EWCA Civ 1282; [2008] 1 Lloyd's Rep 239.

[54] e.g. *Surefire Systems Ltd* v. *Guardian ECL Ltd* [2005] EWHC 1860 (TCC); [2005] BLR 534, at [21], *per* Jackson J; see also Steyn LJ in *Geogas SA* v. *Trammo Gas Ltd ('The Baleares')* [1993] 1 Lloyd's Rep 215, cited in *London Underground Ltd* v. *Citylink Telecommunications Ltd* [2007] EWHC 1749 (TCC); [2007] 2 All ER (Comm) 694; [2007] BLR 391; 114 Con LR 1, at [61].

[55] *London Underground Ltd* v. *Citylink Telecommunications Ltd* [2007] EWHC 1749 (TCC); [2007] 2 All ER (Comm) 694; [2007] BLR 391; 114 Con LR 1, at [52] to [66], *per* Ramsey J for a detailed collection of relevant cases.

8.4 Exclusion of Appeal on Points of English Law

8.21 Parties can contract out of the curial appeal process on points of English law and thus, by agreement, exclude the possibility of one party pursuing the section 69 route to the High Court. But careful wording must be adopted. This seems to strike the right balance between general community interest and private autonomy. However, Schmitthoff, 30 years before the 1996 Act, suggested that there should be a reverse presumption in the English legislation: that section 69 should not apply unless the parties positively opt for it by agreement.[56]

8.22 Under the 1996 Act, where the possibility of appeal under section 69 must be positively excluded, in *Shell Egypt West Manzala GmbH* v. *Dana Gas Egypt Ltd* (2009) Gloster J held that the formula 'final, conclusive and binding', contained in the arbitration agreement, and clearly intended to bestow some form of finality on an award, did not exclude that appeal route on a point of law.[57] The words 'final, conclusive and binding' merely indicated that the award would be final and binding as a matter of *res judicata*, with the result that there should be no further litigation on the same factual matters between the same parties. This still leaves the door open to the award being subject to appeal to the High Court on a point of English law (if permission to appeal to the High Court can be obtained from a judge under section 69(2)(3), Arbitration Act 1996).

8.23 Successful express exclusion can be achieved by adopting certain institutional rules. For example, Article 26.8 of the LCIA Rules (2014) (London Court of International Arbitration) provides:

> '*Every award (including reasons for such award) shall be final and binding on the parties. The parties undertake to carry out any award immediately and without any delay (subject only to Article 27 [which concerns correction of awards by the arbitration tribunal on request by a party or on the initiative of the tribunal]; and the parties also waive irrevocably their right to any form of appeal, review or recourse to any state court or other legal authority, insofar as such waiver shall not be prohibited under any applicable law.*'

8.24 Similarly, Article 34.6 of the ICC (2012) rules (International Chamber of Commerce) provides:

> '*Every award shall be binding on the parties. By submitting the dispute to arbitration under these Rules, the parties undertake to carry out any award without delay and shall be deemed to have waived their rights to any form of recourse insofar as such waiver can validly be made.*'

8.25 However, a clear express clause in a dispute resolution agreement, stipulating that an aggrieved party can bring an appeal before the English High Court in respect of an award concerning an alleged error of substantive English law applied by the tribunal, will be given effect, even though institutional rules, incorporated into the same agreement, contain a conflicting rule which purports to oust such a

---

[56] CM Schmitthoff, 'Finality of Arbitral Awards and Judicial Review', in JDM Lew (ed), *Contemporary Problems in International Arbitration* (London, 1986), 230, 237.

[57] [2009] EWHC 2097 (Comm).

section 69 appeal. Walker J so decided in *Royal & Sun Alliance Insurance plc* v. *BAE Systems (Operations) Ltd* (2008), where the relevant express clause stated: '*Any party to the Dispute may appeal to the court on a question of law arising out of an award made in the arbitral proceedings.*'[58] In that case the applicable institutional rules were those of the LCIA (London Court of International Arbitration). As mentioned, the LCIA provision was held to be overridden by the parties' express clause conferring a right to a section 69 appeal.

8.26 Furthermore, issues of incorporation of terms can arise. The Court of Appeal in *Sukuman Ltd* v. *Commonwealth Secretariat* (2007)[59] held that an exclusion of appeal clause, accompanying an arbitration agreement, had been validly incorporated into the parties' overall agreement. The exclusion of appeal was effected by this clause[60]: '*The judgment of the tribunal shall be final and binding on the parties and shall not be subject to appeal. This provision shall constitute an 'exclusion agreement' within the meaning of the laws of any country requiring arbitration or as those provisions may be amended or replaced.*' This clause had the effect that the arbitration award could not be challenged under section 69 of the Arbitration Act 1996, because the parties' written agreement had excluded that possibility. The process of incorporation was by express reference. Exclusion of section 69 of the Arbitration Act 1996 could not be characterised as an 'onerous or unusual' term for the purpose of Common Law doctrine.[61] The decision contains a thorough review of other case law on this topic. It was also held that such exclusion was not contrary to Article 6 of the European Convention on Human Rights.[62]

8.5 Effect of the High Court Appeal Under Section 69

8.27 Section 69(7) of the Arbitration Act 1996 states that the High Court can uphold the award, or vary it, or set it aside, or remit the award to the (same) arbitral tribunal. In the case of a remittal, the tribunal must normally make a fresh award within three months.[63]

8.28 The Arbitration Act 1996 does not make clear whether the arbitral tribunal is prevented from continuing proceedings during the currency of a challenge

[58] [2008] EWHC 743 (Comm); [2008] 1 Lloyd's Rep 712; [2008] 1 CLC 711, at [22].

[59] [2007] EWCA Civ 243; [2007] 3 All ER 342; [2007] 2 Lloyd's Rep 87.

[60] *ibid,* at [36].

[61] *ibid,* at [44] to [52], and [61], deciding that the doctrine permitting the courts to lean against incorporation of 'onerous or unusual' clauses is inapplicable to such a clause: *Interfoto Picture Library Ltd* v. *Stiletto Visual Programmes Ltd* [1989] QB 433, CA; and see current text below at **13.14**, at paragraph (ii); see also Neil Andrews, *Contract Law* (2nd edn, Cambridge University Press, 2015), 15.02.

[62] [2007] EWCA Civ 243; [2007] 3 All ER 342; [2007] 2 Lloyd's Rep 87, at [58] to [60], *per* Waller LJ.

[63] Section 71(3), Arbitration Act 1996.

under section 69, for example, when the award is a partial award and there are other matters still before the arbitral tribunal. By contrast, when a challenge to an award is being made before the High Court on the issue of substantive jurisdiction under section 67, statute makes clear that the arbitral tribunal 'may' continue its proceedings and make a further award.[64]

8.29 The explanation for this silence is that the draftsman assumed that section 69 challenges would arise only in respect of final awards, so that the arbitral tribunal would thereafter have become inactive in accordance with the *functus officio* principle. This assumption is revealed when section 45 is compared. That provision concerns applications to the court for determinations of points of law at a preliminary stage of the proceedings. Section 45(4) explicitly addresses the impact on the arbitral proceedings of such a section 45 application: *Unless otherwise agreed by the parties, the arbitral tribunal may continue the arbitral proceedings and make an award while an application to the court under this section is pending.*

8.30 But there might be some instances, admittedly rare, when a section 69 challenge occurs in respect of a partial award, and proceedings are still on foot, because the arbitral tribunal has further decision-making to complete. It is submitted that section 45(4) should be applied by analogy to this context.

8.31 In *Sheffield United Football Club Ltd* v. *West Ham United Football Club plc* (2008),[65] Teare J held that an arbitration agreement which expressly excludes '*recourse, review or appeal before a court of law*' does not by implication *create a right of appeal to an upper level arbitration tribunal which has a review or appellate* function. The High Court has power to issue an anti-suit injunction to restrain resort to this unauthorised further stage of arbitration, provided there is 'urgency', and it is not practicable to leave the question of breach to the arbitral tribunal itself. The European Court of Justice's prohibition on anti-suit relief in the *West Tankers* case (2009) (*Allianz SpA* v. *West Tankers Inc C-185-07)*[66] is confined to injunctions concerning intra-Europe court proceedings. And so there is no prohibition upon anti-suit relief aimed at halting or precluding unauthorised arbitration proceedings.

8.6 International Controversy Concerning Section 69 Challenges

8.32 By contrast with English law, in most legal systems, and soft-law provisions, judicial review of arbitral awards is not possible by reference to alleged errors of substantive law.[67] However, the 2006 report on the Arbitration Act 1996 states that a majority of respondents considered that appeals from arbitral tribunals to the

[64] Section 67(2), *ibid.*

[65] [2008] EWHC 2855 (Comm); [2009] 1 Lloyd's Rep 167.

[66] *Allianz SpA etc.* v. *West Tankers* (C-185/07) [2009] 1 AC 1138.

[67] *Redfern and Hunter on International Arbitration* (6th edn, Oxford University Press, 2015), 10.64 ff.

High Court on points of English law should be retained.[68] The 2006 report also rejected the proposition that the restrictive criteria for permission to appeal, specified at section 69 of the Arbitration Act 1996, might be 'starving English Contract Law of nourishment' and 'hindering its development.'[69]

8.33 At the Tokyo arbitration symposium (19 June 2012), it was suggested, however, that an annual average of 12 out of 50 grants of permission is 'high' (for these figures, see this note).[70] High Court review under section 69 is regarded by some foreign lawyers as a quite aberrant feature of English arbitration It is a major contrast with the Model Law system under which appeal to a national court is unavailable from an arbitral award on a point of substantive law (of course the Model Law is not applicable in England).[71]

8.7 Concluding Remarks

8.34 If a reform body were asked to reconsider section 69, what might be taken to be the leading considerations in this field? Six aspects dominate:

(i) arbitral awards should be accorded finality (but, of course, this must not become a slogan precluding consideration of other factors);
(ii) market forces dictate that the English law of arbitrate should be arranged so that it does not alienate potential international commercial custom; however, the 2006 report on the Arbitration Act 1996 states that a majority of respondents considered that appeals from arbitral tribunals to the High Court on points of English law should be retained;[72]
(iii) arbitration is a consensual mechanism; accordingly, due weight should be given to freedom of contract; this means that prospective parties to arbitration should remain free to choose non-English law as the applicable law,[73] or to exclude the section 69 judicial appeal on a point of English law,[74] or positively to create a right of reference under section 69[75];

---

[68] 'Report (2006) on the Arbitration Act 1996', at [66] to [69]: www.idrc.co.uk/aa96survey/Report_on_Arbitration_Act_1996.pdf.

[69] 'Report (2006) on the Arbitration Act 1996', *ibid,* at [70] to [75].

[70] Figures provided in the report by VV Veeder and A Sander (2009), Schedule A, p 8; report available at: http://www.lmaa.org.uk/uploads/documents/First%20Interim%20Report%20Mance%2024%2005%202009.pdf.

[71] Article 34(2), UNCITRAL Model Law on International Commercial Arbitration 1985 (as amended in 2006).

[72] 'Report (2006) on the Arbitration Act 1996', at [66] to [69]: www.idrc.co.uk/aa96survey/Report_on_Arbitration_Act_1996.pdf.

[73] Section 82(1), Arbitration Act 1996; affecting scope of section 69, Arbitration Act 1996; choice of substantive law covered by section 46(1), Arbitration Act 1996.

[74] *Shell Egypt West Manzala GmbH* v. *Dana Gas Egypt Ltd* [2009] EWHC 2097 (Comm).

[75] *Royal & Sun Alliance Insurance plc* v. *BAE Systems (Operations) Ltd* [2008] EWHC 743 (Comm); [2008] 1 Lloyd's Rep 712, *per* Walker J: '*parties to an arbitration may take the view that, as regards questions of law, finality should come from the court rather than from the arbitral tribunal.*'

(iv) the absence of a true jurisdictional basis, or a failure of procedural fairness must be accorded greater weight than an error of law; this is reflected in the fact that the rights of challenge to an award under sections 67 and 68 cannot be excluded by agreement;

(v) an error of law might be regarded as more deserving of correction than an error of fact;

(vi) appeals to the courts from commercial arbitration has proved a fertile source of enrichment of English contract law; many seminal cases have arisen into the daylight from the subterranean tunnels of the arbitral process.[76]

8.35 It is submitted that section 69 strikes a sound balance. However, as explained below, the forum for judicial appeal should be the Court of Appeal, specially constituted to draw upon commercial expertise.

8.36 Under section 69, freedom of contract is respected in two respects: (i) parties can exclude this mechanism by clear language; (ii) conversely, parties can positively stipulate that appeal to the High Court should be a right if one party is tribunal's decision on a point of English law. In the absence of (ii), the High Court is not bound to accede to an application for appeal on a point of English law. Instead the court must take into account the chances of the appeal succeeding and the importance of the relevant point.[77] Statistics show that only roughly a quarter of such applications are in fact successful.[78]

8.37 However, the institutional mechanisms for appeal to the English courts might be refined. The reality is that in a major commercial arbitration the sole arbitrator or chairman of the arbitral tribunal will be an experienced commercial lawyer, often a QC (a senior barrister), or a former English judge of distinction. Even if not a former judge, the individual might often be of sufficient calibre to have decided not to apply to become a High Court judge, even though he or she is manifestly highly likely to have gained such promotion if an application had been made (in fact many such senior barristers sit as part-time High Court judges for a number of weeks each year). It is questionable, therefore, whether on points of real legal difficulty sufficient to pass the test prescribed by the 'filter' of section 69 an appeal to a Commercial Court judge, sitting alone, will be perceived as conferring additional weight to the award, or capable of convincingly repudiating it on legal grounds. All too often, where the point of law is fundamental and highly contentious, the Commercial Court's decision will prove to be merely a procedural stepping-stone, the Commercial Court judge readily acknowledging the need for a re-think by a higher appellate court and thus giving permission for a second appeal.

---

[76] Notable examples include: *Schuler (L) AG* v. *Wickman Machine Tool Sales Ltd* [1974] AC 235, HL (contractual terms; conditions); *Davis Contractors Ltd* v. *Fareham UDC* [1956] AC 696, HL (frustration); *Transfield Shipping Inc* v. *Mercator, 'The Achilleas'* [2008] UKHL 48; [2009] 1 AC 61 (remoteness of damages in contract law).

[77] Section 69(3)(c), Arbitration Act: '*that, on the basis of the findings of fact in the award—(i) the decision of the tribunal on the question is obviously wrong, or (ii) the question is one of general public importance and the decision of the tribunal is at least open to serious doubt...*'

[78] Figures provided in the report by VV Veeder and A Sander (2009), Schedule A, p 8; report available at: http://www.lmaa.org.uk/uploads/documents/First%20Interim%20Report%20Mance%20 24%2005%202009.pdf.

8.38 Might it not be better to adopt a more pragmatic approach, and to take a bold leap, eliminating the first instance stepping-stone? For the reality is that the arbitral tribunal has already provided the equivalent of first instance High Court 'intellectual input'.

8.39 The author's suggestion is that the primary route for an appeal under section 69 should be to the Court of Appeal, once the individual Commercial Court judge has given permission under that provision for such an appeal. Given the paucity of appeals under section 69 (always less than 20 a year within the Commercial Court filter system), it would not over-burden the Court of Appeal for the matter to be automatically assigned to the Master of the Rolls. He (or she) should have power to co-opt current members of the Commercial Court (either two such members, or four, in the case of obviously momentous points of law) to hear the appeal as adjunct Lords Justices of Appeal. Only in quite exceptional circumstances—to be prescribed by rules—would the Supreme Court of the United Kingdom consider it appropriate to grant permission for a second and final appeal.

8.40 In this way the law-making potential of section 69 might be refined. A Court of Appeal decision will be binding not only on all lower courts but on the Court of Appeal itself. The fact that the Court of Appeal would be the relevant court for substantive matters under section 69 of the Arbitration Act 1996 would tend to inhibit still further the 'gateway' decision-maker. It is unlikely that more than a trickle of cases would find their way to the Court of Appeal, and only an occasional case would proceed higher to the Supreme Court. Anxiety concerning judicial involvement would be met by retaining the current rule that appeals under section 69 can be excluded by the parties, using clear language or by adopting institutional rules containing such an exclusion.

Chapter 9
Refusal to Give Effect to Foreign Awards

Abstract Cross-border enforcement of commercial awards under the New York Convention (1958) remains a major force in the expansion of arbitration. The Convention prescribes a narrow set of situations in which the enforcing court can legitimately refuse recognition and enforcement. Within this topic there are two matters of special interest: first, there is the issue whether a national court's annulment of the award at the seat of the arbitration will preclude such cross-border enforcement or whether the enforcing court can still give effect to the award, even if has been annulled locally at the seat; secondly, there is the issue whether the enforcing court can reliably obtain evidence of the foreign law applicable to the arbitration agreement. In the *Dallah* case (section 9.3 of this chapter) the English courts became embroiled in such a difficult issue.

9.1 The Scheme of the New York Convention (1958)[1]

9.01 The arbitral tribunal cannot administer coercive or physical assistance in securing enforcement of its awards. Instead the successful party must invoke the enforcement powers of the relevant judicial system, whether this be within the jurisdiction where the arbitration had its seat or within a foreign jurisdiction.

[1] D Di Pietro and M Platte, *Enforcement of International Arbitration Awards: The New York Convention of 1958* (London, 2001); *ICCA's Guide to the Interpretation of the 1958 New York Convention (1958)* (2011) (International Council for Commercial Arbitration) (available online); D Joseph, *Jurisdiction and Arbitration Agreements and their Enforcement* (3rd edn, London, 2015), 16.57 ff; H Kronke, et al., *Recognition and Enforcement of Foreign Arbitral Awards: A Global Commentary on the New York Convention* (Kluwer, Deventer, 2010); *Redfern and Hunter on International Arbitration* (6th edn, Oxford University Press, 2015), 11.40 ff; AJ van den Berg, *50 Years of the New York Convention* (Kluwer, 2009). Other selected comment: E Gaillard, 'Enforcement of Awards Set Aside in the Country of Origin' (1999) 14 ICSID Rev 16; J Paulsson, '"May" or "Must" Under the New York Convention: An Exercise in Syntax and Linguistics' (1998) 14 Arb Int 227; A Pullé, 'Securing Natural Justice in Arbitration Proceedings' (2012) 20 Asia Pacific L Rev 63; L Radicati di Brozolo, 'The Control System of Arbitral Awards' (2011) ICCA Congress Series 74; H Smit, 'Annulment and Enforcement of International Arbitral Awards: A Practical Perspective', in LW Newman and RD Hill (eds), *The Leading Arbitrators' Guide to International Arbitration* (3rd edn, New York, 2014), chapter 38; S Wilske, L Shore and J-M Ahrens, 'The "Group of Companies Doctrine" – Where Is It Heading?' (2006) 17 Am Rev Int Arb 73.

N. Andrews, *Arbitration and Contract Law*, Ius Gentium: Comparative Perspectives on Law and Justice 54, DOI 10.1007/978-3-319-27144-6_9

9.02 Enforcement includes the possibility that the English High Court of interest might award interest on a foreign arbitral award. In *Yukos Capital Sarl* v. *OJSC Rosneft Oil Co* (2014)[2] Simon J held that the English courts can award interest (under section 35A, Senior Courts Act 1981) on a foreign arbitral award and that a foreign award could be recognised in this manner even though it had been annulled by the courts of the seat, provided the foreign judicial annulment is itself invalid under English conflict of laws principles (see **9.27**).

9.03 National systems provide for enforcement of domestic arbitration awards, but these details are too large and fragmentary[3] to justify separate discussion here. And so attention is confined here to judicial recognition and enforcement of foreign arbitral awards under the New York Convention on the Recognition and Enforcement of Foreign Arbitral Awards (1958).

9.04 Foreign awards are enforceable in over 140 different countries in accordance with the New York Convention (1958). This instrument is the greatest success of modern international commercial arbitration: '*It has made the greatest single contribution to the internationalisation of international commercial arbitration.*'[4]

9.05 *Main Mechanism for Enforcement of Foreign Awards.* The primary mechanism for enforcement of a NYC (1958) award is under section 101(2) of the 1996 Act, namely obtaining the court's leave that the award 'be enforced in the same manner as a judgment or order of the court'.

9.06 *Other Mechanisms.* But section 104 of the Act recognises two alternative routes, namely enforcement of the award 'at Common Law' or under section 66 of the 1996 Act.

> *Action on the Award at Common Law.*[5] This is involves recognition and enforcement of the award-debtor's breach of agreement in not honouring the award. A successful action on the award can result, dependent on the claimant's pleading, in a money award (debt, or damages, plus interest), or specific performance, or an injunction, or a declaration, plus interest.
>
> *Section 66.* This grants the court power to give leave for the award to be 'enforced in the same manner as a judgment or order of the court' (section 66(1)) and for judgment to be 'entered in terms of the award'. Section 66(4) makes clear that Part III of the Act, concerning NYC (1958) awards subsists separately. However, as mentioned, there is some circularity because section 104 (within Part III) preserves the alternative routes of Common Law actions on the award and applications under section 66.

9.07 *Grounds for Non-Recognition or Non-Enforcement.* The grounds (which are permissive—'may'—so that the enforcement court is not obliged[6] to deny

---

[2] [2014] EWHC 2188 (Comm); [2014] 2 Lloyd's Rep 435; 155 Con LR 221.

[3] For analysis, in English, of the Brazilian law concerning enforcement of domestic or internal arbitration awards, G Marques de Campos and M Desteffeni (2012) 208 *Revista de Processo* 343.

[4] *Redfern and Hunter on International Arbitration* (6th edn, Oxford University Press, 2015), 11.62.

[5] *Mustill & Boyd, Commercial Arbitration* (2nd edn, London, 1989), 417–418.

[6] Hence the decisions (generally on this topic, **9.27**) which have allowed recognition/enforcement in foreign state X even though the relevant award has been annulled in state Y where the award was made under the domestic arbitral law: *Redfern and Hunter, ibid,* 11.94 ff. The famous triad of cases comprises: *Hilmarton* (1994)—France state X, Switzerland state Y, English excerpts in (1995) XX Ybk Comm Arb 663); *Chromalloy* (1996) – USA state X, Egypt state Y, 939 F Supp 907 (DDC 1996); and the *Putrabali* case, France state X, England state Y, (2007) Revue de l'Arbitrage.

recognition or refuse enforcement) for the refusal of recognition and enforcement of an arbitration award under Article V of the New York Convention (1958) are as follows[7] (Article V is enacted as section 103 of the Arbitration Act 1996):

(1) Recognition and enforcement of the award may be refused, at the request of the party against whom it is invoked, only if that party furnishes to the competent authority where the recognition and enforcement is sought, proof that:

(a) The parties to the arbitration agreement referred to in article II were, under the law applicable to them, under some incapacity, or the said agreement is not valid under the law to which the parties have subjected it or, failing any indication thereon, under the law of the country where the award was made;
(b) The party against whom the award is invoked was not given proper notice of the appointment of the arbitrator or of the arbitration proceedings or was otherwise[8] unable to present its case;
(c) The award deals with a difference not contemplated by or not falling within the terms of the submission to arbitration, or it contains decisions on matters beyond the scope of the submission to arbitration, provided that, if the decisions on matters submitted to arbitration can be separated from those not so submitted, that part of the award which contains decisions on matters submitted to arbitration may be recognised and enforced;
(d) The composition of the arbitral authority or the arbitral procedure was not in accordance with the agreement of the parties or, failing such agreement, was not in accordance with the law of the country where the arbitration took place; or
(e) The award has not yet become binding on the parties, or has been set aside or suspended by a competent authority of the country in which, or under the law of which, that award was made.

(2) Recognition or enforcement of an arbitral award may also be refused if the competent authority of the country in which enforcement is sought finds that: (a) *The subject-matter of the difference is not capable of settlement by arbitration under the law of that country[9]; or (b) The recognition or enforcement of the award would be contrary to the public policy of that country.*[10]

[7] Most of these grounds were judicially considered in *Honeywell International Middle East Ltd* v. *Meydan Group LLC* [2014] EWHC 1344 (TCC); [2014] 2 Lloyd's Rep 133; [2014] BLR 401, Ramsey J (permission for appeal has been granted on certain aspects of this case: *Honeywell International Middle East Ltd* v. *Meydan Group LLC* [2014] EWCA Civ 1800).

[8] e.g., *Kanoria* v. *Guinness* [2006] EWCA Civ; [2006] Arb LR 513 (Indian arbitration award rendering individual, Mr G, personally liable for debt; but during the arbitration proceedings G had not been informed of the basis for this claim; English enforcement court, acting under section 103(2)(c), Arbitration Act 1996 (adopting the New York Convention (1958)), entitled to refuse recognition and enforcement; authorities also cited were *Minnmetals Germany* v. *Ferco Steel* [1999] 1 All ER (Comm) 315, 326; (1999) XXIV Ybk Comm Arb 739, Colman J; and *Irvani* v. *Irvani* [2000] 1 Lloyd's Rep 412, 426, CA, *per* Buxton LJ). A Pullé, 'Securing Natural Justice in Arbitration Proceedings' (2012) 20 Asia Pacific L Rev 63.

[9] *Redfern and Hunter on International Arbitration* (6th edn, Oxford University Press, 2015), 11.101 ff.

[10] *Westacre Investments Inc* v. *Jugoimport-SPDR Holding Co Ltd* [1999] 2 Lloyd's Rep 65, CA; Rogers and Kaley, 'The Impact of Public Policy in International Commercial Arbitration' (1999) 65 J Chartered Inst of Arbitrators 4; *Soleimany* v. *Soleimany* [1999] QB 785, CA; *Redfern and Hunter on International Arbitration* (6th edn, Oxford University Press, 2015), 11.105 ff.

9.08 The English courts respect the narrowness of the exceptions to enforcement prescribed by the NYC (1958) and recognise the commercial and transnational interest in upholding and enforcing arbitral awards.[11]

9.09 Lord Steyn in *dicta* in the *Lesotho* case (2005) noted a tendency to accept that the New York Convention does not enable the enforcing court to re-consider the merits of the arbitral tribunal's factual and legal assessment of the substance of the dispute[12]:

> *'It is well established that Article V(1)(c) must be construed narrowly and should never lead to a re-examination of the merits of the award: Parsons & Whittemore Overseas Co Inc* v. *Sociéte Générale de l'Industrie du Papier (RAKTA) (1974) 508 F 2d 969 (2nd Circuit); Albert van den Berg, The New York Arbitration Convention of 1958 (1981), pp 311–318; Di Pietro and Platte, Enforcement of International Arbitration Awards: The New York Convention of 1958 (London, 2001), pp 158–162.'*

Similar *dicta* were made by Lord Collins in the *Dallah* case (2010).[13]

9.10 However, in a separate discussion, contributed to a collection of essays, Albert Jan van den Berg[14] contended that a conspicuously erroneous failure to apply the contract might justify refusal to enforce on the basis that:

(i) Article V(1)(c) of the New York Convention (1958) applies: '*The award deals with a difference not contemplated by or not falling within the terms of the submission to arbitration, or it contains decisions on matters beyond the scope of the submission to arbitration*'; or

(ii) Article V(1)(d) applies: *'The composition of the arbitral authority* ***or the arbitral procedure was not in accordance with the agreement of the parties*** *or, failing such agreement, was not in accordance with the law of the country where the arbitration took place.'* In this respect, van den Berg's contention is that such an award would entail violation of the arbitral tribunal's duty to reach a decision which is in accordance with the applicable law governing the main transaction; and that applicable law requires the arbitral tribunal to give effect to the parties' main contract.

9.11 *Public Policy.*[15] For reasons of space, this discussion will mostly (but see **9.12** below on Advocate General Wathelet's Opinion in the *Gazprom* case) concentrate on the position in England. The experience of the 1958 Convention within other systems is collected in specialist works.[16] Section 103(3) of the Arbitration

---

[11] e.g., Colman J's reference in *Westacre Investments Inc* v. *Jugoimport SDPR Holding Co Ltd* [1999] QB 740, 773 to 'the public policy of sustaining international arbitration awards'.

[12] *Lesotho Highlands Development Authority* v. *Impreglio SpA* [2005] UKHL 43; [2006] 1 AC 22, at [30].

[13] [2010] UKSC 46; [2011] 1 AC 763, at [102].

[14] AJ van den Berg, 'Failure by Arbitrators to Apply Contract Terms from the Perspective of the New York Convention', in G Aksen, et al. (eds), *Global Reflections on International Law, Commerce and Dispute Resolution: Liber Amicorum in Honour of Robert Briner* (ICC Publications, Paris, 2005), 63–71.

[15] A Tweedale, 'Enforcing Arbitration Awards Contrary to Public Policy in England' (2000) 17 International Construction Law Review 159.

[16] e.g. *Redfern and Hunter on International Arbitration* (6th edn, Oxford University Press, 2015), 11.420 ff; AJ van den Berg, *The New York Arbitration Convention of 1958* (1981); D Di Pietro and

Act 1996 (incorporating Article V of the NYC (1958), states: 'Recognition or enforcement of the award may also be refused if the award is in respect of a matter which is not capable of settlement by arbitration, or if it would be contrary to public policy to recognise or enforce the award.' The public policy is that applicable in England.[17] But this must include matters of EU law.[18] For this purpose, public policy[19] includes illegality.[20] English courts have adopted a narrow approach to matters of non-legislative public policy.[21] For centuries judicial recognition of public policy has been regarded as a potential source of controversy, an 'unruly horse'.[22] The courts have been restrained, acknowledging the triple dangers of subjectivity, of usurping legislative decision-making, and of fettering freedom of contract in the name of debatable perceptions of general interest. And so Sir John Donaldson MR said in *Deutsche Schachtbau- und Tiefbohrgesellschaft mbH* v. *Ras Al-Khaimah National Oil Co* (1990)[23]:

> '*Considerations of public policy can never be exhaustively defined, but they should be approached with extreme caution. As Burrough J remarked in Richardson* v. *Mellish (1824) 2 Bing 229, 252, "It is never argued at all, but when other points fail."*'

Donaldson MR continued:

> '*It has to be shown that there is some element of illegality or that the enforcement of the award would be clearly injurious to the public good or, possibly, that enforcement would be wholly offensive to the ordinary reasonable and fully informed member of the public on whose behalf the powers of the state are exercised.*'

M Platte, *Enforcement of International Arbitration Awards*: *The New York Convention of 1958* (London, 2001).

[17] *Westacre Investments Inc* v. *Jugoimport SDPR Holding Co Ltd* [1999] QB 740, 751, *per* Colman J, noting that Article V.2(b) of the New York Convention states 'the recognition or enforcement of the award would be contrary to the public policy *of that country*.' (Emphasis added.)'

[18] *Eco Swiss China Time Ltd* v. *Benetton International NV* C-126/97 [1999] ECR I-3055 (ECJ holding that national rules for review of domestic arbitral awards must allow investigation of the allegation that the award is inconsistent with EU competition law).

[19] For wider perspectives, A Chong, 'Transnational Public Policy in Civil and Commercial Matters' (2012) 128 LQR 88–113.

[20] *Omnium de Traitement et de Valorisation SA* v. *Hilmarton Ltd* [1999] 2 All ER (Comm) 146; [1999] 2 Lloyd's Rep 222, *per* Timothy Walker J, citing the *Westacre* case, [1999] 1 All ER (Comm) 865 at 876, *per* Waller LJ; and Colman J [1998] 4 All ER 570 at 601B–C.

[21] *Honeywell International Middle East Ltd* v. *Meydan Group LLC* [2014] EWHC 1344 (TCC); [2014] 2 Lloyd's Rep 133; [2014] BLR 401, at [180] to [182], citing Parke B in *Egerton* v. *Brownlow* (1853) 4 HLC 1 at 123: '*[it] is the province of the statesman, and not the lawyer, to discuss, and of the legislature to determine, what is best for the public good, and to provide for it by proper enactments*'; also citing *Fender* v. *St John-Mildmay* [1938] AC 1, 12, HL, *per* Lord Atkin: '*[public policy] should only be invoked in clear cases in which the harm to the public is substantial, incontestable, and does not depend upon the idiosyncratic inferences of a few judicial minds.*'

[22] Lord Denning, *Enderby Town FC Ltd* v. *Football Association* [1971] Ch 591, 606–7, CA, was not slow to proclaim his equestrian skills, for this purpose: '*With a good man in the saddle, the unruly horse can be kept in control. It can jump over obstacles. It can leap the fences put up by fictions and come down on the side of justice.*'

[23] [1990] 1 AC 295, 316, CA (reversed by HL but on a different point).

It should also be noted that the 'separability' principle (**2.47**) enables an arbitral tribunal to inquire whether the main transaction is illegal. It follows, as the Court of Appeal in the *Harbour Assurance* case (1993) recognised,[24] that if illegality (and/or its impact) is disputed, that issue can form the subject matter (or one of the issues) referred to the tribunal by the parties.

9.12 Although the European Court of Justice in the *Gazprom* case (2015)[25] did not endorse the main contention made in Advocate General Wathelet's Opinion (**4.24**), the Court did not challenge his discussion of public policy as a ground for non-recognition under Article V(2)(b) of the NYC (1958). The main points of his analysis are as follows[26]:

(a) it is established that this ground of non-recognition should receive a narrow application; and this tendency in transnational jurisprudence is manifested by American,[27] French,[28] German,[29] British,[30] and other Member State cases,[31] as well as by UNCITRAL[32];
(b) the European Court of Justice has indicated[33] that Member State courts, when applying this provision, must not derogate from the fundamental consumer control of EU law;
(c) beyond (b), Advocate General Wathelet suggests a very cautious approach, confining relevant norms to those which are mandatory and which form the essential bed-rock of an EU community which respects democracy and the rule of law[34];
(d) it follows from the suggestion at (c) that it cannot be enough that the relevant arbitral award contains a prohibition on litigating before a Member State court; in other words, an arbitral award which purports to mirror the effect of a judicial

[24] *Harbour Assurance Co (UK) Ltd* v. *Kansa General International Insurance Co Ltd* [1993] QB 701, CA, *per* Ralph Gibson LJ, at 712c-f, Leggatt LJ, at 719 and Hoffmann LJ, at 723f-724e; explained by Colman J in *Westacre Investments Inc* v. *Jugoimport SDPR Holding Co Ltd* [1999] QB 740, 756–757.

[25] *Gazprom OAO* case (Grand Chamber, ECJ, 13 May 2015) (Case C-536/13).

[26] Opinion of Advocate General Wathelet (delivered 4 December 2014), at [130] to [152], at [167] to [188].

[27] *ibid*, at [167], note 95.

[28] *ibid*, at [168], note 96.

[29] *ibid*, at [169], note 97.

[30] *ibid*, at [170], note 98, citing *Deutsche Schachtbau- und Tiefbohrgesellschaft mbH* v. *Ras Al-Khaimah National Oil Co* [1990] 1 AC 295, 316, CA (reversed by HL, but on a different point).

[31] *ibid*, at [167], note 95.

[32] *ibid*, at [167] note 94, citing *UNCITRAL Guide on the Convention on the Ecognition and Enforcement of Foreign Awards* (New York, 1958), guide on Article V(2)(b), paragraph 4, available on the UNICTRAL website.

[33] *ibid*, at [181], citing the *Exo Swiss* case (EU C 1999/269), at [36], and the *Mostaza Claro* case (EU C2006/675), at [37].

[34] *ibid*, at [184] and [185].

anti-suit injunction is not within the narrow compass of public policy contemplated by Article V(2)(b) of the NYC (1958)[35];

(e) in the present case it is possible[36] that the appropriate ground of non-recognition would have been Article V(2)(a), namely the (suggested) non-arbitrability of the corporate investigation before the Lithuanian courts (on that issue see further **3.27**).

9.13 The English courts' approach to the 'public policy' exception to enforcement of NYC (1958) awards is summarised in the ensuing paragraphs.

9.14 *Narrow Scope of Public Policy*. English courts have adopted a narrow approach to matters of non-legislative public policy.[37] Sir John Donaldson MR said in *Deutsche Schachtbau- und Tiefbohrgesellschaft mbH* v. *Ras Al-Khaimah National Oil Co* (1990)[38]: '*Considerations of public policy can never be exhaustively defined, but they should be approached with extreme caution…*' Donaldson MR continued:

> '*It has to be shown that there is some element of illegality or that the enforcement of the award would be clearly injurious to the public good or, possibly, that enforcement would be wholly offensive to the ordinary reasonable and fully informed member of the public on whose behalf the powers of the state are exercised.*'

9.15 *High Level of Proof.* If a foreign arbitral award's enforcement is resisted on the ground of public policy, English courts require a very high level of proof that there has been a violation of public policy. In particular, allegations that the relevant foreign arbitral award was procured by perjury will be subject to strict controls at the enforcement stage in England.[39] Similarly, allegations of bribery will be considered with caution. In the *Honeywell* case (2014)[40] Ramsey J sitting in London examined various objections concerning a Dubai award (raised under the New York Convention (1958) but technically an application to set aside an order granting a party leave to enforce a foreign award).[41] The main objection was that the relevant

---

[35] *ibid*, at [185] to [188].

[36] *ibid*, at [165].

[37] *Honeywell International Middle East Ltd* v. *Meydan Group LLC* [2014] EWHC 1344 (TCC); [2014] 2 Lloyd's Rep 133; [2014] BLR 401, at [180] to [182].

[38] [1990] 1 AC 295, 316, CA (the case concerned enforcement in England of a Swiss award; the Court of Appeal's decision was reversed by the House of Lords, but not on the point concerning the definition of public policy in this context).

[39] *Westacre Investments Inc* v. *Jugoimport SDPR Holding Co Ltd* [2000] QB 288, 309, CA, *per* Waller LJ: '*where perjury is…alleged…the evidence must be so strong that it would reasonably be expected to be decisive at a hearing, and if unanswered must have that result*'); see also [1999] QB 740, 784, *per* Colman J; *Honeywell International Middle East Ltd* v. *Meydan Group LLC* [2014] EWHC 1344 (TCC); [2014] 2 Lloyd's Rep 133; [2014] BLR 401, at [166] to [172], *per* Ramsey J; as for failure to object to allegedly perjured evidence during the conduct of English arbitration proceedings, *Thyssen Canada Ltd* v. *Mariana Maritime SA* [2005] EWHC 219 (Comm); [2005] 1 Lloyd's Rep 640, [39], [43], [60] to [66], *per* Cooke J.

[40] *Honeywell International Middle East Ltd* v. *Meydan Group LLC* [2014] EWHC 1344 (TCC); [2014] 2 Lloyd's Rep 133; [2014] BLR 401.

[41] The position regarding domestic awards in England is clear: *David Taylor & Son* v. *Barnett Trading Co* [1953] 1 WLR 562, 572, CA, *per* Hodson LJ (the other judges agreed): '*it is clear that, once the illegality is made plain, the award can, and should be, set aside.*'

underlying transaction had been infected with bribery (but there were many other suggested defences to enforcement). The application to set aside failed for these reasons. First, the procedural test for determining whether the New York Convention (1958)'s grounds for non-recognition were met is the usual test on summary judgments, namely whether there was a real prospect of successfully establishing the ground alleged; in applying that test, the court had to assess the material before it critically, particularly where a party had not raised a matter which could have been raised before the tribunal.[42] Secondly, even if the allegation of bribery has a prospect of success, the court must be cautious; although bribery was clearly contrary to English public policy (see the Bribery Act 2010), contracts procured by bribes (as distinct from contracts to pay or arrange a bribe) are not unenforceable; instead the innocent party is simply given the opportunity to avoid the contract, at its election, provided counter-restitution can be made.[43]

9.16 *Manifestly Illicit Activity.* Arbitral awards will not be enforced if they plainly (notably 'on the face' of the arbitral award) concern illicit activities and are contrary to English public policy. In a case not concerned with the New York Convention (1958) (but nevertheless indicating the likely response of the English courts to a New York Convention (1958) award) the Court of Appeal in *Soleimany* v. *Soleimany* (1999) held that where it was apparent from the face of the award that the arbitral tribunal was dealing with an illicit enterprise in which both parties were principals, an award requiring payment by one of these malefactors to the other should not be enforced.[44]

In this case the parties to the arbitration were a father (defendant) and son (plaintiff) who had engaged in a scam to smuggle carpets out of Iran, in breach of Iranian law. The dispute came before the Beth Din, a London domestic and religious arbitral tribunal which hears civil disputes between orthodox Jews. Under Jewish law, the law chosen to govern the transaction, the arbitral tribunal held that a valid payment obligation arose (£576,574), despite the plain unlawfulness of the underlying contracts.[45] However, the (English) Court of Appeal held that, although the arbitration agreement was not void, this award, because contrary to English public policy, should not be enforced. Waller LJ (giving the court's judgment) said[46]: '*we are dealing with a case where it is apparent from the face of the award that …the arbitrator was dealing with what he termed an illicit enterprise under which it was the joint intention that carpets would be smuggled out of Iran illegally.*' He concluded[47]: '*It is clear that it is contrary to public policy for an English award (i.e. an award*

---

[42] [2014] EWHC 1344 (TCC); [2014] 2 Lloyd's Rep 133, at [65] to [69], [71], [88], [89], [94], [211].

[43] *ibid,* at [173] to [185], [211].

[44] [1999] QB 785, CA.

[45] A Tweedale, 'Enforcing Arbitration Awards Contrary to Public Policy in England' (2000) 17 International Construction Law Review 159, 164, noting A Cohen, *An Introduction to Jewish Civil Law* (Feldheim Publishers, New York, 1991), 186–7.

[46] [1999] QB 785, 794, CA.

[47] *ibid,* at 799.

following an arbitration conducted in accordance with English law) to be enforced if it is based on an English contract which was illegal when made.'

9.17 *Court's Response when Illegality Emerges during Proceedings.* The court is entitled, indeed required, to refuse to give contractual effect to an illegal transaction even if its illegal nature only emerges incidentally during the conduct of the case: see *Birkett* v. *Acorn Business Machines Ltd* (1999)[48]; and Scrutton LJ in *Re Mahmoud and Ispahani* (1921)[49]: see also *Skilton* v. *Sullivan* (1994).[50]

9.18 *Governing Law is English, or Place of Performance is England.* If the transaction which underpins the foreign arbitral award is governed by English law, or its place of performance is in England, the English courts will not enforce the foreign arbitral award if this would infringe English public policy.[51]

9.19 *Award Involves no Violation of English Public Policy.* If a foreign arbitral award arises from a contract infringing the public policy of a foreign state but not the public policy of England, the arbitral award will be enforced.[52]

9.20 *Award Stating that has been no Violation of Foreign Governing Law.* English courts will normally (see next but one paragraph for exceptions) enforce under the New York Convention (1958) a foreign arbitral award which includes a finding that there has been no breach of public policy under the relevant governing law of the transaction (even if performance of the relevant contract involved illegality or breach of public policy in a third jurisdiction).

9.21 Walker J in *Omnium de Traitement et de Valorisation SA ('OTV')* v. *Hilmarton Ltd* (1999) upheld a Swiss award concerning a contract governed by Swiss law in which the tribunal had concluded that there had been no infringement of Swiss public policy.[53] This was so even though there had been an infringement of Algerian law at the place of performance. The arbitration concerned a claim by Hilmarton for unpaid fees in respect of a consultancy agreement. Hilmarton had successfully procured a public works contract for a drainage project in Algiers. The Swiss tribunal held that the contract had not involved bribery or any similarly corrupt practices for the purpose of the governing law, Swiss law, even though Algerian procurement law had been breached (that is, the law of the place of performance within the third jurisdiction). In the English High Court, the enforcing jurisdiction, Timothy Walker J's decision to enforce the Swiss award involved these four steps[54]: (1) the issue whether there had been a violation of public policy under the governing

---

[48] [1999] 2 All ER 429, 433, *per* Colman J, sitting with Sedley LJ; applied in *Pickering* v. *Deacon* [2003] EWCA Civ 554; *The Times*, 19 April 2003.

[49] [1921] 2 KB 716, 729, CA.

[50] *The Times*, 25 March 1994 (end of Beldam LJ's judgment).

[51] Supported by A Tweedale, 'Enforcing Arbitration Awards Contrary to Public Policy in England' (2000) 17 International Construction Law Review 159, 173 at proposition (2).

[52] *Westacre Investments Inc* v. *Jugoimport SDPR Holding Co Ltd* [2000] QB 288, 304, CA, *per* Waller LJ.

[53] [1999] 2 All ER (Comm) 146, Timothy Walker J.

[54] *ibid*, at 148–9.

law had been specifically addressed by the Swiss tribunal[55]; (2) it mattered not that a more fastidious view might have been adopted on the same facts under English law[56]; (3) the English courts should acknowledge that the parties had chosen Swiss substantive law and Swiss arbitration to regulate these matters[57]; (4) the English courts would not go behind the findings of fact which underpin the conclusion mentioned at (1).[58] This last factor was also emphasised by the majority, Mantell LJ[59] and Sir David Hirst,[60] in the *Westacre* case (2000). In the *Westacre* case the award-debtor unsuccessfully contended before the English enforcing court (Colman J in the High Court, and later the Court of Appeal) that there should be no enforcement of a Swiss award because the main agreement, a consultancy arrangement, involved bribery of Kuwaiti officials in order to procure an arms contract. The Swiss tribunal had investigated this allegation and concluded that no bribery was involved and this finding had been upheld on appeal before the Swiss Federal Court.

9.22 *'Super-Norm' of Public Policy: Terrorism, Drug Trafficking, Prostitution, or Paedophilia.* Especially opprobrious violations of English public policy will not be condoned by an English enforcing court. And so, if it becomes apparent that the underlying contract involves a serious form of illicit conduct, such as 'terrorism, drug trafficking, prostitution, paedophilia,'[61] the English court will not give effect to a foreign award which declares that the relevant activity is not illegal or contrary to public policy under the law of the transaction or the place where performance occurred. Waller LJ in the *Westacre* case (2000) identified this 'super-norm' of English public policy (the other members of the (English) Court of Appeal agreed): '*there are some rules of public policy which if infringed will lead to non-enforcement by the English court whatever their proper law and wherever their place of performance.*'[62]

9.23 *Award Set Aside in Foreign Jurisdiction.* The setting aside or suspension of the foreign arbitral award might justify the English courts in refusing to enforce the arbitral award (but the foreign annulment decision might itself be vitiated: see further **9.34** below). This proposition follows from section 103(2)(f) of the 1996 Act, embodying Article V.1(e) of the New York Convention (1958). The English provision (section 103(2)(f)) states: '... the award has not yet become binding on

[55] *ibid,* at 149.

[56] *ibid: per* Timothy Walker J: '*it seems to me that (absent a finding of fact of corrupt practices which would give rise to obvious public policy considerations) the fact that English law would or might have arrived at a different result is nothing to the point.*'

[57] *ibid.*

[58] *ibid,* at 148.

[59] *Westacre Investments Inc* v. *Jugoimport SDPR Holding Co Ltd* [2000] QB 288, 317, CA.

[60] *ibid,* at 317.

[61] *Westacre* case [2000] QB 288, 302, CA.

[62] *ibid,* at 305, CA; noting also at 315, *Lemenda Trading Co Ltd* v. *African Middle East Petroleum Co Ltd* [1988] QB 448, Phillips J, and Neill LJ in *ED & F Man (Sugar) Ltd* v. *Yani Haryanto (No 2)* [1991] 1 Lloyd's Rep 429.

the parties, or has been set aside or suspended by a competent authority of the country in which, or under the law of which, it was made.'

9.24 *Foreign Challenge to Award Still Pending.* The fact that foreign proceedings are pending does not preclude English enforcement under the New York Convention (1958). In the *Honeywell* case (2014) Ramsey J held[63] that the court was not bound to withhold enforcement under the New York Convention (1958) just because the relevant award is currently subject to challenge before the relevant foreign courts.

9.25 *Separability Principle.* The fact that arbitration agreements are separate from the main agreement, in accordance with the principle of 'separability', does not insulate an arbitral award from issues of public policy arising from the main transaction. It follows, as the (English) Court of Appeal in the *Harbour Assurance* case (1993) recognised,[64] that if illegality (and/or its impact) is disputed, that controversy can form the issue (or one of the issues) referred to the tribunal by the parties. As Colman J observed in the *Westacre* case (1999) (the English Court of Appeal (2000) did not disturb this),[65] despite the 'separability' of the arbitration agreement, a court will acknowledge its 'parasitic' or 'ancillary' nature in relation to the main transaction when determining issues of public policy affecting that award:

> '*For an agreement to arbitrate within an underlying contract is in origin and function parasitic. It is ancillary to the underlying contract for its only function is to provide machinery to resolve disputes as to the primary and secondary obligations arising under that contract. The primary obligations under the agreement to arbitrate exist only for the purpose of informing the parties by means of an award what are their rights and obligations under the underlying contract.*' [66]

9.26 *English Municipal Law concerning Bribery, etc.* This topic is now dominated by the Bribery Act 2010[67] (although there have been transitional prosecutions

---

[63] *Honeywell International Middle East Ltd* v. *Meydan Group LLC (No 2)* [2014] BLR 599, Ramsey J.

[64] *Harbour Assurance Co (UK) Ltd* v. *Kansa General International Insurance Co Ltd* [1993] QB 701, CA, *per* Ralph Gibson LJ, at 712c-f, Leggatt LJ, at 719 and Hoffmann LJ, at 723f-724e; explained by Colman J in *Westacre Investments Inc* v. *Jugoimport SDPR Holding Co Ltd* [1999] QB 740, 756–757.

[65] *Westacre Investments Inc* v. *Jugoimport SDPR Holding Co Ltd* [1999] QB 740, 755, *per* Colman J and not disturbed by the CA ([2000] QB 288, CA).

[66] *ibid, per* Colman J.

[67] Bribery Act 2010; E O'Shea, *The Bribery Act 2010: A Practical Guide* (Jordans, Bristol, 2011); N Cropp [2011] Crim L Rev 122–141; S Gentle [2011] Crim L Rev 101–110; J Horder (2011) 74 MLR 911–931 and (2011) 127 LQR 37–54; C Monteith [2011] Crim L Rev 111–121; G Sullivan [2011] Crim L Rev 87–100; A Wells (2011) Business Law Review 186; C Wells [2012] JBL 420–431.

under the preceding legislation).[68] This creates offences[69] concerning the offer, giving, requesting or receipt of a bribe, contrary to reasonable expectations,[70] for the purpose of causing a function (not confined to public functions)[71] to be exercised 'improperly'.[72] The 2010 Act also addresses the problem of bribery of foreign public officials,[73] and makes provision for the problem of foreign customs and expectations.[74] In addition to the statutory predecessors[75] to the Bribery Act 2010, the Common Law had invalidated certain forms of agreements involving corruption. In *Amalgamated Society of Railway Servants* v. *Osborne* (1910), the House of Lords held that an MP cannot contract with a third party that he will cast his vote in Parliament in a particular way.[76] And in *Parkinson* v. *College of Ambulance Ltd* (1925),[77] an agreement foundered under this head because it involved payment for a knighthood. This type of sordid practice is now an offence.[78]

9.2 National Court's Annulment of a Domestic Award: The Position of a Foreign Enforcing Court

9.27 *The 'New Fashion'.* Alan Uzelac (Croatia) has referred to the 'new fashion' for some state courts to adopt the approach that a foreign award, even though annulled in the jurisdiction where the arbitration had its seat, might still be recognised or enforced in another jurisdiction. This possibility exists, according to the

[68] *R* v. *J* [2013] EWCA Crim 2287; [2014] 1 WLR 1857; [2014] 1 Cr App R 21, on the Prevention of Corruption Act 1906 (see Lord Thomas CJ's judgment at [9] ff concerning the Public Bodies Corrupt Practices Act 1889, the 1906 Act just mentioned, and the Prevention of Corruption Act 1916).

[69] Sections 1 and 2, Bribery Act 2010; *Hansard*, HL Vol 715, col 1086 (December 9, 2009) states: '*[The Act] creates two general offences of bribery, a third specific offence of bribing a foreign public official and finally a new corporate offence of failing to prevent bribery....The general offences, in [sections 1 and 2], cover on one side of the coin the offer, promise and giving of a financial or other advantage, and on the flip side the request, agreeing to receive or acceptance of such an advantage. These offences focus on the conduct of the payer or the recipient of a bribe and describe six scenarios, each involving the improper performance of a function, where one or other offence would be committed. These new offences will apply to functions of a public nature as well as in a business, professional or employment context.*'

[70] Section 5, Bribery Act 2010.

[71] Section 3, *ibid.*

[72] Section 4, *ibid.*

[73] Section 6, *ibid.*

[74] Section 5(2), *ibid* (Phillips J had grappled with this problem in *Lemenda Trading Co Ltd* v. *African Middle East Petroleum Co Ltd* [1988] QB 448).

[75] For these statutes, note 68 above concerning *R* v. *J* [2013] EWCA Crim 2287; [2014] 1 WLR 1857, at [9] ff.

[76] [1910] AC 87, HL.

[77] [1925] 2 KB 1, Lush J.

[78] Honours (Prevention of Abuse) Act 1925.

jurisprudence of certain national systems, but it is too early to declare that this is likely to become the predominant possibility amongst leading trading nations. This topic has inspired a large literature,[79] including the remarkable study by Emmanuel Gaillard, *Legal Theory of International Arbitration* (2010).[80]

9.28 *Annulment Not Decisive: the Enforcing Court's Apparent Choice Under the New York Convention (1958).* Article V(1)(e) of the New York Convention (1958) (**9.07**) states that an enforcing court can choose not to recognise or enforce a foreign award if it has been annulled in the courts of the relevant seat. But this is not regarded as a mandatory ground for refusing to recognise or enforce such an award. The relevant text of Article V(1) states:

> *'Recognition and enforcement of the award may be refused, at the request of the party against whom it is invoked, only if that party furnishes to the competent authority where the recognition and enforcement is sought, proof that:*
> *[grounds (a) to (d) omitted here]*
> *(e) The award has not yet become binding on the parties, or has been set aside or suspended by a competent authority of the country in which, or under the law of which, that award was made.'*

9.29 *The Enforcing Court's Election to Uphold the Award Despite that Award having been Annulled at the Seat.* In extensive (and agnostic) *dicta*, Lord Collins in the *Dallah* case (2010), noted the French and Swiss approach (domestic annulment does not preclude foreign court from recognising or enforcing the award).[81] In the *Dallah* case (2010) Lord Collins also noted that the basis for this generous approach is not the 'discretion' whether to enforce an award under Article V(1) of the New York Convention (1958), but Article VII(1) of the same document preserves any wider powers of recognition and enforcement observed by the local law of the relevant enforcing court.[82]

9.30 Christian Koller (Austria) notes that the Austrian Supreme Court has adopted the French/Swiss approach (domestic annulment does not preclude foreign

---

[79] H Kronke, et al., *Recognition and Enforcement of Foreign Arbitral Awards: A Global Commentary on the New York Convention* (Kluwer, Deventer, 2010), 10, and (notably) 324 ff; *Mustill & Boyd, Commercial Arbitration: Companion Volume* (London, 2001), 85 ff; WW Park, *Arbitration of International Business Disputes: Studies in Law and Practice* (Oxford University Press, 2006), 185 ff; 189–92.

[80] (Martinus Nijhoff, Leiden, and Boston, 2010).

[81] [2010] UKSC 46; [2011] 1 AC 763, at [129].

[82] *ibid,* at [129], citing (France) *Pabalk Ticaret Sirketi* v. *Norsolor*, Cour de cassation, 9 October 1984, 1985 Rev Crit 431*; Hilmarton Ltd* v. *OTV,* Cour de cassation, 23 March 1994 (1995) 20 Yb Comm Arb 663, 665; *République arabe d'Egypte* v. *Chromalloy Aero Services,* Paris *Cour d'appel,* 14 January 1997 (1997) 22 Yb Comm Arb 691; *Soc PT Putrabali Adyamulia* v. *Soc Rena Holding,* Cour de cassation, 29 June 2007 (2007) 32 Yb Comm Arb 299 (*award in an arbitration in England which had been set aside by the English court (see PT Putrabali Adyamulia* v. *Soc Est Epices [2003] 2 Lloyd's Rep 700) was enforced in France, on the basis that the award was an international award which did not form part of any national legal order);* also citing (Netherlands) *Yukos Capital SARL* v. *OAO Rosneft,* 28 April 2009, Amsterdam Gerechtshof.

court from recognising or enforcing the award), but in a case not falling within the New York Convention (1958).[83]

9.31 *Foreign Judicial Independence and the Yukos Saga: Non-Recognition of a Domestic Court's Annulment of an Arbitral Award on Basis of Local Court's Lack of Independence.* The following propositions emerge from this saga: (i) A foreign court's annulment of a domestic arbitral award (an award made within that foreign jurisdiction and which is subject to the regulation of the relevant foreign court) will not prevent the English court from recognising or enforcing the impugned arbitral award where the foreign court's annulment was made in circumstances inconsistent with English rules for the recognition of foreign decisions. (ii) Where the issue just mentioned falls for decision by the English courts, the latter are not bound by any third jurisdiction's decision concerning the annulment judgment's effects.

9.32 In the *Yukos* litigation four Russian awards had been annulled by a Russian court. But when the matter of enforcing the awards was received by the Dutch courts, it was held (by the Court of Appeal, Amsterdam) that the Russian court which had purportedly annulled the award had in fact lacked judicial independence.[84] The Dutch courts proceeded to enforce the Russian arbitral awards. As a result of the Dutch enforcement proceedings, the principal sum ($US 425 million) had been paid in (partial) satisfaction of the awards. But interest payable under the awards remained outstanding. The present English proceedings were brought to seek recovery of interest of $US 160 million, namely additional compensation attributable to the dilatory satisfaction by the award-debtor of the award.

9.33 The English Court of Appeal in the *Yukos* case (2012)[85] held that the questions whether the Russian court's decision had been vitiated by extraneous pressure and whether that court lacked impartiality and independence had been resolved by the Amsterdam Court of Appeal applying a **Dutch test of public policy**. This meant that the issue before the English court was not the same because it required the English court to apply independently and afresh **English public policy in this regard**.

9.34 Later in the *Yukos* litigation, Simon J held in *Yukos Capital Sarl* v. *OJSC Rosneft Oil Co* (2014)[86] that the English courts (i) can award interest (under section 35A, Senior Courts Act 1981) on a foreign arbitral award and (ii) that a foreign award could be recognised in this manner even though it had been annulled by the courts of the foreign seat provided (iii) the foreign Russian judicial annulment is itself invalid under English conflict of laws principles. As for point (iii), he held that

[83] Koller (Austria: National Report for the Heidelberg conference, summer 2011): noting OGH 3 Ob 117/93 and 3 Ob 115/95, Ybk Comm Arb 1999, 919.

[84] [2011] EWHC 1461 (Comm); [2012] 1 All ER (Comm) 479; [2011] 2 Lloyd's Rep 443; [2011] 2 CLC 129, examining, among other decisions: *Carl Zeiss Stiftung* v. *Rayner & Keeler Ltd (No 2)* [1967] 1 AC 853, HL; *Carl Zeiss Stiftung* v. *Rayner & Keeler Ltd (No 3)* [1970] Ch 506; *'The Sennar' (No 2)* [1985] 1 WLR 490, 499, HL; P Rogerson, 'Issue Estoppel and Abuse of Process in Foreign Judgments' (1998) CJQ 91.

[85] [2012] EWCA Civ 855; [2013] 1 All ER 223; [2012] 2 Lloyd's Rep 208.

[86] [2014] EWHC 2188 (Comm); [2014] 2 Lloyd's Rep 435; 155 Con LR 221.

the Russian judicial annulment proceedings would not be recognised, applying 'conventional English conflict of law principles', where, for example, the annulment judgments were obtained by fraud, or it would be contrary to public policy to enforce the judgments, or the judgments were obtained in breach of the rules of natural justice.[87] (There was no appeal from Simon J's decision.)

9.35 *Converse Approach: Annulment at the Seat Precluding Enforcing Court from Recognising or Enforcing the Award.* Lord Collins in the *Dallah* case (2010), noted the American approach (domestic annulment is conclusive for foreign purposes).[88] Rolf Stürner (Germany) suggests that the French/Swiss approach (domestic annulment does not preclude foreign court from recognising or enforcing the award) would not be possible in Germany, where the fate of the foreign award would be conclusively determined if it had been annulled by the courts of the relevant seat.[89]

9.3 The *Dallah* Saga: English Court's Refusal to Enforce the French Award

9.36 The Supreme Court of the United Kingdom in *Dallah Real Estate & Tourism Holding Co* v. *Pakistan* (2010)[90] held that a Paris award could not be recognised in England, under the New York Convention (1958), because the French arbitral tribunal had incorrectly determined that the Pakistan Government was a party to the relevant arbitration agreement.[91] It was somewhat embarrassing for the Supreme Court of the United Kingdom that a French court (Paris *Cour d'appel*, 2011), admittedly applying French internal law, as distinct from the New York Convention (1958), reached the opposite conclusion, that this award was satisfactory.[92] These

---

[87] *ibid,*, at [12]; and [15] to [22] is an illuminating discussion.

[88] [2010] UKSC 46; [2011] 1 AC 763, at [130], citing *Baker Marine (Nigeria) Ltd* v. *Chevron (Nigeria) Ltd,* 191 F 3d 194 (2d Cir 1999); *TermoRio SA ESP* v. *Electranta SP,* 487 F 3d 928 (DC Cir 2007); also noting that an Egyptian award which had been set aside by the Egyptian court was enforced because the parties had agreed that the award would not be the subject of recourse to the local courts: *Chromalloy Aeroservices* v. *Arab Republic of Egypt,* 939 F Supp 907 (DDC 1996) (as noted in *Karaha Bodas Co* v. *Perusahaan Pertambangan Minyak Dan Gas Bumi Negara,* 335 F 3d 357, 367, 5th Cir 2003); whether it was correctly decided was left open in the *TermoRio* case 487 F 3d 928, 937 (DC Cir 2007).

[89] Rolf Stürner (Freiburg) (national report for the Heidelberg congress, 2011).

[90] [2010] UKSC 46; [2011] 1 AC 763; for comment, Jan Kleinheisterkamp, 'Lord Mustill and the courts of tennis – *Dallah* v. *Pakistan* in England, France and Utopia' (2012) 75 MLR 639, 640 at n 2 listing various comments on this decision.

[91] Generally on the issue of third parties and joinder or consolidation arbitration, see the abundant literature cited in chapter 2 section XI, at **2.54**.

[92] *Gouvernement du Pakistan* v. *Société Dallah Real Estate & Tourism Holding Co, Cour d'appel de Paris, Pôle 1 – Ch 1, n° 09/28533* (17 February 2011) (www.practicallaw.com/8-505-0043). On which see both the next note and the comment by White & Case: http://www.whitecase.com/insight-03022011/

events show that the New York Convention (1958) is not always the fast route to cross-border enforcement of arbitral awards that enthusiasts for commercial arbitration had expected. The enforcing court, acting under the NYC (1958), is obliged to consider afresh the resisting party's allegation that it was not truly a party to the arbitration agreement (and nor has it become a party to it by acquiescence; of course, it will be crucial that the resisting party has consistently opposed the arbitrators' jurisdiction). The enforcing court under the NYC (1958) will be obliged to make such a fresh determination even though the arbitral tribunal has pronounced on this very issue.

9.37 Under the New York Convention (1958),[93] enacted as section 103 of the Arbitration Act 1996, the question whether a person was in fact party to an arbitration agreement falls to be determined in accordance with either the parties' chosen law (but in the *Dallah* case the arbitration agreement did not contain any such choice of law), or the law of the jurisdiction in which the award was made (here French law). Accordingly, French law applied here. Applying the relevant French test for this purpose, the Supreme Court of the United Kingdom *Dallah Real Estate & Tourism Holding Co* v. *Pakistan* (2010),[94] and, below, the Commercial Court and the (London) Court of Appeal, concluded that the Paris arbitral tribunal had adopted faulty reasoning, and had not applied correctly French law on this point, when concluding that Pakistan was a party to the agreement (even though it had not been named as a party within the arbitration agreement, nor had it signed that clause). The Pakistan Government had neither signed the arbitration agreement, nor had it been named as a party to that agreement. Instead that Government had structured the relevant substantive transaction (including, the literal terms of the arbitration agreement) by using a trust. The English court held that the Pakistan Government should not be regarded as a party to the arbitration agreement, and that the arbitration award was, therefore, flawed in deciding that this Government should be regarded as a party. According to the English courts, the correct approach, founded on French law, required investigation whether the parties' dealings disclosed a common subjective intention (express or implied), shared by Pakistan and the named arbitration parties, that Pakistan would be treated as party to the arbitration agreement. The English courts considered that the Paris arbitral tribunal, had erred by invoking more general notions of 'good faith' and that these nebulous notions were insufficiently tied to the question of common intention.[95]

9.38 The English Court of Appeal (this point was not pursued on further appeal to the Supreme Court) also rejected Dallah's further argument that the French arbitral tribunal's decision on the question whether Pakistan was party to the arbitration agreement was binding as a matter of issue estoppel. It was not binding because the French arbitral tribunal had not applied French law to this question, as it should have. Furthermore, the English court considered that it was inconsistent with the

---

[93] For the text of Article V(1), NYC (1958), **9.07**.

[94] [2010] UKSC 46; [2011] 1 AC 763 (where the lower courts' decisions are also cited).

[95] [2009] EWCA Civ 755, at [24] and [25] for the Court of Appeal's summary of this curious aspect.

New York Convention and section 103 of the Arbitration Act 1996 for the enforcing court to be precluded by issue estoppel from rehearing this question concerning the arbitration agreement's validity and effect. In the Court of Appeal, Moore-Bick LJ said that the structure of the New York Convention (1958) presupposes that the foreign enforcing court must examine whether the award is correct in declaring a person or entity to be party to the arbitration agreement. That question is not one which is exclusively ceded by that Convention to the arbitral tribunal (subject only to the supervisory jurisdiction of the court of the seat).[96] Instead the matter must be tested at the recognition or enforcement stage in a non-seat jurisdiction under the NYC (1958).

9.39 Similarly, the English court held that the fact that Pakistan had chosen not to challenge the French arbitration award within the French supervisory court system did not raise an estoppel against the Government of Pakistan (and so that Government of Pakistan was not precluded by raising this issue during concerning enforcement under the New York Convention, 1958).[97]

9.40 The *Dallah* case (2010) shows the extensive scope during foreign enforcement proceedings under the New York Convention (1958) for the enforcing court to rehear the question concerning the validity, party scope, or material scope, of the arbitration agreement. Thus the enforcing court can and must investigate fully On that question, the enforcing court is to investigate fully: (i) whether the arbitration panel has correctly ascertained the applicable law governing the arbitration award's existence, validity, and effectiveness; (ii) the enforcing court must determine whether the test derived from that applicable law has been correctly formulated; (iii) the enforcing court must then decide for itself whether that test, when meticulously applied to the facts of the case, establishes that the relevant putative party was truly a party to the arbitration agreement. At this third stage it is not enough merely to rubber-stamp the arbitral tribunal's analysis, because it is possible for the party resisting enforcement to show that there was in fact no proper factual or legal support for the conclusion drawn by the arbitral panel.

9.41 Furthermore, consideration in England of the *Dallah* enforcement application involved three levels of judicial review: High Court, Court of Appeal, and Supreme Court. At each level the relevant court carried out a full review itself of that evidence, rather than merely deferring to the first instance decision on this point by Aikens J in the Commercial Court. The delay and costs generated by these further enforcement processes can be considerable. This episode shows that the New York Convention (1958) is not always the fast route to foreign recognition and enforcement which its architects had hoped to create.

9.42 It is right that there should be the opportunity for such a 'final check' on the fundamental preliminary issue whether a party is indeed truly a party to the relevant arbitration before the relevant enforcing courts can validly authorise enforcement against the award-debtor's assets under the New York Convention (1958). The enforcing court's capacity to conduct a searching review of this matter will have the effect of

---

[96] On this [2009] EWCA Civ 755, at [18], *per* Moore-Bick LJ.

[97] ibid, at [56], *per* Moore-Bick LJ.

injecting much greater rigour and accuracy into this fundamental threshold issue. Given the explicit hesitation of two members of the Paris arbitral tribunal in this case on this very jurisdictional issue, it was inevitable that the enforcing court's searchlight would be trained closely at this possible weakness.

9.43 *The French Judicial Decision to Uphold the Paris Arbitration Award.* But the twist in the *Dallah* litigation was when a French court (Paris *Cour d'appel*: the French court nominated to review arbitral awards) later reached the opposite conclusion: that the Paris award was sound (at least according to French arbitration principles), so that the Pakistan Government should be regarded as a party to the arbitration agreement.[98] This decision was made pursuant to Article 1502(1) of the French Code of Civil Procedure. This permits the court to refuse to enforce an award *'if the arbitrator has ruled upon the matter without an arbitration agreement or [the putative arbitration agreement is in fact] a void and lapsed agreement'*. The French court's perspective involved posing different criteria (independent of French national law) compared with the criteria adopted by the English courts when purporting to apply French law to the relevant arbitration agreement.[99] The Paris *Cour d'appel* decision in the *Dallah* case (2011) follows the *Dalico* doctrine[100] which involves a loosening of conflicts rules in the case of international arbitration. The French court then focused on the parties' dealings between the parties. It noted that the Pakistan Government negotiated the contract, and that the Trust created by the Government was merely a signatory. The Paris *Cour d'appel* also noted that the Government was involved in the performance of the contract, and that it effectively controlled the same transactions' termination. And so the Paris *Cour d'appel* concluded that the Trust was 'purely formal' and that the Government was the true Pakistani party to the transaction.

9.44 By contrast the English courts had given very considerable weight to these elements: (a) the legal separateness of the Trust; (b) that the arbitration agreement had been signed only by the Trust and not by the Government; and to the fact that the arbitration agreement made no mention of the Government as an additional party; and, finally, the English courts had been persuaded that there was no true consensus between the members of this triangle that the Government should be treated as a party to the arbitration agreement.

---

[98] *Gouvernement du Pakistan* v. *Société Dallah Real Estate & Tourism Holding Co, Cour d'appel de Paris, Pôle 1 – Ch 1, n° 09/28533* (17 February 2011) (www.practicallaw.com/8-505-0043). On which see both the next note and the comment by White & Case: http://www.whitecase.com/insight-03022011/.

[99] James Clark, http://www.practicallaw.com/4-504-9971?q=&qp=&qo=&qe=: '…*the French court did not focus on French law principles and proceeded to a factual enquiry to determine whether the parties had actually consented to go to arbitration [an approach which reflects the French courts'] desire…to develop …rules for international arbitration that ensure that the outcome of a dispute does not depend on the particularities of a national law. This solution is also consistent with French case law on the extension of arbitration agreements to parties that are non-signatories but have participated in its negotiation and performance.*'

[100] *Cour de Cassation*, First Civil Chamber, *Municipalité de Khoms El Mergeb* v. *Dalico*, 20 December 1993, JDI 1994, 432, note E Gaillard.

9.45 How does this difference of analysis and result leave the relevant award? If a third jurisdiction were to be asked to enforce the *Dallah* award (made by the arbitral tribunal in Paris), it seems highly likely that it would defer to the French court's decision, rather than be guided by the Supreme Court of the United Kingdom's conflicting decision. This is because (a) the French court is situated in the seat of the relevant arbitration and (b) it seems likely that the French court's flexible and transnational reasoning in this matter would be regarded as more attractive; and in fact it appears that the English courts had fallen into error concerning the true question to be posed when applying French arbitration law to determine party membership.

9.46 *Concluding Remarks on the Dallah Case*. The enforcing court's investigation whether the award-debtor is a true party to the arbitration agreement can require sophisticated expert evidence. The English courts, it appears mistakenly, concluded, on the basis of party-appointed expert evidence, that the test under French law for determining whether a person or entity was truly party to an arbitration agreement was a rather formal and traditional criterion of consensus. In fact the Paris *Cour d'appel*'s decision (explained above) reveals that a much more fluid test applies under French arbitral practice when the arbitration has a transnational character. In future cases greater rigour will be required so that the enforcing court can ascertain with confidence the foreign test applicable at the relevant seat.

9.47 Although the *Dallah* case (that is, the Supreme Court of the United Kingdom's decision in the *Dallah* case (2010)[101] just examined in detail) is 'bad news' for the marketability of international commercial arbitration, it is not a complete disaster. It seems unlikely that this development will seriously damage the overall attractiveness of international commercial arbitration when compared to court litigation. Many commercial parties perceive that the advantages of confidentiality and selection of jurisdictionally 'neutral' arbitrators firmly tip the balance in favour of preferring arbitration to state court proceedings.

9.48 However, if jurisdictional wrangles of this scale become more common, it might be considered appropriate to consider whether the New York Convention (1958) should be modified to secure a 'lighter touch' style of recognition and enforcement. Even if consensus among interested states were to emerge, the process of implementing such a revision of this international instrument (to which many countries have acceded) will be long and difficult.

9.49 In the absence of formal variation of the terms of the NYC (1958), perhaps the practice will emerge (at least between jurisdictions enjoying friendly and mature relations) that the enforcing court will suspend proceedings and recommend to a party seeking enforcement that vexed problems (as distinct from straightforward and clear-cut issues) concerning jurisdiction should be tested in the court of the seat, if this is still practicable, provided also that this postponement of the enforcing court's decision will not involve excessive delay and expense. This will avoid a 're-run' of the expensive and slow enforcement process in the *Dallah* litigation. As we have seen, it is most unfortunate that the English courts seem to have

[101] [2010] UKSC 46; [2011] 1 AC 763.

been barking up the wrong tree (from the perspective of the subsequent proceedings in the Paris *Cour d'appel*, see above) when they approached the central jurisdictional issue of which legal analysis to apply when determining whether the Government of Pakistan could be correctly treated as party to the arbitration agreement (and hence subject to the arbitral award). A foreign court which attempts to identify and apply foreign law, especially within the mercurial topic of 'party scope', might be wholly out of its depth, despite the assistance of rival party-appointed foreign law evidence. But this last suggestion must not be misunderstood. It is not recommended that in all circumstances the enforcing court must refer as a preliminary issue such a question to the courts of the seat. To render this practice mandatory would be a disaster for the NYC (1958) system. Flexibility and commercial common-sense require that each situation should be assessed on its merits in order to determine the preferable course.

Part III
Central Contractual Doctrines

Chapter 10
Sources and General Principles of English Contract Law

Abstract After explaining the sources of English contract law, predominantly the case law system of precedent, this chapter sets out four established principles of English contract law and suggests that there is a fifth principle, waiting in the wings, which is the principle of good faith and fair dealing.

10.1 Sources of English Contract Law

10.01 In England the main source of law in the field of substantive contract law is judicial precedent, that is, the decisions of (i) the High Court (sitting in London or other parts of England and Wales), (ii) the Court of Appeal (sitting in London), and (iii) the (former) House of Lords (sitting in Westminster, London), now the Supreme Court of the United Kingdom (sitting in Westminster, London). Decisions of these courts are binding sources of English law. Decisions at level (iii) are binding on all courts below; decisions at level (ii) are binding on the Court of Appeal and on all courts below; decisions at level (i) are binding on courts inferior to the High Court, and will tend to be followed by other High Court decisions, unless demonstrably erroneous in law. Decisions of the Privy Council (the Judicial Committee of the Privy Council), on appeal from non-United Kingdom jurisdictions, tend to be highly influential (on the basis that they are clear statements of Common Law principle), although technically Privy Council case law is not binding on the English courts. For a discussion of (i) failed attempts to codify the general part of English contract law, (ii) the 'good faith' debate in English law, and (iii) the differences between English contract law and soft-law codes, see the author's discussion elsewhere.[1]

10.02 There is relatively little statutory provision within the general part of contract law, although the topics of exclusion clauses (**13.12**) and unfair terms in consumer contracts (**13.20**) are now dominated by legislation. The Civil Liability (Contribution) Act 1978 (**17.42** at paragraph (iv)); the Contracts (Rights of Third Parties) Act 1999 (for example, **12.62**); the Consumer Rights Act 2015 (**13.17** and **13.20**); the Law Reform (Frustrated Contracts) Act 1943 (**16.02** at paragraph (ix));

[1] Neil Andrews, *Contract Law* (2nd edn, Cambridge University Press, 2015), respectively, chapters 22, 21, 23.

N. Andrews, *Arbitration and Contract Law*, Ius Gentium: Comparative Perspectives on Law and Justice 54, DOI 10.1007/978-3-319-27144-6_10

the Law Reform (Contributory Negligence) Act 1945 (**17.26**); the Limitation Act 1980 (**17.39 ff**); the Misrepresentation Act 1967 (**12.13**); the Sale of Goods Act 1979 (for example, **13.04**) (as amended by the CRA 2015); the Supply of Goods And Services Act 1982 (**13.04**) (as amended by the CRA 2015); the Unfair Contract Terms Act 1977 (non-consumer contracts) (as amended by the Consumer Rights Act 2015, 'CRA 2015') (**13.17**).

10.03 In this Part of this work the reference to 'tribunals' is intended to embrace both courts and arbitral tribunals.

10.2 Principle 1: Freedom of Contract

10.04 *THE FREEDOM OF CONTRACT PRINCIPLE IN ENGLISH CONTRACT LAW*

(i) *Nature of the Principle*. This fundamental principle is greatly respected in English commercial practice. Freedom of contract comprises a set of powers exercisable by individuals and other legal entities, notably:

   (a) parties have a general freedom to enter into transactions which are intended (explicitly or otherwise) to create legal obligations; conversely, parties are free to 'walk away' from a proposed deal, provided they have not already committed themselves to a binding agreement;
   (b) parties to a contract can stipulate that it will not be legally binding (**11.14** at (ii));
   (c) the parties have the power to formulate individual terms within such a transaction, or to acquiesce in 'default' terms whether these are 'implied' by statute or Common Law (**13.03**).

(ii) *Freedom of contract*: *qualifications*. Exercise of the various powers mentioned at (i) above is subject to these overarching limitations:

   (a) public policy (**9.11** and **11.17**);
   (b) the parties' inability to exclude liability for fraud at Common Law (**13.15**);
   (c) statutory regulation of adhesion clauses (clauses presented on a take-it-or-leave-it basis, **13.12** and **13.20**); and
   (d) matters of personal capacity (age restrictions, mental disability, or an artificial legal entity's formal capacity: on these matters see **10.05–10.07**);
   (e) freedom of contract presupposes that the parties' purported agreement is the exercise of a free decision and not the product of, for example, duress or other vitiating factors (**12.19**).

10.05 *Capacity*: *Age*. Persons aged 18 or more have legal capacity if they are of sound mind. Those under 18 are called 'minors'. The leading propositions concerning minors are as follows:

(1) a minor is liable for 'necessaries' purchased[2];
(2) a minor is bound by a contract of employment or apprenticeship as long as it is on the whole beneficial to him; but this does not extend to a contract to promote the prospects of a talented footballer[3];
(3) contracts for the sale or purchase of land, or the grant or acquisition of a lease, or for the onerous acquisition of shares, can be repudiated by a minor or, after he reaches 18, repudiated within a reasonable time[4];
(4) all other types of contract (for example, a contract of insurance or a trading contract, or a contract for a luxury item not within the scope of 'necessaries', see proposition (1) above) are not binding on the minor unless he ratifies the transaction after reaching 18;
(5) section 3 of the Minors' Contracts Act 1987 permits the court to order restitution of 'any property acquired by the [minor] under the contract, or any property representing it', even if the minor had not lied about his age, and this provision applies to all contracts other than those at (1) and (2).

10.06 *Capacity*: *Mental Capacity*. The Privy Council in *Hart* v. *O'Connor* (1985) held that a contract will arise if a party's insanity is not known to the other party.[5]

10.07 *Capacity*: *Other Legal Entities*. A company or other legal entity (such as a local authority)[6] must have capacity to enter into the relevant transaction.[7]

---

[2] Section 3, Sale of Goods Act 1979; *Nash* v. *Inman* [1908] 2 KB 1, CA; 'necessaries' can include certain services.

[3] *Proform Sports Management Ltd* v. *Proactive Sports Management Ltd* [2006] EWHC 2903 (Ch); [2007] 1 All ER 542 (the 'Wayne Rooney' case).

[4] On the problematic grant of a lease to a minor, see *Hammersmith and Fulham London Borough Council* v. *Alexander-David* [2009] EWCA Civ 259; [2009] 3 All ER 1098.

[5] *Hart* v. *O'Connor* [1985] 2 All ER 880, PC (the 'rule in *Imperial Loan Co* v. *Stone* [1892] 1 QB 599', see *Blankley* v. *Central Manchester and Manchester Children's University Hospitals NHS Trust* [2014] EWHC 168; [2014] 1 WLR 2683, at [30], *per* Phillips J); however, where the *incapax*'s property is subject to the control of the court under sections 15 ff of the Mental Capacity Act 2005, transactions which would be inconsistent with the court's control of those assets will be void as against that party.

[6] *Hazell* v. *Hammersmith & Fulham LBC* [1992] 2 AC 1, HL, and the flood of 'swaps' litigation resulting from this decision (on which *Haugesund Kommune* v. *Depfa ACS Bank* (*No 1*) [2010] EWCA Civ 579; [2011] 1 All ER 190; [2010] 1 CLC 770).

[7] *Haugesund* case, preceding note, decided in the context of restitution of a void loan, and with discussion of the difference between English and foreign notions of corporate incapacity.

10.3 Principle 2: The Objective Principle

10.08 *THE OBJECTIVE PRINCIPLE IN ENGLISH CONTRACT LAW*[8]

(i) *Nature of the Principle*. The parties' language and conduct must be assessed according to their apparent and reasonable meaning and appearance.
(ii) *Scope*. The principle of objectivity applies to any communication or interaction between parties, or between parties and third parties or remoter non-parties, concerning the relevant contractual dealings or their negotiation.
(iii) *Detached Objectivity*. In general, the tribunal will consider matters from the perspective of a detached observer (detached objectivity).
(iv) *Objectivity by Reference to the Parties' Particular Circumstances*. The approach of detached objectivity at (iii) might not always be appropriate. Instead the tribunal might consider matters from the reasonable and objective perspective of the relevant party (or parties), taking into account that party's particular circumstances. Normally that party will be a promisee or representee, but sometimes the objective inquiry might concern more than one party.
(v) *Objective Principle Qualified: Bad Faith Failure to Point out Special Types of Error*. Party B cannot take advantage of party A's error if B knows (or ought reasonably to have realised) that A has made an apparent offer in error, or that A has presented the terms of the offer erroneously (for example, the price). It is not enough, however, that B was aware of A's error concerning the quality of the relevant subject matter, or its unwarranted value.

10.09 McLauchlan has lucidly distinguished (although this distinction has a long lineage) (1) the 'promisee'-based form of objectivity from (2) the 'detached observer' or 'fly-on-the-wall' form of objectivity. The preferred or presumptive form is (1).[9]

10.10 A's error must not only be known to B, but the error must relate to the supposed *terms of the contract*: *Smith* v. *Hughes* (1871)[10] and *Hartog* v. *Colin &*

---

[8] J Cartwright, *Formation and Variation of Contracts* (London, 2014), 3–01 ff; J Cartwright, *Misrepresentation, Mistake and Non-Disclosure* (3rd edn, London, 2012), 13–04 ff; G McMeel, *The Construction of Contracts: Interpretation, Implication and Rectification* (2nd edn, Oxford University Press, 2011), chapter 3, containing trenchant examination of the case law concerning detached objectivity, Proposition (i), and 'promisee objectivity', Proposition (ii).

[9] The passage, too long to quote here, merits close attention: D McLauchlan, 'Refining Rectification' (2014) 130 LQR 83, at 88–90. See also: D Friedmann, (2003) 119 LQR 68; J R Spencer, [1974] CLJ 104; W Howarth, (1984) 100 LQR 265; J Vorster, (1987) 103 LQR 274; M Chen-Wishart, in JW Neyers, R Bronaugh and SGA Pitel (eds), *Exploring Contract Law* (Hart, Oxford, 2009), 341; T Endicott, 'Objectivity, Subjectivity and Incomplete Agreements' in J Horder (ed), *Oxford Essays in Jurisprudence* (Fourth Series, Oxford University Press, 2000), 159; see also, from an American perspective, L DiMatteo, Q Zhou, S Saintier, K Rowley (eds), *Commercial Contract Law: Transatlantic Perspectives* (Cambridge University Press, 2014), chapter 3 (by T Joo). And for other references, G McMeel, *The Construction of Contracts: Interpretation, Implication and Rectification* (2nd edn, Oxford University Press, 2011), chapter 3, n 1.

[10] (1871) LR 6 QBD 597.

Shields (1939).[11] For this purpose, 'knowledge' extends to imputed knowledge: in *OT Africa* v. *Vickers plc* (1996),[12] Mance J ('knowledge' to include imputed knowledge). The restrictive approach adopted in *Smith* v. *Hughes* (1871) was re-stated by Lord Atkin in *Bell* v. *Lever Bros* (1932).[13] In *BCCI* v. *Ali* (2002) Lord Hoffmann took the opportunity to re-affirm the general merits of the *Smith* v. *Hughes* doctrine: '*there is obviously room in the dealings of the market for legitimately taking advantage of the known ignorance of the other party.*'[14]

10.4 Principle 3: Pacta Sunt Servanda (The Binding Force of Agreement)

10.11 *PRINCIPLE 3: PACTA SUNT SERVANDA (THE BINDING NATURE OF CONTRACTS IN ENGLISH LAW)*

(i) The fact that a contract becomes more difficult or expensive to perform is not enough to exonerate or release a party from his obligation or to cause the contract to be terminated for frustration (**16.01**). More generally, the tribunal has no power to release parties from their obligations or to modify their contracts because of hardship or difficulty encountered during performance. Under the strict approach of English law, parties cannot escape bargains except in extreme circumstances where the contract becomes impossible, illegal, or its very foundation has been annihilated by a change of circumstance (**16.02**). In this sense, the principle of the binding force of contract is strongly supported in English law: *pacta sunt servanda.*

(ii) Provision can be made in the contract, by insertion of *force majeure* clauses (**15.01**), to achieve a consensual modification of this strict regime.

(iii) The tribunal must respect the terms of a contract entered into freely by consenting parties of full capacity (**10.12** and **14.13**).

(iv) A party is not at liberty unilaterally to revise the terms or content of the agreement for that party's benefit unless there is a term (express or implied) permitting this[15] (**10.13**).

10.12 *Tribunal to Respect the Terms of a Contract.* The following leading statements emphasise this fundamental tenet of English contract law. In *Arnold* v. *Britton* (2015) Lord Neuberger said[16]: '*it is not the function of a court when interpreting an agreement to relieve a party from the consequences of his imprudence or*

---

[11] [1939] 3 All ER 566, Singleton J.

[12] [1996] 1 Lloyd's Rep 700, 703.

[13] [1932] AC 161, 224, HL.

[14] [2002] 1 AC 251, HL at [70].

[15] K Lewison, *Interpretation of Contracts* (6th edn, London, 2015), 14.04, 14.05.

[16] [2015] UKSC 36; [2015] 2 WLR 1593, at [20].

poor advice. Accordingly, when interpreting a contract a judge should avoid re-writing it in an attempt to assist an unwise party or to penalise an astute party.' Lord Mustill in *Charter Reinsurance Co Ltd* v. *Fagan* (1997) spoke of the illegitimacy of *'forcing upon the words a meaning which they cannot fairly bear'*, since this would be *'to substitute for the bargain actually made one which the court believes could better have been made.'*[17] He added[18]: *'Particularly in the field of commerce, where the parties need to know what they must do and what they can insist on not doing, it is essential for them to be confident that they can rely on the court to enforce their contract according to its terms. Lord Radcliffe in Bridge v. Campbell Discount Co Ltd (1962) noted that an English judge is not empowered to serve as a general adjuster of men's bargains.'*[19] In *Procter and Gamble Co* v. *Svenska Cellulosa Aktiebolaget SCA* (2012) Moore-Bick LJ said: *'in the case of a carefully drafted agreement of the present kind the court must take care not to fall into the trap of re-writing the contract in order to produce what it considers to be a more reasonable meaning.'*[20]

10.13 *Party's Inability to Alter Unilaterally Contractual Terms*. The Consumer Rights Act 2015 indicates that a term will be unfair if it confers unilateral powers exercisable by a trader and which operate to the prejudice of a consumer.[21] Some agreements expressly permit a party unilaterally to vary rate of payment, etc., but such powers will be subject to implied constraints.[22] There is a special rule in respect of written contracts: a deed or guarantee or other written instrument which is unilaterally and 'materially' altered without the other party's permission is rendered void.[23]

10.5 Principle 4: Good Faith and Fair Dealing (A Principle in Waiting)

10.14 *GOOD FAITH AND FAIR DEALING: THE PIECEMEAL APPROACH WITHIN ENGLISH LAW*

---

[17] [1997] AC 313, 388, HL.

[18] *ibid.*

[19] [1962] AC 600, 626, HL.

[20] [2012] EWCA Civ 1413, at [22]

[21] Schedule 2, Part 1, paragraphs 3, 7, 8, 11 to 17.

[22] *Paragon Finance plc* v. *Nash* [2001] EWCA Civ 1466; [2002] 1 WLR 685, at [32] and [36] (implied term that the lender must exercise an express power to vary the rate of interest payable by its customer *without dishonesty, capriciousness or for an improper purpose*); R Hooley, 'Controlling Contractual Discretion' [2013] CLJ 65–90; K Lewison, *Interpretation of Contracts* (6th edn, London, 2015), 14.04, 14.05; Neil Andrews, *Contract Law* (2nd edn, Cambridge, 2015), 13.14.

[23] *Habibsons Bank Ltd* v. *Standard Chartered Bank (Hong Kong) Ltd* [2010] EWCA Civ 1335; [2011] QB 943, at [34], *per* Moore-Bick LJ; G McMeel, *The Construction of Contracts: Interpretation, Implication and Rectification* (2nd edn, Oxford University Press, 2011), 27.14 ff.

(see also *Estoppel*, at **10.15**)

(i) English law does not apply a general doctrine requiring contracting parties to perform their contracts in good faith (but for doctrines rooted in such a broad concept, see (iii) below). For a discussion of the 'good faith' debate in English law, see the author's discussion elsewhere.[24]

(ii) Similarly, in the pre-formation sphere, protection of negotiating parties is achieved using a miscellany of doctrines rather than a single and overarching concept of good faith bargaining.

(iii) English contract law intervenes in numerous respects in the interest of ensuring a minimal level of fair dealing between the parties and in adjustment of their contractual rights and duties. But such intervention occurs under specific doctrinal headings. There are many contexts in which English courts (see (iv) below for statutory examples) have implicitly acted on a principle of good faith or fair dealing when introducing, shaping, and applying a particular doctrine:

(a) the doctrines of promissory estoppel, estoppel at Common Law, estoppel by convention (**10.15**, paragraph (iii) (c) above), and waiver (**13.26**);
(b) protection where one party has unconscionably acquiesced in the other's mistake (**10.08** to **10.10**, **12.20**, **14.45** (i) (b) and (iii));
(c) specific duties to disclose (**12.18**);
(d) fiduciary duties: the duties of fair dealing imposed on agents and other fiduciaries when they contract with their principals, beneficiaries, or other protected persons;
(e) an implied duty on the part of the invitor to conduct the tender process in good faith (**13.03**);
(f) the penalty jurisdiction (**17.33**);
(g) equitable relief against forfeiture of proprietary or possessory interests (**15.27**);
(h) decisions denying that a party has a right to terminate a contract where this would be a wholly disproportionate or severe response to the relevant breach (**15.22** at paragraph (d), **15.23**);
(i) the general principle that equitable relief will be withheld if the applicant has behaved shabbily and lacks 'clean hands' (**17.27** at paragraph (vii)).

(iv) As for statute, the Consumer Rights Act 2015, Part II (**13.20**) contains 'good faith' as one of the criteria for determining the validity of a standard clause in a contract for the supply of goods or services affecting a consumer (see also section 15A of the Sale of Goods Act 1979 (**15.23**), which prevents a buyer's termination for breach of implied terms where the relevant breach is trivial).

---

[24] Neil Andrews, *Contract Law* (2nd edn, Cambridge University Press, 2015), chapter 21.

10.6 Principle 5: Estoppel – Protection Against a Party's Inconsistency

10.15 *THE VERSATILE CONCEPT OF ESTOPPEL*[25]
(venire contra factum proprium)

(i) Estoppel comprises various Common Law and equitable doctrines (see (iii) for these doctrines in outline) which ensure in a flexible manner that, in the interest of commercial fair dealing or 'good faith' (see **10.14**), party A cannot unfairly derogate from party B's assumption or understanding which: (a) party A has induced or encouraged, or of which he has been aware; or (b) both parties have informally assumed or explicitly agreed.

(ii) Estoppel by representation (see (iii) below for summary of other types of estoppel) applies if:

(a) party B makes a statement (at Common Law this must be a statement of past or present fact; but in Equity the doctrine of 'promissory estoppel' encompasses promises, see further (iii) (a) and (b) below);
(b) the statement leads party A to assume that this statement is indeed the case (or will be the case), and so that party relies on that assumption; and
(c) if elements (a) and (b) are shown, it is possible that party B might be prevented by law ('estopped') from acting inconsistently with the statement; or, at least, B's legal rights might be adjusted to accommodate party A's reliance.

(iii) The main[26] types of estoppel are:

(a) *Estoppel by Representation*. This involves a representation by words (or sometimes by non-verbal conduct) indicating that the representee should be assured that something has happened or is presently the case. Common Law estoppel requires a representation of a past or present fact and does not extend to promises of future conduct or future abstention (contrast (b) below). *Jorden v. Money* (1854) is regarded as House of Lords authority that Common Law estoppel requires a representation of a past or present

---

[25] J Cartwright, *Formation and Variation of Contracts* (London, 2014), Part IV; G Spencer Bower and AK Turner, *Estoppel by Representation* (4th edn, London, 2003); KR Handley, *Estoppel by Conduct and Election* (2nd edn, London, 2014); E Cooke, *The Modern Law of Estoppel* (Oxford University Press, 2000); S Wilken and K Ghalys, *The Law of Waiver, Variation and Estoppel* (3rd edn, Oxford University Press, 2012).

[26] For illuminating discussion (too long to cite here) of the fertile and versatile concept of estoppel, see Lord Denning MR in *McIlkenny* v. *Chief Constable of the West Midlands* [1980] QB 283, 316–7, CA (the case proceeded to the HL as '*Hunter* v. *Chief Constable of the West Midlands* [1982] AC 529). For the separate status of estoppel by deed, see *Prime Sight Ltd* v. *Lavarello* [2013] UKPC 22; [2014] AC 436, at [30], *per* Lord Toulson.

fact and does not extend to promises of future conduct or future abstention.[27] For an illustration, see *Shah* v. *Shah* (2001).[28]

(b) *Promissory Estoppel.* This applies mostly in respect of assurances that a debtor (or another person owing a subsisting obligation) will have more time or will be (or has already been) relieved from the remainder of his debt (or other obligation). This type of estoppel can concern the *future* and is not confined to *past or present* facts. However, this form of estoppel does *not* found a ground of claim (cause of action), but is merely a 'shield' (defensive). Promissory estoppel is rooted in principles of Equity.[29]

(c) *Estoppel by Convention.* Its essence is coincident patterns of conduct indicating that the parties have concurred in treating a subsisting transaction as having a particular effect or application, or that it is valid. This type of estoppel does not require a specific representation.[30] *The outward course of conduct evidences or varies an agreement.*[31] It requires some *pattern of visible conduct* which indicates a shared assumption.[32] And no such *conduct* can arise merely from a pair of matching assumptions lodged metaphysically in the parties' minds. For judicial summaries: Carnwath LJ in *ING Bank NV* v. *Ros Roca SA* (2011)[33]; Bingham LJ in '*The Vistafjord*' (2008)[34] (noted by Burton J in *Durham* v. *BAI (Run Off) Ltd*, 2008).[35] Estoppel by convention cannot be used to circumvent a statutory prohibition upon contracting out of a protective set of rules.[36] Estoppel by convention *does not give rise to a cause of action*, but it can clear the way for a contractual, or other, cause of action to be made out[37]: see *Amalgamated Investment & Property Co Ltd (in liquidation)* v. *Texas Commerce International Bank Ltd* (1982).[38]

---

[27] (1854) 5 HL Cas 185; 10 ER 868; including representations of law, *Re Gleeds*, *Briggs* v. *Gleeds* [2014] EWHC 1178 (Ch); [2015] Ch 212, at [26] to [35], *per* Newey J.

[28] [2001] EWCA Civ 527; [2002] QB 35, at [30] to [33].

[29] B McFarlane, 'Understanding Equitable Estoppel: From Metaphors to Better Laws' (2013) 66 CLP 267–305.

[30] Lord Steyn, 'Contract Law: Fulfilling the Reasonable Expectations of Honest Men' (1997) 113 LQR 433, 440; T Dawson, (1989) 9 LS 16; KR Handley, *Estoppel by Conduct and Election* (2nd edn, London, 2014), chapter 8; S Wilken and K Ghalys, *The Law of Waiver, Variation and Estoppel* (3rd edn, Oxford University Press, 2012), chapter 10; G McMeel, *The Construction of Contracts: Interpretation, Implication and Rectification* (2nd edn, Oxford University Press, 2011), chapter 18.

[31] *Republic of India* v. *India Steamship Co Ltd* ('*The Indian Endurance*') (*No 2*) [1998] AC 878, 914–15, HL, *per* Lord Steyn, clarifying the Court of Appeal's formulation of the doctrine.

[32] *ibid*, at 914–15; *Bridgewater* v. *Griffiths* [2000] 1 WLR 524, 530, *per* Burton J.

[33] [2011] EWCA Civ 353; [2012] 1 WLR 472, at [55] to [73] (Stanley Burnton LJ agreed at [75]); the third judge, Rix LJ, at [85] and [86], preferred to reach the same result by use of promissory estoppel/representation by estoppel.

[34] '*The Vistafjord*' [1988] 2 Lloyd's Law Rep 343, 352, CA.

[35] [2008] EWHC 2692 (QB); [2009] 4 All ER 26, at [267] and [268], *per* Burton J.

[36] *Keen* v. *Holland* [1984] 1 WLR 251 (protection under the agricultural holdings legislation).

[37] *Amalgamated Investment & Property* case, [1982] 1 QB 84, 132, CA, *per* Brandon LJ.

[38] [1982] 1 QB 84, CA.

(d) *Contractual Estoppel*. This enables parties to agree (normally in writing) that specified past facts or events have not occurred. This form of estoppel can cover statements expressed as acknowledgments, representations or agreements. A party to such an estoppel is then precluded from making assertions or claims inconsistent with the agreed denial of events. Therefore, this operates as an evidential bar. Unlike (a) to (c), there is no need to show that there has been reliance on the representation concerning the present or past events. There is the limitation that the estoppel cannot be used as a device contrary to public policy.[39] Leading examinations are by the Court of Appeal in the *Springwell* case (2010),[40] and the Privy Council in the *Prime Sight* case (2013).[41]

(e) *Proprietary Estoppel*. This is the exceptional category: this type of estoppel is alone in furnishing a basis of claim (a cause of action). It arises where A spends money improving (or otherwise acts to his detriment *vis-à-vis*) B's land (or other property) in the mistaken assumption that A has, or will acquire, rights in that land (or other property), and either: B makes a representation which induces that error; or B acquiesces (or even if B, at that point, shares A's error, but perhaps B also makes representations which fortify A's belief) in A's error. Good illustrations are *Crabb* v. *Arun District Council* (1976)[42] and *Thorner* v. *Major* (2009).[43]

(f) *Estoppel by Silence or Acquiescence*. It is possible that estoppel by silence or acquiescence might arise where a particular context imports a duty to point out to the other a misapprehension concerning their legal rights. See Rix LJ's remarks in *ING Bank NV* v. *Ros Roca SA* (2011).[44]

---

[39] *Springwell Navigation Corporation* v. *JP Morgan Chase* [2010] EWCA Civ 1221; [2010] 2 CLC 705, at [144], *per* Aikens LJ; see also *Prime Sight Ltd* v. *Lavarello* [2013] UKPC 22; [2014] AC 436, at [47], *per* Lord Toulson (noted A Trukhtanov, (2014) 130 LQR 3–8).

[40] *Springwell* case, *ibid* (following *Peekay Intermark Ltd* v. *Australia and New Zealand Banking Group Ltd* [2006] EWCA Civ 386; [2006] 2 Lloyd's Rep 511, at [56], [57]); G McMeel, 'Documentary fundamentalism in the Senior Courts: the myth of contractual estoppel' [2011] LMCLQ 185–207; and D McLaughlan, 'The Entire Agreement Clause…' (2012) 128 LQR 521, 536–539.

[41] *Prime Sight Ltd* v. *Lavarello* [2013] UKPC 22; [2014] AC 436, at [30], [46] and [47], *per* Lord Toulson.

[42] [1976] Ch 179, CA (Lord Denning MR, Lawton and Scarman LJJ).

[43] [2009] UKHL 18; [2009] 1 WLR 776 (noted by B McFarlane and A Robertson, (2009) 125 LQR 535–42).

[44] [2011] EWCA Civ 353; [2012] 1 WLR 472, at [93], referring to the possibility (citing Bingham J's examination in *Tradax Export SA* v. *Dorada Cia Naviera SA* ('*The Lutetian*') [1982] 2 Lloyd's Rep 140, 157, of Lord Wilberforce's analysis of estoppel by silence in *Moorgate Mercantile Co Ltd* v. *Twitchings* [1977] AC 890, 903, HL).

(g) *Res Judicata*. This concerns 'claim or issue preclusion'.[45] The leading English decision is *Virgin Atlantic Airways Ltd* v. *Zodiac Seats UK Ltd* (2013).[46] The three elements are: (i) judgments (or awards, see (iii) below) are binding upon the parties (and their privies[47] or successors)[48]; (ii) if made in a civil matter (a final decision,[49] or consent order)[50]; and (iii) if made by a competent civil court or tribunal[51] (including courts recognised under English rules of private international law)[52] or in arbitration proceedings.[53]

---

[45] This terminology, current in the USA and in Canada, has been adopted in ALI/UNIDROIT's *Principles of Transnational Civil Procedure* (Cambridge, 2006), Principles 28.2 and 28.3.

[46] The leading decision is *Virgin Atlantic Airways Ltd* v. *Zodiac Seats UK Ltd* [2013] UKSC 46; [2014] AC 160, *per* Lord Sumption, at [17], [20], [22], [26], considering *Arnold* v. *National Westminster Bank plc* [1991] 2 AC 93; for general background (ante-dating this decision), G Spencer Bower, A K Turner and KR Handley, *The Doctrine of Res Judicata* (4th edn, London, 2009); *Andrews on Civil Processes* (Intersentia, Cambridge, Antwerp, Portland, 2013), vol 1, *Court Proceedings*, chapter 16; generally on this topic, N Andrews, '*Res Judicata* and Finality: Estoppel in the Context of Judicial Decisions and Arbitral Awards', in K Makridou and G Diamantopoulos (eds), *Issues of Estoppel and Res Judicata in Anglo-American and Greek Law* (Nomine Bibliothiki, Athens, 2013), 17–39.

[47] *McIlkenny* v. *Chief Constable of the West Midlands* [1980] 1 QB 283, CA; *House of Spring Gardens Ltd* v. *Waite* [1991] 1 QB 241, CA; *Black* v. *Yates* [1992] 1 QB 526, 545–9.

[48] e.g., *Green* v. *Vickers Defence Systems Ltd* [2002] EWCA Civ 904; *The Times*, 1 July 2002.

[49] Including a final decision of an interim application: *R* v. *Governor of Brixton Prison, ex parte Osman* [1991] 1 WLR 281; *Possfund* v. *Diamond* [1996] 2 All ER 774, 779; for an example of a non-final decision, see *Buehler AG* v. *Chronos Richardson Ltd* [1998] 2 All ER 960, CA.

[50] e.g., *Palmer* v. *Durnford Ford* [1992] 1 QB 483, Simon Tuckey QC sitting as a Deputy High Court Judge; *Green* v. *Vickers Defence Systems Ltd* [2002] EWCA Civ 904; *The Times*, 1 July 2002; *Gairy* v. *Attorney-General of Grenada* [2001] UKPC 30; [2002] 1 AC 167, at [27].

[51] *Green* v. *Hampshire County Council* [1979] ICR 861; *Crown Estate Commissioners* v. *Dorset County Council* [1990] Ch 297, Millett J.

[52] PR Barnett, *Res Judicata, Estoppel and Foreign Judgments: The Preclusive Effects of Foreign Judgments in Private International Law* (Oxford University Press, 2001); P Rogerson, (1998) *Civil Justice Quarterly* 91.

[53] *Andrews on Civil Processes* (Intersentia, Cambridge, Antwerp, Portland, 2013), vol 2, *Arbitration and Mediation*, chapter 17; notably, *Associated Electric & Gas Insurance Services Ltd* v. *European Reinsurance Co of Zurich* [2003] UKPC 11; [2003] 1 WLR 1041, PC; *R (Coke-Wallis)* v. *Institute of Chartered Accountants in England and Wales* [2011] UKCS 1; [2011] 2 AC 146, at [31], *per* Lord Clarke, citing G Spencer Bower, A K Turner and KR Handley, *The Doctrine of Res Judicata* (4th edn, London, 2009), 2.05, and noting *Fidelitas Shipping Co Ltd* v. *V/O Exportchleb* [1966] 1 QB 630, 643 C, CA, *per* Diplock LJ; generally on this topic, N Andrews, '*Res Judicata* and Finality: Estoppel in the Context of Judicial Decisions and Arbitral Awards', in K Makridou and G Diamantopoulos (eds), *Issues of Estoppel and Res Judicata in Anglo-American and Greek Law* (Nomine Bibliothiki, Athens, 2013), 17–39.

Chapter 11
Validity

Abstract The main requirements for a valid contract in English law are: the contract must be certain; there are further requirements of consideration, intent to create legal relations, and compatibility with tests of illegality and public policy.

11.1 Certainty

11.01 *THE REQUIREMENT OF CERTAINTY*[1]

(i) Problems of 'uncertainty' involve either an initial failure to agree ('vagueness' and 'ambiguity') or a postponement of agreement and eventual failure to agree ('incompleteness').

(ii) A contract (and individual terms) must satisfy a practical, objective, and commercial standard of certainty, for example when determining the subject-matter of an agreement or the amount of payment.[2] In *May & Butcher v. R* (1927)[3] an agreement to sell a defined subject matter but at a price on which the parties had merely agreed to agree was held not to create a binding contract of sale. There had been no performance. But this decision was distinguished in *Foley* v. *Classique Coaches* (1934)[4] on the basis that the parties in the latter case had already satisfactorily enjoyed dealings and a three-year course of supply had worked out well already. Aikens LJ in the *Barbudev* case (2012)[5] acknowledged that *Walford* v. *Miles* is binding authority for the proposition that an agreement to agree is not binding, and it makes no difference

[1] J Cartwright, *Formation and Variation of Contracts* (London, 2014), 3-13 to 3-17; G McMeel, *The Construction of Contracts*: *Interpretation, Implication and Rectification* (2nd edn, Oxford University Press, 2011), chapter 14.

[2] K Lewison, *Interpretation of Contracts* (6th edn, London, 2015), 8.15.

[3] [1934] 2 KB 17 n, HL (decided in 1927, but not reported until 1934).

[4] [1934] 2 KB 1.

[5] *Barbudev* v. *Eurocom Cable Management Bulgaria Eood* [2012] EWCA Civ 548; [2012] 2 All ER (Comm) 963, at [46]; see also *Shaker* v. *Vistajet* [2012] EWHC 1329 (Comm); [2012] 2 All ER (Comm) 1010; [2012] 2 Lloyd's Rep 93, Teare J (deposit repayment conditional on payor having negotiated in good faith; purported condition precedent to repayment; condition held to be void for uncertainty; therefore, deposit repayable without this fetter; [8] to [18]).

N. Andrews, *Arbitration and Contract Law*, Ius Gentium: Comparative Perspectives on Law and Justice 54, DOI 10.1007/978-3-319-27144-6_11

that the negotiation agreement is couched as one to negotiate in good faith or reasonably. But Teare J in *Emirates Trading Agency LLC* v. *Prime Mineral Exports Private Ltd* (2014)[6] (**2.41**) recognised an exception to *Walford* v. *Miles* (1992) in the context of dispute resolution clauses. The relevant negotiation clause was restricted to a fixed period of 4 weeks and it required the parties to conduct 'friendly' negotiations as the mandatory prelude to commencing arbitration proceedings. Teare J decided that the negotiation clause operates as a condition precedent to valid arbitral proceedings and that it imports the implied obligation to conduct '*fair, honest and genuine discussions aimed at resolving a dispute*'.[7]

(iii) Lack of certainty can affect a contract in different ways: (a) by invalidating the whole contract; (b) by rendering inoperative only part of the contract; or (c) by entitling the tribunal to withhold the remedy of specific performance.

(iv) It is normally sufficient that the agreement discloses consensus on all essential matters.

(v) Uncertainty has no impact on a contract if: (a) the relevant uncertainty leaves a gap which can be filled easily by a statutory or judicial default rule; or (b) the vague words can be simply ignored, leaving no gap at all.

(vi) The tribunal will strive to resolve problems of uncertainty in favour of finding an agreement[8] (see next paragraph for illustrations).

(vii) Furthermore, the tribunal will be especially keen to find an agreement when there has been significant performance under a purported agreement (or if there has been a compromise).[9] For example, in *Didymi Corporation* v. *Atlantic Lines and Navigation Co Inc.* (1988)[10] the Court of Appeal upheld a hire payment variation clause in a 5-year charterparty, which permitted the hire to be raised or reduced to reflect the ship's speed and efficiency. Adjustment should be 'mutually agreed' according to what was 'equitable'. It was held that the word 'equitable' was a clear enough criterion to permit objective assessment of the disputed hire payment. The parties had enjoyed significant dealings by the time this dispute arose (see **11.02** ff for illustrations).

(viii) The tribunal will not override the negotiating parties' clear reservation of the right to negotiate terms or a particular term. The principle of 'freedom of contract' (**10.04**) will then preclude the tribunal from imposing a contract. But restitutionary relief might be available if goods have been delivered or services performed.

---

[6] [2014] EWHC 2104 (Comm), at [64].

[7] *ibid*, at [64].

[8] K Lewison, *Interpretation of Contracts* (6th edn, London, 2015), 8.12, 8.13.

[9] *ibid*, 8.14.

[10] [1988] 2 Lloyd's Rep 108, CA (noted by Reynolds, (1988) 104 LQR 353), considering *Sudbrook Trading Estate Ltd* v. *Eggleton* [1983] 1 AC 444, HL; *Brown* v. *Gould* [1972] Ch 53, Megarry J (both contracts certain); and *Courtney* v. *Tolaini* [1975] 1 WLR 297, CA and *Mallozzi* v. *Carapelli SpA* [1976] 1 Lloyd's Rep 407, CA (both contracts uncertain).

(ix) Where the parties stipulate that a third party (or set of third parties) can fill a blank (for example, fix the price), it is a question of construction, assessed by reference to the commercial context, whether the specified third party resolution is essential to the parties' relations (if it is, the court cannot substitute its own objective determination).

11.02 *Examples of Sufficient Certainty*. In *Hillas & Co* v. *Arcos Ltd* (1932) the House of Lords upheld a 'repeat' contract.[11] Specification of timber delivered successfully in 1930 disclosed sufficient commercial guidance to regulate the repeat deal in 1931.

11.03 In *Malcolm* v. *University of Oxford* (1994)[12] a majority of the Court of Appeal held that a publisher's casual telephone commitment to publish an academic study was sufficiently certain even though the parties had yet to agree in writing on the detailed provisions of the publishing agreement and even though it was clear in the relevant context that final decisions about publications would normally be made by the senior advisors to the university press (known as 'The Delegates'). The decision is a surprisingly generous and extreme example of the courts heroically filling in large gaps in an oral agreement to publish a book.

11.04 The Court of Appeal held in *Durham Tees Valley Airport Ltd* v. *bmibaby Ltd* (2010),[13] despite the extreme brevity of the relevant undertaking, that the defendant's agreement to run a low-cost flight service at the claimant's airport for a period of 10 years by 'establishing a 2 based aircraft operation' was not void for uncertainty. Similarly, in *Jet2.com Ltd* v. *Blackpool Airport Ltd* (2012)[14] the Court of Appeal held that an airport was contractually committed to use best endeavours to promote a low-cost airline (Jet2's) business in running a service at BAL's airport. The contract should be construed (a) to prevent BAL from restricting Jet2's aircraft movements to (that provincial airport's) normal opening hours.

11.05 Another illustration is *Attrill* v. *Dresdner Kleinwort Ltd* (2013)[15] where the Court of Appeal held that the investment bank's assurance in the late summer of 2008 that in January 2009 traders would be entitled, on an individual discretionary basis, to a minimum bonus pool of Euros 400 million did not lack certainty.

11.06 *Examples of Insufficient Certainty*. The Court of Appeal in *Sulamerica Cia Nacional de Seguros SA* v. *Enesa Engenharia SA* (2012)[16] established that a mediation agreement will be valid in English law only if (i) the mediation clause is

---

[11] (1932) 147 LT 503; [1932] All ER 494, HL; Lord Thankerton's reference to an 'objective yardstick' was cited by Sir Andrew Morritt V-C in *Baird Textile Holdings Ltd* v. *Marks and Spencer plc* [2001] EWCA Civ 274; [2002] 1 All ER (Comm) 737, at [26] to [30].

[12] [1994] EMLR 17, CA.

[13] [2010] EWCA Civ 485; [2011] 1 All ER (Comm) 731; [2011] 1 Lloyd's Rep 68.

[14] [2012] EWCA Civ 417; [2012] 2 All ER (Comm) 1053; [2012] 1 CLC 605; Moore-Bick and Longmore LJJ (Lewison LJ dissenting).

[15] [2013] EWCA Civ 394; [2013] 3 All ER 807.

[16] [2012] EWCA Civ 638; [2013] 1 WLR 102; for criticism, Neil Andrews, 'Mediation Agreements: Time for a More Creative Approach by the English Courts' (2013) 18 Revue de droit uniforme 6–16 (also known as *Uniform Law Review*).

final and thus does not require any further negotiation over its own terms; (ii) the clause nominates a mediation provider or indicates how one is to be appointed; and (iii) the mediation process should be either already finalised under the rules of the agreed mediation provider or the parties must themselves supply minimum details. (No problem of certainty will arise if the mediation clause refers to a well-established institutional 'model' set of mediation rules, as in *Cable & Wireless* v. *IBM United Kingdom Ltd* (2002), where the mediation clause incorporated an institutional set of mediation rules,[17] containing a detailed process).[18]

11.07 In *Raffles* v. *Wichelhaus* (1864)[19] the purchase of a cargo of cotton was held probably to be void (following an appeal, the case was remitted to trial by jury) because there seemed to be no objective means of distinguishing between identical cargoes arriving from the same port and which were to be delivered to Liverpool on ships having the same name.

11.08 In *Scammell* v. *Ouston* (1941)[20] the House of Lords held that a very sketchy hire-purchase arrangement was void for uncertainty. it could not discern a clear enough transaction, only the shadowy beginnings of a real contract.

11.2 Writing

11.09 *EXCEPTIONAL NEED FOR WRITING*[21]

(i) *Most contracts are valid without writing.* The main exceptional situations, where the agreement needs[22] to be in writing, are:

(a) certain land transactions, in accordance with the Law of Property (Miscellaneous Provisions) Act 1989, section 2[23]; (b) guarantees of debts

---

[17] [2002] EWHC 2059 (Comm); [2002] 2 All ER (Comm) 1041; [2002] CLC 1319; [2003] BLR 89, at [21] *per* Colman J.

[18] *ibid.*

[19] (1864) 2 H & C 906; G Gilmore, *The Death of Contract* (Columbus, Ohio, 1974), 35 ff; AWB Simpson, *Leading Cases in the Common Law* (Oxford University Press, 1995), 135 ff; C MacMillan, *Mistakes in Contract Law* (Hart, Oxford, 2010), 186 ff; G Spark, *Vitiation of Contracts* (Cambridge University Press, 2013), chapter 7; on this 1864 decision, see '*The Great Peace*' [2003] QB 679, CA, at [28] and [29].

[20] [1941] AC 251, HL.

[21] J Cartwright, *Formation and Variation of Contracts* (London, 2014), Part II.

[22] For miscellaneous contexts where a written set of terms is required, but their absence does not invalidate the agreement itself: J Cartwright, *Formation and Variation of Contracts* (London, 2014), 5–39.

[23] J Cartwright, *Formation and Variation of Contracts* (London, 2014), 5–05 ff.

(see further **11.10**)[24]; (c) cheques and bills of exchange[25]; and bills of sale[26]; (d) certain credit agreements[27]; (e) arbitration agreements for the purpose of the Arbitration Act 1996 (England); (f) a contract of marine insurance[28]; (g) agreements in these contexts[29]: estate agents, claims management, distance or doorstep contracts affecting consumers, package travel contracts, timeshare and certain types of holiday accommodation.

(ii) *Unilateral Alteration of Deeds or Guarantees.* A deed or guarantee or other written instrument which is unilaterally and 'materially' altered without the other party's permission is rendered void.[30]

11.3 Guarantees (Surety Agreements): Nature

11.10 *CHARACTERISTICS OF GUARANTEES (SURETY AGREEMENTS)*[31]

(On the need for writing in this context, **11.09**; on the problem of unilateral alteration by the principal, **11.09**, at paragraph (ii); on setting aside of contracts of guarantee, **12.26**)

(i) A contract of guarantee, involving a surety agreement, arises where the primary debtor B owes money to the creditor C, and A, the guarantor or surety, undertakes to guarantee B's liability towards C. If B fails to pay C in full, C will be entitled to call upon A to pay C. The guarantor's liability is in damages for failure to ensure that B pays, or fully pays, C.

---

[24] Section 4, Statute of Frauds 1677; *Actionstrength Ltd* v. *International Glass Engineering INGLEN SpA* [2010] EWCA Civ 1477; [2012] 1 WLR 566. J Cartwright, *Formation and Variation of Contracts* (London, 2014), chapter 6; G Andrews and R Millett, *Law of Guarantees* (6th edn, London, 2011), chapter 3; JC Phillips, *The Modern Contract of Guarantee* (2nd edn, English edn, London, 2010), chapter 3; J Cartwright, *Formation and Variation of Contracts* (London, 2014), 6–07 ff. O *Gordon Ramsay* v. *Love* [2015] EWHC 65 (Ch), Morgan J, see text below **11.11**, at paragraph (ii) (relevant signature was an **automated** facsimile, using a fine nib and ink, of the human signatory's autograph; the autograph machine had been activated by Ramsay's manager with the principal's authority; and so the deed was effective).

[25] J Cartwright, *Formation and Variation of Contracts* (London, 2014), 5–36.

[26] On the Bills of Sale Act 1878 (as amended), *Online Catering Ltd* v. *Acton* [2010] EWCA Civ 58; [2011] QB 204 (applicable only to individuals and not to companies).

[27] J Cartwright, *Formation and Variation of Contracts* (London, 2014), 5–32.

[28] *ibid*, 6–19.

[29] J Cartwright, *Formation and Variation of Contracts* (London, 2014), 5-33, 5-34, 5-35, 5-37, 5-38.

[30] *Habibsons Bank Ltd* v. *Standard Chartered Bank (Hong Kong) Ltd* [2010] EWCA Civ 1335; [2011] QB 943, at [34], *per* Moore-Bick LJ.

[31] G Andrews and R Millett, *Law of Guarantees* (6th edn, London, 2011); JC Phillips, *The Modern Contract of Guarantee* (2nd edn, English edn, London, 2010).

(ii) A fundamental concept[32] is that the amount of the guarantor's duty to pay cannot exceed the amount of the outstanding balance between B and C. This was confirmed by the English High Court in 2010: '*The guarantor is only generally liable to the same extent that the principal is liable to the creditor.*'[33]

(iii) To the extent that A, the guarantor, pays C in discharge or partial discharge of B's liability to C, A will be entitled to recover from B

(iv) Such a guarantee must be in writing and signed by the guarantor.[34]

Range of Guarantees. When C makes a loan to B and A guarantees this loan, the obligation assumed by the guarantor, A, to the creditor, C, can take one of four forms[35]:

(a) A will be liable in damages on the basis that the guarantee is a 'see to it' type (A is promising that B will perform his obligations to C, and if he defaults that A will provide compensation);
(b) a conditional liability in debt (if B defaults, A will be liable to C for quantified or quantifiable sums);
(c) an indemnity (where A expressly promises to indemnify C for losses arising if B defaults); and
(d) a primary debtor obligation.

The first three forms of guarantor obligation are secondary obligations. This means that the guarantor is only obliged to compensate the creditor to the extent that the creditor has demonstrated liability on the part of the debtor. The general principle is that the guarantor is only liable to the extent, and in the event that, and subject to the same defences as, the principal (on the facts of this case, the Seller).

---

[32]The so-called co-extensiveness principle requires the guarantee payment to match the primary debt: (1) '*...the surety's liability is no greater and no less than that of the principal, in terms of amount, time for payment and the conditions under which the principal is liable*', G Andrews and R Millett, *Law of Guarantees* (6th edn, London, 2011), paragraph 6-002. (2) '*The surety's liability must not be different in kind or greater in extent debtor than that of the principal debtor*': see JC Phillips, *The Modern Contract of Guarantee* (2nd edn, English edn, London, 2010), paragraph 1-25; see also paragraphs 5.-152 to 5-171; (3) the same principle is examined in two articles in the English literature: J Steyn 'Guarantees—the Co-Extensiveness Principle' (1974) 90 LQR 246; R Else-Mitchell (1947) 63 LQR 355.

[33]*Vossloh AG* v. *Alpha Trains (UK) Ltd* [2010] EWHC 2443; [2011] 2 All ER (Comm) 307; 132 Con LR 32, at [24], *per* Sir William Blackburne; see also, eg, Goulding J in *Barclay* v. *Prospect Mortgages Ltd* [1974] 1 WLR 837, at 844.

[34]Section 4, Statute of Frauds 1677; *Actionstrength Ltd* v. *International Glass Engineering INGLEN SpA* [2010] EWCA Civ 1477; [2012] 1 WLR 566. J Cartwright, *Formation and Variation of Contracts* (London, 2014), chapter 6; G Andrews and R Millett, *Law of Guarantees* (6th edn, London, 2011), chapter 3; JC Phillips, *The Modern Contract of Guarantee* (2nd edn, English edn, London, 2010), chapter 3; J Cartwright, *Formation and Variation of Contracts* (London, 2014), 6–07 ff.

[35]*McGuinness* v. *Norwich and Peterborough Building Society* [2011] EWCA Civ 1286; [2012] BPIR 145, at [7].

The fourth form of obligation is a primary obligation. This means that the creditor can have primary recourse against the guarantor without having any obligation to exhaust his remedies against the debtor; and the liability owed by the guarantor is characterised as a debt. A creditor may pursue the guarantor described in a contract as a 'primary debtor' on the same grounds and under the same conditions as those applicable to the primary debtor (e.g. the seller). And so the guarantor will not be liable when general or special defences are available to the primary debtor under the contract.

Distinction between Accessory Liability and Joint Liability. Where A, although described as a 'primary debtor', is in fact merely a surety for B's liability towards C, A will be entitled to seek a *full indemnity* from B if A pays B's debt. This reflects the fact that B is the primary debtor and A is merely an accessory or secondary debtor. By contrast, where Y and Z are jointly and severally liable to X for £1 million, and Y pays £1 million to X, Y is entitled only to a contribution from Z (on these facts, £500,000, which is Z's share of the debt).

Nature of Primary Debtor Guarantee. If A is primary debtor surety vis-à-vis C, this has these effects: (i) the arrangement enables C to sue A without first having recourse to B, the principal debtor[36]; (ii) A remains liable in the situation where C in some minor way modifies or waives enforcement of the primary debt[37] (displacing the general and technical law[38] which would exonerate the guarantor if B and C alter the primary agreement.

Performance Bonds Distinguished. A primary debtor obligation should also be distinguished from a performance bond, which creates an autonomous obligation for the bond-grantor, nearly always a bank, to pay the bond-holder a sum in respect of an underlying transaction between the bond-holder and a third party. English law will give effect to a clear promise by A that it will pay C on a performance bond (or similar payment bond)[39] irrespective of the merits of the primary transaction between B and C.[40] But such a performance bond

---

[36] See remarks at first instance by Hoffmann LJ (sic) (too long to quote here) in *MS Fashions Ltd* v. *Bank of Credit and Commerce International SA* (*In Liquidation*) [1993] Ch 425, 436, upheld by the Court of Appeal.

[37] In *Berghoff Trading Ltd* v. *Swinbrook Developments Ltd* [2009] EWCA Civ 413; [2009] 2 Lloyd's Rep 233, at [25], Rix LJ explained: '*In the case of guarantors, the contract of guarantee with the creditor may often make the guarantor into a primary obligor,* ***in order to avoid the pitfalls of guaranties, such as their discharge by waiver and so on****. In the normal case, however, the fact that the guarantor is a primary obligor vis-a-vis the creditor does not ordinarily mean that he ceases to have only a secondary liability vis-a-vis the debtor.*'

[38] *Halsbury's Laws of England* (5th edn, London, 2008), vol 49, at paragraph [1214] summarises that technical law as follows: '[*Any*] *variation of the principal contract made without his consent discharges* [*the gurantor*] *from his guarantee, unless the variation is clearly insubstantial or obviously cannot prejudice him.*'

[39] e.g., advance payment bonds, as in *Kookmin Bank* v. *Rainy Sky SA* [2011] UKSC 50; [2011] 1 WLR 770.

[40] *Halsbury's Laws of England* (5th edn, London, 2008), vol 49, paragraphs 1271 ff.

does not sit alongside a guarantee.[41] Such bonds are made available for a fee, typically by banks or insurance companies.[42] The Court of Appeal in *Wuhan Guoyu etc* v. *Emporiki Bank of Greece SA* (2012) considered that it is easy to distinguish an on-demand instrument from a traditional guarantee.[43]

11.4 Deeds or Covenants

11.11 *DEEDS TO FORMALISE GRATUITOUS PROMISES*[44]

(i) A gratuitous promise can be rendered legally binding as a deed (also known as a 'covenant'). The requirements for a valid deed are[45]:

  (a) the document containing the relevant undertaking is signed by 'the covenantor', the promisor;
  (b) this signature is witnessed by a third party ('attestation'); and
  (c) the document is then activated by 'delivery' (this normally, but not necessarily, involves the document's physical transfer to the covenantee).

  Elements (b) and (c), especially element (b), distinguish a deed from an ordinary contract in writing which is signed (a so-called 'contract under hand') but not intended to operate as a deed.

(ii) As for element (i) (a), in *Gordon Ramsay* v. *Love* (2015)[46] Morgan J held that the celebrity chef had validly made a deed in which he had given a personal guarantee in respect of a lease to his company. The relevant signature was an automated facsimile, using a fine nib and ink, of the human signatory's autograph. That automated signature had been activated physically by the signatory's manager. The parties had conceded[47] that, provided Ramsay's manager had received authorisation to use the signature machine on this particular occasion, there would be a legally effective signature (the concession extended to the validity of the signature witness' attestation on these facts). Morgan J found

---

[41] *WS Tankship II BV* v. *The Kwangju Bank Ltd, Seoul Guarantee Insurance Company* [2011] EWHC 3103 (Comm); [2012] CILL 3155, at paragraphs [109] ff, Blair J.

[42] e.g., the insurance company in *General Surety & Guarantee Co Ltd* v. *Francis Parker Ltd* (1977) 6 BLR 18, which provided a performance bond in respect of a building contract.

[43] [2012] EWCA Civ 1629; [2013] 1 All ER (Comm) 1191, at [25] to [28], *per* Longmore LJ.

[44] J Cartwright, *Formation and Variation of Contracts* (London, 2014), chapter 7.

[45] Section 1(2)(3) Law of Property (Miscellaneous Provisions) Act 1989 (as amended by the Regulatory Reform (Execution of Deeds and Documents) Order 2005 (SI 2005/1906, art 7(3)); GH Treitel, *The Law of Contract* (12th edn, by E Peel, London, 2007), 3–164 ff; *Bolton MBC* v. *Torkington* [2004] Ch 66, CA.

[46] [2015] EWHC 65 (Ch), Morgan J.

[47] *ibid*, at [7].

that there had been such a specific authorisation. And so the deed was effective, even though an automated signature had been applied by the signatory's agent.

(iii) As for element (i) (b), there must be some attempt at attestation (the witness making a written declaration that he actually purported to have perceived the signature when it took place). And so, if the attestation was defective (the covenantor signed without the attesting party being present and the attesting was made too late), the deed might be regarded as operative by virtue of estoppel. In *Shah* v. *Shah* (2001), the Court of Appeal held that the covenantor's act of delivering an imperfect deed (imperfect because the deed was invalidly witnessed) to the covenantee created an estoppel by representation.[48] Here the relevant witness had not been in the same room at the time of the covenantor's signature, and that meant that there had been no contemporaneous witnessing of the act of signature. This involved non-compliance with section 1(3) of the Law of Property (Miscellaneous Provisions) Act 1989. This estoppel rendered effective the technically invalid deed. The covenantee's 'reliance' on the representation was his assumption that the deed was legally valid.

By contrast, estoppel cannot save a purported deed which, although signed by the covenantor, has not been attested by a witness in any manner. Here the deed is fatally flawed because there has been no attempt to obtain a witness' confirmation of the covenantor's having signed. And so the *Shah* case was distinguished in *Re Gleeds* (2014) where the relevant document did not contain any attempt at attestation by a witness of the covenantor's signature.[49]

11.5 The Consideration Doctrine

11.12 *CONSIDERATION: TESTING FOR BARGAINS*[50]

(i) *Bargain Needed in the Absence of a Deed.* Unless made as a deed, a gratuitous promise is not enforceable. There must be an element of 'bargain' supporting the relevant promise: the claimant must promise or do something, at the other's request, in order to earn and become entitled to sue the defendant on a promise. This is the Common Law test of 'consideration'. (The contract must also satisfy the requirement of 'intent to create legal relations' **11.14** and certainty **11.01**, and must not be illegal or contrary to public policy, **11.17**).

---

[48] [2001] 4 All ER 138, CA, at [30] ff.

[49] *Re Gleeds, Briggs* v. *Gleeds* [2014] EWHC 1178 (Ch); [2015] Ch 212, Newey J, at [40], [43]; and cf *Actionstrength Ltd* v. *International Glass Engineering In. Gl.En SpA* [2003] UKHL 17; [2003] 2 AC 541, HL (oral guarantee ineffective and does not give rise to an estoppel: see [8] to [9], [26] to [29], [34] to [35] and [51], distinguishing *Shah* v. *Shah*).

[50] J Cartwright, *Formation and Variation of Contracts* (London, 2014), chapter 8.

(ii) *Anatomy of a Bargain*. Consideration (see (i) above) to support the defendant's promise to the claimant can arise:

(a) where the parties exchange valid promises (an 'executory' bilateral contract); or
(b) where the claimant has incurred some detriment requested by the defendant; or
(c) at the defendant's request, the claimant has conferred a benefit on the defendant or on a third party.

11.13 *NOMINAL CONSIDERATION*[51]

(i) There is no testing of the adequacy of consideration: parties can make a bargain by use of nominal consideration. The latter is a token item given or promised in exchange for the defendant's promise as a symbolic exchange or bargain (provided there is an 'intent to create legal relations': **11.14**).
(ii) Therefore, by resort to *nominal* consideration it is possible to bypass the formalities of a deed and convert a gratuitous promise (a promise given without anything of substance being exchanged) into a binding agreement.

11.6 Intent to Create Legal Relations

11.14 *NATURE OF THE 'INTENT TO CREATE LEGAL RELATIONS' REQUIREMENT*[52]

The 'intent to create legal relations' doctrine operates in tandem with the doctrine of consideration (**11.12**). In the absence of a deed (**11.11**), the claimant must show not only that the promise satisfies the notion of a bargain (the element of 'consideration', **11.12**), but that the promise was made and received in circumstances objectively consistent with an 'intent to create legal relations'.

11.15 *INTENT TO CREATE LEGAL RELATIONS READILY INFERRED WITHIN COMMERCIAL CONTEXTS*

(i) There is a strong presumption that a commercial agreement is intended to create legal relations, but consideration must also be shown (**11.12**) (see **11.16** for the qualification that the presumption exists only if there is a manifest promise). Megaw J in *Edwards* v. *Skyways Ltd* (1964) expressed this as the starting point,[53] and Aikens LJ echoed this in *Barbudev* v. *Eurocom Cable Management Bulgaria Eood* (2012)[54]: '*In a commercial context, the onus of demonstrating that there was a lack of intention to create legal relations lies on the party*

[51] *ibid*, 8-25 to 8-35.

[52] *ibid*, 3-09 to 3-12.

[53] [1964] 1 WLR 349, 354-5.

[54] [2012] EWCA Civ 548; [2012] 2 All ER (Comm) 963, at [30].

asserting it and it is a heavy one.' For example, the Court of Appeal in *Attrill* v. *Dresdner Kleinwort Ltd* (2013)[55] held that an investment bank's announcement to its workforce that the bank would be creating a guaranteed minimum 400 million Euro bonus chest disclosed an objective intent to create legal relations. The bank's workforce had reasonably concluded that this was a binding commitment.[56]

(ii) This presumption can be rebutted in any of the following ways:
(a) use of the formula 'subject to contract' (see (iii) and (iv) below), or (b) use of 'honour clauses' or (c) statute might reverse the presumption, as in the case of collective agreements between trade unions and employers or employers' associations.[57]

(iii) *Express use of 'subject to contract'*. If parties to negotiation agree, or one party notifies clearly to the other, that their current dealings are 'subject to contract' (or a similar expression), this will preclude the finding of a contract in relation to those dealings.[58] For a qualification, see (iv) below.

(iv) The Supreme Court in *RTS Flexible Systems Ltd* v. *Molkerei Alois Müller GmbH* (2010) held that the parties' conduct can objectively manifest an intention to displace the 'subject to contract' reservation, notably when there have been substantial dealings which are commercially inconsistent with survival of the 'subject to contract' provision and it is clear that the parties have resolved all points of negotiation.[59]

11.16 *ABSENCE OF A REAL CONTRACTUAL COMMITMENT*

The Court of Appeal's decision in *Baird Textile Holdings Ltd* v. *Marks & Spencer plc* (2001)[60] shows that the 'commercial' presumption of enforceability cannot apply unless the court can first identify an 'explicit' or 'apparent' promise. that is, a clear commitment. For example: (a) a 'letter of comfort' (a parent company's vague indication of its current policy to satisfy its subsidiary's debts, as examined in *Kleinwort Benson* v. *Malaysian Mining*, 1989)[61] does not disclose such a promise. (b) Nor will an open-ended and non-committal pattern of dealings between merchants disclose a hard-edged commitment to maintain legal relations.

---

[55] [2013] EWCA Civ 394; [2013] 3 All ER 807.

[56] *ibid*, at [61], [62], [86], [87], *per* Elias LJ.

[57] Section 178, Trade Union and Labour Relations (Consolidation) Act 1992.

[58] J Cartwright, *Formation and Variation of Contracts* (London, 2014), 2-08; K Lewison, *Interpretation of Contracts* (6th edn, London, 2015), 16-03 to 16-05; G McMeel, *The Construction of Contracts: Interpretation, Implication and Rectification* (2nd edn, Oxford University Press, 2011), 14.14 ff.

[59] [2010] UKSC 14; [2010] 1 WLR 753.

[60] [2001] EWCA Civ 274; [2002] 1 All ER (Comm) 737, at [59] to [70], *per* Mance LJ.

[61] [1989] 1 All ER 785, CA.

11.7 Illegality and Public Policy

11.17 For reasons of space the reader is referred to the author's detailed analysis of this topic elsewhere.[62] For the particular issue concerning refusal of recognition and enforcement of arbitral awards on grounds of public policy, see the present text at **9.11**.

11.8 Third Parties and Assignment

11.18 The Contracts (Rights of Third Parties) Act 1999 (England and Wales) enables third parties to acquire rights of action and other contractual benefits under contracts to which they are not party.[63] The 1999 Act creates a large statutory exception to the Common Law doctrine of 'privity of contract'. That Common Law doctrine does not recognise or give effect to such third party rights or contractual benefits.[64] For discussion of section 8(1) and section 8(2) of the 1999 Act concerning rights to arbitrate, see **2.62–2.65**. It is important to note that the Act does not wholly abrogate the Common Law position, although the Common Law is now substantially tempered by the Act. The 1999 Act does not disturb the rights and remedies exercisable by the promisee as against the promisor.[65] It should also be noted that X's promise to, and for the benefit of, Y might be assigned by Y to Z (Y is then the assignor and Z the assignee who has a direct claim against X, the promisor, for example, a claim in debt).[66]

[62] Neil Andrews, *Contract Law* (2nd edn, Cambridge University Press, 2015), chapter 20.

[63] **M Furmston and G Tolhurst, *Privity of Contract* (Oxford University Press, 2015).**

[64] *ibid.*

[65] *ibid.*

[66] AG Guest, *Guest on the Law of Assignment* (2nd edn, London, 2015); M Smith and N Leslie, *The Law of Assignment* (2nd edn, Oxford University Press, 2013); G Tolhurst, *The Assignment of Contractual Rights* (Hart, Oxford, 2006).

Chapter 12
Misrepresentation and Coercion

Abstract The most common basis for seeking to set aside ('rescind') a contract is pre-contractual misrepresentation, which forms the heart of this chapter. There are exceptional duties to disclose. Other grounds of vitiation (forming the basis of setting aside, that is, rescinding a contract) are duress, undue influence, and unconscionability.

12.1 Misrepresentation

12.01 *THINGS SAID BEFORE THE CONTRACT'S FORMATION.* The main vitiating factor is misrepresentation (**12.04** below) but in practice that topic overlaps with the issue whether a pre-contractual statement gives rise to a binding contractual assurance enabling the promisee to obtain contractual damages. And so, before addressing misrepresentation, it is necessary to consider the criteria governing the possible treatment of such assurances as collateral warranties or contractual terms. It is also possible that a particular assurance or statement might be concurrently classified as a contractual term (or a collateral warranty) and a misrepresentation (see the next paragraph).

12.02 *MISREPRESENTATIONS AND BINDING ASSURANCES*

(i) A pre-formation statement might give rise to contractual liability if it is classified as (a) a collateral contract ('collateral warranty')[1] (that is, a side contract subsisting independently of the main contract) or (b) if it becomes a term of the main contract.[2]

(ii) A misrepresentation can subsist concurrently as a misrepresentation and a contractual term of the main contract. According to section 1(a) of the Misrepresentation Act 1967, even if (as occasionally occurs) a misrepresentation becomes a term of the eventual contract (allowing contractual damages to

[1] KW Wedderburn, 'Collateral Contracts' [1959] CLJ 58; Paterson, *Collateral Warranties Explained* (London, 1991); DW Greig, (1971) 87 LQR 179.

[2] J Cartwright, *Misrepresentation, Mistake and Non-Disclosure* (3rd edn, London, 2012), chapter 8; *Spencer Bower, Turner and Handley's Actionable Misrepresentation* (5th edn, London, 2014), 2.12.

N. Andrews, *Arbitration and Contract Law*, Ius Gentium: Comparative Perspectives on Law and Justice 54, DOI 10.1007/978-3-319-27144-6_12

be awarded), it can simultaneously subsist as a misrepresentation for the purpose of the remedy of rescission.[3]

(iii) Rescission of the main contract precludes a claim to compensation for breach of contract, unless (see (i)(a) above) there is a collateral contract ('collateral warranty').[4]

12.03 *Criteria for Finding 'Contractual Assurances'*. The test governing the finding of a collateral warranty remains strict (despite Lord Denning's suggestion in *Howard Marine* v. *Ogden* (1978) that a more flexible approach be adopted).[5] *Business Environment Bow Lane Ltd* v. *Deanwater Estates Ltd* (2007)[6] (below) exemplifies this strict approach. There the Court of Appeal cited Lord Moulton's seminal comment in the *Heilbut, Symons* case (1913)[7]: '*Such collateral contracts, the sole effect of which is to vary or add to the terms of the principal contract, are therefore viewed with suspicion by the law. They must be proved strictly. ...Any laxity on these points would...have the effect of lessening the authority of written contracts.*' In fact the courts have now watered down Lord Moulton's remarks. In particular, the courts will apply the following criteria[8]:

(1) was the representee entitled reasonably to assume that the statement was being warranted, that is, guaranteed to be contractually binding[9] (see, for example, *Yam Seng Pte Ltd* v. *International Trade Corp Ltd*, 2013)[10];
(2) did the representee made plain that the matter was crucial to him[11];
(3) was it obvious from the circumstances that the matter was crucial to the representee; for example, in *City & Westminster Properties (1934) Ltd* v. *Mudd* (1959), the landlord had assured a prospective tenant that he would be free to sleep in the demised business premises at night, despite the prohibition contained in one of the written covenants in the lease; Harman J, noting that

---

[3] J Cartwright, *Misrepresentation, Mistake and Non-Disclosure* (3rd edn, London, 2012), 4-38; *Spencer Bower, Turner and Handley's Actionable Misrepresentation* (5th edn, London, 2014), 15-03.

[4] J Cartwright, *Misrepresentation, Mistake and Non-Disclosure* (3rd edn, London, 2012), 2-12; *Spencer Bower, Turner and Handley's Actionable Misrepresentation* (5th edn, London, 2014), 14-08, 14-09.

[5] *Howard Marine and Dredging Co Ltd* v. *A Ogden & Sons (Excavations) Ltd* [1978] QB 574, 590G, CA.

[6] [2007] EWCA Civ 622; [2007] L & TR 26, at [23].

[7] *Heilbut, Symons & Co* v. *Buckleton* [1913] AC 30, 47, HL (see also Lord Haldane at 37–9); citing *Chandelor* v. *Lopes* (1603) Cro Jac 4; explained by Denning LJ in the *Oscar Chess* case, [1957] 1 WLR 370, CA; see also *Hopkins* v. *Tanqueray* (1854) 15 CB (NS) 130.

[8] Cf the farrago of factors successfully enumerated by counsel in the *Howard Marine* case, [1978] QB 574, 583, CA.

[9] *Thake* v. *Maurice* [1986] QB 644, CA (3.71); reasonableness is also a factor in the tort of negligent mis-statement: *Williams* v. *Natural Life & Health Foods* [1998] 1 WLR 830, 837, HL.

[10] [2013] EWHC 111 (QB); [2013] 1 All ER (Comm) 1321; [2013] 1 Lloyd's Rep 526, at [98].

[11] e.g., *Bannerman* v. *White* (1861) 10 CB (NS) 844 (prospective buyer asking whether sulphur had been used in cultivation of hops; seller saying 'no'; but it was clear that the purchaser would have walked away if the hops had been sulphurated; therefore the assurance had contractual effect).

inability to sleep on site had been a potential 'deal-breaker', gave effect to this oral assurance by preventing the landlord from terminating the lease for breach of the written non-residential covenant[12];

(4) what was the relative skill, knowledge and expertise of the parties[13]; in *Dick Bentley Productions* v. *Harold Smith (Motors)* (1965),[14] the Court of Appeal held that a car dealer's statement that a car had covered 20,000 miles since a new engine had been fitted was a contractual warranty; but the car's true mileage since that engine had been fitted was 100,000 (see also *Esso Petroleum Ltd* v. *Mardon* (1976))[15]; by contrast, in *Oscar Chess Ltd* v. *Williams* (1957),[16] no warranty was established when a private vendor, basing himself on a logbook which had been forged by a third party, said in good faith that a car was a 1948 model, when in fact it was a 1939 model; the buyer was an experienced car dealer;
(5) had the representor asked the representee to verify the matter for himself[17];
(6) did the representor assure the other that such verification was unnecessary?[18]

12.04 *ESSENCE OF A MISREPRESENTATION*[19]

A misrepresentation is an inaccurate statement of past or present fact or 'law'[20] concerning a material matter (that is, a comment which, objectively, is apt to influence a reasonable person)[21] which induces the other party to enter into the contract.

---

[12] [1959] Ch 129, 145–6, Harman J.

[13] *Harlingdon & Leinster Enterprises* v. *Christopher Hull Fine Article* [1991] 1 QB 564, CA (where the purchaser was an expert and placed no reliance on the seller's attribution of a work of art to a particular painter).

[14] [1965] 1 WLR 623, CA.

[15] [1976] QB 801, CA.

[16] [1957] 1 WLR 370, CA (Morris LJ dissenting).

[17] *Ecay* v. *Godfrey* [1947] Lloyd's Rep 286, Lord Goddard CJ (seller of second-hand boat making clear his belief that the purchaser would have it surveyed first); cf (see next note) in *Schawel* v. *Reade* [1913] 2 IR 64, HL.

[18] *Schawel* v. *Reade* [1913] 2 IR 64, HL ('you need not look for anything; the horse is perfectly sound. If there were anything the matter with the horse, I should tell you.').

[19] J Cartwright, *Misrepresentation, Mistake and Non-Disclosure* (3rd edn, London, 2012), chapters 2 and 3; D O'Sullivan, S Elliott and R Zakrzewski, *The Law of Rescission* (Oxford University Press, 2008), chapter 4; *Spencer Bower, Turner and Handley's Actionable Misrepresentation* (5th edn, London, 2014).

[20] Misstatements of law will count: *Re Gleeds [2014] EWHC 1178 (Ch); [2015] Ch 212, at [35], per Newey J, Brennan* v. *Bolt Burdon* [2004] EWCA Civ 1017; [2005] QB 303 approving Judge Rex Tedd QC in *Pankhania* v. *Hackney London Borough Council* [2002] EWHC 2441 (Ch), at [58]; J Cartwright, *Misrepresentation, Mistake and Non-Disclosure* (3rd edn, London, 2012), 3.20 ff.

[21] *Museprime Properties Ltd* v. *Adhill Properties Ltd* (1991) 61 P & CR 111, CA; Mance LJ in *MCI Worldcom International Inc* v. *Primus Telecommunications plc* [2004] EWCA Civ 957; [2004] All ER (Comm) 833, at [30].

12.05 *MISREPRESENTATION BY WORDS OR CONDUCT*[22]

The misrepresentation is normally a statement by words but can be a representation by conduct, or a combination of these.

12.06 *MERE OPINION*[23]

(i) The inaccurate statement (unless fraudulent, **12.07**) should not involve the assertion of a mere matter of opinion.

(ii) But a person's statement (even if not made fraudulently) might imply that he is not aware of current facts (matters known to him) which tend to contradict the impression made by that statement. If so, that implication can give rise to a misrepresentation. In *Smith* v. *Land and House Property Co* (1884),[24] a vendor of a property which was subject to a commercial tenancy misleadingly declared that the tenant was 'most desirable' but in fact this tenant had recently been very slow indeed to pay the rent on this property. The Court of Appeal found this to be a statement of fact. As for lack of experience, the clearest example is *Bisset* v. *Wilkinson* (1927)[25] which concerned a vendor's statement concerning a farm in New Zealand (in that jurisdiction sheep greatly outnumber the human population). In that case the vendor said that the land to be sold would have a capacity to support 2,000 sheep, if the land were converted to a sheep-farm. The Privy Council held that this did not count as a representation of fact. The court emphasised that it was apparent to the representee that the vendor was making a guess and not relying on any knowledge, skill, experience or expert report from a third party source.

12.07 *Fraudulent Statements of Opinion.* Where the representor fraudulently states that he holds an opinion (and so he lies about his current belief), a misrepresentation of fact occurs with respect to the representor's state of mind or belief. As Bowen LJ said in *Edgington* v. *Fitzmaurice* (1885): '*...the state of a man's mind is as much a fact as the state of his digestion. It is true that it is very difficult to prove what the state of a man's mind at a particular time is, but if it can be ascertained it is as much a fact as anything else.*'[26]

---

[22] J Cartwright, *Misrepresentation, Mistake and Non-Disclosure* (3rd edn, London, 2012), 3-03; *Spencer Bower, Turner and Handley's Actionable Misrepresentation* (5th edn, London, 2014), 4-23.

[23] J Cartwright, *Misrepresentation, Mistake and Non-Disclosure* (3rd edn, London, 2012), 3-14 to 3-19, 3-45 ff; *Spencer Bower, Turner and Handley's Actionable Misrepresentation* (5th edn, London, 2014), 2-18 to 2-023.

[24] (1884) 28 Ch D 7, CA (considered in *IEE Fund SA* v. *Goldman Sachs International* [2007] EWCA Civ 811; [2007] 2 Lloyd's Rep 449, citing also *Hummingbird Motors Ltd* v. *Hobbs* [1986] RTR 276, CA, and *Sumitomo Bank Ltd* v. *BBL* [1997] 1 Lloyd's Rep 487, Langley J; and see *Dimmock* v. *Hallett* (1866) LR 2 Ch App 21).

[25] [1927] AC 177, PC; similarly, *Economides* v. *Commercial Union Assurance Co plc* [1998] QB 587, CA (noted MA Clarke, [1998] CLJ 24 and H Bennett, (1998) 61 MLR 886–98); *Royal Bank of Scotland plc* v. *Chandra* [2011] EWCA Civ 192; [2011] NPC 26; [2011] Bus LR D149, notably at [36] and [37].

[26] *Edgington* v. *Fitzmaurice* (1885) 29 Ch D 459, 483, CA, *per* Bowen LJ.

12.08 *IMMATERIAL FALSITY*[27]

The allegedly misleading statement must not be false in a trivial sense, having regard to the totality of the pre-formation information supplied by the representor.

12.09 *STATEMENT BECOMING FALSE BEFORE FORMATION*[28]

Where, before the contract is formed, an initially accurate statement becomes false because of a change of circumstances, the representor will be treated as having made a misrepresentation if (also before formation) he became aware of the falsification but failed to draw any necessary correction to the representee's attention.

One view (adopted by Romer LJ and Clauson J, and supported by Lord Wright MR, in *With* v. *O'Flanagan*, 1936)[29] is that the representor becomes liable if he discovers the change before the contract's formation but fails to correct his earlier statement. Many cases have emphasised the element of bad faith.[30] This can be analysed as breach of a continuing implied representation that the representor honestly continues to believe his statement.[31]

12.10 *RELIANCE*[32]

The representee must be both (a) aware of the statement and (b) decisively influenced by the representation. There is, however, an exception to (b) if the statement was made fraudulently: in the case of a fraudulent misrepresentation, it is enough that the information affected the mind of the representee without necessarily having any causal influence on his decision to enter the contract (but this fraud exception applies only where the relief sought is rescission, as distinct from damages for deceit).

12.11 *REMEDIAL CONSEQUENCES*[33]

---

[27] J Cartwright, *Misrepresentation, Mistake and Non-Disclosure* (3rd edn, London, 2012), 3-05 to 3-08; *Spencer Bower, Turner and Handley's Actionable Misrepresentation* (5th edn, London, 2014), 4-04, 4-05.

[28] J Cartwright, *Misrepresentation, Mistake and Non-Disclosure* (3rd edn, London, 2012), 4-27, 4-28; *Spencer Bower, Turner and Handley's Actionable Misrepresentation* (5th edn, London, 2014), 4-10, 4-11.

[29] [1936] Ch 575, 586, CA, and supported by R Bigwood, [2005] CLJ 94.

[30] In *Banks* v. *Cox* [2002] EWHC (Ch) 2166, at [4], Lawrence Collins J held that this is a case of fraud; see also *Fitzroy Robinson Ltd* v. *Mentmore Towers Ltd* [2009] EWHC 1552 (TCC); [2009] EWHC 1552 (TCC); [2009] BLR 505; 125 Con LR 171; [2009] NPC 90, at [173], *per* Coulson J (knowledge that a vital project manager, despite earlier statement, would no longer be available); *Foodco Uk LLP* v. *Henry Boot Developments Limited* [2010] EWHC 358 (Ch), at [208] to [215], *per* Lewison J; *Erlson Precision Holdings Ltd* v. *Hampson Industries plc* [2011] EWHC 1137 (Comm), at [43], *per* Field J (sufficient that party A knows that there has been a change; no further requirement that A should know that there is a legal duty for A to correct the false impression).

[31] *IFE Fund SA* v. *Goldman Sachs* [2007] EWCA Civ 811; [2007] 2 Lloyd's Rep 449; [2007] 2 CLC 134, at [74], *per* Gage LJ; and at first instance, Toulson J in [2006] EWHC 2887 (Comm); [2007] 1 Lloyd's Rep 264; [2006] 2 CLC 1043, at [60].

[32] J Cartwright, *Misrepresentation, Mistake and Non-Disclosure* (3rd edn, London, 2012), 3-50 ff; *Spencer Bower, Turner and Handley's Actionable Misrepresentation* (5th edn, London, 2014), chapter 6.

[33] J Cartwright, *Misrepresentation, Mistake and Non-Disclosure* (3rd edn, London, 2012), chapters 4–7; *Spencer Bower, Turner and Handley's Actionable Misrepresentation* (5th edn, London, 2014), chapters 12–17.

(i) The two remedies which might (depending on the facts) be applicable following a misrepresentation are: (a) the mutual dismantling of the parties' benefits received under the contract (known as 'rescission *ab initio*'); and/or (b) damages.
(ii) As for (i)(a), rescission is available whether or not the representation was culpable (but on the possible 'bars' to rescission, see **12.14** below).
(iii) As for (i)(b), damages are available as of right only if (1) the misrepresentation is fraudulent (the tort of deceit, **12.12**), or (2) the misrepresentation is negligent at Common Law (the tort of negligent misstatement), or (3) the representor is liable under section 2(1) of the Misrepresentation Act 1967, a statutory tort (because of its pro-representee strategic importance, section 2(1) is explained separately at **12.13** below).

12.12 *DECEIT*

The tort of deceit requires a representation to be made without an honest belief in its accuracy. Failure to take care to verify is not enough to constitute deceit, provided the representor has the honest belief that what he asserts is true. In *Derry* v. *Peek* (1889), the House of Lords made clear that the *absence of an honest belief* is the essence of a fraudulent misrepresentation.[34] As for the measure of damages for deceit,[35] Lord Browne-Wilkinson explained in the leading decision, the *Smith New Court* case (1997)[36]: '*[T]he defendant is bound to make reparation for all the damage directly flowing from the transaction; although such damage need not have been foreseeable, it must have been directly caused by the transaction ... In addition, the plaintiff is entitled to recover consequential losses caused by the transaction.*'[37]

12.13 *STATUTORY DAMAGES FOR CULPABLE MISREPRESENTATION*[38]

Section 2(1) of the Misrepresentation Act 1967 (a statutory tort) is the representee's favoured source of compensation for two reasons: (a) damages awarded are equivalent to those available for deceit (**12.12** above); and (b) once the claimant shows that the statement is false, the burden of proof rests on the representor to show he had reasonable grounds for making the statement.

---

[34] *Derry* v. *Peek* (1889) 14 App Cas 337, 374, HL.

[35] For the criticism that damages for deceit are too robustly defined and computed, J Devenney, 'Re-Examining Damages for Fraudulent Misrepresentation', in L DiMatteo, Q Zhou, S Saintier, K Rowley (eds), *Commercial Contract Law: Transatlantic Perspectives* (Cambridge University Press, 2014), chapter 17.

[36] *Smith New Court Securities Ltd* v. *Scrimgeour Vickers (Asset Management) Ltd* [1997] AC 254, 266–7, HL, *per* Lord Browne-Wilkinson; *Banks* v. *Cox* [2002] EWHC (Ch) 2166, at [13] ff, *per* Lawrence Collins J.

[37] e.g., the facts of *Doyle* v. *Olby (Ironmongers) Ltd* [1969] 2 QB 158, CA.

[38] J Cartwright, *Misrepresentation, Mistake and Non-Disclosure* (3rd edn, London, 2012), chapter 7; *Spencer Bower, Turner and Handley's Actionable Misrepresentation* (5th edn, London, 2014), chapter 13.

As for element (a), the Court of Appeal in *Royscot* v. *Rogerson* (1991)[39] held that the courts must give effect to the so-called 'fiction of fraud' contained in section 2(1) of the 1967 Act (namely, the parenthetical phrase within section 2(1) which reads: '*if the person making the misrepresentation would be liable in respect thereof had the misrepresentation been made fraudulently* ...'). This curious 'fiction' dispenses with the general remoteness test applicable to negligence claims in tort (the 'reasonable foreseeability' formulation of a remoteness test).[40] And so the representee can recover his loss, however unforeseeable, provided this loss is causally related to the misrepresentation; in other words, provided 'the chain of causation' has not been broken. In *Yam Seng Pte Ltd* v. *International Trade Corp Ltd* (2013) Leggatt J said that he did not consider that the *Royscot* case's interpretation of section 2(1) was correct, but he acknowledged that it is binding Court of Appeal authority on the need to quantify such damages as though fraud had been established.[41]

> *Section 2(1) reads: Where a person has entered into a contract after a misrepresentation has been made to him by another party thereto and as a result thereof he has suffered loss, then, if the person making the misrepresentation would be liable in respect thereof had the misrepresentation been made fraudulently, that person shall be so liable notwithstanding that the misrepresentation was not made fraudulently, unless he proves that he had reasonable ground to believe and did believe up to the time the contract was made that the facts represented were true.*

12.14 *RESCISSION BARRED*[42]

Rescission is subject to the following four general equitable 'bars', any of which will be sufficient to preclude rescission:

(i) inability to restore the parties in a practical sense to the pre-formation position ('*restitutio in integrum* impossible');
(ii) the subject matter of the contract between A and B has been acquired in good faith by a sub-purchaser;
(iii) affirmation of the contract by the representee; or
(iv) lapse of time rendering it unjust for the contract to be dismantled by rescission.

12.15 *STATUTORY DISCRETION TO WITHHOLD RESCISSION*[43]

---

[39] [1991] 2 QB 297, CA.

[40] *'The Wagon Mound'* [1961] AC 388, PC (summarised by Lord Rodger in *Simmons* v. *British Steel plc* [2004] UKHL 20; [2004] ICR 585, at [67]).

[41] [2013] EWHC 111 (QB); [2013] 1 All ER (Comm) 1321; [2013] 1 Lloyd's Rep 526, at [206].

[42] J Cartwright, *Misrepresentation, Mistake and Non-Disclosure* (3rd edn, London, 2012), 4-38 ff; *Spencer Bower, Turner and Handley's Actionable Misrepresentation* (5th edn, London, 2014), 17-08 ff; D O'Sullivan, S Elliott and R Zakrewski, *The Law of Rescission* (Oxford University Press, 2007), chapters 13 ff; Neil H Andrews, MA Clarke, AM Tettenborn, G Virgo, *Contractual Duties: Performance, Breach, Termination and Remedies* (London, 2012), chapters 3 and 4 (by G Virgo).

[43] J Cartwright, *Misrepresentation, Mistake and Non-Disclosure* (3rd edn, London, 2012), 4-61 ff; *Spencer Bower, Turner and Handley's Actionable Misrepresentation* (5th edn, London, 2014), 15-07 ff.

Even if the misrepresentation is wholly innocent, the tribunal has discretion to award damages instead of allowing the contract to be rescinded (section 2(2) of the 1967 Act). However, this discretion does not apply if the statement was fraudulent.

Section 2(2) reads: Where a person has entered into a contract after a misrepresentation has been made to him otherwise than fraudulently, and he would be entitled, by reason of the misrepresentation, to rescind the contract, then, if it is claimed, in any proceedings arising out of the contract, that the contract ought to be or has been rescinded, the court or arbitrator may declare the contract subsisting and award damages in lieu of rescission, if of opinion that it would be equitable to do so, having regard to the nature of the misrepresentation and the loss that would be caused by it if the contract were upheld, as well as to the loss that rescission would cause to the other party.

12.2 Misrepresentation and Exclusion Clauses

12.16 *EXCLUSION CLAUSES CONCERNING MISREPRESENTATION*

(i) The Common Law prevents a party from excluding or limiting liability for fraudulent misstatements.[44]

(ii) There is also a statutory control upon exclusion clauses which purport to exclude or restrict liability in respect of a misrepresentation.[45]

(iii) **The following clauses (in non-consumer contracts) are subject to the resonableness test contained in section 3(1) of the Misrepresentation Act 1967** (the Court of Appeal in the *Springwell* case confirms that (a) to (c) are covered by section 3(1) of the 1967 Act)[46]:

(a) a 'no representations made clause' (that is, a clause providing that there have not been any representations made by a party concerning the relevant transaction);

(b) a 'mere opinion/non-verification clause' (that is, a clause stating that a party has not assumed any responsibility for any representations made); and

(c) a 'non-reliance clause' (that is, a clause providing that there has been no reliance on any representation).

---

[44] J Cartwright, *Misrepresentation, Mistake and Non-Disclosure* (3rd edn, London, 2012), 9.13, 9.14; *Spencer Bower, Turner and Handley's Actionable Misrepresentation* (5th edn, London, 2014), 11.10 see also 8.10, 18.13 ff.

[45] As for Propositions (ii) to (iv): J Cartwright, *Misrepresentation, Mistake and Non-Disclosure* (3rd edn, London, 2012), 9.18 ff; K Lewison, *Interpretation of Contracts* (6th edn, London, 2015), 3.16; G McMeel, *The Construction of Contracts: Interpretation, Implication and Rectification* (2nd edn, Oxford University Press, 2011), chapter 26; *Spencer Bower, Turner and Handley's Actionable Misrepresentation* (5th edn, London, 2014), 13.08 to 13.12.

[46] *Springwell Navigation Corporation* v. *JP Morgan Chase* [2010] EWCA Civ 1221; [2010] 2 CLC 705.

(iv) The following clauses (appearing in non-consumer contracts) are not subject to the reasonableness test contained in section 3(1) of the Misrepresentation Act 1967:

(e) an entire agreement clause: such a clause states that the parties' contractual obligations are to be found only within the four corners of the written contract[47] and not in any side or prior agreement. Such a clause does not fall within the scope of section 3 of the Misrepresentation Act 1967 because that provision concerns only attempts to exclude or restrict liability *for 'misrepresentation'* as distinct from contractual liability arising from breach of warranty[48]; but a clause could be hybrid, and be intended simultaneously (a) to preclude collateral warranties and (b) to exclude or restrict liability for a misrepresentation. Element (b) must be spelt out clearly, as Rix LJ explained in the *AXA* case (2011).[49]

(f) A 'lack of agent's authority' clause: Brightman J in *Overbrooke Estates* v. *Glencombe Properties Ltd* (1974) held that section 3(1) of the 1967 Act does not cover a clause which denies that a party's agent has authority to make statements affecting the principal.[50] (This point should be revisited: the better view is that section 3(1) should apply because otherwise the salutary statutory control will be too readily evaded.)

Section 3(1) of the Misrepresentation Act 1967 is applicable to all types of contract except (1) consumer contracts[51] and (2) contracts for the international supply of goods.[52] Section 3(1) (as reformulated by section 75 and Schedule 4 paragraph 1 of the Consumer Rights Act 2015) states:

> *Avoidance of provision excluding liability for misrepresentation: If a contract contains a term which would exclude or restrict—(a) any liability to which a party to a contract may be subject by reason of any misrepresentation made by him before the contract was made or (b) any remedy available to another party to the contract by reason of such a misrepresentation, that term shall be of no effect except in so far as it satisfies the requirement of*

---

[47] *Deepak Fertilisers & Petrochemicals Corp* v. *ICI Chemicals and Polymers Ltd* [1999] 1 Lloyd's Rep 387, 395, CA (noted by Gloster J in *Six Continents Hotels Inc* v. *Event Hotels GmbH* [2006] EWHC 2317 (QB), at [49]); D McLaughlan, 'The Entire Agreement Clause…' (2012) 128 LQR 521–540; M Barber, 'The Limits of Entire Agreement Clauses' [2012] JBL 486–503.

[48] *Inntrepreneur Pub Company (GL)* v. *East Crown Ltd* [2000] 2 Lloyd's Rep 611, Lightman J, adopting *McGrath* v. *Shah* (1987) 57 P & CR 452 (Chadwick QC sitting as a Deputy High Court judge); *Six Continents Hotels Inc* v. *Event Hotels GmbH* [2006] EWHC 2317 (QB), at [49], *per* Gloster J, citing *Deepak Fertilisers* v. *ICI Chemicals* [1999] 1 Lloyd's Rep 387, 395, CA, *per* Stuart-Smith LJ; and *Witter* v. *TBP Industries Ltd* [1996] 2 All ER 573, 595, *per* Jacob J.

[49] [2011] EWCA Civ 133; [2011] 2 Lloyd's Rep 1; [2011] 1 CLC 312, at [94]; noted A Trukhtanov, (2011) 127 LQR 345–350.

[50] [1974] 1 WLR 1335 or [1974] 3 All ER 511, Brightman J; approved in *Museprime Properties Ltd* v. *Adhill Properties Ltd* (1990) 61 P & CR 111, CA.

[51] Section 75 and Schedule 4 paragraph 1 of the Consumer Rights Act 2015.

[52] *Trident Turboprop (Dublin) Ltd* v. *First Flight Couriers* [2009] EWCA Civ 290; [2010] QB 86, at [15] ff *per* Moore-Bick LJ; *Air Transworld Ltd* v. *Bombadier Inc* [2012] EWHC 243 (Comm); [2012] 2 All ER (Comm) 60; [2012] 1 Lloyd's Rep 349, Cooke J.

reasonableness as stated in section 11(1) of the Unfair Contract Terms Act 1977 and it is for those claiming that the term satisfies that requirement to show that it does.

12.17 *Misrepresentation and Exclusion Clauses in Consumer Contracts.*
This topic is governed by Part 2 of the Consumer Rights Act 2015.[53] As indicated by section 75 and Schedule 4 paragraph 1 of the Consumer Rights Act 2015, that statute's test of unfairness will catch a term or notice which restricts a consumer's rights arising from a misrepresentation made by a trader in respect of the supply of 'goods, digital content or service'.[54] The four steps necessary to invalidate the relevant term or notice in a consumer contract are: (i) the term or notice operates 'contrary to the requirement of good faith'; (ii) if the term or notice were valid this would cause '*a significant imbalance in the parties' rights and obligations*' either (a) (simply) because the exclusion or restriction will weigh the transaction heavily in favour of the representor 'trader'; or (b) because that notice or term will tend to be asymmetrical, operating only to affect the trader; (iii) the phrase '*rights and obligations under the contract*' is to be applied broadly so as to include all rights and obligations arising with respect to the consumer transaction, thus including pre-contractual misrepresentation; (iv) the term or notice will manifestly operate '*to the detriment of the consumer*'.

In *Shaftsbury House (Developments) Limited* v. *Lee* (2010),[55] Proudman J considered (without deciding) that the 1999 Regulations[56] (ante-dating the Consumer Rights Act 2015) would catch an entire agreement clause or a non-reliance clause,[57] although the judge doubted that such a clause would then be invalidated on the present facts.[58]

12.3 Exceptional Duties to Disclose

12.18 *DUTIES TO DISCLOSE*[59]

(i) There is no general positive duty for a prospective party to reveal information which might be relevant to the transaction or to negotiations concerning the contract's contents. Nor does English law require a prospective party to point

---

[53] Replacing the Unfair Terms in Consumer Contracts Regulations 1999 (SI 1999 No 2083) (which is replaced by the Consumer Rights Act 2015).

[54] These three categories of supply are covered by Part 2 of the Consumer Rights Act 2015, in the light of sections 64(1)(b) and 76(2).

[55] [2010] EWHC 1484 (Ch).

[56] Unfair Terms in Consumer Contracts Regulations 1999 (SI 1999 No 2083).

[57] [2010] EWHC 1484 (Ch), at [61] to [67].

[58] *ibid*, at [64].

[59] J Cartwright, *Misrepresentation, Mistake and Non-Disclosure* (3rd edn, London, 2012), Part 3; D O'Sullivan, S Elliott, R Zakrzewski, *The Law of Rescission* (Oxford University Press, 2008), chapter 5; H Beale, *Mistake and Non-Disclosure of Facts* (Oxford University Press, 2012); *Spencer Bower, Turner and Sutton: Actionable Non-Disclosure* (2nd edn, London, 1990).

out to the other an imminent and ordinary bargaining mistake (but see the qualifications at **10.22, 12.20, 14.45** at (iii)): a person cannot take unfair advantage of the other's confusion concerning the supposed terms of the agreement).

(ii) However, in specific (narrowly confined) situations, notably contracts of insurance, the law imposes a positive duty to reveal relevant information.

12.4 Other Grounds of Vitiation: Mistake, Duress, Undue Influence, and Unconscionability

12.19 *MISTAKE, DURESS, UNDUE INFLUENCE, AND UNCONSCIONABILITY.* For reasons of space, these doctrines are not considered in detail here. It is enough to note these doctrines in outline in the ensuing text.

12.20 *UNILATERAL ERROR*

(i) *General Position.* In accordance with the objective principle (**10.08**), a contract is not invalid if only one party was mistaken as to the subject-matter of the proposed contract (for qualifications, see immediately below).[60]

(ii) *Situations where Unilateral Error Becomes 'Operative'.* A unilateral error becomes 'operative' only in one of the following four situations[61]:

(a) party B made a material misrepresentation (**12.04**) and this induced party A to be mistaken; or

(b) party B did not speak out to disabuse party A of his error even though party B was at that stage aware of A's error *as to the existence or meaning of an oral or written term*; if this is shown, party A at Common Law will be excused from performing the supposed agreement; or

(c) in the case of written contracts, party A can *obtain rectification of the agreement*, so that party A's 'version' of the agreement will be incorporated by equitable judicial order into the final text, if party B is aware of party A's error concerning the terms of the final form of the document but B fails to disabuse A of this error; or

(d) a unilateral error can also justify 'refusal of specific performance', if party B is aware of the other's error but (again) B fails to disabuse party A of this error.

12.21 *SHARED FUNDAMENTAL MISTAKE*

(i) *Test for Shared Mistake.*

(a) 'Common mistake' (or 'shared mistake') applies where the parties to a supposed agreement share a 'fundamental' error which deprives one party

---

60 J Cartwright, *Misrepresentation, Mistake and Non-Disclosure* (3rd edn, London, 2012), 13–19.

61 *ibid*, 13–44 ff.

(or both) of the benefits which he tried to obtain from the agreement.[62] The test for Common Law mistake, based on the parties' shared erroneous assumption, was formulated by Lord Atkin in *Bell* v. *Lever Bros* (1932) and by the Court of Appeal in '*The Great Peace*' (2002), the two leading cases. Lord Atkin said in *Bell* v. *Lever Bros* (1932): '*...a mistake will not affect assent unless it is the mistake of both parties, and is as to the existence of some quality which makes the thing without the quality essentially different from the thing as it is believed to be.*'[63]

(b) It follows from (a) that a contract will be void for initial impossibility or shared fundamental mistake if the subject-matter has never existed, or no longer exists (so-called *res extincta*: the subject matter disappeared), or the subject matter is already owned by the purchaser/proposed tenant (so-called cases of *res sua*: the inability to buy what you already own).[64]

(ii) *Mistake of Law*. A shared mistake concerning a pure point of law can vitiate a contract.[65]

(iii) *No Parallel Equitable Doctrine of Shared Mistake.* There is no separate doctrine in English law of rescission in Equity for shared fundamental error.[66]

(iv) *'Non est Factum': Fundamental Error in Signed Documents.* This Common Law doctrine invalidates a deed or other signed written agreement when the document's contents are wholly or radically different from those which the signatory assumed them to be.[67] This doctrine renders the apparent agreement void (rather than merely voidable).

12.22 *ERROR AS TO IDENTITY*[68]

Background: Issues of 'identity error' normally arise following a party's fraudulent impersonation; the leading discussion is by the House of Lords in Shogun Finance Ltd v. Hudson (2004).[69]

(i) The identity of parties to a written agreement is established by the names stated in that agreement. It follows that in dealings between persons who are not face-to-face there might be a failure to achieve consensus because the supposed offeree cannot validly accept the offer intended for another (the 'contract' is a nullity and void *ab initio*).

---

[62] J Cartwright, *Misrepresentation, Mistake and Non-Disclosure* (3rd edn, London, 2012), 15–19 ff.

[63] [1932] AC 161, 218, HL (for a similarly strict Common Law decision, cited in the present decision at 207, 218, 233, Blackburn J in *Kennedy* v. *Panama, New Zealand and Australian Royal Mail Co* (1867) L R 2 QB 580, 586–8).

[64] J Cartwright, *Misrepresentation, Mistake and Non-Disclosure* (3rd edn, London, 2012), 15–26.

[65] *ibid*, 15–24.

[66] *ibid*, 15–29 ff.

[67] *ibid*, 13–55 ff.

[68] *ibid*, chapter 14.

[69] [2004] 1 AC 919, HL.

(ii) Face-to-face transactions are unlikely to be regarded as void for error as to person, and instead will normally be voidable. This is because one party normally intends to deal with the other who is physically opposite, and the error concerns that person's good faith and credit-worthiness.

12.23 *DURESS (COMMON LAW DOCTRINE)*[70]

(i) Common law duress involves unlawful or illegitimate pressure which renders the relevant contract, or contractual modification, unsafe.
(ii) (a) The pressure will normally involve a threatened unlawful act (crime, tort, breach of contract, etc); but (b) exceptionally it might be the threat of a lawful act (such as reporting a person to the police or some other authority). In situation (b), the law might regard the threat as 'illegitimate', that is, an unacceptable or morally reprehensible use of pressure; but this involves a value-judgement to be made by the tribunal.
(iii) The effect of duress is to render the relevant transaction voidable (on the remedy of rescission, and possible 'bars' to rescission, **12.11**, **12.14**).

12.24 *Judicial Definitions of Duress.* There are two leading judicial definitions of duress. In *Universe Tankships Inc. of Monrovia* v. *International Transport Workers Federation ('The Universe Sentinel')* (1983), Lord Scarman said[71]: '*[T]he law regards the threat of unlawful action as illegitimate, whatever the demand. Duress can, of course, exist even if the threat is one of lawful action: whether it does so depends upon the nature of the demand.*' And, in *Dimskal Shipping Co SA* v. *International Transport Workers Federation ('The Evia Luck No 2')* (1992), Lord Goff said: '*[E]conomic pressure may be sufficient to amount to duress ... provided at least that the economic pressure may be characterised as illegitimate and has constituted a significant cause inducing the plaintiff to enter into the relevant contract.*'[72]

12.25 *UNDUE INFLUENCE (EQUITABLE DOCTRINE)*[73]
(See also the position concerning contracts of loan and guarantees, **12.26**)

(i) This is an equitable doctrine: The leading case is the House of Lords discussion in the *Etridge* case (2002).[74] The effect of undue influence is to render the

---

[70] N Enonchong, *Duress, Undue Influence and Unconscionable Dealing* (2nd edn, London, 2012), Part I (chapters 2 to 5); *Goff and Jones, The Law of Unjust Enrichment* (8th edn, London, 2011), chapter 10; AS Burrows, *The Law of Restitution* (3rd edn, Oxford University Press, 2012), chapter 10.

[71] [1983] 1 AC 366, 400–1, HL.

[72] [1992] 2 AC 152, 165G, HL.

[73] N Enonchong, *Duress, Undue Influence and Unconscionable Dealing* (2nd edn, London, 2012), Part II (notably, chapters 6 to 12); *Goff and Jones, The Law of Unjust Enrichment* (8th edn, London, 2011), chapter 11; AS Burrows, *The Law of Restitution* (3rd edn, Oxford University Press, 2012), chapter 11.

[74] *Royal Bank of Scotland* v. *Etridge (No 2)* [2002] 2 AC 773, HL, at [8] (generally on undue influence, Lord Nicholls [6] to [89]; and Lord Scott at [139] to [192]); M Oldham [2002] CLJ 29–32 and D O'Sullivan (2002) 118 LQR 337–51.

relevant contract (or gift) voidable (on the remedy of rescission, and possible 'bars' to rescission, **12.11**, **12.14**).

(ii) Undue influence is broader than coercion (see Duress at **12.23**), although undue influence can take the form of coercion.

(iii) In most cases undue influence can be made out as an inference drawn in respect of a relationship of vulnerability. The inference drawn will be that there has been abuse of a relationship by someone occupying a superior or dominant position (see further (v) below).

(iv) If undue influence is established, the effect is to render the relevant transaction (or gift) voidable (on the remedy of rescission, and possible 'bars' to rescission, **12.11**, **12.14**).

(v) The presumption that one party has the potential to influence the other unduly can arise within two categories (see (a) and (b) below):

(a) intrinsically unequal relationships, namely, solicitor/client, teacher/pupil, spiritual advisor/follower, trustee/beneficiary. Here the law acknowledges that the danger of abuse necessarily exists. If, furthermore, the relevant transaction 'calls for explanation', there is a presumption that undue influence has occurred;

(b) in other situations, the claimant must show that, on the particular facts of the case, he 'looked up to' and so placed 'trust and confidence' in the other; if this is shown and provided also the relevant transaction 'calls for explanation', the presumption of undue influence is triggered;

(c) in both categories (a) and (b), the requirement that a transaction 'calls for explanation' means that the contract (or gift) has occurred in circumstances where objectively there is suspicion that the weaker party was not acting spontaneously, freely, and emancipated from any external influence of a sinister or objectionable nature.

12.26 *SETTING ASIDE GUARANTEES (SURETY AGREEMENTS)*[75]

(On the nature of guarantees, see also **11.10**)

Background: Here the triangular connections are as follows: X lends to Y, the borrower, and Z acts as guarantor (also known as a surety) of this debt, Z entering into a contract of guarantee with borrower Y, whether or not Z also provides real security to support the guarantee.

If the guarantor and borrower are in a non-commercial relationship, the contract of guarantee will become voidable by the guarantor (subject to the usual 'bars' to rescission (**12.14**), and any supporting real security will not be available for enforcement by the lender) in the following circumstances (again, the *Etridge* case (2002) is the leading discussion)[76]:

[75] N Enonchong, *Duress, Undue Influence and Unconscionable Dealing* (2nd edn, London, 2012), Part IV; D O'Sullivan, S Elliott and R Zakrzewski, *The Law of Rescission* (Oxford University Press, 2008), chapter 9.

[76] *Royal Bank of Scotland* v. *Etridge (No 2)* [2002] 2 AC 773, HL.

(a) the guarantor was the victim of a legal wrong or impropriety committed by the borrower; and
(b) any one of the following three situations applies: (1) the lender had asked the borrower as agent to procure the guarantee; or (2) the lender had actual knowledge of the wrong or impropriety; or (3) the lender had constructive notice of the wrong or impropriety (constructive notice arises because of the intrinsically onerous nature of a guarantee of a loan, provided the lender is aware of the non-commercial nature of the relationship between the borrower and the guarantor); and
(c) the lender did not take appropriate steps to ensure that the guarantor received independent legal advice; and furthermore no such adequate and independent legal advice was in fact obtained.

12.27 *UNCONSCIONABILITY (EQUITABLE DOCTRINE)*[77]

(Care must be taken because within some legal systems, such as Australia, Hong Kong, and the USA, statute has rendered unconscionability much broader than in English law.)

(i) This doctrine (sometimes referred to as 'exploitation') is another equitable doctrine. The essence of unconscionability is that a stronger party has taken unacceptable advantage of the other party's weakness or vulnerability in a 'shocking' fashion. As a result, the relevant transaction is severely weighted in favour of the stronger party. Even so, the transaction might be upheld if the claimant received independent legal advice before acceding to the agreement. There are judicial summaries in *Alec Lobb (Garages) Ltd* v. *Total Oil GB Ltd* (1983), by Peter Millett QC[78]; in *Strydom* v. *Vendside Ltd* (2009), by Blair J;[79] by Lord Templeman in the Privy Council in *Boustany* v. *Pigott* (1995)[80]; and by Buxton LJ in *Irvani* v. *Irvani* (2000).[81]
(ii) If unconscionability is established, the effect is to render the relevant transaction (or gift) voidable (on the remedy of rescission, and possible 'bars' to rescission, **12.11**, **12.14**).

---

[77] N Enonchong, *Duress, Undue Influence and Unconscionable Dealing* (2nd edn, London, 2012), Part III; *Goff and Jones, The Law of Unjust Enrichment* (8th edn, London, 2011), chapter 11; AS Burrows, *The Law of Restitution* (3rd edn, Oxford University Press, 2012), chapter 12.

[78] [1983] 1 WLR 87, 94–5 (not disturbed on appeal [1985] 1 WLR 173, CA); note also the Australian doctrine of 'unconscionability': *Commercial Bank of Australia Ltd* v. *Amadio* (1983) 151 CLR 447; *Louth* v. *Diprose* (1992) 175 CLR 621, H Ct Aust; *Garcia* v. *National Australia Bank Ltd* (1998) 194 CLR 395, H Ct Aust (on last two cases, AS Burrows, *The Law of Restitution* (2nd 2002) at 266–7); and see *Nichols* v. *Jessup* [1986] NZLR 226.

[79] [2009] EWHC 2130 (QB); [2009] 6 Costs LR 886, at [36].

[80] (1995) 69 P & CR 298, 303.

[81] [2000] 1 Lloyd's Rep 412, CA.

Chapter 13
Terms and Variation

Abstract Terms can be express or implied. A party's attempt to impose exclusion clauses continues to be subject to Common Law doctrine (although here the law has been largely ineffective). But statute now dominates such matters. The commercially significant topic of warranties and indemnities in share purchase agreements, and similar transactions, must be considered. Finally, the chapter notes the intricate rules governing variation of contracts.

13.1 Overview of Contractual Terms

13.01 *THE RANGE OF TERMS*

On incorporation of terms, see **13.14** concerning exclusion clauses.

(i) Breach of a collateral contract or contractual term gives the promisee the right to recover damages aimed at placing him in the position which he would occupy if the contractual assurance had been true or not broken (on this measure of damages, **17.17**). By contrast, a misrepresentation enables the representee to rescind the contract and/or it is possible that the representee might obtain damages aimed at indemnifying against the loss incurred as a result of relying on a tortious misrepresentation (fraud or negligence) or a misrepresentation giving rise to damages under statute.

(ii) A pre-contractual statement might sometimes be analysed both as a misrepresentation and a collateral warranty (or term).

(iii) Terms are promissory or non-promissory (see (iv) and (v) below), express[1] or implied (on the latter **13.03**). (On the topic of interpretation of written contracts and rectification, **14.45**).

(iv) There are three types (**15.21**) of promissory terms: conditions (**15.22**); intermediate terms (**15.28**) (also known as an 'innominate term'), and warranties (**15.21**).[2]

[1] K Lewison, *Interpretation of Contracts* (6th edn, London, 2015),16-01, 16-02, 16-13.

[2] G McMeel, *The Construction of Contracts: Interpretation, Implication and Rectification* (2nd edn, Oxford University Press, 2011), chapter 20.

N. Andrews, *Arbitration and Contract Law*, Ius Gentium: Comparative Perspectives on Law and Justice 54, DOI 10.1007/978-3-319-27144-6_13

(v) Non-promissory terms do not impose primary duties on the contractual parties concerning the main operation of the contract but instead perform various ancillary functions, such as:

(a) preventing the contract from operating ('condition precedent');
(b) causing the contract to terminate on the occurrence of a supervening event ('condition subsequent')[3];
(c) enabling a party to terminate the contract (termination clauses) (**15.29**);
(d) restricting or excluding a party's liability for breach, including in respect of non-contractual misrepresentations (exclusion clauses) (**12.16** and **013.12**).

13.2 Written Agreements and the Parol Evidence Rule

13.02 *WRITTEN AGREEMENTS (THE 'PAROL EVIDENCE RULE')*[4]

(i) *Main Rule.* A cannot adduce evidence (oral or written) outside the written agreement ('extrinsic evidence') for the purpose of seeking to add to, subtract from, vary, or contradict the written terms. But this rule applies only if a contract is wholly contained in writing and not if it is oral or partly written and partly oral. (There is a separate rule, **14.01**, element (vi), which bars extrinsic evidence of negotiations or subjective intent in the context of *interpretation* of written contracts.)
(ii) *Qualifications upon the Rule.* Even if a contract is wholly in writing, the parol evidence rule excluding extrinsic evidence does not preclude reference to outside evidence in these circumstances:

(a) the doctrine of *rectification*, **14.45**;
(b) *collateral warranties* (**12.02** and **12.03**, normally based on oral assurances, a collateral warranty is a free-standing agreement);
(c) *issues of contractual invalidity* etc. Extrinsic evidence is admissible to show that the supposed written contract is invalid, void, vitiated, or otherwise inoperative for any of these reasons:

mistake (**12.21**); lack of consideration (**11.12**); statutory non-compliance (**11.09**); illegality (**11.17**); fraud (**12.12**); misrepresentation (**12.01**); duress (**12.23**); the agreement is subject to a condition precedent; the agreement has been subsequently varied or discharged by consensus

[3] As for Proposition (v)(a),(b): K Lewison, *Interpretation of Contracts* (6th edn, London, 2015),16-01, 16-02, 16-13; Neil Andrews, *Contract Law* (2nd edn, Cambridge University Press, 2015), 12.06(2).

[4] K Lewison, *Interpretation of Contracts* (6th edn, London, 2015), 3.16; (for a sceptical discussion, G McMeel, *The Construction of Contracts: Interpretation, Implication and Rectification* (2nd edn, Oxford University Press, 2011), 15.08 ff).

(**13.22**); to show that it is one type of agreement (for example a mortgage rather than a conveyance); to reveal the identity of the parties; or to discover the subject matter of the agreement.

13.3 Implied Terms

13.03 *THREE TYPES OF IMPLIED TERM*[5]

(i) As explained by Lord Wright in *Luxor (Eastbourne) Ltd* v. *Cooper* (1941),[6] there are three types of implied terms[7]:

  (a) terms implied *by law* to govern well-recognised transactions (such regulation is achieved by statute or declaration of the Common Law by judicial decision) (**13.05**);
  (b) terms implied on the basis of custom or trade usage (**13.07**); and
  (c) terms implied *in fact* (on the basis of obvious tacit assent) (**13.08**).

(ii) Recognition of terms under the preceding three rubrics permits contract law to reflect implicit standards of fair dealing. The vitality of the implied term doctrine is the main reason why English law has not traditionally employed an express general principle of commercial good faith in the performance of contracts (**10.14**).

13.04 *STATUTORY TERMS IMPLIED BY LAW*[8]

A term implied *by law* can arise under statute, for example, certain provisions of the Sale of Goods Act 1979, Supply of Goods and Services Act 1982, and Consumer Rights Act 2015.

13.05 *JUDICIALLY RECOGNISED TERMS IMPLIED BY LAW*

(i) Judicial precedent is another source of terms implied *by law*. The High Court or higher courts, in exercise of their law-making power to pronounce binding decisions, can find such an implied term. Terms implied in law by the courts[9]

---

[5] R Austen-Baker, *Implied Terms in English Contract Law* (Edward Elgar, Cheltenham, 2011), chapters 1 and 2; K Lewison, *Interpretation of Contracts* (6th edn, London, 2015), chapter 6; G McMeel, *The Construction of Contracts: Interpretation, Implication and Rectification* (2nd edn, Oxford University Press, 2011), chapter 10.

[6] [1941] AC 108, 137–8, HL.

[7] On the many types of implied terms, see the reviews in *Bank of Nova Scotia* v. *Hellenic Mutual War Risks, 'The Good Luck'* [1989] 3 All ER 628, 665-8, CA, and in *Philips Electronique Grand Publique SA* v. *British Sky Broadcasting Ltd* [1995] EMLR 472, CA.

[8] R Austen-Baker, *Implied Terms in English Contract Law* (Edward Elgar, Cheltenham, 2011), chapter 6 (but see now the Consumer Rights Act 2015); 1.33 ff (history of this type of term); G McMeel, *The Construction of Contracts: Interpretation, Implication and Rectification* (2nd edn, Oxford University Press, 2011), 10.15 ff.

[9] R Austen-Baker, *Implied Terms in English Contract Law* (Edward Elgar, Cheltenham, 2011), chapter 3; K Lewison, *Interpretation of Contracts* (6th edn, London, 2015), 6-01, 6-02; G McMeel,

prescribe the essential incidents of well-established transactions (as Lord Steyn said in *Equitable Life Assurance Co Ltd* v. *Hyman* (2002), these are *'incidents impliedly annexed to particular forms of contracts...such standardised implied terms operate as general default rules'*).[10] Such a term will reflect wide-ranging policy considerations and matters of general exigency.[11] The decision to recognise such a term, therefore, is not based on a single criterion of the parties' tacit joint intention, although the overall consideration is the court's perception of what is 'reasonable' in transactions of a common type[12]: the 'existence and scope of standardised implied terms raise questions of reasonableness, fairness and the balancing of competing policy considerations'.[13]

(ii) In many professional relationships involving the provision of services, and in other contractual contexts, there might be overlapping liability in the tort of negligence and in contract, the latter being based on an implied term that the defendant must exercise reasonable care or display customary skill.[14]

13.06 *Illustration.* In *Liverpool City Council* v. *Irwin* (1977) the issue was whether there should be an implied term to govern the incidents of a tenancy of a local authority's 'high-rise' flats.[15] The tenants had complained that the local authority had failed to maintain the stairways and lifts. Most tenants were elderly or parents of young children. The House of Lords held that a term should be implied in law to require the landlord to exercise reasonable care to keep the common parts in reasonable repair (although, on the facts, it was held that the obligation had not been breached). The House of Lords regarded themselves as searching for an obligation essential to the relations between a landlord and tenants inhabiting a block of flats.[16]

13.07 *IMPLIED TERMS BASED ON CUSTOM OR TRADE USAGE*[17]

The Construction of Contracts: Interpretation, Implication and Rectification (2nd edn, Oxford University Press, 2011), 10.36 ff.

[10] [2002] 1 AC 408, 458–9 HL; *Lister* v. *Romford Ice & Cold Storage Co* [1957] AC 555, 598, HL; for overt gap-filling and explicit reference to fairness, in the context of credit card payments, *Re Charge Card Services Ltd* [1989] Ch 497, 513, CA.

[11] Lord Wright in *Luxor (Eastbourne) Ltd* v. *Cooper* [1941] AC 108, 137, HL; Viscount Simonds and Lord Tucker in *Lister* v. *Romford Ice & Cold Storage Co* [1957] AC 555, 576, 594, HL. Elizabeth Peden, 'Policy Concerns Behind Implication of Terms in Law' (2001) 117 LQR 459–76.

[12] Lord Steyn (1997) 113 LQR 433, 442.

[13] *Crossley* v. *Faithful & Gould Holdings Ltd* [2004] ICR 1615, CA at [34] and [36], *per* Dyson LJ; *Geys* v. *Société Générale, London Branch* [2012] UKSC 63; [2013] 1 AC 523, at [55] to [60], *per* Baroness Hale.

[14] K Lewison, *Interpretation of Contracts* (6th edn, London, 2015), 6–019; R Austen-Baker, *Implied Terms in English Contract Law* (Edward Elgar, Cheltenham, 2011), 4.47, 4.48.

[15] [1977] AC 239, HL, cited in *Tai Hing Cotton Mill Ltd* v. *Liu Chong Hing Bank Ltd* [1986] AC 80.

[16] *ibid*, at 163; cited by Lord Scarman in *Tai Hing Cotton Mill Ltd* v. *Liu Chong Hing Bank Ltd* [1986] AC 80, 105, PC, and by Coulson J in *Jani-King (GB) Ltd* v. *Pula Enterprises Ltd* [2007] EWHC 2433 (QBD); [2008] 1 Lloyd's Rep 305, at [47].

[17] R Austen-Baker, *Implied Terms in English Contract Law* (Edward Elgar, Cheltenham, 2011), chapter 5; K Lewison, *Interpretation of Contracts* (6th edn, London, 2015), 6-012; G McMeel, *The*

(i) For a term to be implied on the basis ofcustom or trade usage, the suggested term must be very clearly supported by settled practice.[18]

(ii) The relevant custom or trade usage must satisfy the following criteria[19]: (a) it must be 'notorious', that is, so readily ascertainable that the parties can be taken to have assented to it (not satisfied in *Turner* v. *Royal Bank of Scotland plc*, 1999)[20]; (b) 'certain', that is, clearly established; (c) 'reasonable'[21]; (d) consistent with the contract's written terms (as the maxim states, *expressum facit cessare tacitum:* 'what is spelt out overrides what is implicit')[22]; (e) perceived as binding in law; mere regularity of conduct is not enough, because it might be an expression of courtesy or concession.[23]

(iii) A term can be implied to reflect the custom of a locality or the usage of a particular trade even though the contract is in writing or it is a formal deed, as *Hutton* v. *Warren* (1836) shows.[24]

(iv) Terms implied on the basis of custom are normally incorporated on the basis of Common Law recognition of the relevant custom. But statute might declare that custom can support an implied term. Examples are to be found in the Consumer Rights Act 2015: section 10(5) states: *in a contract to supply goods a term about the fitness of the goods for a particular purpose may be treated as included as a matter of custom.*[25]

13.08 *IMPLIED TERMS IN FACT: CAUTIOUS APPROACH*

Construction of Contracts: Interpretation, Implication and Rectification (2nd edn, Oxford University Press, 2011), chapter 12.

[18] *Liverpool CC* v. *Irwin* [1977] AC 239, 253, HL, *per* Lord Wilberforce; *Baker* v. *Black Sea & Baltic General Insurance Co Ltd* [1998] 1 WLR 974, 983–4, HL, 979–80, 982–4, HL; *Turner* v. *Royal Bank of Scotland plc* [1999] 2 All ER (Comm) 664, CA; R Goode 'Usage and Its Reception in Transnational Commercial Law' (1997) 46 ICLQ 1–36; and R Goode *Commercial Law* (3rd edn, 2004), 13, and 88; HG Collins, 'Implied Terms: the Foundation in Good Faith and Fair Dealing' (2014) 67 CLP 297, 303–4, contending that this category of implied terms might be dropped.

[19] *Cunliffe-Owen* v. *Teather & Greenwood* [1967] 1 WLR 1421, 1438–9, Ungoed-Thomas J (concerning customs of the London Stock Exchange); *Baker* v. *Black Sea & Baltic General Insurance Co Ltd* [1998] 1 WLR 974, 983–4, HL, *per* Lord Lloyd, cited in *Hyundai Engineering & Construction Co Ltd* v. *UBAF (Hong Kong) Ltd* [2013] HKEC 1368.

Cunliffe-Owen case, *ibid.*

[20] [1999] 2 All ER (Comm) 664, CA.

[21] *Robinson* v. *Mollett* (1875) LR 7 HL 802, 836–8, HL.

[22] *Les Affréteurs Réunis SA* v. *Leopold Walford (London) Ltd* [1919] AC 801, HL (cf 808 for Lord Birkenhead's doubt concerning this custom); considered by the Hong Kong Court of Appeal in *Leslie Deak* v. *Deak Perera Far East Ltd* [1991] 1 HKLR 551; [1990] 2 HKC 198; [1991] HKCU 389.

[23] *General Reinsurance Corporation* v. *Forsakringsaktiebologet Fennia Patria* [1983] QB 856, 874, CA, *per* Slade LJ (custom in insurance market merely matter of 'grace' and so non-binding).

[24] (1836) 1 M & W 466; 150 ER 517.

[25] Section 9(8) of the Act contains a parallel provision concerning quality of goods; sections 34(8) and 35(5) make similar provision concerning contracts for 'digital content'.

(i) *Nature of Terms Impliedin Fact*. Here the tribunal seeks to identify retrospectively, assessed at the time of formation, the parties' unexpressed common intention. And so this type of implied term involves imputing to the parties a readily acknowledged tacit understanding ('obviousness', see below).

(ii) *A Residual Category*. Terms 'implied *in fact*' form a residual category. They are applicable only if the term is neither implied by law (**13.04** and **13.05**) nor included as a matter of custom or trade usage (**13.07**).

(iii) *Cautious Approach*. Finding a term on the basis that it is implied *in fact* requires a high threshold of 'obviousness'. One test (see paragraph (v) below) is objective obviousness (the so-called 'officious bystander' test of obviousness). A slightly less exacting (and hence potentially problematic) test is whether the term's recognition is necessary to give the contract 'business efficacy' (see paragraph (vi) below).[26] The English approach tends towards a minimalist level of judicial regulation. For example, in *Paragon Finance plc* v. *Nash* (2002)[27] the lender had an express power to vary the rate of interest payable by its borrower. The court held that there was an implied term that this power would be used *without dishonesty, capriciousness or for an improper purpose*.[28] This restriction would prevent the lender from increasing interest levels in a way, or to an extent, that would be inconsistent with others' activity in this commercial sector.[29] The court drew back from stating that the implied term further outlawed any allegedly 'unreasonable' exercise of this power.[30] This narrow approach is attractive. It satisfies the need for the courts to provide minimal protection of a disadvantaged party (but compare *Mid Essex Hospital Services NHS Trust* v. *Compass Group UK and Ireland Ltd*, 2013).[31] Furthermore, because this approach is not too 'interventionist', the courts will avoid the charge that they have constructed an entirely new contract for the parties. The *Paragon* v. *Nash* test is not confined to discretions concerning financial modification.[32] Hooley's careful study[33] notes, in particular, the

---

[26]As for Propositions (iii) and (iv): K Lewison, *Interpretation of Contracts* (6th edn, London, 2015), 6–04; G McMeel, *The Construction of Contracts: Interpretation, Implication and Rectification* (2nd edn, Oxford University Press, 2011), 11.53.

[27]*Paragon Finance plc* v. *Nash* [2001] EWCA Civ. 1466; [2002] 1 WLR 685, at [36] to [42], *per* Dyson LJ, reviewing earlier case law, notably *Gan Insurance Co Ltd* v. *Tai Ping Insurance Co Ltd (No 2)* [2001] 2 All ER (Comm) 299, CA (V Sims and R Goddard [2002] CLJ 269–71).

[28]*Paragon* case, *ibid*, at [32] and [36].

[29]*ibid*, drawing upon *Gan* case, *ibid*, at [64] to [73], *per* Mance LJ (implied term that reinsurer's discretion to approve proposed settlement must not be absurdly unreasonable or based on extraneous and non-commercial considerations).

[30]*Paragon* case, *ibid*, at [37] to [42].

[31][2013] EWCA Civ 200; [2013] BLR 265, at [92].

[32]*Ludgate Insurance Co Ltd* v. *Citibank NA* [1998] Lloyds LR 221, CA, at [35]; general survey in *Barclays Bank plc* v. *Unicredit Bank AG* [2012] EWHC 3655 (Comm); [2012] EWHC 3655 (Comm); [2013] 2 Lloyd's Rep 1; [2014] 1 BCLC 342, at [56] to [67], *per* Popplewell J.

[33]R Hooley, 'Controlling Contractual Discretion' [2013] CLJ 65–90; see also M Arden, 'Coming to Terms with Good Faith' (2013) 30 JCL 199, 204–5.

restrictive comments of Cooke J in *SNCB Holding* v. *UBS AG* (2012),[34] and of Rix LJ in *Socimer International Bank Ltd* v. *Standard Bank London Ltd* (2008).[35]

(iv) *Approaches to be Avoided by the Tribunal.* The test of 'obviousness' is objective and demanding, as explained at (iii) above, and so the tribunal will not adopt any of the following approaches in order to find an implied term *in fact*:

(a) it is not enough that the term would be 'reasonable' or 'fair'; Lord Hoffmann in *Attorney-General for Belize* v. *Belize Telecom Ltd* (2009) noted that terms implied in fact are not found by reference to the test of reasonableness, but by reference to a more demanding criterion of necessity[36]; in the *Strydom* case (2009),[37] Blair J explained that the business efficacy test is not a licence for the court to exercise a benevolent discretion, or to 'to introduce terms to make the contract fairer or more reasonable';

(b) nor will the tribunal embark on reconstruction of the agreement on equitable principles; as Lord Wright said in the *Luxor* case (1941): *'[the courts will not] embark on a reconstruction of the agreement on equitable principles, or on a view of what the parties should, in the opinion of the Court, reasonably have contemplated*'; and he said, *'judges...have no right to make contracts for the parties.'*[38]

(c) nor should the process of finding implied terms in fact become policy-orientated, for this would unacceptably conflate the distinction between terms implied *in fact* and terms implied *by law* (**13.03 ff**);

(d) nor would it be acceptable to loosen the criteria for discovering an implied term *in fact* by referring to the objective standard of hypothetical parties' 'reasonable expectations'.

(v) *Objective Obviousness Test.* The main criterion adopted by the courts for the finding of a term implied *in fact* is the 'officious bystander' test: whether, just before entering (or renewing or extending) the relevant contract, and following the inquiry of an imaginary neutral, the prospective contractual parties would have readily assented to the term suggested for the sake of absolute clarification by the bystander. This strict approach is consistent with the principle of freedom of contract (**10.04**), that is, the need to respect the parties' general

---

[34] [2012] EWHC 2044 (Comm), at [72] and [112] (avoidance of dishonesty); Hooley, [2013] CLJ 65., at 75.

[35] [2008] EWCA Civ 116; [2008] 1 Lloyd's Rep 558, at [66]: contractual discretion to be exercised honestly ('honesty, good faith and genuineness') and without objective 'arbitrariness, capriciousness, perversity and irrationality'), on which Hooley, [2013] CLJ 65, at 68–69, 73, 76.

[36] [2008] EWCA Civ 116; [2008] 1 Lloyd's Rep 558, at [19].

[37] *Strydom* v. *Vendside Ltd* [2009] EWHC 2130 (QB); [2009] 6 Costs LR 886, at [33].

[38] *Luxor (Eastbourne) Ltd* v. *Cooper* [1941] AC 108, 137, HL.

liberty to fix their own terms.[39] MacKinnon LJ formulated the 'officious bystander' test in *Shirlaw* v. *Southern Foundries Ltd* (1939)[40]: '*that which in any contract is left to be implied and need not be expressed is something so obvious that it goes without saying; so that, if, while the parties were making their bargain, an officious bystander were to suggest some express provision for it in their agreement, they would testily suppress him with a common "Oh, of course!"*'

(vi) *Business Efficacy Test.* The older and vaguer criterion for finding a term implied *in fact* is the 'business efficacy' test, the so-called '*Moorcock* test' (1889)[41]: without the suggested term, the contract would not make any real business sense.[42] This approach can become unruly, for it might be misapplied as a pretext or licence to create a term to which the parties had not implicitly agreed, and to which they would never jointly have assented. An even wider amalgam of factors was assembled by Lord Simon in *BP Refinery (Westernport) Pty Ltd* v. *Shire of Hastings* (1978), giving the Privy Council's judgment, noting that the 'business efficacy' test is not a sufficient criterion, and identifying this range of factors[43]: '*(1) it must be reasonable and equitable; (2) it must be necessary to give business efficacy to the contract, so that no term will be implied if the contract is effective without it; (3) it must be so obvious that "it goes without saying"; (4) it must be capable of clear expression*[44]*; (5) it must not contradict any express term of the contract.*'[45]

13.09 The English approach, which is cautious, is to be contrasted with the more open-textured criteria espoused in the (non-binding) codes: PECL, *Principles of European Contract Law,* Article, 6:102 and UNIDROIT's *Principles of International Commercial Contracts* (2010), Article 5.1.2. Both 'soft law codes' refer to 'good faith and fair dealing', and the UNIDROIT principle includes

---

[39] R Austen-Baker, *Implied Terms in English Contract Law* (Edward Elgar, Cheltenham, 2011), 7.34 to 7.43; K Lewison, *Interpretation of Contracts* (6th edn, London, 2015), 6–09; G McMeel, *The Construction of Contracts: Interpretation, Implication and Rectification* (2nd edn, Oxford University Press, 2011), chapter 11.

[40] *Shirlaw* v. *Southern Foundries (1926) Ltd* [1939] 2 KB 206, 227–8, CA (affmd [1940] AC 701, HL).

[41] (1889) 14 PD 64, 68, CA; A Phang, 'Implied Terms, Business Efficacy and the Officious Bystander–A Modern History' [1998] JBL 1.

[42] R Austen-Baker, *Implied Terms in English Contract Law* (Edward Elgar, Cheltenham, 2011), 7.01 to 7.38; K Lewison, *Interpretation of Contracts* (6th edn, London, 2015), 6–08; G McMeel, *The Construction of Contracts: Interpretation, Implication and Rectification* (2nd edn, Oxford University Press, 2011), chapter 11.

[43] (1978) 52 ALJR 20, 26, PC; these factors were applied in *Jim Ennis Construction Ltd* v. *Premier Asphalt Ltd* [2009] EWHC 1906 (TCC); 125 Con LR 141, at [22] to [25], *per* HHJ Stephen Davies.

[44] A vague and uncertain term is unlikely to be accepted: *Shell* v. *Lostock* [1977] 1 All ER 481, 491G, CA; *Luxor (Eastbourne) Ltd* v. *Cooper* [1941] AC 108, 115–18, HL.

[45] *County Homesearch Co (Thames & Chilterns) Ltd* v. *Cowham* [2008] EWCA Civ 26, at [19]; [2008] 1 WLR 909. As for factor (5), an express power to award or deny performance points was held not to be regulated by an implied term in *Mid Essex Hospital Services NHS Trust* v. *Compass Group UK and Ireland Ltd* [2013] EWCA Civ 200; [2013] BLR 265, at [92].

'reasonableness'. Furthermore, these 'soft-law' codes contain an explicit general requirement that each party must co-operate to perform and fulfil the contract: PECL, Article 1.102 and UNIDROIT, Articles 5.1.3.

13.10 *IMPLIED TERMS AND WRITTEN CONTRACTS*[46]

(i) Sometimes it will be apparent, applying the officious bystander test or the business efficacy test (on these, **13.08**) that the only way to make sense of a commercial document is to infer the need for an implied term. A good example is the Supreme Court's decision in *Aberdeen City Council* v. *Stewart Milne Group Ltd* (2012)[47] (on that case see also **14.23**). The purchaser had bought land from a local authority, but the latter retained a share of the land's open market value. Accordingly, the authority was to receive an uplift payment on the occurrence of any of the following disposals: a buy-out by the purchaser of the local authority's share; or a lease to a third party by the purchaser; or an outright sale by the purchaser to a third party. This last mode of disposal in fact occurred. But the twist was that, in effecting this disposal, the purchaser sold the property *to an associated company for a sum well below its open market value*. The issue was whether that small sum should form the basis of the uplift or whether the property's open market value should be taken into account. The absence of any express reference to open market value with respect to the third form of disposal was a manifest *lacuna* in the contract. The Supreme Court held that this gap should be filled by inferring from the express language applicable to the first two modes of disposal (the buy-out and lease 'triggers') an overall intention that open market value should govern. Lord Clarke, with the agreement of a majority, preferred to conceptualise this result as founded on an implied term,[48] rather than an exercise in interpretation of subsisting words. The commercial imperative of reaching that result in this way was not in real doubt.

But in other situations the suggested implied term will wreak havoc. As *Philips Electronique Grand Publique SA* v. *British Sky Broadcasting Ltd* (1995) shows,[49] the courts are wary of implying a term of fact into a detailed contract which represents a 'closely negotiated compromise between…conflicting objectives…'[50] It would be perilous and potentially intrusive to impute a common intention in this context and so the law imposes strict constraints on the exercise of this extraordinary power.

---

[46] R Austen-Baker, *Implied Terms in English Contract Law* (Edward Elgar, Cheltenham, 2011), 7.44 to 7.48; K Lewison, *Interpretation of Contracts* (6th edn, London, 2015), 6–05; G McMeel, *The Construction of Contracts: Interpretation, Implication and Rectification* (2nd edn, Oxford University Press, 2011), chapter 11.

[47] [2011] UKSC 56; 2012 SC (UKSC) 240; 2012 SLT 205; 2012 SCLR 114 (for comments on this case, *Arnold* v. *Britton* [2015] UKSC 36; [2015] AC 1619, at [22], [71], and [113] to [115]).

[48] *ibid*, at [30].

[49] [1995] EMLR 472, CA; Sir Bernard Rix, 'Lord Bingham's Contributions to Commercial Law', in M Andenas and D Fairgrieve, *Tom Bingham and the Transformation of the Law: A Liber Amicorum* (Oxford University Press, 2009), 675.

[50] *Ali* v. *Christian Salvesen* [1997] 1 All ER 721, 726, CA (in the context of a collective agreement governing employment relations).

(ii) It has been suggested (in *Yam Seng Pte Ltd* v. *International Trade Corp Ltd*, 2013) that implied terms will be more readily discovered if the written contract is 'skeletal',[51] that is, skimpy rather than finely detailed.
(iii) Implied terms *in fact* involve discovery of terms to deal with matters for which the parties themselves have made no provision. The better view is that an implied term *in fact*, as an addition to a written text, must be independently supported by reference to the established objective 'obviousness' test (**13.08** at paragraph (v) above). To permit implied terms *in fact* to be implied by applying the abstract notion of reasonable construction of the document would cross the line between giving legal meaning to pre-existing text and inserting new text under the guise of 'construction'. Such an intrusive method of implying terms has been rejected.

13.11 The Supreme Court in *Marks & Spencer plc* v. *BNP Paribas* [2015] UKSC 72; [2015] 3 WLR 1843 rejected Lord Hoffmann's suggestion, in the Privy Council in *Attorney-General for Belize* v. *Belize Telecom Ltd* (2009),[52] that the true test for determining whether an implied term should be found in this context should be this: the **written contract** should be construed in the manner in which it would be understood by its reasonable addressee, so as to give effect to the overall purpose of the document, but eschewing judicial discovery of implied terms of fact on the basis of reasonableness. Instead the Supreme Court held that implied terms must be found cautiously if the parties have committed their agreement in detailed terms in written form. The traditional criteria for implying terms apply, therefore, and these criteria must be applied in a circumspect manner. But, even before the Marks and Spencer rejection, it was reasonably clear that Lord Hoffmann's remarks were unlikely to prevail.[53] In *Mediterranean Salvage & Towage Ltd* v. *Seamar Trading & Commerce Inc ('The Reborn')* (2009),[54] Sir Anthony Clarke MR was not impressed by Lord Hoffmann's discussion in the *Belize* case (see above), and instead emphasised orthodoxy.[55] However, in *Re Coroin Ltd* (2013) Arden LJ had been more positive concerning Lord Hoffmann's remarks in the *Belize* case.[56]

[51] [2013] EWHC 111 (QB); [2013] 1 All ER (Comm) 1321; [2013] 1 Lloyd's Rep 526, at [161], *per* Leggatt J.

[52] [2009] UKPC 10; [2009] 2 All ER 1127; [2009] BCC 433, at [16] to [27]; noted K Low and K Loi (2009) 125 LQR 561–7 (earlier, A Kramer, 'Implication in fact as an instance of contractual interpretation' (2004) CLJ 384).

[53] R Ahdar, 'Contract Doctrine, Predictability and the Nebulous Exception' [2014] CLJ 39, 43, noting Singaporean rejection of the *Belize* suggestion, in *Foo Jong Peng* [2012] SGCA at [43], and *Sembcorp Marine Ltd* v. *PPL Holdings Ltd* [2013] SGCA 43, at [76] to [101]; Paul S Davies, 'Recent Developments in the Law of Implied Terms' [2010] LMCLQ 140 and in 'Construing Commercial Contracts: No Need for Violence', in M Freeman and F Smith (eds), *Law and Language: Current Legal Issues 2011*, vol 15 (Oxford University Press, 2013), 434; J McCaughran, 'Implied Terms: The Journey of the Man on the Clapham Omnibus' [2011] CLJ 607–622; E MacDonald, 'Casting Aside "Officious Bystanders" and "Business Efficacy"' (200(0 26 JCL 97; for a positive reception, R Hooley, 'Implied Terms after *Belize* '[2014] CLJ 315–349.

[54] [2009] EWCA Civ. 531; [2009] 2 Lloyd's Rep 639, at [18].

[55] *ibid*, at [18].

[56] [2013] EWCA Civ 781; [2014] BCC 14; [2013] 2 BCLC 583, at [84] (and citing her longer discussion in *Stena Line Ltd* v. *Merchant Navy Ratings Pension Fund Trustees Ltd* [2011] EWCA Civ 543; [2011] Pens LR 223, at [36] to [41]).

13.4 Exclusion Clauses in General

13.12 *NATURE OF EXCLUSION CLAUSES*[57]

There are three main types:

(i) total exclusion: 'X Co will not be liable to you at all for breach of any of these obligations', sometimes known as an 'exemption clause';
(ii) time restriction: 'if you want to claim compensation you must notify your claim within [a specified period] of the alleged harm'; or
(iii) financial cap: 'liability to pay compensation shall not exceed £ x'.[58]

13.13 There are also elaborate definitions of exclusion clauses in the English statutes: for example, section 13(1), Unfair Contract Terms Act 1977.[59]

To the extent that this Part of this Act prevents the exclusion or restriction of any liability it also prevents—

(a) *making the liability or its enforcement subject to restrictive or onerous conditions;*
(b) *excluding or restricting any right or remedy in respect of the liability, or subjecting a person to any prejudice in consequence of his pursuing any such right or remedy;*
(c) *excluding or restricting rules of evidence or procedure;*

and (to that extent) sections 2 and 5 to 7 also prevent excluding or restricting liability by reference to terms and notices which exclude or restrict the relevant obligation or duty.

13.14 *INCORPORATING EXCLUSION CLAUSES*[60]

(i) The document purporting to include the exclusion clause must be objectively intended to have contractual effect. In *Chapelton* v. *Barry UDC* (1940)[61] the English Court of Appeal held that the defendant council's written exclusion clause – contained on the back of his receipt for the chairs—was not objectively intended to affect contractual rights.
(ii) A clause will be incorporated within the contract, and so bind party B, in any of these situations: party B knew that there was writing which contained terms and conditions; or party B knew that the document referred to such terms and conditions; or party A, the party raising the exclusion clause, took reasonably sufficient steps to give party B notice of the terms and conditions. Bingham LJ

---

[57] R Lawson, *Exclusion Clauses and Unfair Contract Terms* (11th edn, 2014); J Cartwright, *Misrepresentation, Mistake and Non-Disclosure* (2nd edn, 2007), chapter 9.

[58] K Lewison, *Interpretation of Contracts* (6th edn, London, 2015), 12.17.

[59] Similarly, sections 31(2) to (4), 47 (2) to (4), 57(4) to (6), Consumer Rights Act 2015.

[60] K Lewison, *Interpretation of Contracts* (6th edn, London, 2015), 3.10, 3.12, 3.13; G McMeel, *The Construction of Contracts: Interpretation, Implication and Rectification* (2nd edn, Oxford University Press, 2011), 15.51 ff (and 27.25 ff on the *non est factum* doctrine).

[61] [1940] 1 KB 532, CA.

in *Interfoto* v. *Stiletto* (1989)[62] noted that this test applies not just to exclusion clauses but to all 'onerous or unusual' clauses (perhaps only if 'particularly onerous or unusual').[63]

(iii) If a party has signed a document, he is taken objectively to have assented to the exclusion clause, even if in fact he had not read it, nor understood its effect. This was affirmed in *L'Estrange* v. *F Graucob Ltd* (1934),[64] where the court added that there are various exceptions to this, notably fraud and misrepresentation. or the signatory was wholly mistaken as to the nature of the document he was to sign (for example, believing it to be a mere acknowledgement of receipt rather than containing contractual terms: the *non est factum* doctrine. Although English law has not yet taken this step, it is arguable that this incorporation by signature rule will not apply if party A was aware that party B (party B is the party signing) had not read the relevant material.

(iv) The exclusion clause will have no effect if it comes to a party's notice only after the contract has been formed. In *Olley* v. *Marlborough Court Ltd* (1949), the defendant hotelier tried to escape liability for this negligence by relying on an exclusion clause placed in the hotel room. But this exclusion clause had not come to the claimant's notice until she had gone upstairs to her room.[65] The court held that this clause had no effect because it had come to the claimant's notice too late. Similarly, in *Thornton* v. *Shoe Lane Parking* (1971), the English Court of Appeal held that notice of an exclusion clause came too late to be binding on the plaintiff, because the contract had already been formed once he had driven his car through the automated entrance of the defendant's car-park.[66]

(v) A term can be incorporated by a consistent course of dealing between the parties· or on the basis of trade usage.[67]

13.15 *EXCLUSION CLAUSES INEFFECTIVE IF DEFENDANT GUILTY OF FRAUD*[68]

---

[62] [1989] QB 433, CA; considered in *DBS Bank (Hong Kong) Ltd* v. *San Hot HK Industrial Co Ltd & Another* [2013] HKCU 565; H McLean [1988] CLJ 172; Chandler and Holland (1988) 104 LQR 359; Sir Bernard Rix, 'Lord Bingham's Contributions to Commercial Law', in M Andenas and D Fairgrieve, *Tom Bingham and the Transformation of the Law: A Liber Amicorum* (Oxford University Press, 2009), at 668–71.

[63] *HIH Casualty & General Insurance Ltd* v. *New Hampshire Insurance Co* [2001] EWCA Civ 735; [2001] 2 All ER (Comm) 39, at [211], *per* Rix LJ; Gloster J in *JP Morgan Chase Bank* v. *Springwell Navigation Corp.* [2008] EWHC 1186, at [578] ff; affirmed [2010] EWCA Civ 1221; [2010] 2 CLC 705.

[64] [1934] 2 KB 394 Div Ct; JR Spencer, 'Signature, Consent and the Rule in *L'Estrange* v. *Graucob*' [1973] CLJ 104; cited in *Landale Development Ltd* v. *Zhum Heng Development Ltd* [1990] 1 HKC 274.

[65] [1949] 1 KB 532, CA.

[66] [1971] 2 QB 163, CA.

[67] *British Crane Hire Corporation Ltd* v. *Ipswich Plant Hire Ltd* [1975] QB 303, CA.

[68] G McMeel, *The Construction of Contracts: Interpretation, Implication and Rectification* (2nd edn, Oxford University Press, 2011), 21.57 ff.

A party cannot exclude or restrict liability (including rescission by the other party) in respect of that party's fraud[69] (that is, 'fraud or wilful, reckless or malicious damage' but not an ordinary 'intentional' breach of contract).[70]

13.16 *INTERPRETING EXCLUSION CLAUSES*[71]

(i) Ambiguous or unclear language contained in an exclusion clause will be construed against the party (the *proferens*) in breach who had inserted the relevant exclusion clause (interpretation '*contra proferentem*').

(ii) Although express exclusion or restriction of liability for negligence is possible (subject to **13.17**, paragraphs (iv) and (v) below), such a clause will be ineffective if the relevant wording does not explicitly refer to negligence and if the language is wide enough to cover a 'head of damage other than that of negligence...which is not so fanciful or remote that the *proferens* cannot be supposed to have desired protection against it' (the so-called *Canada Steamships* case's (1952) principles of construction).[72] Furthermore, European consumer protection legislation (implemented as Part 2 of the Consumer Rights Act 2015) extends the *contra profentem* style of interpretation in favour of consumers who are subject to written terms contained in consumer contracts for the supply of goods or services.[73]

13.17 *STATUTORY CONTROL OF EXCLUSION CLAUSES*

The Consumer Rights Act 2015, which took effect in October 2015, substantially changed the complex statutory rules governing these matters. The result is that a dichotomy emerges: the Unfair Contract Terms Act 1977 governing non-consumer transactions and the 2015 Act applying to consumer contracts.

---

[69] *S Pearson & Son Ltd* v. *Dublin Corporation* [1907] AC 351, 353, 362, HL; considered in *HIH Casualty and General Insurance Ltd* v. *Chase Manhattan Bank* [2003] UKHL 6; [2003] 1 All ER (Comm) 349; [2003] 2 Lloyd's Rep 61; [2003] 1 CLC 358, at [16] *per* Lord Bingham, [98] *per* Lord Hobhouse, [78] and [81], *per* Lord Hoffmann, and [122] *per* Lord Scott) (leaving open the possibility that a principal might exclude liability in respect of an agent's fraud; although that point is said to be covered by authority, not cited to the courts in the *HIH* litigation, precluding such exclusion, KR Handley, (2003) 119 LQR 537–41); *Granville Oils & Chemicals Ltd* v. *Davis Turner & Co Ltd* [2003] EWCA Civ 570; [2003] 1 All ER (Comm) 819; [2003] 2 Lloyd's Rep 356, at [13] ff.

[70] *Regus (UK) Ltd* v. *Epcot Solutions Ltd* [2008] EWCA Civ 361; [2009] 1 All ER (Comm) 586, at [33] ff.

[71] R Calnan, *Principles of Contractual Interpretation* (Oxford University Press, 2014); K Lewison, *Interpretation of Contracts* (6th edn, London, 2015), chapter 12; G McMeel, *The Construction of Contracts: Interpretation, Implication and Rectification* (2nd edn, Oxford University Press, 2011), 21-09 ff.

[72] *HIH Casualty and General Insurance Ltd* v. *Chase Manhattan Bank* [2003] 2 Lloyd's Rep 61, HL, at [11], [59]–[63], [95], citing *Canada Steamship Lines Ltd* v. *R* [1952] AC 192, 208, PC, *per* Lord Morton; and see Lord Hope in *Geys* v. *Société Générale, London Branch* [2012] UKSC 63; [2013] 1 AC 523, at [37] to [40].

[73] Section 69, Consumer Rights Act 2015 provides a statutory version of the *contra proferentem* rule in favour of consumers; and sections 64 and 68 emphasise the need for a term's presentation by traders to be 'transparent' and 'prominent'.

(i) In non-consumer contracts, liability arising from breach of the implied term that the seller (or party supplying goods under hire-purchase) has good title cannot be excluded: section 6(1), Unfair Contract Terms Act 1977.
(ii) In non-consumer contracts, in relation to other relevant implied terms by law, a party can only exclude or restrict liability 'in so far as the term satisfies the requirement of reasonableness': sections 6(1A), 7(1A) Unfair Contract Terms Act 1977.
(iii) In the case of consumer contracts for sale of goods, section 31 of the Consumer Rights Act 2015 invalidates any term which purports to exclude or restrict liability for breach of a statutory implied term arising under sections 9–17, 28, 29 (similarly, section 47 concerning attempts to exclude or restrict liability with respect to consumer contracts for 'digital content'; and section 57 with respect toconsumer contracts for the supply of services).
(iv) An exclusion clause (or notice) cannot exclude or restrict liability for death or personal injury arising from negligence. In the case of consumer services this bar appears in section 65, Consumer Rights Act 2015.[74] In other contractual contexts, see section 2(1), Unfair Contract Terms Act 1977.
(v) If, in the case of a non-consumer agreement, the relevant contractual negligence has caused other types of loss or harm, the relevant exclusion clause is subject to a reasonableness test: see section 2(2), Unfair Contract Terms Act 1977 (in the case of a consumer contract the clause will fall for examination under the 'unfairness' provision within section 62, Consumer Rights Act 2015).
(vi) Exclusion clauses inserted into non-consumer contracts and appearing within the defendant's standard written terms of business are subject to a reasonableness test: section 3, Unfair Contract Terms Act 1977.

13.18 In *Watford Electronics Ltd* v. *Sanderson CFL Ltd* (2001)[75] Chadwick LJ said that the courts should be 'very cautious' before deciding to invalidate under a statutory reasonableness test (at that time the Unfair Contracts Terms Act 1977, now the 2015 Act) an exclusion clause made between 'experienced businessmen' of equal bargaining strength unless '*one party has, in effect, taken unfair advantage of the other or [the court is satisfied] that a term is so unreasonable that it cannot properly have been understood or considered..*' Similar remarks are collected by Gloster J in *JP Morgan Chase* v. *Springwell Navigation Corp* (2008),[76] collecting such endorsements in various cases; and see also the Court of Appeal in the *Regus* case (2008).[77] First instance decisions concerning the statutory test of reasonableness are unlikely to be rejected on appeal: '*...the appellate court should treat the original decision with the utmost respect and refrain from interference with it unless*

[74] There are exceptions: a contract of employment or apprenticeship (section 61(1)), or a contract of insurance (section 66(1)(a)), including annuities payable on human life, or they relate to the creation or transfer of an interest in land (section 66(1)(b)); or harm arising from recreational use of premises due to the dangerous state of the premises and outside the occupier's trade, business, craft or profession.

[75] [2001] 1 All ER (Comm) 696; [2001] BLR 143, CA; noted E Peel (2001) 117 LQR 545.

[76] [2008] EWHC 1186, Gloster J, at [603] ff.

[77] *Regus (UK) Ltd* v. *Epcot Solutions Ltd* [2008] EWCA Civ 361; [2009] 1 All ER (Comm) 586, at [40].

satisfied that it proceeded upon some erroneous principle or was plainly and obviously wrong.'[78]

13.19 *Stewart Gill Ltd* v. *Horatio Myer & Co Ltd* (1992)[79] establishes that if part of an exclusion clause fails to satisfy the test of reasonableness, or it is otherwise invalid under Unfair Contract Terms Act 1977, the courts will not re-write the clause in order to preserve any 'reasonable' part. But a clause might be severable, and then at least part might then survive.[80] In *Watford Electronics Ltd* v. *Sanderson CFL Ltd* (2001)[81] the Court of Appeal held that the following composite clause was severable, and that each sentence should be considered as a separate exclusion clause: '*Clause 7.3 Neither the Company nor the Customer shall be liable for any claims for indirect or consequential losses whether arising from negligence or otherwise. In no event shall the Company's liability under the Contract exceed the price paid by the Customer to the Company for the [software] connected with any claim.*'[82]

13.5 Consumers Contracts: Control of Unfair Terms

13.20 UNFAIR TERMS IN CONSUMER CONTRACTS: *PART 2 OF THE CONSUMER RIGHTS ACT 2015*

These statutory rules (replacing a set of Regulations) cover many types of 'unfair' terms and not just exclusion clauses: see this note.[83] The protection is, however, confined to consumers: see this note.[84]

13.6 Warranties and Indemnities in Sales of Businesses

13.21 *WARRANTIES AND INDEMNITIES*[85]

---

[78] *George Mitchell (Chesterhall) Ltd* v. *Finney Lock Seeds Ltd* [1983] 2 AC 803, 810, HL, *per* Lord Bridge.

[79] [1992] QB 600, CA; *Thomas Witter Ltd* v. *TBP Industries Ltd* [1996] 2 All ER 573, 597–8, Jacob J.

[80] *Edmund Murray* v. *BSP International Foundations Ltd* (1993) 33 Const LR 1, CA (remitting the severance issue to the trial judge).

[81] [2001] 1 All ER (Comm) 696; [2001] BLR 143, CA; noted E Peel (2001) 117 LQR 545.

[82] This case was applied in *Regus (UK) Ltd* v. *Epcot Solutions Ltd* [2008] EWCA Civ 361; [2009] 1 All ER (Comm) 586, at [44] ff.

[83] Section 62(1), Consumer Rights Act 2015, referring to any 'unfair term'; see also section 61(4), section 63(1), Schedule 2, Part 1.

[84] Sections 2(3), 76(2), Consumer Rights Act 2015.

[85] A Stilton, *Sale of Shares and Businesses: Law, Practice and Agreements* (3rd edn, London, 2011), 177–178; R Thompson (ed), *Sinclair on Warranties and Indemnities on Share and Asset Sales* (8th edn, London, 2011); W Courtney, *Contractual Indemnities* (Hart, Oxford, 2014).

(i) *Warranties in Share Purchase Agreements or Business Sales.* A Seller's warranty, as used in sale and purchase agreements, is a promise or undertaking that the relevant subject-matter corresponds in nature and quality to the description contained in the warranty. The purpose of a Seller's warranty is to guarantee that the Buyer will be protected against potential loss arising from matters which are within the knowledge of the Seller or which the Seller is better placed to assess.

(ii) An unqualified warranty imposes strict liability, which means that the Seller will be liable even if it was not responsible for the inaccuracy of the warranty. A qualified warranty will impose a level of obligation less demanding than strict liability. For example, the warranty might be qualified to require merely that the Seller is offering assurances 'to the best of its knowledge' or 'after taking reasonable care to check the assurance's accuracy'. A warranty will not be breached if it states that accounts have been prepared in accordance with professional standards and in fact the accounts have been prepared to that standard.[86]

(iii) If the warranty is strict, (see (ii) above), a breach of warranty will arise if the subject-matter does not correspond to the terms of the warranty. If a warranty is breached, the innocent party is entitled to recover contractual damages. The purpose of those damages is to place the promisee in the financial position in which that party would have been if the warranty had not been breached. In the case of share purchase agreements, the measure of damages is the difference between the actual value of the relevant shares, assessed at the date of completion, and the (higher) value which those shares would have had if, at that date, they had corresponded to the relevant warranty.[87] That calculation will require careful evaluation by experts. A claim under the agreement must be notified to the Seller within that agreed time limit, otherwise it will be invalid.[88] However, in order for damages under a warranty to be recoverable, there must be a causal link between the alleged breach of contract and the claimant's loss. The breach of contract must be the "effective" or "dominant" cause of the loss, and there must therefore have been no intervening act or omission by the claimant. Such an intervening act or omission is more likely to be found where the claimant had knowledge of the breach: '*he more the claimant has actual knowledge of the breach...and of the need to take appropriate remedial measures, the greater the likelihood that the chain of causation will be broken.*'[89] Therefore, if the claimant has actual knowledge of the circumstances which led to an alleged breach of contract, he bears the burden

---

[86] The Court of Appeal held that no breach of warranty had occurred on the facts of *Macquarie Internationale Investments Ltd* v. *Glencore UK Ltd* [2010] EWCA Civ 697; [2011] 1 BCLC 561; [2010] 1 CLC 1035.

[87] *Sycamore Bidco Ltd* v. *Breslin* [2012] EWHC 3443 (Ch), at [390] to [466].

[88] *Laminates Acquisition Co* v. *BTR Australia Ltd* [2003] EWHC 2540 (Comm); [2004] 1 All ER (Comm) 737, Cooke J.

[89] *Borealis AB* v. *Geogas Trading SA* [2010] EWHC 2789, at [46].

of proof and must demonstrate that it was the breach of contract, and not the claimant's own intervening act or omission, that was the "dominant" or "effective" cause of loss. Furthermore, in order to recover damages the claimant must demonstrate that the loss suffered consists of either:

(a) such losses that arise naturally in ordinary course of things from the breach of contract itself; or
(b) losses that may fairly and reasonably have been contemplated by the parties, at the time of entering into the contract, as the probable result of the breach of it.[90]

(iv) The English Court of Appeal in *Eurocopy plc* v. *Teesdale* (1992) acknowledged that a Seller can validly plead a defence that the Buyer's knowledge concerning matters covered by a warranty may make it unjust to require the Seller to pay compensation under the warranty.[91] Similarly, the Court of Appeal in *Infiniteland Ltd* v. *Artisan Contracting Ltd* (2005) held that there will be no breach of a warranty concerning a company's assets when the process of disclosure has enabled the Buyer, acting through its accountants, to make an informed assessment of the company's financial position.[92] Mann J in *Sycamore Bidco Ltd* v. *Breslin* (2012) acknowledged that knowledge held by a Buyer would defeat a claim by that party for breach of warranty where (i) the evidence demonstrates that such knowledge has been acquired because of matters properly disclosed by the Seller or (ii) the Buyer has acquired such knowledge from specific sources as a result of its inquiries so that at the date of completion the Buyer knows the true state of affairs concerning matters covered by the warranty.[93]

(v) *Repeated Warranties.* A sale and purchase agreement might also provide that the Seller's initial set of warranties, as made at the date of contract, are to be repeated at the date of completion. The effect is to create two successive waves of protection, the latter wave superseding the earlier wave. In the interval between the date of contract and completion (but only during that period), the Buyer will enjoy protection under the first set of warranties. Provided the transaction is completed, the Buyer will gain protection under the second set of warranties. Upon completion, it is the second set of warranties which will exclusively govern. The Buyer cannot claim that a breach of warranty has occurred in respect of the second set of warranties where the Buyer had knowledge that these warranties were inaccurate, nor can the Buyer then rely on the first set of warranties.

---

[90] *Hadley* v. *Baxendale* (1854) 9 Ex 341.

[91] *Eurocopy plc* v. *Teesdale* [1992] BCLC 1067, CA (Nourse and Lloyd LJJ).

[92] *Infiniteland Ltd* v. *Artisan Contracting Ltd* [2005] EWCA Civ 758; [2006] 1 BCLC 632 (see also on this case, A Stilton, *Sale of Shares and Businesses: Law, Practice and Agreements* (3rd edn, London, 2011), 177–178).

[93] *Sycamore Bidco Ltd* v. *Breslin* [2012] EWHC 3443 (Ch), per Mann J, at [359].

(vi) *Nature of Indemnities.*[94] It is common for commercial agreements, for example, a sale and purchase agreement concerning shares or a business, to contain indemnities. The indemnity agreement is a promise that the indemnifier will pay money to the promisee (the indemnifiee) for the purpose of nullifying a loss, that is, to make the beneficiary of the indemnity 'financially whole'. And so, under an indemnity, A agrees to render B free from loss. Normally that loss will arise from B's liability to a third party. A true indemnity imposes primary liability on A to pay a sum protecting B from loss *whether or not B is a primary debtor.* This contrasts with a guarantee (**11.10**) where A (the surety or guarantor) guarantees T that, if primary debtor B (the principal) defaults, A will indemnify T.[95]

(vii) *Mechanics of Satisfying the Obligation to Indemnify.* Under a true contract of indemnity, the duty to indemnify might be expressly defined to require that the indemnifiee should first have paid money to the third party, as distinct from merely incurring liability to pay the third party. If the duty is expressly restricted in this way the courts will respect this limitation.[96] In the absence of such a provision, the payment of A's indemnity on B's behalf might take one of three forms: (1) Where A has agreed to indemnify B against loss, and B has already incurred the relevant loss by paying a sum to T, A's payment to B to indemnify B is strictly classified as a claim for damages. (2) Where A's protection of B takes the form of a direct payment to T. This seems to be based on the equitable right of B to demand specific performance of A's duty to indemnify by requiring A to pay T directly. And so that form of money payment by A to T is an equitable money payment. (3) There is also the possibility that A might be required to pay the relevant 'indemnity' sum directly to B even before the latter has incurred the relevant loss because he has yet to pay T.[97]

(viii) *Express Restrictions on the Duty to Indemnify.* An indemnity is a purely contractual instrument. Parties to a contract are free to agree on the division of risk and liability, and English courts will respect the terms that they agreed. More generally, Lord Sumption in the Supreme Court in *ENE Kos 1 Ltd* v. *Petroleo Brasileiro SA (No 2)* (2012) noted[98] that the court must determine '*the intended scope of the indemnity as a matter of construction, which is necessarily informed by its purpose.*' Thus, an indemnity might specify the limits of the obligation to indemnify and import expressly, for example, defences based on 'acts of the Buyer' or the Buyer's failure to mitigate, or by reference to the risk of subsequent changes in the law, etc., and these terms

---

[94] W Courtney, *Contractual Indemnities* (Hart, Oxford, 2014).

[95] On these points see *Halsbury's Laws of England* (5th edn, London, 2008), vol 49, paragraph 1021.

[96] *Firma C-Trade SA* v. *Newcastle Protection and Indemnity Association (The Fanti)* [1991] 2 AC 1, HL.

[97] *ibid* [1991] 2 AC 1, 28, HL, *per* Lord Brandon.

[98] [2012] UKSC 17; [2012] 2 AC 164, at [12].

would be upheld by an English court. All of these restrictions apply on the present facts, as will be noted in detail below.

(ix) *Indemnifiee's Own Responsibility for the Loss and the Relevance of the Indemnifiee's Negligence.* The House of Lords in *Smith* v. *South Wales Switchgear Co Ltd* (1978)[99] held that an indemnity should not be construed to expose the indemnifier to liability based on the indemnifiee's own negligence. The general rule of construction, acknowledged by the House of Lords in *Smith* v. *South Wales Switchgear Co Ltd* (1978)[100] is that the indemnifiee's negligence will not be covered by an indemnity. This general rule was acknowledged in the House of Lords by Lord Bingham in *Caledonia North Sea* v. *BT* (2002),[101] and by the Court of Appeal in *EE Caledonia* v. *Orbit Valve* (1995).[102] In *Total Transport Corp* v. *Arcadia Petroleum Ltd ('The Eurus')* (1991) Rix J concluded that indemnities will not be construed as requiring the indemnifier to cover all losses suffered by the indemnifiee[103]: '*indemnity is curtailed by a process of construction. It is only consequences that are proximately caused that are covered. The indemnity, absent express language, will not cover consequences caused or contributed to by the negligence of the party in whose favour the indemnity is given.*' But in *Campbell* v. *Conoco (UK) Ltd* (2003)[104] the Court of Appeal acknowledged that the express and clear language of the indemnity extended the scope of the indemnity so that the indemnifier was liable for loss resulting from the indemnifiee's own negligence. But this is quite exceptional and turns on the clear and specific language of an indemnity.

(x) *Damages for Breach of Indemnity.* If an indemnity is breached, the amount of money awarded for breach of an indemnity will be the amount of loss as defined by the terms of the indemnity to the extent that the indemnifier has not already satisfied that loss.[105] This will generally require the indemnifier to reimburse the indemnifiee for all loss suffered as a result of the breach in question. Further propositions made with respect to damages for breach of warranty at (ii) above apply also to the present type of claim.

---

[99] *Smith* v. *South Wales Switchgear Co Ltd* [1978] 1 WLR 165, HL.

[100] *ibid.*

[101] *Caledonia North Sea* v. *BT* [2002] 1 Lloyd's Rep 553, at [10].

[102] *EE Caledonia* v. *Orbit Valve* [1995] 1 All ER 174, 182F-182H, 184H-185 D, *per* Steyn LJ.

[103] *Total Transport Corp* v. *Arcadia Petroleum Ltd (The Eurus)* [1996] CLC 1084, 1114 (also reported at [1996] 2 Lloyd's Rep 408); the decision was upheld by the Court of Appeal at [1998] 1 Lloyd's Rep 351; [1998] CLC 90.

[104] *Campbell* v. *Conoco (UK) Ltd* [2003 1 All ER (Comm) 35, CA.

[105] The inability to recover twice for the same loss is a general feature of English private law: A Stilton, *Sale of Shares and Businesses: Law, Practice and Agreements* (3rd edn, London, 2011), 208.

13.7 Variation of Contracts

13.22 *VARIATION PROMISES TO PAY MORE OR IMPROVE TERMS*[106]

(i) Consideration (**11.12**) must be shown to support a promise to increase payment (or otherwise render the defendant's obligation more onerous). But consideration has been whittled down in this context almost to vanishing point. It is enough in this context that any 'practical benefit' results for the party who promises to increase the other party's rate of payment or to improve other terms. The most common practical benefit is that the party was promised such enhanced terms will remain constant and not abandon the contract.

(ii) Subject to the two conditions (a) and (b) below [and possibly subject to a third condition (c), although this last point awaits clarification], the defendant's promise to pay more than the originally agreed payment creates an enforceable 'increasing pact', even though the claimant's obligations are not intensified or increased. The two conditions mentioned are: (a) in exchange for the increasing pact the claimant must confer on the other party the 'practical benefit' of continuing to perform or at least promising to continue to perform (and so no enforceable increasing pact will arise if it is made after the party giving the pact has already completed performance); and (b) even if element (a) is satisfied, the increasing pact will be voidable if procured by the claimant's fraud, misrepresentation, duress, undue influence, or unconscionability (see **12.01** ff for each of these doctrines).

13.23 The development just summarised (**13.22**) is commercially welcome. It affords parties greater scope to agree binding increasing pacts even if nothing in reality is added to 'buy' the right to enhanced payment. This expresses an attractively common-sense and commercial perspective. a renegotiation freely agreed to ensure timely and proper performance is 'in everyone's interests'. Indeed it might be that, following the lead of New Zealand,[107] English law will go even further and declare that consideration is no longer required in this context of *increasing pacts*. In this context few will mourn its passing.

13.24 The background to the English law on this topic is as follows. The Court of Appeal in *Williams* v. *Roffey & Nicholls (Contractors)* (1991)[108] loosed the process of upholding variation agreements entailing an increase in the promisor's obligation ('increasing pacts'). That decision established this proposition: the

---

[106] J Cartwright, *Formation and Variation of Contracts* (London, 2014), 9-08 to 9-16, 9-23.

[107] This was the response in the New Zealand case, *Antons Trawling Co Ltd* v. *Smith* [2002] NZCA 331; [2003] 2 NZLR 23; noted B Coote (2004) 120 LQR 19-23. (2003), where the apparatus of consideration was excised from this context, increasing pacts becoming enforceable, even though gratuitous, unless procured by fraud or duress.

[108] [1991] 1 QB 1, CA.

promise to pay more is enforceable if the promisor receives any single 'practical benefit'; that will provide consideration; and this includes a bare promise by the recipient of the increasing pact to carry on with precisely the same job. *Williams* v. *Roffey & Nicholls (Contractors)* is a liberal decision reflecting other advances in the law of contract. The concept of 'practical benefits' was the key chosen to unlock the door to that new approach. That door had seemed to be locked by the authority of *Stilk* v. *Myrick* (1809),[109] which had obstructed enforcement of such an increasing pact.

13.25 *VARIATION PROMISES TO PAY LESS*[110]

(i) *Common law*. In the following situation a promise or assurance that a debt will be reduced or even terminated will be upheld at Common Law (if the debtor receives protection at Common Law the debtor need not invoke the doctrine of promissory estoppel, see (ii) below):

(a) *Common Law Protection by Bargain*: protection of the debtor arises when the debtor, at the creditor's request, supplies consideration (**11.12**) to support the creditor's promise to accept part-payment and to forego the remainder (or some agreed portion) of the debt (such as an arrangement to pay part in return for earlier payment (or similar revisions favourable to the creditor); or

(b) *Common Law Protection by Deed*: the creditor entered into a deed or covenant to accept part-payment as full discharge or to extinguish the debt; or

(c) *Common Law Protection by Intervention of a Third Party Part-payment.* Here a third party (with the debtor's consent) pays part of the debt to the creditor and the latter agrees with the payor that such partial payment will discharge the entire contract (or at least that the debt will be reduced beyond the amount of the third party's payment), that is, the creditor assented on these terms to this permanent discharge or reduction.

(ii) *Protection of the Debtor in Equity ('Promissory Estoppel').*

Equity, adopting the doctrine of promissory estoppel, offers protection even if the conditions summarised at (i) above (the position at *Common Law*) are not satisfied. Equitable protection requires the debtor to establish the following:

---

[109] (1809) 2 Camp 317, Lord Ellenborough CJ.

[110] The Common Law Rule in *Pinnel's Case* (1602), (1602) 5 Co Rep 117a (entire Court of Common Pleas); affirmed by the House of Lords in *Foakes* v. *Beer* (1884) 9 App Cas 605, HL; and for the position in Equity, see *Collier* v. *P & MJ Wright (Holdings) Ltd* [2007] EWCA Civ 1329; [2008] 1 WLR 643, which is the leading case concerning promissory estoppel (the Court of Appeal approved the suggestion in *High Trees* case [1947] 1 KB 130, 133-5, *per* Denning J that a decreasing pact will be given effect in Equity). Generally, J Cartwright, *Formation and Variation of Contracts* (London, 2014), 9-17 to 9-22, and chapter 10.

(a) the creditor agreed to release his debtor from the remainder of a debt, or to forego part of a debt ('creditor's assurance');
(b) *prima facie* the creditor's assurance will become binding if the debtor sufficiently acts on this assurance (acting on this assurance can include making a partial payment to the creditor);
(c) but the debtor will not enjoy Equitable protection mentioned at (b) if the assurance was procured by the debtor's fraud, misrepresentation, duress, undue influence, or unconscionability (see **12.01** ff for each of these doctrines).

13.26 *WAIVER AND ESTOPPEL*[111]

(i) The doctrines mentioned below at (ii) might sometimes bind party A to a variation of the contract if party B has relied on that promised variation, even if party B cannot show consideration (**11.12**), such as some step or abstention by party B and requested by party A.
(ii) The following doctrines can apply in the context of variation:[112] (a) estoppel (**10.15**), (b) 'accord and satisfaction' (variations binding because they are supported by consideration), (c) deeds of variation (a formal agreement to vary the contract, such a variation becoming binding because the agreement is couched as a deed, **11.11**), (d) waiver, (e) compromises of *bona fide* disputed points, and (f) third party discharge.
(iii) The variation of an agreement is to be distinguished from the replacement of an agreement between the same parties (agreement one replaced by agreement two). Here there are successive agreements (not necessarily on the same terms). Here one of the parties to the original contract is substituted by a new third party. And so a contract between A and B is replaced by a contract between A and C, a new party. B falls out of the picture because B is not a party to the new contract. The position, therefore, is that the A/B contract disappears and is replaced by the A/C contract. Lord Selborne's statement in *Scarf* v. *Jardine* (1882)[113] distinguishes novation of A/B contract Number 1 by A/B contract Number 2, and the novation of a contract between A and B by the creation of a contract between A and C, where C is a new party. In the latter case, novation involves A's duty to B being extinguished and a fresh contract arising between A and C. This is not the same mechanism, therefore, as a transfer, by assignment, from B to C of B's right against A. Where the new party, C, assumes an obligation under the novated contract, the obligation can relate to matters pre-

[111] J Cartwright, *Formation and Variation of Contracts* (London, 2014), 9-06, 9-07, 10-01 to 10-13.

[112] *Specialist works*: *compromise*: D Foskett, *The Law and Practice of Compromise* (8th edn, London, 2015); *waiver, and related matters*: KR Handley, *Estoppel by Conduct and Election* (2nd edn, London, 2014) G Spencer Bower and AK Turner, *Estoppel by Representation* (4th edn, London, 2003) S Wilken and K Ghalys, *The Law of Waiver, Variation and Estoppel* (3rd edn, Oxford University Press, 2012); G Spencer Bower and AK Turner, *Estoppel by Representation* (4th edn, London, 2003); E Cooke, *The Modern Law of Estoppel* (Oxford University Press, 2000).

[113] (1882) LR 7 App Cas 345, 351, HL.

ceding the date of the novation, as *CMA SA* v. *Hyundai MIPO Dockyard Co Ltd* (2008)[114] shows. In that case Burton J held that a party to a shipbuilding company (that party having joined as a party to this agreement following novation) had breached an arbitration clause requiring that disputes arising from this substantive agreement should be referred only to London arbitrators. That party, in breach of this arbitration clause, continued French court proceedings which had been wrongly commenced before the novation. It was a breach of the arbitration clause for the novated party (the party added by way of substitution) not to discontinue the French proceedings, once it had become privy to this contractual set of arrangements, including the arbitration clause.[115]

[114] [2008] EWHC 2791 (Comm); [2009] 1 All ER (Comm) 568; [2009] 1 Lloyd's Rep 213; [2008] 2 CLC 687.

[115] In reaching his decision concerning proposition (ii), Burton J said, *ibid*, at [23]: '*The Novation Agreements are not self-standing, they simply repeople the original contracts*'.

Chapter 14
Interpretation of Written Contracts

Abstract The topic of interpretation of written contracts is of central importance in arbitration practice. The English principles have developed fast in recent decades and the law remains in a state of radical, hectic, and sometimes perplexing development or doctrinal re-examination. However, some points have survived this wave of change. For example, English law does not, in general, permit a party to adduce evidence of pre-contractual negotiations in an attempt to illuminate the final text, but such evidence is regularly admitted if the same party adds a claim for rectification of the document. Another controversy is whether, even without resorting to the doctrine of rectification, the ordinary system of interpretation should permit the adjudicator to alter the text in order to give effect to the clear double conclusion (drawn simply from within the four corners of the document) that the text is obviously defective and obviously capable of being patched up.

14.1 Principles for the Interpretation of Written Contracts

14.01 *LEADING JUDICIAL SUMMARY*[1]

Lord Neuberger's Synopsis in Arnold v. Britton (2015):[2]

'When interpreting a written contract, the court is concerned to identify the intention of the parties by reference to "what a reasonable person having all the background knowledge which would have been available to the parties would have understood them to be using the language in the contract to mean", to quote Lord Hoffmann in Chartbrook Ltd v. Persimmon Homes Ltd [2009] AC 1101, at [14]. And it does so by focussing on the meaning of the relevant words...in their documentary, factual and commercial context. That meaning has to be assessed in the light of (i) the natural and ordinary meaning of the clause, (ii) any other relevant provisions of the [document], (iii) the overall purpose of the clause and the [document], (iv) the facts and circumstances known or assumed by the parties at the time that the document was executed, and (v) commercial common sense, but (vi) disregarding subjective evidence of any party's intentions.'

[1] See literature cited in note at **14.02**.

[2] [2015] UKSC 36; [2015] AC 1619, at [15]; substantially reproducing his synopsis in *Marley* v. *Rawlings* [2014] UKSC 2; [2015] AC 129, at [19].

N. Andrews, *Arbitration and Contract Law*, Ius Gentium: Comparative Perspectives on Law and Justice 54, DOI 10.1007/978-3-319-27144-6_14

14.02 The technique of construing written contracts is probably the most important topic within commercial contract law.[3] Remarkably, all the rules and principles are the creature of judicial precedent. The arrangement is facilitated by the overarching principle that interpretation of a written contract is a point of law. Such points tend to ascend within the appellate hierarchy, regularly reaching the House of Lords, now the Supreme Court. If English law governs the relevant agreement, interpretation of (wholly) 'written contracts' (including electronic documents) is a question of law, whereas interpretation of contracts not wholly contained in writing (whether oral, or part written and part oral) is a 'matter of fact'. Appeal courts have power to review first instance errors of law, but in general defer to findings of fact.[4]

14.03 In general, the modern law of interpretation has fallen back in step with sensible business expectations (but on the controversial exclusion of pre-formation negotiation evidence, see **14.24** ff below). In England this subject is dominated by the principles enunciated by Lord Hoffmann in the *Investors Compensation Scheme* case (1998)[5] (see **14.04** below for full quotation). In essence, the courts must give objective[6] effect to the language, consistent with sensible business expectations (so-called commercial common-sense), but without reference to the parties' actual negotiations or subsequent dealings.[7] Under this Common Law scheme, the pre-contractual history of the written contract is ancient history locked in the archives and hence invisible to the court. In this sense, the Common Law position is that the chosen words are King. But Equity can have the last word by opening the doors to the archives and poring over the pre-formation drafts or other discussions: the

---

[3] *Main textbooks*: R Calnan, *Principles of Contractual Interpretation* (Oxford University Press, 2014); K Lewison, *Interpretation of Contracts* (6th edn, London, 2015); G McMeel, *The Construction of Contracts: Interpretation, Implication and Rectification* (Oxford University Press, 2nd edn 2011); for comments by the author, Neil Andrews, *Contract Law* (2nd edn, Cambridge University Press, 2015), chapter 14 (and citing a vast bibliography on this topic); 'Judicial Interpretation of Written Contracts: A Civilian Lawyer's Guide to the Principles of English Law' (2012) 205 *Revista de Processo,* 163–180; 'La interpretación de los contratos por escrito en Inglaterra' (2014) XLII Revista de Derecho (Chile) 39–46; 'Interpretation of Written Contracts' (2014) 2 Russian LJ 12–28; and 'Interpretation of Written Contracts in England' (2013) *Lis International* (Italy) 156–162; 'The Devil is in the Detail: Procedural and Substantive Aspects of the Interpretation of Written Contracts in England', in Jens Adolphsen, Joachim Goebel, Ulrich Haas, Burkhard Hess, Stephan Kolmann, Markus Würdinger (eds), *Festschrift für Peter Gottwald zum 70. Geburtstag* (CH Beck, 2014), 23–32.

[4] *Andrews on Civil Processes* (Intersentia, Cambridge, Antwerp, Portland, 2013), vol I, *Court Proceedings*, at 15.12 and 15.72 ff.

[5] *Investors Compensation Scheme Ltd* v. *West Bromwich Building Society* [1998] 1 WLR 896, 912–13, HL; this statement was treated by the UK Supreme Court as canonical in *Re Sigma Finance Corporation (in administrative receivership)* [2009] UKSC 2; [2010] 1 All ER 571; [2010] BCC 40, at [10]. For an attractive analysis of the entire bundle of rules, Lord Grabiner, 'The Iterative Process of Contractual Interpretation' (2012) 128 LQR 41.

[6] *Kirin-Amgen Inc* v. *Hoechst Marion Roussel Ltd* [2004] UKHL 46; [2005] 1 All ER 667; [2005] RPC 9, at [32], *per* Lord Hoffmann, noting that: 'I have discussed these questions at some length in *Mannai Investment Co Ltd v. Eagle Star Life Assurance Co Ltd [1997] AC 749* and *Investors Compensation Scheme Ltd v. West Bromwich Building Society [1998] 1 WLR 896.*'

[7] See **14.26** on the five rationales for this bar.

equitable doctrine of Rectification (see **14.45** below) permits the court to revise the text to remedy a mismatch between the parties' pre-formation settled intention and the wording in fact adopted[8] (a second ground of rectification is where the court substitutes language to reflect one party's mistaken understanding of the contract's effect, provided the opposing party was aware of that mistake but in bad faith failed to point it out prior to formation (see **14.45**, paragraph (iii) below). Furthermore, even without resort to Rectification, the courts are at liberty to reconstruct phrases if it is obvious that something has gone wrong in the contractual formulation and it is also evident what is necessary to cure the textual defect (see **14.34** below) (this rule has been applied many times,[9] but it is controversial, notably because of its close, and hence problematic, relationship with rectification). And so in this field the objective principle (**10.08**) of contract law operates strongly. But there are various interpretative rules designed to avoid arid literalism:[10]

(i) the transaction's factual matrix, that is, commercial background,[11] must be kept in view;
(ii) words must be construed to promote business common-sense;[12]
(iii) the whole contractual text must be read in a harmonising fashion, rather than odd phrases being read in isolation;[13]
(iv) bungled language can be straightened out if it is obvious how the contract should properly read;[14]

---

[8] *Daventry District Council* v. *Daventry & District Housing Ltd* [2011] EWCA Civ 1153; [2012] 1 WLR 1333, at [227], *per* Etherton LJ.

[9] eg, *Chartbrook Ltd* v. *Persimmon Homes Ltd* [2009] UKHL 38; [2009] 1 AC 1101; *Pink Floyd Music Ltd* v. *EMI Records Ltd* [2010] EWCA Civ 1429; [2011] 1 WLR 770.

[10] See Lord Hoffmann in *Investors Compensation Scheme Ltd* v. *West Bromwich Building Society* [1998] 1 WLR 896, 912–3, HL, which he traced to decisions in the 1970s: *Prenn* v. *Simonds* [1971] 1 WLR 1381, 1384–6, HL and *Reardon Smith Line Limited* v. *Hansen Tangen* [1976] 1 WLR 989, HL; in the *Prenn* case, at 1384, Lord Wilberforce traced the 'anti-literal' approach to mid-nineteenth century case law.

[11] *Reardon Smith Line Limited* v. *Hansen Tangen* [1976] 1 WLR 989, 995–6, HL; *Charter Reinsurance Co Ltd* v. *Fagan* [1997] AC 313, 384, HL, *per* Lord Mustill: '*The words must be set in the landscape of the instrument as a whole.*'

[12] *Rainy Sky SA* v. *Kookmin Bank* [2011] UKSC 50; [2011] 1 WLR 2900, at [20], [21], [40]; and note *Procter and Gamble Co* v. *Svenska Cellulosa Aktiebolaget SCA* [2012] EWCA Civ 1413, at [22] and at [38], *per* Moore-Bick and Rix LJJ.

[13] *In Re Sigma Finance Corporation (in administrative receivership)* [2009] UKSC 2; [2010] 1 All ER 571; [2010] BCC 40; Lord Mustill in *Charter Reinsurance Co Ltd* v. *Fagan* [1997] AC 313, 384, HL, quoted in the *Sigma* case, *ibid,* at [9].

[14] *Investors Compensation Scheme* case [1998] 1 WLR 896, 912–3, HL (propositions (iv) and (v)); Arden LJ in *Cherry Tree Investments Ltd* v. *Landmain Ltd* [2012] EWCA Civ 736; [2013] Ch 305, at [63]; AS Burrows, 'Construction and Rectification' in AS Burrows and E Peel (eds), *Contract Terms* (Oxford University Press, 2007), 77; R Buxton, '"Construction" and Rectification After *Chartbrook*' [2010] CLJ 253; D Hodge, *Rectification: The Modern Law and Practice Governing Claims of Rectification* (2nd edn, London, 2015); G McMeel, *The Construction of Contracts: Interpretation, Implication and Rectification* (Oxford University Press, 2nd edn 2011), chapter 17; G McMeel, 'The Interplay of Contractual Construction and Civil Justice...' (2011) European Business L Rev 437–449.

(v) *in extremis* the text can be rewritten using the criteria, as explained above, of equitable Rectification.

14.04 *The Investors Compensation Scheme* (1998) P*rinciples:*[15]

(i) '*Interpretation is the ascertainment of meaning which the document would convey to a reasonable person having all the background knowledge which would reasonably have been available to the parties in the situation in which they were at the time of the contract.*

(ii) *The background [has been described] as the 'matrix of fact', but this phrase is, if anything, an understated description of what the background may include, subject to the requirement that it should have been reasonably available to the parties and to the exception to be mentioned next, it includes absolutely anything which would have affected the way in which the language of the document would have been understood by a reasonable man.*

(iii) *The law excludes from the admissible background the previous negotiations of the parties and the declarations of subjective intent.*[16] *The law makes this distinction for reasons of practical policy and, in this respect only, legal interpretation differs from the way we would interpret utterances in ordinary life. The boundaries of this exception are unclear. But this is not the occasion on which to explore them.*

(iv) *The meaning which a document (or any other utterance) would convey to a reasonable man is not the same thing as the meaning of words. The meaning of words is a matter of dictionaries and grammars; the meaning of the document is what the parties using those words against the relevant background would reasonably have been understood to mean. The background may not merely enable the reasonable man to choose between the possible meanings of words which are ambiguous but even (as occasionally happens in ordinary life) to conclude that the parties must, for whatever reason, have used the wrong words or syntax.*

(v) (a) *The 'rule' that words should be given their 'natural and ordinary meaning' reflects the common sense proposition that we do not easily accept that people have made linguistic mistakes, particularly in formal documents. (b) On the other hand, if one would nevertheless conclude from the background that something must have gone wrong with the language, the law does not require judges to attribute to the parties an intention which they plainly could not have had'* (letters (a) and (b) added here).

As for points (i) to (iv), the seeds for this contextual approach had been sown by Lord Wilberforce in the 1970s, as Lord Hoffmann acknowledged.[17]

14.05 The most recent re-examination of the principles just cited is by the Supreme Court in *Arnold* v. *Britton* (2015).[18] Earlier restatements include the following: (1) Longmore LJ in *Absalon* v. *TRCU Ltd* (2005) (approving the four-fold

---

[15] [1998] 1 WLR 896, 912–13, HL; and this statement was treated by the UK Supreme Court as canonical in *Re Sigma Finance Corporation (in administrative receivership)* [2009] UKSC 2; [2010] 1 All ER 571; [2010] BCC 40, at [10].

[16] *Prenn* v. *Simonds* [1971] 1 WLR 1381, 1383 G, HL.

[17] Lord Hoffmann in *Kirin-Amgen Inc* v. *Hoechst Marion Roussel Ltd* [2004] UKHL 46; [2005] 1 All ER 667; [2005] RPC 9 (for a magisterial overview at [27] to [35]), noting at [30]: '*The speeches of Lord Wilberforce in Prenn v. Simmonds [1971] 1 WLR 1381 and Reardon Smith Line Ltd v. Yngvar Hansen-Tangen [1976] 1 WLR 989 are milestones along this road.*'

[18] [2015] UKSC 36; [2015] AC 1619, notably at [[15] to [22], *per* Lord Neuberger.

summary adopted by Aikens J at first instance);[19] (2) Simon J in *HHR Pascal BV* v. *W2005 Puppet II BV* (2009);[20] (3) Walker J in *British American Insurance (Kenya) Ltd* v. *Matelec SAL* (2013);[21] (4) Peter Prescott QC (sitting as a Deputy High Court judge) in the *Oxonica* case (2008)[22] (attractively surveying this topic's development); and (5) Aikens LJ in the *Barbutev* case (2012).[23]

14.06 *CRITERIA OF OBJECTIVITY AND COMMERCIAL COMMON SENSE*[24]

(i) The criteria by which the tribunal must interpret a written contract are 'objectivity' and 'commercial common-sense'.
(ii) But the second criterion, 'commercial common-sense', is not to be abused in order to rewrite contracts in the interests of abstract fairness.

14.07 *Criterion (1): Objectivity.* On this fundamental topic the English approach is in vivid contrast with that adopted within other jurisdictions where the search is for the parties' actual, as distinct from imputed, intention.[25] Words count,

---

[19] *Absalon* v. *TRCU Ltd* [2005] EWCA Civ 1586; [2006] 1 All ER (Comm) 375; [2006] 2 Lloyd's Rep 129 approving Aikens J in *Absalon* v. *TRCU Ltd* [2005] EWHC 1090 (Comm); [2005] 2 Lloyd's Rep 735, at [24] and [25].

[20] [2009] EWHC 2771 (Comm); [2010] 1 All ER (Comm) 399, at [35]

[21] [2013] EWHC 3278 (Comm), at [46].

[22] [2008] EWHC 2127 (Patents Court); not disturbed on appeal, [2009] EWCA Civ 668.

[23] *Barbudev* v. *Eurocom Cable Management Bulgaria Eood* [2012] EWCA Civ 548; [2012] 2 All ER (Comm) 963, at [31], noting *Rainy Sky* v. *Kookmin Bank* [2011] 1 WLR 2900 at [21] *per* Lord Clarke of Stone-cum-Ebony JSC.

[24] K Lewison, *Interpretation of Contracts* (6th edn, London, 2015), 2–03 ff (objectivity); 2–07 ff (business common-sense); G McMeel, *The Construction of Contracts: Interpretation, Implication and Rectification* (2nd edn, Oxford University Press, 2011), chapter 3 (objectivity); 1.70 to 1.72f and 1.158 (business common-sense).

[25] For comparative observations on interpretation of contracts, MJ Bonell, 'The UNIDROIT Principles and CISG – Sources of Inspiration for English Courts?' [2006] 11 Uniform Law Review 305; MJ Bonell (ed), *The UNIDROIT Principles in Practice: Case Law and Bibliography on the UNIDROIT Principles of International Commercial Contracts* (2nd ed, Ardsley, New York, USA, 2006), 144; Eric Clive in H MacQueen and R Zimmermann (eds), *European Contract Law: Scots and South African Perspectives* (Edinburgh University Press, 2006), chapter 7 at 183; E Allan Farnsworth, 'Comparative Contract Law' in M Reimann and R Zimmermann (eds), *The Oxford Handbook of Comparative Law* (Oxford University Press, 2006), chapter 28, at 920 ff.; C Valke, 'On Comparing French and English Contract Law: Insights from Social Contract Theory' (2009) Jo of Comparative Law 69–95 (cited as 'illuminating' by Lord Hoffmann in the *Chartbrook* case [2009] UKHL 38; [2009] 1 AC 1001, at [39]); 'Contractual Interpretation: at Common Law and Civil Law: An Exercise in Comparative Legal Rhetoric' in JW Neyers, R Bronaugh, SGA Pitel (eds), *Exploring Contract Law* (Hart, Oxford, 2009), 77–114; S Vogenauer, 'Interpretation of Contracts: Concluding Comparative Observations', in AS Burrows and E Peel (eds), *Contract Terms* (Oxford University Press, 2007), chapter 7; S Vogenauer and J Kleinheisterkamp (eds), *Commentary on the UNIDROIT Principles of International Commercial Contracts* (Oxford University Press, 2009), 311; K Zweigert and H Kötz, *An Introduction to Comparative Law* (trans Tony Weir, 3rd edn, Oxford University Press, 1998), chapter 30 (although their discussion of English law is now out-of-date, because of the developments in the present text).

and they must be read objectively. In *Arnold* v. *Britton* (2015) Lord Neuberger said:[26]

'The exercise of interpreting a provision involves identifying what the parties meant through the eyes of a reasonable reader, and, save perhaps in a very unusual case, that meaning is most obviously to be gleaned from the language of the provision. Unlike commercial common sense and the surrounding circumstances, the parties have control over the language they use in a contract.'

14.08 In *Kirin-Amgen Inc* v. *Hoechst Marion Roussel Ltd* (2004) Lord Hoffmann elaborated upon objective ascertainment of meaning:[27]

'Construction...is of course not directly concerned with what the author meant to say. There is no window into the mind of the patentee or the author of any other document. Construction is objective in the sense that it is concerned with what a reasonable person to whom the utterance was addressed would have understood the author to be using the words to mean. Notice, however, that it is not, as is sometimes said, "the meaning of the words the author used", but rather what the notional addressee would have understood the author to mean by using those words.'

14.09 Lord Hoffmann continued in *Kirin-Amgen Inc* v. *Hoechst Marion Roussel Ltd* (2004):[28]

'The meaning of words is a matter of convention, governed by rules, which can be found in dictionaries and grammars. What the author would have been understood to mean by using those words is not simply a matter of rules. It is highly sensitive to the context of, and background to, the particular utterance. It depends not only upon the words the author has chosen but also upon the identity of the audience he is taken to have been addressing and the knowledge and assumptions which one attributes to that audience.'

14.10 *Criterion (2): Commercial Common-sense.* The courts need not wait until confronted by an extremely unreasonable or absurd documentary provision before adopting this perspective.[29] In the *Rainy Sky* case (2011)[30] Lord Clarke said:[31]

'It is not in my judgment necessary to conclude that, unless the most natural meaning of the words produces a result so extreme as to suggest that it was unintended, the court must give effect to that meaning....

.. If there are two possible constructions, the court is entitled to prefer the construction which is consistent with business common sense and to reject the other...'

14.11 There are many other statements supporting this need to consider business common-sense.

(1) Lord Diplock said in *Antaios Cia Naviera SA* v. *Salen Rederierna AB* (1985):[32] *'if detailed semantic and syntactical analysis of words in a commercial contract is going*

---

[26] [2015] UKSC 36; [2015] AC 1619, at [17].

[27] In *Kirin-Amgen Inc* v. *Hoechst Marion Roussel Ltd* [2004] UKHL 46; [2005] 1 All ER 667; [2005] RPC 9, at [32].

[28] *ibid.*

[29] *Rainy Sky SA* v. *Kookmin Bank* [2011] UKSC 50; [2011] 1 WLR 2900, at [20].

[30] *ibid.*

[31] *ibid*, respectively at [20], [21], [40]; cited in *L Batley Pet Products Ltd* v. *North Lanarkshire Council* [2014] UKSC 27; [2014] 3 All ER 64, at [18].

[32] [1985] AC 191, 201, HL.

to lead to a conclusion that flouts business common sense, it must be made to yield to business common sense.'

(2) Lord Steyn said in *Mannai Investment Co* v. *Eagle Star Life Assurance* (1997):[33] '*Words are …interpreted in the way in which a reasonable commercial person would construe them. And the standard of the reasonable commercial person is hostile to technical interpretations and undue emphasis on niceties of language.*'

(3) Lord Bingham said in *'The Starsin'* (2003):[34] '*The court must of course construe the whole instrument before it in its factual context, and cannot ignore the terms of the contract. But it must seek to give effect to the contract as intended, so as not to frustrate the reasonable expectations of businessmen. If an obviously inappropriate form is used, its language must be adapted to apply to the particular case.*'

(4) Lord Hope endorsed this approach in the Supreme Court in *Multi-Link Leisure* v. *North Lanarkshire* (2010),[35] noting that this was consistent with Lord Hoffmann's principles in *Investors' Compensation Scheme Ltd* v. *West Bromwich Building Society* (1998).[36]

14.12 *Commercial Common-sense: Not a Warrant to Re-write the Contract in the Interest of Abstract Fairness.* (There are important comments on the limits of the courts' capacity to discern and take into measured account the notion of 'commercial purpose' in *Lewison on the Interpretation of Contracts* (6th edn. London, 2015), page 69, end of 2.08 (section entitled 'The Limits of Business Common Sense'.) Lord Neuberger in *Arnold* v. *Britton* (2015) re-emphasised the need to resist the temptation to re-write imprudent contracts under the guise of business common-sense:[37] '*commercial common sense is not to be invoked retrospectively. …Commercial common sense is only relevant to the extent of how matters would or could have been perceived by the parties, or by reasonable people in the position of the parties, as at the date that the contract was made.*' Earlier, the Court of Appeal in *Procter and Gamble Co* v. *Svenska Cellulosa Aktiebolaget SCA* (2012) also made clear that the *Rainy Sky* case is not a warrant for re-writing a contract to achieve a 'fairer result' (even assuming that this can be perceived): where there is no ambiguity, the court should give effect to the contract's clear meaning.[38] Christopher Clarke LJ in *Wood* v. *Sureterm Direct Ltd and Capital Insurance Services Ltd* [2015] EWCA Civ 839 warned against the danger that 'business common-sense' might seduce the court into adopting at an interpretation at variance with the parties' true common ground expressed by them in a way which at first provokes surprise but which is in fact a compromise choice of wording resulting from tough negotiation. He said, first, '*what may appear...as lacking in business common sense may be the product of a compromise which was the only means of reaching agreement*' (at [29]); secondly, '*it is not the function of the court to improve [the parties'] bargain or to make it more reasonable by a process of interpretation which amounts to rewriting it*' (at [30]).

---

[33] [1997] AC 749, HL (a majority decision concerning a rent notice); PV Baker (1998) 114 LQR 55–62.

[34] [2003] UKHL 12; [2004] 1 AC 715, at [12]; and see similar remarks at [10] (Lord Bingham noted *The Okehampton'* [1913] P 173, 180, *per* Hamilton LJ, later Lord Sumner).

[35] [2010] UKSC 47; [2011] 1 All ER 175, at [21]; decision criticised D McLaughlan, 'A Construction Conundrum' [2011] LMCLQ 428–448.

[36] [1998] 1 WLR 896, 913, HL.

[37] [2015] UKSC 36; [2015] AC 1619, at [19].

[38] [2012] EWCA Civ 1413, at [22] and at [38], *per* Moore-Bick and Rix LJJ.

14.13 *TRIBUNAL NOT TO OVERSTRETCH ITS POWERS*[39]

(On the possibility that the text might be re-cast in accordance with 'corrective construction', **14.34**; on the use of rectification, **14.45**; and on the connection with the principle of freedom of contract, **10.04**, Proposition (iv)).

A fundamental tenet of English contract law (reflecting the principle of freedom of contract, **10.04**) is that the courts will respect the terms of a contract entered into by two consenting parties. Tribunals are in fact bound to give effect to a contractual text: they must not illegitimately ignore, modify, or rewrite the contract if its meaning is clear and does not lead to commercial absurdity. In *Arnold* v. *Britton* (2015) Lord Neuberger said:[40]

> '......*it is not the function of a court when interpreting an agreement to relieve a party from the consequences of his imprudence or poor advice. Accordingly, when interpreting a contract a judge should avoid re-writing it in an attempt to assist an unwise party or to penalise an astute party.*'

Lord Radcliffe in *Bridge* v. *Campbell Discount Co Ltd* (1962) noted that an English judge is not empowered 'to serve as a general adjuster of men's bargains'.[41]

Lord Mustill in *Charter Reinsurance Co Ltd* v. *Fagan* (1997) warned that it is illegitimate for courts or arbitrators to 'force upon the words a meaning which they cannot fairly bear', since this would be 'to substitute for the bargain actually made one which the court believes could better have been made.'[42]

Similarly, Rix LJ said in *ING Bank NV* v. *Ros Roca SA* (2011):[43] '*Judges should not see in Chartbrook Ltd v. Persimmon Homes Ltd [2009] AC 1101 an open sesame for reconstructing the parties' contract, but an opportunity to remedy by construction a clear error of language which could not have been intended.*' See also at **14.12** the important quotations from *Wood* v. *Sureterm* (2015), cautioning against an injudicious over-use of the concept of 'business common sense'.

14.14 *WHOLE TEXT*[44]

It is a cardinal principle of interpretation that the whole contract must be considered when interpreting a particular word, phrase, clause, or part of a document etc. For example, as noted at **15.22**, paragraph (c), the House of Lords in *Schuler (L) AG* v. *Wickman Machine Tool Sales Ltd* (1974) held that, on proper construction of the contract, the word 'condition' (contained in clause 7(b)) had not been intended to operate in a technical sense.[45] This construction was based on the need to harmonise conflict-

---

[39] K Lewison, *Interpretation of Contracts* (6th edn, London, 2015), 2-07(d), 2–08.

[40] [2015] UKSC 36; [2015] AC 1619, at [20].

[41] [1962] AC 600, 626, HL.

[42] [1997] AC 313, 388, HL.

[43] [2011] EWCA Civ 353; [2012] 1 WLR 472.

[44] K Lewison, *Interpretation of Contracts* (6th edn, London, 2015), 7–02, 7–03; G McMeel, *The Construction of Contracts: Interpretation, Implication and Rectification* (2nd edn, Oxford University Press, 2011), 4–01 ff.

[45] [1974] AC 235, HL; noted by JH Baker, [1973] CLJ 196, R Brownsword, (1974) 37 MLR 104, and FA Mann, (1973) 89 LQR 464.

ing clauses. The innocent party could not invoke clause 7(b) (containing the word 'condition') in order to by-pass clause 11(a)(1) which provided that the innocent party must first serve notice on the other party requiring the latter to take remedial steps.

14.15 Also instructive is the House of Lords' decision in *Charter Reinsurance Co Ltd* v. *Fagan* (1997),[46] which demonstrates the pitfall of becoming attached to one's 'first blush' and seemingly 'common-sense' reading of commercial words, without pausing more carefully to consider the entire contractual document. The question was whether (1) a reinsurer had agreed to indemnify the reinsured only if the latter's liability had accrued, been quantified, and been discharged by payment (the so-called 'actual disbursement' interpretation) or (2) whether it was enough that the liability to indemnify had arisen and been quantified, without actual discharge of that liability (the liability to pay or finalised quantification interpretation). The semantic battle was fought over the words 'actually paid'. The House of Lords held that (2) was the correct contextual construction of that phrase within the whole agreement (admittedly surprising, because it appears to be the very opposite of one's first understanding).

14.16 *FACTUAL MATRIX (BACKGROUND)*[47]

(i) Tribunals are not tied to the literal wording of the written contract, but can consider the parties' common intention against the background of the transaction.
(ii) In making this extended search, however, parties should not be permitted to adduce excessive quantities of background information.
(iii) The background material must have been available to the parties to the relevant transaction at the time of its formation.

The English courts will adopt a contextual approach to interpretation rather than a narrow 'dictionary meaning' approach: see Lord Hoffmann's seminal statement in *Investors Compensation Scheme Ltd* v. *West Bromwich Building Society* (1998)[48] (which he traced to decisions in the 1970s).[49] The courts permit the parties to refer to the contractual setting, expressed variously as the transaction's 'commercial purpose', 'genesis', 'background', 'context', its location in the relevant 'market',[50] or its 'landscape'.[51] But it must be emphasised that 'background' **does not extend to pre-contractual negotiations** (on that, see **14.24**; however, in the case of applications for rectification, there is an exception to the bar on evidence of

[46] [1997] AC 313, HL.

[47] K Lewison, *Interpretation of Contracts* (6th edn, London, 2015), 3–17, 3–18; G McMeel, *The Construction of Contracts: Interpretation, Implication and Rectification* (2nd edn, Oxford University Press, 2011), 5.40 ff.

[48] [1998] 1 WLR 896, 912–3, HL; E McKendrick, in S Worthington (ed) *Commercial Law and Commercial Practice* (London, 2003) 139–62.

[49] *Prenn* v. *Simonds* [1971] 1 WLR 1381, 1384–6, HL and *Reardon Smith Line Limited* v. *Hansen Tangen* [1976] 1 WLR 989, HL; in the *Prenn* case, at 1384, Lord Wilberforce traced the 'anti-literal' approach to mid-nineteenth century case law.

[50] The leading comment is by Lord Wilberforce in *Reardon Smith Line Limited* v. *Hansen Tangen* [1976] 1 WLR 989, 995–6, HL; see Sir Christopher Staughton [1999] CLJ 303 on the problem of the 'factual matrix'.

[51] *Charter Reinsurance Co Ltd* v. *Fagan* [1997] AC 313, 384, HL, *per* Lord Mustill: '*The words must be set in the landscape of the instrument as a whole.*'

pre-contractual negotiations: see further **14.45** below). The courts are alert to the need for a contextual approach: 'No one has ever made an "acontextual" statement. There is always some context to any utterance, however meagre.'[52] And 'courts will never construe words in a vacuum…'[53]

14.17 In *Arnold* v. *Britton* (2015)[54] Lord Neuberger indicated that 'context' concerns the state of affairs at the time of the contract ('the facts and circumstances known or assumed by the parties at the time that the document was executed') and 'the overall purpose of the clause and the [document]' (whole passage cited at **14.01** above).

14.18 Lord Hoffmann in the *BCCI* case (2001) said that the courts and arbitral tribunals, rather than encouraging an uncontrolled 'trawl' through all background material, should curb attempts by parties to adduce excessive quantities of background information.[55]

14.19 Rix LJ *Procter and Gamble Co* v. *Svenska Cellulosa Aktiebolaget SCA* (2012)[56] noted that the Common Law tool of pre-trial disclosure of documents[57] is an important procedural support for the construction of documents.

14.20 *Accessibility of Background Material.* The relevant 'background' must have been accessible to the present parties, as noted in the S*igma* case (2009).[58] Berg notes that reconstruction of the 'background' can be expensive, pain-staking, and even impossible, when the 'parties' are complex organisations, represented by legal and other professions 'teams', and the parties' successors are now required retrospectively and minutely to examine the transaction's pre-formation landscape in order to capture its tacit nuances.[59] Berg notes the Chief Justice of New South Wales' condemnation of the Lord Hoffmann's 'background' principle: 'it is not a schema that can be applied to a substantial range of commercial contractual relationships'.[60]

14.21 *ORIGINAL ASSUMPTIONS*[61]

---

[52] *Marley* v. *Rawlings* [2014] UKSC 2; [2015] AC 129, at [20], Lord Neuberger citing Lord Hoffmann in *Kirin-Amgen Inc* v. *Hoechst Marion Roussel Ltd* [2004] UKHL 46; [2005] 1 All ER 667; [2005] RPC 9, at [64].

[53] *Marley* v. *Rawlings* [2014] UKSC 2; [2015] AC 129, at [20], Lord Neuberger citing Sir Thomas Bingham MR in *Arbuthnott* v. *Fagan* [1995] CLC 1396, 1400.

[54] [2015] UKSC 36; [2015] AC 1619, at [15]; substantially reproducing his synopsis in *Marley* v. *Rawlings* [2014] UKSC 2; [2015] AC 129, at [19].

[55] [2001] 1 AC 251, at [39], HL.

[56] [2012] EWCA Civ 1413, at [38].

[57] The leading rules are codified at CPR Part 31: for comment on these procedural rules, *Andrews on Civil Processes* (Intersentia, Cambridge, Antwerp, Portland, 2013), vol I, *Court Proceedings*, at chapter 11.

[58] *Sigma* case, [2009] UKSC 2; [2010] 1 All ER 571; [2010] BCC 40, at [35] to [37], Lord Collins (with the support of Lords Mance and Hope); and for the problem of rectification of public documents, *Cherry Tree Investments Ltd* v. *Landmain Ltd* [2012] EWCA Civ 736; [2013] Ch 305, noted Paul S Davies, (2013) 129 LQR 24–27; M Barber and R Thomas, (2014) 77 MLR 597–618.

[59] A Berg (2008) 124 LQR 6, 12–14.

[60] *ibid,* at 14, citing an address given by this Australian judge in March 2007.

[61] K Lewison, *Interpretation of Contracts* (6th edn, London, 2015), 5.15.

(i) Objectively determined, the original assumptions, including the parties' 'purposes and values', are relevant when seeking to give effect to the contract.
(ii) The tribunal must give effect to the purposes and values which are expressed in, or at least implicit within, the document and adopt an interpretation which applies that document to the relevant changed circumstances in a manner consistent with them.
(iii) But the tribunal will not apply the original language in an unmodified way if it is obvious that, at the time of the original agreement, the parties could not possibly have contemplated a novel and drastic development.

14.22 In *Lloyds TSB Foundation for Scotland* v. *Lloyds Group plc* (2013)[62] a deed of covenant, dated 1997, stated that the Lloyds Banking Group would pay to a charitable foundation, the appellants ('the Foundation'), (a) £38,920 or (b) (if higher) a specified percentage of the group's pre-tax profits, as defined in the deed. The Supreme Court held that an item creating the mirage of an enhanced or actual profit, based on an accountancy change (this change having been made by statute 8 years after the deed), could be safely disregarded. The parties could not reasonably have contemplated the radical change in accountancy practice implemented 8 years after the 1997 deed.

14.23 As noted in *Arnold* v. *Britton* (2015), the Supreme Court in *Aberdeen City Council* v. *Stewart Milne Group Ltd* (2012) (on that case see also **13.10**) construed a provision for a payment in a development contract by reference to the parties' original assumptions. In the *Arnold* case (2015) Lord Neuberger commented:[63]

> '*...in some cases, an event subsequently occurs which was plainly not intended or contemplated by the parties, judging from the language of their contract. ... An example...is the Aberdeen City Council [case]*[64] *..where the,... conclusion was based on what the parties "had in mind when they entered into" the contract...*'.

14.24 *NEGOTIATION EVIDENCE GENERALLY BARRED*

(i) When seeking to interpret written contracts, a party cannot adduce, without his opponent's permission, the parties' prior negotiations.[65]
(ii) This evidential bar does not apply if:[66]

(a) an application is made for the equitable remedy of rectification (**14.45**); or

[62] [2013] UKSC 3; [2013] 1 WLR 366, at [19], *per* Lord Mance, citing the first instance judge; similarly, *ibid*, at [22] and [25].

[63] [2015] UKSC 36; [2015] AC 1619, at [22].

[64] [2011] UKSC 56; 2012 SC (UKSC) 240; 2012 SLT 205; 2012 SCLR 114.

[65] K Lewison, *Interpretation of Contracts* (6th edn, London, 2015), 1–05, 3–09; G McMeel, *The Construction of Contracts: Interpretation, Implication and Rectification* (2nd edn, Oxford University Press, 2011), 5.60 ff.

[66] G McMeel, *The Construction of Contracts: Interpretation, Implication and Rectification* (2nd edn, Oxford University Press, 2011), 5.98 ff.

(b) the pre-formation dealings disclose a settled understanding based on the doctrine of estoppel by convention, that is, a consensual understanding manifested in their dealings; or
(c) the parties (including possibly a special group or sect of which they are members) habitually use the relevant word or phrase in an unusual manner (unlike (a) or (b) this special usage subsists independently of the negotiations, although those negotiations might evidence the fact that the parties have adopted this special usage).

14.25 The English rule (confirmed by the House of Lords in *Chartbrook Ltd* v. *Persimmon Homes Ltd*, 2009)[67] is that, when seeking to interpret written contracts (as distinct from oral or partly written contracts), a party cannot adduce, without his opponent's permission, evidence of the parties' prior negotiations.

14.26 The five rationales for this bar are[68]: (i) avoidance of 'uncertainty and unpredictability', (ii) the fact that interested third parties cannot be guaranteed access to such negotiation history, (iii) such dealings are notoriously shifting and so such evidence would be unhelpful, (iv) one-sided impressions might contaminate the inquiry so that the objective approach to interpretation would be undermined, and (v) 'sophisticated and knowledgeable negotiators would be tempted to lay a paper trail of self-serving documents'.[69]

14.27 The unwillingness of English courts to consider pre-contractual negotiations is odd from a comparative perspective. The case in favour of this distinctive English approach is a complex argument, which turns on issues or perceptions of efficiency, certainty, and predictability (see the preceding paragraph). Not many non-English lawyers will find the English approach to be convincing. Certainly, English law is doctrinally inconsistent: this is because parties regularly plead Rectification in order to open the door to the court's reception of pre-formation negotiation evidence.[70]

14.28 The Supreme Court's decision in *Oceanbulk Shipping and Trading SA* v. *TMT Asia Ltd* (2010)[71] only just remained faithful to the present bar. It was held (i) that 'objective facts communicated by one party to the other in the course of the

[67] *Chartbrook Ltd* v. *Persimmon Homes Ltd* [2009] UKHL 38; [2009] 1 AC 1101; noted D McLaughlan (2010) 126 LQR 8–14.

[68] As collected by Briggs J at first instance in *Chartbrook Ltd* v. *Persimmon Homes Ltd* [2007] EWHC 409 (Ch), at [23], drawing upon Lord Nicholls' famous lecture, 'My Kingdom for a Horse: the Meaning of Words' (2005) 121 LQR 577; in his note on the House of Lords' decision in the *Chartbrook* case, D McLaughlan (2010) 126 LQR 8, 9–11 rejects these various suggested justifications; see also G Yihan, 'A Wrong Turn in History: Re-understanding the Exclusionary Rule Against Prior Negotiations in Contractual Interpretation' [2014] JBL 360–387.

[69] *Chartbrook* v. *Persimmons* [2008] EWCA Civ 183; [2008] 2 All ER (Comm) 387, at [111], *per* Collins LJ; this argument is described as unconvincing by D McLaughlan (2010) 126 LQR 8, 11.

[70] For expansion of the points made in this paragraph, Neil Andrews, *Contract Law* (2nd edn, Cambridge University Press, 2015), 14.16, 14.41, 14.42.

[71] [2010] UKSC 44; [2011] 1 AC 662; noted PS Davies [2011] CLJ 24–7 noting the artificial distinction between resort to negotiation evidence for discovery of background facts (allowed) and of the trend of negotiations (not allowed).

negotiations' can be taken into account as background factual matrix evidence to determine the scope of the settlement agreement; and (ii) that 'without prejudice' negotiations, which result in a settlement agreement, can be admitted for this purpose. Point (i) turns on the difficult distinction between objective fact and subjective one-sided opinion. As for point (ii), to decide otherwise would be to create an unprincipled distinction between interpretation of all other commercial contracts and interpretation of settlement agreements.[72]

14.29 *Three Exceptions to the Bar on Negotiation Evidence.* However, in the *Chartbrook* case (2009) Lord Hoffmann noted that it is acceptable to adduce extrinsic evidence of negotiations in the following three situations.[73]

14.30 (1) *Rectification.* Such claims (**14.45**) are often brought in conjunction with a pleading based on ordinary 'interpretation'.[74] In this way the adjudicator gains access to pre-formation negotiations for the purpose of that *equitable doctrine*. It follows that the adjudicator will not be blind to the pre-formation negotiations. To this extent, the doctrinal contrast between English law and civilian systems is a matter of no great practical significance.[75]

14.31 (2) *'Estoppel by Convention'.* This exception arises where the parties have outwardly reached an agreement concerning words in the written contract so that each is estopped from denying the non-literal construction which they wish to place on those words. This is 'estoppel by convention' (**10.15**, paragraph (iii)(c) above), which requires proof that an implicit agreement was manifested in the parties' pattern of behaviour and interaction, namely, proof that, *the parties had implicitly agreed on how the written terms should be interpreted or modified.*[76] Normally such an argument arises by reference to dealings subsequent to formation. But Lord Hoffmann contemplated that such an estoppel might arise with respect to their pre-formation dealings.

14.32 (3) *Habitual Unusual Usage by the Parties.* This exception arises if the contract contains words or phrases that have been used in a quite unusual sense by the parties in a course of dealing or the relevant wording is used in a special sense by, for example, members of a particular trade, etc. Lord Hoffmann said in the *Chartbrook* case (2009):[77] '*evidence may always be adduced that the parties habitually used words in an unconventional sense in order to support an argument that words in a contract should bear a similar unconventional meaning…*' But

---

[72] *ibid*, at [40].

[73] For acute analysis of each of these exceptions, D McLaughlan, 'Common Intention and Contract Interpretation' [2013] LMCLQ 30–50.

[74] On this two-pronged approach, G McMeel (2011) European Business L Rev 437–449, and R Buxton, '"Construction" and Rectification After *Chartbrook*' [2010] CLJ 253 and AS Burrows, 'Construction and Rectification', in AS Burrows and E Peel (eds), *Contract Terms* (Oxford University Press, 2007), 88 ff.

[75] E Clive, in H MacQueen and R Zimmermann (eds), *European Contract Law: Scots and South African Perspectives* (Edinburgh, 2006), chapter 7 at 183.

[76] *Amalgamated Investment & Property Co Ltd* v. *Texas Commerce International Bank Ltd* [1982] QB 84, 120, CA, *per* Lord Denning MR.

[77] [2009] UKHL 38; [2009] 1 AC 1101, at [45].

McLaughlan (2010)[78] has suggested that this qualification is troublesome because there is no workable concept of an 'unusual' meaning.

14.33 *POST-FORMATION CONDUCT*[79]

A written contract should not be construed by reference to the parties' conduct subsequent to the contract's formation, unless (1) it can be shown that the parties had specifically agreed to vary or discharge the agreement; or (2) the doctrine of estoppel by convention (**10.15**, paragraph (iii)(c) above) applies (based here on the parties' post-formation dealings).

14.34 *OBVIOUS ERROR, OBVIOUS SOLUTION: 'CORRECTIVE CONSTRUCTION'*[80]

(i) Unless the document is irredeemably defective, the tribunal can construe a manifestly defective text so as to correct a problem of drafting, provided the following tests are satisfied: (a) it is clear that the text is indeed defective; and (b) it is also obvious how the text should be repaired in order to reflect the parties' objective true meaning.
(ii) The technique of 'corrective construction' enables the tribunal to 'construe' a written contract by recasting a relevant phrase or portion of a written contract when it is obvious that the drafting is defective and the parties' true pre-formation shared meaning can be ascertained by consideration of the commercial purpose of the agreement and internal hints in the text.
(iii) But care must be taken that the tribunal does not substitute for the bargain actually made one which the tribunal believes could better have been made.

14.35 The House of Lords in *Chartbrook Ltd* v. *Persimmon Homes Ltd* (2009)[81] held that a judge can 'construe' a contract by wholly recasting a relevant phrase or portion of a written contract when (i) it is obvious that the drafting has gone awry and (ii) it is also obvious, as a matter of objective interpretation, what was the parties' true meaning.[82]

14.36 In the *Chartbrook* case (2009), Lord Hoffmann summarised the governing principles as follows:[83]

> '*In East v. Pantiles (Plant Hire) (1981), Brightman J stated the conditions for what he called "correction of mistakes by construction": "...first, there must be a clear mistake on the face of the instrument; secondly, it must be clear what correction ought to be made in order to cure the mistake. If those conditions are satisfied, then the correction is made as a matter of construction.*"'

---

[78] D McLaughlan (2010) 126 LQR 8, 12 (case note).

[79] *Whitworth Street Estates (Manchester) Ltd* v. *James Miller & Partners Ltd* [1970] AC 583, 603, HL, *per* Lord Reid.

[80] K Lewison, *Interpretation of Contracts* (6th edn, London, 2015), chapter 9; G McMeel, *The Construction of Contracts: Interpretation, Implication and Rectification* (2nd edn, Oxford University Press, 2011), chapter 17.

[81] [2009] UKHL 38; [2009] 1 AC 1101; noted D McLaughlan (2010) 126 LQR 8–14.

[82] Arden LJ in *Cherry Tree Investments Ltd* v. *Landmain Ltd* [2012] EWCA Civ 736; [2013] Ch 305, at [63].

[83] [2009] UKHL 38; [2009] 1 AC 1101, at [22] to [25].

14.37 Lord Hoffmann continued (also in the *Chartbrook* case, 2009):[84]

> '*[In] deciding whether there is a clear mistake, the court is not confined to reading the document without regard to its background or context. As the exercise is part of the single task of interpretation, the background and context must always be taken into consideration.*'

14.38 Lord Hoffmann added in the *Chartbrook* case:[85]'there is not, so to speak, a limit to the amount of red ink or verbal rearrangement or correction which the court is allowed. All that is required is that it should be clear that something has gone wrong with the language and that it should be clear what a reasonable person would have understood the parties to have meant.'

14.39 However, in *Marley* v. *Rawlings* (2014), in *dicta* (the case concerned rectification of wills under statutory powers), Lord Neuberger noted that the second sentence of this principle is 'controversial' (*per* Lord Hoffmann in *ICS*: '*On the other hand, if one would nevertheless conclude from the background that something must have gone wrong with the language, the law does not require judges to attribute to the parties an intention which they plainly could not have had*').[86] And Lord Neuberger noted[87] the criticism of Sir Richard Buxton (2010) in the *Cambridge Law Journal* (2010)[88] (see below), which was approved by *Lewison on the Interpretation of Contracts* (2015).[89]

14.40 *Examples of Corrective Construction.* There are many examples of the courts invoking this style of interpretation: *Holding & Barnes plc* v. *Hill House Hammond Ltd (No 1)* (2001);[90] *Littman* v. *Aspen Oil (Broking) Ltd* (2005);[91] *KPMG LLP* v. *Network Rail Infrastructure Ltd* (2007);[92] *Chartbrook Ltd* v. *Persimmon Homes Ltd* (2009);[93] *Multi-Link Leisure* v. *North Lanarkshire* (2010);[94] *Springwell Navigation Corporation* v. *JP Morgan Chase* (2010);[95] *Pink Floyd Music Ltd* v. *EMI Records Ltd* (2010);[96] the *Caresse Navigation* case (2014).[97]

---

[84] *ibid*, at [24].

[85] *Chartbrook Ltd* v. *Persimmon Homes Ltd* [2009] AC 1101, at [25].

[86] [2014] UKSC 2; [2015] AC 129, at [37].

[87] *ibid*, at [39].

[88] '"Construction" and Rectification after *Chartbrook*' [2010] CLJ 253.

[89] *Lewison on The Interpretation of Contracts* (6th edn, London, 2015), at 9.03 n 80.

[90] [2001] EWCA Civ 1334; [2002] L & TR 103.

[91] [2005] EWCA Civ 1579; [2006] 2 P & CR 2; [2006] L & TR 9; [2005] NPC 150.

[92] [2007] EWCA Civ 363; [2007] Bus LR 1336.

[93] [2009] UKHL 38; [2009] 1 AC 1101; noted D McLaughlan (2010) 126 LQR 8–14.

[94] [2010] UKSC 47; [2011] 1 All ER 175; for observations on this case, Lord Grabiner, 'The Iterative Process of Contractual Interpretation' (2012) 128 LQR 41, 52–3.

[95] [2010] EWCA Civ 1221; [2010] 2 CLC 705, at [132] to [140].

[96] [2010] EWCA Civ 1429; [2011] 1 WLR 770.

[97] [2014] EWCA Civ 1366; [2015] QB 366.

14.41 In *Littman* v. *Aspen Oil (Broking) Ltd* (2005)[98] a lease contained a mutual break clause exercisable by either party upon giving 6 months' written notice. The landlord had intended that the contract should permit the tenant to exercise this break clause only if the tenant had complied with its covenants at the relevant time. But the botched text (see the words in bold below) stated: '*that up to the Termination Date in the case of a notice* ***given by the Landlord*** *[emphasis inserted] the Tenant shall have paid the rents…and shall have duly observed and performed the Tenant's covenants…and the conditions herein contained….*' The Court of Appeal upheld Hart J's decision that the words highlighted above should be construed to read: 'given by the Tenant'. There is no need for the corrupted text to be grammatically or syntactically wrong. Such 'construction' could cure a manifest slip. Otherwise, the final text would be commercial nonsense.

14.42 In *Pink Floyd Music Ltd* v. *EMI Records Ltd* (2010)[99] Lord Neuberger MR and Laws LJ held that an agreement for exploitation of the 'records' of Pink Floyd could be construed as embracing digital recordings by the same band. To decide otherwise would run counter to the obvious commercial purpose of the transaction (but Carnwath LJ dissented, finding no such obvious mistake).

14.43 In the *Caresse Navigation* case (2014) a bill of lading purported to incorporate from a charterparty 'All terms…including the law and arbitration clause…'[100] In fact the charterparty contained no arbitration clause and instead provided for the exclusive jurisdiction of the English courts. It was held that the jurisdiction clause was validly incorporated. This was an occasion for 'corrective construction' because there was an evidently mistaken formulation, the incorporation clause ('and arbitration clause') being plainly intended to incorporate 'any arbitration clause or jurisdiction clause'.

14.44 *No Possibility of 'Corrective Construction'.*[101] This form of construction is unavailable if:

(1) *The Only Real Complaint is that Both Parties have Misunderstood the Extent of the Subject-matter. Bashir* v. *Ali* (2011), where Etherton LJ said:[102]

> '*…The wording of the documentation in the present case is clear…It may have resulted in a good bargain for one of the parties, but, as Lord Hoffmann pointed out in Chartbrook at [20], that is not itself a sufficient reason for supposing that the contract does not mean what it says.*'

[98] [2005] EWCA Civ 1579; [2006] 2 P & CR 2; [2006] L & TR 9; [2005] NPC 150.

[99] [2010] EWCA Civ 1429; [2011] 1 WLR 770.

[100] *Caresse Navigation Ltd* v. *Office National de l'Electricité* [2014] EWCA Civ 1366; [2015] QB 366.

[101] The phrase adopted by Lewison LJ in *Cherry Tree Investments Ltd* v. *Landmain Ltd* [2012] EWCA Civ 736; [2013] Ch 305, at [97] and also used in Arden LJ's judgment.

[102] [2011] EWCA Civ 707; [2011] 2 P & CR 12, at [39].

Etherton J added[103] '*There may be a case in which the commercial advantage would be so great that it moves the case into the sphere of irrationality and arbitrariness. That, however, is not the present case.*'

(2) *A Clause is Flawed but does not Contain an Inner Solution.* In *Arnold* v. *Britton* (2015) Lord Hodge said:[104]

> '*The court must be satisfied as to both the mistake and the nature of the correction: Pink Floyd Music Ltd v. EMI Records Ltd [2010] EWCA Civ 1429 at [21], per Lord Neuberger of Abbotsbury MR. This is not an unusual case, such as KPMG [2007] Bus LR 1336 in which a mistake was obvious on the face of the contract and the precise nature of the correction had no effect on the outcome.*'

For this reason, the Court of Appeal in *ING Bank NV* v. *Ros Roca SA* (2011)[105] found it impossible, on the facts, to apply 'constructive interpretation' to re-write a clause concerning an investment bank's 'additional fee'.

(3) *The Contract is beyond Verbal Redemption.* This was the position in *Fairstate Ltd* v. *General Enterprise & Management Ltd* (2010),[106] where the judge said:[107] '*the defects in the agreement recorded in the Guarantee Form are so fundamental and extensive that they cannot sufficiently be cured, either by purposive construction, or by rectification, or by any combination of those approaches.*' (Here rectification also failed because there had been no clear prior consensus concerning the effect and scope of the guarantee.)

(4) *Public Registers.* The Court of Appeal in *Cherry Tree Investments Ltd* v. *Landmain Ltd* (2012)[108] held that corrective interpretation could not be used to change a public document (a land registration) to reflect a special clause concerning the operation of the relevant registered interest. The majority (Lewison and Longmore LJJ) held that it was necessary to insulate such public registers from corrective interpretation by reference to collateral information inaccessible to third parties (instead they gave priority to the statutory process of rectification which has been introduced in that particular context under the land registration legislation;[109] but no application for statutory rectification had been made in this case). In her dissent in the *Cherry Tree* case, Arden LJ contended that, corrective interpretation should be permitted because the present case did not in fact involve prejudice to third parties.[110]

---

[103] *ibid*, at [40].

[104] [2015] UKSC 36; [2015] AC 1619, at [78].

[105] [2011] EWCA Civ 353; [2012] 1 WLR 472 (but the court was able to achieve a favourable outcome for the bank by employing the doctrine of estoppel by convention to take account of post-formation dealings).

[106] [2010] EWHC 3072 (QB); [2011] 2 All ER (Comm) 497; 133 Con LR 112 (Richard Salter QC, Deputy).

[107] *ibid*, at [94].

[108] [2012] EWCA Civ 736; [2013] Ch 305, at [121].

[109] *ibid*, at [117] ff (notably at [121]), noting Schedule 4 to the Land Registration Act 2002.

[110] *ibid*, at [54] to [60]; here argument was rejected by Lewison LJ at [122].

14.2 Equitable Doctrine of Rectification of Written Agreements

14.45 RECTIFICATION (EQUITABLE ORDER)[111]

(i) *Outline.* Rectification[112] is an equitable order concerning written contracts (and 'instruments').[113] There are two separate grounds for rectifying written contracts:

(a) common intention rectification: here the tribunal responds to a mismatch between the objectively agreed version of the transaction, subsisting immediately prior to the written form, and the parties' final instrument which purports to give unaltered effect to that agreed version; or
(b) unilateral mistake: here party B has reprehensibly failed to point out to party A that the written terms of their imminent transaction will not accord with party A's mistaken understanding concerning the contents of that written agreement.

(ii) *Common Intention Rectification.* This equitable remedy allows the tribunal to declare that a written contract should be reconstituted because by joint mistake it fails to reflect the parties' pre-formation 'common continuing intention'. The elements are:

(a) the parties had a common intention at the time of formation (it is possible that the relevant common intention superseded an earlier common intention, especially where negotiations have been protracted and the proposed deal has proceeded through numerous phases);
(b) the existence and content of that common intention will be established objectively (**10.08**); that is to say by reference to what an objective observer would have thought the intentions of the parties to be during the relevant negotiations;
(c) the relevant common intention must have subsisted at the moment of formation;
(d) by mistake, the written contract (or other 'instrument') did not accurately and fully reflect that common intention.

(iii) *Unilateral Error Accompanied by the Other Party's Misconduct or Reprehensible Silence.* Mere unilateral error does not support a claim for rec-

---

[111] D Hodge, *Rectification: The Modern Law and Practice Governing Claims of Rectification* (2nd edn, London, 2015); G McMeel, *The Construction of Contracts: Interpretation, Implication and Rectification* (2nd edn, Oxford University Press, 2011), chapter 17.

[112] D Hodge, *Rectification: The Modern Law and Practice Governing Claims for Rectification for Mistake* (2nd edn, London, 2015).

[113] e.g., nominations of pensions beneficiaries: *Collins* v. *Jones and Jones* 3 February 2000 *The Times* (Stanley Burnton QC); and for other unilateral instruments (such as leasehold notices or patents), see *Marley* v. *Rawlings* [2014] UKSC 2; [2015] AC 129, at [21], [22], [27], [77].

tification, unless the other party's position is wholly unmeritorious, in particular, because he has dishonestly acquiesced in the other's mistake.

(iv) *Standard of Proof.* In all claims for rectification, the party seeking rectification must satisfy a high standard of proof, especially where both parties have been professionally advised.

(v) *Third Party Rights.* Rectification will not be awarded if this would harm a third party who has, in good faith and for consideration, acquired rights in the relevant subject matter.[114] But there must be good faith.[115] Consider the case where the document which is to be rectified was between A and B, but the present dispute is between A and D. In this situation, rectification in favour of A, and to D's disadvantage, is available provided D is not a *bona fide* purchaser (as where it is shown that a portion of land was not intended to be included in the A/B transaction, and D knew that, following a blunder in the drafting of the A/B document, the literal terms of the A/D transaction purported to give D the same portion of land; rectification can be ordered of the A/B and A/D transactions; and D is in fact the trustee of the wrongly conveyed portion for the benefit of A, the original vendor).[116]

(vi) *Rectification is Retroactive to Date of Formation.* But where there is no third party good faith purchaser, and rectification is granted, the effect of the rectification order is that the document operates in its rectified form from the formation of the document: it is treated as having always operated in its rectified form.[117]

(vii) *Rectification barred by prejudicial delay ('laches'), acquiescence, or affirmation.* A party must take prompt action by applying to the tribunal for rectification: rectification will be denied if a party 'sleeps on his rights'.[118]

14.46 *Common Intention Rectification.* In the *Daventry* case (2011) Etherton LJ summarised the law of common intention rectification (a statement approved by Lord Neuberger MR in the same case)[119] as follows:[120]

---

[114] *Smith* v. *Jones* [1954] 1 WLR 1089, 1091–3, *per* Upjohn J; A Berg (2008) 124 LQR 6, 12.

[115] *Craddock Bros* v. *Hunt* [1923] 2 Ch 136, 151, 154–5, 158–9, CA, *per* Lord Sterndale MR and Warrington LJ (Younger LJ dissenting).

[116] *ibid*

[117] See G McMeel, *The Construction of Contracts: Interpretation, Implication and Rectification* (2nd edn, Oxford University Press, 2011), 17.93 *Craddock Bros Ltd* v. *Hunt* [1923] 2 Ch 136, 151–2, CA, *per* Lord Sterndale MR (citing *Johnson* v. *Bragge* [1901] 1 Ch 28, 37, *per* Cozens-Hardy J); and [1923] 2 Ch 136, 160, *per* Warrington LJ.

[118] G McMeel, *The Construction of Contracts: Interpretation, Implication and Rectification* (2nd edn, Oxford University Press, 2011), 17.93.

[119] *Daventry District Council* v. *Daventry & District Housing Ltd* [2011] EWCA Civ 1153; [2012] 1 WLR 1333, at [227]; noted Paul S Davies, 'Rectifying the Course of Rectification' (2012) MLR 412–426.

[120] *ibid*, at [80].

(1) 'the parties had a common continuing intention, whether or not amounting to an agreement, in respect of a particular matter in the instrument to be rectified;
(2) which existed at the time of execution of the instrument sought to be rectified;
(3) such common continuing intention to be established objectively, that is to say by reference to what an objective observer would have thought the intentions of the parties to be; and
(4) by mistake, the instrument did not reflect that common intention.'

14.47 The *Need for an Unbroken Continuing Intention.* If the earlier stage of the negotiations involves the parties agreeing a set of terms 'A, B, and C', but the final version is a set of terms 'X, Y, and Z', it might be clear that the parties have substituted for elements 'A, B and C' new elements 'X, Y and Z'. If that is the case, there should be no scope for rectifying the contract to restore the terms 'A, B, and C'.

14.48 A troublesome development is the Court of Appeal's majority decision in *Daventry* case (2011).[121] During the negotiations, the original version of the document had allocated the financial burden for a pension shortfall to DDH ('Housing') rather than DDC ('Council'). But Housing clearly introduced into the second phase of the negotiations a competing clause which placed the burden on Council. Council, on legal advice, seemed to have accepted this change, which was reflected in the final agreement. Council sought rectification under both the common intention and unilateral mistake heads. Vos J at first instance denied rectification under both heads. The appeal focused on the common intention head. By a majority (Etherton LJ dissenting) the Court of Appeal granted common intention rectification on these facts. Toulson LJ[122] and Lord Neuberger MR[123] held that the subsequent change had not been clearly enough signalled to Council. This was a surprising conclusion because (i) this final wording clearly contradicted the earlier version and (ii) and that final version was available to be read by Council's officials and their lawyers.

14.49 The difference between the majority (Toulson LJ and Lord Neuberger MR) and Etherton LJ (dissenting) was whether one party's last minute change of the terms (reflected in the final wording) had been sufficiently absorbed by the other so that the final text was accurate (the dissenting judge's analysis, and that adopted by Vos J at first instance, both refusing rectification) or whether rectification should be granted because the last minute change was introduced without a joint decision to change the contract's provision and even involved the objective appearance of a mistake (as preferred by the majority). It is submitted that: (1) the relevant 'common continuing intention' must be established, on the balance of probabilities, as an objectively subsisting matter; for this purpose the court will draw objective inferences when determining whether such a common intention existed, its scope and content, and whether that common intention continued or was revised or abandoned; and (2) where it is clear that the parties had a shared intention which does not match the objective analysis, it should be the parties' actual shared belief which prevails.

---

[121] *Daventry* case.

[122] *ibid*, at [178].

[123] *ibid*, at [213] to [225].

Chapter 15
Breach

Abstract The rules concerning breach are fundamental but complex. This is a topic which requires careful analysis because one party's assertion that his conduct was a legitimate response to the other's default might in fact misfire if the tribunal concludes that there was no default, or at least an insufficiently serious default. English law classifies obligations as (i) terms which invariably permit termination if breached (conditions); or (ii) terms which potentially, but not necessarily, allow termination if breached (intermediate terms); or (iii) minor terms breach of which does not justify termination, and which instead merely give rise to the liability to pay damages (warranties). There are also subtleties concerning anticipatory breach, renunciation, repudiation, and the process of bringing the contract to an end by virtue of breach.

15.1 Nature of Breach

15.01 *DEFINITION*[1]

Breach of contract involves unexcused default. Sources of possible excuses might be: (i) an exclusion clause (**13.12**); or (ii) a *force majeure* clause[2] (stipulating that a party will be released from his obligations by reason of freak and excusable supervening events); or (iii) frustration of the contract or of part of the contract (**16.01**); (iv) the fact that the other party's default excuses the current party from

[1] Neil H Andrews, MA Clarke, AM Tettenborn, G Virgo, *Contractual Duties: Performance, Breach, Termination and Remedies* (London, 2012) (breach and performance section by Neil Andrews), 5–001 ff; see also Q Liu, *Anticipatory Breach* (Hart, Oxford, 2011); JE Stannard and D Capper, *Termination for Breach of Contract* (Oxford University Press, 2014). (From an Australian perspective, JW Carter, *Carter's Breach of Contract* (Hart, Oxford, 2012), reviewed by Neil Andrews [2013] CLJ 214–7).

[2] K Lewison, *Interpretation of Contracts* (6th edn, London, 2015), chapter 13; E McKendrick (ed), *Force Majeure and Frustration of Contract* (2nd edn, London, 1995); G McMeel, *The Construction of Contracts: Interpretation, Implication and Rectification* (2nd edn, Oxford University Press, 2011), 22.35 ff; GH Treitel, *Frustration and Force Majeure* (3rd edn, London, 2014); important cases include*: Tennants (Lancashire) Ltd* v. *CS Wilson & Co Ltd* [1917] AC 495, HL; *Tandrin Aviation Holdings Ltd* v. *Aero ToyStore LLC* [2010] EWHC 40 (Comm); [2010] 2 Lloyd's Rep 668 at [40], generally on this topic, [38] to [51], per Hamblen J; *Great Elephant Corpn v. Trafigura Beheer BV ('The Crudesky')* [2013] EWCA Civ 905; [2013] 2 All ER (Comm) 992; [2014] 1 Lloyd's Rep 1.

N. Andrews, *Arbitration and Contract Law*, Ius Gentium: Comparative Perspectives on Law and Justice 54, DOI 10.1007/978-3-319-27144-6_15

performing (**15.38**); or (v) the innocent party has waived his rights to complain about the relevant breach (**15.25**).

15.02 *RENUNCIATION OR ACTUAL DEFAULT*[3]

Breach can occur by declaration ('renunciation') (**15.04**) or actual default (by misconduct or omission, see **15.05**).

15.03 *ADVANCE DEFAULT AND PERFORMANCE DEFAULT*[4]

(i) Breach by actual default can arise before or at the time of expected performance. Accordingly, breach can be categorised under the following three headings:

(a) *Renunciation, Explicit or Implicit. Renunciation occurs if*, either before or at the time of performance, a party declares ('explicit renunciation') or indicates by conduct ('implicit renunciation') that he does not intend to perform.

(b) *Advance Default*: *Culpable Impossibility*. Before the performance is due, a party might have culpably (that is, without lawful excuse) prevented the contract from being performed.

(c) *Defective Performance*. Performance might be defective in various ways, including: total non-performance; the tender or supply of wrong or sub-standard subject-matter, or useless or unsatisfactory services; performance might be delayed or too slow; or the guilty party might do that which he promised not to do, for example, by working for a rival company in breach of an obligation to perform exclusively for the claimant's benefit.

(ii) *Innocent Party's Position*. In the face of (i)(a) or (i)(b) the other party ('innocent party') can 'elect' to terminate the contract straightaway and sue for compensation. If breach takes the form of defective performance, as in (i)(c), the innocent party can terminate for breach only if the breach is serious (a serious breach is one which goes to the root of the transaction). See further **15.20** below on situations where breach justifies the innocent party terminating the contract.

(iii) *Terminology*: *Distinguishing Renunciation and Repudiation*. The expression 'repudiation' (or 'repudiatory breach') is sometimes used in a generic sense to embrace any form of breach (by renunciation or otherwise) justifying termination. However, 'renunciation' (see further **15.04**) is a clearer way of expressing the type of breach mentioned at (i)(a).

---

[3]Neil H Andrews, MA Clarke, AM Tettenborn, G Virgo, *Contractual Duties*: *Performance, Breach, Termination and Remedies* (London, 2012) (breach and performance section by Neil Andrews), chapter 5.

[4]Neil H Andrews, MA Clarke, AM Tettenborn, G Virgo, *Contractual Duties*: *Performance, Breach, Termination and Remedies* (London, 2012) (breach and performance section by Neil Andrews), chapters 5 to 8, and chapter 13.

15.04 *RENUNCIATION*[5]

(i) *Renunciation*. Renunciation is the communication of an intention that the renouncing party no longer wishes to be bound by the contract. In *Federal Commerce & Navigation Co* v. *Molena Alpha Inc*, *'The Nanfri'* (1979)[6] Lord Wilberforce cited Lord Cockburn CJ in *Freeth* v. *Burr* (1874): 'a*n intimation of an intention to abandon and altogether to refuse performance of the contract…*' or '*to evince an intention no longer to be bound by the contract.*'[7]

(ii) The renunciation might be total (absolute unwillingness to perform at all) or substantial (unwillingness to comply except defiantly, on a new and unauthorised basis which is inconsistent with the contract).

(iii) The renunciation can be either (a) by words ('explicit renunciation') or (b) implication from conduct ('implicit renunciation').

(iv) It is not enough for renunciation to be evidenced; it must be communicated to, or reach, the other party; and so the other party must be notified, or at least receive clear evidence, of renunciation.

(v) *Explicit Renunciation*.[8] The following definition has been judicially approved: '*A renunciation of a contract occurs when one party by words or conduct evinces an intention not to perform, or expressly declares that he is or will be unable to perform, his obligations under the contract in some essential respect. The renunciation may occur before or at the time fixed for performance. An absolute refusal* [*will count*]*… as will also a clear and unambiguous assertion by one party that he will be unable to perform when the time for performance should arrive.*'

(vi) *Implicit Renunciation*.[9] The following definition has been judicially approved: '[*such implicit renunciation arises where the*] *actions of the party in default are such as to lead a reasonable person to conclude that he no longer intends to be bound by its provisions. The renunciation is then evidenced by conduct.*'

---

[5] Neil H Andrews, MA Clarke, AM Tettenborn, G Virgo, *Contractual Duties: Performance, Breach, Termination and Remedies* (London, 2012) (breach and performance section by Neil Andrews), chapter 6.

[6] [1979] AC 757, 778–9, HL.

[7] (1874) LR 9 CP 208, 213, *per* Lord Coleridge CJ (Court of Common Pleas); cited by Earl of Selborne LC in *Mersey Steel and Iron Co (Limited)* v. *Naylor, Benzon & Co* (1883–84) L.R 9 App Cas 434, 438–9, HL; Lord Salmon collected various formualtions of the test in *Woodar Investment Development Ltd* v. *Wimpey Construction UK Ltd* [1980] 1 WLR 277, 287–8, HL.

[8] Endorsed in *Ampurius Nu Homes Holdings Ltd* v. *Telford Homes (Creekside) Ltd* [2013] EWCA Civ 577; [2013] 4 All ER 377, at [70].

[9] Also endorsed in *Ampurius* case, see preceding note.

15.05 *REPUDIATION*[10]

This involves an actual breach of contract by conduct (or sometimes by omission) which is grave enough that it 'goes to the root of the contract', that is, the breach is really serious.

15.06 *IRRELEVANT THAT BREACH IS DELIBERATE*[11]

(i) The fact that breach is deliberate makes no difference, except:

  (a) exclusion clauses might not be construed to extend to deliberate breach; and
  (b) deliberate breach might indicate (as part of a wider inquiry) that the guilty party has manifested an intention no longer to be bound by the contract (renunciation: **15.04**).

(ii) Deliberate breach does not give rise to liability for exemplary damages in English contract law (more generally, exemplary damages are unavailable for breach of contract).

15.07 *DEFAULTING PARTY'S GOOD FAITH*[12]

(i) In general (for qualifications, see (ii) below) breach will arise despite the guilty party's belief that he is not acting, or proposing to act, wrongly. And so, *prima facie* a party's refusal or failure to perform, although occurring or proposed in good faith, will constitute a renunciation or repudiation if the contract does not in fact justify that party's stance. The fundamental decision is *Federal Commerce & Navigation Co* v. *Molena Alpha Inc*, '*The Nanfri*' (1979).[13] A shipowner, acting on incorrect legal advice, refused to issue pre-paid bills of lading. The House of Lords unanimously held that the breach justified termination and that the owner's good faith was irrelevant: such good faith does not 'cleanse' a renunciation or repudiation. There were three salient factors: (i) *clarity*-the repudiation was clear and emphatic; (ii) *danger*- the innocent charterer was placed in a very tight corner because the charterer's clientele, namely third-party cargo dealers in the relevant trade, as noted by later decisions;[14] (iii) *lack of time*-- there was no time to spare, no commercial 'window' within which to sort out this difference.

---

[10] Neil H Andrews, MA Clarke, AM Tettenborn, G Virgo, *Contractual Duties: Performance, Breach, Termination and Remedies* (London, 2012) (breach and performance section by Neil Andrews), chapter 8.

[11] Neil H Andrews, MA Clarke, AM Tettenborn, G Virgo, *Contractual Duties: Performance, Breach, Termination and Remedies* (London, 2012) (breach and performance section by Neil Andrews), 5–023.

[12] *ibid*, 6–068 ff.

[13] [1979] AC 757, HL.

[14] *Dalkia Utilities Services plc* v. *Celtech International Ltd* [2006] EWHC 63 (Comm); [2006] 1 Lloyd's Rep 599, at [148], *per* Christopher Clarke J; *Gulf Agri Trade FZCO* v. *Aston Agro Industrial AG* [2008] EWHC 1252 (Comm); [2009] 1 All ER (Comm) 991; [2008] 2 Lloyd's Rep 376, at [43], *per* Aikens J.

(ii) The proposition at (i) above is subject to these exceptions (in each of these three situations party A's position is unjustified, even though presented in good faith; and in each situation party B will not be justified in terminating the contract by reason of A's statements or behaviour): (a) it should have been apparent to party B that the circumstances provided a reasonable opportunity for the validity of party A's stance to be referred to a neutral third-party for determination (*Woodar Investment Development Ltd* v. *Wimpey Construction UK Ltd*, 1980;[15] or (b) party B could have checked the position with party A in order to discover whether the latter was really prepared to provide party B with the right to terminate the contract for breach (*Vaswani* v. *Italian Motors (Sales & Services) Ltd*, 1996),[16] or (c) party B could and should have corrected party A's obvious error (*Eminence Property Developments Ltd* v. *Heaney*, 2010).[17]

15.08 *WRONG REASON GIVEN FOR JUSTIFIED TERMINATION*

Where one party has renounced or repudiated the contract (or otherwise acted so as to justify termination for breach, see **15.20** on these situations), the other party will have validly brought the contract to an end, even if he gives the wrong reason for doing so or gives no reason at all.[18]

15.09 *REPETITIVE BREACH*[19]

(i) Repetitive breach of a serious nature (whether categorised as implicit renunciation (**15.04**) or repudiation (**15.05**) might justify termination.
(ii) *Repeated breaches* might justify the other party in terminating the contract even though there has been neither a breach of a 'condition', nor a clear renunciation (communication of unwillingness to honour the contract) nor a one-off repudiatory breach (a single default striking at the root of the contract).
(iii) For this purpose, the tribunal will assess whether a party's repeated default is grave enough, presently and prospectively, so as to strike at the root of the other party's contractual expectations.

---

[15] [1980] 1 WLR 277, HL (but time seldom permits this to occur: *James Shaffer Ld.* v. *Findlay Durham & Brodie* [1953] 1 WLR 106, 118, CA, *per* Singleton LJ).

[16] [1996] 1 WLR 270, 277, PC (Lord Woolf).

[17] [2010] EWCA Civ 1168; [2011] 2 All ER (Comm) 223, generally at [61] to [65], notably, at [65] sub-para (4); approved in *Oates* v. *Hooper* [2010] EWCA Civ 1346, [2010] N.P.C. 119 and *Samarenko* v. *Dawn Hill House Ltd* [2011] EWCA Civ 1445; [2013] Ch 36.

[18] *Force India Formula One Team Ltd* v. *Etihad Airways PJSC* [2010] EWCA Civ 1051; [2011] ETLR 10, at [116]; *Tele2 International Card Company SA* v. *Post Office Ltd* [2009] EWCA Civ 9, at [30] n 17, *per* Aikens J, noting *Boston Deep Sea and Ice Co* v. *Ansell* (1888) 39 Ch D 339, 364, CA, *per* Bowen LJ; *British and Benningtons Ltd* v. *NorthWestern Cahar Tea Co Ltd* [1923] AC 48, 71–72, HL, *per* Lord Sumner; and see '*The Mihalis Angelos*' [1971] 1 QB 164, 193, 195, CA.

[19] Neil H Andrews, MA Clarke, AM Tettenborn, G Virgo, *Contractual Duties: Performance, Breach, Termination and Remedies* (London, 2012) (breach and performance section by Neil Andrews), 8–007 ff.

15.10 *TYPES OF ANTICIPATORY BREACH*[20]

(i) *Two types*. Such breach can take one of two forms:

(a) *Advance Renunciation*: for example, an airline might notify passengers that it has cancelled a flight several weeks in advance; or

(b) *Destruction of the Chance to Perform* (*Culpable Inevitable Default*): prevention of future performance, again when the date for performance has not arrived.

(ii) *Advance Renunciation*. As for (i)(a), party B commits an anticipatory breach by renunciation only if he has expressed unwillingness to perform or his conduct demonstrates clearly that he did not intend to proceed with the contract[21]: see '*The Simona*' (1989) for Lord Ackner's survey of the doctrine's development,[22] noting, in particular, the seminal nineteenth-century cases of *Hochster* v. *De La Tour* (1853)[23] and *Frost* v. *Knight* (1872).[24]

(iii) *Destruction of the Chance to Perform* (*Culpable Inevitable Default*). As for (i)(b), here the guilty party incapacitates himself, or prevents performance, before the scheduled date. This need not involve deliberate sabotaging of the contract. It is enough that the default involves breach of an express or implied term.

(iv) *Innocent Party's Need to Demonstrate Inevitable Default by the Other*. In situation (i)(b), a high standard of proof applies: the tribunal must be satisfied that there is proof of inevitable future default. It is not enough that something was done (or there has been a failure to prepare) which made future performance uncertain, or unlikely, or even very unlikely. For this reason, advance renunciation under (i)(a) above is the much safer platform for establishing entitlement to terminate for breach. Devlin J noted in *Universal Cargo Carriers Corporation* v. *Citati* (1957)[25] that termination on this basis involves the 'serious risk' that the court might find that in fact the other party's inability to perform had not been shown to be inexorable or sufficiently probable. Popplewell J in *Geden Operations Ltd* v. *Dry Bulk Handy Holdings Inc* ('*The Bulk Uruguay*') (2014)

---

[20] Neil H Andrews, MA Clarke, AM Tettenborn, G Virgo, *Contractual Duties: Performance, Breach, Termination and Remedies* (London, 2012) (breach and performance section by Neil Andrews), chapter 7; Q Liu, *Anticipatory Breach* (Hart, Oxford, 2011).

[21] M Mustill, *Anticipatory Breach: Butterworths Lectures 1989–90* (London, 1990) (and (2008) 124 LQR 569, at 576 ff); JC Smith in E Lomnicka and CJG Morse (eds), *Contemporary Issues in Commercial Law: Essays in Honour of AG Guest* (1994), 175.

[22] *Fercometal SARL* v. *Mediterranean Shipping Co SA* ('*The Simona*') [1989] AC 788, 797–805, HL.

[23] (1853) 2 E & B 678; 22 LJ (QB) 455.

[24] (1872) LR 7 Ex 111.

[25] [1957] 2 QB 401, 436–8 (not disturbed on appeal on this point: [1957] 1 WLR 979, CA and [1958] 2 QB 254, CA); MJ Mustill, *Anticipatory Breach: Butterworths Lectures 1989–90* (1990), 69 ff; MJ Mustill (2008) 124 LQR 569, 580 n 23 notes the galaxy of commercial talent employed in arguing this case.

referred to the need for inevitable default.[26] In *Alfred Toepfer International GmbH* v. *Itex Itagrani Export SA* (1993)[27] the seller prematurely calculated that the buyer would be unable to load a cargo in full. In fact it was not at all certain that the buyer would have failed to do so. And so the seller was held to have repudiated. Saville J commented[28]: '... *[In] the present case there was only a chance that the buyers would be unable to perform.*'

(v) *Date for Assessment of Damages*: see further **17.13** below: the House of Lords in *Golden Strait Corporation* v. *Nippon Yusen Kubishika Kaisha* ('*The Golden Victory*')[29] held that damages for anticipatory breach should reflect post-breach events if they reduce or eliminate the claimant's loss.

15.11 *SEEKING REASSURANCE*[30]

(i) A party (the 'anxious party') who is concerned that the other party will in due course default has no general contractual right (for qualifications see (ii) below) to place the other party in immediate jeopardy by issuing a precautionary demand requiring an assurance that the other party remains able and willing to perform without default.

(ii) The anxious party must wait and see whether default in fact eventually occurs unless: (a) the contract contains an express contractual right to demand such an assurance; or (b) there has been a clear advance renunciation (**15.04**); or (c) there are facts constituting destruction of the chance to perform (culpable inevitable default) (**15.10**, paragraph (iii) above); or (d) the anxious party obtains an injunction against the other party (as explained below at **15.12**).

---

[26] [2014] EWHC 885 (Comm), at [18] (see also [17]).

[27] [1993] 1 Lloyd's Rep 360, Saville J; similarly *Continental Contractors Ltd and Ernest Beck & Co Ltd* v. *Medway Oil & Storage Co Ltd* (1926) 25 Lloyd's Rep 288DOUBLEHYPHEN-suppliers of kerosene had not 'wholly and finally disabled' themselves, even though they had encountered difficulties in procuring a supply; the *Toepfer* case and other authorities were considered by Proudman J in *Ridgewood Properties Group Ltd* v. *Valero Energy Ltd* [2013] EWHC 98 (Ch); [2013] Ch 525, at [30], [31], [107], considering *Synge* v. *Synge* [1894] 1 QB 466; *Ogdens Ltd* v. *Nelson* [1905] AC 109; *Fratelli Sorrentino* v. *Buerger* [1915] 1 KB 307; *Omnium d'Enterprises* v. *Sutherland* [1919] 1 KB 618, CA.

[28] [1993] 1 Lloyd's Rep 360, Saville J.

[29] [2007] UKHL 12, [2007] 2 AC 353; noted Lord Mustill (2008) 124 LQR 569; J Morgan [2007] CLJ 263; C Nicholls (2008) JBL 91; B Coote (2007) 123 LQR 503; Sir Bernard Rix, in M Andenas and D Fairgrieve (eds), *Tom Bingham and the Transformation of the Law: A Liber Amicorum* (Oxford University Press, 2009), 679–83.

[30] Neil H Andrews, MA Clarke, AM Tettenborn, G Virgo, *Contractual Duties: Performance, Breach, Termination and Remedies* (London, 2012) (breach and performance section by Neil Andrews), 7–079 ff.

15.12 *ANTICIPATORY BREACH: INJUNCTION*[31]

(i) In appropriate circumstances, a party might obtain an injunction to prevent a party taking a step which would preclude him from complying in due course with an obligation.

(ii) An injunction might be granted even where that party's capacity to execute fully the relevant obligation is contingent on a third party's permission, such as planning permission. In *Berkeley Community Villages Ltd* v. *Pullen* (2007)[32] P, a landowner, proposed to sell part of the land to a third party. That would deprive B, with whom P had entered into a development contract, of its right to commission. The proposed sale would involve a breach. P had conceded[33] that an injunction would be available if Morgan J found that the proposed sale would involve breach. The judge added *dicta*[34] (not necessary for his decision in view of this concession) that an injunction would have been available for anticipatory breach of an obligation (here, clause 10).[35] The injunction would prevent a party taking a step which would preclude him from complying in due course with that obligation even where that party's capacity to execute fully the relevant obligation is contingent on a third party's permission (such as planning permission).

15.13 *STRICT AND NON-STRICT OBLIGATIONS*[36]

(i) Breach of contract can involve failure to satisfy a strict obligation (for example, a seller's statutory obligations to supply goods which correspond to their contractual description, and are of satisfactory quality, and are reasonably fit for their intended purpose: sections 13 to 15 of the Sale of Goods Act 1979; sections 9 to 32 (goods) and 33 to 47 (digital content agreements) of the Consumer Rights Act 2015. Strict liability can also arise under a judicially recognised implied term. For example, strict liability was imposed for bug bites suffered by a visitor to the Turkish baths in *Silverman* v. *Imperial London Hotels Ltd* (1927).[37]

(ii) Some contractual obligations require only the exercise of reasonable care, or the meeting of the relevant professional level of diligence (for example, section 13 of the Supply of Goods and Services Act 1982 and sections 48 to 57 of the Consumer Rights Act 2015). The law is highly pragmatic in this respect. In a contract for professional services (doctors receiving remuneration, lawyers not

[31] Neil H Andrews, MA Clarke, AM Tettenborn, G Virgo, *Contractual Duties: Performance, Breach, Termination and Remedies* (London, 2012) (breach and performance section by Neil Andrews), 7–022, 7–023.

[32] [2007] EWHC 1330 (Ch); [2007] 3 EGLR 101; [2007] 24 EG 169 (CS); [2007] NPC 71.

[33] *ibid*, at [142].

[34] *ibid*, at [79] to [83].

[35] clause 10.

[36] This literature antedates the Consumer Rights Act 2015; Neil H Andrews, MA Clarke, AM Tettenborn, G Virgo, *Contractual Duties: Performance, Breach, Termination and Remedies* (London, 2012) (breach and performance section by Neil Andrews), 5–015 ff.

[37] 137 LT 57; [1927] All ER 712, 714; 43 TLR 260.

acting *pro bono*, surveyors, vets, etc), the professional will normally owe merely a duty to exercise due care (but even in such relationships the contractual obligation might exceptionally involve strict liability, in accordance with the specific terms of the agreement or assurances given by the professional in the course of his performance, or based on the relevant context). Atkinson J in *Aerial Advertising Co* v. *Batchelors Peas Ltd* (*Manchester*) (1938) held that performance of an aerial advertising campaign on behalf of a dried peas company[38] imported an implied term to use reasonable skill and care not to harm the company's interests, and certainly not to fly advertising planes on occasions which will bring its customer into hatred and contempt. In breach of that term the advertiser flew over a town during the Armistice service just before 11 am on the 11th of November. This provoked public outrage and the advertising was a commercial disaster. As the Court of Appeal noted in *Urban 1* (*Blonk Street*) *Ltd* v. *Ayres* (2013), contractual obligations to perform within a reasonable time are particularly troublesome because the issue whether there has been breach will raise a range of imponderable factors.[39]

(iii) The House of Lords affirmed in *Henderson* v. *Merrett Syndicates Ltd* (1995)[40] that, when a contractual duty of care overlaps with an essentially similar duty of care imposed by the tort of negligence (a case of 'concurrent' obligations), a claimant can select whichever cause of action he prefers, or indeed plead both.

15.2 Effects of Breach

15.14 *BREACH AND NOMINAL DAMAGES*[41]

Every breach entitles the innocent party to recover at least 'nominal damages' (a token sum signifying the fact that there has been a technical legal wrong, for example, sums of £5 or £10). Breach might expose the guilty party to a claim for substantial damages, or debt, or specific performance, or an injunction, or at least a declaration that breach has occurred (on remedies for breach of contract see Chap. 16). The innocent party can recover substantial damages if a recognised type of loss is shown (for the various tests applicable to such damages claims, **17.21**).

---

[38] [1938] 2 All ER 788, 792.

[39] *Urban 1* (*Blonk Street*) *Ltd* v. *Ayres* [2013] EWCA Civ 816 [2014] 1 WLR 756, at [49], *per* Sir Terence Etherton C (citing *Hick* v. *Raymond & Reid* [1893] AC 22, 32–33, HL, *per* Lord Watson, and the fuller discussion by Maurice Kay LJ in *Peregrine Systems Ltd* v. *Steria Ltd* [2005] EWCA Civ 239; [2005] Info TLR 294, at [15], noting Judge Richard Seymour QC in *Astea* (*UK*) *Ltd* v. *Time Group Ltd* [2003] EWHC 725 (TCC), at [144]).

[40] [1995] 2 AC 145, HL.

[41] *McGregor on Damages* (19th edn, 2014), chapter 12; Neil H Andrews, MA Clarke, AM Tettenborn, G Virgo, *Contractual Duties*: *Performance*, *Breach*, *Termination and Remedies* (London, 2012) (breach and performance section by Neil Andrews), 5–005.

15.15 *TERMINATION FOR BREACH NOT AUTOMATIC*[42]

Even a serious breach (as explained in detail at **15.31** below) does not automatically cause the contract to be terminated. Instead the innocent party has this choice: (i) to 'accept the renunciation or repudiation' and thus terminate the contract and sue for damages or (ii) to affirm the contract and sue for damages.

15.16 *CONTRAST BETWEEN TERMINATION FOR BREACH AND RESCISSION AB INITIO ON (FOR EXAMPLE) THE GROUND OF MISREPRESENTATION*

(i) A contract can be brought to an end either because there is some initial defect in the consensus (it is 'vitiated') or because something occurs subsequent to formation which causes or justified termination.[43] The term 'rescission' must be used only to describe the process of setting aside retrospectively a contract which is vitiated by reason of misrepresentation, or another ground of initial invalidity. Termination for breach operates to end the contract from that point in time, but only prospectively; it does not annihilate the contract retrospectively.

(ii) The main result of this analysis is that the innocent party retains the right to sue in respect of preceding breaches. By contrast, 'rescission' (for example, for misrepresentation) is the avoidance, that is, the setting aside, of voidable contracts. Such avoidance involves returning the parties to the original position as though the contract never existed. Thus 'rescission' involves the contract being dismantled with retroactive effect, with a mutual restoration of benefits. That analysis precludes actions for breach of contract: the contract is dead.

15.17 *DISTINCTION BETWEEN TERMINATION FOR BREACH AND NON-OCCURRENCE OF A DEPENDENT OBLIGATION ('ENTIRE OBLIGATION' DOCTRINE)*

The process of termination for breach should also be distinguished from the right to refuse performance if the other side has failed to complete performance of an obligation, that is, where the parties' obligations are 'dependent': see **15.38**).[44]

15.18 *EFFECTS OF TERMINATION FOR BREACH*[45]

The following consequences flow from the fact that termination for breach operates only to terminate the contract in a prospective manner (elements (a) and (b) concern the 'ledger' of accrued liabilities between the parties, and element (c) concerns clauses which survive termination):

(a) The innocent party retains the right to sue:

[42] Neil H Andrews, MA Clarke, AM Tettenborn, G Virgo, *Contractual Duties: Performance, Breach, Termination and Remedies* (London, 2012) (breach and performance section by Neil Andrews), chapter 10 to 14.

[43] *ibid*, chapter 13.

[44] *ibid*, chapter 15.

[45] *ibid*, chapter 13.

(1) in respect of preceding breaches (in so far as these have not become statute-barred) as well as holding the guilty party liable in damages for breach which led to termination of the contract;
(2) for any unpaid sums (other than liability to pay damages under (1) above) which have 'accrued' before termination, for example, a partner's liability to make contributions to partnership expenses or a purchaser's liability to pay accrued instalments under a contract for construction of a ship.

(b) Conversely (on the other side of the ledger), the guilty party retains the right to sue the innocent party for unpaid accrued sums (that is, debts or other liabilities which became payable prior to the date of termination, but which were not paid by that date). Such sums and damages will be set-off against the guilty party's total liabilities to pay damages, etc. If the innocent party's liabilities exceed the guilty party's liabilities, the latter can recover this balance.
(c) Furthermore, various ancillary obligations will continue to apply, notably: exclusion clauses;[46] liquidated damages clauses; choice of law clauses,[47] jurisdiction clauses,[48] mediation clauses,[49] arbitration clauses;[50] a consensual time bar;[51] a stipulation for a retainer in an agency contract;[52] a software supplier's undertaking to provide continuing support and maintenance;[53] and a clause allowing inspection of documents.[54]

However, restrictive covenants (inserted into partnership or employment contracts) do not survive in favour of the guilty party[55] (this remains[56] the law

---

[46] *Photo Production* case [1980] AC 827, HL.

[47] This follows *a fortiori* from *Mackender* v. *Feldia AG* [1967] 2 QB 590, CA (rescission for non-disclosure under an insurance contract does not wipe out a (i) jurisdiction and (ii) a choice of law clause: especially, Diplock LJ at 603–4).

[48] See *Mackender* case, preceding note; generally, *Port Jackson Stevedoring Pty* v. *Salmond & Spraggon (Australia) Pty* (*'The New York Star'*) [1981] 1 WLR 138, 145, PC.

[49] *Cable & Wireless plc* v. *IBM United Kingdom Ltd* [2002] 2 All ER (Comm) 1041, Colman J; *Sulamerica Cia Nacional de Seguros SA* v. *Enesa Engenharia SA* [2012] EWCA Civ 638; [2013] 1 WLR 102.

[50] *Heyman* v. *Darwins Ltd* [1942] AC 356, 374, HL.

[51] *Port Jackson Stevedoring Pty* v. *Salmond & Spraggon (Australia) Pty*, *'The New York Star'* [1981] 1 WLR 138, 145, PC, *per* Lord Wilberforce.

[52] *Duffen* v. *FRA BO Spa (No 2)* [2000] 1 Lloyd's Rep 180 (Judge Hallgarten QC, Central County Court, London).

[53] *Harbinger UK Ltd* v. *GE Information Services Ltd* [2000] 1 All ER (Comm) 166 (severable clause, surviving termination of main contract, that company 'in perpetuity' would provide support and maintenance of software supplied to a customer; the customer would not everlastingly be prepared to use this soft-ware; so long as it did, the supplier's obligation would endure).

[54] *Yasuda Fire & Marine Insurance Co of Europe Ltd* v. *Orion Marine Insurance Underwriting Agency Ltd* [1995] QB 174, Colman J.

[55] *General Billposting Co Ltd* v. *Atkinson* [1909] AC 118, HL (for Commonwealth cases, F Dawson, (2013) 129 LQR 508–513).

[56] *Group Lotus plc* v. *1Malaysia Racing Team SDN BHD* [2011] EWHC 1366 (Ch), at [364] to [371], *per* Peter Smith J.

although Lord Phillips criticised this analysis).[57] As Lord Wilson noted in *Geys* v. *Société Générale* (2012),[58] this point is open to 'debate', but the law is nevertheless settled. The position concerning confidentiality clauses is not settled.[59]

15.19 *TERMINATION OF A SEVERABLE PART*

In an instalment contract, party A might repudiate only *vis-à-vis* a severable part of the contract, justifying termination by B of that part, but not justifying termination of the whole contract.[60]

15.20 *NO AUTOMATIC RIGHT TO TERMINATE FOR BREACH*[61]

The innocent party is entitled to terminate a contract for breach in any of the following situations: (a) the other party has shown a clear unwillingness to satisfy his contract ('renunciation)'; or (b) default by the guilty party has rendered performance impossible (**15.10**, paragraph (iii) above); or (c) the contract has been breached in a serious manner going to the root of the innocent party's contractual expectations ('repudiation'); or (d) there has been a breach of an important term (a 'condition', on which see **15.22** below); or (e) the facts disclose a serious breach of an intermediate term (also known as an 'innominate term').

15.21 *CONDITIONS, INTERMEDIATE TERMS, AND WARRANTIES*[62]

(i) There are three types of promissory obligation: conditions; intermediate terms (also known as 'innominate terms'); and warranties.
(ii) Breach of a condition entitles the other party to obtain damages and to terminate for breach of contract.
(iii) Breach of an intermediate term also entitles the innocent party to claim damages; whether it also justifies termination of the contract depends on an assessment of the breach's gravity in the relevant set of circumstances.
(iv) Breach of a warranty gives rise only to a duty to pay damages.

15.22 *CONDITIONS*[63]

A term is a condition, rather than an intermediate term or a warranty, in any of the following five situations:

---

[57] *Campbell* v. *Frisbee* [2002] EWCA Civ 1374; [2003] ICR 141, at [22], *per* Lord Phillips.

[58] [2012] UKSC 63; [2013] 1 AC 523, at [68] (see F Dawson, (2013) 129 LQR 508–513 for Commonwealth cases).

[59] [2002] EWCA Civ 1374; [2003] ICR 141, at [22].

[60] *Friends Provident Life & Pensions Ltd* v. *Sirius International Insurance Corp.* [2005] EWCA Civ 601; [2005] 2 Lloyd's Rep 517, at [31]; Neil H Andrews, MA Clarke, AM Tettenborn, G Virgo, *Contractual Duties: Performance, Breach, Termination and Remedies* (London, 2012) (breach and performance section by Neil Andrews), 13–011.

[61] Neil H Andrews, MA Clarke, AM Tettenborn, G Virgo, *Contractual Duties: Performance, Breach, Termination and Remedies* (London, 2012) (breach and performance section by Neil Andrews), 5–026.

[62] *ibid*), chapters 10 to 12; K Lewison, *Interpretation of Contracts* (6th edn, London, 2015), 16.10.

[63] Neil H Andrews, MA Clarke, AM Tettenborn, G Virgo, *Contractual Duties: Performance, Breach, Termination and Remedies* (London, 2012) (breach and performance section by Neil Andrews), 10–009 ff; K Lewison, *Interpretation of Contracts* (6th edn, London, 2015), 16.12.

(a) statute explicitly classifies the term in this way (for example, sections 12(5A), 13(1A), 14(6) and 15(3) of the Sale of Goods Act 1979 (as amended); sections 13 to 15 must be read subject to section 15A (as amended by Schedule 1, paragraph 15, Consumer Rights Act 2015);
(b) there is a binding judicial decision supporting classification of a particular term as a 'condition'; examples abound;
(c) a term is described in the contract as a 'condition' and, upon construction, it has that technical meaning;

Category (c) might be problematic; this is because 'condition' might sometimes be construed as a synonym for 'term'; but the better view is that this construction should be adopted only if there is another provision in the contract which clearly indicates that 'condition' was exceptionally being used as a synonym for the neutral word 'term'; by a majority, the House of Lords in *Schuler (L) AG* v. *Wickman Machine Tool Sales Ltd* (1974) held that, on proper construction of the contract, the word 'condition' (contained in clause 7(b)) might not have been intended to operate in a technical sense; therefore, breach of the relevant obligation does not necessarily justify termination;[64] the majority's decision turns on the need to harmonise different clauses within the contract; there was tension between those clauses; it was held that the innocent party could not invoke clause 7(b) (containing the word 'condition') in order to bypass clause 11(a)(1) which provided that the innocent party must first serve notice on the other party requiring the latter to take remedial steps;
(d) the parties have explicitly agreed that breach of the relevant term, no matter what the factual consequences, or perhaps breach of any term (again irrespective of the consequences), will entitle the innocent party to terminate the contract for breach; but careful drafting indeed is required if the innocent party is to achieve an unobstructed right to terminate (see *Rice* v. *Great Yarmouth Borough Council* (2000);[65] this decision and later cases are examined at **15.29** below in connection with termination clauses); nevertheless, tribunals will respect clear drafting between commercial parties which grants such an unqualified right to terminate for a nominated type of breach, or a particular range of breaches, or even for any breach (if that is clearly intended);

or

(e) the relevant term as a matter of general construction of the contract (whether written or not) requires it to be treated as sufficiently serious so as to be a condition, even though the contract has not explicitly stipulated this; in making this evaluation a tribunal will consider whether 'the parties must, by necessary implication, have intended that the innocent party would be discharged from further performance of his obligations in the event that the term was not fully

---

[64] [1974] AC 235, HL; noted by JH Baker, [1973] CLJ 196, R Brownsword, (1974) 37 MLR 104, and FA Mann, (1973) 89 LQR 464; see also Beatson LJ's comments in *Tullow Uganda Ltd* v. *Heritage Oil and Gas* [2014] EWCA Civ 1048; [2014] 2 CLC 61, at [33] ff.

[65] *The Times*, 26 July 2000; (2001) 3 LGLR 4, CA; S Whittaker, 'Termination Clauses', in AS Burrows and E Peel (eds), *Contract Terms* (Oxford University Press, 2007), chapter 13, at 273–83; for Australian case law, JW Carter, *Carter's Breach of Contract* (Hart, Oxford, 2012), 5.04 ff.

and precisely complied with.' An instructive decision is *PT Berlian Laju Tanker TBK v, Nuse Shipping Ltd* ('*The Aktor*') (2008).[66] The seller of a ship had agreed to receive a 10 *per cent* deposit at a Singapore bank. But the full price, 100 *per cent* payment, had to be paid at a Greek bank. The buyer had paid the 10 *per cent* deposit into a joint account held at a Singaporean bank. Christopher Clarke J held that it was a condition that a 100 *per cent* payment should be made in Greece.

15.23 *OVER-TECHNICAL TERMINATION*[67]

Under section 15A[68] of the Sale of Goods Act 1979, a buyer is confined to damages, and cannot reject the goods, if (i) the breach is so 'slight' that it would be 'unreasonable' to reject the goods; (ii) the contract neither expressly nor impliedly precludes this conclusion.[69] This result is expressed as follows: '[T]he breach is not to be treated as a breach of condition but may be treated as a breach of warranty.' The seller bears the burden of proving (i).[70] The test stated at (i) is an objective inquiry: there is no need to prove subjective bad faith on the buyer's part. The same provision states that it will not apply if 'a contrary intention appears in, or is to be implied from, the contract'.[71] Section 15A will not, therefore, apply where the parties have *expressly categorised the relevant term as a condition*, thereby permitting termination, no matter how slight the breach, or where the parties have expressly stated that termination is justified no matter how slight the defective performance might be. Section 15A does not render the seller's obligation an intermediate term in the Common Law sense. Instead, this provision permits the buyer to terminate unless the breach is 'slight'. If the breach is not slight, the *second* issue of reasonableness does not arise. Section 15A of the 1979 Act applies whether or not the purchaser is a consumer (the Consumer Rights Act 2015, section 60 and Schedule 1 paragraph 15, has extended section 15A to consumer contracts; it was previously confined to contracts where the buyer was not a consumer).

15.24 *Two Cases Ante-dating Section 15A*. In *Re Moore & Co and Landauer & Co* (1921),[72] the commercial buyer was held to be entitled to reject goods (some of which were) sent in boxes of twenty-four rather than in boxes of thirty, the contract

---

[66] [2008] EWHC 1330 (Comm); [2008] 2 All ER (Comm) 784; [2008] 2 Lloyd's Rep 246.

[67] Neil H Andrews, MA Clarke, AM Tettenborn, G Virgo, *Contractual Duties: Performance, Breach, Termination and Remedies* (London, 2012) (breach and performance section by Neil Andrews), 10–056.

[68] Section 30(2A) of the 1979 Act adopts a similar approach where goods delivered are less than, or greater than, the quantity contracted for, but this quantitative deviation is 'so slight that it would be unreasonable' for the buyer to reject the goods; for comparative analysis (comparing the UN 'Vienna' Convention on the International Sale of Goods, 'CISG'), D Saidov, in L DiMatteo, Q Zhou, S Saintier, K Rowley (eds), *Commercial Contract Law: Transatlantic Perspectives* (Cambridge University Press, 2014), chapter 18.

[69] On this last factor, see section 15A(2) of the Sale of Goods Act 1979.

[70] *ibid*, section 15A(3).

[71] *ibid*, section 15A(2).

[72] [1921] 2 KB 519, CA.

having required boxing in quantities of thirty (such boxing would be form a binding feature of a sale by description under section 13(1) of the Sale of Goods Act 1979). Scrutton LJ said that the boxing stipulation might matter if the buyer had agreed to a sub-sale on the same terms.[73] This discrepancy looks 'slight' and it seems unlikely that the commercial buyer would remain entitled to reject under the section 15A. What of deviations from the agreed substance of the goods? Would section 15A would change the result in *Arcos* v. *Ronaasen* (1933) where the supply of timber of 9/16ths of an inch was held not to be equivalent to the contractually stipulated dimension of half an inch (8/16ths)? Perhaps a 1/16th discrepancy is not necessarily 'slight'. If so, the commercial buyer would remain entitled to reject the goods.

15.25 *WAIVER OF BREACH OF CONDITION*

A party can waive a breach of condition, or, in the case of sales of goods, a buyer can be treated under statutory rules as having 'accepted' the goods (for 'acceptance' in the context of sales of goods, see sections 11(4), 35, 35A and 36 of the Sale of Goods Act 1979). Furthermore, the innocent party might be estopped from terminating because his conduct has caused the other party to change his position.

15.26 *'TIME OF THE ESSENCE'*[74]

(i) Such a clause denotes that timely performance is a condition of the contract and, therefore, delay in performance is treated as going to the root of the contract, without regard to the magnitude of the breach.
(ii) An *ex facie* neutral time stipulation might be construed by the tribunal as neither a mere warranty nor an intermediate term (also known as an 'innominate term') but instead as a condition.
(iii) In commercial arrangements, the tendency is to give effect to strict time stipulations, whether or not couched expressly as 'conditions', if the tribunal perceives that commercial certainty is important in that context.
(iv) *Time Not of Essence, but Dilatory Party Receives Notice of the Need for Prompt Performance*. Here the following propositions apply:
    (a) If the time stipulation is not a condition (as explained above), but a party has already been guilty of delay, the other party can give notice requiring the contract to be performed within a reasonable time.
    (b) Such a notice does not elevate the obligation to the level of a condition.
    (c) Instead the notice operates as evidence of the date by which the promisee considers it reasonable to require the contract to be performed.

---

[73] *ibid*, at 524.

[74] Neil H Andrews, MA Clarke, AM Tettenborn, G Virgo, *Contractual Duties: Performance, Breach, Termination and Remedies* (London, 2012) (breach and performance section by Neil Andrews), chapter 12; J.E. Stannard, *Delay in the Performance of Contractual Obligations* (Oxford University Press, 2007); K Lewison, *Interpretation of Contracts* (6th edn, London, 2015), 15.12 ff; G McMeel, *The Construction of Contracts: Interpretation, Implication and Rectification* (2nd edn, Oxford University Press, 2011), chapter 26.

(d) And so the innocent party must show that any post-notification delay constitutes serious default justifying termination, namely any of these possibilities:

1. failure to comply with the notice is repudiatory because it goes to the 'root' of the contract (including the possibility that there has been breach of an intermediate term going to the root of the expected performance); or
2. the dilatory party's default manifests a renunciation, that is, an implicit 'intimation' to abandon the contract.

15.27 *RELIEF AGAINST FORFEITURE*[75]

(i) This equitable doctrine[76] enables the tribunal to exercise a discretion to relieve borrowers or tenants against forfeiture following non-payment of mortgage debts or of rent.
(ii) This jurisdiction applies in respect of all forms of property including money held under a trust[77] (but not money[78] more generally).
(iii) This jurisdiction does not apply in these circumstances: (a) in favour of a prospective purchaser of an interest in land who pays late causing the vendor to cancel the proposed purchase); (b) nor does this jurisdiction apply to mere *in personam* rights (non-proprietary rights created by simple obligation, for example, under a license[79] or a 'time charterparty').[80] As for element (a), the Privy Council in *Union Eagle Ltd* v. *Golden Achievement Ltd* (1997)[81] held that the doctrine does not operate in favour of a purchaser of land who pays late: vendors must be free to walk away from the deal if the purchase money is paid late when punctual performance 'is of the essence'. This case concerned the purchase of a flat in Hong Kong. The buyer tendered the price only ten minutes late, but the vendor decided to terminate the contract and forfeit the deposit (the market price was rising). The buyer unsuccessfully contended

---

[75] Neil H Andrews, MA Clarke, AM Tettenborn, G Virgo, *Contractual Duties: Performance, Breach, Termination and Remedies* (London, 2012) (breach and performance section by Neil Andrews), 10–068 ff.

[76] Robert Walker LJ in *On Demand plc* v. *Gerson plc* [2001] 1 WLR 155, 163G–172, CA (reversed on another basis at [2003] 1 AC 368, HL); L Gullifer, in AS Burrows and E Peel (eds), *Commercial Remedies: Current Issues and Problems* (Oxford University Press, 2003), 191, at 212 ff.

[77] *Nutting* v. *Baldwin* [1995] 1 WLR 201, 209, *per* Rattee J.

[78] *UK Housing Alliance (North West) Ltd* v. *Francis* [2010] EWCA Civ 117; [2010] 3 All ER 519, at [14], *per* Longmore LJ (loss of contingent right to a payment; noted by C Conte, (2010) 126 LQR 529–34).

[79] *Sport Internationals Bussum BV* v. *Inter-Footwear Ltd* [1984] 1 WLR 776, HL; considered in *Celestial Aviation 1 Ltd* v. *Paramount Airways Private Ltd* [2010] EWHC 185 (Comm); [2010] 1 CLC 15, Hamblen J; noted by L Aitken, (2010) 126 LQR 505–7; see also *UK Housing Alliance (North West) Ltd* v. *Francis* [2010] EWCA Civ 117; [2010] 3 All ER 519, at [14]; noted by C Conte, (2010) 126 LQR 529–34.

[80] *'The Scraptrade'* [1983] 2 AC 694, HL.

[81] *Union Eagle Ltd* v. *Golden Achievement Ltd* [1997] AC 514, 520, PC.

that, even before attempting to pay, he had acquired an inchoate equitable title to the property and that Equity would relieve against such forfeiture in the interests of fairness.

(iv) It will be too late to seek relief if the relevant subject-matter has already been sold to an innocent third party.[82]

15.28 *INTERMEDIATE TERMS*[83]

(i) Breach of an intermediate term (also known as an 'innominate term') entitles (a) the innocent party to claim damages; whether (b) it also justifies termination of the contract depends on an assessment of the breach's gravity on the particular facts. The leading decision is *Hongkong Fir Shipping Co Ltd* v. *Kawasaki Kisen Kaisha Ltd* (1962)[84] (although Lord Wilberforce in the *Schuler* case (1974) [85] and Lord Denning in '*The Hansa Nord*' (1976)[86] suggested that the broad notion of an intermediate term ante-dated the *HongKong Fir* decision).

(ii) As for the issue whether termination is justified, as mentioned at (i)(b), the better view is that it is enough that the breach is serious and 'goes to the root'; that is, breach depriving the innocent party of 'a substantial part of the contract' or a breach producing serious or substantially adverse consequences for the innocent party so that termination is a proportionate and reasonable response. A rival, but unpersuasive, formulation of the test is to consider whether the breach's effect has been to 'deprive the [innocent party] of substantially the whole benefit which it was the intention of the parties that he should obtain'. As for the case law, Diplock LJ[87] (but not Upjohn LJ)[88] in the *Hongkong Fir* case (1962) suggested that the true test is to consider whether the breach's effect has been to '*deprive the [innocent party] of substantially the whole benefit which it was the intention of the parties that he should obtain*'. That is a very high threshold. Should it be enough that the breach is serious and 'goes to the root'? There has been inconclusive re-examination of this issue.[89]

---

[82] *ibid.*

[83] Neil H Andrews, MA Clarke, AM Tettenborn, G Virgo, *Contractual Duties: Performance, Breach, Termination and Remedies* (London, 2012) (breach and performance section by Neil Andrews), chapter 12.

[84] [1962] 2 QB 1, CA; JE Stannard and D Capper, *Termination for Breach of Contract* (Oxford University Press, 2014), chapter 6; D Nolan, in C Mitchell and P Mitchell (eds), *Landmark Cases in the Law of Contract* (Hart, Oxford, 2008), 269 ff; and, for Lord Diplock's own account of this decision, see 'The Law of Contract in the Eighties' (1981) 15 *University of British Columbia Law Review* 371.

[85] [1974] AC 235, 262 F, HL: '*I do not think this was anything new.*'

[86] '*The Hansa Nord*' [1976] 1 QB 44, 60, CA.

[87] [1962] 2 QB 1, at 69–70, CA.

[88] [1962] 2 QB 1, 64.

[89] *Ampurius Nu Homes Holdings Ltd* v. *Telford Homes (Creekside) Ltd* [2013] EWCA Civ 577; [2013] 4 All ER 377, at [38] to [50], *per* Lewison LJ; *Urban 1 (Blonk Street) Ltd* v. *Ayres* [2013] EWCA Civ 816 [2014] 1 WLR 756, at [57], *per* Etherton C.

Attractively, the High Court of Australia in *Koompahtoo Local Aboriginal Land Council* v. *Sanpine Pty Ltd* (2007)[90] said that the innominate term doctrine permits termination for 'serious and substantial breaches of contract'. The same court appeared to treat the phrase 'breach going to the root of the contract' and breach depriving the innocent party of 'a substantial part of the contract' as synonymous.[91]

(iii) *Sale of Goods*. In '*The Hansa Nord*' (1976), the Court of Appeal held that an express term in a sale of goods contract might be classified as an intermediate term even though the statute (then the 1893 Sale of Goods Act, now the 1979 Act) does not include that expression and instead refers (in its classification of terms) to the dichotomy of conditions and warranties.[92]

15.29 *TERMINATION CLAUSES AND RIGHTS*[93]

(i) There are three possible types of termination right but only the third of these is a response to breach:

(a) express rights to cancel without showing the other party's breach (that is, the termination right applies even in the absence of a Common Law right to terminate for breach);
(b) implied rights to serve notice to cancel without showing the other party's breach;
(c) express rights to terminate in respect of the other party's breach.

A party needs to act in an unequivocal manner when purporting to exercise a termination clause or other unilateral notice clause.[94]

(ii) As for (i)(a), a contract might expressly permit a party to terminate a contract in specified circumstances, even in the absence of a Common Law right to terminate for breach. Where this occurs, the party who terminates might be entitled to obtain damages in respect of past breaches, but he will not be able to obtain damages for loss of the remaining period of the contract *unless the*

---

[90] [2007] HCA 61; (2007) 82 ALJR 345; (2008) 241 ALR 88, H Ct Aust (Gleeson CJ, Gummow, Heydon, Crennan JJ), at [52].

[91] *ibid*, at [54] and [71].

[92] '*The Hansa Nord*' [1976] QB 44, CA, noted by A Weir, [1976] CLJ 33.

[93] Neil Andrews, *Contract Law* (2nd edn, Cambridge University Press, 2015), 17.25 ff; Neil H Andrews, MA Clarke, AM Tettenborn, G Virgo, *Contractual Duties: Performance, Breach, Termination and Remedies* (London, 2012) (breach and performance section by Neil Andrews), chapter 9; K Lewison, *Interpretation of Contracts* (6th edn, London, 2015), 17.15 to 17.17; G McMeel, *The Construction of Contracts: Interpretation, Implication and Rectification* (2nd edn, Oxford University Press, 2011), 23.02 ff; E Peel, 'The Termination Paradox' [2013] LMCLQ 519–543; J Randall, 'Express Termination Clauses' [2014] CLJ 113–141; R Hooley, 'Express Termination Clauses', in G Virgo and S Worthington (eds), *Commercial Remedies: Resolving Controversies* (Cambridge University Press, 2016); JE Stannard and D Capper, *Termination for Breach of Contract* (Oxford University Press, 2014), chapter 8; S Whittaker, 'Termination Clauses', in AS Burrows and E Peel (eds), *Contract Terms* (Oxford University Press, 2007), chapter 13 (discussion of many related decisions concerning 'material breach' and similar contract drafting).

[94] *Geys* v. *Société Générale* [2012] UKSC 63; [2013] 1 AC 523, at [52], *per* Baroness Hale.

facts disclose that there has been a repudiatory breach in respect of which the innocent party has terminated the contract.

(iii) As for (i)(b), in contracts of indefinite duration, the courts might find an *implied term* that either party can terminate the contract, without breach of contract, by giving the other reasonable notice *Staffordshire Area Health Authority* v. *South Staffordshire Waterworks Co* (1978).[95]

(iv) As for (i)(c), where the scope of the obligation is narrow and the wording is water-tight, effect must be given to the termination provision, notably a termination clause within a sophisticated financial instrument. In such a context, when parties have spelt out the capacity to terminate following breach of condition, this cannot be re-cast by the tribunal as a warranty or an intermediate term because that would conflict with the principle of freedom of contract (**10.04**). For example, in *BNP Paribas* v. *Wockhardt EU Operations (Swiss) AG* (2009) the judge said[96]: '*the parties have… spelt out the consequences which result from a breach of condition. It is unrealistic to suppose that, having done so, they are to be taken to have intended that a failure to pay should be regarded as a warranty or an innominate term…*' Similarly, in *Kuwait Rocks Co* v. *AMN Bulkcarriers Inc* ('*The Astra*') (2013) Flaux J declared that the following clause gave the owner a right to terminate the contract and to recover damages for breach: '*failing the punctual and regular payment of the hire, or bank guarantee…the Owners shall be at liberty to withdraw the vessel from the service of the Charterers, without prejudice to any claim they (the Owners) may otherwise have…*'[97]

By contrast, in *Rice* v. *Great Yarmouth Borough Council* (2000),[98] which concerned a 4-year contract for the claimant to maintain the defendant's sports and parks facilities, the contract gave the defendant local authority the right to terminate for 'breach of any of [Rice's] obligations under the Contract'. The defendant terminated the contract because of shortcomings in performance. But the Court of Appeal held that 'any' should not be taken to mean 'any at all', otherwise the parties would have created a 'draconian' contractual regime,[99] and that extreme interpretation would 'fly in the face of commercial sense'. Instead 'any' meant 'any repudiatory' breach.[100] And so termination would be

---

[95] [1978] 1 WLR 1387, CA.

[96] [2009] EWHC 3116 (Comm); 132 Con LR 177, at [33], *per* Christopher Clarke J).

[97] *Kuwait Rocks Co* v. *AMN Bulkcarriers Inc* ('*The Astra*') [2013] EWHC 865 (Comm); [2013] 2 Lloyd's Rep 69, Flaux J; noted J Shirley (2013) 130 LQR 185–188 (charterer's duty to pay hire punctually a condition; so expressed in relevant clause).

[98] *The Times*, 26 July 2000; (2001) 3 LGLR 4, CA; S Whittaker, 'Termination Clauses', in AS Burrows and E Peel (eds), *Contract Terms* (Oxford University Press, 2007), chapter 13, at 273–83; for Australian case law, JW Carter, *Carter's Breach of Contract* (Hart, Oxford, 2012), 5.04 ff.

[99] *The Times*, 26 July 2000; (2001) 3 LGLR 4, CA, at [22], *per* Hale LJ.

[100] Adopting *Antaios Compania Naviera SA* v. *Salen Rederierna AB* [1985] AC 191, 200–1, HL (clause entitling owner to terminate the charterparty for 'any' breach did not cover minor breach, but only a repudiatory breach); on which *Multi-Link Leisure* v. *North Lanarkshire* [2010] UKSC 47; [2011] 1 All ER 175, at [21], *per* Lord Hope.

justified only if there had been 'repudiation' of the overall contract by a pattern of breaches.[101] But, on the facts, the breaches had not been cumulatively serious enough.

It is submitted that Kitchin J was correct in *Dominion Corporate Trustees Ltd* v. *Debenhams Properties Ltd* (2010)[102] to suggest that the *Rice* case (2000), and its precursor, *Antaios Cia Naviera SA* v. *Salen Rederierna AB* (1985),[103] should be understood to turn on the extremely varied range of possible breaches capable of being committed by the service provider on the facts of those two cases.

15.30 '*MATERIAL' BREACH*[104]

(i) Breach will be material if it is 'substantial' (that is, not trivial) or 'a serious matter'[105] (but it need not be so serious as to justify termination, applying the criterion of Common Law termination for breach).
(ii) The courts do not use the concept of 'material breach', but contractual draftsmen often use this phrase.
(iii) Commercial agreements often provide that the innocent party cannot terminate before giving the guilty party the opportunity to try to remedy the matter (for example in the leading case, *Schuler* v. *Wickman* 1974).[106]

In some situations it might be enough that the default could be stopped, as for the future. But some breaches are not 'remediable'.[107] For example, the Court of Appeal in *Force India Formula One Team Ltd* v. *Etihad Airways PJSC* (2010),[108] considered that the harm could not be undone[109] when a 'formula one' racing team had breached their sponsorship agreement (i) by re-styling the team so as to excise reference to their Abu Dhabi sponsors, (ii) by changing the livery logo of the team. Rix LJ held that the genie could not be put back into

[101] *The Times*, 26 July 2000; (2001) 3 LGLR 4, CA, at [17], *per* Hale LJ.

[102] *Dominion Corporate Trustees Ltd* v. *Debenhams Properties Ltd* [2010] EWHC 1193 (Ch); [2010] NPC 63, at [32], *per* Kitchin J ('*a multitude of obligations, many of which are of minor importance and which can be broken in many different ways*').

[103] [1985] AC 191, 201, HL.

[104] Neil Andrews, *Contract Law* (2nd edn, Cambridge University Press, 2015), 17.30 and on 'remediable breach', 17.31; Neil H Andrews, MA Clarke, AM Tettenborn, G Virgo, *Contractual Duties: Performance, Breach, Termination and Remedies* (London, 2012) (breach and performance section by Neil Andrews), 9–018 ff; G McMeel, *The Construction of Contracts: Interpretation, Implication and Rectification* (2nd edn, Oxford University Press, 2011), 23.25.

[105] *Mid Essex Hospital Services NHS Trust* v. *Compass Group UK and Ireland Ltd* [2013] EWCA Civ 200 [2013] BLR 265 at [126], *per* Jackson LJ.

[106] [1974] AC 235, 248–9, HL (clause 11(a)(i)).

[107] See further N Andrews, MA Clarke, AM Tettenborn, G Virgo, *Contractual Duties: Performance, Breach, Termination and Remedies* (London, 2012) (breach and performance section by N Andrews), 9–029 ff.

[108] [2010] EWCA Civ 1051; [2011] ETLR 10, at [100] to [109].

[109] *ibid*, at [108]: where, *per* Rix LJ, 'the breach or breaches are repeated, cumulative, continuing and repudiatory.'

the bottle, nor could the clock be put back.[110] But in other situations (Lord Reid in *Schuler* v. *Wickman* (1974)[111] suggested that this is the more usual usage) it might be enough that the default could be stopped, as for the future (as noted by Lords Reid, Simon, and Kilbrandon in that case).[112]

15.3 The Process of Terminating for Breach

15.31 *INNOCENT PARTY'S CHOICE*[113]

(i) Faced by the other party's serious breach (renunciation, repudiation or other breach which justifies termination, on which **15.20**), the innocent party has a choice: he can respond to the serious breach by choosing to terminate the contract and sue for damages, or he can affirm the contract and sue for damages.
(ii) This choice between termination or affirmation (the latter involves keeping the contract alive) is known as 'the right to elect'.

15.32 *THE DECISION TO TERMINATE FOR BREACH*[114]

(i) The innocent party's decision whether to affirm or to terminate the contract requires no particular form. This decision must be successfully communicated, or the other party must be left in no doubt from the circumstances concerning the innocent party's decision.
(ii) There must be a real and conscious manifestation of a decision to bring the contract to an end, or the doing of something that is inconsistent with its continuation.
(iii) The decision to affirm or to terminate can be manifested (a) expressly or (b) impliedly.
(iv) In the latter case (situation (iii)(a)), t*he innocent party's* decision might occasionally be inferred from conduct, even from silence, but only if the inference can be safely drawn from the relevant context. As for this last point, Lord Steyn in the House of Lords in *Vitol SA* v. *Norelf Ltd* (1996) explained that *conduct* can be effective to communicate a decision to terminate the contract: '*An act of acceptance of a repudiation requires no particular form…It is sufficient that*

[110] [2010] EWCA Civ 1051; [2011] ETLR 10, at [108].

[111] [1974] AC 235, 249–250, HL.

[112] [1974] AC 235, 249–250, 265, 271, HL (as noted in the *Force India* case, [2010] EWCA Civ 1051; [2011] ETLR 10, at [104] to [107]).

[113] Neil H Andrews, MA Clarke, AM Tettenborn, G Virgo, *Contractual Duties: Performance, Breach, Termination and Remedies* (London, 2012) (breach and performance section by Neil Andrews), 14–001 ff.

[114] Neil H Andrews, MA Clarke, AM Tettenborn, G Virgo, *Contractual Duties: Performance, Breach, Termination and Remedies* (London, 2012) (breach and performance section by Neil Andrews), 14–037 ff.

the communication or conduct clearly and unequivocally conveys to the repudiating party that that aggrieved party is treating the contract as at an end.'[115] Lord Steyn added that context might support an inference that a repudiatory breach or renunciation *has been accepted by the innocent party*, as where an employer wrongfully dismissed an employee, and the latter fails to reappear for work on the following day or indeed thereafter.[116] Lord Steyn's statement is concerned not with the innocent party's mental decision to 'call off the contract' but with the 'conveying' of that decision to the other party.

15.33 *DECISION IS FINAL*[117]

(i) The decision is final once the innocent party has communicated to the other party the decision to terminate or to affirm the contract (the 'election').
(ii) If the innocent party has elected to terminate the contract for breach, that party cannot revive the contract by a unilateral decision, but only by the parties' joint decision.
(iii) Similarly, once the innocent party decides to affirm the contract, he cannot change his mind, at least where, at the time of that affirmation, he had full knowledge of the relevant facts and of his right to terminate.

15.34 *NO THIRD CHOICE*[118]

(i) The innocent party's choice is to affirm the contract or to terminate (as explained above at **15.15**). The innocent party has no 'third' choice. He cannot affirm the contract and yet be absolved from tendering further performance unless and until the other party gives reasonable notice that he is once again able and willing to perform. As Lord Ackner explained in '*The Simona*' (1989)[119]: '*such a [third] choice would negate the contract being kept alive for the benefit of both parties and would deny the party [party A] who [attempted to repudiate], the right to take advantage of any supervening circumstance which would justify him in declining to complete.*'[120]
(ii) If follows from (i) that, once the innocent party decides to continue with the contract, he must comply with his contractual obligations as they remain or arise.

---

[115] *Vitol SA* v. *Norelf Ltd* ('*The Santa Clara*') [1996] AC 800, 810–11, *per* Lord Steyn, noted by S Hedley, [1996] CLJ 430–2.

[116] *ibid*, at 811, *per* Lord Steyn; similarly, *Force India Formula One Team Ltd* v. *Etihad Airways PJSC* [2010] EWCA Civ 1051; [2011] ETLR 10, at [112], *per* Rix LJ; *Melli Bank plc* v. *Holbud Ltd* [2013] EWHC 1506 (Comm), at [27] (silience and inactivity, on the facts, not indicating acceptance of alleged repudiation).

[117] Neil H Andrews, MA Clarke, AM Tettenborn, G Virgo, *Contractual Duties*: *Performance, Breach, Termination and Remedies* (London, 2012) (breach and performance section by Neil Andrews), 14–004 ff.

[118] Neil H Andrews, MA Clarke, AM Tettenborn, G Virgo, *Contractual Duties*: *Performance, Breach, Termination and Remedies* (London, 2012) (breach and performance section by Neil Andrews), 14–017 ff.

[119] *Fercometal SARL* v. *Mediterranean Shipping Co SA* ('*The Simona*') [1989] AC 788, 805E–F, HL.

[120] *ibid.*

15.35 *INNOCENT PARTY PAUSING TO CONSIDER OPTIONS*[121]

(i) Although the innocent party must 'elect' whether to affirm or terminate the contract (as explained at **15.15** above), the tribunal will recognise that the innocent party should have a reasonable but short period for assessing the situation, as noted by Rix LJ in the *Stocznia* case (2003).[122] In most commercial contexts, the time for assessment will be quite short. Such a period for reflection is commercially attractive, provided the parties realise that the tribunal will normally require only a short period (see (ii) below for a qualification).

(ii) Sometimes, even in a commercial context, the circumstances might permit an innocent party to have a decent interval within which to assess whether to terminate. This was held to be the situation in one case where the decision whether to terminate a sponsorship contract by reason of the sponsored party's default fell to be made by the sponsor within the fallow period between racing seasons: see Rix LJ's further examination of this topic in *Force India Formula One Team Ltd* v. *Etihad Airways PJSC* (2010).[123]

15.36 *INNOCENT PARTY DECIDING TO PERFORM*[124]

As explained in greater detail at **17.10**, the innocent party is sometimes in a position to keep open the contract ('electing to affirm the contract'), and complete his side of the bargain. He can then sue for the agreed price.[125] But (also see **17.10**) there are two restrictions: (a) the claimant cannot succeed in suing for debt if his performance requires the other party's co-operation; and (b) the tribunal must be satisfied (as it generally will be) that it was not so commercially unacceptable that it would be grotesque for the claimant to have pursued his unwanted performance (the case law presents this from the perspective of the performing party lacking a 'legitimate interest' in maintaining the contract in play). Consistent with the principle of *pacta sunt servanda* (**10.04**), requirement (b) will be applied generously in favour of the claimant who has performed in these circumstances.

15.37 *NEW OPPORTUNITY TO TERMINATE*[126]

(i) A party gains a fresh right to elect to terminate the contract if the other party commits a fresh repudiation.

---

[121] Neil H Andrews, MA Clarke, AM Tettenborn, G Virgo, *Contractual Duties: Performance, Breach, Termination and Remedies* (London, 2012) (breach and performance section by Neil Andrews), 14–026 ff.

[122] *Stocznia Gdanska SA* v. *Latvian Shipping Co (No. 3)* [2002] EWCA Civ 889; [2002] 2 All ER (Comm) 768, at [87].

[123] [2010] EWCA Civ 1051; [2011] ETLR 10, at [122].

[124] Neil Andrews, *Contract Law* (2nd edn, Cambridge University Press, 2015), 18–03 ff; Neil H Andrews, MA Clarke, AM Tettenborn, G Virgo, *Contractual Duties: Performance, Breach, Termination and Remedies* (London, 2012) (breach and performance section by Neil Andrews), 7–092.

[125] *White & Carter* v. *McGregor* [1962] AC 413, HL: see **17.10** for detailed discussion.

[126] Neil H Andrews, MA Clarke, AM Tettenborn, G Virgo, *Contractual Duties: Performance, Breach, Termination and Remedies* (London, 2012) (breach and performance section by Neil Andrews), 14–032 ff.

(ii) A party also gains a fresh right to elect to terminate the contract if the breach is continuous, such as a failure to pay money.
(iii) As for situation (ii), the innocent party will not have made a final election to affirm the contract if he maintains the contract in being for the moment, while reserving his right to treat it as repudiated if the other party persists in his repudiation.

15.4 Incomplete Performance

15.38 *NO DUTY TO PAY FOR INCOMPLETE PERFORMANCE*[127]

(i) In contracts for services, or for goods and services, payment might be postponed expressly or impliedly until performance is completed. The 'entire obligation' rule will then prevent the contractor from becoming entitled to payment until conclusion of the job.
(ii) The 'substantial performance' doctrine might enable the performer to claim the agreed sum (debt, **17.10**) even if performance has not been perfect. Then the innocent party's protection is confined to a cross-claim or deduction in respect of defective performance.[128]
(iii) Substantial performance will not apply if the failure to perform is significant[129]: this depends on questions of proportionality, reasonableness and fairness.[130] The doctrine is traceable to the eighteenth century.[131] The three leading[132] modern decisions are *Sumpter* v. *Hedges* (1898),[133] *Bolton* v. *Mahadeva* (1972)[134] and *Hoenig* v. *Isaacs* (1952)[135]

---

[127] Neil H Andrews, MA Clarke, AM Tettenborn, G Virgo, *Contractual Duties: Performance, Breach, Termination and Remedies* (London, 2012) (breach and performance section by Neil Andrews), chapter 15.

[128] *Hoenig* v. *Isaacs* [1952] 2 All ER 176, CA (discussed Neil H Andrews, MA Clarke, AM Tettenborn, G Virgo, *Contractual Duties: Performance, Breach, Termination and Remedies* (London, 2012) (breach and performance section by Neil Andrews), 17.56).

[129] *Sumpter* v. *Hedges* [1898] 1 QB 673 (17.54).

[130] As mentioned in *Bolton* v. *Mahadeva* [1972] 1 WLR 1010, CA.

[131] *Boone* v. *Eyre* (1779) 1 Hy Bl 273n (summarised in the notes to *Cutter* v. *Powell* (1795) 6 Term Rep 320; *Smith's Leading Cases* (13th edn 1929); Lord Denning MR in '*The Hansa Nord*' [1976] 1 QB 44, 60, CA).

[132] Other modern decisions: *Vigers* v. *Cook* [1919] 2 KB 475, 482, CA, *Williams* v. *Roffey & Nicholls (Contractors) Ltd* [1991] 1 QB 1, 17, CA; *Pilbrow* v. *Pearless de Rougemont & Co* [1993] 3 All ER 355, 361B, 360, CA; *Systech International Ltd* v. *PC Harrington Contractors Ltd* [2012] EWCA Civ 1371; [2013] 2 All ER 69, at [17], [31], [32] (Adjudicator in construction dispute not entitled to fee if his decision is unenforceable).

[133] [1898] 1 QB 673, CA.

[134] [1972] 1 WLR 1010, CA.

[135] [1952] 2 All ER 176, CA.

Chapter 16
Frustration and Termination by Notice

Abstract The central proposition is that mere hardship or difficulty or increased expense will not form the basis for terminating the contract under general law. Instead the doctrine of frustration is confined to supervening impossibility, (non-culpable and non-elective) incapacitation, or illegality. Another topic treated here is contracts of indefinite duration. These are normally capable of being terminated by one party giving reasonable notice to the other.

16.1 The Frustration Doctrine

16.01 For reasons of space, the doctrine of frustration will be briefly noted here. For greater detail the reader is referred to specialist discussion.[1]

16.02 *NARROW SCOPE*

(i) The general test for frustration is whether, without default of either party, a contractual obligation has become incapable of being performed because the circumstances in which performance is required would render it a thing radically different from that which was undertaken by the contract. Aggravating circumstances, even a commercial crisis for the relevant party, will not constitute frustration[2] unless Lord Radcliffe's test in the *Davis Contractors Ltd* v. *Fareham UDC* (1956)[3] can be satisfied: '*frustration occurs whenever the law*

[1] GH Treitel, *Frustration and Force Majeure* (3rd edn, London, 2014); E McKendrick (ed), *Force Majeure and Frustration of Contract* (2nd edn, London, 1995); Clarke in Neil H Andrews, MA Clarke, AM Tettenborn, G Virgo, *Contractual Duties*: *Performance, Breach, Termination and Remedies* (London, 2012), Part III, chapters 16 to 18.

[2] *Pioneer Shipping Ltd* v. *B T P Tioxide Ltd*, '*The Nema*' [1982] AC 724, 752, HL, *per* Lord Roskill; '*The Super Servant Two*', *J Lauritzen AS* v. *Wijsmuller BV*. [1990] 1 Lloyd's Rep 1, 8, CA, *per* Bingham LJ.

[3] *Davis Contractors Ltd* v. *Fareham Urban District Council* [1956] AC 696, 729, HL, *per* Lord Radcliffe; considered in *Pioneer Shipping Ltd* v. *BTP Tioxide Ltd* ('*The Nema*') [1982] AC 724, 744, 751–2, HL (at 753, noting the weak chances of a successful appeal if the right test has been applied; see also '*The Mary Nour*' [2008] EWCA Civ 856; [2008] 2 Lloyd's Rep 526, at [11]); The current approach is to follow the guidance of Rix LJ's 'multi-factorial' approach in '*The Sea Angel*' [2007] EWCA Civ 547; [2007] 2 Lloyd's Rep 517, at [111], see also [110], [112], and [132]. This test focuses on (a) whether the event falls within the scope of the established categories of

N. Andrews, *Arbitration and Contract Law*, Ius Gentium: Comparative Perspectives on Law and Justice 54, DOI 10.1007/978-3-319-27144-6_16

recognises that without default of either party a contractual obligation has become incapable of being performed because the circumstances in which performance is called for would render it a thing radically different from that which was undertaken by the contract. Non haec in foedera veni. It was not this which I promised to do.'

(ii) It is now clear that the doctrine of frustration operates as an exceptional release of both parties, based on a rule of law.[4] The earlier theory that the doctrine rests on an implied term was repudiated in *Davis Contractors Ltd* v. *Fareham Urban District Council* (1956)[5] (and this repudiation was confirmed by Lord Denning MR in '*The Eugenia*', 1964).[6]

(iii) Frustration is a narrow doctrine: it is not enough that a contract becomes unexpectedly difficult or more expensive to perform.[7] In the absence of express provision, the tribunal under English principles has no power to absolve contracting parties from their obligations on grounds of hardship arising after formation.[8] In the absence of frustration, the courts have no power of 'equitable adjustment' of the contract *Lloyds TSB Foundation for Scotland* v. *Lloyds Group plc* [2013] UKSC 3; [2013] 1 WLR 366, at [47], *per* Lord Hope.

frustration (b) whether the risk of the event is allocated, expressly or impliedly, to one of the parties and (c) whether a finding of frustration would be consistent with commercial conceptions of fairness. This case was cited by Flaux J in *Bunge SA v. Kyla Shipping Co Ltd (No 2)* [2012] EWHC 3522 (Comm); [2013] 1 Lloyd's Rep 565, at [39] to [41]; *Bunge SA v. Kyla Shipping Co Ltd (No 1)* [2013] EWCA Civ 734; [2013] 3 All ER 1006; [2013] 2 All ER (Comm) 577; [2013] 2 Lloyd's Rep 463, at [7], per Longmore LJ; *Melli Bank plc v. Holbud Ltd* [2013] EWHC 1506 (Comm), at [15], per Deputy High Court judge Robin Knowles QC; *Islamic Republic of Iran Shipping Lines v. Steamship Mutual Underwriting Association (Bermuda) Ltd* [2010] EWHC 2661 (Comm); [2011] 1 Lloyd's Rep 195; [2011] 2 All ER (Comm) 609, at [105], per Beatson J. See also the NZ Supreme Court's discussion in *Planet Kids Ltd v. Auckland Council* [2013] NZSC 147; [2014] 1 NZLR 149, at [60] to [62]; Mustill LJ in *FC Shepherd* v. *Jerrom* [1987] QB 301, 321–2, CA, attractively chronicled the evolution of the frustration doctrine; there is a careful analysis of the leading authorities in *Islamic Republic of Iran Shipping Lines* v. *Steamship Mutual Underwriting Association (Bermuda) Ltd* [2010] EWHC 2661 (Comm); [2011] 1 Lloyd's Rep 195; [2011] 2 All ER (Comm) 609, at [101] to [107], *per* Beatson J.

[4] GH Treitel, *Frustration and Force Majeure* (3rd edn, London, 2014), chapter 16.

[5] [1956] AC 696, HL.

[6] [1964] 2 QB 226, 238, CA.

[7] *British Movietonews Ltd* v. *London & District Cinemas Ltd* [1952] AC 166, 183–4, 188, HL, *per* Viscount Simon and Lord Simonds; '*The Mary Nour*' [2008] EWCA Civ 856; [2008] 2 Lloyd's Rep 526, at [14], [23], [27] (supplier's duty to procure suppoly of goods; embargo by cartel of cement producers not an excuse).

[8] *British Movietonews* case [1952] AC 166, 185, HL (repudiating Denning LJ's unorthodox leniency in the lower court, at [1951] 1 KB 190, 201–2, CA); cf no repentance shown by Lord Denning MR in his minority judgment in *Staffordshire A H A* v. *S Staffordshire WW Co* [1978] 1 WLR 1387, 1397–8, CA.

(iv) Frustration operates only if the relevant risk is not allocated to a party[9] in accordance with (1) an express[10] term, or (2) a pre-existing rule,[11] or (3) an implied allocation based on the court's assessment of the particular context. Rix LJ noted in '*The Sea Angel*' (2007) that this requires close examination of the relevant commercial context, always bearing in mind that contractual excuses on the basis of frustration are not to be handed out like confetti[12] (and see the summary by Beatson J in *Islamic Republic of Iran Shipping Lines* v. *Steamship Mutual Underwriting Association (Bermuda) Ltd*, 2010).[13]

(v) When determining the issue of whether the relevant supervening event is a risk borne by a party, the fact that the relevant risk is foreseeable is relevant but not decisive: foreseeable or foreseen risks can sometimes give rise to frustration. This was noted by Rix LJ in '*The Sea Angel*' (2007[14] and earlier by Lord Denning MR in '*The Eugenia*' (1964).[15] Although some decisions, for example, the Privy Council in the *Maritime National* case (1935), had adopted the proposition that foreseeability precludes any chance of frustration,[16] the better view, now accepted, is that foresight and foreseeability are not free-standing impediments to frustration.[17] Instead they are factors concerning the issue whether one party has impliedly assumed the risk of the relevant event's occurrence. This 'better view' is traceable to Lord Denning MR's discussion in *The Eugenia* (1964).[18] Furthermore, frustration does not arise if (a) the relevant impediment results from breach or other blameworthy conduct (b) or the suggested inability to perform is traceable to a choice made by the party who now invokes frustration as a defence ('*The Superservant Two*' [1990] 1 Lloyd's Rep 1, 10, CA; *Melli Bank plc* v. *Holbud* [2013] EWHC 1506 (Comm), at [15] to [21]).

(vi) The modern frustration doctrine concerns three main situations: (1) supervening illegality, that is, performance of the contract becomes illegal because of

[9] *National Carriers Ltd* v. *Panalpina (Northern) Ltd* [1981] AC 675, 712, HL, *per* Lord Simon.

[10] For cases where express terms were construed not to preclude frustration, see *Metropolitan Water Board* v. *Dick, Kerr & Co* [1918] AC 119, HL; and *Bank Line Ltd* v. *Arthur Capel & Co* [1919] AC 435, HL.

[11] '*The Great Peace*' [2002] EWCA Civ 1407; [2003] QB 679, at [74], *per* Lord Phillips CJ.

[12] *Edwinton Commercial Corporation* v. *Tsavliris Russ Ltd* ('*The Sea Angel*') [2007] EWCA Civ 547; [2007] 2 Lloyd's Rep 517, at [111].

[13] [2010] EWHC 2661 (Comm); [2011] 1 Lloyd's Rep 195; [2011] 2 All ER (Comm) 609, at [105]; see also *Bunge SA* v. *Kyla Shipping Ltd* [2012] EWHC 3522 (Comm); [2013] 1 Lloyd's Rep 565, at [69] *per* Flaux J.

[14] *Edwinton Commercial Corporation* v. *Tsavliris Russ Ltd* ('*The Sea Angel*') [2007] EWCA Civ 547; [2007] 2 Lloyd's Rep 517, at [127].

[15] '*The Eugenia*' [1964] 2 QB 226, CA; cf C Hall, (1984) 4 LS 300 (proposing a recklessness basis).

[16] *Maritime National Fish Ltd* v. *Ocean Trawlers Ltd* [1935] AC 524, PC.

[17] Generally on these factors, GH Treitel, *Frustration and Force Majeure* (3rd edn, London, 2014), chapter 13.

[18] '*The Eugenia*' [1964] 2 QB 226, CA; C Hall (1984) 4 LS 300 (proposing a recklessness basis).

a legal change subsequent to the contract's formation,[19] (2) physical impossibility or (3) severe obstruction of contractual performance ((a) frustrating delay and (b) 'frustration of the venture', referred to as 'frustration of the purpose' by some modern commentators). On delay, category (3)(a), see Lord Roskill's remarks in '*The Nema*' [1982] AC 724, 752-3, House of Lords. However, category (3)(b) is very seldom successfully pleaded (see further (vii) below).

(vii) As for category (vi)(3)(b), an unusual instance is *Krell* v. *Henry* (1903), in which the hire of a room for 1 day overlooking the ceremonial Coronation procession of King Edward VII had been frustrated because the event had to be postponed when the King fell ill.[20] It was clear that the hire was for the specific purpose of witnessing a one-off event on a special occasion: the licensee could not sensibly be expected to languish in this room if the procession did not take place that day. The risk that the Coronation would be postponed could not fairly be allocated to the licensee. *Krell* v. *Henry* (1903) was distinguished by the Court of Appeal in *Herne Bay Steam Boat Co* v. *Hutton* (1903). In the latter case, the 'foundation' of the contract had not wholly disappeared. Indeed, a large part of it remained.[21] The *Herne Bay Steam Boat* case (1903) concerned the commercial hire of a craft to be offered to members of the public so that, on payment, they could inspect the great naval review at Spithead. These events were to take place after the Coronation of Edward VII. The Court of Appeal held that his illness, and the postponement of the Coronation, did not render the contract of hire a 'complete waste of time' (to use modern parlance). And so there was no frustration. The King's absence at the review did not destroy the public's opportunity to see the magnificent array of warships at anchor. This decision is sound. The King's presence would have enhanced the sense of occasion (because he would have been recently crowned). But his absence did not turn the naval review into a 'non-event'. It would perhaps have been different if the purpose of the hire had been specifically advertised in these terms: 'Vessel available for hire during King's review of the Fleet'. However, objectively, this was not the sole or predominant purpose of the hire on the facts of the case. The risk of slight public disappointment (and consequently a reduction in the public's interest in trips to view the fleet) was rightly allocated to the party who hired the craft.

(viii) The House of Lords in *National Carriers Ltd* v. *Panalpina (Northern) Ltd* (1981) held that leases (of interests in land) could be frustrated (although this will be quite exceptional).[22]

---

[19] Section 1(1), Law Reform (Frustrated Contracts) Act 1943 refers to contracts which have become 'impossible of performance or been otherwise frustrated'.

[20] [1903] 2 KB 740, CA (Lord Wright in the *Maritime National Fish* case, [1935] AC 524, 529, PC, noting the exceptional nature of *Krell* v. *Henry*).

[21] [1903] 2 KB 683, CA.

[22] [1981] AC 675, HL (e.g., a lease would be terminated if there were a 99 year lease and after only a couple of years the demised premises, situated on a cliff-top, fell into the sea as a result of coastal erosion); generally, GH Treitel, *Frustration and Force Majeure* (3rd edn, London, 2014), chapter 11.

(ix) If a contract becomes frustrated, money already paid is repayable, and money owed ceases to be payable, unless the court in its discretion decides to make an allowance in favour of the payee in respect of the latter's expenses in performance of the contract: section 1(2), Law Reform (Frustrated Contracts) Act 1943.[23] Secondly, section 1(3) of the same Act enables the court to award the performing party ('P') a sum in respect of the valuable benefit gained by the other party.[24] Such an award will be in respect of party P's supply of goods or services, taking into account what is 'just' in all the circumstances.[25]

16.2 Termination by Notice: Contracts of Indefinite Duration

16.03 *INDEFINITE CONTRACTS*[26]
(See also **15.29** on Termination Clauses and Rights)

(i) Indefinite contracts (that is, contracts of indefinite duration) are often, as a matter of construction, subject to an implied term enabling one party to give reasonable notice to the other that the contract will be terminated. The leading modern case is *Staffordshire Area Health Authority* v. *South Staffordshire Waterworks Co* (1978). A majority of the Court of Appeal held that a 1929 agreement to supply 5,000 gallons of water a day free of charge, thereafter at seven old pence per 1,000 gallons 'at all times hereafter', was neither a perpetual contract nor (as was evident) a contract of fixed duration. Since the contract was of indefinite duration, the Court of Appeal held that, on construction, it was terminable by the giving of reasonable notice.[27] The water company

---

[23] *Gamerco SA* v. *ICM/Fair Warning (Agency) Ltd* [1995] 1 WLR 1226, Garland J.

[24] *BP Exploration Co (Libya) Ltd* v. *Hunt (No 2)*: main discussion by Robert Goff J is at [1979] 1 WLR 783, 799; subsidiary aspects are examined in successive appeals, [1981] 1 WLR 232, CA; [1982] 2 AC 352, HL.

[25] Generally on the 1943 Act, GH Treitel, *Frustration and Force Majeure* (3rd edn, London, 2014), chapter 15; E McKendrick (ed), *Force Majeure and Frustration of Contract* (2nd edn, London, 1995); *Goff and Jones, The Law of Unjust Enrichment* (8th edn, London, 2011), chapter 15; E McKendrick, 'Frustration, Restitution and Loss Adjustment', in AS Burrows (ed), *Essays on Restitution* (Oxford, 1991), 147; GL Williams, *Law Reform (Frustrated Contracts) Act 1943* (1944).

[26] K Lewison, *Interpretation of Contracts* (6th edn, London, 2015), 6.18; Malcolm Clarke in Neil H Andrews, MA Clarke, AM Tettenborn, G Virgo, *Contractual Duties: Performance, Breach, Termination and Remedies* (London, 2012), 17–083 ff.

[27] [1978] 1 WLR 1387, CA, *per* (Reginald) Goff and Cumming-Bruce LJJ; at *ibid*, 1397–8, Lord Denning MR, in a minority opinion, reached the same conclusion by the heterodox route of finding frustration to be satisfied by inflation; T A Downes, (1985) 101 LQR 98, 104–8; K Dharmananda and L Firios (eds), *Long Term Contracts* (Federeation Press, Sydney, 2013) (collection of comparative essays); McKendrick, 'The Regulation of Long-Term Contracts in English Law', in J Beatson and D Friedmann (eds), *Good Faith and Fault in Contract Law* (Oxford, 1995), 305.

was prepared to continue the supply, charging, for daily usage in excess of 5,000 gallons, the 1970s price for commercial supply. Goff LJ, having examined the authorities, formulated this test[28]:

> '*the [party seeking to establish a right to terminate by giving reasonable notice has] to show, and the onus is upon them, why, there being no express power to determine this agreement, one should be inferred, but there is no presumption either way; the onus is not the heavy one of rebutting a presumption to the contrary. This being so, one has to consider the surrounding circumstances as well as what the parties have said or left unsaid in the agreement itself.*'

(ii) It was held in *ServicePower Asia Pacific Pty Ltd* v. *ServicePower Business Solutions Ltd* (2009) that the court will not construe a contract as being subject to an implied termination clause if an express term already covers the giving of notice.[29]

(iii) *Contracts of Fixed Duration*. Where the contract is of a *fixed duration*, there will be no implied term that a party can terminate it by giving reasonable notice, as *Jani-King (GB) Ltd* v. *Pula Enterprises Ltd* (2007) shows.[30]

(iv) '*Perpetual' Clause Not Truly Intended to be Permanent. BMS Computer Solutions Ltd* v. *AB Agri Ltd* (2010)[31] shows that a clause purporting to confer on a licensee a 'perpetual' entitlement might be construed as merely creating an entitlement of no fixed duration; if so, the licensor can give reasonable notice to terminate the entitlement.[32]

(v) '*Perpetual' Clause Expiring as a Practical Commercial Matter*. A clause in which a soft-ware supplier undertook to provide permanent support for the user of the product was held to be perpetual, surviving the termination of the main contract. But the parties' relationship would in practice end when advances in technology would render that particular product commercially obsolete.[33]

---

[28] [1978] 1 WLR 1387, 1399–1400, CA, *per* (Reginald) Goff; Goff LJ's judgment and supporting authorities were followed by Buxton LJ in *Colchester and East Essex Co-Operative Society Ltd* v. *The Kelvedon Labour Club and Institute Ltd* [2003] EWCA Civ 1671, at [9].

[29] [2009] EWHC 179 (Ch); [2010] 1 All ER (Comm) 238, at [25] ff (William Trower QC).

[30] [2007] EWHC 2433 (QBD); [2008] 1 Lloyd's Rep 305, at [60] to [66], *per* Coulson J.

[31] [2010] EWHC 464 (Ch), Sales J.

[32] See his cogent articulation of supporting reasons, *ibid*, at [18].

[33] *Harbinger UK Ltd* v. *GE Information Services Ltd* [2000] 1 All ER (Comm) 166 (severable clause, surviving termination of main contract, that company 'in perpetuity' would provide support and maintenance of software supplied to a customer; the reality was that the customer would not everlastingly be prepared to use this soft-ware; so long as it did, the supplier's obligation would endure).

Chapter 17
Remedies for Breach of Contract

Abstract This chapter embraces all the remedies applicable if there has been a breach of contract. Discussion covers the judicial remedies of debt, damages, specific performance, injunctions, and declarations. It should be noted that English law will not enforce an agreement for the payment of a sum which will act as a penalty, that is, the amount agreed to be paid (or other stipulated detriment) is not an acceptable forecast of the actual loss likely to arise from the relevant default and instead the stipulated payment or detriment is disproportionate to the innocent party's interest in compensation or other legitimate interests. Nor will the courts award punitive damages for breach of contract. The process of forfeiting deposits is also noted. Other topics covered are set-off and limitation of actions.

17.1 Money Claims in General

17.01 Discussion in this chapter concerns matters where the governing law concerning the substance is English contract law.[1]

17.02 *CURRENCY*[2]

The currency of the judgment or award for payment of money (whether as damages, including liquidated damages, or debt, or otherwise) will often, but need not invariably, be that of the forum (in England and Wales pound Sterling).[3]

[1] On the application of remedies and procedure where the law governing the contract is non-English, Louise Merrett, 'Commercial Remedies in International Cases', in G Virgo and S Worthington (eds), *Commercial Remedies: Resolving Controversies* (Cambridge University Press, 2016).

[2] Adam Kramer, *The Law of Contract Damages* (Hart, Oxford, 2014), section 1.5; *McGregor on Damages* (19th edn, 2014), 19–025 ff.

[3] *Miliangos v. Frank (Textiles) Ltd [1976] AC 443, HL; Services Europe Atlantique Sud v. Stockholms Rderiaktie SVEA ('The Folias' and 'The Despina R') [1979] AC 685, HL (also considering Federal Commerce and Navigatons Co Ltd v. Tradax Export SA [1977] 1 QB 324, CA); 'The Kafalonia Wind' [1986] 1 Lloyd's Rep 273, Bingham J; 'The Dione' [1980] 2 Lloyd's Rep 577, Lloyd J; 'The Federal Huron' [1985] 2 Lloyd's Rep 189, Bingham J; Metaalhandel JA Magnus BV* v. *Ardfields Transport* [1988] 1 Lloyd's Rep 197; *'The Texaco Melbourne' [1994] 1 Lloyd's Rep 473, HL; Kinetics Technology International SpA* v. *Cross Seas Shipping Corp (The Mosconici)* [2001] 2 Lloyd's Rep 313, David Steel J; *Virani v. Marcel Revert y Compagnia SA [2003] EWCA Civ 1651; [2004] 2 Lloyd's Rep 14; Carnegie v. Giessen* [2005] EWCA Civ 191; [2005] 1 WLR 2510; *Milan Nigeria Ltd* v. *Angeliki B Maritime Co* [2011] EWHC 892 (Comm); [2011] Arb LR

N. Andrews, *Arbitration and Contract Law*, Ius Gentium: Comparative Perspectives on Law and Justice 54, DOI 10.1007/978-3-319-27144-6_17

17.03 *In Milan Nigeria Ltd* v. *Angeliki B Maritime Co* (2011) *Gloster J formulated this summary*[4]*:*

> *[62] ...[T]he legal principles to be applied to the issue of the currency in which an award is to be made are well-established and clearly identifiable...[The court or tribunal] must act in accordance with the principles identified by Lord Wilberforce in 'The Folias' (1979)* [5] *and restated by Lord Goff in 'The Texaco Melbourne' (1994):*[6]
>
> > *'First, it is necessary to ascertain whether there is an intention, to be derived from the terms of the contract, that damages for breach of contract should be awarded in any particular currency or currencies. In the absence of any such intention, "the damage should be calculated in the currency in which the loss was felt by the plaintiff" or "which most truly expresses his loss".'*
>
> *[63] The currency in which a claimant feels its loss is a question of fact to be determined by the tribunal having regard to all the circumstances of the case before it: see 'The Texaco Melbourne' (supra at pages 478–480). The decision-maker's function is to identify "the currency which most justly expresses the loss that has been suffered by the claimants"...*[7] *... [C]aution must be taken not to elevate factual observations made in one case into statements of principle to be applied generally in other cases.*

17.04 *Arbitral Tribunals.* Section 48(4) of the Arbitration Act 1996 permits the arbitral tribunal to make an order for payment of a sum in any currency. This was considered in *Lesotho Highlands Development Authority* v. *Impreglio SpS* (2005), where it was held that the matter might arise for appeal under section 69 of that Act (that right had been excluded, however, by the relevant contract).[8] This decision provides majority support for the proposition that the tribunal does not have a complete discretion in the matter but must apply the established rules summarised above.

17.05 As Andrews has noted[9]:

> *'the House of Lords rejected the radical opinion of Lord Steyn that this matter lies within the tribunal's discretion*[10] *(his approach was rejected explicitly by the other four judges, Lords Hoffmann,*[11] *Phillips,*[12] *Scott,*[13] *and Rodger).*[14] *Instead the majority construed section*

24, Gloster J. The question whether a debt is payable in a foreign currency was examined in *Addax Bank BSC* v. *Wellesley Partners LLP* [2010] EWHC 1904 (QB), Eady J; and for waiver of the currency see *Alan* v. *El Nasr* [1972] 2 QB 189, CA.

[4] *Milan Nigeria Ltd* v. *Angeliki B Maritime Co* [2011] EWHC 892 (Comm); [2011] Arb LR 24, at [62] and [63], *per* Gloster J.

[5] *Services Europe Atlantique Sud v. Stockholms Rderiaktie SVEA ('The Folias' and 'The Despina R') [1979] AC 685, 697–698, HL.*

[6] *[1994] 1 Lloyd's Rep 473,* at 477–478, HL.

[7] Citing, *Kinetics Technology International SpA* v. *Cross Seas Shipping Corp ('The Mosconici')* [2001] 2 Lloyd's Rep 313, 316, David Steel J.

[8] *Lesotho Highlands Development Authority* v. *Impreglio SpS* [2005] UKHK 43; [2006] 1 AC 221.

[9] *Andrews on Civil Processes* (Intersentia, Cambridge, Antwerp, Portland, 2013), vol 2 ('*Arbitration and Mediation*'), 15-07 and 15-08.

[10] *Lesotho Highlands Development Authority* v. *Impreglio SpS* [2005] UKHK 43; [2006] 1 AC 221, at [22].

[11] *ibid,* at [42].

[12] *ibid,* at [50].

[13] *ibid,* at [56].

[14] *ibid,* at [55].

48(4) as entitling the tribunal to award payment (a) in the currency chosen by the parties or (b) in the currency which can be ascertained from the parties' transaction or (in the absence of (a) or (b)), in (c) the currency which the tribunal considers most appropriate. There is no general licence to proceed straight to approach (c) and thus select a currency at random in the name of abstract justice. Instead constraints (a) and (b) must first be observed.'

17.06 The contract in the *Lesotho* case stated that payments would be made in the Lesotho currency ('Maloti'). The agreement also provided that the payment could be calculated by reference to various foreign currencies (the 'foreign proportions'), which could be used to calculate specified percentages of the sum to be paid. The exchange rate for making this calculation was that prevailing at the Central Lesotho bank 42 days prior to the start date ('historic exchange rate'). The arbitral tribunal made an award in European currencies. It arrived at these figures after determining the amount of Maloti which should have been paid (there were several tranches which had not been paid), and then applying both the 'foreign proportions' and 'the historic exchange rate'. Because the Maloti had fallen in value significantly since that date, the effect was to grant an enhanced sum in favour of the payee. The tribunal did not complete the task of revalorising its Maloti award by expressing the final amount in Maloti, but instead issued an award expressed in European currencies, contrary to the parties' main transaction (the section 69, Arbitration Act 1996, route to appeal to the High Court had been excluded in this contract; and the House of Lords held that section 68 (serious irregularity) did not cover this type of issue).

17.07 It is submitted that no objection would have been taken if the award in the *Lesotho* case had been expressed in Maloti (the contractually nominated currency of account and payment) by (1) taking the amount of the Maloti not paid by the employer to the contractor; (2) subjecting that sum to revalorisation under the main contract, by combining the 'foreign proportions' and 'the historic exchange rate'; and (3) stating the final amount of Maloti produced after steps (1) and (2). This process of calculation would have accurately reflected the agreement's specification that Maloti should be the currency of account and that, in valuing the amount of payment, there should be reference to both the 'foreign proportions' and the 'historic exchange rate'. Interest could be validly added.

17.08 *INTEREST*[15]

The *court* (as for arbitral tribunals where England and Wales or Northern Ireland is the seat of the proceedings, see the next paragraph) has these powers to award interest:

(i) 'when giving judgment on the principal sum' (for damages or debt), the court can award *simple* interest under section 35A of the Senior Courts Act 1981;
(ii) *simple* interest can also be awarded where the principal sum was (fully) paid only after commencement of formal proceedings but before judgment was obtained (section 35A of the Senior Courts Act 1981); and

[15] Adam Kramer, *The Law of Contract Damages* (Hart, Oxford, 2014), chapter 7 (and related issues); *McGregor on Damages* (19th edn, 2014), chapter 18. Andrew Burrows, 'Of Interest' in G Virgo and S Worthington (eds), *Commercial Remedies: Resolving Controversies* (Cambridge University Press, 2016).

(iii) *Sempra Metals Ltd* v. *Inland Revenue Commissioners* (2007)[16] decides that *simple and compound*[17] interest can be awarded at Common Law for breaches of contract,[18] provided the contractual remoteness test is satisfied[19];

(iv) even where no proceedings were commenced with respect to the principal sum, the Late Payment of Commercial Debts (Interest) Act 1998 (as amended)[20] confers a right to *simple* interest (at a specified level) on the unpaid price of goods or services *if the supplier and recipient are both acting in the course of business* (section 2).[21]

17.09 *As for interest and arbitral tribunals where the seat is England and Wales or Northern Ireland,* Andrews has noted[22]:

> '*Under the English legislation the arbitral tribunal can grant monetary relief.*[23] *..including interest*[24] *(which can be compound).*[25] *Interest can be awarded in respect of the principal sum(s) mentioned in the award,*[26] *or the sum(s) claimed and which were only paid after commencement of the proceedings;*[27] *post-award interest can also be awarded,*[28] *and this can be compound.*[29] *In the Lesotho case (2005)*[30] *the House of Lords held that the power to*

[16] [2007] UKHL 34; [2008] 1 AC 561, at [94] to [100], *per* Lord Nicholls; at [16], *per* Lord Hope; at [164] and [165], *per* Lord Walker; at [226], *per* Lord Mance; at [140], *per* Lord Scott; noted by G Virgo, [2007] CLJ 510; C Nicholl, (2008) 124 LQR 199; *McGregor on Damages (19th edn, London, 2014)*, chapter 18; and, for fuller discussion, see P Ridge, 'Pre-Judgment Compound Interest' (2010) 126 LQR 279–301; the *Sempra* case was considered in *Parabola Investments Ltd* v. *Browallia Cal Ltd* [2010] EWCA Civ 486 at [51] ff. The *Sempra* decision renders otiose recommendations made by Law Commission, '*Pre-Judgment Interest on Debts and Damages*' (Law Commission Report No 287, London, 2004); earlier, Law Commission, '*Compound Interest*' (Law Commission Consultation Paper No 167, London, 2002).

[17] Also available in arbitral proceedings: section 49(3) of the Arbitration Act 1996.

[18] [2007] UKHL 34; [2008] 1 AC 561, at [216], *per* Lord Mance, on the relevance of remoteness.

[19] *ibid*, at [216], *per* Lord Mance, on the relevance of remoteness.

[20] Late Payment of Commercial Debts Regulations 2002 (SI 2002 No 1674); Late Payment of Commercial Debts Regulations (SI 2013 No 395); Late Payment of Commercial Debts (No 2) Regulations (SI 2013 No 908); *Martrade Shipping & Transport GmbH* v. *United Enterprises Corpn* [2014] EWHC 1884 (Comm); [2015] 1 WLR 1 (section 12(1) of the 1998 Act renders that statute inapplicable where the main transaction lacks 'significant connection' with the UK).

[21] As for the dates when interest becomes payable, sections 4(3)(4), Late Payment of Commercial Debts (Interest) Act 1998.

[22] *Andrews on Civil Processes* (Intersentia, Cambridge, Antwerp, Portland, 2013), vol 2 ('*Arbitration and Mediation*'), 15-04 to 15-06.

[23] *X Ltd* v. *Y Ltd* [2005] BLR 341 on the issue of contribution orders under the Civil Liability (Contribution) Act 1978 (on which Neil Andrews, *English Civil Procedure* (Oxford University Press, 2003), 11.76 ff).

[24] Section 49, Arbitration Act 1996.

[25] Section 49(3),(4), *ibid.*

[26] Section 48(5)(b), *ibid.*

[27] Section 48(5)(a), *ibid.*

[28] Section 49(4), *ibid.*

[29] *ibid.*

[30] *Lesotho Highlands Development Authority* v. *Impreglio SpS* [2005] UKHK 43; [2006] 1 AC 221.

> *make awards of interest is unconstrained. Lord Phillips noted*[31] *that the phrase 'as it considers meets the justice of the case' confers a broad discretion.*'

But what if the parties have agreed to exclude compound interest and yet the arbitral tribunal goes on to award compound interest? There is a passage in Lord Steyn's speech[32] in the *Lesotho* case (2005) where he appears to assent to Lord Phillips' suggestion, made in argument during the hearing, that this would involve not an erroneous exercise of the power to award interest but the unjustified arrogation of a power to award a type of interest plainly barred by the parties' agreement and hence an excess of power. If so, this might give rise to 'substantial injustice': section 68(2). Section 68(3) allows the court to remit the award, set it aside in whole or in part, or to declare it to be invalid in whole or in part.

17.2 The Claim in Debt

17.10 *DEBT CLAIMS*[33]

(i) *Action for an Agreed Sum.* A contracting party's failure to pay a debt (a sum fixed by agreement or ascertainable in amount) will entitle the creditor to bring a Common Law claim for payment of that sum (also known as the action for an agreed sum) (for supplementary claims for interest, see **17.08**). The remedy is not discretionary and is instead available as of right. Examples are: the price in a sale of goods transaction or in an agreement to buy real property; a premium in an insurance agreement; rent in a lease; hire in a charterparty (hire of a vessel) or other contract for borrowing goods or equipment; fees, salary, wages, commission, agreed sums by way of contribution, etc; sums invoiced for services rendered; and fares.

(ii) *Debt Obligations and Specific Performance.* Exceptionally, payment of a debt is enforced by an injunctive order, sanctioned by contempt of court. This might be appropriate if the debt comprises a series of periodic payments. As explained at **17.27**, specific performance is an equitable and discretionary remedy. It is only available if the Common Law pecuniary remedies (debt and damages) are inadequate in the relevant context.

(iii) *Penal Sums.* The 'penalty doctrine' (**17.33**) renders unenforceable an agreement requiring the debtor to pay a sum exceeding the principal and interest owed.

(iv) *Rejection of a Party's Attempt to Cancel a Contract.* Here the situation is that one party (the eventual debtor) attempts to call off the job (or relevant performance), but this suggested cancellation is rejected by the other party (an unaccepted renunciation, also known as an attempted anticipatory breach). The

[31] *ibid*, at [50].

[32] *ibid*, at [29].

[33] Tettenborn, in Neil H Andrews, MA Clarke, AM Tettenborn, G Virgo, *Contractual Duties: Performance, Breach, Termination and Remedies* (London, 2012), chapter 19.

latter party might be in a position to complete performance. If so, he will acquire the right to claim in debt (the so-called 'agreed sum'). This possibility was confirmed by a majority, the House of Lords in *White & Carter* v. *McGregor* (1962).[34] The decision was to allow an innocent party to perform (the provision of advertising services, including physical display on bill-boards) and charge[35] the other party the agreed sum even though the other party had declared that he no longer wanted the relevant performance. But there are two restrictions upon this possibility of completing performance and suing in debt:

(a) performance by the claimant must not require the other party's co-operation (as where property is made available for the other's use under a contract of hire or under a lease, or the performance takes the form of advertising or manufacture without the other needing to collaborate or assist);[36] and
(b) the tribunal must be satisfied (as it generally will be) that it was not so commercially unacceptable that it was or would be extremely or wholly unreasonable or perverse for the claimant to cling to the contract and present such an unwanted performance (the case law presents this from the perspective of the performing party lacking a 'legitimate interest' in maintaining the contract in play). Consistent with the principle of *pacta sunt servanda* (**10.11**), requirement (b) will be applied generously in favour of the claimant who has performed in these circumstances. Cooke J in *Isabella Shipowner SA* v. *Shagang Shipping Co Ltd ('The Aquafaith')* (2012)[37] said: *'an innocent party will have no legitimate interest in maintaining the contract if damages are an adequate remedy and his insistence on maintaining the contract can be described as "wholly unreasonable", "extremely unreasonable" or, perhaps, in my words, "perverse".'*[38]

The case law has consistently (subject to one isolated reported exception) upheld the creditor's claim for the relevant debt:

---

[34] [1962] AC 413, HL (Lords Reid, Hodson and Tucker; dissenting, Lords Keith and Morton); AS Burrows, *Remedies for Torts and Breach of Contract* (3rd edn, Oxford University Press, 2004), 435–44.

[35] In fact, the pursuer part-performed and the defender failed to pay the relevant instalment; an acceleration clause (Neil Andrews, *Contract Law* (2nd edn, Cambridge University Press, 2015), 19.18; G McMeel, *The Construction of Contracts: Interpretation, Implication and Rectification* (2nd edn, Oxford University Press, 2011), 24.06) rendered the defendant liable for all the instalments in the event of non-payment of one instalment.

[36] As for the co-operation requirement, Neil Andrews, *Contract Law* (2nd edn, Cambridge University Press, 2015), 18.04; A Dyson, 'What do the *White & Carter* "Limitations" Limit?' in G Virgo and S Worthington (eds), *Commercial Remedies: Resolving Controversies* (Cambridge University Press, 2016).

[37] [2012] EWHC 1077 (Comm); [2012] 2 All ER (Comm) 461; [2012] 2 Lloyd's Rep 61, at [44].

[38] *ibid*, at [49]. See also *MSC Mediterranean Shipping Co* v. *Cottonex Anstalt* [2015] EWHC 283 (Comm); [2015] 1 Lloyd's Rep 359; and see J O'Sullivan 'Unaccepted Repudiation and the Protection of the Performance Interest' in G Virgo and S Worthington (eds), *Commercial Remedies: Resolving Controversies* (Cambridge University Press, 2016).

(1) Most charterparty cases have acknowledged the owner's legitimate interest in keeping the vessel on hire[39] (see below for the lone exception in *The Alaskan Trader'*, 1984).
(2) In *Barclays Bank plc* v. *Unicredit Bank AG* (2012) Popplewell J held that a bank was entitled to claim charges for providing a facility even when the commercial party had sought to cancel the arrangement.[40]
(3) In *Ministry of Sound (Ireland)* v. *World Online Ltd* (2003),[41] Nicholas Strauss QC held that the claimant had a legitimate interest in continuing to provide publicity for the defendant[42] (the facts are analogous to the unwanted advertising in the *White & Carter* case, see above).
(4) In *Reichman* v. *Beveridge* (2006)[43] the Court of Appeal confirmed that a landlord is entitled to claim rent accruing (quarterly) during the residue of a business tenancy (the case is analogous to the cases concerning hire from charterparties).

An isolated case where the creditor lacked a 'legitimate interest is *Clea Shipping Corporation* v. *Bulk Oil International ('The Alaskan Trader')* (1984).[44] Lloyd J upheld, but without enthusiasm, the arbitrator's decision that a shipowner was not entitled to keep a time-chartered vessel on hire, with full crew, for 8 months and to charge this to the charterer (later Cooke J said in '*The Aquafaith*' (2012), commenting on this 1984 case, that a 8 month dormant period would be a 'commercial absurdity').[45]

17.3 Compensation Claims

17.11 *AGREED COMPENSATION*

(see, for greater detail, *PROTECTION AGAINST PENALTY CLAUSES,* **17.33**)

Liquidated Damages Agreed ex ante. A liquidated damages clause can fix in advance of breach the measure of damages which the innocent party will receive in the event of breach (the clause will be upheld unless the sum is punitive: see main discussion at **17.33**).

---

[39] *Gator Shipping Corporation* v. *Trans-Asiatic Oil Ltd SA and Occidental Shipping Establishment ('The Odenfeld')* [1978] 2 Lloyd's Rep 357, 373–4, Kerr J; *Ocean Marine Navigation Ltd* v. *Koch Carbon Inc ('The Dynamic')* [2003] EWHC 1936; [2003] 2 Lloyd's Rep 693, at [23], *per* Simon J; *Isabella Shipowner SA* v. *Shagang Shipping Co Ltd ('The Aquafaith')* [2012] EWHC 1077 (Comm); [2012] 2 All ER (Comm) 461; [2012] 2 Lloyd's Rep 61, at [51, [52], [56].

[40] *Barclays Bank plc* v. *Unicredit Bank AG* [2012] EWHC 3655 (Comm); [2012] EWHC 3655 (Comm); [2013] 2 Lloyd's Rep 1; [2014] 1 BCLC 342, at [110] and [111].

[41] [2003] EWHC 2178; [2003] 2 All ER (Comm) 823.

[42] *ibid*, at [64] to [66].

[43] [2006] EWCA Civ 1659; [2007] 1 P & CR 20; [2007] L & TR 18.

[44] [1984] 1 All ER 129, 136–7, Lloyd J.

[45] [2012] EWHC 1077 (Comm); [2012] 2 All ER (Comm) 461; [2012] 2 Lloyd's Rep 61, at [44].

17.12 *DAMAGES 'ONCE FOR ALL': NO SECOND CLAIM*[46]

Damages will be assessed and awarded on a one-off basis in respect of the whole of the relevant loss and not determined in instalments or reviewed from time to time. And so a claimant cannot obtain damages in successive actions in respect of the same cause of action: '*Damages resulting from one and the same cause of action must be assessed and recovered once and for all.*'[47]

17.13 *DATE FOR ASSESSING DAMAGES*[48]

(i) The starting-point is that, in general,[49] damages are assessed with regard to the facts as they subsisted at the time of breach,[50] notably in the cases of failure to accept or to deliver goods in contracts of sale.[51]

(ii) However, regard will be had to facts subsequent to the breach which have occurred and which inevitably reduce the value of the damages claim.

In *Golden Strait Corporation* v. *Nippon Yusen Kubishika Kaisha ('The Golden Victory')* (2007)[52] a bare majority of the House of Lords held that damages for anticipatory breach be reduced to reflect post-breach events inevitably reduced the value of the damages claim if they reduce or eliminate the claimant's loss. However, Lords Bingham and Walker dissented, the latter saying[53]: '*In this case an objective and well-informed observer, looking at the matter [at the time of the renunciation] would have thought...that the prospect of the war clause option being exercised... was a mere possibility carrying little or no weight in commercial terms.*' Lord Mustill in the *Law Quarterly Review* supported the dissentients, suggesting that the cause of action based on anticipa-

---

[46] Adam Kramer, *The Law of Contract Damages* (Hart, Oxford, 2014), section 1.2 C; *McGregor on Damages* (19th edn, 2014), chapter 11.

[47] *Brunsden* v. *Humphrey* (1884) 14 QBD 141, 147, CA, *per* Bowen LJ; *Conquer* v. *Boot* [1928] 2 KB 336; *Republic of India* v. *India Steamship Co Ltd ('The Indian Grace')* [1993] AC 410, 420–1, HL; L A Collins, (1992) 108 LQR 393, 394; *Jaggard* v. *Sawyer* [1995] 1 WLR 269, 284, CA; *Deeny* v. *Gooda Walker Ltd* [1995] 1 WLR 1206, 1214; Adam Kramer, *The Law of Contract Damages* (Hart, Oxford, 2014), section 1.2C; G Spencer Bower, AK Turner and KR Handley, *The Doctrine of Res Judicata* (4th edn, London, 2009), chapter 21; Neil Andrews, *Andrews on Civil Processes* (vol 1, *Court Proceedings*), (Intersentia, Cambridge, Antwerp, Portland, 2013),16.84; AS Burrows, *Remedies for Torts and Breach of Contract* (3rd edn, Oxford University Press, 2004), 174 ff.

[48] Adam Kramer, *The Law of Contract Damages* (Hart, Oxford, 2014), chapter 17; *McGregor on Damages* (19th edn, 2014), 10–112 ff.

[49] Cf Lord Wilberforce in *Johnson* v. *Agnew* [1980] 367, 401, HL: 'not an absolute rule ... the court has power to fix such other date as may be appropriate.'

[50] S Waddams, 'The Date for the Assessment of Damages' (1981) 97 LQR 445–61; Adam Kramer, *The Law of Contract Damages* (Hart, Oxford, 2014), chapter 17; against the existence of this approach, A Dyson and Adam Kramer, 'There is No "Breach Date Rule"...' (2014) 130 LQR 259–281.

[51] Respectively, sections 50(3) and 51(3) of the Sale of Goods Act 1979.

[52] *'The Golden Victory'* [2007] UKHL 12; [2007] 2 AC 353; noted Lord Mustill (2008) 124 LQR 569;; Sir Bernard Rix, 'Lord Bingham's Contributions to Commercial Law', in M Andenas and D Fairgrieve (eds), *Tom Bingham and the Transformation of the Law: A Liber Amicorum* (Oxford, 2009), at 679–83.

[53] [2007] UKHL 12, [2007] 2 AC 353, at [46].

tory breach should be conceptualised as loss of the value of contractual rights, assessed as the market value of those rights at the time of discharge, with appropriate adjustment to reflect contingencies *then also affecting* the value of those rights.[54] Critics of this decision seem now to be chasing a lost cause because the Supreme Court in *Bunge SA* v. *Nidera BV* ([2015] UKSC 43; [2015] 3 All ER 1082, at [21] to [23], *per* Lord Sumption, and at [83], *per* Lord Toulson) has endorsed the majority decision in 'The *Golden Victory*'.

(iii) The breach date is unlikely to apply in respect of land transactions. In *Hooper* v. *Oates* (2013) held[55] the purchaser had defaulted in 2008 when the property was worth £605,000, and the vendor had then unsuccessfully tried to sell it, eventually deciding to retain the property. At that stage the value had fallen to £495,000. The court held that there had been no failure to take reasonable steps to mitigate its loss. And so the vendor was entitled to damages (£110,000) measured by the difference between the price and the property's value at the date when the vendor had decided to retain the property.

17.14 DEFENDANT'S LEAST ONEROUS MODE OF PERFORMANCE[56]

Durham Tees Valley Airport Ltd v. *bmibaby Ltd* (2010)[57] confirms both propositions (i) and (ii) set out below:

(i) Damages will only be awarded if the claimant is entitled to recover compensation in respect of benefits which the defendant was legally obliged to confer. However, where it is clear that the claimant has suffered loss in respect of a legally protected right, but the defendant had a choice between two or more ways to perform, the claimant will be awarded damages on the less or least onerous basis, tilting matters in favour of the defendant.

(ii) Where, however, the defendant's performance involves a single obligation, within which he enjoys elements of discretion, tribunals are prepared to regulate this by reference to standards of reasonableness, where necessary and appropriate.

17.15 *CLAIMANT'S POVERTY IRRELEVANT*[58]

A claimant cannot be prevented from recovering loss merely because that loss stems from his lack of funds.[59]

---

[54] Lord Mustill (2008) 124 LQR 569.

[55] [2013] EWCA Civ 91; [2014] Ch 287, notably at [34] to [40], *per* Lloyd LJ (noted, A Dyson and Adam Kramer, 'There is No "Breach Date Rule"...' (2014) 130 LQR 259–281).

[56] Adam Kramer, *The Law of Contract Damages* (Hart, Oxford, 2014), section 13.3 B; *McGregor on Damages* (19th edn, 2014), 10–104 ff; Tettenborn, in Neil H Andrews, MA Clarke, AM Tettenborn, G Virgo, *Contractual Duties: Performance, Breach, Termination and Remedies* (London, 2012), 21.76 to 21.84; K Lewison, *Interpretation of Contracts* (5th edn, London, 2011), 8.09.

[57] [2010] EWCA Civ 485; [2011] 1 All ER (Comm) 731; [2011] 1 Lloyd's Rep 68, at [79], *per* Patten LJ (Toulson and Mummery LJJ agreed, [147], [150]).

[58] Adam Kramer, *The Law of Contract Damages* (Hart, Oxford, 2014), section 16.7 B.

[59] The *Liesbosch* case (*Liesbosch* v. *Owners of the Steamship Edison ('The Edison')* [1933] AC 449, HL 1933) had imposed an 'impecuniosity' restriction, but the decision is now regarded as bad law *Lagden* v. *O'Connor* [2004] 1 AC 1067, at [62].

17.16 *LITIGATION COSTS AND DAMAGES*[60]

Costs incurred in bringing or defending a claim against the other party are recoverable only under the costs regime of the procedural rules,[61] unless (i) party B's breach led to party A incurring litigation expenses *vis-à-vis* a third party[62]; or (ii) party B's breach led party A to incur litigation costs in a *foreign jurisdiction.*[63]

17.17 *EXPECTATION LOSS AND RELIANCE LOSS*[64]

(i) The main[65] aim of compensatory damages for breach of contract is to place the innocent party in the position he would have been in if the contract had been properly performed.[66] This is the so-called 'expectation' or 'loss of bargain' measure.

(ii) But if loss of profit is too hard to prove, a 'fall-back' type of damages is to restore the claimant monetarily to the position he enjoyed before the contract was breached. This is the so-called 'reliance loss' measure.[67] For example, in *Anglia Television Ltd* v. *Reed* (1972)[68] an actor failed to attend the claimant's film-shoot. The claimant company could not show loss of profit and so it received damages for expenses wasted when the project had to be scrapped. But there are two restrictions on the reliance loss claim:

(1) the defendant might show (the burden being upon that party)[69] that the claimant had no chance of 'covering his expenses' even if the contract had not been breached; in other words, that the contract was inherently loss-making for the innocent party.[70] If so, the defendant need only pay 'nominal damages'. This restriction can be justified for two reasons: first,

[60] *McGregor on Damages* (19th edn, 2014), chapter 20; L Merrett, 'Costs as Damages' (2009) 125 LQR 468; Adam Kramer, *The Law of Contract Damages* (Hart, Oxford, 2014), sections 20.2 to 20.4; for a judicial review of the authorities, *Carroll* v. *Kynaston* [2010] EWCA Civ 1404; [2011] QB 959 at [14] to [31].

[61] Notably, CPR Part 44; *Andrews on Civil Processes* (vol 1, *Court Proceedings*), (Intersentia, Cambridge, Antwerp, Portland, 2013), chapters 18–20.

[62] e.g., *British Racing Drivers Club* v. *Hextall Erskine & Co* [1996] BCC 727, Carnwath J.

[63] e.g., *Union Discount Co Ltd* v. *Zoller* [2001] EWCA Civ 1755; [2002] 1 WLR 1517.

[64] Adam Kramer, *The Law of Contract Damages* (Hart, Oxford, 2014), section 1.3; *McGregor on Damages* (19th edn, 2014), 4–02 ff; Tettenborn, in Neil H Andrews, MA Clarke, AM Tettenborn, G Virgo, *Contractual Duties: Performance, Breach, Termination and Remedies* (London, 2012), 21.034 ff.

[65] Similarly, Law Commission, *Contract Code* (1972), Article 434.

[66] Parke B, in *Robinson* v. *Harman* (1848) 1 Exch 850, 855; on the claimant's expectation or performance interest, Fuller and Perdue, 'The Reliance Interest in Contract Damages' (1936) 46 *Yale Law Journal* 52 and 373 (in two parts);.

[67] Similarly, Law Commission, *Contract Code* (1972), Article 435.

[68] [1972] 1 QB 60, CA.

[69] *CCC Films* v. *Impact Quadrant Ltd* [1985] QB 16, Hutchison J; considered in *Grange* v. *Quinn* [2013] EWCA Civ 24; [2013] 1 P & CR 18.

[70] The seminal case is *C & P Haulage* v. *Middleton* [1983] 1 WLR 1461, CA.

as a matter of causation, the claimant would have been impoverished by the contract even if everything had been performed perfectly, and so he suffered no loss as a result of the breach; and, secondly, an award of substantial damages would be punitive if no loss has been shown.

(2) The second restriction is that reliance loss might be eliminated because the claimant has successfully mitigated its loss. In *Omak Maritime Ltd* v. *Mamola Challenger Shipping Co Ltd, 'The Mamola Challenger'* (2010)[71] the owner had incurred nearly US$ 90,000 fitting out a vessel to suit the charterer, under a lengthy time charterparty. Although the charterer then repudiated, the owner quickly recouped the expenditure because the market rate had risen well above the level of the contract rate.

(iii) Compensatory damages for breach of contract are awarded normally on Common Law principles, but the court has a statutory power to award (compensatory) damages instead of, or in addition to, specific performance or an injunction (section 50, Senior Courts Act 1981).[72] The leading cases are: *Johnson* v. *Agnew* (1980)[73]; *Oakacre Ltd* v. *Claire Cleaners (Holdings) Ltd* (1982)[74]; and *Jaggard* v. *Sawyer* (1995).[75] Such damages are the same as those at Common Law, except that damages can be awarded under this provision even before breach has occurred.

(iv) Contractual damages are intended to compensate the claimant, rather than to punish the defendant.[76]

---

[71] [2010] EWHC 2026 (Comm); [2011] Bus LR 212; [2011] 1 Lloyd's Rep 47; [2010] 2 CLC 194, at [59]; noted David McLauchlan (2011) 127 LQR 23–7; A Tettenborn [2011] LMCLQ 1–4.

[72] Section 50, Senior Courts Act 1981); Adam Kramer, *The Law of Contract Damages* (Hart, Oxford, 2014), section 1.2 B(iii); GH Jones and W Goodhart, *Specific Performance* (2nd edn, London, 1996), 275 ff; *McGregor on Damages* (19th edn, London, 2014), 11–29; JA Jolowicz [1975] CLJ 224.

[73] [1980] AC 367, HL.

[74] [1982] Ch 197, Mervyn-Davies J (damages awarded instead of specific performance; latter sought in good faith before breach had occurred).

[75] [1995] 1 WLR 269, CA (injunction refused; circumstances in which injunction will be withheld; damages in lieu awarded under section 50 of the Senior Courts Act 1981).

[76] *Addis* v. *Gramophone Co Ltd* [1909] AC 488, HL (considered in *Ruxley Electronics and Construction Ltd* v. *Forsyth* [1996] 1 AC 344, 365, HL and *Edwards* v. *Chesterfield Royal Hospital NHS Foundation Trust* [2011] UKSC 58; [2012] 2 AC 22, noted C Barnard and L Merrett (2013] CLJ 313); Adam Kramer, *The Law of Contract Damages* (Hart, Oxford, 2014), section 23.3; R Cunnington, 'Should Punitive Damages be Part of the Judicial Arsenal in Contract Cases?' (2006) 26 LS 369; J Morgan, *Great Debates in Contract Law* (2nd edn, Palgrave, Basingstoke, 2015), 252–7; S Rowan (2010) 30 OxJLS 495; J Goudkamp, 'Punishment in the Shadows', in G Virgo and S Worthington (eds), *Commercial Remedies: Resolving Controversies* (Cambridge University Press, 2016); otherwise in Canada, *Royal Bank of Canada* v. *Got* (2000) 17 DLR (4th) 385 (Supreme Court of Canada), noted by J Edelman (2001) 117 LQR 539; *Whiten* v. *Pilot Insurance Co* [2002] SCC 18; [2002] 1 SCR 595 (Supreme Court of Canada); *Honda Canada Inc* v. *Keays* [2008] SCC 39; (2008) 294 DLR (4th) 371 (Supreme Court of Canada), noted by M McInnes (2009) 125 LQR 16, at 19–20; as for punitive damages in English *tort* law, see *Kuddus* v. *Chief Constable of Leicestershire* [2002] 2 AC 122, HL, and *A* v. *Bottrill* [2003] 1 AC 449, PC.

17.18 *COST OF CURE OR REINSTATEMENT DAMAGES*[77]

Such damages are designed to fund substitute performance and thus rectify breach (where the innocent party has already paid for substitute performance such damages provide reimbursement of that party's expenses in financing such substitute performance). For example, Oliver J awarded the cost of cure measure in *Radford* v. *De Froberville* (1977), where the defendant's failure to construct a wall could be remedied by the claimant paying a third party to construct the wall on the claimant's side of the relevant boundary.[78]

(i) However, such damages might exceed the diminution in value of the relevant subject matter. And so tribunals will not award cost of cure damages if they appear pointless,[79] excessive, disproportionate, or the claim is unacceptably vindictive rather than a genuine request for compensation (see further (iii) below).

(ii) The leading discussion is *Ruxley Electronics and Construction Ltd* v. *Forsyth* (1996),[80] where a wealthy homeowner had commissioned a company to install a swimming pool to agreed specifications. But at one end the pool was 18 in. less deep than specified and putting it right would cost £21,560. There had been no market diminution in the owner's property value. The House of Lords held that the cost of cure measure would here be 'unreasonable' (according to Lord Jauncey)[81] and 'disproportionate' (as noted by Lord Lloyd of Berwick).[82] The trial judge's findings were: (1) the customer had no real intention of reconstructing the pool; (2) 'flat' diving was still safe, even taking account of the fact that X was quite tall; (3) there was no market diminution of value. The House of Lords upheld an award of £2500 for loss of amenity (a claim for intangible loss, including overall disappointment). Lords Jauncey and Lloyd said that the customer's (tactical) willingness to give an undertaking to spend the cost of cure damages on repairs made no difference,[83] because the trial judge had

---

[77] Adam Kramer, *The Law of Contract Damages* (Hart, Oxford, 2014), sections 4.3, 4.4; *McGregor on Damages* (19th edn, 2014), 25–044, 26–052; Tettenborn, Neil H Andrews, MA Clarke, AM Tettenborn, G Virgo, *Contractual Duties: Performance, Breach, Termination and Remedies* (London, 2012), 21.65 to 21.75.

[78] [1977] 1 WLR 1262, 1268–88, 1284E, Oliver J; D Harris, A Ogus and J Phillips, (1979) 95 LQR 581, at 581–2, 590; GH Jones, (1983) 99 LQR 443, 450; H Beale, in PBH Birks (ed), *Wrongs and Remedies in the Twenty-First Century* (Oxford, 1996), 231; for Australian discussion, see *Tabcorp Holdings Ltd* v. *Bowen Investments Pty Ltd* [2009] HCA 8; (2009) ALJR 390 (cost of cure damages for tenant's breach of a no-alteration clause).

[79] e.g., *Sunrock Aircraft Corp.* v. *Scandinavian Airlines Systems* [2007] EWCA Civ 882; [2007] 2 Lloyd's Rep 612 (no justification to finance removal of 'scabs' on an aircraft; imperfections made no difference to aircraft's value, reliability, etc).

[80] [1996] AC 344, HL; D Winterton, 'Money Awards Substituting for Performance' [2012] LMCLQ 446–470.

[81] *ibid*, at 357, HL.

[82] *ibid*, at 366, HL (noting Cardozo J in the Court of Appeals of New York in *Jacob & Youngs* v. *Kent* 129 NE 889, 1921).

[83] *ibid*, at 359C, 373E.

found that the customer had no real intention of rebuilding the pool.[84] The customer's proffered undertaking was transparently an attempt to obtain a substantial award of damages for vindictive purposes.

17.19 *AGGRAVATION AND INTENSE DISAPPPOINTMENT*[85]

(i) In general, a defendant is not[86] liable for mental distress caused by breach of contract, even though the distress is not too remote a consequence of the breach.[87]

(ii) However, damages are available under these heads[88]: (1) 'physical' discomfort (including noise), which engenders such negative feelings[89]; or (2) consumer disappointment ('consumer surplus' compensation)[90]: such a claim is for 'loss' which, although palpable to consumers, is not reflected concretely in the 'market'[91]; or (3) the contract has as one of its main[92] purposes (a) the avoidance of aggravation (such as liability of surveyors commissioned to inspect property or the liability of lawyers retained to obtain injunctive relief against violent or

[84] *ibid*, at 372H.

[85] Adam Kramer, *The Law of Contract Damages* (Hart, Oxford, 2014), chapter 19; *McGregor on Damages* (19th edn, 2014), 5–015 ff; Tettenborn, Neil H Andrews, MA Clarke, AM Tettenborn, G Virgo, *Contractual Duties: Performance, Breach, Termination and Remedies* (London, 2012), chapter 22.

[86] Contrast, Article 7.4.2(2), UNIDROIT, PICC (3rd edn, Rome, 2010).

[87] *Addis* v. *Gramophone Co Ltd* [1909] AC 488, HL; *Watts* v. *Morrow* [1991] 1 WLR 1421, 1445, CA, *per* Bingham LJ; *Johnson* v. *Gore, Wood & Co* [2002] 2 AC 1, 37–8, HL; *Hamilton Jones* v. *David and Snape* [2003] EWHC 3147 (Ch); [2004] 1 All ER 657, at [52] ff, Neuberger J; see also *Ashworth* v. *Royal National Theatre* [2014] EWHC 1176; [2014] 4 All ER 238, Cranston J, at [30].

[88] *Farley* v. *Skinner* [2001] UKHL 49; [2002] 2 AC 732, HL, noted D Capper, (2002) 118 LQR 193 and E McKendrick and M Graham, [2002] LMCLQ 161; cf Canada: *Fidler* v. *Sun Life Assurance Co of Canada Ltd* [2006] SCC 30; [2006] 2 SCR 3 (Supreme Court of Canada), noted by M Clapton and M McInnes, (2007) 123 LQR 26–9; and *Honda Canada Inc* v. *Keays* [2008] SCC 39; (2008) 294 DLR (4th) 371 (Supreme Court of Canada), noted by M McInnes, (2009) 125 LQR 16.

[89] e.g., *Farley* v. *Skinner* [2001] UKHL 49; [2002] 2 AC 732, HL, and *Hobbs* v. *London and South Western Railway Co* (1875) LR 10 QB 111, CA (physical inconvenience of late-night walk in the rain; considered in *Milner* v. *Carnival plc (trading as Cunard)* [2010] EWCA Civ 389; [2010] 3 All ER 701, at [31] ff); breach of landlord's repairing obligation, *English Churches Housing Group* v. *Shine* [2004] EWCA Civ 434.

[90] *Ruxley Electronics and Construction Ltd* v. *Forsyth* [1996] AC 344, HL; D Harris, A Ogus and J Phillips, (1979) 95 LQR 581, cited by Lord Mustill in the *Ruxley* case.

[91] The leading discussion of the 'consumer surplus' concept is *Ruxley Electronics and Construction Ltd* v. *Forsyth* [1996] AC 344, HL.

[92] *Farley* v. *Skinner* [2001] UKHL 49; [2002] 2 AC 732, at [24], *per* Lord Steyn: 'a major or important object of the contract is to give pleasure, relaxation or peace of mind.'

threatening persons); or (b) conferment of pleasure (holiday companies[93] or photographers at 'one-off' special occasions).[94]

17.20 *AWARD FOR FAILURE TO NEGOTIATE RELEASE FEE ('HYPOTHETICAL BARGAIN DAMAGES')*[95]

This award is made after-the-event to simulate a notional fee which might have been exacted from the defendant if he had sought permission to 'buy out', wholly or partially, the claimant's contractual rights as against the defendant (such as a restriction on the capacity of the defendant to build on land subject to a restrictive covenant in favour of the claimant). Such an award is available where there is no other identifiable financial loss,[96] the main criterion being that 'it would be manifestly unjust to leave the claimants with an award for no or nominal damages'.[97]

This involves the attempt to re-write history: the courts try to mimic possible negotiation for a fee to be paid in return for relaxing the claimant's restrictive covenant.[98] In *Wrotham Park Estate Co* v. *Parkside Homes* (1974),[99] in breach of a restrictive covenant, the defendant had built some houses on its land. Brightman J chose not to award the innocent party the whole of the gain made from this breach. Instead, he awarded the claimant a rather modest percentage (5 %) of the defendant's profit. Stadlen J in the *Giedo* case (2010) cited judicial support for the compensatory analysis[100]; and he noted that relevant criteria are: either (a) a portion of the defendant's gain or (b) (unusually, as in the *Giedo* case) the defendant's savings by not having performed.[101]

---

[93] *Milner* v. *Carnival plc (trading as Cunard)* [2010] EWCA Civ 389; [2010] 3 All ER 701, at [32] ff (noting parsimonious awards for bad holiday –perhaps because many lawyers are too busy to take holidays – at [54] ff; and disappointment damages for a most unhappy 'luxury cruise' were pegged at £4,500 for the wife and £4,000 for the husband).

[94] *Farley* v. *Skinner* [2001] UKHL 49; [2002] 2 AC 732, at [52] to [69]; solicitors have been liable under this heading: *Heywood* v. *Wellers* [1976] QB 446, CA, and *Hamilton Jones* v. *David & Snape* [2003] EWHC 3147 (Ch); [2004] 1 WLR 921, Neuberger J.

[95] Adam Kramer, *The Law of Contract Damages* (Hart, Oxford, 2014), chapters 10 and 22; *McGregor on Damages* (19th edn, 2014), 25–052 ff; Tettenborn, in Neil H Andrews, MA Clarke, AM Tettenborn, G Virgo, *Contractual Duties: Performance, Breach, Termination and Remedies* (London, 2012), 26–016 ff.

[96] *Giedo Van Der Garde BV* v. *Force India Formula One Team Limited* [2010] EWHC 2373 (QB), at [499] to [559] (noted D Winterton and F Wilmot-Smith (2012) 128 LQR 23); where Stadlen J reviewed the scope for awarding '*Wrotham Park*' damages; see especially at [533], *per* Stadlen J; noting also, at [525] ff, notably at [535], *Pell Frischmann Engineering Ltd* v. *Bow Valley Iran Ltd* [2009] UKPC 45; [2011] 1 WLR 2370.

[97] *Giedo* case [2010] EWHC 2373 (QB), at [538], *per* Stadlen J.

[98] This is a problematic hypothetical exercise: P Devonshire, 'The hypothetical negotiation measure: an untenable fiction?' [2012] LMCLQ 393–411.

[99] [1974] 1 WLR 798, Brightman J; Adam Kramer, *The Law of Contract Damages* (Hart, Oxford, 2014), chapter 22, and section 23.2; *McGregor on Damages* (19th edn, 2014), chapter 14.

[100] *Giedo* case [2010] EWHC 2373 (QB), at [540] to [548], citing *Att-Gen* v. *Blake* [2001] 1 AC 268, 281 letter G, and 298 HL, *per* Lords Nicholls and Hobhouse.

[101] *Giedo* case [2010] EWHC 2373 (QB), *ibid*, at [549].

17.21 *RESTRICTIONS UPON DAMAGES*[102]

The following restrictions upon recovery of damages for breach of contract apply to any claim for substantial damages (damages which are not nominal):

(a) *Certainty of Loss (loss must not be too speculative)*: the loss must be proved sufficiently ('loss of chance' damages are available only if the relevant chance was 'real' or 'substantial') (**17.22**);
(b) *Causation*: the loss should be causally connected to the breach (**17.23**);
(c) *Remoteness*: the loss must not be too remote (**17.24**);
(d) *Mitigation*: the claimant must not have failed to mitigate loss (**17.25**).

(Contributory negligence, allowing damages to be reduced on a percentage basis, is not a general defence: see **17.26** below).

17.22 *LOSS OF A CHANCE*[103]

Loss of chance damages are available only if the relevant chance was 'real' or 'substantial'. For example, in the leading contract case on this type of claim, *Allied Maples Group* v. *Simmons & Simmons* (1995), the defendant firm of City solicitors, acting for a purchaser, negligently failed to try to reinsert a protective 'warranty', in favour of the buyer, into a prospective agreement. The case raised the problem of calibrating the level of chance that the defendant lawyers, if they had bothered, might have persuaded the opposing party, that is, the vendor's advisors, to re-insert this warranty. The test laid down in this case is that damages can be awarded for such a missed opportunity only if what has been lost is a 'real' or 'substantial' chance. On these facts the majority[104] held that the chance was strong enough (but Millett LJ dissented on this question of assessment, taking the view that the chance was too flimsy, although he did not disagree concerning the applicable test of a 'real' or 'substantial' possibility).[105]

As for lost future business, in *Jackson* v. *Royal Bank of Scotland* (2005), the House of Lords upheld a trial judge's award of 4 years of lost future business between the claimant and X. The claimant had been selling imported 'doggie chews' to X.[106] Disaster struck when the defendant bank let slip to X, in breach of contract, details of the claimant's 'mark-up' (the difference between the purchase price in the Far East and the much higher on-sale price in the UK). After this disclosure, X bought directly from the Far East, cutting out the middle-man (the claimant).

---

[102] Adam Kramer, *The Law of Contract Damages* (Hart, Oxford, 2014), chapters 14 to 16; *McGregor Damages* (19th edn, 2014), chapters 6 to 10; Tettenborn, in Neil H Andrews, MA Clarke, AM Tettenborn, G Virgo, *Contractual Duties: Performance, Breach, Termination and Remedies* (London, 2012), chapters 23, 24.

[103] Adam Kramer, *The Law of Contract Damages* (Hart, Oxford, 2014), section 13.5; *McGregor on Damages* (19th edn, 2014), chapter 10; Tettenborn, Neil H Andrews, MA Clarke, AM Tettenborn, G Virgo, *Contractual Duties: Performance, Breach, Termination and Remedies* (London, 2012), 24–028 ff.

[104] Stuart-Smith and Hobhouse LJJ.

[105] Millett LJ, dissenting, would instead have ordered that the matter be re-opened for further evidence.

[106] [2005] UKHL 3; [2005] 1 WLR 377, at [43].

The 4 year award of damages reflected the chance that transactions between the claimant and the wholesaler might well have petered out in due course, even if the defendant bank had not committed its breach of contract.

17.23 *CAUSATION*[107]

The defendant's breach must have been the 'effective cause' of the claimant's loss. It is not enough in contract law that the connection between breach and loss satisfied a 'but for' inquiry.[108] In the *Galoo* case (1994)[109] (which concerned financial loss) Glidewell LJ said that the court, applying common sense, must determine whether the contractual breach was the 'effective' or 'dominant' cause of the loss.[110] It will not be this if the breach merely provided the occasion or opportunity for the claimant to sustain loss. In that case the defendant accountancy firm breached its contract by negligently failing to carry out an audit of two companies. Those companies later became insolvent, whereupon their shareholders and liquidators sought compensation against the defendants. The claim foundered on the question of causation because the Court of Appeal held that the defendant's breach had not been a sufficient factor in the companies' subsequent commercial activity. Instead, the loss involved an independent set of decisions by the companies' directors to continue to trade.

In the other major modern contract case on this topic, *Supershield* case (2010),[111] the defendant, the Supershield company, had breached a contract by failing to tighten a nut controlling a sprinkler system. This led to a flood in a building. Supershield failed to invoke causation in order to pass the responsibility for the flood to those responsible for three 'back-up' systems (an overflow tank which had become blocked; a warning system which had failed; routine maintenance during which the loose nut had not been spotted). Toulson LJ said[112] that the defective valve '*was an effective cause of the flood' and 'the blockage of the drains did not take away the potency of the overflow to cause damage, but rather failed to reduce it.*'

17.24 *REMOTENESS*[113]

---

[107] Adam Kramer, *The Law of Contract Damages* (Hart, Oxford, 2014), chapters 15 and 16; *McGregor on Damages* (19th edn, 2014), 8–137 ff; Tettenborn, Neil H Andrews, MA Clarke, AM Tettenborn, G Virgo, *Contractual Duties: Performance, Breach, Termination and Remedies* (London, 2012), 24.02–24.26.

[108] The two leading modern cases are *Galoo* v. *Bright Grahame Murray* [1994] 1 WLR 1360, CA and *Supershield Ltd* v. *Siemens Building Technologies FE Ltd* [2010] EWCA Civ 7; [2010] NPC 5.

[109] [1994] 1 WLR 1360, CA; AS Burrows, *Remedies for Torts and Breach of Contract* (3rd edn, Oxford University Press, 2004), 107.

[110] [1994] 1 WLR 1360, 1374–5, *per* Glidewell LJ (Evans and Waite LJJ agreed); a causation defence also failed in *Elephant Corpn* v. *Trafigura Beheer BV ('The Crudesky')* [2013] EWCA Civ 905; [2013] 2 All ER (Comm) 992; [2014] 1 Lloyd's Rep 1.

[111] [2010] EWCA Civ 7; [2010] NPC 5.

[112] *ibid*, at [32] and [33].

[113] Neil Andrews, *Contract Law* (2nd edn, Cambridge University Press, 2015) 18.16 ff; Adam Kramer, *The Law of Contract Damages* (Hart, Oxford, 2014), chapter 14; *McGregor on Damages*

(i) The defendant in breach of contract is only liable to pay damages if the relevant type of loss was reasonably contemplated by both parties at the time of the contract's formation as a serious possibility,[114] taking into account (a) ('limb 1') the ordinary course of things and (b) ('limb 2')[115] any special knowledge which caused the defendant to have assumed a wider responsibility than in (a).[116]
(ii) Subject to (iii), there is no need to have contemplated the scale of the relevant loss: it is enough that the type (or 'head') of loss has been contemplated for the purpose of proposition (i): *H Parsons (Livestock) Ltd* v. *Uttley Ingham & Co Ltd* (1978)[117] and *Brown* v. *KMR Services Ltd* (1995).[118]
(iii) The exception concerns claims for lost profits: tribunals distinguish between ordinary levels of profit and unusually high levels of profit and the latter might be held to be too remote: the *Victoria Laundry* case (1949).[119]
(iv) The remoteness doctrine, summarised at (i) above, allocates the scope of the defaulting party's compensatory risk. The remoteness doctrine is flexible and must be applied with commercial sensitivity to each relevant context. But '*the question [of remoteness] is not simply one of probability, but of what the contracting parties must be taken to have had in mind, having regard to the nature and object of their business transaction.*'[120] And so, when applying the remoteness doctrine, exceptionally it will be necessary for the tribunal to place the transaction in its objective context and give effect to any assumptions within the relevant market which demonstrate that the defendant is to bear a scale or measure of loss different from that generated by applying the ordinary

(19th edn, 2014), 8–155 ff; Tettenborn, Neil H Andrews, MA Clarke, AM Tettenborn, G Virgo, *Contractual Duties: Performance, Breach, Termination and Remedies* (London, 2012), chapter 23.

[114] Lord Walker in the *Transfield* case, [2008] UKHL 48; [2009] 1 AC 61, at [76].

[115] The two limbs are parts of a composite rule or 'principle': *per* Lord Mance in *Sempra Metals Ltd* v. *Inland Revenue Commissioners* [2007] UKHL 34; [2008] 1 AC 561, at [215]; and *per* Lord Walker in *Jackson* v. *Royal Bank of Scotland plc* [2005] 1 WLR 377, HL, at [46] to [48].

[116] *Mulvenna* v. *Royal Bank of Scotland plc* [2003] EWCA Civ 1112, at [24] and [25], *per* Waller LJ.

[117] [1978] QB 791, CA.

[118] [1995] 4 All ER 598, CA.

[119] [1949] 2 KB 528, CA; similarly, Thomas J in *North Sea Energy Holdings* v. *Petroleum Authority of Thailand* [1997] 2 Lloyd's Rep 418, 4378, would have been prepared to disallow on the ground of remoteness a seller's claim for a very high level of lost profits (the seller alleged that it had agreed with its supplier to buy cheap; the seller's buyer repudiated; the potential loss was enormous and would have been too remote; but in fact the trial judge was not satisfied that the seller would have procured the oil from this supplier; and the Court of Appeal, [1999] 1 Lloyd's Rep 483, affirmed the decision that damages were nominal); see also *Cory* v. *Thames Ironwork Co* (1868) LR 3 QB 181; *Hall* v. *Pim* (1928) 33 Com Cas 324, 330, 33, HL, *per* Lord Dunedin ('extravagant and unusual bargains') and Lord Shaw; similarly *Household Machines* v. *Cosmos Exporters* [1947] 1 KB 217, Lewis J; *Coastal International Trading* v. *Maroil* [1988] 1 Lloyd's Rep 92; *McGregor on Damages* (19th edn, London, 2014), 23-030, 23-129.

[120] *Supershield Ltd* v. *Siemens Building Technologies FE Ltd* [2010] EWCA Civ 7; [2010] NPC 5, at [42], *per* Toulson LJ. cf exclusive reference to issue of foreseeability in Article 7.4.4, UNIDROIT, PICC (3rd edn, Rome, 2010).

remoteness test. Within that perspective it might exceptionally be concluded that it is necessary to reduce (or perhaps expand) the scope of the defendant's liability.

This remoteness of law defence[121] has a long history. The fundamental decisions are *Transfield Shipping Inc.* v. *Mercator ('The Achilleas',* 2008)[122] *Hadley* v. *Baxendale* (1854)[123]; the *Victoria Laundry* case (1949)[124]; *C Czarnikow Ltd* v. *Koufos ('The Heron II')* (1969)[125]; *H Parsons (Livestock) Ltd* v. *Uttley Ingham & Co Ltd* (1978)[126]; *Balfour Beatty Construction Ltd* v. *Scottish Power* (1994)[127]; and *Brown* v. *KMR Services Ltd* (1995).[128]

An attractive development is that the Court of Appeal In *Wellesley Partners LLP* v. *Withers LLP* (2015) made clear that where a contractual and tortious duty of care overlap on the facts of the case the relevant remoteness test governing a claim for economic loss is the contractual remoteness test (that is, the rule in *Hadley* v. *Baxendale*). The Court of Appeal explained this as follows.: 'where … contractual and tortious duties to take care in carrying out instructions exist side by side, the test for recoverability of damage for economic loss should be the same, and should be the contractual one. The basis for the formulation of the remoteness test adopted in contract is that the parties have the opportunity to draw special circumstances to each other's attention at the time of formation of the contract. Whether or not one calls it an implied term of the contract, there exists the opportunity for consensus between the parties, as to the type of damage (both in terms of its likelihood and type) for which it will be able to hold the other responsible. The parties are assumed to be contracting on the basis that liability will be confined to damage of the kind which is in their reasonable contemplation. It makes no sense at all for the existence of the concurrent duty in tort to upset this consensus, particularly given that the tortious duty arises out of the same assumption of responsibility as exists under the contract' ([2015] EWCA Civ 1146, at [80], per Floyd LJ; similarly Roth J at [147] and Longmore LJ at [186]).

---

[121] Similarly, Law Commission, *Contract Code* (1972), Article 437.

[122] [2008] UKHL 48; [2009] 1 AC 61; B Coote, (2010) 26 JCL 211; D Foxton, [2009] LMCLQ 461–87; VP Goldberg (2013) 66 CLP 107–130; G Gordon, (2009) 13 *Edinburgh Law Review* 125–30; Lord Hoffmann, (2010) 14 *Edinburgh Law Review* 47–61; H Hunter, (2014) 31 JCL 120–130; Adam Kramer, (2009) 125 LQR 408–15; PCK Lee [2010] LMCLQ 150; D McLaughlan, (2009) 9 *Oxford University Commonwealth Law Journal* 109–39; SS Naravane, [2012] JBL 404–418; J O'Sullivan, [2009] CLJ 34–7; E Peel, (2009) 125 LQR 6–12; M Stiggelbout, [2012] LMCLQ 97–121; P C K Wee, [2010] LMCLQ 150–76.

[123] (1854) 9 Exch 341.

[124] [1949] 2 KB 528, CA.

[125] [1969] 1 AC 350, HL.

[126] [1978] QB 791, CA.

[127] 1994 SLT 807; *The Times*, 23 March 1994 (a Scots case taken on final appeal to the House of Lords).

[128] [1995] 4 All ER 598, CA.

17.25 *MITIGATION*[129]

(i) *General Rule.* An innocent party must take reasonable[130] steps to reduce or eliminate the loss resulting from the other party's breach of contract (and the same requirement applies to loss arising from tortious misconduct). To the extent that this party fails to take such steps, the claim for compensation will fail.[131] *The leading decision is British Westinghouse Electric Co Ltd* v. *Underground Electric Railways (1912).*[132] The defendant bears the burden of proving that there has been a failure to mitigate.[133] 'Reasonable steps' do not require a claimant to engage in litigation,[134] unless that course is exceptionally predictable and risk-free[135] Certainly, the claimant is not required to sue third parties if this will injure its commercial reputation.[136] Where it is cheaper to repair rather than to replace, the mitigation principle will confine the innocent party to recovering the cost of cure measure of compensation rather than suing for the larger sum necessary to purchase a complete replacement.[137]

(ii) *Mitigation in fact Achieved.*[138] The innocent party must adjust his compensatory claim to reflect losses avoided and any benefits which in fact accrue to him as a result of steps taken by him in response to the relevant breach. [139] It will be different if the claimant's gain or saving has no sufficient connection with the

---

[129] Adam Kramer, *The Law of Contract Damages* (Hart, Oxford, 2014), section 15.3; *McGregor on Damages* (19th edn, 2014), chapter 9; Tettenborn, Neil H Andrews, MA Clarke, AM Tettenborn, G Virgo, *Contractual Duties: Performance, Breach, Termination and Remedies* (London, 2012), 24–038 ff.

[130] Consistent with the English approach is Article 7.4.8(1), UNIDROIT, PICC (3rd edn, Rome, 2010).

[131] Similarly, Law Commission, *Contract Code* (1972), Article 439(1)(4).

[132] [1912] AC 673, 691, HL.

[133] *Geest plc* v. *Lansiquot* [2002] UKPC 48; [2002] 1 WLR 3111, PC; *Roper* v. *Johnson* (1873) LR 8 CP 167, 178, 181–2.

[134] *Pilkington* v. *Wood* [1953] Ch 770, Harman J.

[135] *Horsfall* v. *Haywards* [1999] PNLR 583, 588, CA, considering *Western Trust & Savings Ltd* v. *Travers & Co* [1997] PNLR 295, CA and *Walker* v. *Geo. H Medlicott* [1999] 1 All ER 685, CA (application for rectification of a will under section 20 of the Administration of Justice Act 1982).

[136] *James Finlay & Co* v. *Kwik Hoo Tong* [1929] 1 KB 400, CA; *London and South of England Building Society* v. *Stone* [1983] 3 All ER 105, CA.

[137] *Ruxley Electronics and Construction Ltd* v. *Forsyth* [1996] 1 AC 344, 366 D, HL, Lord Lloyd.

[138] Similarly, Law Commission, *Contract Code* (1972), Article 439(2).

[139] *British Westinghouse Electric Co Ltd* v. *Underground Electric Railways* [1912] AC 673, 691, HL (For close re-examination of the case, A Dyson, [2012] LMCLQ 412–425, preferring to explain the case as concerned with benefits accruing in course of steps taken in pursuance of a duty to mitigate); subsequent cases reviewed in *Primavera* v. *Allied Dunbar Assurance plc* [2002] EWCA Civ 1327; [2003] PNLR 276, CA; see also the sale of defective goods case law, where the purchaser succeeds in re-selling without suffering pecuniary loss, KE Barnett, (2014) 130 LQR 387, examining the English and Australian authorities); see also *Fulton Shipping Inc of Panama* v. *Globalia Business Travel SAU* [2015] EWCA Civ 1299.

defendant's breach other than an 'historical connection'.[140] For this purpose the tribunal will consider the following factors: (1) the interval between the initial wrong and the claimant's subsequent benefit (the *Hussey* (1990)[141] and *Gardner* (1997)[142] cases); (2) inconvenience or disruption to the claimant occurring during that interval; (3) the claimant's effort (including complex negotiations with third parties), determination, and ingenuity, in achieving that benefit; (4) whether the achievement of that benefit involved a deviation from the intended use of the subject matter of the relevant contract (real estate redeveloped, rather than use as a residence, as in the *Hussey* case); and (5) whether, as a matter of commercial prudence, it was appropriate for the innocent party to use a different product in the interest of achieving an economy (as in the *British Westinghouse* case).[143]

(iii) *Recovery of Extra Loss for Attempts to Mitigate.*[144] The innocent party is entitled to recover from the defendant any expense or additional loss incurred when taking reasonable steps to mitigate the loss,[145] even if the attempt at mitigation was unsuccessful,[146] provided this attempt was reasonable.[147]

17.26 *CONTRIBUTORY NEGLIGENCE*[148]

The defence of contributory negligence applies only[149] where the relevant contractual obligation is (a) to exercise reasonable care (in fact many contractual obligations are *strict*)[150] and (b) the relevant breach of contract occurs within a

[140] *Primavera* v. *Allied Dunbar Assurance plc* [2002] EWCA Civ 1327; [2003] PNLR 276, CA, at [52], *per* Latham LJ; H McGregor, 'The Role of Mitigation in the Assessment of Damages', in D Saidov and R Cunnington (eds), *Contract Damages: Domestic and International Perspectives* (Oxford, 2008), chapter 14, at 336 ff.

[141] *Hussey* v. *Eels* [1990] 2 QB 227, 241 CA, *per* Mustill LJ, noted by AJ Oakley, [1990] CLJ 394; *Primavera* v. *Allied Dunbar Assurance plc* [2002] EWCA Civ 1327; [2003] PNLR 276, CA.

[142] *Gardner* v. *Marsh & Parsons (a firm)* [1997] 1 WLR 489, CA.

[143] *British Westinghouse Electric Co Ltd* v. *Underground Electric Railways* [1912] AC 673, 691, HL.

[144] Similarly, Law Commission, *Contract Code* (1972), Article 439(3).

[145] H McGregor, 'The Role of Mitigation in the Assessment of Damages', in D Saidov and R Cunnington (eds), *Contract Damages: Domestic and International Perspectives* (Oxford, 2008), chapter 14, at 336.

[146] Consistent with the English approach is Article 7.4.8(2), UNIDROIT, PICC (3rd edn, Rome, 2010).

[147] *Esso Petroleum Co Ltd* v. *Mardon* [1976] QB 801, CA.

[148] Adam Kramer, *The Law of Contract Damages* (Hart, Oxford, 2014), section 15.5; *McGregor on Damages* (19th edn, London, 2014), 7–009 ff; Tettenborn, Neil H Andrews, MA Clarke, AM Tettenborn, G Virgo, *Contractual Duties: Performance, Breach, Termination and Remedies* (London, 2012), 24.70 to 24.76.

[149] cf much broader approach in Article 7.4.7, UNIDROIT, PICC (3rd edn, Rome, 2010).

[150] Proposition (a) reflects the wording of sections 1(1) and 4 of the Law Reform (Contributory Negligence) Act 1945:

Where any person suffers damage as the result partly of his own fault and partly of the fault of any other person or persons, a claim in respect of that damage shall not be defeated by reason of the fault of the person suffering the damage, but the damages recoverable in respect thereof shall

relationship where the defendant *is also liable to the claimant in the tort of negligence for the same default* (that is, where there is 'concurrent' liability in contract and tort).[151]

17.4 Coercive Orders: Specific Performance and Injunctions

17.27 *SPECIFIC PERFORMANCE*[152]

(i) Specific performance is a final and mandatory order to compel performance of a positive obligation. A party who fails to comply with such an order will be in contempt of court.[153] (and become a 'contemnor'). As Lord Hoffmann said in *Co-operative Insurance Services* v. *Argyll Stores Ltd* (1998): '*the ...procedure of punishment for contempt...is a powerful weapon.*'[154] A 'contemnor' can be committed for contempt of court,[155] a quasi-criminal wrong for which the standard of proof is 'beyond reasonable doubt' rather than the lower civil standard of proof 'on the balance of probabilities'.[156] The civil court, when hearing proceedings for committal of a contemnor, can apply the following sanctions to the contemnor: imprisonment for up to 2 years[157]; a fine; or, in the

---

be reduced to such extent as the court thinks just and equitable having regard to the claimant's share in the responsibility for the damage.

Fault is defined in section 4 as: 'negligence, breach of statutory duty or other act or omission which gives rise to a liability in tort or would, apart from this Act, give rise to the defence of contributory negligence'.

[151] Proposition (b) was established in *Forsikringsaktieselskapet Vesta* v. *Butcher* (affirmed on other points by the House of Lords, [1989] AC 852, 860, where the Court of Appeal's decision is also reported).

[152] GH Jones and W Goodhart, *Specific Performance* (2nd edn, London, 1996); AS Burrows, *Remedies for Torts and Breach of Contract* (3rd edn, Oxford University Press, 2004), chapter 20; Tettenborn, in Neil H Andrews, MA Clarke, AM Tettenborn, G Virgo, *Contractual Duties: Performance, Breach, Termination and Remedies* (London, 2012), chapter 27;D Ong, *Ong on Specific Performance* (Sydney, 2013); ICF Spry, *The Principles of Equitable Remedies: Specific Performance, Injunctions, Rectification and Equitable Damages* (9th edn, Thomson Reuters, Australia, 2013); Mindy Chen-Wishart and Owen Lloyd, 'Specific Performance', in G Virgo and S Worthington (eds), *Commercial Remedies: Resolving Controversies* (Cambridge University Press, 2016).

[153] *Arlidge, Eady and Smith on Contempt* (4th edn, London, 2011).

[154] [1998] AC 1, 15.

[155] RSC Order 52 in Schedule 1 to the CPR; and CCR Order 29 in Schedule 2 to the CPR.

[156] *Z Bank* v. *D1* [1974] 1 Lloyd's Rep 656, 660, Colman J.

[157] *Harris* v. *Harris* [2001] EWCA Civ 1645; [2002] Fam 253, CA, at [12] to [14], noting section 14(1) of the Contempt of Court Act 1981, restricting the period to a maximum of two years' imprisonment.

case of both individuals[158] and companies, 'sequestration' of assets[159] ('sequestrators', officers of the court, appointed specially, can then seize the contemnor's property and sell it).[160]

(ii) Specific performance is available only if the contractual promise is supported by consideration (**11.12**), and provided also that Common Law remedies, of debt (**17.10**) or damages (**17.11**), are inadequate in the relevant case. An illustration is *Beswick* v. *Beswick* (1968),[161] where the debtor had agreed to pay periodic sums to the promisee's wife, a third party. The promisee's estate successfully claimed that the debtor should be compelled, by order of specific performance, to continue paying periodical sums to this third party.

(iii) Specific performance is an equitable remedy: the Common Law does not award specific performance, and instead the principles governing this remedy remain the product of the parallel system of Equity. Because the remedy is founded on equitable principles, it is technically not available as of right (unlike Common Law claims for debt or damages). Accordingly, specific performance is discretionary. However, there is a considerable uniformity in the judicial application of this remedy, the courts making consistent reference to established factors (see the list of such factors at (vii) below).

(iv) *Personal Services.* There can be no specific performance of contracts for personal services[162] (statute specifically renders the remedy unavailable to compel an individual to work for an employer).[163]

(v) *Seldom Available for Transfers of Movables.*[164] Specific performance is not awarded to compel transfers of chattels unless they are special, indeed 'unique' (for example, 'Princess Diana's wedding dress' or Bobby Moore's World Cup winner's medal).[165] The duty to mitigate requires the disappointed party to re-enter the market and find a substitute supplier. Unless the subject matter is 'unique' (a criterion which Burrows finds too rigid),[166] the disappointed buyer is confined to his remedy in damages. This is so even if he can show a convincing 'sentimental attachment' to the relevant chattel. Reported cases have

[158] *Raja* v. *Van Hoogstraten* [2004] EWCA Civ 968; [2004] 4 All ER 793, at [71] ff.

[159] RSC Order 45, rules 3(1)(c), 4(2)(c) and 5(1)(b)(i)(ii); RSC Order 46, rule 5; on the court's inherent power, see *Webster* v. *Southwark London Borough Council* [1983] QB 698.

[160] *IRC* v. *Hoogstraten* [1985] QB 1077, CA; *Raja* v. *Van Hoogstraten* [2007] EWHC 1743 (Ch).

[161] [1968] AC 58, HL.

[162] Similarly, Law Commission, *Contract Code* (1972), Article 407.

[163] In the case of contracts of employment, this restriction is enshrined in section 236, Trade Union and Labour Relations (Consolidation) Act 1992. Generally, GH Jones and W Goodhart, *Specific Performance* (2nd edn, London, 1996), 169–83; P Saprai, 'The Principle against Self-Enslavement in Contract Law' (2009) 26 *Journal of Contract Law* 25–44.

[164] GH Jones and W Goodhart, *Specific Performance* (2nd edn, London, 1996), 143–54.

[165] The history of English performances since 1966 underlines the continuing 'uniqueness' of that medal.

[166] AS Burrows, *Remedies for Torts and Breach of Contract* (3rd edn, Oxford University Press, 2004), 464, suggesting that the 'consumer surplus' factor might be borne in mind here.

produced an eclectic collection: unusual china jars[167]; stones from old Westminster Bridge[168]; an Adam-style door[169]; and a 'practically unique' ship.[170]

Sometimes the fact that fungibles have become alarmingly scarce can justify exceptional relief. Thus, in *Sky Petroleum Ltd* v. *VIP Petroleum Ltd* (1974), Goulding J recognised that exceptional market conditions can render damages an inadequate remedy for default even in the supply of a commodity (wholesale petrol).[171] As a result of steps taken by the OPEC cartel during the 1970s 'oil crisis', wholesale petrol supplies had become scarce. Unless it gained the present remedy, the claimant would have been forced out of business.[172] Goulding J awarded an interim injunction, equivalent to specific performance, to compel an oil supplier to deliver petrol to a retailer.[173]

But even that extreme case is open to doubt, in light of the later (but now rather dated) Court of Appeal decision in *Société des Industries Metallurgiques SA* v. *Bronx Engineering Co Ltd* (1975).[174] The court held that damages would be adequate when a seller refused to supply machinery, even though it would take almost a year for an alternative manufacturer to supply the claimant. However, Burrows attractively contends that 'commercial uniqueness' should lead to specific performance if 'an accurate assessment of the claimant's losses is so difficult that [he] is likely to be incorrectly compensated'.[175]

There is a modern line of first instance decisions in which the courts have granted orders (before, or even at,[176] trial) to compel delivery of goods in con-

[167] *Falcke* v. *Gray* (1859) 4 Drew 651.

[168] *Thorn* v. *Public Works Commissioners* (1863) 32 Beav 490.

[169] *Phillips* v. *Lamdin* [1949] 2 KB 33, 41, Croom-Johnson J.

[170] *Behnke* v. *Bede Shipping Co Ltd* [1927] 1 KB 649, Wright J; this test was not satisfied in *'The Stena Nautica' (No 2)* [1982] 2 Lloyd's Rep 336, Parker J; cf the wide *dictum* of Browne-Wilkinson V-C in *Bristol Airport plc* v. *Powdrill* [1990] Ch 744, 759 CA (lease of an aircraft is specifically enforceable; every aircraft is unique; but ship cases not cited).

[171] [1974] 1 WLR 576, Goulding J, where the goods were not even 'specific or ascertained' for the purpose of section 52 of the Sale of Goods Act 1979; *Re Wait* [1927] 1 Ch 606, CA (specific performance unavailable outside the limits of that provision); generally, see Treitel, [1966] JBL 211, AS Burrows, *Remedies for Torts and Breach of Contract* (3rd edn, Oxford University Press, 2004), 462 ff.

[172] [1974] 1 WLR 576, 578–9, Goulding J.

[173] *ibid.*

[174] [1975] 1 Lloyd's Rep 465, CA.

[175] AS Burrows, *Remedies for Torts and Breach of Contract* (3rd edn, Oxford University Press, 2004), 463.

[176] See *Thames Valley Power Ltd* v. *Total Gas & Power Ltd* [2005] EWHC 2208 (Comm); [2006] 1 Lloyd's Rep 441, at [63], *per* Christopher Clarke J (supply of gas under long-term contract), where the order was named as specific performance.

texts where supply is crucial to a commercial party's economic interest and the parties are (at least for a time)[177] locked into a relationship.[178]

(vi) Apart from agreements to transfer land (where specific performance is the primary remedy), or agreements concerning shares in private companies, English law is right to confine this remedy to a residual role, for three main reasons.[179]

(1) Specific performance is a heavy-handed remedy, sanctioned by contempt of court powers. It should be narrowly confined, otherwise it threatens to become a remedial sledgehammer.

(2) The mitigation principle requires that, in general, an innocent party should be required to act straightaway in order to reduce or even eliminate his loss, and he should not be at liberty to wait for the court to order the guilty party to perform.[180] In the *Co-operative Insurance* case (1998) Lord Hoffmann noted that an order to compel someone to carry on a business at a loss 'cannot be in the public interest' because 'it is not only a waste of resources but yokes the parties together in a continuing hostile relationship', whereas damages would allow the parties to `go their separate ways and the wounds of conflict can heal.'[181]

(3) Parties can insert liquidated damages clauses[182] (**17.33**) or require payment of a deposit[183] (**17.34**) to apply leverage to induce performance (on agreed protection of this type).

The House of Lords in the *Co-operative Insurance Services* case *(1998)*[184] confirmed the residual function of specific performance. Specifically, it was there held that specific performance is not available to

---

[177] But that period was potentially for many years in the case just cited.

[178] R Halson, *Contract Law* (2nd edn, London, 2013), 444–445, noting *Land Rover Group Ltd* v. *UPF (UK) Ltd* [2002] EWHC 3183; [2003] BCLC 222 (mandatory injunction against insolvent company to compel supply until trial of Land Rover parts); similar order made in *Aston Martin Lagonda Ltd* v. *Automobile Industrial Partnerships Ltd* (Birmingham, High Court, 2009, unreported); and in *SSL International plc* v. *TTK LIG Ltd* [2011] EWHC 1695 (Ch); (2011) 108(28) LSG 21, Mann J (supply of condoms); *Thames Valley Power Ltd* v. *Total Gas & Power Ltd* [2005] EWHC 2208 (Comm); [2006] 1 Lloyd's Rep 441, at [63], *per* Christopher Clarke J (supply of gas under long-term contract).

[179] SM Waddams, 'The Choice of Remedy for Breach of Contract', in J Beatson and D Friedmann (eds), *Good Faith and Fault in Contract Law* (Oxford University Press, 1995), 471 ff, provides a compelling defence of the residual role of coercive specific relief.

[180] D Friedmann, 'Economic Aspects of Damages and Specific Performance Compared', in D Saidov and R Cunnington (eds), *Contract Damages: Domestic and International Perspectives* (Oxford, 2008), chapter 2, at 86 ff.

[181] *Co-operative Insurance Society Ltd* v. *Argyll Stores (Holdings) Ltd* [1998] AC 1, 15–16, HL, *per* Lord Hoffmann.

[182] Neil Andrews, *Contract Law* (2nd edn, Cambridge University Press, 2015), 19.02 ff.

[183] Neil Andrews, *Contract Law* (2nd edn, Cambridge University Press, 2015), 19.27 ff.

[184] *Co-operative Insurance Society Ltd* v. *Argyll Stores (Holdings) Ltd* [1998] AC 1, HL.

compel a tenant to honour a long-running covenant to 'keep open' a business.

The case concerned a thirty-five lease, to run from 1979 to 2014, for a supermarket site in a shopping mall. The tenant covenanted that it would continue trading for the same period (a so-called 'keep open' clause). In 1994, when the tenancy still had more than 19 years to run, the defendant supermarket chain handed back the keys to the landlord (the defendant had made a loss of £70,000 in the previous year).[185] The claimant landlord sought specific performance to force the defendant to trade at this site until 2014, or until it sublet or assigned to another supermarket company.

The House of Lords held that the relevant clause was insufficiently precise.[186] And, in any event, specific performance could not[187] be granted to compel a party to run a business, otherwise, the courts will become embroiled in a litany of minor complaints and counter-arguments. Lord Hoffmann commented on the 'constant supervision' problem: '*[One must] distinguish between orders which require a defendant to carry on an activity, such as running a business over a more or less extended period of time, and orders which require him to achieve a result [such as, building contracts and repairing covenants*].'[188]

(vii) Even if the relevant context is *prima facie* amenable to this remedy, various subsidiary factors regulate the court's 'discretion' to order specific performance[189]: (1) whether the claimant's conduct has been unmeritorious ('lack of clean hands'); (2) delay and acquiescence;[190] (3) 'mutuality' (that is, when the claimant, who is seeking specific performance, has yet to satisfy his side of the bargain, and the court must consider whether the defendant is protected against the risk[191] of default by the claimant)[192]; (4) vagueness[193]; (5) problems of

---

[185] [1998] AC 1, 10, HL

[186] [1998] AC 1, 17, HL.

[187] Such 'keep open' clauses are specifically enforced in Scotland: but D Campbell and R Halson, in L DiMatteo, Q Zhou, S Saintier, K Rowley (eds), *Commercial Contract Law: Transatlantic Perspectives* (Cambridge University Press, 2014), chapter 12, contend that the English position is preferable.

[188] [1998] AC 1, at 40.

[189] *Co-operative Insurance Society* v. *Argyll Stores (Holdings) Ltd* [1998] AC 1, HL, noted by GH Jones, [1997] CLJ 488; *Rainbow Estates Ltd* v. *Tokenhold Ltd* [1999] Ch 64, 68G–74; *Beswick* v. *Beswick* [1968] AC 58, HL; *Price* v. *Strange* [1978] Ch 337, CA; *Tito* v. *Waddell (No 2)* [1977] Ch 106, 321–8, Megarry V-C; *Verrall* v. *Great Yarmouth District Council* [1980] 1 All ER 839, CA; *Posner* v. *Scott-Lewis* [1987] Ch 25, Mervyn-Davies J, noted by GH Jones, [1987] CLJ 21–3.

[190] Claims for injunctive relief or specific performance are subject to the equitable bars of laches and acquiescence, and the statutory periods of limitation do not apply: *P&O Nedlloyd BV* v. *Arab Metals Co* [2006] EWCA Civ 1717; [2007] 1 WLR 2288; *Andrews on Civil Processes* (Intersentia, Cambridge, Antwerp, Portland, 2013), vol 1 (*Court Proceedings*), chapter 8; A McGee, *Limitation Periods* (7th edn, 2014).

[191] Similarly, Law Commission, *Contract Code* (1972), Article 409.

[192] *Price* v. *Strange* [1978] Ch 337, CA.

[193] Similarly, Law Commission, *Contract Code* (1972), Article 405.

continuing supervision[194]; and (6) hardship[195] (and courts have had regard to a wide range[196] of factors).

17.28 *INJUNCTIONS*[197]

(i) An injunction can be awarded either to prevent the anticipated breach ('prohibitory' relief) or to reverse the relevant wrong (a 'mandatory' injunction).
(ii) The party who fails to comply with an injunction will be in contempt of court (**17.27**, paragraph (i) above) (and so will a party who breaches a formal 'undertaking' given by that party in court in substitution for a formal injunctive order).
(iii) There is a discretion to award damages 'in lieu' of an injunction[198] (for example, when the relevant undertaking requires construction using building material 'X', and instead material 'Y' has been wrongly used, but it would be draconian and wasteful to require demolition to ensure eventual compliance). Such compensatory damages in Equity can be awarded, under section 50 of the Senior Courts Act 1981,[199] instead of, or in addition to, an injunction or specific performance: the leading cases are: *Johnson* v. *Agnew* (1980)[200]; *Oakacre Ltd* v. *Claire Cleaners (Holdings) Ltd* (1982)[201]; and *Jaggard* v. *Sawyer* (1995).[202]
(iv) A final injunction is an order to refrain from breaching a duty not to do something (such as a restrictive covenant in a conveyance restricting or even prohibiting the purchaser from constructing buildings on the relevant land).
(v) An interim injunction can be either prohibitory (preventing prohibited performance which would be contrary to a negative undertaking) or mandatory (compelling performance of a positive obligation).

---

[194] Similarly, Law Commission, *Contract Code* (1972), Article 406.

[195] *Patel* v. *Ali* [1984] Ch 283, Goulding J; Law Commission, *Contract Code* (1972), Article 408.

[196] *Ashworth* v. *Royal National Theatre* [2014] EWHC 1176; [2014] 4 All ER 238, Cranston J.

[197] Tettenborn, in Neil H Andrews, MA Clarke, AM Tettenborn, G Virgo, *Contractual Duties: Performance, Breach, Termination and Remedies* (London, 2012), chapter 28; ICF Spry, *The Principles of Equitable Remedies: Specific Performance, Injunctions, Rectification and Equitable Damages* (9th edn, Thomson Reuters, Australia, 2013); Paul Davies, 'Injunctions in Tort and Contract', in G Virgo and S Worthington (eds), *Commercial Remedies: Resolving Controversies* (Cambridge University Press, 2016).

[198] e.g., *Oxy-Electric Ltd* v. *Zaiduddin* [1991] 1 WLR 115, Hoffmann J (application for striking out refused; case to proceed to trial); *Jaggard* v. *Sawyer* [1995] 1 WLR 269, CA (injunction refused; damages in lieu awarded under section 50 of the Senior Courts Act 1981).

[199] Section 50, Senior Courts Act 1981); Adam Kramer, *The Law of Contract Damages* (Hart, Oxford, 2014), section 1.2 B(iii); GH Jones and W Goodhart, *Specific Performance* (2nd edn, London, 1996), 275 ff; *McGregor on Damages* (19th edn, London, 2014), 11–29; JA Jolowicz [1975] CLJ 224.

[200] [1980] AC 367, HL.

[201] [1982] Ch 197, Mervyn-Davies J (damages awarded instead of specific performance; latter sought in good faith before breach had occurred).

[202] [1995] 1 WLR 269, CA (injunction refused; circumstances in which injunction will be withheld; damages in lieu awarded under section 50 of the Senior Courts Act 1981).

(vi) When a final injunction is mandatory, English law labels the order as one for 'specific performance' (this species of final injunction is examined at **17.27** above).

(vii) Injunctions (interim or final) are readily[203] awarded to prevent a defendant breaching a 'negative' promise, that is, an undertaking not to do something. In such a case, an injunction is not[204] subject to the restriction (which governs specific performance) that damages would be an inadequate remedy. But no such injunction will be granted if its indirect effect will be to coerce a person into performing a contract for personal services (see **17.29** below). The principle that mandatory (as distinct from prohibitory) injunctions (including specific performance) are unavailable 'unless damages are inadequate' is not to be applied mechanistically: clauses limiting or excluding damages for breach do not oust the court's capacity to award interim or final injunctive relief.[205]

17.29 *INJUNCTION: DANGER OF INDIRECT PERSONAL COERCION*[206]

(i) *Warren* v. *Mendy* (1989)[207] confirmed that injunctions will not be awarded if the indirect effect will be to apply such compulsion to require a person (contrast companies, see (ii) below) to perform personal relations or remain in a close relationship between mutual confidence (just as specific performance will not be granted to compel direct performance of such an obligation, **17.27**, paragraph (iv) above). For example, if a defendant actor, manager, employee, or sportsman has agreed not to work for anyone other than the claimant for a specified period, an injunction to enforce this negative undertaking might indirectly impose compulsion on the defendant to work for, or with, the claimant. (See (iii) below for other cases considered in this leading decision).

---

[203] *Doherty* v. *Allman* (1878) 3 App Cas 709, 720, HL, *per* Lord Cairns LC; see also *Araci* v. *Fallon* [2011] EWCA Civ 668; [2011] LLR 440 at [30], *per* Elias LJ (adequacy of damages does not preclude award of prohibitory injunction); and at [39], *per* Jackson LJ: '*Where the defendant is proposing to act in clear breach of a negative covenant, in other words to do something which he has promised not to do, there must be special circumstances (eg restraint of trade contrary to public policy) before the court will exercise its discretion to refuse an injunction.*' See too *Att-Gen* v. *Barker* [1990] 3 All ER 257 at 262, *per* Nourse LJ.

[204] *Araci* v. *Fallon* [2011] EWCA Civ 668; [2011] LLR 440 at [30], *per* Elias LJ.

[205] *AB* v. *CD* [2014] EWCA Civ 229; [2014] 3 All ER 667; [2014] 2 All ER (Comm) 242; [2014] CP Rep 27; [2014] BLR 313, notably *per* Underhill LJ at [25] to [30]; noted PG Turner [2014] CLJ 493–6 (CA following Mance LJ in *Bath & NE Somerset DC* v. *Mowlem plc* [2004] EWCA 722; [2004] BLR 153, CA, at [15]).

[206] Tettenborn, in Neil H Andrews, MA Clarke, AM Tettenborn, G Virgo, *Contractual Duties: Performance, Breach, Termination and Remedies* (London, 2012), 28–027 ff.

[207] *Warren* v. *Mendy* [1989] 1 WLR 853, CA, noted by H McLean, [1990] CLJ 28, noting *Lumley* v. *Wagner* (1852) 1 De GM & G 604, and *Warner Bros Pictures Inc* v. *Nelson* [1937] I KB 209, and *Page One Record Ltd* v. *Britton* [1968] 1 WLR 157 ('The Troggs' case); Mance LJ in *LauritzenCool AB* v. *Lady Navigation Inc* [2005] EWCA Civ 579; [2006] All ER 866, CA (18.22); P Saprai, 'The Principle against Self-Enslavement in Contract Law' (2009) 25 *Journal of Contract Law* 26.

(ii) But, as the Court of Appeal in the *LauritzenCool* case (2006)[208] acknowledged, the liberal principle that *individuals* should not be compelled (directly or indirectly) to work for others does not apply if the defendant is a company (nor, relatedly be yoked within relationships of trust and confidence when the relationship has fallen down or is in a precarious state). And so in that case it was legitimate to issue an injunction to prevent a company from removing its two ships from the charterer. Similarly, in *Regent International Hotels (UK) Ltd* v. *Pageguide Ltd* (1985)[209] Ackner LJ contrasted a personal relationship between a pop group and a manager (where an injunction would be inappropriate)[210] and the commercial context of a company's undertaking to manage a hotel (where an injunction would be appropriate, as in the *Regent International Hotel* case itself).

(iii) *Warren* v. *Mendy* (1989)[211] examined these cases (see also Lord Wilson's remarks in *Geys* v. *Société Générale*, 2012)[212]:

(1) *Lumley* v. *Wagner* (1852),[213] where Lord St Leonards, LC, granted an injunction against an opera singer. Although the defendant could not be compelled to sing, she could be restrained, for 3 months—a relatively short engagement–, from singing for a rival impresario, in breach of her express negative undertaking not to sing for a rival during this period.

(2) In *Whitwood Chemical Co* v. *Hardman* (1891)[214] the Court of Appeal held that no injunction should be granted to enforce the defendant's express negative undertaking, and so require the defendant to concentrate all his employment energies and time on the plaintiff company, as he had agreed. There were still over 4 years of employment still to run.[215]

(3) Branson J in *Warner Bros Pictures Inc* v. *Nelson* (1937)[216] enforced an exclusivity clause by issuing an injunction against the actress, Bette Davis, for 3 years from 1936 **within England and Wales**. Although Nourse LJ in *Warren* v. *Mendy* (1989)[217] doubted this decision, the territorial restriction just mentioned makes the result palatable: for she might still have worked for a rival outside the UK and USA (the contract would have enabled the claimant to obtain an injunction within the USA).

---

[208] *LauritzenCool AB* v. *Lady Navigation Inc* [2005] EWCA Civ 579; [2006] All ER 866, CA, at [30].

[209] *The Times*, 13 May 1985, CA.

[210] *Page One Record Ltd* v. *Britton* [1968] 1 WLR 157.

[211] [1989] 1 WLR 853, 860–8, CA, *per* Nourse LJ.

[212] [2012] UKSC 63; [2013] 1 AC 523, at [70] ff.

[213] (1852) 1 De GM & G 604.

[214] [1891] 2 Ch 416, CA.

[215] Lindley LJ at 427–8 said that an express negative clause is essential; similarly, Kay LJ at 431.

[216] [1937] I KB 209.

[217] [1989] 1 WLR 853, 865, CA.

(4) In *Page One Records Ltd* v. *Britton* (1968),[218] Stamp J refused an injunction to require a pop group, 'The Troggs', to stay loyal to their manager, with whom they had fallen out. The contract was for 5 years. Stamp J noted that the need for mutual confidence in such a close-working relationship.[219]

17.5 Declarations, Accounts, and Stays

17.30 *DECLARATIONS*[220]

(i) This is a non-coercive remedy. In making a declaration, the tribunal states definitively the facts and legal result in the proceedings. A declaration might be the only relief sought. For example, in *Lock* v. *Bell* (1931), a vendor obtained a declaration that the deposit of £120 on the sale of a public house had been forfeited validly.[221]

(ii) 'Negative declarations' (applications to gain a binding declaration that the claimant *is not legally liable to the other party*) are often sought in English civil proceedings as a tactic to preclude proceedings by a defendant against a claimant in another jurisdiction.[222]

(iii) Another example, although lacking the cross-border feature mentioned at (ii), is *Patten* v. *Burke Publishing Co Ltd* (1991) where the applicant, a writer, was proposing to deal with publisher B To clear the ground for this, the applicant sought a declaration that he could safely do so because he was no longer contractually committed to write for publisher A.[223]

17.31 *TARGETING THE GAIN MADE BY BREACH ('ACCOUNT')*[224]

(i) *Gain-based Relief.* This remedy requires the defendant to 'disgorge' ('account for') a gain made as a result of the bare breach of contract. The defendant's gain forms the basis of the claim. The remedy is granted regardless of whether the claimant has suffered substantial loss.

---

[218] [1968] 1 WLR 157.

[219] *ibid*, at 165, *per* Stamp J.

[220] Zamir and Woolf, *The Declaratory Judgment* (4th edn, London, 2011); *Dicey, Morris and Collins on the Conflicts of Laws* (15th edn, London, 2012), 12–048 ff.

[221] [1931] 1 Ch 35, Maugham J.

[222] *Dicey, Morris and Collins on the Conflicts of Laws* (15th edn, London, 2012), 12–048 ff.

[223] [1991] 1 WLR 541.

[224] K Barnett, *Accounting for Profit for Breach of Contract* (Hart, Oxford, 2012); J Edelman, *Gain-Based Damages* (Oxford, 2002), chapter 5; E McKendrick in AS Burrows and E Peel (eds), *Commercial Remedies: Current Issues and Problems* (Oxford University Press, 2003), 93–119; AS Burrows, *Remedies for Torts and Breach of Contract* (3rd edn, Oxford University Press, 2004), 395–407; Tettenborn, in Neil H Andrews, MA Clarke, AM Tettenborn, G Virgo, *Contractual Duties: Performance, Breach, Termination and Remedies* (London, 2012), chapter 26.

(ii) *Exceptional Power to Award Gain-stripping in respect of a Bare Breach of Contract.* Exceptionally, the court might grant the equitable remedy of an account of profits for a bare breach of contract, that is, even though the contractual breach has involved neither a breach of fiduciary duty of a proprietary right. *Attorney-General* v. *Blake* (2001) is the leading case.[225]

(iii) *Constraining Factors.* The remedy of account for a bare breach of contract, as summarised at (ii), is granted only in exceptional situations (and the pattern of the English decisions has been to refuse such relief, see (iv) below). The remedy is equitable and hence discretionary. An account in respect of a bare breach of contract will be granted only if all four of the following criteria are satisfied: first, the claimant can show a legitimate interest in seeking this remedy; secondly, all other remedies are inadequate; thirdly, the tribunal, in its discretion, regards this as an appropriate response to the breach; and, fourthly, the gain is attributable to that breach.

(iv) As for p*ost-Blake* case law,[226] the *Blake* case has produced no deluge, indeed hardly a drop of consequence. Sales J in the *Vercoe* case (2010) emphasised the non-negotiable nature of the contractual rights in the *Blake* case, and the non-commercial context of that case, contrasting the post-*Blake* judicial preference for awarding (the less generous measure of) 'loss of bargaining opportunity' (so-called 'user principle') damages (**17.20**).[227]

An isolated application is Morritt V-C's *pre-Trial* decision in *Esso Petroleum Ltd* v. *Niad Ltd* (2001) not to strike out a claim for an account of profits made by a petrol retailer in breach of the supplier's contractual requirement that retailers should reduce pump prices to match local competitors' prices. The decision to allow this claim to proceed in this commercial context is unconvincing. However, because this was not a final decision on the merits at trial,[228] the decision has little, if any, binding effect.

(v) *Supplementing the Main Order.* Where an account would be available, applying the preceding propositions, but the party in breach has yet to acquire or receive the relevant gain (or the full extent of the gain), a supplementary remedy might be available, such as an injunction to prevent such enrichment from occurring or at least from recurring.

[225] [2001] 1 AC 268 HL (the literature is enormous); specialist works are K Barnett, *Accounting for Profit for Breach of Contract* (Hart, Oxford, 2012); J Edelman, *Gain-Based Damages* (Oxford, 2002), chapter 5.

[226] Summarised by Arden LJ in *Devenish Nutrition Ltd* v. *Sanofi-Anetis SA* [2008] EWCA Civ 1086; [2009] Ch 390, at [40] and [62] to [70]; see also *Vercoe* v. *Rutland Fund Management* [2010] EWHC 424 (Ch); [2010] Bus LR D141, Sales J.

[227] *Vercoe* v. *Rutland Fund Management* [2010] EWHC 424 (Ch); [2010] Bus LR D141, at [340]; more generally, [339] to [346] (noted by P Devonshire, (2010) 126 LQR 526); for an example of a refusal of a *Blake*-acount for breach of a non-competition covenant, even though the breach was deliberate, *One Step (Support) Ltd* v. *Morris-Garner* [2014] EWHC 2213 (QB); [2015] IRLR 215, Phillips J.

[228] *The Times*, 19 April 2003, Morritt V-C.

17.32 *STAYING PROCEEDINGS TO PREVENT BREACH OF CONTRACT*[229]

(i) This is a decision by the court to place proceedings in suspense, until the 'stay' is lifted.[230] A 'stay' is sometimes a contractual remedy, in the sense that it can be a judicial response to a breach of contract.[231]

(ii) The main context has been the staying of civil proceedings commenced prematurely in breach of a mediation agreement (**2.46**). For example, in *Cable & Wireless plc* v. *IBM United Kingdom Ltd* (2002) the parties had agreed (in a multi-tier resolution clause)[232]: (1) to negotiate disputes; and (2) thereafter, if necessary, to conduct a mediated negotiation; (3) if necessary, the aggrieved party could finally resort to formal litigation. Colman J held that failure by one party to proceed to stage (2) involved breach, for which the discretionary 'remedy' was to issue a stay of the High Court proceedings brought at stage (3), prematurely on these facts, in breach of the dispute-resolution agreement.[233]

(iii) In some contexts a court can go further and, rather than stay proceedings, dismiss a claim, where such a final disposal of the matter is appropriate: *Snelling* v. *John Snelling Ltd* (1973) (not concerned with a mediation clause, but with a 'no claim to be commenced' clause).[234]

17.6 Protection Against Penalty Clauses

17.33 *PENALTIES*[235]

(i) *Basic Test.* The 'penalty doctrine' regulates a clause which stipulates that the party in breach shall pay a sum that is 'extravagant and unconscionable' in

---

[229] *Andrews on Civil Processes* (Intersentia, Cambridge, Antwerp, Portland, 2013), vol 2 ('*Arbitration and Mediation*'), 10.03 ff.

[230] Section 49(3), Senior Court Act 1981 acknowledges the court's inherent power to issue a stay; *Andrews on Civil Processes* (Intersentia, Cambridge, Antwerp, Portland, 2013), vol 2, *Arbitration and Mediation*, 10.03 ff; *Reichhold Norway ASA* v. *Goldman Sachs International* [2000] 1 WLR 173, CA.

[231] Conversely, when an exclusive jurisdiction clause nominates England, but related proceedings are on foot in another jurisdiction, the court might even so stay the English proceedings: *Nomura International plc* v. *Banca Monte dei Paschi Di Siena Spa* [2013] EWHC 3187 (Comm); [2014] 1 WLR 1584 at [16], [17], [80] to [83], Eder J.

[232] D Joseph, *Jurisdiction and Arbitration Agreements and their Enforcement* (2nd edn, London, 2010), chapter 8.

[233] [2002] 2 All ER (Comm) 1041.

[234] [1973] QB 87, 99, Ormrod J.

[235] *McGregor on Damages* (19th edn, 2014), chapter 15; Tettenborn, in Neil H Andrews, MA Clarke, AM Tettenborn, G Virgo, *Contractual Duties: Performance, Breach, Termination and Remedies* (London, 2012), chapter 25; K Lewison, *Interpretation of Contracts* (5th edn, London, 2011), 17.01 ff; S Worthington, 'Penalties and Agreed Damages Clauses', in G Virgo and S Worthington (eds), *Commercial Remedies: Resolving Controversies* (Cambridge University Press, 2016).

comparison with the greatest loss that could be contemplated at the time the contract was formed as likely to flow from breach of the relevant substantive term.

In *Cavendish Square Holdings BV v. El Makdessi* [2015] UKSC 67; [2015] 3 WLR 1373 Lords Neuberger and Sumption said: 'The true test is whether the impugned [contractual] provision is a secondary obligation [that is, one which does not define the parties' primary obligations independent of breach] which imposes a detriment on the contract-breaker out of all proportion to any legitimate interest of the innocent party in the enforcement of the primary obligation. The innocent party can have no proper interest in simply punishing the defaulter. His interest is in performance or in some appropriate alternative to performance. In the case of a straightforward damages clause, [the innocent party's relevant] interest will rarely extend beyond compensation for the breach, and we therefore expect that Lord Dunedin's four tests [in *Dunlop v. New Garage* (1915): and see text below] would usually be perfectly adequate to determine its validity. But compensation is not necessarily the only legitimate interest that the innocent party may have in the performance of the defaulter's primary obligations.' (Lords Neuberger and Sumption ([2015] UKSC 67; [2015] 3 WLR 1373, at [32]; supported by Lords Clarke and Carnwath; similarly, Lord Mance at [152]).Thus the criterion to identify an invalid penalty is whether the relevant clause prescribes a sum (or other detrimental consequence) which is 'extravagant and unconscionable', that is, the sum (or other specified detrimental consequence) is disproportionate ('out of all proportion') either to the loss likely to be suffered or to some wider commercial or non-commercial interest which the innocent party wishes to protect. And this test must be applied at the time the contract was formed and not at the stage when the relevant breach has occurred.

This 2015 decision substantially endorses but slightly modifies Lord Dunedin's statement in *Dunlop* v. *New Garage* (1915).[236] Lord Dunedin's statement (which concerned a damages clause) was an incomplete statement of the penalty doctrine because it concentrated only on the issue of punishment from the perspective of palpable financial loss or other concrete damage. That left out of account the innocent party's possibly wider legitimate commercial or non-commercial interest in securing proper performance of the contractual obligation. In other words, the penalty jurisdiction must be applied with sensitivity to the possibility that the innocent party is not seeking merely to protect himself against the risk of incurring financial loss but against a wider risk of harm or disappointment for which monetary relief is not readily quantifiable (as noted by Lord Atkinson in the *Dunlop case* ([1915] AC 70, 9093, HL, 1915), who was quoted by Lords Neuberger and Sumption in the *Cavendish* case ([2015] UKSC 67; [2015] 3 WLR 1373, at [23]).

---

[236] *Dunlop Pneumatic Tyre Co Ltd* v. *New Garage and Motor Co Ltd* [1915] AC 70, 86–8, HL.

Paragraph 4 of Lord Dunedin's list of criteria in the Dunlop case (1915) states:

('a) It will be held to be a penalty if the sum stipulated for is extravagant and unconscionable in amount in comparison with the greatest loss that could conceivably be proved to have followed from the breach. (b) It will be held to be a penalty if the breach consists only in not paying a sum of money, and the sum stipulated is a sum greater than the sum which ought to have been paid... This though one of the most ancient instances is truly a corollary to the last test ...(c) There is a presumption (but no more) that it is a penalty when "a single lump sum is made payable by way of compensation, on the occurrence of one or more or all of several events, some of which may occasion serious and others but trifling damage". On the other hand: (d) It is no obstacle to the sum stipulated being a genuine preestimate of damage, that the consequences of the breach are such as to make precise pre-estimation almost an impossibility. On the contrary, that is just the situation when it is probable that pre-estimated damage was the true bargain between the parties.'

In the *Alfred McAlpine* case (2005),[237] Jackson J said that the test is whether there is '*a substantial discrepancy between the level of damages stipulated in the contract and the level of damages which is likely to be suffered*'. Similarly, in the *BNP Paribas* case (2009) Christopher Clarke J said: '*the court may look to see whether or not the sum is disproportionate to the least important of the contractual undertakings to which it applies and thus whether it represents an extravagant or unconscionable sum in relation to such a breach.*'[238]

(ii) *Deterrent Purpose?* (This discussion is overtaken by the Cavendish case, but is preserved here as background information.) The Court of Appeal in the *Murray* case (2007) said that the real issue is whether the innocent party's main *purpose* was to insert a payment clause containing a sum *so large that it would deter the other from breaching*, rather than to provide compensation.[239] The court said that there should be no automatic conclusion that a non-compensatory element renders the clause 'deterrent' in aim and hence invalidates the clause. Otherwise, Buxton LJ said, the approach would become unacceptably 'rigid and inflexible'.[240] Burton J followed this approach in the *M & J Polymers* case (2008).[241]

---

[237] *Alfred McAlpine Capital Projects Ltd* v. *Tilebox Ltd* [2005] EWHC (TCC) 281; [2005] BLR 271, 280, at [48], *per* Jackson J.

[238] *BNP Paribas* v. *Wockhardt EU Operations (Swiss) AG* [2009] EWHC 3116 (Comm), 132 Con LR 177, 132 Con LR 177, at [26], *per* Christopher Clarke J.

[239] *Murray* v. *Leisureplay plc* [2005] EWCA 963; [2005] IRLR 946, at [110] to [118], especially at [106], *per* Clarke and Buxton LJJ (noting *Cines Bes Filmclik ve Yapincilik AS* v. *United International Pictures* [2003] EWCA Civ 1669, at [13], *per* Mance LJ, and *Lordsvale Finance plc* v. *Bank of Zambia* [1996] QB 752, 762G, Colman J).

[240] *Murray* v. *Leisureplay plc* [2005] EWCA 963; [2005] IRLR 946, at [42].

[241] [2008] EWHC 344 (Comm); [2008] 1 Lloyd's Rep 541, at [40] to [48], especially at [46].

But the criterion of a 'deterrent purpose' was a controversial change of emphasis, although it was repeated in the Court of Appeal in *Makdessi* v. *Cavendish Square Holdings BV* (2013).[242] The test in the seminal *Dunlop* case (above) refers to an 'extravagant and oppressive' difference between 'the greatest possible loss' and the amount stipulated for. This is an objective test. There is no need to obscure matters by referring to the payee's intention in procuring the relevant clause: after all, no real monetary threat can be made unless the stipulated sum greatly exceeds the ordinary Common Law measure of compensation (so that emphasis on the clause's function or intent becomes rather jejune).[243] The search for a *deterrent purpose* is unhelpful, as Lord Radcliffe noted in *Bridge* v. *Campbell Discount* (1962).[244] And this criterion would require the court to determine what the common intention of the parties was, who inserted the relevant clause, and what the purpose of its insertion was. Instead the law should be kept simple and objective: whether the stipulated sum is 'extravagant and unconscionable'.

(iii) *Impact Penalty Clauses are Invalid.* The *Cavendish* case has repudiated the suggestion that a penalty clause can be relied upon in any manner. Instead a penalty clause is invalid and so cannot be enforced or relied upon in any way. Lords Neuberger and Sumption, in *Cavendish Square Holdings BV v. El Makdessi* [2015] UKSC 67; [2015] 3 WLR 1373, at [87] rejected the suggestion in *Jobson v. Johnson* ([1989] 1 WLR 1026, CA) that the court can re-write or revise a penal clause by either providing for relief 'on terms' or by deciding that the penal clause can be enforced partially, the punitive element having been excised. Instead the true proposition is that the penalty doctrine operates to invalidate completely the relevant clause. The innocent party, in the absence of an effective liquidated damages clause, will need to claim compensation (or other relief) under general remedial principles.

According to the pre- *Cavendish* law it was (wrongly) considered that it would be possible to bring an action on a 'scaled down' penalty clause (its penal element having been excised) is technically a debt claim, rather than one for damages.[245] But, even before the *Cavenish* case (2015), the penalty clause was regarded as a dead letter and the claim was instead framed as one for Common Law damages based on general compensatory principles.[246]

(iv) *Need to Show Breach.* The Supreme Court's decision in *Cavendish Square Holdings BV v. El Makdessi* [2015] UKSC 67; [2015] 3 WLR 1373 confirms that the penalty doctrine only invalidates clauses which operate subsequent to breach of contract. This follows established law: *Export Credits Guarantee*

[242] [2013] EWCA Civ 1539; [2014] BLR 246, at [120], [121], [124], *per* Christopher Clarke LJ (an appeal is outstanding).

[243] *ibid*, at [120], *per* Christopher Clarke LJ (an appeal is outstanding).

[244] [1962] AC 600, 621–2, HL.

[245] *Jobson* v. *Johnson* [1989] 1 WLR 1026, 1039–41, CA, Nicholls LJ.

[246] *Jobson* case, *ibid.*; R Halson, *Contract Law* (2nd edn, London, 2012), 514.

Department case (1983)[247] and the Court of Appeal in the *Euro London Appointments* case (2006).[248] If there is a different trigger, the relevant clause will not be a penalty. In *Office of Fair Trading* v. *Abbey National plc* (2008)[249] Andrew Smith J held[250] that the penalty doctrine cannot apply to the banking practice (supported by written terms) of charging a fee for unauthorised loans granted by the bank when a customer exceeds his credit limit on his current account. In that situation, the customer does not commit a breach of his contract towards the bank. And so the fee cannot be regarded as a penalty at Common Law.

(v) *Commercial Parties.* English courts are reluctant to upset liquidated damages clauses if they have been agreed between non-consumers.[251] As the Court of Appeal's decision in the *Jeancharm* case (2003) shows, even between commercial parties of roughly equal bargaining strength, an intrinsically 'extravagant and unconscionable' clause (on the facts, one which required payment of interest on a commercial debt of 260 % a year) will be struck down.[252] However, Jacob LJ said in the *Jeancharm* case: '[O]ne should be careful before deciding whether or not a clause is a penalty when the parties are of equal bargaining power.'[253]

(vi) *Penalty in the Context of Debts.* A clause stipulating that non-payment of £ x will require payment of £ x and £ y is a penalty (unless £ y is a sum by way of interest set at a commercially acceptable level.[254] As Lord Dunedin said in the *Dunlop* case (1915)[255]: '*It will be held to be a penalty if the breach consists only in not paying a sum of money, and the sum stipulated is a sum greater than the sum which ought to have been paid.*' But, in the modern cases, some flexibility has been shown. Thus, Colman J in the *Lordsvale* case (1996) upheld a

---

[247] *Export Credits Guarantee Department* v. *Universal Oil Products Co* [1983] 1 WLR 399, HL (applied in *Jervis* v. *Harris* [1996] Ch 195, CA, and in *Euro London Appointments Ltd* v. *Claessens International Ltd* [2006] EWCA Civ 385; [2006] 2 Lloyd's Rep 436); for earlier criticism, see *Bridge* v. *Campbell Discount* [1962] AC 600, 631, HL, *per* Lord Denning; Law Commission, *Penalty Clauses and Forfeiture of Monies Paid* (Law Commission Consultation Paper No 61, London, 1975), Part III.

[248] *Euro London Appointments Ltd* v. *Claessens International Ltd* [2006] EWCA Civ 385; [2006] 2 Lloyd's Rep 436, at [29]; also supported by *Export Credits Guarantee Department* v. *Universal Oil Products Co* [1983] 1 WLR 399, HL (19.09) (applied in *Jervis* v. *Harris* [1996] Ch 195, CA), both cited by Andrew Smith J in *Office of Fair Trading* v. *Abbey National plc* [2008] EWHC 875 (Comm), at [295] ff.

[249] [2008] EWHC 875 (Comm); M Chen-Wishart, (2008) 124 LQR 501–8; PS Davies, [2008] CLJ 466–9.

[250] [2008] EWHC 875 (Comm), at [295] to [323].

[251] *Philips Hong Kong Ltd* v. *Attorney-General for Hong Kong* (1993) 61 BLR 41, 61.

[252] *Jeancharm Ltd* v. *Barnet Football Club Ltd* [2003] EWCA Civ 58; 92 Con LR 26.

[253] *ibid*, at [15].

[254] *Jeancharm* case.

[255] *Dunlop* case, [1915] AC 70, 87, HL, *per* Lord Dunedin; similarly, *Jobson* v. *Johnson* [1989] 1 WLR 1026, 1041, CA, *per* Nicholls LJ.

clause in a loan agreement which stipulated that the borrower's default in making repayments would trigger a *prospective* and 'modest' increase of one *per cent* in the level of interest.[256]

17.7 Deposits

17.34 *NATURE*[257]

(i) A deposit is a sum paid (or payable) to secure performance by the payor: it is an 'earnest' payment.[258] That sum is validly forfeited if the payor has contractually defaulted and the transaction has been justifiably terminated for this reason (that is, when the purchaser manifestly abandons the contract, or clearly defaults, or if he delays in completing the sale to such a degree that the court can conclude that he has repudiated his contract).[259] Conversely, if the transaction goes smoothly, without the payor defaulting, the deposit will be put towards the purchase money. The payee must hand back the deposit if the contract came to an end as a result of his own default[260] (but where that payee cannot return the deposit, because he has become insolvent the payor's lawyer is not liable for his client's loss because the lawyer owes no duty to investigate the depositee's creditworthiness risk, nor, it would seem, a duty to advise payment of the deposit to a stake-holder).[261]

(ii) A prepayment cannot be forfeited if it was not paid as a deposit. In *Mayson* v. *Clouet* (1924), the Privy Council held that forfeiture was restricted to a deposit of 10 %. The purchaser had made two further instalments, each of a further 10 %. He had then defaulted. The court held that only the first 10 % was a deposit, and that the further payments should be returned.[262]

---

256 *Lordsvale Finance plc* v. *Bank of Zambia* [1996] QB 752, 763–7, Colman J (consistent with Canadian, Australian and New York banking law).

257 *Goff and Jones on the Law of Unjust Enrichment* (8th edn, London, 2011), chapter 14; K Lewison, *Interpretation of Contracts* (5th edn, London, 2011), 17.11 ff; Carmine Conte, 'Deposit Clauses' in G Virgo and S Worthington (eds), *Commercial Remedies: Resolving Controversies* (Cambridge University Press, 2016).

258 *Goff and Jones on the Law of Unjust Enrichment* (8th edn, London, 2011), chapter 14; L Gullifer, in AS Burrows and E Peel (eds), *Commercial Remedies: Current Issues and Problems* (Oxford University Press, 2003), 191, 205 ff; R Halson, *Contract Law* (2nd edn, London, 2012), 517–521; Law Commission, *Penalty Clauses and Forfeiture of Monies Paid* (Law Commission Consultation Paper No 61, London, 1975); GH Treitel, *Remedies for Breach of Contract: A Comparative Account* (Oxford University Press, 1988), 234 ff.

259 *Howe* v. *Smith* (1884) 27 Ch D 89, CA (delay justified forfeiture); cf the facts of *Cole* v. *Rose* [1978] 3 All ER 1121, 1129, at letter 'H'.

260 *Cole* v. *Rose* [1978] 3 All ER 1121; C Harpum, [1984] CLJ 134, 170.

261 On the absence of a duty to conduct a creditworthiness search, *Kandola* v. *Mirza Solicitors* [2015] EWHC 460 (Ch), at [50] to [53], *per* Cooke J.

262 [1924] AC 980, PC.

(iii) The innocent party is entitled to seek compensation in excess[263] of the deposit if such additional loss can be shown (unless the deposit is intended to place a cap on the payor's liability for breach and provided the claimant can satisfy the various rules governing the recovery of compensation, see the list at **17.21**). When calculating the amount of compensation for a breach, the fact that the innocent party has forfeited a deposit in relation to that breach must be taken into account when fixing the amount of compensation, otherwise the imposition of the deposit would be wholly penal and the award of compensation would be excessive because it would not accurately reflect the true extent of the loss.[264]

(iv) The 'penalty jurisdiction' (**17.33**) does not govern deposits.[265] And so the entire deposit can be validly forfeited even though the innocent party's actual loss is less than the amount of the deposit, provided the deposit is not vulnerable to challenge on the grounds mentioned at (vii).[266]

(v) A deposit which is owed (the duty to pay having 'accrued'), but not paid, can be subject to forfeiture principle if the contract has in fact ended through the payor's default'.[267]

(vi) Failure to pay a deposit can constitute a repudiatory breach of the contract, itself justifying termination of the contract,[268] including the situation where the vendor has re-notified the purchaser of the need to make this agreed payment.[269] Upon termination for breach in the situation just mentioned, the innocent party can obtain damages, and these can include the amount of the deposit.[270]

(vii) There are controls (**17.35**), statutory and judge-made, on excessive deposits, notably in the field of contracts for the purchase of land.

---

[263] *Lock* v. *Bell* [1931] 1 Ch 35, Maugham J; *Shuttleworth* v. *Clews* [1910] 1 Ch 176.

[264] *Ng* v. *Ashley King (Developments) Ltd* [2010] EWHC 456 (Ch); [2011] Ch 115, at [17] ff, especially at [51], *per* Lewison J.

[265] *Workers Trust & Merchant Bank Ltd* v. *Dojap Investments Ltd* [1993] AC 573, 579, PC, *per* Lord Browne-Wilkinson; followed in *Polyset Ltd* v. *Panhandat Ltd* [2003] 3 HKLRD 319 (35% deposit on commercial property held to be penal; compensation award substituted); L Ho, (2003) 119 LQR 34.

[266] *Workers Trust & Merchant Bank Ltd* v. *Dojap Investments Ltd* [1993] AC 573, 578 F, PC.

[267] *Damon Cia Naviera SA* v. *Hapag-Lloyd International SA* [1985] 1 WLR 435, 449G, 456 F, CA; *Griffon Shipping LLC* v. *Firodi Shipping Ltd ('The Griffon')* [2013] EWCA Civ 1567; [2014] 1 All ER (Comm) 593; [2014] 1 Lloyd's Rep 471; *Hardy* v. *Griffiths* [2014] EWHC 3947 (Ch); [2015] Ch 417, Deputy High Court judge Amanda Tipples QC, at [107], [109], [117].

[268] *Damon* case, [1985] 1 WLR 435, 446 E, 456; *Samarenko* v. *Dawn Hill House Ltd* [2011] EWCA Civ 1445; [2013] Ch 36, at [24] to [27], [52] to [54], [60] and [64] (contract for the sale of land; buyer's failure to pay a 10 % deposit on the stipulated day and on the revised deadline for payment) (case noted JW Carter (2013) 129 LQR 149–152).

[269] AJ. Oakley [1994] Conv 41, 44, citing *Millichamp* v. *Jones* [1982] 1 WLR 1422, and *John Willmott Homes* v. *Read* [1985] 51 P & CR 90.

[270] *Damon* case, [1985] 1 WLR 435, 449, 457, CA (Robert Goff LJ dissented).

17.35 *DEPOSITS WHICH ARE EXCESSIVE OR UNJUSTIFIABLY FORFEITED*[271]

(i) There is a Common Law power to regulate excessive deposits. Deposits of ten *per cent* or less of the price in contracts for the sale of land (or of a leasehold[272] interest) are acceptable, but larger deposits are *normally*[273] invalid. Exceptionally, a larger deposit in a land transaction might be justified if there are 'special circumstances'. If a deposit is excessive at Common Law, the deposit must be repaid, 'less any damage actually proved to have been suffered as a result of non-completion'.[274]

(ii) In the case of contracts for the sale or exchange of land in England and Wales, there is a statutory discretion to relieve against forfeiture of deposits in such contracts: Law of Property Act 1925, section 49(2). This provision allows a court 'if it thinks fit' to 'order the repayment of any deposit'.[275] But this control applies only to contracts for the 'sale or exchange of any interest of land'. The parties cannot by agreement oust the court's jurisdiction to apply this control.[276] It will not be enough that the loss suffered by the vendor is less than the amount of the deposit, nor that the vendor has subsequently been successful in selling the property to a third party for a profit following a market price rise.[277] But it is possible (the matter might require more careful consideration by the courts) that relief might be granted if the deposit-holder has forfeited for no sound economic reason, in a situation where the defaulting party was able to offer good economic protection, and the court infers that the forfeiture involved unjustified pique or defiance and suffered no economic harm (see the Court of Appeal's approval in the *Midill* case (2008) of Neuberger J's decision in the *Tennaro* case (2003)[278] to relieve the defaulting purchaser from forfeiture of his deposit in respect of flat 31, where the seller had received the opportunity to complete at the contract price, but had refused to do so, and had not come forward with any explanation for this refusal; and in respect of flat 32, where the

[271] *Goff and Jones on the Law of Unjust Enrichment* (8th edn, London, 2011), chapter 14.

[272] e.g., *Sheikha Maryam Bint Rashid Al Maktoum* v. *South Lodge Flats Ltd, The Times* 21 April, 1980.

[273] *Omar* v. *El-Wakil* [2001] EWCA Civ. 1090; [2002] 2 P & CR 3 (at pp 36 ff), CA (upholding deposit of over 30% in a conveyance of a business, both at Common Law and under section 49(2), Law of Property Act 1925; no citation of the *Workers Trust* case, see next note).

[274] *Workers Trust & Merchant Bank Ltd* v. *Dojap Investments Ltd* [1993] AC 573, 582, PC (citing *Commissioner of Public Works* v. *Hills* [1906] AC 368, PC).

[275] Section 49(2)(3), 1925 Act.

[276] *Aribisala v. St James Homes etc No 1 [2007] EWHC 1694 (Ch) (*Alan Steinfield QC, sitting as a Deputy High Court judge).

[277] *Midill (97PL) Limited and Park Lane Estates Limited and Gomba International* [2008] EWCA Civ 1227; [2009] 1 WLR 2460 (considering, especially, *Omar* v. *El-Wakil* [2001] EWCA Civ 1090; [2002] 2 P & CR 3 (at pp 36 ff), CA; *Tennaro Ltd* v. *Majorarch* [2003] EWHC 2601; [2004] 1 P & CR 13, Neuberger J; and *Bidaisee* v. *Sampath* (1995) 46 WIR 461, PC, a case which had languished in obscurity).

[278] *Tennaro Ltd* v. *Majorarch* [2003] EWHC 2601; [2004] 1 P & CR 13, Neuberger J.

vendor had mysteriously refused to accept an attractive offer, much higher than the contract price, from the depositor's assignee, a third party).[279]

(iii) *Deposits and Consumer Contracts for the Supply of Goods, Digital Content, or Services*. In this consumer context the Consumer Rights Act 2015 (Schedule 2, Part 1, paragraph 4) presumptively provides that a trader cannot validly forfeit a deposit in a contract concerning such matters if the forfeiture rests on a 'term which has the object or effect of permitting the trader to retain sums paid by the consumer where the consumer decides not to conclude or perform the contract, without providing for the consumer to receive compensation of any equivalent amount from the trader where the trader is the party cancelling the contract'.[280] This definition, contained in Schedule 2, Part 1, of the Act, is not exhaustive.

17.8 Restitution and Unjust Enrichment

17.36 *TYPES OF RESTITUTIONARY CLAIM*[281]

(i) Restitutionary claims are based on the defendant's unjust enrichment. The claim is not for the claimant's loss, but for the defendant's enrichment at the claimant's expense. The relevant enrichment can be money or services or goods. This cause of action can take various forms: it might be that the benefit was conferred as a result of the claimant's mistake of fact or law, or that there was a (total) failure of consideration, or duress, or undue influence, or abuse of fiduciary relationship, or an unjustified tax demand.

(ii) There are three main forms of restitutionary relief relevant to contract law: (a) money recovered for a total failure of consideration; (b) recovery in respect of goods or services; and (c) disgorgement of gains made in breach of contract. Most restitutionary remedies arise independently of breach.[282] However, breach of contract is an essential element in one restitutionary remedy, namely, the remedy of 'equitable account' (*Attorney-General* v. *Blake (2001)* ***17.31***). Categories (a) and (b) are now explained further.

(iii) *Money Recovered for a Total Failure of Consideration*. A payor is entitled to recover money where there has been a 'total[283] failure of consideration'.

---

[279] As explained by Carnwath LJ in the *Midill* case, [2008] EWCA Civ 1227; [2009] 1 WLR 2460*ibid,* at [54].

[280] Sch 2, Part 1, paragraph 4, Consumer Rights Act (UK) 2015.

[281] AS Burrows, *The Law of Restitution* (3rd edn, Oxford University Press, 2011); *Goff and Jones on the Law of Unjust Enrichment* (8th edn, London, 2011).

[282] See also T Baloch, *Unjust Enrichment and Contract* (Hart, Oxford, 2009); AS Burrows, E McKendrick and J Edelman, *Cases and Materials on the Law of Restitution* (2nd edn, Oxford University Press, 2007).

[283] For comment or criticism, F Wilmot-Smith. 'Reconsidering "total" failure' [2013] CLJ 414; PBH Birks, in FD Rose (ed), *Consensus ad Idem: Essays on the Law of Contract in Honour of Guenter Treitel* (London, 1996), chapter 9.

The *Fibrosa* case (1942)[284] provides an example (which must suffice, for reasons of space).[285] The *Fibrosa* case concerned an agreement (subject to English law) for an English supplier to sell machinery to be delivered to a Polish port. The foreign buyer paid £1000 in advance. The contract was frustrated because the (supervening) German occupation of Poland in 1939 rendered performance illegal (the contract then terminated by operation of law in accordance with the rule that there can be no trading with the enemy: it had become, as a result of supervening events, illegal to perform. The House of Lords held that the prepayment should be repaid because the payor had not received any of the promised 'consideration', that is, none of the machinery had been delivered. The House of Lords overruled the decision in *Chandler* v. *Webster* (1904),[286] where the Court of Appeal had fallaciously barred recovery of payments whenever the payee had made to the payor a promise of performance. As the House of Lords noted in *Fibrosa*, although 'consideration' relevant to the formation of contracts can consist in the making of a promise, what counts in the context of the restitutionary claim for 'failure of consideration' is not the promise but actual performance of that promise. Furthermore, the House of Lords in the *Fibrosa* case held that, in this transaction, the relevant performance was delivery of machinery, and that preparation for its delivery did not count. For this reason, non-delivery involved total failure of performance.

In the context of frustrated contracts, however, recovery of money is now subject to the Law Reform (Frustrated Contracts) Act 1943 (**16.02**). Section 1(2) of the Act allows money to be recovered even in the absence of a 'total failure'. But such recovery under the 1943 Act is subject to adjustment between the parties.[287] Apart from frustrated contracts, where this Act applies, the Common Law claim for repayment based on 'total failure' (see above) still applies to various other contexts.

(iv) *Recovery in respect of Goods or Services*. This is illustrated by the *British Steel* case (1984)[288] (see also the *Whittle* case, 2009).[289] In the *British Steel* case (1984), Goff J held that there had been no true agreement because negotiations had not resolved the issue of potential liability for late delivery of building materials to the defendant's order. The question of restitutionary relief arose

[284] [1943] AC 32, HL.

[285] An important survey is *Giedo Van Der Garde BV* v. *Force India Formula One Team Limited* [2010] EWHC 2373 (QB), at [233] ff, notably at [323], [354], [359] to [361], [366], [377] (noted D Winterton and F Wilmot-Smith (2012) 128 LQR 23).

[286] [1904] 1 KB 493, CA.

[287] Section 1(2) of the Law Reform (Frustrated Contracts) Act 1943.

[288] *British Steel Corporation* v. *Cleveland Bridge* [1984] 1 All ER 504, Goff J.

[289] *Whittle Movers Ltd* v. *Hollywood Express Ltd* [2009] EWCA Civ 1189; [2009] CLC 771, Waller, Dyson and Lloyd LJJ; noted by P S Davies, (2010) 126 LQR 175–9.

because British Steel had supplied steel to the defendant company, which had used it in its building project. It was plainly just that the building company should pay a fair market sum to the claimant. This award was based on restitutionary or unjust enrichment principles. The *British Steel* case concerned goods, but a similar award is available in the case of services performed to the order of the defendant, even though there is no agreement or no valid contract.[290] Here, a restitutionary sum of recompense, conferring a reasonable sum, can be awarded (known as a *quantum meruit*) for the performing party's benefit, as in *Planché* v. *Colburn* (1831) (recompense for work done in composing material no longer required by the defendant publisher),[291] *Craven-Ellis* v. *Canons Ltd* (1936) (services performed under void contract),[292] *William Lacey* v. *Davis* (1957) (work carried out in anticipation of contract; risk of abortive negotiations with defendant).[293]

The Supreme Court held in *Benedetti* v. *Sawiris* (2013) that a restitutionary award for services (*quantum meruit*) should be calculated on the basis of the objective value of services, reflecting the normal 'market value'. This mode of quantification does not permit the figure to be augmented to reflect figures used in negotiations concerning performance of the work. There are also *dicta* that the valuation might be below the objective level in some circumstances.[294]

On this last point, a figure lower than market rate was awarded in *Whittle Movers Ltd* v. *Hollywood Express Ltd* (2009)[295] to reflect the fact that the contemplated agreement (which did not become operative) imposed a preliminary tranche of low prices, which would be augmented over time.

---

[290] *Goff and Jones on the Law of Unjust Enrichment* (8th edn, London, 2011), chapter 16; *MSM Consulting Ltd* v. *United Republic of Tanzania* [2009] EWHC 121 (QB), at [171], *per* Clarke J (distilling principles, with the assistance of Nicholas Strauss QC's decision in *Countrywide Communications Ltd* v. *ICL Pathway Ltd* [2000] CLC 324, 349: noted by P Jaffey, [2000] *Restitution Law Review* 270–5).

[291] (1831) 8 Bing 14.

[292] [1936] 2 KB 403, CA.

[293] [1957] 1 WLR 932, Barry J (see 12.04).

[294] [2013] UKSC 50; [2014] AC 938 (noted M McInnes (2014) 130 LQR 8–13; G Virgo [2013] CLJ 508–11; C Mitchell [2013] LMCLQ 436); see also *Littlewoods Retail Ltd* v. *Revenue and Customs Commissioners* [2014] EWHC 868 (Ch) and *Harrison* v. *Madejski* [2014] EWCA Civ 361.

[295] [2009] EWCA Civ 1189; [2009] CLC 771 (Waller, Dyson and Lloyd LJJ); noted by P S Davies, (2010) 126 LQR 175–9.

17.9 Set-Off

17.37 *TYPES OF SET-OFF*[296]

General Remarks. The effect of set-off is to diminish (even to extinguish) a claim. For example, where a claimant sues for £7000 and the defendant has a claim against that claimant for £3000, the defence of set-off will enable the defendant to reduce judgment to the value of the difference, that is, £4000.

The Civil Procedure Rules ('CPR')[297] preserve the pre-existing law. Four main[298] types of set-off might arise (see Morris LJ in *Hanak* v. *Green* (1958) on ((i) to (iii) below).[299] Abatement and equitable set-off (see (ii) and (iii) below) can be jointly described as 'transactional' forms of set-off.[300] Unlike adjustment of mutual debts between the parties (category (i)), transactional forms of set-off (categories (ii) and (iii)) are based on some strong factual connection between the claim and defence.

(i) *Mutual Debts: 'Independent' or 'Statutory' Set-off.*[301] When party A brings proceedings against party B, there can be set-off of mutual debts or ascertained sums. There is no need for any factual connection between the obligations owed by the parties to the relevant litigation. Set-off in this context occurs at judgment. This form of set-off is not discretionary.

Founded on legislation of 1729 and 1735, and the oldest type,[302] this is 'the set-off of reciprocal claims which are unconnected and independent of each other.'[303] Suppose that B owes A £10,000 on a loan which has now accrued. A

---

[296] *Andrews on Civil Processes* (Intersentia, Cambridge, Antwerp, Portland, 2013), vol 1, 7.05 to 7.45; *Derham on the Law of Set-off* (4th edn, Oxford University Press, 2010); G McMeel, *The Construction of Contracts: Interpretation, Implication and Rectification* (2nd edn, Oxford University Press, 2011), 23.57 ff; P Pichonnaz and L Gullifer, *Set-off in Arbitration and Commercial Transactions* (Oxford University Press, 2014); Peter Turner, 'Current Controversies in the Law of Set-off', in G Virgo and S Worthington (eds), *Commercial Remedies: Resolving Controversies* (Cambridge University Press, 2016).

[297] CPR 16.6; set-off is referred to in the contexts of (i) statements of case (statement of claim's value), CPR 16.3(6)(c) and (ii) interim payments, CPR 25.7(5)(b); but, remarkably, not referred to in Part 24 (summary judgment).

[298] As for a fifth type, 'banker's set-off', *Derham on the Law of Set-off* (4th edn, Oxford University Press, 2010), chapter 15 ('combination of bank accounts'); S McCracken, *The Banker's Right of Set-Off* (3rd edn, London, 2010); P Wood, *English and International Set-off* (London, 1989).

[299] *Hanak* v. *Green* [1958] 2 QB 9, 23, CA, *per* Morris LJ; *Eller* v. *Grovecrest Investments Ltd* [1995] QB 272, CA (injunction to prevent a creditor asserting the self-help remedy of distraint against goods).

[300] P Wood, *English and International Set-off* (London, 1989) 31; Hoffmann LJ in *Aectra Refining and Manufacturing Inc* v. *Exmar NV* [1994] 1 WLR 1634, 1648–9, CA, adopted this terminology.

[301] *Derham on the Law of Set-off* (4th edn, Oxford University Press, 2010), chapter 2.

[302] These statutes have been replaced: *per* Morritt C in *Re Kaupthing Singer & Friedlander Ltd (In Administration)* [2009] EWHC 740 (Ch); [2009] 2 Lloyd's Rep 154; [2009] 2 BCLC 137, at [10] on the history of this form of set-off, P Wood, *English and International Set-off* (London, 1989), 2–9.

[303] P Wood, *English and International Set-off* (London, 1989), 32.

also owes B £4000 as 'liquidated damages' which became payable on a contract wholly unconnected with the loan agreement. A sues B for £10,000. B can set off the £4000 against this main claim; A's judgment will be for £6000.

The principal sum which the claimant seeks in the main claim must be ascertained.[304] Independent set-off is available in respect of debts or other sums owed to the defendant provided these are ascertainable at the date of pleading (that is, once the 'statements of case' are finalised).[305]

The Court of Appeal in 1994 held that independent set-off applies even where the sum claimed by the defendant ('B') is not yet precisely ascertained, since it is the subject of a dispute between the parties.[306] It suffices that B's claim is 'liquidated', that is, it is a definite sum of money and arises from a debt, a liquidated damages clause or a *quantum meruit/valebat* claim. Eady J summarised the position in *Addax Bank BSC v. Wellesley Partners LLP* [2010] EWHC 1904 (QB), at [39]: '*It is clear that the Statutes of Set-Off, of 1729 and 1735, apply in the case of mutual debts. Those debts need not be connected in any way, but there must be mutuality. The law is succinctly stated in the words of Cockburn CJ in Stooke v Taylor (1880) 5 QBD 569, 575, to the effect that a statutory plea of setoff "is available only where the claims on both sides are in respect of liquidated debts, or money demands which can be readily and without difficulty ascertained". More recently, the principle was reformulated by Lord Hoffmann in Stein v Blake [1996] AC 243, 251, who stated that the relevant debts must be " ... either liquidated or in sums capable of ascertainment without valuation or estimation".*'

Independent set-off does not affect the parties' substantive rights until judgment, and in this sense this species of set-off is 'procedural'[307] (see *Fearns* v. *Anglo-Dutch Paint & Chemical Co Ltd*, 2010).[308] By contrast, bankruptcy[309] and transactional forms of set-off operate so that the parties' rights are (provisionally) affected without waiting for judgment.[310]

(ii) *Abatement*.[311] A claim for the price in respect of goods or services is subject to set-off in respect of the claimant's defective supply or performance. This form of set-off is not discretionary. This Common Law set of rules was

---

304 *Axel Johnson Petroleum AB* v. *MG Mineral Group AG* [1992] 1 WLR 270, 274, *per* Leggatt LJ, citing *Henriksens Rederi A/S* v. *THZ Rolimpex* [1974] QB 233, 246, CA, *per* Lord Denning.

305 *Axel* case [1992] 1 WLR 270, 272–4, CA; CPR 12.4(1)(a) and 26.2(1)(a) now refers to a liquidated or ascertainable sum as a 'specified amount of money'.

306 *Aectra Refining and Manufacturing Inc* v. *Exmar NV* [1994] 1 WLR 1634, CA.

307 *ibid,* at 1650, CA; *Stein* v. *Blake* [1996] AC 243, 251, HL, *per* Lord Hoffmann; *Fuller* v. *Happy Shopper Markets Ltd* [2002] 1 WLR 1681, at [23], *per* Lightman J.

308 [2010] EWHC 2366 (Ch); [2011] 1 WLR 366, at [15], citing *Stein* v. *Blake* [1996] AC 243, 251, HL, *per* Lord Hoffmann, and *ibid,* at [16], citing *Axel Johnson Petroleum AB* v. *MG Mineral Group AG* [1992] 1 WLR 270, CA, and *Stein* v. *Blake* [1996] AC 243, 251, HL, *per* Lord Hoffmann.

309 For example, notably *Re Bank of Credit and Commerce International SA (No 8)* [1998] AC 214, HL.

310 R Derham 'A Critique of *Muscat* v. *Smith*' (2006) 122 LQR 469, 470–1.

311 R Goode, *Legal Problems of Credit and Security* (4th edn, London, 2008), 7.72 ff.

partially codified by the Sale of Goods Act 1979.[312] In this way the principal claim suffers an 'abatement'.[313] Lord Diplock provided a lucid summary of this doctrine in *Gilbert-Ash Ltd* v. *Modern Engineering (Bristol) Ltd* (1974).[314] But abatement cannot be used to provide a basis for reducing or extinguishing a claim for freight (carriage of goods by sea and/or land).[315]

(iii) *Transactional or Equitable Set-off.*[316] Where A sues B (normally, but not necessarily, for an ascertained sum), B can raise a set-off if B's cross-claim is 'so *closely connected with the [main demand] that it would be manifestly unjust to allow [the claimant] to enforce payment without taking into account the cross-claim.*' This form of set-off is discretionary. This is not available as of right but is discretionary.[317] The Court of Appeal in *Geldorf Metaalconstructie NV* v. *Simon Carves Ltd* (2010) held that the claim and the putative set-off should be '*so closely connected with the [claimant's] demands that it would be manifestly unjust to allow him to enforce payment without taking into account the cross-claim*'[318] This decision is now authoritative, as noted in *Fearns* v. *Anglo-Dutch Paint & Chemical Co Ltd* (2010).[319] Set-off on this basis was held inapplicable in *Esso Petroleum Co Ltd* v. *Milton* (1997)[320] (primary claim for petrol supplied, and cross-claim for alleged breach of the solus agreement by the supplier; latter insufficiently related to the claim for non-payment and that it was not enough that the two claims arose out of the same broad transaction).[321]

The Court of Appeal in *Eller* v. *Grovecrest Investments Ltd* (1995)[322] recognised set-off in respect of a landlord's self-help (non-judicial) distraining for rent. The tenant was complaining that the landlord had committed a nuisance and breached his covenant to ensure quiet enjoyment of the premises. The court noted the absurdity if the tenant's cross-claim could be recognised,

---

[312] Section 53(1), Sale of Goods Act 1979.

[313] *Mondel* v. *Steel* (1841) 8 M & W 858, 870–1, *per* Parke B; cited in *Hanak* v. *Green* [1958] 2 QB 9, 17–8, CA; now section 53(1) Sale of Goods Act 1979.

[314] [1974] AC 689, 717, HL.

[315] *Aries Tanker Corpn* v. *Total Transport Ltd ('The Aries')* [1977] 1 WLR 185, HL.

[316] *Derham on the Law of Set-off* (4th edn, Oxford University Press, 2010), chapters 3 and 4; R Goode, *Legal Problems of Credit and Security* (4th edn, London, 2008), 7.55 ff.

[317] On the non-discretionary nature of 'abatement', *Gilbert-Ash Ltd* v. *Modern Engineering (Bristol) Ltd* [1974] AC 689, 717, HL; for an example of equitable set-off, see *Esso Petroleum Ltd* v. *Milton* [1997] WLR 938, CA.

[318] [2010] EWCA Civ 667; [2010] 4 All ER 847; [2011] 1 Lloyd's Rep 517; at [43] sub-para (vi).

[319] [2010] EWHC 2366 (Ch); [2011] 1 WLR 366, at [20].

[320] *Esso Petroleum Co Ltd* v. *Milton* [1997] WLR 938, CA; see also *Intreprenneur Pub Company (CPC)* v. *Sweeney, The Times* 26 June 2002, Park J.

[321] *ibid,* at 951, *per* Simon Brown LJ; 954, *per* Sir John Balcombe; the third judge, in the *Esso* case, Thorpe LJ, did not examine this aspect of the case: see *ibid,* 953, and 951.

[322] [1995] QB 272, CA.

as it now plainly is, when the landlord is suing in an action for non-payment of rent,[323] but not if he were deploying the extra-judicial remedy of distraint.[324]

In *Muscat* v. *Smith* (2003)[325] a landlord's action for rent was held to be subject to set-off in respect of the landlord's assignor's (the previous landlord's) failure to repair the premises.

(iv) *Insolvency Set-off*.[326] Where A, a creditor, is insolvent, and A's trustee in bankruptcy or liquidator sues B, who is solvent, B can set-off in full the sum owed by A to B Insolvency set-off cannot be excluded by agreement.

If A, a creditor, is insolvent and A's trustee in bankruptcy or liquidator sues B, the latter can set off the entire sum which A owes to B.[327] B's set-off is not scaled down to take account of A's insolvency. Conversely, if B owes £3 million to A, and A (the party in liquidation) owes B £1 million, the statutory balance for which B can prove is £2 million, the difference between these sums. Either way, insolvency form of set-off enables the solvent party, B, to get much more by set-off from A than B would otherwise receive in a direct claim against A's trustee or liquidator.[328] This is an exception to the normal insolvency regime of *pari passu* distribution of funds, but the English position is not followed in every foreign jurisdiction.[329]

(v) *Consensual Exclusion of Set-off*. [330] Insolvency set-off (category (iv) above) cannot be excluded by agreement.[331] But the parties can agree to exclude a prospective right of set-off from their dealings in respect of categories (i) to

[323] R Goode, *Legal Problems of Credit and Security* (4th edn, London, 2008), 7.60.

[324] *British Anzani (Felixstowe) Ltd* v. *International Marine Management Ltd* [1980] QB 137 established that equitable set-off is available in an action brought by the landlord against the tenant (and see the following two notes).

[325] [2003] EWCA Civ 962; [2003] 1 WLR 2853; challenged by R Derham 'A Critique of *Muscat* v. *Smith*' (2006) 122 LQR 469.

[326] Section 323, Insolvency Act 1986 (bankruptcy); in the case of insolvent companies, see rr 2.85 (administration), and 4.90 (liquidation and winding-up), Insolvency Rules 1986 (SI 1986, No 1925) (as amended).

[327] Generally on insolvency set-off, *Derham on the Law of Set-off* (4th edn, Oxford University Press, 2010), chapters 6 ff; R Goode, *Legal Problems of Credit and Security* (4th edn, London, 2008), 7.76 ff.

[328] *MS Fashions Ltd* v. *Bank of Credit and Commerce International SA* [1993] Ch 425, 432 ff, *at first instance*, where Hoffmann LJ discussed the main principles; *Stein* v. *Blake* [1996] AC 243, HL.

[329] P Wood, *English and International Set-off* (London, 1989), 7.2 ff.

[330] *Derham on the Law of Set-off* (4th edn, Oxford University Press, 2010), chapter 16.

[331] As acknowledged by Vinelott J in *Re Maxwell Communications (No 2)* [1993] 1 WLR 1402, 1407 ff, citing *Halesowen Presswork & Assemblies Ltd* v. *National Westminster Bank Ltd* [1972] AC 785, HL (in which, 4 to 1, the House had approved *Rolls Razor Ltd* v. *Cox* [1967] 1 QB 552, CA).

(iii),[332] (whether this be independent (statutory) set-off,[333] or transactional set-off, equitable set-off and abatement).[334]

The Court of Appeal in the *AXA* case (2011)[335] held that a clause creating or preserving a right of set-off in favour of party A to a transaction but excluding a reciprocal right of set-off in favour of party B was unreasonable under the Unfair Contract Terms Act 1977 (clause inserted as a written standard term by the main creditor[336]; and not shown that it was reasonable, according to the 1977 Act's criteria).

(vi) Categories (ii) and (iii) of set-off do not apply to the claim for freight under a voyage charterparty.

(vii) *Letters of Credit, Bills of Exchange (including Cheques) and Direct Debit Agreements.* Categories (ii) and (iii) of set-off do not apply to claims based on the following special modes of payment: letters of credit, bills of exchange[337] (including cheques) and direct debit agreements.[338] Each of these is treated by the business community as equivalent to cash: '*It is elementary that as between the immediate parties to a bill of exchange, which is treated in international commerce as the equivalent of cash, the fact that the defendant may have a counterclaim for unlimited damages arising out of the same transaction forms no sort of defence to an action on the bill of exchange and no ground on which he should be granted a stay of execution of the judgment in the action for the proceedings of the bills of exchange.*'[339] Cancellation of a direct debit, without legal right, is equivalent to dishonouring a cheque[340]: and

---

[332] *Crédit Suisse International* v. *Ramot Plana OOD*, [2010] EWHC 2759 (Comm), Hamblen J, at [43]; *Hong Kong & Shanghai Bank Corpn* v. *Kloeckner & Co AG* [1990] 2 QB 514, Hirst J; *Coca-Cola Financial Corpn* v. *Finsat International Ltd* [1998] QB 43, CA; *Re Kaupthing Singer & Friedlander Ltd (In Administration)* [2009] EWHC 740 (Ch); [2009] 2 Lloyd's Rep 154; [2009] 2 BCLC 137, Morritt C.

[333] *Re Kaupthing* case, *ibid.*

[334] *Coca-Cola Financial Corpn* v. *Finsat International Ltd* [1998] QB 43, CA.

[335] *AXA Sun Life Services plc* v. *Campbell Martin Ltd* [2011] EWCA Civ 133; [2011] 2 Lloyd's Rep 1; [2011] 1 CLC 312.

[336] This gives the court jurisdiction to consider the clause's 'reasonableness' under section 3, Unfair Contract Terms Act 1977, even though both parties are engaged in business, viz neither is a consumer.

[337] A cheque is included within the category of bills of exchange, section 73, Bills of Exchange Act 1882: '*A cheque is a bill of exchange drawn on a banker payable on demand. Except as otherwise provided in this Part, the provisions of the Act applicable to a bill of exchange payable on demand apply to a cheque.*'

[338] R Goode, *Legal Problems of Credit and Security* (4th edn, London, 2008), 7.58; 7.59.

[339] *Montechi* v. *Shimco Ltd* [1979] 1 WLR 1180, 1183, CA, *per* Bridge LJ; *Power Curber International Ltd* v. *National Bank of Kuwait SAK* [1981] 1 WLR 1233, 1241, CA, *per* Lord Denning MR; in *Montrod Ltd* v. *Grundkotter Fleischvertriebs GmbH* [2002] 1 WLR 1975, CA, at [27], [37], [38], *per* Potter LJ; R Goode, *Legal Problems of Credit and Security* (4th edn, London, 2008), 7.58; 7.59.

[340] *Esso Petroleum Co Ltd* v. *Milton* [1997] 1 WLR 938, CA; *ibid*, at 952, *per* Thorpe LJ; at 954, *per* Sir John Balcombe; at 948 Simon Brown LJ dissented on this point.

so the arrangement must be honoured, and set-off in respect of an *unliquidated* sum[341] is not possible, in the absence of fraud[342] or the creditor's insolvency.[343] However, where the putative set-off is liquidated is possible both in respect of bills of exchange and letters of credit (and, one assumes, direct debit arrangements)[344] (and see remarks of Lord Wilberforce in the *Nova (Jersey) Knit* case, 1977).[345]

In *Simon Carves Ltd* v. *Ensus UK Ltd* (2011) Akenhead J noted judicial reluctance[346] to interfere with a bank's payments to a beneficiary of a letter of credit or performance bond, but he noted the 'fraud' exception,[347] where the bank realises, or it must be obvious to it, that the beneficiary is making a forged or other bad faith claim to payment; and there is further exception[348] when the beneficiary's demand on a performance bond is in clear breach of a contractual restriction (such as failure to satisfy a condition precedent to a valid demand) established between the provider of the bond (as distinct from the bank) and the beneficiary (see the remarks by Akenhead J).[349]

(viii) *Carriage of Goods.*[350] Payment of 'freight' under a voyage charterparty cannot be reduced by pleading alleged damage to cargo caused during the

---

[341] Bills of exchange: *Nova (Jersey) Knit Ltd* v. *Kammgarn Spinnerei GmbH* [1977] 1 WLR 713, 721, HL, *per* Lord Wilberforce; letters of credit: *Power Curber International Ltd* v. *National Bank of Kuwait SAK* [1981] 1 WLR 1233, CA.

[342] *cf* in *Montrod Ltd* v. *Grundkotter Fleischvertriebs GmbH* [2002] 1 WLR 1975, CA, (the court reviewed at [38] ff the case law concerning 'fraud' and held that this required bad faith by C, which was not shown here).

[343] e.g., *Willment Bros Ltd* v. *North West Thames Regional Health Authority* (1984) 26 BLR 51, 59, CA.

[344] Bills of exchange: *Nova (Jersey) Knit Ltd* v. *Kammgarn Spinnerei GmbH* [1977] 1 WLR 713, HL; *Hong Kong & Shanghai Bank Corpn* v. *Kloeckner & Co AG* [1990] 2 QB 514, 524; letters of credit, *Hong Kong & Shanghai Bank* case, *ibid,* at 526.

[345] *Nova (Jersey) Knit Ltd* v. *Kammgarn Spinnerei GmbH* [1977] 1 WLR 713, 721, HL; cited, for example, *Esso Petroleum Co Ltd* v. *Milton* [1997] 1 WLR 938, 946, 954, CA.

[346] [2011] EWHC 657 (TCC); [2011] BLR 340; 135 Con LR 96, at [28], where Akenhead J cited *Edward Owen Engineering Ltd* v. *Barclays Bank International Ltd* [1978] QB 159, 171, CA, *per* Lord Denning MR (and the CA in this 1978 case considered Kerr J in *RD Harbottle (Mercantile) Ltd* v. *National Westminster Bank Ltd* [1978] QB 146, 155–6).

[347] [2011] EWHC 657 (TCC); [2011] BLR 340; 135 Con LR 96, at [28], Akenhead J; and see Lord Denning MR in *Edward Owen Engineering Ltd* v. *Barclays Bank International Ltd* [1978] QB 159, 169, CA.

[348] *Simon Carves Ltd* v. *Ensus UK Ltd* [2011] EWHC 657 (TCC); [2011] BLR 340; 135 Con LR 96, at [30] to [32], where Akenhead J cited *Sirius International Insurance Co* v. *FAI General Insurance Ltd* [2003] 1 WLR 2214, CA (which was also considered, as noted at [35] by Akenhead J in the *Simon Carves* case, by Ramsey J in *Permasteelisa Japan KK* v. *Bouyguesstroi and Banca Intesa SpA* [2007] EWHC 3508 (TCC), at [51] and [52]).

[349] *Simon Carves Ltd* v. *Ensus UK Ltd* [2011] EWHC 657 (TCC); [2011] BLR 340; 135 Con LR 96, at [33].

[350] R Goode, *Legal Problems of Credit and Security* (4th edn, London, 2008), 7.61.

carrier's performance of the charterparty[351] (but set-off is permitted in relation to time charterparties).[352] The 'freight' rule has been retained so that insurance arrangements are not unsettled.[353] This maritime freight rule has been extended to carriage of goods by land, including international road and rail carriage.[354]

(ix) *The Crown.* A taxpayer cannot raise set-off in response to a claim by the Crown for 'any taxes, duties or penalties'.[355]

17.10 Limitation of Actions (Prescription of Claims)

17.38 *STATUTORY AND EQUITABLE LIMITATION OF ACTIONS*[356]

'... there are few areas where clarity is as important as it is in the law of limitation, whose whole object is to foreclose argument on what ought to be well defined categories of ancient dispute.'[357]

General Remarks. In many tort and contract-based actions the period of limitation runs from when the claimant's cause of action accrues.[358] 'Cause of action' denotes the set of material facts, or core factual matrix, which supports a recognised legal ground of claim; for example, a cause of action might be the facts which have produced a claim that a defendant has breached his contract or breached a tortious duty of care which he owed to the claimant.[359] In *Berezovsky* v. *Abramovich* (2011),

---

[351] *Aries Tanker Corpn* v. *Total Transport Ltd ('The Aries')* [1977] 1 WLR 185, HL; *'The Dominique'* [1989] AC 1056, HL.

[352] *Federal Commerce & Navigation Co Ltd* v. *Molena Alpha Inc ('The Nanfri')* [1978] 1 QB 927, CA (affirmed on other grounds at [1979] AC 757, HL).

[353] *ibid,* 195, HL, *per* Lord Salmon.

[354] *United Carriers Ltd* v. *Heritage Food Ltd* [1996] 1 WLR 375 (where May J, collected many authorities; at 378 he reluctantly extended this rule).

[355] CPR, Schedule 1, RSC Ord 77, r 6.

[356] *Andrews on Civil Processes* (Intersentia, Cambridge, Antwerp, Portland, 2013), vol 1, chapter 8; A McGee, *Limitation Periods* (7th edn, 2014).

[357] *Test Claimants in the FII Group Litigation* v. *Revenue and Customs Commissioners* [2012] UKSC 19; [2012] 2 AC 337, at [185], *per* Lord Sumption.

[358] Sections 2, 5, Limitation Act 1980; see also *Seaton* v. *Seddon* [2012] EWHC 735 (Ch); [2012] 1 WLR 3637, Roth J (a non-fraudulent breach of fiduciary duty also falls within section 2, 1980 Act).

[359] *Cooke* v. *Gill* (1873) LR 8 CP 107; *Brunsden* v. *Humphrey* (1884) 14 QBD 141, CA; *Letang* v. *Cooper* [1965] 1 QB 232, 243, CA; *Republic of India* v. *India Steamship Co Ltd* [1993] AC 410, 419, HL; *Walkin* v. *South Manchester Health Authority* [1995] 1 WLR 1543, 1547, CA; *Brown* v. *KMR Services Ltd* [1995] 4 All ER 598, 640, CA; *Paragon Finance* v. *DB Thakerar & Co* [1999] 1 All ER 400, 405–6, CA; *Roberts* v. *Gill & Co* [2010] UKSC 22; [2011] 1 AC 240, at [41]; *Berezovsky* v. *Abramovich* [2011] EWCA Civ 153; [2011] 1 WLR 2290, at [59] ff (see text immediately following).

Longmore LJ said, in the context of amendment of pleadings[360]: '*a cause of action is that combination of facts which gives rise to a legal right.*' Applying this to a straightforward contract case, the accrual of the cause of action is when the defendant's repudiatory breach is accepted by the innocent party.

17.39 Commencement of English civil proceedings does not suspend the limitation period. Consider this example. Suppose in a contract case governed by section 5 of the Limitation Act 1980, which prescribes a 6 year limitation period, the claimant issues a claim form 5 years after the cause of action arose, and so 12 months before the time bar falls. The claimant will be out-of-time for limitation purposes if, more than 12 months after commencement of proceedings, this case is either discontinued by the claimant or struck out by the court. The 6 year period will then have elapsed and any further claim will be statute-barred.

17.40 Generally, a limitation defence does not automatically extinguish the claimant's right. Such a defence must be pleaded in the defendant's statement of case. If the defence is not raised, the action is sound.[361] However automatic extinction occurs in a few exceptional contexts.[362] One of these exceptions arises when the case concerns a foreign limitation period and that foreign prescriptive bar operates extinctively.[363]

17.41 *Concurrence of Contractual and Tortious Claims for Failure to Exercise Reasonable Care.* The question of concurrence between contract law and tort, that is the possibility of more than one cause of action arising on the same facts, gives rise to a well-known anomaly in this field. The defendant's contractual liability will become time-barred 6 years after his breach, but the tort claim for negligence will not arise until the claimant suffers damage or loss. Therefore, the 6 year period applicable to such a tort claim will sometimes be time-barred later than the parallel contractual cause of action. Lord Nicholls has commented: '*As every law student knows, causes of action for breach of contract and in tort arise at different times. In cases of breach of contract the cause of action arises at the date of the breach of contract. In cases in tort the cause of action arises, not when the culpable conduct occurs, but when the plaintiff first sustains damage.*'[364] In *Henderson* v. *Merrett*,

---

[360] [2011] EWCA Civ 153; [2011] 1 WLR 2290, at [59] ff.

[361] *Ketteman* v. *Hansel Properties* [1987] AC 189, 219, HL, *per* Lord Griffiths; 'Limitation of Actions' (L Com No 270, 2001), 2.93, also citing *Ronex Properties Ltd* v. *John Laing Construction Ltd* [1983] 1 QB 398, 404–5, CA.

[362] PD (16), 16.1; for exceptions, 'Limitation of Actions' (L Com CP No 151, 1998), 9.4, notably consensual limitation periods; the rules of certain conventions, for example, *Payabi* v. *Armstel Shipping Corpn* [1992] QB 907 (the Hague Rules); claims made under the Consumer Protection Act 1987; the tort of conversion, section 3(2), 1980 Act; recovery of land, section 17, 1980 Act.

[363] Foreign Limitation Periods Act 1984; e.g., *Gotha City* v. *Sotheby's, The Times* 8 October, 1998; noted in *Garcia* v. *De Aldama* [2002] EWHC 2087 (Ch); [2003] ECDR CN1, at [252], [253], *per* Peter Smith J.

[364] *Nykredit Mortgage Bank plc* v. *Edward Erdman Group Ltd (No 2)* [1997] 1 WLR 1627, 1630, HL, *per* Lord Nicholls; *Bell* v. *Peter Browne & Co* [1990] 2 QB 495, CA.

(1995) which is the leading decision on this question, Lord Goff said that this aspect cannot be altered by the courts.[365]

17.42 (i) *General Regime.*

(a) In general (see below for qualifications) the period of limitation governing debt (including recovery of rent)[366] or damages claims for breach of contract is 6 years[367] from the date when the cause of action (ground of claim) arises, but 12 years if the claim is based on a deed,[368] that is, from the date when the cause of action accrues, for example, when the covenantor's promise to pay a sum of money first becomes subject to demand.[369] In *Green* v. *Eadie* (2011)[370] it was held in the Chancery Division that an action for damages under section 2(1) of the Misrepresentation Act 1967 does not fall within the category of a 'specialty', and therefore the 12 year rule applicable to a 'specialty' did not apply. Instead the claim was convincingly categorised as founded upon a statutory tort, to which the normal 6 year period contained in section 2 of the Limitation Act 1980 applied.

(b) The Contracts (Rights of Third Parties) Act 1999 applies the 6- and 12-year periods mentioned at (a) to third party claims upon simple contracts and contracts founded upon deeds.[371]

(ii) The parties can agree to extend or reduce the limitation period. However, agreements which reduce a limitation period might be invalidated under the statutory unfair contractual terms regime.[372] Alternatively such an agreement might increase the period beyond the normal period. Agreements which modify the limitation rules are nearly always express. However, exceptionally, they might be implied. The courts will require strong persuasion that it is appropriate to imply such agreement, especially if the suggested agreement would reduce the normal period of limitation.[373]

(iii) In very clear circumstances a party might be estopped from relying on the limitation period, provided A has made a representation to B, on which the

---

[365] *Henderson* v. *Merrett Syndicates Ltd* [1995] 2 AC 145, 184–194, HL.

[366] Section 19, 1980 Act.

[367] Section 5, 1980 Act.

[368] Section 8(1), 1980 Act.

[369] Section 8, 1980 Act, for example, *Rahman* v. *Sterling Credit Ltd* [2001] 1 WLR 496, 500–2, CA; in *West Bromwich Building Society* v. *Wilkinson* [2005] UKHL 44; [2005] 1 WLR 2303 the House of Lords assumed, without specific decision, that section 8 applied to a repayment obligation contained in a mortgage.

[370] [2011] EWHC B24 (Ch); [2012] PNLR 9 (Deputy High Court judge, Mark Cawson QC).

[371] Section 7(3), Contracts (Rights of Third Parties) Act 1999; generally on the Act, Neil Andrews 'Strangers to Justice No Longer…' [2001] CLJ 353–81.

[372] Acknowledged in the *Ronex* case [1983] 1 QB 398, 404 D, CA; see now Part II, Consumer Rights Act 2015, on which **13.20**.

[373] L Com No 270 (2001), 2.96 citing *Lade* v. *Trill* (1842) 11 LJ Ch 102; for greater detail, L Com CP No 151 (1998), 9.7 to 9.11, citing also *Lubovsky* v. *Snelling* [1944] KB 44; for a restrictive approach to implied agreements, see case law cited in L Com CP No 151 (1998), 9.8.

latter has relied detrimentally, that A will not rely on the limitation period.[374] The Court of Appeal in *Ace Insurance SA* v. *Seechurn* (2002) accepted that the doctrine of promissory estoppel can apply to prevent a defendant from asserting a limitation defence, provided the following three factors are satisfied[375]: (a) the defendant made to the claimant a clear and unequivocal promise or representation, assessed objectively[376]; mere inactivity by the prospective defendant is not normally enough to constitute such an implied representation[377]; (b) the defendant thereby indicated that he would not rely on a limitation defence[378]; (c) the claimant relied detrimentally on this, so that it would be 'unconscionable for the defendant to seek to take advantage of the claimant's mistake.'[379]

(iv) The periods mentioned at (i) (see *General Regime* above) do not apply in the following special situations:

(a) a claim in respect of personal injury or death (the period is instead 3 years); for such a claim the limitation period is 3 years from the date of damage or from the date when the claimant acquired 'knowledge' of the wrong.[380] On 'knowledge' see the Supreme Court in *AB* v. *Ministry of Defence* (2012).[381] The 3 year rule applies to personal injury arising from breach of contract, even when the obligation breached is strict.[382] There is a discretionary power to lift the statutory bar in the case of actions for personal injury or fatal accidents.[383]

In tort claims for negligently inflicted loss, other than personal injury actions, the limitation period is (a) 6 years from the date at which the cause of action accrued *or* (b) 3 years from the 'starting date'; this last phrase refers to the date when claimant acquired knowledge of the claim and capacity to bring it.[384] As for (b), the latent damage provision applies only to negligence pleaded in tort (and not in contract).[385]

---

[374] Besides *Ace Insurance SA NV* v. *Seechurn* (CA, 6 February 2002); [2002] EWCA Civ 67; K Lewison, *Interpretation of Contracts* (5th edn, London, 2011), 12.17.

[375] *Ace Insurance* case, *ibid*, at [17] to [26].

[376] *ibid*, at [18], [19], [26] (ii).

[377] *ibid*, at [20].

[378] *ibid*, at [21].

[379] *ibid*, at [25].

[380] Sections 11, 12 to 14, 1980 Act.

[381] [2012] UKSC 9; [2013] 1 AC 78.

[382] *Foster* v. *Zott GmbH & Co* (CA, unreported, 24 May 2000); noted 'Limitation of Actions' (L Com No 270, 2001), 2.10.

[383] Section 33, 1980 Act; leading cases include: *Thompson* v. *Brown* [1981] 1 WLR 744, HL; *Donovan* v. *Gwentoys Ltd* [1990] 1 WLR 472, HL; *Halford* v. *Brookes* [1991] 1 WLR 428, CA; *Hartley* v. *Birmingham CC* [1992] 1 WLR 969, CA (helpful guidelines at 979–80).

[384] Section 14A, 1980 Act (added by Latent Damage Act 1986); Janet O'Sullivan, 'Limitation, latent damage and solicitors' negligence' (2004) 20 PN 218, 237 ('penetrating' discussion, *per* Lord Nicholls in *Haward* v. *Fawcetts* [2006] UKHL 9; [2006] 1 WLR 682, at [15]).

[385] *Iron Trade Mutual Insurance Co Ltd* v. *J K Buckenham Ltd* [1990] 1 All ER 808, QBD; affirmed *Société Génerale de Réassurance* v. *Eras (International) Ltd (note)* [1992] 2 All ER 82, CA.

(b) recovery of the proceeds of sale of land (12 years);[386]
(c) mortgagee's recovery of the principal sum (12 years),[387] but the Court of Appeal held in *Gotham* v. *Doodes* (2007) that this provision does not apply to a charge imposed on property in favour of a trustee in bankruptcy under the insolvency legislation.[388]
(d) contribution claims: for a claim for contribution under the Civil Liability (Contribution) Act 1978,[389] the period is 2 years[390] (on which, *Aer Lingus plc* v. *Gildacroft Ltd*, 2006).[391] As for contribution claims outside this Act, notably between co-sureties and co-insurers,[392] this is governed by the 6 year period applicable to contractual claims.[393]

(v) A 6-year period of limitation applies to restitutionary claims[394] for recovery of money paid by the claimant under mistake of fact or law, or for total failure of consideration.[395] In the case of claims for re-payment of money in respect of contracts which have become frustrated by supervening illegality or some other drastic event, the cause of action accrues at the date of the frustrating event.[396] Similarly, the starting date for an action based on total failure of consideration at Common Law is the date when the consideration fails.[397]
(vi) The limitation periods mentioned at (i), (iv) and (v) above are subject to statutory exceptions based on fraud, deliberate concealment, or mistake.[398] The

---

386 Section 20(1)(b), 1980 Act.

387 Section 20(1)(a), 1980 Act: the mortgagor has twelve years to claim in order to redeem a mortgage once the mortgagee has taken possession of the property: section 16, 1980 Act; *West Bromwich Building Society* v. *Wilkinson* [2005] UKHL 44; [2005] 1 WLR 2303, at [12].

388 [2006] EWCA Civ 1080; [2007] 1 WLR 86, at [36] to [38], and [40], considering section 313, Insolvency Act 1986.

389 On the 1978 Act, see Neil Andrews, *English Civil Procedure* (Oxford University Press, 2003), 11.71–11.134.

390 Section 10, 1980 Act; 'Limitation of Actions' (L Com CP No 151, 1998), 7.22–7.25.

391 [2006] EWCA Civ 4; [2006] 1 WLR 1173.

392 On Common Law contribution, Neil Andrews, *English Civil Procedure* (Oxford University Press, 2003), 11.71–11.134.

393 *Hampton* v. *Minns* [2002] 1 WLR 1 (the judge concluded that the guarantee in the present case created a debt and that section 5, 1980 Act applied (6 years) rather than section 10, 1980 Act (2 years if claim had been covered by the Civil Liability (Contribution) Act 1978)).

394 'Limitation of Actions' (L Com No 270, 2001), 2.48–2.51; AS Burrows, *The Law of Restitution* (3rd edn, Oxford University Press, 2011), 604 ff; *Goff and Jones, The Law of Unjust Enrichment* (8th edn, 2011), chapter 33; Hazel McLean, 'The Limitation of Actions in Restitution' [1989] CLJ 472–506 (still valuable); M West (2011) 30 CJQ 366.

395 *Kleinwort Benson Ltd* v. *Sandwell BC* [1994] 4 All ER 890, 942–3, *per* Hobhouse J; *BP Exploration Co (Libya) Ltd* v. *Hunt (No 2)* [1983] 2 AC 352, 373–4, *per* Lord Brandon.

396 AS Burrows, *The Law of Restitution*, *ibid*, 608, citing *BP Exploration Co (Libya) Ltd* v. *Hunt (No 2)* [1983] 2 AC 352, 373–4, HL.

397 AS Burrows, *ibid*, citing *Guardian Ocean Cargoes Ltd* v. *Brasil* [1994] 2 Lloyd's Rep 152 (*dictum* of Hirst J).

398 Section 32(1)(a), (b), (c), Limitation Act 1980: 'Limitation of Actions' (L Com No 270, 2001), 2.78–2.90 and *ibid*, L Com CP No 151 (1998), paragraphs 8.1–8.48.

limitation period is postponed: (1) when the action is based on the defendant's fraud[399]; or (2) a fact relevant to the right of action has been deliberately concealed by the defendant; or (3) the action is one for relief from the consequences of mistake (whether of fact or law).[400] In these situations, the limitation period only runs from the date when the claimant discovers the fraud, deliberate concealment or mistake, or could with reasonable diligence have discovered it.[401] Discovery of the fraud is not the same as merely having a suspicion that fraud has occurred.[402]

A person under a disability, including a minor, has the benefit of the full limitation period applicable to the relevant type of claim (for example, 6 years in an ordinary contractual claim). This period runs from the date the disability ceases, or the date of death, or from his 18th birthday (in the case of 'minority').[403] Mental capacity occurring while a party is a minor gives rise to postponement of the limitation period until that person acquires mental capacity.[404]

(vii) Provided the right of action has not already become time-barred, the limitation period recommences if the defendant acknowledges, in written and signed form, the claimant's claim or title,[405] or if he makes a payment in respect of it.[406] This applies to debt claims or other ascertained amounts, claims to recover a share or interest in a deceased person's personal estate, actions for the recovery of land, and claims in relation to mortgages. The limitation period can be repeatedly extended in this way. But acknowledgment or part-payment cannot revive a right of action once it has become time-barred.[407] The House of Lords in *Bradford & Bingley plc* v. *Rashid* (2006)[408] held that an acknowledgment of a debt does not attract the protection of 'without prejudice' negotiation privilege on the question of liability or the amount of the debt, if the statement is intended merely to propose terms for re-payment of the debt over an extended period. Lord Brown explained[409]:

---

399 *Cattley* v. *Pollard* [2006] EWHC 3130 (Ch); [2007] Ch 353 (Richard Sheldon QC); *Beaman* v. *ARTS Ltd* [1949] 1 KB 550; *Barnstable Boat Co* v. *Jones* [2007] EWCA Civ 727; [2008] 1 All ER 1, at [31].

400 On mistake of law, *Kleinwort Benson Ltd* v. *Lincoln CC* [1999] 2 AC 349, HL.

401 Section 32(1), 1980 Act.

402 *Barnstable Boat Co* v. *Jones* [2007] EWCA Civ 727; [2008] 1 All ER 1, at [34] to [36].

403 Sections 28, 38(2), (3), 1980 Act; *Headford* v. *Bristol & District Health Authority* [1995] PIQR P180, CA.

404 *Seaton* v. *Seddon* [2012] EWHC 735 (Ch); [2012] 1 WLR 3637, at [94], *per* Roth J.

405 For a case where the admission was held not to be effective because it was privileged, *Ofulue* v. *Bossert* [2009] UKHL 16; [2009] 1 AC 990.

406 Sections 29 to 31, 1980 Act; 'Limitation of Actions' (L Com No 270, 2001), 2.91 and 2.92; *ibid,* (L Com CP No 151, 1998), 8.27 to 8.48.

407 Section 29(7), 1980 Act.

408 [2006] UKHL 37; [2006] 1 WLR 2066.

409 *ibid,* at [73].

'... the without prejudice rule has no application to apparently open communications, such as those here, designed only to discuss the repayment of an admitted liability rather than to negotiate and compromise a disputed liability'.

(viii) Claims for injunctions or specific performance are subject to the principles of 'laches' and 'acquiescence', rather than the statutory limitation periods mentioned above. The tribunal will have regard to the claimant's conduct or acquiescence and any detriment or unfairness to the defendant. These are equitable bars upon grant of certain remedies, such as injunctive relief or specific performance. They are based upon a long line of case law.[410] The essence of laches is prejudicial delay: lapse of time by a prospective claimant who has knowledge of his entitlement, *coupled with circumstances rendering it inequitable to enforce the claim:* see *Cattley* v. *Pollard* (2006) and the *T & N* case (2003)[411] and Moore-Bick LJ said in the *P & O Nedlloyd* case (2006).[412]

> *'The defence of 'acquiescence' arises if a claimant has knowledge of his rights and nevertheless acquiesces in the defendant's breach of those rights in circumstances which render it unconscionable for the claimant to rely on them.[413] In some contexts, Equity imposes a limitation period upon an equitable remedy by analogy with statutory limitation periods applicable to Common Law remedies.[414] However, extension by analogy does not apply to the remedy of specific performance,[415] nor does extension by analogy apply to injunctions: and so claims for injunctive relief or specific performance are only subject to the equitable bars of 'laches' and acquiescence, and that the statutory periods of limitation do not apply.'[416]*

(ix) There is a statutory discretion to disapply a foreign limitation period if it will lead to undue hardship. The Foreign Limitation Periods Act 1984 confers on a court power not to apply a foreign limitation period if it will lead to undue

---

[410] Chadwick LJ in *re Loftus decd, Green* v. *Gaul* [2006] EWCA Civ 1124; [2007] 1 WLR 591, at [42]; *Lindsay Petroleum Co* v. *Hurd* (1874) LR 5 PC 221, 239–40, PC, *per* Sir Barnes Peacock, cited and glossed by Lord Blackburn in *Erlanger* v. *New Sombrero Phosphate Co* (1878) 3 App Cas 1218, 1279–80, HL.

[411] *T & N Ltd* v. *Royal & Sun Alliance plc* [2003] EWHC 1016 (Ch); [2003] 2 All ER (Comm) 939, at [140].

[412] *P & O Nedlloyd BV* v. *Arab Metals Co* [2006] EWCA Civ 1717; [2007] 1 WLR 2288, 2310.

[413] 'Limitation of Actions' (L Com No 270, 2001), 2.99, citing *Shaw* v. *Applegate* [1977] 1 WLR 970, 978, 980, CA; defendant must have relied to his detriment on claimant's positive conduct, words or inaction, *Jones* v. *Stones* [1999] 1 WLR 1739, 1742–4, *per* Aldous LJ, CA.

[414] Section 36(1), 1980 Act notes this; 'Limitation of Actions' (L Com CP No 151, 1998), 9.22; a leading statement is by Lord Westbury in *Knox* v. *Gye* (1872) LR 5 HL 656, 674–5, HL.

[415] W Goodhart and GH Jones, *Specific Performance* (2nd edn, 1996), 109–112; J Beatson, 'Limitation Periods and Specific Performance' in E Lomnicka and CGJ Morse (eds), *Contemporary Issues in Commercial Law* (1997), 9–23.

[416] *P & O Nedlloyd BV* v. *Arab Metals Co* [2006] EWCA Civ 1717; [2007] 1 WLR 2288; *Heath* v. *Heath* [2009] EWHC 1908 (Ch); [2010] FSR 610, at [27] ff; 'Limitation of Actions', Law Commission Report No 270 (HC 23, 2001), 2.97 to 2.99.

hardship.[417] The Court of Appeal in *Harley* v. *Smith* (2011)[418] held that this will not be shown merely because the foreign period is shorter than the parallel English period. The Court of Appeal in *Bank St Petersburg* v. *Arkhangelsky* (2014) upheld a ('multi-factorial') decision to grant relief under the 1984 Act in respect of a Russian limitation period of 3 years.[419]

[417] Section 2(1), Foreign Limitation Periods Act 1984; *Gotha City* v. *Sotheby's, The Times* 8 October, 1998; noted in *Garcia* v. *De Aldama* [2002] EWHC 2087 (Ch); [2003] ECDR CN1, at [252], [253], *per* Peter Smith J.

[418] [2010] EWCA Civ 78; [2010] CP Rep 33 (final paragraph of judgment).

[419] [2014] EWCA Civ 593; [2014] 1 WLR 4360, at [15] to [25].

Index

N. Andrews, *Arbitration and Contract Law*, Ius Gentium: Comparative Perspectives on Law and Justice 54, DOI 10.1007/978-3-319-27144-6

CPSIA information can be obtained at www.ICGtesting.com
Printed in the USA
BVOW06*0212280416

445951BV00005B/8/P

9 783319 271422